THE

PUBLICATIONS

OF THE

SURTEES SOCIETY

VOL. 216

THE

\ PUBLICATIONS

OF THE

SURTEES SOCIETY

ESTABLISHED IN THE YEAR
M.DCCC.XXXIV

\ VOL. CCXVI

THE
RELIGIOUS CENSUS
OF 1851

NORTHUMBERLAND
AND
COUNTY DURHAM

EDITED
BY
ALAN MUNDEN

THE BOYDELL PRESS

First published 2012

A Surtees Society Publication
published by The Boydell Press
an imprint of Boydell & Brewer Ltd
PO Box 9, Woodbridge, Suffolk IP12 3DF, UK
and of Boydell & Brewer Inc.
Mt Hope Avenue, Rochester, NY 14620–2731, USA
website: www.boydellandbrewer.com

ISBN 978–0–85444–071–9

ISSN 0307–5362

A catalogue record for this book is available
from the British Library

Details of other Surtees Society volumes are available
from Boydell & Brewer Ltd

The publisher has no responsibility for the continued existence or
accuracy of URLs for external or third-party internet websites
referred to in this book, and does not guarantee that any content
on such websites is, or will remain, accurate or appropriate

Papers used by Boydell & Brewer Ltd are natural, recyclable products
made from wood grown in sustainable forests

Printed and bound in Great Britain by
CPI Group (UK) Ltd, Croydon, CR0 4YY

CONTENTS

Cumberland

Appendices

Indices

ILLUSTRATIONS

The editor and publishers are grateful to all the institutions and persons listed for permission to reproduce the materials in which they hold copyright. Every effort has been made to trace the copyright holders; apologies are offered for any omission, and the publishers will be pleased to add any necessary acknowledgement in subsequent editions.

ACKNOWLEDGEMENTS

I am greatly indebted to numerous archivists and local studies staff in the north-east for their assistance and in particular to the staff of the Special Collections of the University of Durham; the staff of the Literary and Philosophical Society of Newcastle upon Tyne; and to the staff of the Newcastle Central Library. Early on in the research I valued the brief contact with the late Dr Rob Lee of the University of Teeside. Many individuals have provided local information and helped to clarify for me factual issues and have corrected my numerous errors and inconsistencies. Where known, I have provided supplementary information on churches, chapels and individuals, and local detailed knowledge would enrich this even more.

My family were aware that I was working on what they disparagingly referred to as 'the list of names' without fully realising what the undertaking was all about, and sadly (but understandably) they never caught my enthusiasm for this absorbing piece of historical research. Perhaps this publication of the Religious Census might encourage some of them to read it.

The census returns held at the National Archives at Kew under class HO129 are Crown Copyright, and are reproduced by permission of the Controller of Her Majesty's Stationery Office, using microfilms held at Newcastle Central Library.

Alan Munden
Newcastle upon Tyne

ABBREVIATIONS

Arch. Ael.   *Archaeologia Aeliana*
B   Baptisms
CPAS   Church Pastoral Aid Society
DUL   Durham University Library
NRO   Northumberland Record Office
ODCC   *Oxford Dictionary of the Christian Church*
ODNB   *Oxford Dictionary of National Biography*
OPE   Other Permanent Endowment
SS   Sunday scholars

INTRODUCTION

This volume contains an edited version of the national religious census for Northumberland and County Durham. In 1851 three national censuses were conducted – the Civil Census, the Education Census and the Religious Census. The first recorded that the population of England and Wales had reached 17,927,609, and the third discovered that of that number only 7,261,032 individuals had attended a place of worship on the Sunday of the Census. After allowances were made for children, the sick, domestic servants and public employees it was calculated that there were 5,288,294 people who had chosen not to attend one of the 34,467 places of worship. However, even with the vast amount of statistical information that became available from the Religious Census, 'the number of habitual non-attenders cannot be precisely stated'[1] for they might not always have been the same individuals: they might have attended irregularly or intermittently. It was recognised at the time that the practice of religion was greater amongst the middle and upper classes, and weakest among the working class, and that the Church of England was strongest in the south of England and nonconformity was strongest in the north and in Wales.

In their book, *Rival Jerusalems*, K.D.M. Snell and P.S. Ell have provided a comprehensive study of the background and context of the Religious Census together with a regional overview of fifteen counties (one of which is Northumberland)[2] and the Census in County Durham was touched on too by Robert Lee in his book on the Church of England and the Durham coalfield.[3] But apart from

---

1   *Census of Great Britain. Religious Worship. England and Wales. Report and Tables* (London, 1853) (hereafter *Religious Worship. England and Wales*), p. cliii. Reprinted in the Irish University Press series of *British Parliamentary Papers. Population*, vol. 10, 1970. The report for Scotland was published in 1854.
2   K.D.M. Snell and P.S. Ell, *Rival Jerusalems. The Geography of Victorian Religion* (Cambridge, 2000).
3   R. Lee, *The Church of England and the Durham Coalfield, 1810–1926* (Woodbridge, 2007).

these two works and the research of Geoffrey Milburn[4] and Robin Gill,[5] no detailed study has yet been published on the Religious Census for the two north-east counties.

The Census was concerned with *Sunday attendance* (or Saturday for the Jews) but not with *religious profession*. Clearly mere attendance in a place of worship did not necessarily imply a believing faith, simply an allegiance to a particular denomination or religious group. There are instances where chapel-going and church-going related more to keeping in with the colliery management and feeling obliged to follow the dictates of an authoritarian manager.[6] Children attending the schools provided by London Lead Mining Company were expected to attend either church or chapel every Sunday.[7] During the course of the day of the Census individuals might have attended more than one service, so their attendance would have been recorded once, twice or three times. To allow for this a rough and ready calculation was devised which was based on the number of worshippers attending in the morning, together with a half in the afternoon and a third in the evening. This method was to the advantage of some denominations but also unfair to others. Generally the Church of England had larger congregations in the morning, fewer in the afternoon and fewest in the evening; and nonconformists had the most in the evening, fewer in the morning and least in the afternoon. Some worshippers might not have been present for personal and practical reasons like sickness, the poor weather, or where their usual place of worship might not have held a service on Census day. This would have been the case with the Church of England in a multi-benefice situation, for example, and for Methodists where there were numerous places of worship within the circuit. Obviously the published figures have to be interpreted with some care but they do give some indication of the number of worshippers on a given day mid-way through the nineteenth century.

---

4   G.E. Milburn, 'Church-going in Northumberland in the Period just prior to the Foundation of the Diocese', in W.S.F. Pickering (ed.), *A Social History of the Diocese of Newcastle 1882–1982* (Stocksfield, 1981), pp. 79–103. G.E. Milburn, *Religion in Sunderland in the mid-Nineteenth Century* (Sunderland, 1982).

5   R. Gill, *Competing Convictions* (London, 1989). R. Gill, *The Myth of the Empty Church* (London, 1993), pp. 35–51.

6   R. Lee, *The Church of England and the Durham Coalfield 1810–1926* (Woodbridge, 2007), p. 44.

7   S. Bruce, 'Methodism and Mining in County Durham, 1881–1991', *Northern History*, xlviii (2011), p. 342.

Nationally thirty-five separate denominations were identified in the Census, most of which were found throughout the north-east. The majority of the denominations subscribed to a *Trinitarian* faith (Church of England, Presbyterian, Baptist; Methodist, Countess of Huntingdon's Connexion, Brethren and Roman Catholic) and a minority to a *non-Trinitarian* faith (Unitarian, Swedenborgian and Latter-day Saints) and somewhere in between was the ambiguous position of the Society of Friends. In the mid-nineteenth century the divisions between the denominations were theological, with clear distinctions between Anglican and nonconformist, Episcopalian and Presbyterian, Protestant and Roman Catholic, Christian and Jew and between the majority who practised infant baptism and the minority who baptised only adults. Some of the denominations were centuries old, while others were still in their infancy. Some, like the Salvation Army, were yet to be born. In addition to the thirty-five denominations the only other world faith to be included in the Census was the Jewish. The adherents of other faiths would have been widely scattered and were certainly insufficient to have their own places of worship.

THE RELIGIOUS CENSUS OF 1851

The individual responsible for conducting the Census was the young barrister Horace Mann who in 1855 became the registrar and then in 1875 the secretary of the Civil Service Commission.[8] For the purposes of the Census, the area of England and Wales was divided into 30,610 districts, each of which was under an enumerator who was responsible to one of the 2,190 local registrars of births and deaths.[9] A week before Census day (Sunday, 30 March 1851) the enumerators had to identify the names and addresses of the persons responsible for each denomination within his district. It would have been straightforward to identify the Anglican clergy, but more difficult to locate a small congregation of independent dissenters meeting in an isolated house or cottage.

There were three main forms to be completed. First, for the Church of England (printed in black on pale blue paper). Second, for other religious bodies (printed in red on pale blue paper). Third, for the

8 'Horace Mann (1823–1917)', *ODNB*, vol. 36, pp. 440–441.
9 For the organisation and publication of the Census see Snell and Ell, *Rival Jerusalems*, pp. 28–35.

Society of Friends (printed in black on white paper). However the colour of the paper and ink still did not prevent the wrong denominational forms from being issued and completed, and seven examples of this error are found in this publication.[10] In addition there were two simplified forms for the Church of England and for other religious bodies. The day after the forms had been completed the enumerators collected them and gave them to the local registrar who returned them to the Census office in London. The 34,000 or so forms were then numbered, filed and analysed by the statisticians. Those individuals who had not completed their form were then issued with a replacement from the Census office, and if this also failed to elicit a response the local registrar was expected to obtain and record as much information as he could. This whole process was a lengthy affair and some information from the defaulters was still being collected well into 1852. This accounts for the sometimes uneven presentation of information recorded in the following pages where it can be either very detailed or very sparse.

The Census of Religious Worship in England and Wales was published as a parliamentary paper in December 1853, and after publication the findings were widely debated in the national and regional press. This was the only census of its kind and the experiment was never repeated. The published Census included both commentary and summaries of the returns for large towns, registration districts and counties but did not give the details of individual places of worship. It is this more detailed information for Northumberland and County Durham that is provided in this publication.

The Census of religious worship consisted of a detailed discussion of the thirty-five denominations followed by a section on 'spiritual provision and destitution'. In examining the provision of sittings in places of worship, Horace Mann recommended that it should be possible for 58% of the population to be accommodated in a place of worship. Obviously there was no uniform pattern of attendance or denominational support throughout England and Wales. In rural areas most, if not all, worshippers could easily be accommodated, but in urban areas this was impossible. Mann discovered that

---

10 Nonconformist and Roman Catholic on a Church of England form **4.23**, **10.44**, **16.86**, **18.51**; and Church of England and Quaker on a nonconformist form **16.22**, **21.62**, **21.63**. Throughout the introduction, the first figure in references such as this relates to the *district* and the *second* to the *place of worship* within the district. Thus **4.23** in this note refers to registration district 4, i.e. Berwick, and place of worship 23, i.e. the English Presbyterian church at Tweedmouth.

throughout England and Wales 66.5% of the population could be accommodated in rural parishes but only 46.0% in urban parishes. He found that there were 'widely varying condition[s] of particular localities: some fortunately basking in excess of spiritual privileges, others absolutely "perishing for lack of knowledge"'.[11] For him the solution was obvious. More places of worship were required, particularly in the larger towns, 'for relieving such deplorable deficiency'.[12] It was found that only in nine out of seventy-two large towns and boroughs could 58% and more of the population be accommodated. The highest provision was in Colchester (73.2%), followed by Wakefield (70.9%) and York (65.1%), and the lowest was in Lambeth (24.8%) and Tower Hamlets (25.6%) in London. Overall, the average provision for England and Wales was 37.3%. In the north-east the greatest provision was in York and the least in Newcastle. In the five urban areas of Northumberland and County Durham the figures were: Newcastle (34.5%), Gateshead (35.5%), Tynemouth (44.1%), Sunderland (48.9%) and South Shields (49.0%). From these findings it was calculated that many more sittings were required in Newcastle (20,596), Gateshead (5,748), Tynemouth (4,065), Sunderland (5,796) and South Shields (2,607). Across the two counties, Durham had the lowest proportion of sittings to population (17.6%) and Northumberland was only slightly better (18.1%). Horace Mann remarked that 'the destitute condition of this vast proportion of our countrymen appeals to the benevolence of Christians indiscriminately', but especially to the Church of England 'to whose care the spiritual welfare of these myriads is particularly entrusted'. Furthermore, 'doubtless, the *ill*-taught and the *wrong*-taught demand her as well as the *un*taught, but the utterly neglected evidently claim her *first* exertions'.[13]

Looking in broad terms across the counties the total attendances as a percentage of the population (known as the index of attendance) revealed some wide variations. The average figure for England and Wales was 58.1%. For the northern counties the index of attendance was: Cheshire 52.3%, Lancashire 44.1%, Cumberland 37.3%, Westmorland 50.1%, Yorkshire – East Riding 58.8%, West Riding 52.9% and North Riding 63.6%. For the two north-east counties the index

---

11   *Religious Worship. England and Wales*, p. cxxvii.
12   *Ibid.*, p. cxxx.
13   *Ibid.*, p. cxxxviii.

of attendance was much the same with Northumberland 42.0% and Durham 42.6%.[14]

Whilst Mann calculated that about 2,000 more places of worship were required, he suggested that there were other ways in which to accommodate more people. Often churches and chapels were only open for a single service on a Sunday, but during the course of the day additional services could be held and other acts of worship conducted during the week. Where people were hostile and indifferent to clergy, then lay agents could be employed, street preaching should be adopted by the Church of England, and greater use made of school rooms in which to hold services. Of course these suggestions raised practical issues over the number of clergy and ministers who were available, and for the even more contentious issue within the Church of England of using laymen to lead worship. This novelty took years to be implemented, and even after the introduction of Anglican Readers in the 1880s their activities were severely restricted, and they were not permitted to preach from the pulpit until 1941.[15]

Mann did not mince his words and was scathing in his observations. He noted that more money was devoted to overseas missions than to support church building at home. He believed that new churches were often erected in middle-class areas where the population had 'not only the desire to have, but also the ability to get, an adequate provision for religious culture'.[16] Religion had become 'regarded as a purely middle-class propriety or luxury'[17] and, he observed, society was deeply divided, and the working classes were absent due 'to a genuine repugnance to religion itself.'[18] Even where churches and chapels were opened and sermons preached, 'the masses of the population, careless or opposed, will not frequent them'[19] and the buildings remained half empty. But at the same time Mann commended both the Methodists and the Mormons for the obvious success of their evangelistic endeavours.

---

14 B.J. Coleman, *The Church of England in the Mid-Nineteenth Century* (London, 1980), p. 40.
15 R. Hiscox, *Celebrating Reader Ministry* (London, 1991), p. 19.
16 *Religious Worship. England and Wales*, p. cl.
17 *Ibid.*, p. clix.
18 *Ibid.*, p. clxi.
19 *Ibid.*, p. clxi.

THE RELIGIOUS CENSUS IN NORTHUMBERLAND AND COUNTY DURHAM

The Religious Census took place on 30 March 1851. It was Mothering Sunday and because of the festival some members of families were absent from their usual place of worship. Those who completed the Census forms sometimes made reference to the bad weather and illness in contributing towards a lower attendance than usual. Certainly on that day the weather was poor and the precise conditions may be traced across the United Kingdom. The health of the nation was also noted. Some people were suffering from influenza, scarlet fever and measles which meant that a number of women remained at home caring for their sick children. In Stanhope the weather was described as 'unfavourable' (24.30) which depleted the congregation. A Baptist minister in Newcastle noted that 'owing to sickness and the weather the attendance on the 30 March was below the average' (10.21) and similar reasons were given for the poor attendance at St Mary, West Rainton (19.6). At the Bethel chapel in Chester-le-Street the congregation was reduced by an outbreak of influenza (14.11). At Seaham Harbour, the attendance at the Sunday school at St John's church was depleted because of an outbreak of measles (17.9), and at Billingham parish church some of the Sunday school were absent through illness, and because the building was 'imperfectly warmed' (21.1).[20]

Other reasons were given for being absent. At Birdhopecraig chapel the congregation included farmers and shepherds who were otherwise engaged with lambing (3.17). Some of the congregation of the United Presbyterian church at Bishopwearmouth were fishermen and away at sea (22.12). Many of the parishioners of Wingate Grange were also fishermen and the incumbent complained that they were 'a class of people most constantly ignorant' of the Christian faith and 'the greater part of them cannot be persuaded to attend my place of worship' (17.11). At the Roman Catholic church at Wolsingham many of the men could not attend Mass because they were employed at the iron works and had to work on alternate Sundays (24.37). At Berwick upon Tweed the numbers at the Wesleyan Methodist chapel fluctuated depending on the numbers of soldiers stationed in the town

---

20 The Archdeacon of Lindisfarne considered that heating churches was 'a modern indulgence' which necessitated the insurance of churches. R.C. Coxe, *A Charge delivered to the Clergy of the Archdeaconry of Lindisfarne, June 1855* (London, 1855), p. 7.

(4.26). At Crook most of the population of the parish were Primitive Methodists (13.7), at Kyloe the majority were dissenters (4.5) and at Carham (6.2), Ingram (6.9) and Cambo (9.4) they were mostly Presbyterians. At South Hetton the Wesleyan and Primitive Methodist chapels were well supported and this affected the attendance at the Anglican church (17.4). At Collierley, there were a large number of Roman Catholics, and since most of the miners were Wesleyan Methodists few of the population attended the Church of England (16.4), while at the seaside resort of Seaton Carew the parish church was often full and included visitors during the summer bathing season (21.16).

Since the completion of the Census returns was not compulsory critics have questioned the reliability of its findings.[21] In some instances the returns were incomplete and not all of the questions were answered, but the non-compliants were in a minority and of the 34,467 returns made only 390 of them lacked the necessary information on sittings and attendances. Throughout England and Wales there were some Church of England clergy and nonconformist ministers who refused to co-operate and to give any information. There were many reasons for this course of action. Some were suspicious of the whole idea of conducting a Census, while others, anticipating the published findings, were fearful of what might be disclosed. In the north-east the non-compliant clergy included Henry Warkman of Earsdon (12.3), James Brown of Dalton-le-Dale (17.2), John Reed of Newburn (5.9), Christopher Reed of North Shields (12.7), John Besly of Longbenton (12.6) and Henry Carr of Whickham (18.15). George Jenkinson, of Lowick (6.11), who twice refused to give the required information, was at the time under a two-year suspension from his living for drunkenness.[22] John Grey of Houghton-le-Spring completed a form but remarked that the 'numbers are conjectural as I am not in the habit of counting the congregation. I do not go to church for that purpose' (19.2) and neither did Richard Skipsey of St Thomas, Bishopwearmouth (22.4). Numbering the congregation was also a problem for George Sproston of Trimdon (21.25) and John Roberts of Shilbottle (1.12). Richard Blenkinsopp, the incumbent of Shadforth, refused to give any information about the endowment or the attendance (16.23). Samuel Brasher, the incumbent of St Stephen's, South Shields (20.8), objected to supplying any infor-

---

21 For criticisms in general see Snell and Ell, *Rival Jerusalems*, pp. 35–46.
22 DUL, ASC, DDR/EJ/CLD/2, Clergy Discipline 1846–56.

mation and at Dalton-le-Dale 'the vicar refused to fill up a return' (**17.2**). Henry Gipps, who was responsible for Corbridge and Halton, returned incomplete forms (**8.12, 13**), and since Thomas Green, the incumbent of Byker, had already completed two forms, he refused to complete a third (**10.8**). The vicar of St Giles', Durham, completed the return on condition 'that no part of the information contained in it, will ever be made known' (**16.10**). Thomas Boycott, the minister of a Methodist New Connexion chapel in Newcastle, commented 'we think that this return (if required at all) ought to have been obligatory on all parties without exception' (**10.35**).

In churches and chapels the sittings were either *unappropriated* (that is they were free) *or appropriated* (for which a pew rent was charged) and the income was used to provide the stipend for the incumbent or minister and to meet the running costs of the building. The more wealthy worshippers could afford prominent seats where they could see and hear what was happening, and sometimes the provision of their seating was linked to particular properties (**6.11, 11.2, 17.5**). The poor sat on free pews in less prominent positions or on benches in the main aisle. Often the Sunday school children sat on benches; at Winston they were provided in the chancel (**23.7**) and at Ponteland in the gallery (**5.13**). One incumbent noted that 'the poor do not like to enter allotted sittings [even] though empty'.[23] It was the general policy in Presbyterian churches that those individuals who were unable to pay could occupy any seats that were unoccupied after the service had started. Provision was also made for people to stand and reference is made in the nonconformist returns to 'standing room'. At Frosterley the Primitive Methodist chapel could only accommodate 150 people, but on the evening of the Census there were another fifty present, who presumably had to stand during the service. The society steward remarked that 'it is intended to build a larger chapel as soon as the society find it convenient to do so' (**24.28**) and the new chapel was opened in 1861.

The Religious Census recorded the actual *attendances* for each service, but not the number of times that an individual might have attended during the course of the day. In most cases the attendance figures are approximations and rounded up, but some incumbents gave precise figures. At Whitburn parish church those attending were 'counted' (**20.12**) and at St James, Castle Eden, the total attend-

---

23 DUL, ASC, AUC/1/142, St Mary, Lesbury. Clergy returns for the Bishop's first visitation, September 1857.

ance of 415 was made up of 334 individuals (**17.1**). The minister of St George's Presbyterian chapel in Bishopwearmouth who knew that attendance figures were often inflated, made sure that his congregation was accurately counted (**22.15**). Throughout the two counties there was a considerable variation in attendance. With a larger, concentrated population in the towns (particularly in Newcastle, Bishopwearmouth and Sunderland) there was a higher Sunday attendance but some rural churches also had large congregations. At Wooler some of the congregation of the West Chapel Presbyterian church travelled six miles and more to attend services (**6.21**). In some parts of Northumberland there were more Presbyterians than Anglicans, and those attending the Church of England were in a minority. In Berwick upon Tweed, out of a population of just over 10,000, the parish church had a morning attendance of 770 (**4.2**), while in the five Presbyterian churches in the town there was a total attendance of 2,268 (**4.13, 15–18**). At Belford, where the township had a population of 1,226, there was a morning congregation of 230 at the parish church (**2.3**), whereas in the three Presbyterian places of worship there was a total morning congregation of 771 (**2.7–8, 10**).

In Northumberland the largest Anglican congregations were in Newcastle with 1,510 at St Nicholas' (**10.1**), 1,390 at St John's (**10.2**) and 1,292 at St Thomas' (**10.10**). Outside Newcastle there were congregations of 770 in Holy Trinity, Berwick upon Tweed (**4.2**), and 697 in St Mary, Alnwick (**1.1**). The largest average attendances at nonconformist places of worship were 950 at Howard Street, Wesleyan Methodist chapel, North Shields (**12.39**), 904 at the United Presbyterian church in Wooler (**6.16**), 820 at the Brunswick Place Wesleyan Methodist chapel, Newcastle (**10.29**), and 800 at the Golden Square Presbyterian church at Berwick upon Tweed (**4.16**). The largest Roman Catholic congregation was at St Andrew's, Newcastle, with an attendance of 1,689 at the two morning services (**10.47**). At the other end of the spectrum the smallest congregation, with only six adults, was at the parish church of Thockrington where the incumbent was clearly discouraged by his situation. 'The 30 [March] was on a cold and stormy day, and the church stands upon a bleak and an exposed situation. The parishioners are nearly all dissenters except one or two families who live at some distance from the church' (**3.11**). There were eight adults at the independent 'Christian' congregation in Monk Street, Newcastle (**10.43**), and nine Quakers at Wooley, Allendale (**8.95**).

In County Durham the largest Anglican congregations were 1,240 at St Thomas', Stockton on Tees (**21.22**), 1,034 at Holy Trinity, Sunderland (**22.8**), 1,000 at St Mary's, Gateshead (**18.1**), and St Michael's, Bishopwearmouth (**22.1**), and 885 at Holy Trinity, Darlington (**15.4**). The largest evening congregations at nonconformist places of worship were 1,150 at the Flag Lane Primitive Methodist chapel in Sunderland (**22.54**), 1,000 at the Bethesda Free chapel, Bishopwearmouth (**22.27**), 930 at the Wesleyan Reformers place of worship in Bishopwearmouth (**22.60**) and 800 at the Wesleyan Methodist chapel at Bishopwearmouth (**22.28**). The Roman Catholic church at Bishop Auckland was reported to have a potential congregation of 900 (**13.61**). Throughout the county many of the places of worship had modest congregations of between twenty and thirty people. There was a congregation of only twelve at the Anglican schoolroom at Barlow, Winlaton (**18.13**), and the smallest adult attendance, of six people (together with a Sunday school of 35), was at the Wesleyan Methodist chapel at Sedgefield (**21.46**). Apart from the concentration of Quakers at Darlington (but unrecorded in the Census) the Society of Friends had small congregations – fifteen at Staindrop (**23.30**), thirteen at New Shildon (**13.60**) and eleven at Durham (**16.84**).

Mostly the returns were completed by the clergy and ministers of the respective denominations, by the deacons of the Independent chapels, and many of the Methodist returns were made by chapel stewards and class leaders. Unusually, three of the returns were completed by women (**21.31, 21.43, 22.22**). Some of the spelling was poor (particularly among the Primitive Methodists) and this gives an indication of their social status and general level of education. In only one instance (and outside the two north-east counties), Joseph Featherston, a member of the Wesleyan Methodist Association at High Leven, North Yorkshire was unable to write and simply made his mark (**21.87**).

INCREASE IN POPULATION

From the beginning of the nineteenth century there had been a steady rise in the population of England and Wales, from 8,872,980 in 1801 to 17,927,609 in 1851. In the north-east the increases were as shown on the following page:[24]

---

24   In this section the information (and the quotations) are taken from the *Census of Great Britain 1851. Population Tables II, Vol. 2, Numbers of the Inhabitants* (London, 1852). County Durham, pp. 11–23; Northumberland, pp. 23–43.

	Northumberland	County Durham
1801	168,078	159,161
1811	183,269	175,784
1821	212,589	205,194
1831	236,959	251,051
1841	266,020	326,043
1851	303,568	411,679

From 1801 to 1821 the population of Northumberland was greater than that of County Durham, but from 1831 the numbers in County Durham exceeded those in Northumberland. This increase was challenging to all of the denominations, and the Religious Census reflects the response to the situation. In 1831 the ratio of places of worship to population was one to 1,175 and in 1851 it was one to 1,296. In the first half of the nineteenth century many new churches and chapels were opened, and following the publication of the Census this activity continued throughout the rest of the century.

While there was an obvious overall increase in the population the precise number of people could fluctuate in particular localities. The population figures were not recorded in the Religious Census but were given in the Civil Census of the same year. The following paragraphs are taken from the statistics and footnotes provided in the Civil Census. In 1851 large numbers were employed as coal miners. In County Durham there were 28,265 male miners and thirty-eight women, and in Northumberland 10,536 male miners and eight women.[25] In the north-east the increase in population was mainly brought about by the expansion of the mining industry, but it could just as easily decline as coal seams were exhausted and when the miners and their families moved elsewhere to find employment. This regular migration was common and became a hindrance to effective outreach and pastoral supervision by the clergy and ministers. When the railways were under construction the influx of sixty or seventy labourers would increase the population of a small community, but once the work was completed they moved on and the population was immediately depleted. Some communities expanded when stone quarries, lime-kilns, iron works, mills and factories were opened, and by the development of the woollen, linen and flax industries, but declined when they closed. The opening of a railway line or port

25 *Census of Great Britian 1851. Population Tables II, Vol. 2, Ages, Civil Condition,
    Occupations and Birth-place of the People* (London, 1854), pp. 758, 761, 764, 767.

was good for trade, and inevitably brought an increase in the resident population. There was a temporary increase in the number of workmen when specific building work was in progress such as in the construction of new ports and harbours, and in the restoration of the castles at Streatlam and Brancepeth. But when fewer people were employed at Chillingham Castle the population decreased. The population could decrease with the closure of a colliery or quarry; and with the closure of cotton, spinning or paper mills. When coal mining ceased in the townships of East Brunton and Fawdon over half of the houses in the community were empty, and at Black Callerton 'several houses erected for the colliers have been demolished'.[26] At Corsenside half of the inhabitants left the parish and 112 houses were uninhabited when the population fell from 1,108 (in 1841) to 579 (in 1851). In 1851 the colliery was closed at Coundon and 'many coal-miners had left at least thirty houses unoccupied' (**13.6**). The numbers working on the land could also vary. From 1821 to 1851 thirty people left Alwinton due to emigration and distress among sheep farmers. In places where there were a large number of seamen there could be an imbalance between men and women such as at Heworth and South Shields (where there were 1,000 more women than men). In the parish of Whalton the population decreased when more single men were employed than those who were married and had children.

Numbers could increase due to the influx of summer visitors to watering places such as Middleton St George and Benfieldside, or to Cullercoats where the population in 1841 included 'fifty visitors for the benefit of sea bathing',[27] and the Durham Fair of 1851 brought an additional 240 people into the parishes of St Nicholas and St Giles. At Berwick upon Tweed the increase in population was ascribed to the employment of workmen building a new pier and the residents having been vaccinated. An unexpected increase occurred in Gateshead Fell when the number of inmates at the lunatic asylum increased from 210 (in 1841) to 320 (in 1851). Those accommodated in workhouses[28] or confined in prison could also impact upon the local

---

26 *Census of Great Britain 1851. Numbers of the Inhabitants*, Northumberland, p. 27.
27 *Ibid.*, p. 25. In Redcar, Yorkshire, two churches recorded that their congregations increased during the summer when sea bathing attracted visitors to the town. J. Wolffe, *The Religious Census of 1851 in Yorkshire* (York, 2005), p. 17.
28 See Appendix 4.

community.[29] The conversion of the former barracks into homes at Preston, Tynemouth, increased the population, but the closing of a boarding school at Headlam led to its decline.

Some areas were rapidly swamped by new residents and the local services would have been challenged to respond to the increase in population, particularly in housing, shops, schools, churches and chapels. At Thornley near Easington the population increased from 50 (in 1821) to 2,456 (in 1851); at Dawdon from 35 (in 1821) to 3,538 (in 1851) and at Hetton-le-Hole from 919 (in 1821) to 5,664 (in 1851). These situations were not uncommon and were found throughout the north-east. The Anglican response to these expanded communities was slow and ponderous and restricted by legal complexities and yards of red-tape, and the erection of a church or chapel was only at the end of a lengthy process. At Tow Law it was twenty years before a church was provided. In 1841, 'Tow Law' was the name of a house but over the course of the next ten years the community rose to 2,000 people. In 1849 the Anglican schoolroom was made available for worship and in 1857 the minister reported to the bishop that 'a church is required at Tow Law',[30] but the parishioners had to wait until 1869 before it was opened. On the other hand, the nonconformists were able to make an immediate response to an influx of new residents. They could preach in the open air and meet in a private house long before fund-raising for the erection of a chapel. At the same time the nonconformists living in a thinly populated area might well have been prepared to travel further than their Anglican counterparts to hear powerful preaching and to participate in revivalist worship.

THE CONTEXT IN WHICH THE CENSUS TOOK PLACE

Having examined the findings of the Religious Census and setting it alongside the increase in population it is now time to relate this to the contemporary context within the denominations in the northeast. The Census took place in the mid-century and the information it provided gives a useful marker in examining the strengths and weaknesses of the various religious bodies.

---

29 In St James', Benwell (**10.3**), the incumbent referred to 131 children from the Union workhouse attending his church, and noted the need for a chaplain to be responsible for the workhouse.

30 DUL, ASC, AUC/1/142, Tow Law. Clergy returns for Bishop Charles Longley's first visitation, September 1857.

Church of England[31]

Geographically the diocese of Durham consisted of the two counties of Northumberland and Durham together with the parish of Alston (with the chapelries of Garrigill and Nenthead) in Cumberland, which was under the episcopal oversight of the Bishop of Durham.[32] This oversight was extended in January 1836 when Hexham and the parishes of Hexhamshire (Allendale, Allenheads, Bingfield, Carrshields, Ninebanks, St John Lee and Whitley chapel) were transferred from the diocese of York to the diocese of Durham. From at least the twelfth century there was an archdeacon for Durham and Northumberland and their geographical responsibilities remained unchanged until the archdeaconry of Lindisfarne was created in September 1842.[33]

During the eighteenth and nineteenth centuries the fabric of many of the existing Anglican churches and chapels was in such a poor state that they were completely rebuilt or restored.[34] To increase the number of sittings some were enlarged by the building of a new aisle, or more commonly (and particularly in the eighteenth century), by the erection of galleries, only to be later removed by 'restorers'. In the nineteenth century some of the so-called 'restorations' were inspired by the principles of the Church of England Ecclesiologists and by the influential Roman Catholic architect Augustus Pugin. The idea at the time was to restore the buildings to how they were imagined to have been before the Reformation and to create in stone a romanticised Gothic structure that would provide the ritualistic setting for what was believed to be true catholic worship. This meant that the main focus of the building shifted from the pulpit to the altar; that the seating was no longer divided between rented private box-pews and free benches for the poor, but in free open seats for all classes; and that the singers and their musical accompaniment were removed from the west gallery, and in their place a surpliced choir and organ were located in the chancel.

---

31 'Church of England', *ODCC*, pp. 347–351.
32 After the diocese of Newcastle was created in 1882, Northumberland (and Alston) came under the episcopal supervision of the Bishop of Newcastle.
33 Subsequently two more archdeaconries were created – Auckland in May 1882 and Sunderland in March 1997. For the names of the bishops and archdeacons, see Appendix 2.
34 N. Yates, *Buildings, Faith and Worship* (Oxford, 1991), pp. 48–55. B.F.L. Clark, *The Building of the Eighteenth-Century Church* (London, 1963).

Alongside the medieval romance were the practicalities of providing a place of worship for an increasing population, and where the parish church was inconveniently located some distance away from the homes of the parishioners. The result was that from 1791 to 1882 about 234 new churches and chapels were consecrated in the diocese of Durham.[35]

Before 1818 new churches could only be erected, or ruinous churches rebuilt, after the granting of a special Act of Parliament.[36] In this way several new churches were erected in urban centres like Newcastle, Sunderland and Wallsend, and in rural areas like Penshaw, Longbenton and Haydon Bridge. Unique to the region was the division of the extensive parish of Simonburn, whose boundaries had a circumference of over one hundred miles and included a widely scattered population. In 1811, 'An Act for erecting five distinct rectories and parishes within the rectory and parish of Simonburn, in the county of Northumberland'[37] made provision for five churches to be erected. Initially only four were built, at Greystead (**3.7**), Humshaugh (**8.15**), Thorneyburn (**3.12**) and Wark (**3.13**), and the fifth, at Falstone (**3.6**), was rebuilt and opened in 1825. The capital to erect the churches, the residences for the clergy and the endowment for the new benefices was provided by the landowners, the governors of Greenwich Hospital, who stipulated that each incumbent, as well as being a graduate of Oxford or Cambridge, should previously have served as a naval chaplain. Over the course of four days in August 1818[38] the four new churches designed by Henry Hake Seward, the surveyor to Greenwich Hospital, were consecrated by the Bishop of Oxford (Edward Legge). In such a sparsely populated and isolated area the Religious Census revealed that Greystead (**3.7**) had one of the smallest congregations in the whole of the diocese, and since the area was strongly Presbyterian it was not surprising that the Church of England had few adherents.

The Church Building Act of 1818[39] was the first of over twenty Church Building Acts which formed 'an almost impenetrable jungle of laws and orders'[40] that faced prospective builders of new churches.

---

35 See Appendix 1.
36 M.H. Port, *Six Hundred New Churches. The Church Building Commission 1818– 1856* (Reading, 2006), pp. 45–57.
37 51 Geo. III c.194.
38 *Newcastle Courant*, 5 September 1818.
39 58 Geo. III c.45. Port, *Six Hundred New Churches*, pp. 37–43.
40 G.F.A. Best, *Temporal Pillars. Queen Anne's Bounty, the Ecclesiastical Commissioners*

Arguably the most important of these was 'An Act to make better provision for the spiritual care of populous parishes'[41] of 1843 (popularly known as Peel's District Churches Act). This permitted new districts to be created, unconsecrated places of worship to be licensed within existing parishes, and for clergy to be appointed and licensed (invariably a curate from the parish church) to serve the district. A variety of buildings, mostly church schools that were considered 'to be fit and proper for such a purpose',[42] were licensed for worship and became what are known today as church plants of the parish church. This provision permitted a congregation to become established long before a suitable site was obtained and sufficient funds raised for the erection of a permanent building. Such funds that were required might be obtained from wealthy landowners and benefactors, private supporters and parishioners, from the bishop, the dean and chapter and from grant-making bodies such as the Church Building Commissioners, the Incorporated Church Building Society and from the diocesan church building society.

From 1801 to 1851 the population of Newcastle increased from 28,294 to 87,784. Although the town[43] was extended in 1835 to include the growing suburbs of Byker, Elswick, Heaton, Jesmond and Westgate, it still only consisted of the four ancient parishes of St Nicholas, St John, All Saints and St Andrew. In May 1839 the Bishop of Durham (Edward Maltby) wrote to the Ecclesiastical Commissioners. 'I have no doubt that the peculiar situation of Newcastle must have attracted your observation. A very numerous population, with an inadequate number of churches, and comparatively few ministers, who with all their zeal (to which I gladly bear witness) cannot supply the spiritual wants of the people.'[44] Gradually new districts were formed, more churches and chapels were erected and finally new parishes were created. The needs of Newcastle were considerable, but examples of the sequence of district, the provision

---

and the Church of England (Cambridge, 1964), p. 355. These particular Church Building Acts are conveniently listed in Port, *Six Hundred New Churches*, p. 363, with the surprising omission of 'An Act to make better provision for the spiritual care of populous parishes' of 1843 (6 and 7 Vic. c.37).

41 6 and 7 Vic. c.37. Port, *Six Hundred New Churches*, p. 261.
42 6 and 7 Vic. c.37, paragraph xiii.
43 The city of Newcastle upon Tyne was not created until 1882.
44 Church of England Record Centre, St Paul's church, High Elswick, 15977, letter from the Bishop of Durham to the Ecclesiastical Commissioners, 11 May 1839.

of a place of worship and then the creation of a new parish are found throughout the diocese.

Although successive bishops of Durham were acutely aware that more church accommodation was required, their response to the situation was varied. William Van Mildert,[45] who was the Bishop of Durham from 1826 to 1836, was reluctant to license 'schoolrooms and other unconsecrated buildings for the purpose of public worship'.[46] Such places, he maintained, lacked solemnity and reverence and lowered public respect for the Church of England. He much preferred the erection of what he called 'auxiliary chapels' of the simplest sort that were 'set apart exclusively for the Church of England service'.[47] But his successors were less concerned about such niceties and were prepared to recognise the value of using church schools and former nonconformist chapels to accommodate Anglican worshippers. For example, in Sunderland a former Presbyterian chapel in Spring Garden Lane became an Episcopal Chapel (**22.10**) and a former Independent chapel became a chapel of ease to Monkwearmouth (**22.6**). In the widespread parish of Lanchester (**16.15**), three schoolrooms were licensed to serve the outlying areas (**16.16–18**) and in South Shields two former Methodist chapels (**20.10–11**) were licensed, to enable the incumbent 'to do good to the colliery population' (**20.10**). In the hamlet of Mordon, Sedgefield, a room in a farmhouse was licensed for worship (**21.10**). While these venues were only temporary places of worship in many cases they anticipated the erection of permanent buildings. While these unconsecrated buildings were licensed for 'divine service' this did not generally include the administration of the sacraments of baptism and communion,[48] which would continue to take place in the parish church. For convenience the bishop often granted a licence to permit worship to take place in a completed church or chapel some months before it was consecrated. This meant that there was no delay in using a newly erected

---

45 'William Van Mildert (1765–1836)', *ODNB*, vol. 38, pp. 112–114.
46 W. Van Mildert, *A Charge delivered to the Clergy of the Diocese of Durham, 1827* (Oxford, 1828), p. 10.
47 W. Van Mildert, *A Charge delivered to the Clergy of the Diocese of Durham, 1831* (Oxford, 1831), pp. 10, 11.
48 Fees for conducting weddings and funerals were part of the income of the incumbent (and are included in Church of England entries in this publication under 'endowment'). The fees would continue to be paid to the incumbent from a district within his parish, but once a new parish was created he would have to be compensated for loss of fee income.

building before the bishop was in a position to conduct the consecration service. In addition there were also a number of unlicensed places of worship that were intended only to be used for a limited period before other arrangements could be made. In the 1820s only fifteen new churches were erected in the diocese, but the position improved after the Durham Diocesan Church Building Society was formed in September 1827. During the episcopate of Edward Maltby (1836–56)[49] sixty new churches were erected and consecrated, the details of many of which were included in the Religious Census returns. But once the findings of the Census were known it became all too obvious that there was still a pressing need to provide more church accommodation.

The number of Anglican churches consecrated
from 1801 to 1880[50]

1801–10	3
1811–20	7
1821–30	16
1831–40	24
1841–50	39
1851–60	24
1861–70	57
1871–80	55

Bishop Maltby was particularly proactive in the erection of new churches, and in the provision of housing and improved stipends for his clergy. As the diocesan bishop he had assigned thousands of pounds from his large income for 'the building and repairing of churches and parsonage-houses, [and] to giving assistance in establishing schools'.[51] Grants towards the provision of new parsonage houses were provided from the Maltby Fund[52] and authorised by the Ecclesiastical Commissioners. In seventeen years something like £221,900 had gone out from the diocese to the Commissioners and a total of £71,414 from the bishop's purse.

Alongside the diocesan bishops some of the parochial clergy were all too aware of what ought to be done, and were prepared to offer

---

49 'Edward Maltby (1770–1859)', *ODNB*, vol. 36, pp. 361–363.
50 See Appendix 1.
51 E. Maltby, *A Charge delivered to the Clergy of the Diocese of Durham at the Visitation in July and August 1853* (London, 1853), p. 19.
52 See Appendix 5.

their advice and to make recommendations. For John Collinson, the rector of Gateshead from 1810 to 1839, it was all too obvious that more church buildings were required and that the clergy should receive a sufficient stipend. 'The remuneration to the clergy in populous districts is very inadequate: people wish to have among them, and very rightly and laudably, gentlemen of good manners and sound learning as ministers of the gospel; but they will not obtain this supply of able men, unless more inducements are held out of a temporal independence; without which the office is degraded, and the clergyman becomes more the servant of those who choose to give or withhold his salary, than the minister of God and the ambassador of Christ.'[53] Traditionally, poorer clergy had received financial assistance from Queen Anne's Bounty[54] and later from the grant-awarding bodies, the one Evangelical (the Church Pastoral Aid Society, 1836) and the other High Church (the Additional Curates Society, 1837). To secure a reasonable stipend the Peel district clergy received a stipend of £130 a year, increased to £150 once a permanent church building had been erected.

Collinson's successor, John Davies, the rector of Gateshead from 1840 to 1861, pointed out the weakness of the Church of England in the five urban centres of Newcastle, Gateshead, North and South Shields and Sunderland[55] and set out the situation as he saw it. Newcastle, with a population of 72,000, had ten churches served by sixteen clergy; Gateshead, with a population of 15,000, had three churches (able to accommodate 2,000 people) and four clergy; North Shields, with a population of about 25,000 had three churches and four clergy; South Shields, with a population of 25,233, had four churches (able to accommodate 4,780 people) and four clergy; and Sunderland (together with Bishopwearmouth and Monkwearmouth) had a population of 56,107, with eight churches and chapels (able to accommodate 8,265 people) and twelve clergy. While Davies commended the provision of nonconformist places of worship, he

---

53 J. Collinson, *A Farewell Sermon, preached at Gateshead; in the chapel of the Holy Trinity, in the morning and in St Mary's Church, in the evening, on Sunday, 29 December 1839* (Newcastle, 1840), p. 14.

54 Best, *Temporal Pillars*, pp. 11–34. In 1948 the Church Commissioners were formed by the amalgamation of Queen Anne's Bounty (1704) and the Ecclesiastical Commissioners (1836). 'Church Commissioners', *ODCC*, p. 347.

55 J. Davies, *The Ministry of the Church Considered with Respects to its Influence on Society* (London, 1843), pp. 43–44.

was keen to promote the cause of the Church of England. 'I must be allowed to state it as my calm and deliberate conviction that no exertions on their part can compensate for the want of an adequate parochial and ecclesiastical provision.' He was convinced that the national church – 'an orthodox, scriptural and tolerant Church establishment like our own ... is, I am persuaded, the only system which affords any reasonable prospect of overtaking and subduing that torrent of moral evil, which is now so widely desolating our country'.[56] For Davies the solution was obvious: to erect more churches and chapels and to create new districts and parishes.

Two years before the Religious Census was conducted Davies published an open letter to Lord Shaftesbury on *The Subdivision and Re-arrangement of Parishes*.[57] Shaftesbury was a member of a Commission on the parochial system, and Davies responded to its questionnaire. He knew what he was talking about, since he had been the rector of Gateshead 'for nearly ten years, of a very populous parish, and as such having witnessed and felt the grievous evils and inconveniences of the existing state of things, not without some efforts to obviate them'. Taken as a whole in the diocese of Durham 'of which Newcastle and Gateshead may be regarded as the focus', there were also a few maritime and manufacturing towns where there was an inadequate number of churches, 'yet the counties of Durham and Northumberland generally by no means labour under an amount of spiritual destitution, equal of some of the other northern and midland counties'. Much good had been done in the growing towns of 'Newcastle, Gateshead, Sunderland, North and South Shields' and the adjoining parishes, by the respective incumbents with the support of Bishop Maltby and the Dean and Chapter of the cathedral. But still the provision in these towns only amounted to one sixth of the population, and in some cases to only one eighth. In a region with a population of about a quarter of a million people there were an insufficient number of churches and clergy, which meant that barely one half of the population could be accommodated in the Church of England. Within recent years 'a considerable number of chapels of ease have been built, served by curates, [and] paid by the incumbent of the mother church',[58] from the sacrificial giving of the clergy. Once

---

56 *Ibid.*, p. 43.
57 J. Davies, *The Subdivision and Re-arrangement of Parishes. A Letter addressed to the Right Honourable Lord Ashley MP* (London, 1849).
58 *Ibid.*, pp. 7, 20.

these churches had been erected, they should then be given a separate district and become independent of the mother church, able to receive the statutory parochial fees. Any loss of income to the incumbent of the mother church should be made up from another source, and where the parish church could afford to maintain a chapel of ease it should continue to be financially dependent upon the mother church.

The publication of the Religious Census challenged the Church of England to extend its influence by the erection of more churches and chapels and to appoint more clergy. In January 1860, and only months before he became the Archbishop of York, Charles Longley, who had been the Bishop of Durham from 1856, called a public meeting to establish the Durham Diocesan Society for the Employment of Additional Clergy. After he left the diocese little progress was made during the brief episcopate of his successor Henry Villiers (1860–61)[59] but under Charles Baring (1861–79)[60] over one hundred[61] new churches and chapels were erected or rebuilt and more clergy appointed.

In his Primary Charge of 1862,[62] Bishop Baring referred to the Religious Census, which had recommended that there should be accommodation for 58% of the population. Yet if only half of the population were able to be accommodated, this meant that in County Durham there should be sufficient room for 254,000 people and in Northumberland 171,000 people. But in the recent visitation returns made by the clergy it was revealed that there were only 72,068 sittings

---

59 'Henry Montagu Villiers (1813–1861)', *ODNB*, vol. 56, pp. 514–515.

60 'Charles Baring (1807–1879)', *ODNB*, vol. 3, pp. 818–819. He was described as 'a man of deep personal piety and of great kindness … his personal acts of charity, though done in secret were very numerous' p. 819.

61 Baring is credited with having been responsible for the erection of 119 churches, providing additional accommodation for 40,530 people at a cost of £363,830. (Anon.), *Biographical Sketch of the Late Bishop of Durham (the Rt Rev Charles Baring DD)* (Newcastle, 1879), reprinted from the *Newcastle Daily Journal*, 16 September 1879, p. 20. *ODNB*, vol. 3, p. 819.
    In Appendix 1 only *consecrated* churches are listed. As a general rule new churches rebuilt on the site of a demolished building were not re-consecrated (e.g. **7.5**). In addition to the consecrated buildings there were at least sixteen mission chapels and temporary iron churches. Also there were about 116 churches that were enlarged or restored at a cost of £167,878. By 1881 there were an estimated 118 chapels of ease, mission chapels and licensed rooms in the reduced diocese of Durham.

62 C. Baring, *A Charge delivered at his Primary Visitation of the Diocese, October 1862* (Durham, 1862).

available in Durham and 51,230 in Northumberland. 'In other words, throughout the whole diocese, out of every seven persons who ought to go to church, only two could find a sitting; and it would need the building of as many as 300 new churches, each of them containing 1,000 sittings, to supply to the full the present deficiency of church accommodation.'[63] There were still 76,000 people in Durham and 35,000 in Northumberland who had no place in which to worship. But, he said, this was only part of the problem. Pew rents reduced the seating capacity for the poor; and even where there was sufficient room, if the church was remotely situated, the distance from home and bad weather were factors that could discourage attendance. While the number of clergy had steadily increased there were still too few in the diocese. The average was one clergyman for every 2,400 people, whereas for the rest of England there was one clergyman for every 1,100 people. Baring noted that throughout the diocese the Census had revealed that the nonconformists had twice the amount of accommodation than was provided by the Church of England. He commended the accommodation provided by the nonconformists, for the deficiencies of the established church had been supplied by 'the praiseworthy efforts of the Wesleyans and other separatists'.[64] However, their efforts should provoke churchmen to greater zeal for 'we believe our doctrine and discipline to be more perfect and scriptural than theirs'.[65] The challenge to the Church of England was to accommodate a population that had doubled during the previous thirty years. While he recognised that it took time to raise funds to erect a new church, he knew too that the population had become more and more 'wholly estranged from the church of their fathers, and almost hopelessly confirmed in habits of vice and of profane contempt of all religious observances'.[66]

In December 1864 Baring launched his 'Special Church Building Fund' for 'the erection of new churches or mission chapels in new districts or populous parishes'.[67] From this fund forty-one new churches providing 13,851 free sittings were erected at a cost of £92,023, and with mission rooms, the accommodation increased from

63 *Ibid.*, p. 7.
64 *Ibid.*, p. 8.
65 *Ibid.*, p. 8.
66 *Ibid.*, p. 10.
67 *Durham Diocesan Calendar, Clergy List and Church Almanac* (Durham, 1873), p. 132. See also the *Diocesan Calendar* for 1878, pp. 162–164.

11,754 sittings in 1873 to 19,355 in 1883.[68] During the period 1862 to 1877, 116 new churches had been erected at a cost of £353,955, and a further £167,878 had been spent on the enlargement and restoration of churches in the diocese. Yet in spite of the determination of Bishop Baring to provide more churches and chapels it was still impossible to keep pace with the rising population. 'A comparison of the decennial periods will show that church extension has failed to keep pace with the enormous growth of population, and that the proportion of sittings in our churches to people in the diocese has steadily decreased from one in four in the first and second decades of the century, to one in five in the third and fourth, one in six in the fifth and sixth, one in seven in the seventh and eighth, until in the beginning of the ninth decade the lowest point of one in eight is reached.'[69] Following the division of the diocese in 1882 appeals were made to raise funds to erect twenty-five additional churches in the diocese of Durham, and twelve in the diocese of Newcastle.

Old Dissent

Historically 'Old Dissent' included the Presbyterians,[70] Independents,[71] Baptists,[72] Unitarians[73] and the Society of Friends,[74] and the Religious Census revealed that there were about one hundred such places of worship in Northumberland and seventy in County Durham. This was far fewer than the Methodist family of churches, which had about 350 places of worship in County Durham and just under 200 in Northumberland.

The eighteenth-century Evangelical revival or awakening was not confined to what are known as the newly created 'Methodist' churches.[75] 'It was a movement of the spirit that affected churches and individuals without respect for denominational distinctions.'[76] Alongside this there had been a rejuvenation of Presbyterianism, the seeding of the Scottish Secession Church in Northumberland, and

---

68   F. Burnside (ed.), *The Official Yearbook of the Church of England 1885* (London, 1885), pp. 15–18.
69   *Ibid.*, p. 18.
70   'Presbyterian', *ODCC*, pp. 1322–1323.
71   'Independent', *ODCC*, pp. 399–400, 826.
72   'Baptist', *ODCC*, pp. 154–155.
73   'Unitarian', *ODCC*, pp. 1659–1660.
74   'Society of Friends', *ODCC*, pp. 642–643.
75   D.W. Bebbington, *Evangelicalism in Modern Britain* (London, 1989), pp. 27–34.
76   R.T. Jones, *Congregationalism in England 1662–1962* (London, 1962), p. 146.

the opening of a Secession church in Newcastle in 1744.[77] By 1836 there were six presbyteries in Northumberland and the movement was further extended after 1843 following the Disruption in Scotland when 474 ministers left the Church of Scotland and formed the Free Church of Scotland.[78] This schism also had an impact south of the border and a number of new congregations were established or existing ones divided and established elsewhere. From 1844 the Presbyterian Church *in* England became the usual title for those English Presbyterian churches in fellowship with the Church of Scotland, and in 1847 the United Presbyterian Church was formed from the union of two earlier schisms within the Church of Scotland. In the Religious Census there were sixty-five Presbyterian churches in Northumberland[79] and fourteen in County Durham.[80] The Census figures confirm the observation that 'Northumberland has long been the most Presbyterian county in England'.[81]

In the north-east there were far fewer Independent or Congregational chapels, and in the Religious Census only fifteen were recorded in Northumberland and twenty-six in County Durham. Congregationalism was stronger in the urban areas, and in Bishopwearmouth, Monkwearmouth and Sunderland there were six Independent congregations (**22.16–21**). It may well be that where there were few Independents their needs could be satisfied within Presbyterianism.

The Religious Census recorded three Unitarian chapels in Northumberland and three in County Durham. The largest Unitarian chapel was in Newcastle with an average attendance of 460 and with a Sunday school of over 100 children (**10.50**) and the second was in Bishopwearmouth with an average evening congregation of 200 (**22.70**). In the 1770s part of the congregation of the Baptist Chapel in Tuthill Stairs, Newcastle (**10.21**), adopted Unitarian beliefs and from 1788 worshipped in a chapel in Pandon Bank. In 1797 these Unitarian Baptists merged with the Hanover Square congregation.

---

77 A.H. Drysdale, *History of the Presbyterians in England. Their Rise, Decline and Revival* (London, 1889), pp. 567–579.

78 'Disruption', *ODCC*, pp. 489–499.

79 Church of Scotland (7), United Presbyterian (29) and English Presbyterian (29). Throughout England and Wales there were Church of Scotland (18), United Presbyterian (66) and English Presbyterian (76).

80 United Presbyterian (10) and English Presbyterian (4).

81 Drysdale, *Presbyterians in England*, p. 567. In a footnote Drysdale adds that in 1889 there were seventy Presbyterian congregations in the county.

The congregation attending the Unitarian chapel in Stockton-on-Tees (**21.67**) had declined because there was no minister to lead it.

There were thirty-seven Baptist congregations in the two counties, sixteen of which were in Northumberland (with six in Newcastle). In the rest of the county there was a Baptist chapel in Berwick upon Tweed and four in the Tyne Valley. In County Durham there were twenty-one Baptist chapels, with a concentration of six of them in Monkwearmouth, Bishopwearmouth and Sunderland. The Baptist congregation at Maling's Rigg, Sunderland met in a large room over a public house and butcher's shop (**22.26**).

One of the Baptist chapels in Sunderland was led by Arthur Augustus Rees (1814–1884)[82] who had seceded from the Church of England.[83] He trained for ordination at St David's College, Lampeter, where a fellow student, who later became his brother-in- law, was Henry James Prince.[84] Rees was ordained deacon and priest in 1841 and became a curate to William Webb, the rector of Sunderland. When Rees' powerful extempore preaching attracted large congregations the incumbent and the bishop tried unsuccessfully to curtail his activities, and so he was given three months notice to leave. Immediately 1,400 parishioners signed a petition in his favour and they urged him to remain in Sunderland. However, he soon left the town and briefly settled in Bath, and after several bishops refused to offer him preferment he turned from Anglicanism to nonconformity. In March 1844 he returned to Sunderland, and having been left a legacy from his father, erected the Bethesda Free Chapel (**22.23**). In the following year the autocratic and 'somewhat eccentric' Rees was re-baptised by George Muller, the Christian Brethren leader of Bristol.[85] On the day of the Religious Census the morning congregation at Bethesda was 550 and the evening 1,000, making it one of the largest nonconformist congregations in County Durham.

By the time of the Religious Census the Society of Friends (the Quakers) had only four meeting houses in Northumberland and eight in County Durham. The largest congregations were in Newcastle,

82 W. Brockie, *Sunderland Notables: Natives, Residents and Visitors* (Sunderland, 1894), pp. 439–449.

83 For the background to the secessionists, see G. Carter, *Anglican Evangelicals. Protestant Secessions from the Via Media, c.1800–1850* (Oxford, 2001).

84 'Henry James Prince (1811–1899)', *ODNB*, vol. 45, pp. 390–391. Later Prince became the leader of the bizarre sect based in Spaxton, near Bridgwater, Somerset, known as the Church of the Agapemone or Abode of Love.

85 H.H. Rowdon, *The Origins of the Brethren, 1825–1850* (London, 1967), p. 173.

with 207 members present in the morning and 112 in the afternoon (**10.46**), and Bishopwearmouth, with 136 in the morning and 93 in the afternoon (**22.68**). The rural congregations were very small. At Coanwood, Haltwhistle, there were only twelve people at the only service of the day (**7.26**) and at Wooley, Allendale, the meeting house could accommodate 300 people, but on Census day only nine people were present for the morning service (**8.95**).[86] A particular stronghold of the Society of Friends was in Darlington, but no Census return was recorded or survived for that meeting house.[87] Although the Society of Friends was a small denomination it included a number of influential members who were prominent bankers, businessmen and entrepreneurs,[88] of whom the Pease family of Darlington were part of that 'glittering superstructure of great industrialists and financiers' who were part of the upper class in society.[89]

New Dissent

Historically 'New Dissent' was represented mostly by the Methodists,[90] the Countess of Huntingdon's Connexion[91] and by the Calvinistic Methodists.[92] Nationally there was a steady increase in the number of Methodists and this continued even after the numerous schisms following the death of John Wesley and well into the nineteenth century. Within Methodism the main bodies were the Methodist New Connexion (1797),[93] the Primitive Methodists (1811),[94] the Bible Christians (1815),[95] the Wesleyan Methodist Association (1835) and the Wesleyan Reformers (1849).[96]

---

86 In Yorkshire there were also few worshippers, giving 'graphic evidence of the decline of rural and small town Quakerism'. Wolffe, *The Religious Census of 1851*, p. 24.

87 By 1870 there were just under 400 members of the Society of Friends in Darlington. M.W. Kirby, *Men of Business and Politics* (London, 1984), p. 71.

88 E.H. Milligan, *British Quakers in Commerce and Industry 1775–1920* (York, 2007).

89 Kirby, *Men of Business and Politics*, p. 53.

90 'Methodist Churches', *ODCC*, pp. 1077–1079.

91 'Selina, Countess of Huntingdon', *ODCC*, p. 806.

92 'Calvinistic Methodists', *ODCC*, p. 269.

93 'Methodist New Connexion', *ODCC*, pp. 1079–1088.

94 'Primitive Methodist', *ODCC*, p. 1328.

95 'Bible Christian', *ODCC*, p. 204.

96 These factions, together with other smaller groups, were brought together through a series of unions – the United Methodist Free Churches (1857), the United Methodist Church (1907) and finally, the Methodist Church of Great Britain (1932). *ODCC*, pp. 1660–1661, 1077–1079.

In 1790 the total Methodist membership in England was 55,705 and in the next forty years the number rose to 285,530.[97] This steady expansion was reflected in the north-east, and the growth is evident in the number of places of worship that were opened during the decade 1820 to 1830. Such was the appeal of Methodism that members would walk twenty miles to attend services, and in the highly charged atmosphere there were 'deep emotions, loud responses, and sometimes faintings and convulsions, attended the preaching and other religious services among the pitmen'.[98] In the 1840s in the area between Hexham and Tynemouth the Wesleyan Methodists had thirty-eight chapels within half a mile of the banks of the River Tyne. This steady expansion of Methodism was the outcome of the eighteenth-century awakening and it continued well into the following century through a succession of religious revivals. For example, John Wesley[99] described a powerful awakening having taken place in Weardale in June 1772,[100] and fifty years later in the same locality a Primitive Methodist revival took place following the conversion of John Muschamp (**24.24**). So many people were being converted that one observer remarked that 'I think all the people in Weardale are going to be Ranters [Primitive Methodists].'[101] Not untypically, at Bowless in 1851, a revival took place over the course of thirteen weeks.[102]

Primitive Methodism arrived in Sunderland in 1822; a year later 6,000 people attended an open-air 'camp meeting'.[103] In just over a year there were 400 members in Sunderland and Monkwearmouth, and the circuit grew from 1,674 members in 1825 to 6,169 in 1849. Sunderland became an important Primitive Methodist centre. The annual conference was held there in 1825, 1833, 1849, 1868 and 1890, and in 1868 the former infirmary became the Sunderland Theological Institute.[104]

---

97   D. Hempton, *Methodism. Empire of the Spirit* (New Haven, CT, 2005), p. 109.
98   W.M. Patterson, *Northern Primitive Methodism* (London, 1909), p. 310.
99   'John Wesley (1703–1791)', *ODNB*, vol. 58, pp. 182–193.
100 J. Wesley, *The Journal of the Rev John Wesley* (London, 1906), vol. 3, pp. 473–481.
101 Patterson, *Northern Primitive Methodism*, p. 159.
102 For revivals in Weardale, see D. Bebbington, *Victorian Religious Revivals* (Oxford, 2012).
103 Patterson, *Northern Primitive Methodism*, pp. 242–243.
104 *Ibid.*, pp. 242–264.

Wesleyan Methodism prospered, according to its leader Jabez Bunting,[105] by 'repentance towards God, faith in our Lord Jesus Christ, a penny a week and a shilling a quarter'.[106] In other words, the movement was committed to evangelism and to the growth of the Kingdom of God, and the experience of conversion could touch the hearts of all classes. In Hatcase, Sunderland, the small congregation of New Connexion Methodists met in a room in a house. 'In this place we have had services almost every night in the week and sum (*sic*) much good done among abandoned characters, reclaimed and brought to God, and are now good citizens and Christians united to the Christian church, about 100 which some have join[ed] other churches' (**22.48**). Methodism had a particular appeal among the working classes and a number of the local leaders came from humble backgrounds and included farmers, grocers, drapers, butchers, shoemakers and blacksmiths. Few Wesleyan Methodist leaders were coal miners but many more were farmers, grocers and drapers. However, among the Primitive Methodists there were about the same numbers of coal miners, farmers, grocers and drapers.[107] Some chapels, such as at East Hetton (**16.48, 76**), Shotton (**17.28**) and Usworth (**14.25, 34**), were actually located in the colliery buildings where the preachers and stewards were employed. Other classes were also active within Methodism, and the Wesleyan Methodist leadership in County Durham included one gentleman, one landed proprietor, three proprietors of houses and five schoolmasters.

It was the fairly common practice for a small congregation to begin meeting together in a room of a private house or schoolroom, then, as the membership increased and funds became available, a modest chapel was erected and finally later in the century it was replaced by a larger and more commodious building. However, by that time, when across the nation chapel attendance was in decline, these larger chapels were opened in debt and the decreasing membership would have found it difficult to pay their way.[108] After the disparate Meth-

---

105 'Jabez Bunting (1779–1858)', *ODNB*, vol. 8, pp. 696–698.
106 M. Braithwaite, *History of Methodism in the Bishop Auckland Circuit* (Bishop Auckland, 1885), p. 177.
107 From the Religious Census returns, out of the 131 Wesleyan Methodist leaders in County Durham there were 16 farmers, 28 grocers and drapers and 12 coal miners; and of 66 Primitive Methodists there were 6 farmers, 7 grocers and drapers and 12 coal miners. In Northumberland the leadership was diverse and no one occupation dominated the rest.
108 Gill, *Myth of the Empty Church*, pp. 77, 89–90.

odist churches were gradually united there was a surplus of chapels and those not required were sold and the buildings put to a variety of secular uses.

There were significant differences in the leadership style and ethos of the various Methodist bodies, reflected in what was said concerning 'the tyranny of [the] Wesleyan ministers' (**12.69**) compared with the less authoritarian stance adopted by the leaders of the Methodist New Connexion (**12.49**). The contemporary tensions within Methodism were particularly evident with the creation of the Wesleyan Reformers in 1849, and within only two years of the division nineteen places of worship were recorded in Northumberland and seven in County Durham. Former long-standing Wesleyans left that denomination over ministerial heavy-handedness and became Reformers. In Shildon, the Wesleyan Methodist Association chapel had been well attended, but by March 1851 it was reported that 'owing to schism in the church the chapel has nearly been deserted' and only twenty-five worshippers remained (**13.57**).

However, there was not always bitter rivalry between the different factions and there are a some examples of co-operation between the Wesleyans and the Primitives – at Heathery Cleugh (**24.16, 29**), Rupells Houses (**14.22, 33**), Washington Row (**14.27, 35**) and in the collieries at East Hetton (**16.48, 76**) and Usworth (**14.27, 35**). There were also instances where Methodists shared facilities, as at Monkwearmouth Colliery where the Wesleyan Reformers shared with the Primitives (**22.53, 64**); at Monkwearmouth Shore where the Wesleyans shared with Baptists (**22.25, 44**); and at Acomb the Wesleyans shared premises with the Independents (**8.29, 55**).

Two major disruptions within Methodism took place in the northeast, both of which had a profound effect upon the wider movement. One Methodist protagonist, Alexander Kilham,[109] was an outspoken critic of centralism and clerical control and his direct criticism of John Wesley so soon after the founder's death in 1791 did not endear him to his fellow Methodists. When he was stationed at Alnwick he formulated his ideas and published them in 1795 as *The Progress of Liberty amongst the people called Methodists*. The outcome was a three-day examination in Newcastle, followed by his expulsion from the Methodist Conference, after which he formed the Methodist New Connexion in 1797. After his death the following year, the movement

---

109 'Alexander Kilham (1762–1798)', *ODNB*, vol. 31, pp. 546–547.

continued under the leadership of his co-founder, William Thom.[110] The consequence of the schism was evident in Alnwick, where there was an immediate decline in membership of the Wesleyan Methodist chapel (**1.23, 28**).

In the 1840s there was a considerable disruption within the Methodist New Connexion. Joseph Barker,[111] who had served as a minister in the Connexion in Newcastle 1831–32, Sunderland 1832–33 and Gateshead 1839–41, was expelled in 1841 over his increasingly unorthodox theological views. The outcome of his expulsion was the loss to the denomination of twenty-nine societies and 4,348 members. In Newcastle, in August 1845, a ten-day debate took place between Barker (who by then had returned to the town) and William Cooke,[112] an orthodox New Connexion minister. Barker was an immensely popular speaker and a prolific writer who became increasingly radical in his views and gained support from Quakers and Unitarians. In later life he returned to a more orthodox faith. Locally, a number of New Connexion chapels in Newcastle and North Shields were influenced by Barker's teaching and some members became 'Barkerites' and identified with him, while others left and transferred their membership to other Methodist chapels and even joined the Church of England. The Methodist New Connexion congregation at Wallsend was split by Barker's views (**12.51**), and at Alnwick the membership was divided when some of them left and formed a Unitarian congregation (**1.31**). In South Shields, Academy Hill chapel had been 'occupied by Chartists, Socialists and Barkerites' and had been 'the resort of itinerant orators and leaders of mischievous sects, religious and political' before the incumbent of Holy Trinity church acquired it for Anglican use (**20.11**).

In the Religious Census eleven non-denominational congregations are listed in the north-east. Four of them were missions for sailors and were situated in the seaports of Newcastle (**10.45**), Monkwearmouth (**22.66**), Sunderland (**22.67**) and Stockton on Tees (**21.61**). One congregation was associated with the Town Mission in Berwick

---

110 'William Thom (1751–1811)', in J.A. Vickers, *A Dictionary of Methodism in Britain and Ireland* (Peterborough, 2000), p. 348.

111 'Joseph Barker (1806–1875)', *ODNB*, vol. 3, pp. 885–887.

112 'William Cooke (1806–1884)', in Vickers, *Dictionary of Methodism*, p. 79. Cooke wrote over sixty books, most notably his *Christian Theology* (1846). Three times (1843, 1859 and 1869) he was elected as president of the Methodist New Connexion conference. T. Larsen, *A People of One Book. The Bible and the Victorians* (Oxford, 2011), pp. 91–100.

upon Tweed (**4.32**), but there is no reference to the Newcastle Town Mission (began in 1846) or to the Hartlepool Town Mission (began in 1848) that had a congregation of 300 made up mostly of sailors and their families. In the 1840s the missionaries worked alongside the mainstream denominations and had no established congregations or chapels of their own (**10.45, 21.61**).

The Christian Brethren movement began in the late 1820s and in 1849 it divided into the Exclusive Brethren, under the autocratic leadership of John Nelson Darby, and the Open Brethren (usually known as the Christian or Plymouth Brethren).[113] In the north-east the Religious Census revealed that there was at least one congregation associated with the Brethren. At West Holborn, South Shields, the 'Bristol Brethren' met in the old railway station and had a congregation of upwards of 200 people (**20.47**). Other possible Brethren congregations were at Willington Quay (**12.78**), Howdon (**12.77**) and Bishopwearmouth (**22.65**), where they were called the 'Disciples of Jesus Christ'. The movement continued to grow and thirty years later in 1881 there was a congregation of 140 Plymouth Brethren in Gateshead.[114]

Roman Catholic[115]

By the mid-eighteenth century there were some 2,733 Roman Catholics living in County Durham and 2,159 in Northumberland, and the numbers were inflated during the French Revolution when hundreds of Roman Catholic priests sought sanctuary in the north-east. There were an estimated 150 to 200 French priests living in Sunderland and over 100 in Berwick upon Tweed, and 'on one day, 5 October 1796, 295 clergy were landed at Shields'.[116] The next influx came in the 1840s when large numbers of Irish fled from the effects of the potato famine, and men were employed as labourers in the construction of the canals, railways and ports. In Cambo the Anglican incumbent

---

113 'Plymouth Brethren', *ODCC*, pp. 1302–1303. A Brethren historian has concluded that 'the most morbid strains of Darby's teachings, isolated and exaggerated, reached their over-ripe maturity in those developments, which took the teaching of this exclusive group far from the paths of normal Christianity orthodoxy'. R. Coad, *A History of the Brethren Movement* (Exeter, 1968), pp. 212–213.

114 See Appendix 7.

115 'Roman Catholic', *ODCC*, pp. 1407–1409.

116 D. Bellenger, 'The French Exiled Clergy in the North of England', *Arch. Ael.*, fifth series, x (1982), p. 170. J. Bossy, *The English Catholic Community 1570–1850* (London, 1975), pp. 295–365.

reported that 'some Irish are temporarily employed in draining' (**9.4**). In October 1850 it was reported that the collieries around Thornley employed 'a vast number of Irishmen and it is an important fact that from their extensive numbers they are likely to become a very formidable and important portion of the workmen in the coalfield of Durham'.[117] In the period 1841 to 1851 something like 400,000 Irish came into Britain, and the Civil Census recorded that there were 12,666 Irish-born persons living in Northumberland and 18,501 in County Durham.[118] By 1861 there were 42,000 living in the north-east. The Irish community in the north-east was the fourth largest in the country after Lancashire, London and Yorkshire.[119]

Provision was made for the training of priests in 1808 when Ushaw College near Durham was opened (**16.90**), and the creation of the Roman Catholic diocese of Hexham in 1850 strengthened the position of the church in the region and gave it a greater prominence than before. William Hogarth,[120] who had taught at Ushaw, became the parish priest in Darlington in 1823 and was the last vicar apostolic of the Northern district in 1848, before the hierarchy was restored in 1850, when he became the first Bishop of Hexham. Robert Suffield, the parish priest of Thornley and Sedgefield, made reference to the new situation when he referred to 'certain hierarchical arrangements' that were being made (**21.65**).

In the Religious Census twenty Roman Catholic places of worship were recorded in County Durham, and nineteen in Northumberland.[121] There were an estimated 10,000[122] Roman Catholics living in Newcastle, 6,000 of whom were served by one priest based at St Andrew's, Pilgrim Street (**10.47**). In his congregation there were

117 M. Morris and L. Gooch, *Down your Aisles. The Diocese of Hexham and Newcastle 1850–2000* (Hartlepool, 2000), p. 12.
118 F. Neal, 'The Foundations of the Irish Settlement in Newcastle upon Tyne: The Evidence of the 1851 Census', in D.M. MacRaild (ed.), *The Great Famine and Beyond* (Dublin, 2000), p. 73.
119 *Ibid.*, p. 72.
120 'William Hogarth (1786–1866)', *ODNB*, vol. 27, pp. 555–556.
121 The membership numbers given here are from the Religious Census returns; they vary from the figures given for 1852 in R. Cooter, *When Paddy met Geordie. The Irish in County Durham and Newcastle 1840–1880* (Sunderland, 2005), p. 178.
122 In the 1851 Civil Census there were 7,152 Irish-born Roman Catholics living in Newcastle, 57% of of whom lived in the All Saints' district. Neal, 'The Foundations of the Irish Settlement', pp. 75, 90.

1,000 labourers with families back in Ireland.[123] The church was well attended, and at the morning Masses there was an attendance of 1,389 adults together with a Sunday school of 300 children. Most of the 3,000 Roman Catholics living in Gateshead were 'either Irish born or born of I[rish] parents' (**18.64**). There were various temporary places of worship until St Joseph's church was opened in July 1859. In Durham there were an estimated 1,220 Roman Catholics, and since there was insufficient accommodation in St Cuthbert's Chapel, Old Elvet, many of them did not attend Sunday Mass (**16.88**). The Anglican clergy reported that there were a large number of Roman Catholics living at Coniscliffe (**15.2**) and at Collierley (**16.4**), while at Esh 'the greater part of the land in the parish belongs to Roman Catholics' (**16.14**).

Jews,[124] Swedenborgians and Latter-day Saints[125]

In the Religious Census four synagogues were recorded: in Newcastle (**10.49**) and North Shields (**12.82**), Bishopwearmouth (**22.71**) and Sunderland (**22.72**). Sunderland had one of the earliest Jewish communities in the north-east, and Jews first settled there in 1768 and opened a synagogue in 1781.[126] This was known as the 'Polish' synagogue and in 1821 a break-away congregation formed an 'Israelite' synagogue. The difference between them was that the second was more observant and less anglicised than the first. While the Jewish community in Sunderland was 'small but vigorous'[127] it could not sustain two places of worship and the Polish synagogue, already in decline, closed soon after the Religious Census was conducted. When a new synagogue was opened in Sunderland in 1862 there were about 250 Jews living in the area.[128]

The tiny denomination associated with the eccentric Swedish-born Count Emmanuel Swedenborg[129] had only fifty congregations

---

123 In Newcastle, 44% of the Irish migrants were born in the counties of Roscommon, Sligo, Mayo and Galway. Neal, 'The Foundations of the Irish Settlement', p. 90.

124 'Judaism', *ODCC*, pp. 905–907.

125 'Mormons', *ODCC*, pp. 1115–1116.

126 L. Olsover, *The Jewish Communities of North-East England 1755–1980* (Sunderland, 1981), p. 13.

127 B. Susser, 'The Nineteenth-century Constitution of the Sunderland Congregation', *Transactions of the Jewish Historical Society*, 40 (2005), p. 13.

128 In Gateshead (now an important centre of Judaism) the first synagogue was opened in 1883.

129 'Emmanuel Swedenborg (1688–1772)', *ODCC*, pp. 1563–1564.

throughout the country, and only one in the north-east. The followers opened their New Jerusalem Temple in Newcastle in February 1823 and on the day of the Religious Census there were seventy people in the congregation (**10.52**). By 1881 this place of worship had closed. The Count created his own blend of philosophy and Christianity but the movement never gained a large following. After reading his works John Wesley observed that Swedenborg was 'one of the most ingenious, lively, entertaining madmen that ever set pen to paper'.[130]

The Church of Jesus Christ of the Latter-day Saints (usually known as the Mormons) began their English mission in Liverpool in 1837.[131] Initially the Mormon missionaries had no particular plan of campaign and their message was randomly spread by their adherents. Isaac Russell, who was born in Alston, emigrated to Canada and after becoming a Mormon returned to Alston and, much to the ire of the local clergy, gained a few converts.[132] In his introduction to the Census Horace Mann drew attention to the fact that the 222 Mormon places of worship were open for worship in the morning, afternoon and evening, which, when compared with other denominations, 'is much above the average frequency of service'.[133] Furthermore, 'the preachers, it appears, are far from unsuccessful in their efforts to obtain disciples: the surprising confidence and zeal with which they promulgate their creed ... have combined to give the Mormon movement a position and importance with the working classes, which, perhaps, should draw to it much more than it has yet received of the attention of our public teachers'.[134]

In the north-east, as elsewhere, Mormon missionaries initially preached in the open-air and then gathered a congregation together. At Earsdon, near North Shields, where the congregation that began in 1850 met in a converted stable, there was a Sunday attendance of from 20 to 50, with a monthly attendance of 180 (**12.83**). At Bedlington a former Baptist chapel was occupied by the Mormons, with an attendance of between 21 and 38 adults (**9.36**). Further south there were Mormon congregations at Westoe, South Shields with an attendance of between 11 and 41 adults (**20.49**) and at Hartlepool

---

130 Wesley, *Journal*, vol. 3, p. 395.
131 V.B. Bloxham, J.R. Moss and L.C. Porter (eds.), *Truth will Prevail. The Rise of the Church of Jesus Christ of Latter-day Saints in the British Isles 1837–1987* (Solihull, 1987), p. 71.
132 *Ibid.*, pp. 82–83, 117.
133 *Religious Worship. England and Wales*, p. cxlviii.
134 *Ibid.*, p. cxi.

there was an attendance of some 30 to 40 adults (**21.68**). Later in the 1850s Mormons are known to have been active in Newcastle and in Stockton on Tees, and in 1866 they were meeting in Bishopwear-mouth.

CONCLUSION

Writing to *The Times* in July 1861, Horace Mann said that the Religious Census of 1851 had never intended to 'attempt to enumerate the adherents to each denomination' but it was to ascertain first, 'the amount of provision for public worship available throughout the land', and second, 'the extent to which this available provision was made use of … The Census was a census of religious worship, and the compiler therefore confined himself strictly to a statement of the provision for worship, and the number of worshippers on a given day.' Mann believed that the Census was 'both accurate and complete within its professed scope' and that any accusations of falsehood and deliberate misrepresentation were ludicrous. It remained 'a faithful representation of the religious condition of the people, so far that can be represented by attendance upon public worship'.[135] That alone is sufficient justification for us today in using the information recorded in the Census.

Of course it is necessary for us to be wary about comparing the findings of the Religious Census with the number of people who attend a place of worship today. Then church- and chapel-going was often a matter of custom and conformity. Today personal belief and religious practice are probably better connected than they were, and what is believed by individuals is now more closely expressed in their active participation in public worship. The published figures challenge the popular myth that in the past 'the churches were always full'. The detailed returns made for the Census prove that this was certainly not the case and many churches and chapels were more than half empty. In both urban and rural situations some congregations were quite small and then, as now, the Christian church struggled to engage with the local community. Churches were built for potential congregations and with the expectation that a building would attract a congregation. But clearly this was not the case and Robin Gill concludes that following the 1851 Religious Census the Church of England Sunday attendances were in decline, and that

---

135 *The Times*, 11 July 1861.

nonconformity was in 'continuous decline' from the 1880s.[136] In his detailed examination of the Church of England in Newcastle, he found that although the Sunday attendances had *increased* from 12,703 in 1851 to 18,973 in 1887, the percentage of the population attending the Church of England had *decreased* from 14.2% in 1851 to 10.8% in 1887.[137]

John Wolffe has observed that it is crucial to appreciate that the Census is not portraying 'a static picture, but as vividly illuminating a single day in a religious landscape that was in reality changing rapidly week by week, season by season and year by year'.[138] The Methodist historian Geoffrey Milburn concluded that 'the Census is unique … it was taken at an important moment in the evolution of English society and at a time when religion was one of the prime social forces … it stands as a magnificent piece of evidence for a fuller understanding of the strength and deployment of the churches in mid-Victorian England'.[139]

---

136 Gill, *Myth of the Empty Church*, p. 76.
137 *Ibid.*, pp. 85–86, 142, 312.
138 Wolffe, *The Religious Census of 1851*, p. 28.
139 G.E. Milburn, 'The Census of Worship of 1851', *Durham County Local History Society*, 17 (1974), p. 11.

CENSUS OF GREAT BRITAIN, 1851.
(13 & 14 Victoriæ, Cap. 53.)

A RETURN of the several Particulars to be inquired into respecting the under-mentioned Church or Chapel in England, belonging to the United Church of England and Ireland.

A similar Return (*mutatis mutandis*) will be obtained with respect to Churches belonging to the Established Church in Scotland, and the Episcopal Church there, and also from Roman Catholic Priests, and from the Ministers of every other Religious Denomination throughout Great Britain, with respect to their Places of Worship.]

I.	NAME AND DESCRIPTION OF CHURCH OR CHAPEL.

II.	WHERE SITUATED.	Parish, Ecclesiastical Division or District, Township, or Place.	Superintendent Registrar's District.	County and Diocese.

III.	WHEN CONSECRATED OR LICENSED.	UNDER WHAT CIRCUMSTANCES CONSECRATED OR LICENSED.

IV. IN THE CASE OF A CHURCH OR CHAPEL CONSECRATED OR LICENSED SINCE THE 1st JANUARY 1800 ; STATE

HOW OR BY WHOM ERECTED.	COST, HOW DEFRAYED.
	By Parliamentary Grant - - - Parochial Rate - - - Private Benefaction or Subscription, or from other Sources - } Total Cost - - £

V.	VI.
HOW ENDOWED.	SPACE AVAILABLE FOR PUBLIC WORSHIP.
£ Land - - - Tithe - - - Glebe - - - Other Permanent Endowment - - } Pew Rents - - - Fees - - - Dues - - - Easter Offerings - - Other Sources - -	£ Free Sittings - - - Other Sittings - - - Total Sittings -

VII.

ESTIMATED NUMBER OF PERSONS ATTENDING DIVINE SERVICE ON SUNDAY, MARCH 30, 1851.				AVERAGE NUMBER OF ATTENDANTS during Months next preceding March 30, 1851. (See Instruction VII.)			
	Morning.	Afternoon.	Evening.		Morning.	Afternoon.	Evening.
General Congregation - } Sunday Scholars -				General Congregation - } Sunday Scholars -			
Total -				Total -			

VIII.	REMARKS.

I certify the foregoing to be a true and correct Return to the best of my belief.

Witness my hand this_____ day of_____ 1851.

IX. (*Signature*) _____

(*Official Character*) _____ *of the above-named.*

(*Address by Post*) _____

1. Census form for Church of England places of Worship
(Crown Copyright)

FORM B.

CENSUS OF GREAT BRITAIN, 1851.

(13 & 14 Victoriæ, Cap. 53.)

A RETURN of the several Particulars to be inquired into respecting the under-mentioned Place of Public Religious Worship.

[N.B.—A similar Return will be obtained from the Clergy of the Church of England, and also from the Ministers of every other Religious Denomination throughout Great Britain.]

I. Name or Title of Place of Worship.	II. Where situate; specifying the			III. Religious Denomination.	IV. When erected.	V. Whether a separate and entire Building.	VI. Whether used exclusively as a Place of Worship (except for a Sunday School).	VII. Space available for Public Worship.		VIII. Estimated Number of Persons attending Divine Service on Sunday March 30, 1851.			IX. REMARKS.
	Parish or Place.	District.	County.					Number of Sittings already provided.		Morning.	Afternoon.	Evening.	
	(1)	(2)	(3)					Free Sittings.	Other Sittings.				
								(4)	(5)	General Congregation } Sunday Scholars } TOTAL ·			
								Free Space or Standing Room for		Average Number of Attendants during the Months. (See Instruction VIII.) General Congregation } Sunday Scholars } TOTAL ·			

I certify the foregoing to be a true and correct Return to the best of my belief. Witness my hand this _____ day of _____ 1851.

I. (Signature) _____
(Official Character) _____
(Address by Post) _____ of the above-named Place of Worship.

The Particulars to be inserted in Divisions I. to VI. inclusive, and in IX., may be written either along or across the Columns, as may be more convenient.

2. Census form for Nonconformist, Roman Catholic and all other places of worship, apart from the Society of Friends (Crown Copyright)

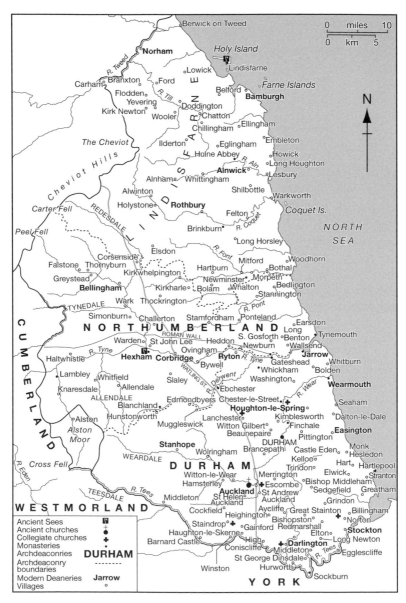

3. Map of the Diocese of Durham
Based on Map of Northumberland and Durham
(from J.L. Low, *Diocesan Histories. Durham* (London, 1881))

EDITORIAL METHOD

A number of counties have already published the returns of the Religious Census[1] and this volume concentrates on Northumberland and County Durham. In the other published returns of the Religious Census the editors have followed the order in which the documents were assembled in the districts and sub-districts, but there is no particular justification for listing the returns in this way, since it does not make it at all easy to locate places and denominations and to evaluate the material. When the denominations are separated it is not possible to make connections between those churches and chapels which have some common association. For these reasons the returns for Northumberland and County Durham have been rearranged. The twenty-four registration districts[2] are listed alphabetically for each county, and for each district the churches and chapels have been rearranged under the various denominations and roughly follow the order given in the Census: Church of England; Church of Scotland; Old Dissent (Presbyterian, Independent and Baptist); New Dissent (mainly Methodist) followed by non-denominational places of worship; Quakers, Roman Catholics and finally others such as Unitarians, Swedenborgians, Jews and Mormons. Places of worship are listed alphabetically, and those churches and chapels that have some obvious connection are put sequentially; for example, where there was the same clergyman or minister, chapels of ease attached to a parish church and chapels and places of worship within the same Methodist circuit are grouped together.

In the original returns it is not always possible to identify the precise location and, in some instances, the denomination of partic-

---

1   These are helpfully listed in C.D. Field, 'The 1851 Religious Census of Great Britain: a Bibliographical Guide for Local and Regional Historians', *The Local Historian*, vol. 27, no. 4 (November 1997), pp. 194–217; J. Wolffe (ed.), *Yorkshire Returns of the 1851 Census of Religious Worship* (York, 2000), vol. 1, p ii; and http://www.brin.ac.uk/ British Religion in Numbers, recent publications on the 1851 Religious Census of England and Wales (accessed November 2011).

2   The registration districts were the same as the existing Poor Law Unions.

ular places of worship, but these details have been found, and the titles are in bold type along with a new reference number. After the title the number from the original returns is given (and may be located in the index of districts and sub-districts). In the nineteenth century the dedications of some parish churches were unknown (or never used), and confusingly some of the dedications were subsequently changed when the churches were rebuilt, so for identification purposes these alternatives are also given.

Several minor editorial changes, additions and amendments have also been made. Immediately under the title of the Anglican churches are given the population figures for the parish and township. This information was not provided in the Religious Census (but is taken from the Civil Census) and is included so that the attendance figures can be related to the population of the parish. Another editorial change has been to give, where known, the full names of the clergy and ministers and the duration of their period in office at their church or chapel. The ministerial careers of the Church of England clergy are taken from the *Clergy List* and *Crockford's Clerical Directory*, and when information about the endowment income was unrecorded in the Religious Census it has been taken from the *Clergy List* of 1851. In some instances the original returns gave the occupations of some of the nonconformist leaders. Where this information was not given, but yet they could be identified, their occupations have been taken from the Civil Census, and from town and county directories. These publications were also used to check the name and address of individuals and in some instances the spelling when the handwriting was unclear. The estimates of the number of Roman Catholics made in 1852 are taken from R. Cooter, *When Paddy met Geordie. The Irish in County Durham and Newcastle 1840–1880* (Sunderland, 2005), p. 178.

In the returns made by the clergy, ministers and other individuals reference is often made to the 'Sabbath'. In the 1850s this was the usual designation for Sunday, when Christians set aside the first day of the week for public worship. In the nineteenth century church and chapel services were generally held in the morning and afternoon (when often the Sunday school assembled) and evening services only became more common after the installation of gas lighting. Obviously the Jewish congregations did not meet for worship on Sunday, 30 March and so their returns were for the previous day, Saturday, 29 March. In a few instances the returns were completed *before* 30 March, perhaps because the minister was to be absent on the Sunday and there was going to be no variation in attendance.

In the summary totals in the published report on the Religious Census, 488 places of worship were given for Northumberland and 621 for County Durham, making a total of 1,109.[3] In this publication the numbers have been refined and from a detailed examination of the returns 475 places of worship have been identified in Northumberland and 617 in County Durham, making a total of 1,092. In addition to these figures, a number of churches and chapels were not included with the returns and were either lost or never recorded. In his footnotes Horace Mann refers to some of them but without giving any identification. Some of the unrecorded churches and chapels are relatively easy to identify, but most are impossible to trace, and so the information found under 'Places of Worship not listed in the Religious Census' must be regarded as incomplete. However, those that have been identified amount to over sixty in Northumberland and over sixty in County Durham. Numbers of those attending services at workhouse chapels (where they existed) and at Newcastle and Morpeth gaols were not recorded, nor at Durham cathedral, since cathedrals were exempt from the Religious Census.[4] Three of the registration districts stray over the boundary of County Durham into North Yorkshire, where there were a further sixty-three places of worship. These are separately listed. The registration district of Alston in Cumberland is included because the ecclesiastical parish of Alston (which included the chapelries of Garrigil and Nenthead) (25.1–3) were part of the diocese of Durham, and from 1882 in the diocese of Newcastle. All Saints, Easington, in the East Riding of Yorkshire (17.33) was incorrectly included in the County Durham return.

In addition to the text of the Religious Census there are seven appendices listing those Anglican churches and chapels that were consecrated between 1791 and 1882; the names of the bishops and archdeacons of the dioceses of Durham and Newcastle; Dissenters' Places of Worship; Workhouse attendance; the Maltby Fund; the Lord Crewe Charity and *The Newcastle Daily Chronicle* census of 1881.

Alongside the Religious Census, the Civil Census of 1851 includes a considerable amount of statistical information, including the total

---

3   *Religious Worship. England and Wales*, pp. cciii, ccxvi.
4   Though in the neighbouring diocese of York, the Minster is included. J. Wolffe (ed.), *Yorkshire Returns of the 1851 Census of Religious Worship* (York, 2000), vol. 1, p. 3. For the returns for Yorkshire, see all four volumes.

number of clergy and teachers in the two counties.[5] In Northumberland there were 160 Anglican clergy, 135 Protestant ministers and 40 priests and other religious teachers. At the same time there were also 399 schoolmasters and 135 other male teachers; together with 397 schoolmistresses and 133 governesses. In County Durham there were 220 Anglican clergy, 113 Protestant ministers and 49 priests and other religious teachers; together with 720 schoolmistresses and 148 governesses. At the same time there were also 488 schoolmasters and 179 other male teachers. Obviously many of these clergy and ministers do not appear in the Religious Census and their identities would have to be traced through clerical and county directories.

Throughout the publication square brackets '[ ]' indicate material that has been added by the editor or where the original is illegible. Round brackets '( )' may have been used in the original returns, and in some instances where for the sake of clarity material has been transposed. Within the curly brackets '{ }' is information given in the Anglican episcopal visitation of 1857.[6] The first figure on the left refers to the attendance and the second to the number of communicants. The figure on the right refers to the return of the number of baptisms conducted in the parish in 1851.[7] Before the second half of the nineteenth century there was very little outward support for sacramentalism among the Anglican clergy in the region, and the only incumbent in the whole of the Durham diocese to hold a weekly communion service was Francis Grey, the rector of Morpeth (9.12).[8] The majority of his fellow clergy only administered communion monthly or less frequently. The number of communicants set against the usual Sunday attendance figures recorded in the Religious

---

5 *Census of Great Britian, 1851, Ages, civil condition, occupations and birth-place of the people, ibid.*, pp. 756, 759, 762, 765.

6 DUL, ASC, AUC/1/142, Extracts from Clergy Returns for the Bishop's First Visitation, September 1857.

7 DUL, ASC, DDR/EA/PBT/5, Return of baptisms in the diocese of Durham, 1851.

8 Walter Hook, the High Church vicar of Leeds, freely gave his advice. 'In Morpeth, Francis Grey, with his family determination, has determined to have a choral service; and when there was one church a tempest began to growl around him. When there were two [from 1846] I advised him to have a plain service in one and a choral service in the other, and now people see that they have no right to complain.' W.R.W. Stephens, *The Life and Letters of Walter Farquhar Hook*, vol. 2 (London, 1878), p. 254. For Walter Farquar Hook (1798–1875), see *ODNB*, vol. 27, pp. 945–948.

Census of 1851 provides another insight into the life of the Church of England in the middle of the nineteenth century.

The first part of the publication covers the twelve registration districts of Northumberland; the second section covers the twelve registration districts of County Durham. In each of the districts the sequence of the denominations is given as Church of England, Church of Scotland, Presbyterian, Independent, Baptist, the Methodist family of churches, non-denominational places of worship, Society of Friends (Quakers), Roman Catholics, Unitarians, Swedenborgians, Jews and Latter-day Saints (Mormons). Places of worship are identified throughout the publication by their registration district number, followed by their number within that registration district. For example, **13.46** refers to the Primitive Methodist Chapel at Crook and Billy Row, the **13** referring to the Auckland district of County Durham, and the **46** to the chapel's listing within that district. The indices of persons and places use these same numerical references.

Each section is followed by an index of districts and sub-districts; a summary of all the places of worship; a total summary; an indication of numerical strength, and a list of those places of worship which for some reason or another were not listed in the religious census.

Some of the registration districts extended into north Yorkshire. These are listed as a separate section, Yorkshire, which included four County Durham registration districts – Darlington, Easington, Stockton, and Teesdale. The area around Alston (registration district 25) was also included in the Durham return, and is listed separately as a fourth section, Cumberland.

For the date of the consecration of an Anglican church refer to Appendix 1.

INDEX OF DISTRICTS AND SUB-DISTRICTS

The twenty-four registration districts, twelve in Northumberland and twelve in County Durham, corresponded to the existing Poor Law Unions. Each district was divided into sub-districts. The Census returns held at the National Archives at Kew are in the Home Office papers as class HO 129 but in the present volume the returns for Northumberland and County Durham have been re-arranged to allow the easiest access for the reader (see p. liii above).

Listed below are the twenty-four registration districts as numbered in the alphabetical ordering used in this volume, together with the Alston registration district, then within the diocese of Durham. Then follow the districts, sub-districts and places of worship as numbered in the Religious Census with the National Archive shelf-mark order and with the numbering of the returns in the present volume.

The Districts as numbered in this Volume

Northumberland

1 Alnwick District (HO 129/559)
2 Belford District (HO 129/560)
3 Bellingham District (HO 129/557)
4 Berwick District (HO 129/561)
5 Castle Ward District (HO 129/554)
6 Glendale District (HO 129/562)
7 Haltwhistle District (HO 129/556)
8 Hexham District (HO 129/555)
9 Morpeth District (HO 129/558)
10 Newcastle upon Tyne District (HO 129/552)
11 Rothbury District (HO 129/563)
12 Tynemouth District (HO 129/553)

County Durham

13 Auckland District (HO 129/542)
14 Chester le Street District (HO 129/548)

15 Darlington District (HO 129/540)
16 Durham District (HO 129/545)
17 Easington District (HO 129/546)
18 Gateshead District (HO 129/551)
19 Houghton le Spring District (HO 129/547)
20 South Shields District (HO 129/550)

21 Stockton District (HO 129/541)
22 Sunderland District (HO 129/549)
23 Teesdale District (HO 129/543)
24 Weardale District (HO 129/544)

Cumberland
25 Alston (HO 129/564)

The Districts, Sub-districts and Places of Worship as numbered in the Religious Census

NORTHUMBERLAND

HO 129/552 Newcastle District (10)
[52 places of worship]

552.i Westgate sub-district
[Population 21,388]
552.1 St James, Benwell Lane, Benwell (10.3)
552.3 Methodist New Connexion, Scotswood (10.34)
552.4 Church of England Schoolroom, High Elswick (10.5)
552.5 St Paul, Westgate Hill (10.4)
552.6 and 552.34 Synagogue, Temple Street (10.49)
552.7 Wesleyan Reformers, Benwell (10.40)
552.8 Particular Baptist, Marlborough Crescent (10.25)

552.ii St Andrew sub-district
[Population 15,643]
552.9 St Thomas' Chapel, Barras Bridge (10.10)
552.11 St Andrew, Newgate Street (10.9)
552.12 United Presbyterian, Carliol Street (10.16)

552.13 Roman Catholic, Pilgrim Street (10.47)
552.14 English Presbyterian, New Bridge Street (10.18)
552.15 Wesleyan Methodist, Brunswick Place, Northumberland Street (10.29)
552.16 [United Presbyterian], High Bridge (10.14)
552.17 Wesleyan Reformers, Grey Street (10.41)
552.18 Primitive Methodist, Nelson Street (10.37)
552.19 Independent, Blackett Street (10.20)
552.20 Methodist New Connexion, Hood Street (10.35)
552.21 Swedenborgian, Percy Street (10.52)
552.22 St Peter, Oxford Street (10.11)
552.23 Church of Scotland, Blackett Street (10.12)
552.24 Non-denominational, Ancrum Street, Spital Tongues (10.44)

COUNTY DURHAM

HO 129/540 Darlington District (15)
[38 places of worship, and in italics 10 in north Yorkshire]

540.i Darlington sub-district
[Population 16,860]
540.2 All Saint's, Manfield (15.42)
540.3 and 540.4 St Cuthbert with St Mary, Barton (15.39)
540.5 St Peter, Cleasby (15.40)
540.6 Wesleyan Methodist Association Schoolroom, Cleasby (15.47)
540.7 Wesleyan Methodist, Barton (15.44)
540.8 Wesleyan Methodist, Stapleton (15.46)
540.9 St Peter, Croft (15.41)
540.10 Wesleyan Methodist Association, Croft (15.48)
540.11 Wesleyan Methodist Schoolroom, Dalton-on-Tees (15.45)
540.12 St Andrew, North Cowton (15.43)
540.13 All Saints, Girsby, Sockburn (15.14)
540.14 St John the Baptist, Low Dinsdale (15.8)
540.14a and 540.15 St George, Middleton St George (15.13)
540.16 All Saints, Hurworth (15.12)
540.17 Wesleyan Methodist, Hurworth (15.25)
540.18 Primitive Methodist, Hurworth (15.33)
540.19 Wesleyan Methodist, Hurworth Place (15.26)
540.20 Wesleyan Methodist Association, Blackwell (15.34)
540.21 St John the Evangelist, Neasham Road, Darlington (15.6)
540.22 St Cuthbert, Darlington (15.3)
540.23 Holy Trinity, Darlington (15.4)
540.24 Roman Catholic, Paradise Row, Darlington (15.38)
540.25 Wesleyan Methodist, Bondgate, Darlington (15.19)
540.26 Baptist, Upper Archer Street, Darlington (15.16)

540.27 Primitive Methodist, Queen Street, Darlington (15.31)
540.28 Wesleyan Methodist, Park Street, Darlington (15.20)
540.29 Wesleyan Methodist Association, Paradise Row, Darlington (15.35)
540.30 Independent, Union Street, Darlington (15.15)
540.31 St Edwin, Coniscliffe (15.2)
540.32 Wesleyan Methodist, High Coniscliffe (15.24)
540.33 Wesleyan Methodist Schoolroom, Piecebridge (15.27)

540.ii Aycliffe sub-district
[Population 4,758]
540.35 Church of England Schoolroom, Cockerton (15.5)
540.36 Wesleyan Methodist Association, Cockerton (15.36)
540.37 Wesleyan Methodist, Cockerton (15.18)
540.38 St Mary the Virgin, Denton (15.7)
540.39 Wesleyan Methodist, Summerhouse (15.29)
540.40 St Michael the Archangel, Heighington (15.11)
540.41 Wesleyan Methodist, Heighington (15.23)
540.42 Primitive Methodist, Redworth, Heighington (15.32)
540.43 Wesleyan Methodist, Redworth, Heighington (15.28)
540.44 St Mary the Virgin, Aycliffe (15.1)
540.45 Primitive Methodist, Aycliffe (15.30)
540.46 Wesleyan Methodist Association, Brafferton (15.37)
540.47 Wesleyan Methodist, Aycliffe (15.17)
540.48 St Andrew, Haughton-le-Skerne (15.9)
540.49 Wesleyan Methodist, Haughton-le-Skerne (15.22)
540.50 St Andrew, Sadberge (15.10)

INDEX OF DISTRICTS AND SUB-DISTRICTS   lxxv

HO 129/546 Easington District (17)
[32 places of worship, and in italics 1 in east Yorkshire]

546.i   Easington sub-district
[Population 21,795]

CUMBERLAND

THE
RELIGIOUS CENSUS
OF 1851

NORTHUMBERLAND

1. Alnwick District
2. Belford District
3. Bellingham District
4. Berwick District
5. Castle Ward District
6. Glendale District
7. Haltwhistle District
8. Hexham District
9. Morpeth District
10. Newcastle upon Tyne District
11. Rothbury District
12. Tynemouth District

1. Alnwick District (HO 129/559)
31 places of worship

1.1 Church of England, St Mary, Bailiffgate, Alnwick (559.17)
Population 1851: 7,319 (parish) 6,057 (township)

Name   St Mary's church. The parish church.
Consecrated   Before 1800. [Restored 1782, 1818, 1863–64.]
Endowment   Land and old house £82. OPE £117 9s 4d.
                Fees £33 19s 4d (average). Payment by Vestry 10s.
                Other £12 (from [the] Crown).
Sittings   Free 44. Other 948. Total 992.
Attendance 30 March   Morning 528 + 169 SS. Total 697.
                Afternoon 273 + 197 SS. Total 470.
Average attendance   [Not given.]
Remarks   The amount of income as given in full. The income tax
                is not deducted.
Dated   31 March 1851.
Signed   Court d'ewes Granville, minister [1846–54].
                Alnwick, Northumberland.
{1857   Attendance 1,200. 180 communicants.}   {B 116.}
[The precise dedication of Alnwick parish church is unclear. In the
Religious Census it is given as St Mary, but in the 19th century it was
also known as St Mary and St Michael, or St Michael and St Mary.
Today it is known as St Michael's church.]

1.2 Church of England, St John the Baptist, Edlingham (559.27)
Population 1851: 742 (parish) 149 (township)

Name   Parish church of Edlingham.
Consecrated   Before 1800. [Restored 1902.]
Endowment   Tithe £400 17s (commutations). Glebe £84.
                OPE £10. Fees £5.
Sittings   Free 130. Other 40. Total 170.
Attendance 30 March   Morning none.
                Afternoon 60 + 20 SS. Total 80.
                Evening none.
Average attendance   Morning 100 + 20 SS. Total 120.
                Afternoon 80 + 20 SS. Total 100.
Remarks   Morning and afternoon services alternately at Bolton
                Chapel in the same parish and Edlingham.

Dated   1 April 1851.
Signed   Matthew Hughes George Buckle, vicar [1839–93].
Edlingham, Morpeth.

{B 7.}
[Previously Matthew Buckle had been the headmaster of Durham Grammar School 1833–39.]

1.3   Church of England, Bolton Chapel, Bolton (559.26)
Population 1851: 165 (township)

Name   Bolton Chapel. Chapel of ease [of Edlingham].
Consecrated   Before 1800. Enlarged about four years ago. Rebuilt this year.
[Restored 1869.]
Endowment   A portion of Edlingham parish.
Sittings   Free about 140. Other about 60. Total 200.
Attendance 30 March   Morning 120 + 12 SS. Total 132.
Morning and afternoon service alternately.
Average attendance   Morning 150 + 18 SS. Total 168.
Afternoon 170 + 18 SS. Total 188.
Remarks   Morning and afternoon services, alternately at Bolton Chapel and the parish church.
Dated   1 April 1851.
Signed   Matthew Hughes George Buckle, vicar [1839–93].
Edlingham, near Morpeth.

1.4   Church of England, St Maurice, Eglingham (559.29)
Population 1851: 2,000 (parish) 357 (township)

Name   Ancient parish church.
Consecrated   Before 1800. [Restored 1837, 1865–67.]
Endowment   [Total] gross value £1,014.
Sittings   Free 160. Other 340. Total 500.
Attendance 30 March   Morning 137 + 70 SS. Total 207.
Afternoon 62. Total 62.
Average attendance   Morning 250 + 80 SS. Total 330.
Afternoon 70. Total 70.
Remarks   The parish of Eglingham is very extensive, being 13 miles in length [and contains sixteen townships] and has only one church. Some of the parishioners therefore attend at the neighbouring churches of Ilderton, Chillingham, Bolton. There are two chapels in

ruins; no service has been performed in them within the memory of men. There are also the sites of two other chapels. [The four chapels were Bewick, Branton, West Lilburn and Wooperton.] (The living of Eglingham is an endowment to the Archdeaconry of Lindisfarne.)

Dated   31 March 1851.
Signed   George Bland, vicar [1844–53].
             Eglingham vicarage, Alnwick.

{B 30.}

[From 1842 the Archdeaconry of Lindisfarne was annexed to Eglingham. George Bland was the Archdeacon of Lindisfarne 1844–53 and Archdeacon of Northumberland 1853–80.

An earlier incumbent, the Evangelical Henry Baker Tristram, 1821–37, described Eglingham as 'this remote wilderness [where] I am very much shut out from society, especially that of my old friends' (vol. 1, p. 424). In March 1829 he reported, 'at present I have no curate; but I do double duty with more ease than the half formerly. Our schools prosper: we have about one hundred Sunday scholars. The congregation fills the church, which is improved in accommodation and comfort. This winter it has been warmed by a stove and flue. My engagements are incessant; for I have to look after everything and do the churchwardens' duty as well as my own, or nothing is done. ... The ministry of God's Word with the poorest maintenance is more honourable than any other situation. As to pupils, I can do little for you. The gentry in this neighbourhood do not send many sons to public schools in the south, and I have very little intercourse with them' (vol. 2, p. 46). C. Hole, *The Life of the Reverend and Venerable William Whitmarsh Phelps MA*, 2 vols. (London, 1871, 1873). His son Henry Baker Tristram became the incumbent of Castle Eden 1849–60. (**17.1**)]

1.5   Church of England, Holy Trinity, Embleton (559.32)
Population 1851: 2,275 (parish) 656 (township)

Name   Trinity Church. An ancient church.
Consecrated Before 1800. [Restored and enlarged 1850, chancel rebuilt 1867.]
Endowment   Tithe commuted at £565. Glebe now let at £350. Fees £3 10s (in 1850).
Sittings   *Free 174. Other 157. Total 331.
Attendance 30 March   Morning 182 + 54 SS. Total 236.

Afternoon 60 + 57 SS. Total 117.

Average attendance   [Not given.]

Remarks   *Of the free sittings, all but 38 are appropriated to the several townships, but are free to any inhabitants of these townships.

Dated   31 March 1851.

Signed   George Rooke, vicar [1830–74].
Embleton, Alnwick.

{B 42.}

[George Rooke was succeeded by Mandell Creighton (1843–1901), vicar of Embleton 1875–84, Dixie Professor at Cambridge 1884–91, Bishop of Peterborough 1891–97, Bishop of London 1897–1901. His biography outlines his ministry at Embleton. L. Creighton, *Life and Letters of Mandell Creighton* (London, 1913), vol. 1, pp. 148–273.]

1.6   Church of England, All Saints, Rennington (559.34)
Population 1851: 269 (township)

Name   All Saints. The church of a district parish, served from the mother
church of Embleton.

Consecrated   Before 1800. [Rebuilt 1831, restored and enlarged 1865.]

Endowment   Land £36 per annum. OPE Payment from vicar of Embleton £1. Queen Anne's Bounty £6 6s 4d. Total £43 6s 4d.

Sittings   Total 208.

Attendance 30 March   Morning 72 + 72 SS. Total 144.
Afternoon – alternately [with Rock].

Average attendance   [Not given.]

Remarks   The perpetual curacy of Rennington is always held together with that   of Rock, and is situated a mile off, and is another district parish served from Embleton. The services are alternate, morning and afternoon.

Dated   31 March 1851.

Signed   Henry Richard Ridley, perpetual curate [1848–51].
Rennington, Alnwick.

{1857   Attendance 120. 34 communicants.}   {B 9.}

1.7   Church of England, St Philip and St James, Rock (559.33)
Population 1851: 250 (township)

Name   St Philip and St James. The church of the district
parish of Rock served from the mother church of
Embleton.

Consecrated   Before 1800. [Rebuilt 1806, restored 1855, enlarged
1866.]

Endowment   Land £36 per annum. OPE Payment of vicar of
Embleton £1. Queen Anne's Bounty £6 6s 4d. Total £43
6s 4d.

Sittings   Free 160. Total 160.

Attendance 30 March   Morning 52 + 63 SS. Total 115.
Afternoon alternately [with Rennington].

Average attendance   [Not given.]

Remarks   The perpetual curacy of Rock is always held with
that of Rennington, situated a mile off, as is another
district parish served from Embleton. The services are
alternate, morning and afternoon.

Dated   31 March 1851.

Signed   Henry Richard Ridley, perpetual curate [1848–51].
Rennington, Alnwick.

{1857   Attendance 110. 34 communicants.}   {B 3.}

1.8   Church of England, St Michael and All Angels, Felton (559.2)
Population 1851: 1,574 (parish) 708 (township)

Name   St Michael. Ancient parish church.
[With a chapel of ease St Lawrence, Longframlington
(**11.5**).]

Consecrated   Before 1800. [Gallery erected 1759, removed 1870.
Building enlarged 1845, restored 1870, 1884, 1900.]

Endowment   Land £104. Tithe £160. Fees £10.

Sittings   Free 40. Other about 500. Total 540.

Attendance 30 March   Morning 250 + 66 SS. Total 316.
Afternoon 90 + 64 SS. Total 154.

Average attendance   Morning 250 + 76 SS. Total 326.
Afternoon 70 + 71 SS. Total 140 (*sic*) [141].

Dated   2 April 1851.

Signed   Thomas Ilderton, minister [1850–71].
Felton, Northumberland.

{B 29.}

[Thomas Ilderton was also responsible for Longframlington (**11.5**).]

1.9   Church of England, St Michael and All Angels, Howick
(559.31)
Population 1851: 315 (parish)

Name   St Michael's. An ancient parish church.
Consecrated Before 1800. [Rebuilt 1746, enlarged 1849.]
Endowment   Tithe £321 (gross value). Glebe £1. Dues 5s.
Sittings   Free 195. Other 24. Total 219.
Attendance 30 March   Morning 59 + 58 SS. Total 117.
                        Afternoon 36 + 54 SS. Total 90.
Average attendance   Morning 85 + 58 SS. Total 143.
                        Afternoon 80 + 54 SS. Total 134.
Remarks   In making the return [on attendance] it is to be
               observed that the Rt. Hon. Earl Grey, family and
               establishment, are not included as his lordship resides
               principally in London.
Dated   31 March 1851.
Signed   Oswald Head, rector [1846–54].
               Howick, near Alnwick.
{1857   Attendance 200. 40 communicants.}   {B 11.}
[The parishes of Howick and Lesbury were held in plurality. Until
1842 Howick was annexed to the Ardeaconry of Northumberland.]

1.10   Church of England, St Mary, Lesbury (559.15)
Population 1851: 1,238 (parish) 750 township

Name   St Mary's. Ancient parish church.
Consecrated Before 1800. [Restored 1849–50.]
Endowment   Tithe £304 16s 1d (gross value). Glebe £7 5s (gross
               value).
               Fees £8 18s 1d.
Sittings   Free 121. Other 152. Total 273.
Attendance 30 March   Morning 83 + 51 SS. Total 134.
                        Afternoon 53 + 53 SS. Total 106.
Average attendance   Morning 90 + 55 SS. Total 145.
                        Afternoon 40 + 55 SS. Total 95.
Dated   31 March 1851.
Signed   Hilkiah Bedford Hall, curate of Lesbury [1848–50].
               Vicarage, Lesbury, Northumberland.
Incumbent   [Oswald Head 1839–54.]
{1857   Attendance 300. 40 communicants.}   {B 19.}
[In June 1846 during repairs to the building, Lesbury School and a
'bathing house' at Alnmouth were licensed for worship.]

1.11   Church of England, St Peter and St Paul, Longhoughton
(559.30)
Population 1851: 861 (parish) 149 (township)

Name   St Peter's, Longhoughton parish church.
Consecrated   Before 1800. [Restored and enlarged 1873.]
Endowment   Tithe £228 2s 6d. Glebe £1 10s. OPE £2 14s.
                Fees £1 4s. Easter offerings 10s.
Sittings   Free 100. Other 145. Total 245.
Attendance 30 March   Morning 160 + 50 SS. Total 210.
                        Afternoon 75 + 25 SS. Total 100.
Average attendance   [Not given.]
Dated   31 March 1851.
Signed   Henry Edward Bell, vicar [1842–71].
                Longhoughton, Alnwick.
{1857   Attendance 180. 40 communicants.}   {B 15.}

1.12   Church of England, St James, Shilbottle (559.6)
Population 1851: 1,298 (parish) 601 (township)

[Summary form]
Name   St James.
Erected   Re-erected about 200 years ago. [Rebuilt and
                consecrated on 14 October 1885.]
Endowment   [£222.]
Sittings   Free 88. Other 119. Total 207.
Usual attendance: Morning (full service) about 140 + 54 SS.
                       Total [194].
                       Afternoon Prayer. Very few.
Dated   [Not given.]
Signed   John Barthrop Roberts, vicar [1849–79].
                [Shilbottle vicarage, Alnwick.]
{1857   Attendance. 'I cannot say. I have never numbered
               them'.}   {B 39.}

1.13   Church of England, St Lawrence, Warkworth (559.12)
Population 1851: 4,439 (parish) 834 (township)

[Summary form]
Name   St Lawrence, Warkworth.
Erected   About 1760 (*sic*). [Restored 1860–61.]
Endowment   [£528.]

Sittings   Free 30. Other 300. Total 330.
Usual attendance   Morning 200 + 70 SS. Total [270].
                        Afternoon 50 + 70 SS. Total [120].
Dated   [Not given.]
Signed   Andrew Robson, registrar.
Incumbent   [Henry Percy 1840–53.]
{1857   Attendance. Unanswered.}   {B 90.}
[Henry Percy was the second son of Hugh Percy, the Bishop of
Carlisle 1827–56.]

1.14   United Presbyterian, Clayport Street, Alnwick (559.20)
Name   United Presbyterian Church
Erected   The congregation has existed about 100 years [since
                1753]. The present church was erected on a new site in
                Clayport Street in 1846. [New chapel opened February
                1847 and cost £1,220.]
Building   A separate and entire building. Exclusively as a place
                of worship.
Sittings   [*None free.] Other between 6[00] and 700. Total
                [600–700].
                No free space or standing room. Isles (*sic*) or passages
                only.
Attendance 30 March   Morning about 500 [including SS]. Total [500].
                        Afternoon from 3[00] to 400 [including SS].
                        Total 300–400.
                        No evening service.
Average attendance   Morning 500 + 117 SS. Total 617.
Remarks   *The poor who cannot pay for a seat are allowed to sit
                where they can find accommodation.
Dated   31 March 1851.
Signed   Michael Paterson, session clerk (draper).
                Alnwick.
Minister   [John Ker 1845–51; William Leamont 1851–89.]
[In 1955 united with St James, Alnwick (**1.17**).]

1.15   United Presbyterian, Embleton (559.35)
Name   None.
Erected   1833.
Building   [Separate and entire. Exclusively used for worship.]
Sittings   Free 12. Other 300. Total [312].
Attendance 30 March   Morning 196. Total 196
                        Evening 68. Total 68.

Average attendance   [Not given.]
Remarks   [Above] is given the average attendance on every
    Sabbath day.
Dated   31 March 1851.
Signed   William Ross, minister [1850–80].
    Embleton, by Alnwick.

1.16   United Presbyterian, Warkworth (559.10)
Name   Warkworth Chapel.
Erected   1828. [Opened 1 May 1828.]
Building   Separate and entire. Exclusively a place of worship.
Sittings   Free 21. Other 265. Total [286].
    Standing room. None, except in the passages.
Attendance 30 March   Morning 184 + 18 SS. Total 202.
    Afternoon no service.
    Evening 65. Total 65.
Average attendance   [Not given.]
Dated   31 March 1851.
Signed   James Duncan, minister [1836–54].
    Warkworth, Northumberland.

1.17   English Presbyterian, Pottergate Street, Alnwick (559.22/23)
Name   St James Church.
Erected   (St James Church dates as far back as the Revolution
    of 1688. It was rebuilt in the year 1796, and in 1838
    the building was again taken down and rebuilt on the
    same site, which building now stands.)
    [Erected 1780. Rebuilt in 1895 as St James, Pottergate.]
Building   An entire building. Used exclusively as a place of
    worship and Sabbath school.
Sittings   [None free.] Other 700. Total [700]. Standing room 180.
Attendance 30 March   Morning 500. Total [500].
    Afternoon 76 SS. Total [76].
    Evening 400. Total [400].
Average attendance   [Not given.]
Dated   31 March 1851.
Signed   John Walker, minister [1851–58].
    St James Manse, Alnwick.
[In 1888 united with Lisburn Street, Alnwick, and in 1955 with
Clayport Street, Alnwick (**1.14**).]

1.18   English Presbyterian, Glanton (559.28)
Name   Glanton Presbyterian Chapel.
Erected   1783. [Altered 1867, 1911.]
Building   Separate building. Used only as a place of worship.
Sittings   Free 10. Other 448. Total [458].
Attendance 30 March   Morning 440. Total [440].
                        Evening 126. Total [126].
Average attendance   Morning 430. Total [430].
Dated   31 March 1851.
Signed   Duncan Lennie, Presbyterian minister [1844–58].
                Glanton, Northumberland.
[From 1781–83 the congregation had worshipped in a granary.]

1.19   Independent [Congregational], St Michael's Place, Alnwick
(559.19)
Name   Sion Chapel. [Sion Meeting House.]
Erected   Before 1800. [Inscription 'Sion Meeting House erected
                1815'. Opened 30 June 1816.]
Building   [Separate and entire. Exclusively used for worship.]
Sittings   [None free.] Other 750. Total [750].
Attendance 30 March   Morning 237. Total [237].
                        Afternoon 97 SS. Total [97].
                        Evening 132. Total [132].
Average attendance   Morning 300. Total [300].
                        Afternoon 97 SS. Total [97].
                        Evening 200. Total [200].
Dated   31 March 1851.
Signed   Robert Greener, minister [1850–65].
                Percy Street, Alnwick.
[Formerly a Presbyterian church and became a Congregational
church in 1843.]

1.20   Independent [Congregational], Amble (559.8)
Name   None.
Erected   1848. [New chapel 1894.]
Building   [Separate and entire. Exclusively used for worship.]
Sittings   [None free.] Other 330. Total [330].
Attendance 30 March   Morning 80 + 30 SS. Total 110.
                        Evening 100. Total 100.
Average attendance   Morning 100 + 90 SS. Total 190.
                        Evening 150 + 10 SS. Total 160.

Remarks   This chapel is without an appointed minister at
              present.
Dated   31 March 1851.
Signed   Alexander Allan, manager (joiner).
              Amble, Northumberland.
[Previous minister David F. Sunderland 1849–51, followed by
Thomas Rogers 1851–53.]

1.21   Wesleyan Methodist, Acklington (559.7)
Name   None.
Erected   Before 1800.
Building   Separate and used as a weekly day-school. Used as a
              weekly day-school, also as a Sunday school.
Sittings   Will seat 45 persons. All free. Total [45].
Attendance 30 March   Afternoon 14 + 31 SS. Total 45.
Average attendance   Afternoon 18 + 27 SS. Total 45.
Dated   31 March 1851.
Signed   David Edgar, Wesleyan minister [1849–51].
              Alnwick, Northumberland.

1.22   Wesleyan Methodist, Alnmouth (559.13)
Name   Alnmouth Chapel.
Erected   1826. [Rebuilt 1892.]
Building   [Separate and entire.] Used for a day school.
Sittings   Free 200. Total [200].
Attendance 30 March   Morning 100 + 15 SS. Total [115].
              Evening 51 + 20 SS. Total [71].
Average attendance   Morning 100. Total [100].
              Evening 100. Total [100].
Dated   30 March 1851.
Signed   David Edgar, Wesleyan minister [1849–51].
              Alnwick, Northumberland.

1.23   Wesleyan Methodist, Clayport Street, Alnwick (559.21)
Name   Old Chapel.
Erected   1786. [Restored 1886.]
Building   [Separate and entire. Exclusively used for worship.]
Sittings   Free 120. Other 600. Total [720].
Attendance 30 March   Morning no service.
              Evening 70. Total [70].
Average attendance   Morning from 40 to 60. Total [40–60].
              Evening 70. Total [70].

Dated   31 March 1851.
Signed   David Edgar, Wesleyan minister [1849–51].
            Alnwick, Northumberland.
[John Wesley laid the foundation stone on 2 June 1786.]

1.24   Wesleyan Methodist, Low Buston (559.11)
Name   Low Buston.
Erected   Before 1800.
Building [Separate and entire, but not exclusively used for
            worship.]
Sittings Free 50. Total [50].
Attendance 30 March   Morning no service.
                        Afternoon [45]. Total 45.
                        Evening no service.
Average attendance   Morning 35. Total [35].
Dated   31 March 1851.
Signed   David Edgar, Wesleyan minister [1849–51].
            Alnwick, Northumberland.

1.25   Wesleyan Methodist, Shilbottle (559.4)
Name   Shilbottle Chapel.
Erected   1841.
Building [Separate and entire. Exclusively used for worship.]
Sittings Free 84. Other 40. Total [124].
Attendance 30 March   Morning no service.
                        Afternoon no service.
                        Evening [88]. Total 88.
Average attendance   Evening 120. Total [120].
Dated   31 March 1851.
Signed   David Edgar, Wesleyan minister [1849–51].
            Alnwick, Northumberland.

1.26   Wesleyan Methodist Schoolroom, Victoria Street, Amble
(559.9)
Name   George Duncan's Schoolroom.
Erected   1848.
Building [Separate and entire, but not exclusively used for
            worship.]
Sittings Free 70. Total [70].
Attendance 30 March   Morning 23 + 24 SS. Total 47.
                        Evening 19 + 15 SS. Total 34.
Average attendance   Morning 30 + 20 SS. Total 50.

Evening 34 + 15 SS. Total 49.

Dated   31 March 1851.
Signed   George Duncan, local preacher (schoolmaster).
    Amble, Northumberland.

1.27   Wesleyan Methodist, Radcliffe Terrace, Warkworth (559.14)
Name   Wesleyan Chapel.
Erected   1842.
Building   [Separate and entire, but not exclusively used for
    worship.]
Sittings   Free 130. Other [Not given]. Standing room, square
    feet 800 yards (*sic*).
Attendance 30 March   Morning 101 SS. Total 101.
    Afternoon 137. Total 137.
    Evening 130. Total 130.
Average attendance   Morning 420 SS. Total 420.
    Afternoon 400. Total 400.
    Evening 460. Total 460.
Dated   30 March 1851.
Signed   David Patterson, steward (coal miner).
    Radcliffe Terrace, [Hauxley], Northumberland.

1.28   Methodist New Connexion, Chapel Lane, Alnwick (559.18)
Name   Bethel Chapel.
Erected   About the year 1803. [Opened 1804.]
Building   [Separate and entire. Exclusively used for worship.]
Sittings   Free 100. Other 200. Total [300].
Attendance 30 March   Morning 97. Total 97.
    Evening 200. Total 200.
Average attendance   [Not given.]
Dated   30 March 1851.
Signed   James Wright, minister.
    South Street, Alnwick.

1.29   Methodist New Connexion, Newton on the Moor (559.5)
Name   None.
Erected   Used as a place of worship since the year 1830.
Building   [Separate and entire. Exclusively used for worship.]
Sittings   Free 70. Other none. Total [70].
Attendance 30 March   Afternoon 44. Total [44].
Average attendance   [Not given.]
Dated   30 March 1851.

Signed   James Wright, minister.
         South Street, Alnwick.

1.30   Roman Catholic, Felton Park, Felton (559.3)

Name   None.
Erected   Before 1800. [Opened after rebuilding, 16 June 1857.]
Building   [Separate] domestic chapel. [Exclusively used for worship.]
Sittings   Free 50. Total [50].
Attendance 30 March   Morning 50. Total [50].
                  Afternoon 25. Total [25].
Average attendance   [Not given.]
Remarks   This chapel is a private one, for the use of Tho[mas] May Riddle Esq., and family etc. The family do not reside here since the mansion is let. All sittings [are] free; those excepted which the family when [resident] require.
Dated   31 March 1851.
Signed   Samuel Day, Catholic chaplain [1849–69].
         Felton, Northumberland.

1.31   Unitarian, Correction House Yard, Alnwick (559.24)

Name   Unitarian Chapel. [Ebenezer Chapel.]
Erected   [2 February] 1817. [Cost £405.]
Building   [Separate and entire. Exclusively used for worship.]
Sittings   Free 30. Other 180. Total [210].
Attendance 30 March   Morning 38. Total [38].
                  Evening 58 (extra service). Total [58].
Average attendance   Morning 26. Total [26].
Dated   31 March 1851.
Signed   James Stott, lay minister [gardener].
         4 Hotspur Place, Alnwick.
[In the trust deed it is called 'The Independent Arminian Meeting House'.]

2. Belford District (HO 129/560)
13 places of worship

2.1 Church of England, St Aidan, Bamburgh (560.2)
Population 1851: 4,545 (parish) 416 (township and 50 at Bamburgh
    Castle)

[Summary form]
Name   St Aidan.
Erected   Not known. [Restored 1830, 1895.]
Endowment   [£200 that included £40 a year from the Lord Crewe
    Charity.]
Sittings   [None free.] Other 400. Total 400 (exclusive of seats for
    Sunday scholars).
Usual attendance   Morning 300 + 160 SS. Total [460].
              Afternoon 100. Total [100].
Dated   [Not given.]
Signed   George Scott [registrar].
Incumbent   [William Darnell 1841–82.]
{1857   Attendance 250. 60 communicants.}   {B 14.}

2.2 Church of England, Beadnell Chapel [later St Ebba], Beadnell (560.4)
Population 1851: 326 (township)

[Summary form]
Name   Beadnell Chapel under Bambro (*sic*).
              [Separated from Bamburgh in August 1766.]
Erected   [Consecrated 10 August 1766.] Rebuilt in the year 1792
    [and enlarged. Restored 1860].
Endowment   [£79.]
Sittings   Free 100. Other 154. Total 254.
Usual attendance   Morning 100 + 20 SS. Total [120].
              Afternoon, no duty.
              Evening, no duty.
Dated   [Not given.]
Signed   Thomas Armstrong [schoolmaster].
Incumbent   [John Ayton Wood 1831–53.]
{1857   Attendance 130. 14 communicants.}   {B 10.}

2.3   Church of England, St Mary, Belford (560.14)
Population 1851: 1,857 (parish) 1,226 (township)

Name   St Mary's. Parish Church.
Consecrated Before 1800. [Rebuilt 1615, 1700. Restored 1828–29,
               1873.]
Endowment   [£147.]
Sittings   Free 142. Other 508. Total [650].
Attendance 30 March Morning 230. Total 230.
                       Afternoon 80. Total 80.
Average attendance   [Not given.]
Dated   31 March 1851
Signed   George Walker, incumbent [1843–77].
               Belford, Northumberland.
{1857   Attendance 400. 90 communicants.}   {B 29.}

2.4   Church of England, St Maurice, Ellingham (560.5)
Population 1851: 936 (parish) 313 (township)

[Summary form]
Name   St Maurice.
Erected   Not known. [Rebuilt 1805, 1862.]
Endowment   [£538.]
Sittings   [None free.] Other 300. Total 300.
Usual attendance   Morning 200 + 60 SS. Total [260].
                       Afternoon 50. Total [50].
Remarks   Information obtained [by] my own observation.
Dated   [Not given.]
Signed   George Scott [registrar].
Incumbent   [Charles Perigal 1803–54.]
                                                             {B 13}

2.5   Church of England, St Hilda the Virgin, Lucker (560.12)
Population 1851: 293 (township)

Name   Lucker Chapel, the chapel of an ancient chapelry [of
               Bamburgh].
Consecrated Before 1800. [Restored 1776. Unsafe building
               demolished and new church consecrated by Bishop
               Vincent William Ryan, 4 November 1874.]
Endowment   Land £54. OPE Queen Anne's Bounty £32. Woods and
               forests £7.

Sittings   [Not given.]
Attendance 30 March   Morning 100 + 30 SS. Total 130.
Average attendance   [Not given.]
Dated   30 March 1851.
Signed   Leonard Shafto Orde, incumbent [1848–54].
        Shoreston Hall, Belford.
{1857   Attendance 95. 24 communicants.}   {B 10.}

2.6   Church of England, St Paul, North Sunderland (560.3)
Population 1851: 1,208 (parish)

[Summary form]
Name   St Paul's. *Erected* 1832. [License granted for newly
        erected chapel 5 June 1833, and consecrated by the
        Bishop of Carlisle, 14 January 1834. Parish created out
        of Bamburgh 8 November 1843.]
Endowment   [Not given.] [£200.]
Sittings   Free 300. Other 16. Total 316.
Usual; attendance   Morning 200 + 60 SS. Total [260].
        Afternoon 100. Total [100].
Remarks   [Information obtained by my own] observation.
Dated   [Not given.]
Signed   George Scott [registrar].
Incumbent   [Frederick Robinson Simpson 1843–86.]
{1857   Attendance 150. 20 communicants.}

2.7   Church of Scotland, West Street, Belford (560.7)
Name   National Scotch Church.
Erected   1766. [1776. Restored 1870, closed 1902 and is now the
        community centre.]
Building   Separate [and entire. Exclusively used for worship].
Sittings   [None free.] Other 500. Total [500].
Attendance 30 March   Morning 300 + 26 SS. Total 326.
        Evening 85. Total [85].
Average attendance   Morning 250 + 30 SS. Total 280.
        Evening [Not given].
Remarks   The number of communicants at the dispensation of
        the sacrament of the Lord's Supper on the 20 October
        1850, was 216.
Dated   31 March 1851.
Signed   Thomas Guthrie, session clerk [grocer and merchant
        tailor].

Belford, Northumberland.
Minister   [William Ettershall 1850–53.]
[Marcus Dods (1786–1838) was the minister 1811–38. His youngest
son, also called Marcus Dods was born at Belford. He became an
influential liberal biblical scholar who from 1889 taught the New
Testament at New College, Edinburgh. In 1907 he was appointed
Principal but was too ill to take up the post. 'Marcus Dodds (1844–
1909)', *ODNB*, vol. 16, pp. 431–432.]

2.8   United Presbyterian, Nursery Lane, Belford (560.9)
Name   United Session Chapel. [Erskine Church.]
Erected   AD 1777. [Rebuilt 1821. Restored 1875 and cost £900.]
Building   Separate entire. Exclusively [used for worship]
    except for S[unday] school, prayer meetings and
    congregational purposes.
Sittings   Free 330. Total [330].
Attendance 30 March   Morning [244]. Total 244.
    Evening [68]. Total 68.
Average attendance   Morning [240]. Total 240.
    Evening [75]. Total 75.
Remarks   I have a morning and an evening service, but many
    of my hearers resident in the country cannot attend in
    the evening.
    Chapel measured to let for about 330, but can contain
    and has contained above 400 persons. Poor members
    have sittings *gratis*
    intermingled with those that are let. J. H.
Dated   31 March 1851.
Signed   John Hunter, minister [1831–66].
    Belford, Northumberland.

2.9   United Presbyterian, North Sunderland (560.10)
Name   United Presbyterian Chapel.
Erected   1810.
Building   [Separate and entire. Exclusively used for worship.]
Sittings   [Information crossed out.]
Attendance 30 March   Morning 320. Total 320.
    Afternoon 60 SS. Total 60.
    Evening 80. Total 80.
Average attendance   Morning from 300 to 400. Total [300–400].
Remarks   [Sunday school] from 90 to 100. This number includes
    certain other Bible classes in addition to that in the

chapel. These includes certain other small Bible classes in addition to that in the chapel.

Dated   31 March 1851.
Signed   Hugh Glover, minister [1842–69].
             North Sunderland, Belford.

[In 1883 this church (known as North Sunderland West) was reunited with North Sunderland East (**2.11**).]

2.10   English Presbyterian, Belford (560.8)

Name   The English Presbyterian Church. [Columba Church.]
Erected   [See remarks.]
Building [Not separate and entire or exclusively used for worship.]
Sittings [None free.] Other 250. Total [250].
Attendance 30 March   Morning 191 + 10 SS. Total 201.
            Evening 58 + 3 SS. Total 61.
Average attendance   Morning 230 + 30 SS. Total 260.
Remarks   This congregation is at present worshipping in a large room of an inn. Our new church is now in course of erection and will be finished in about six months. (This congregation is vacant at present. The minister who has lately been chosen by the people is not yet arrived. The schedule is therefore signed by one of the ruling e[lder]s.)
Dated   31 March 1851.
Signed   James Bromfield, elder [grocer].
            Belford.

[The congregation met in the Long Room of the Black Swan Inn that had been registered for worship on 22 November 1849. DUL, ASC, DDR/EA/NCN/2/18/3, Meeting House Certificates, 1732–1851. Columba Church was opened in the nearby hamlet of Warenton, where the first the minister was David Terras 1851–83.]

2.11   English Presbyterian, North Lane, North Sunderland (560.11)

Name   English Presbyterian Church.
Erected   In 1843.
Building [Separate and entire. Exclusively used for worship.]
Sittings [None free.] Other 360. Total [360].
Attendance 30 March   Morning 150. Total [150].
            Afternoon 20. Total [20].
Average attendance   Morning 200 + 30 SS. Total 230.

Dated   31 March 1851.
Signed   Donald Munro, minister [1844–64].
             North Sunderland, by Belford, Northumberland.
[In 1883 this church (known as North Sunderland East) was reunited with North Sunderland West (**2.9**) and the church closed.]

2.12   English Presbyterian, Warenford (560.13)

Name   Warenford Church.
Erected   Before 1800. [1750, rebuilt 1824.]
Building   A separate and entire building. [Exclusively used for worship.]
Sittings   Free 107. Other 310. Total [417].
Attendance 30 March   Morning 194 + 56 SS. Total 250.
Average attendance   Morning 250 + 50 SS. Total 300.
Remarks   There is only one act of public worship on Sabbath except on extraordinary occasions. No part of the church is set apart for the Sabbath scholars. Their attendance at church is not compulsory.
             They usually sit in the same pews with their parents or other friends. The distance from which the congregation must travel to church prevents from having more acts than one.
Dated   31 March 1851.
Signed   Andrew Hutcheson DD, minister [1816–51].
             Warenford, Belford, Northumberland.

2.13   Roman Catholic, Ellingham Hall, Ellingham (560.6)

Name   Ellingham Chapel.
Erected   [Not given.] [Restored 1897.]
Building   [Not separate and entire, but exclusively used for worship.]
Sittings   Free 70. Total [70]. Standing room 20.
Attendance 30 March   Morning 51. Total [51].
                        Afternoon 12. Total [12].
Average attendance   [Not given.]
Dated   30 March 1851.
Signed   Rev George Meynell, Catholic priest [1848–56].
             Ellingham, Belford, Northumberland.
[In the 18th century the Roman Catholic community in Ellingham were served by the Jesuits.]

3. Bellingham District (HO 129/557)
23 places of worship

3.1 Church of England, St Cuthbert, Bellingham (557.11)
Population 1851: 1,594 (parish) 770 (township)

Name	St Cuthbert. The church of an ancient chapelry in the parish of Simonburn, which was divided in 1814 by Act of Parliament [of 1811 (51 Geo. III c.194)] into six parishes, of which Bellingham is one, and St Cuthbert, its parish church.
Consecrated	Many hundred years before 1800. [Restored 1843, 1885.]
Endowment	Land £15. Tithe £196. Glebe £22. Fees £5.
Sittings	Free 228. Total 228.
Attendance 30 March	Morning 100 + 20 SS. Total 120. Evening 70. Total 70.
Average attendance	Morning 150 + 20 SS. Total 170. Evening 100. Total 100.
Dated	31 March 1851.
Signed	John Marshall, rector [1848–51]. Bellingham, near Hexham.
{1857	Attendance 150. 40 communicants.} {B 23.}

3.2 Church of England, St Giles, Birtley (557.18)
Population 1851: 428 (parochial chapelry)

Name	Birtley Chapelry.
Consecrated	Licensed by the then Bish[op] of Durham, Doctor [Shute] Barrington 1806. By a high dignitary of the church I am informed that our church was built ab[ou]t 200 years ago and licensed to me 1806. [Restored 1884.]
Erected	I cannot answer this question but it has undergone splendid repairs, by the late Duke of North[umberlan]d, the ceiling, moulding etc. etc. are delightful.
Endowment	[£84.] Glebe land. Very trifling fees.
Sittings	Free 200. Other 18. (All the sittings free.) Total 218.
Attendance 30 March	Morning 128. Total [128]. No duty in the afternoon.
Average attendance	[Not given, but written across morning, afternoon and evening]:

	Sometimes when the day is good from 70 [to] 80 and upwards. Till after Easter no Sunday scholars. After that we commence.	
Dated	31 March 1851.	
Signed	Robert Lowther, incumbent [1806–53].	
	Birtley, Hexham.	
{1857	Attendance 50. 15 communicants.}	{B 14.}

3.3   Church of England, St Francis, Byrness (557.6)
Population 1851: [Not given. Part of Elsdon parish 1,643]

Name   Byrness chapel of ease [of St Cuthbert, Elsdon (**11.4**)].
Consecrated Before 1800. [Consecrated 8 July 1801.]
Endowment   [£75.] Land (partly). Glebe (partly).
                     OPE Queen Anne's Bounty. 3 per cent consols £70 a
                     year.
Sittings   Free 60. Total 60.
Attendance 30 March   Morning and afternoon alternately 15.
                     Total 15.
Average attendance   [Not given.]
Remarks   The above chapel has no district assigned to it. The
                     annual income from all sources is about £70 and
                     derived from lands, glebe, Queen Anne's Bounty of
                     3 per. cent.
Dated   31 March 1851.
Signed   John Burrell, minister [1843–59].
                     Byrness parsonage, Elsdon, North[umberlan]d.
{1857   Attendance 10. 8 communicants.}

3.4   Church of England, Holy Trinity, Horsley (557.7)
Population 1851: [Not given. Part of Elsdon parish 1,643]

Name   Trinity Chapel.
                     [Chapel of ease of St Cuthbert, Elsdon (**11.4**).]
Consecrated [18 September] 1844 as an additional church.
Erected   By private benefaction and subscriptions.
                     Cost £770. Total cost £900 [crossed out].
Endowment   No [permanent] endowment.
Sittings   Free 185. Total 185.
Attendance 30 March   Morning and afternoon alternately 50.
                     Total 50.
Average attendance   [Not given.]

Remarks The above is a district chapel under the control of the rector of the parish [of Elsdon] who pays and provides a curate to officiate there.
Dated 31 March 1851.
Signed John Burrell, minister [1843–59].
Byrness, Elsdon, North[umberlan]d.

3.5 Church of England, St Cuthbert, Corsenside (557.14)
Population 1851: 579 (parish)

Name Corsenside Parish Church, an ancient structure.
Consecrated Very remotely consecrated. [Replaced by All Saints, consecrated on 1 November 1907.]
Endowment [Permanent endowment] about £300. Fees perhaps £2.
Sittings Free about 200. Total about 200.
Attendance 30 March Morning 24. Total 24.
Average attendance Morning [about 30]. Total about 30.
Remarks The church is very inconveniently situated in a remote locality at the northern extremity of the parish.
Dated 31 March 1851.
Signed Adam Harry, curate [died 30 May 1851].
Corsenside, Hexham.
Incumbent [William Kell 1843–63.]
{1857 Attendance 110. 14 communicants.} {B 7.}

3.6 Church of England, St Peter, Falstone (557.3)
Population 1851: 562 (parish)

Name Falstone Church: formerly the church of the ancient chapelry of Falstone, now under the provisions of the Act [of Parliament of 1811 (51 Geo. III c.194)] for the division of the parish of Simonburn. The church of the distinct and separate parish of Falstone.
Consecrated In [1 September] 1825 [by the Bishop of Oxford], in lieu of the dilapidated church of the old chapelry. [The new church which cost £955 was burnt down in 1890, and rebuilt 1891–92.]
Endowment Tithe £228. Glebe £100. Fees 7s 6d. Dues 7s 6d. Easter offerings 7s 6d.
Sittings Free 105. Other 65. Total 170.
Attendance 30 March Morning 25 + 8 SS. Total 33.
Average attendance [Not given.]

Remarks   The inhabitants of Falstone are mostly Presbyterians.
The parish is situated on the border of Scotland.
Dated   31 March 1851.
Signed   Thomas Forster, rector [1839–80].
Falstone rectory, near Hexham.

{B 2.}

3.7   Church of England, St Luke, Greystead (557.2)
Population 1851: 251 (parish)

Name   Parish church of the rectory of Greystead, or Gaystead.
Consecrated   In 1818. Consecrated [on 9 August by the Bishop of
Oxford] as an additional church.
Erected   Erected by the Lord's Commissioners of Greenwich
Hospital, the patrons of the living.
Endowment   Tithe (commuted at) £150. Glebe £24. Fees £10.
Sittings   Free 190. Other 10. Total 200.
Attendance 30 March   Morning 22. Total [22].
Afternoon 12. Total [12].
Average attendance   Morning from 20 to 30. Total [20–30].
Afternoon 8 only and upwards. Total [8+].
Remarks   Greystead (or Gaystead) is one of the six subdivisions
of the great living of Simonburn, which were made
distinct rectories by Act of Parliament in 1811 [51 Geo.
III c.194].
Dated   31 March 1851.
Signed   James Edward Surridge MA, rector [1845–67].
Greystead rectory, Hexham.

{B 4.}

3.8   Church of England, St Wilfrid, Kirkharle (557.23)
Population 1851: 170 (parish) 164 (township)

Name   St Wilfrid. An ancient parish church.
Consecrated   Before 1800. [Restored 1771–78, 1884.]
Endowment   Tithe £21 10s. Glebe £152.
Sittings   Free 30. Other 170. Total 200.
Attendance 30 March   Morning 71. Total [71].
Average attendance   Morning 120. Total [120].
Dated   [Not given.]
Signed   John Horsley Newton, minister [1839–55].
Kirkharle, Newcastle upon Tyne.

{1857   Attendance 50. 10 communicants.}   {B 2.}

3.9   Church of England, St Bartholomew, Kirkwhelpington
(557.21)
Population 1851: 679 (parish) 220 (township)

Name   Dedicated to St Bartholomew, and an ancient parish church.
Consecrated   Before 1800. [Restored 1896.]
Endowment   Tithe £174 (net). Glebe and house £178. No permanent endowment.
      Fees £25 (average annual amount).
Sittings   Free 65. Other 260 (appropriated). Total 325.
Attendance 30 March   Morning 70 + 12 SS. Total 82.
Average attendance   Morning 100 + 20 SS. Total 120.
Remarks   Continuation of remarks. Since the last Census was taken the population of two townships previously belonging to this parish, viz. Little Harle and West Harle and amounting to 89 persons became annexed to the adjoining parish of Kirkharle. In exchange I received the township of Hawick (but which has only a population of seven persons) within, and none (if exchange of townships) there will appear a deficiency of 82 persons at Kirkwhelpington and a proportional increase in Kirkharle. J. W.
Dated   31 March 1851.
Signed   John Walker, vicar [1834–67].
      Kirkwhelpington, Newcastle upon Tyne.
{1857   Attendance 60. 40 communicants.}   {B 6.}

3.10   Church of England Schoolroom, Capheaton (557.21a)
[Included as 'remarks' under 3.9]
There is occasional divine service on Sundays at Capheaton village in a licensed schoolroom. The average attendance 100 + 34 SS. Total 134.
Incumbent   John Walker [1834–67].
{1857   Attendance about 90. In use since 1825.}

3.11   Church of England, St Aidan, Thockrington (557.19)
Population 1851: 173 (parish) 36 (township)

Name   No name but Thockrington Church. It is an ancient
             church of Norman architecture and of a distinct and
             separate parish.
Consecrated [Not given. Restored 1876.]
Endowment [Not given.]
Erected   The time of erection not known.
Endowment Tithe £20. Glebe £40.
Sittings   Free 60. Other 12. Total 72.
Attendance 30 March   Morning *6. Total [6].
Average attendance   Morning 30. Total [30].
Remarks   *The 30 [March] was on a cold and stormy day, and
             the church stands upon a bleak and an exposed
             situation. The parishioners are nearly all dissenters
             except one or two families who live at some distance
             from the church.
Dated   1 April 1851.
Signed   Humphrey Brown, perpetual curate [1834–60].
             Kirkheaton, Newcastle upon Tyne.
[Humphrey Brown (junior) was also the incumbent of St Bartholomew,
Kirkheaton (**5.7**).
Until 24 January 1837 the parish of Thockrington was in the diocese
of York, and 'was an ecclesiastical peculiar attached to the York
prebend of Tockerington' (M. McCollum, 'Changes in the Pattern
of Ecclesiastical Jurisdictions in and connected with the Diocese of
Durham during the 19th Century', *Transactions of the Architectural
and Archaeological Society of Durham and Northumberland*, new series
(1982), p. 61).]

3.12   Church of England, St Aidan, Thorneyburn (557.10)
Population 1851: 340 (parish) 167 (township)

Name   Thorneyburn Church. Parish of Thorneyburn.
Consecrated About 1817, 1818 or 1819. A new church on the
             division of the parish of Simonburn by Act of
             Parliament [of 1811] and consecrated on 8 August 1818
             [by the Bishop of Oxford].
Erected   (Erected according to Act of Parliament) 51 Geo. III
             c.194.
Endowment Tithe £200 (commuted). Glebe about 20 acres.

Sittings   Free about 150. Total [about 150].
Attendance 30 March   Morning 21. Total [21].
Average attendance   [Not given.]
Dated   31 March 1851.
Signed   Joseph Littlewood AM, rector [1833–52].
    Thorneyburn, near Hexham, Northumberland.

{B 3.}

[In 1846 the living was sequestrated because of the bankruptcy of Joseph Littlewood. He maintained that it was impossible to support five people on an annual income of £120. DUL, ASC, DDR/EJ/CLD/2.]

3.13   Church of England, St Michael, Wark (557.17)
Population 1851: 865 (parish) 483 (township)

Name   Wark Parish Church. Built under the authority of an
    Act [of Parliament of 1811 (51 Geo. III c. 194)] passed
    for the Commissioners of Greenwich Hospital.
Consecrated   11 August 1818 [10 August 1818, by the Bishop of
    Oxford] as an additional church.
Erected   By Parliamentary grant of the Commissioners of
    Greenwich Hospital.
    Cost by Parliamentary grant to Greenwich Hospital.
    Total cost £4,000.
Endowment   Tithe £330. Glebe £16. Fees £1 10s.
Sittings   Free 40 (pews holding six each). Total 240.
Attendance 30 March   Morning 131 + 21 SS. Total 152.
    Evening 71. Total 71.
Average attendance   Morning 120. Total [120].
    Evening 100. Total [100].
Remarks   The above named church is one of those built at the
    division of the ancient parish of Simonburn into five
    distinct parishes.
Dated   31 March 1851.
Signed   Henry Morton, minister [1851–53].
    Wark, near Hexham, Northumberland.
Incumbent   [Edward Beatty 1848–51.]
{1857   Attendance 150. 30 communicants.}   {B 12.}

3.14   United Presbyterian, Bellingham (557.12)
Name   United Presbyterian Chapel.
Erected   1806. [New chapel opened 19 July 1883.]

Building   [Separate and entire. Exclusively used for worship.]
Sittings   Free 100. Other 280. Total [380].
Attendance 30 March   Morning 206 + 38 SS. Total [244].
Average attendance   Morning 250. Total [250].
Dated   31 March 1851.
Signed   John Young, minister [1829–70].
          Bellingham, Northumberland.

3.15   United Presbyterian, Otterburn (557.8)

Name   Otterburn Chapel.
Erected   1832. [Rebuilt 1885.]
Building   Separate and entire. [Exclusively used for worship.]
Sittings   Free 80. Other 220 (let). Total [300].
Attendance 30 March   Morning 200 + SS (included). Total 200.
Average attendance   Morning 200 + SS (included). Total 200.
Dated   30 March 1851.
Signed   Anthony Leslie Christie, minister.
          Otterburn, via Newcastle upon Tyne.

3.16   English Presbyterian, Great Bavington (557.22)

Name   Presbyterian Church.
Erected   In the year 1735 but in place of the […] and in the time
          of the Con. Union.
Building   [Separate and entire. Exclusively used for worship.]
Sittings   Free 160. Other 140. Total [300]. Standing room (no
          such space).
Attendance 30 March   Morning 130. Total 130.
Average attendance   Morning 130. Total 130.
Remarks   The people attending the Presbyterian Church at Great
          Bavington being widely located in the country cannot
          attend public worship in great numbers, unless when
          the season is fine and so it is that even the general
          congregation is small.
          The Presbyterian Church at Great Bavington existed in
          the time of the conformists and nonconformists. [There
          was a meeting house at Great Bavington in 1693.]
Dated   31 March 1851.
Signed   Alexander Trotter, minister [1824–52].
          Capheaton, by Newcastle upon Tyne.
[In 1803 some of the congregation left and formed the Presbyterian
church at North Middleton (**9.19**).]

3.17   English Presbyterian, Birdhopecraig (557.9)

Name   Birdhopecraig Chapel.
Erected   Before 1800. [1724. Inscription 'Birdhopecraig Scotch
                Church 1826'.]
Building   [Separate and entire. Exclusively used for worship.]
Sittings   [None free.] Other 450. Total [450].
Attendance 30 March   Morning 197 + 23 SS. Total 220.
Average attendance   Morning at least 260 + 29 SS. Total 289.
Remarks   [Sittings] There are no sittings expressly free, but any
                person is at liberty to attend without any charge,
                if he chooses to do so. The chapel is seated for the
                number specified, but it will hold 500 easily enough.
                [Attendance.] We have no interval of public worship.
                There is only one act of service. The people were
                counted on the 30 March. The busy season among the
                shepherds has commenced, and the congregation is
                composed of sheep farmers and shepherds.
Dated   31 March 1851.
Signed   William Menzies Whyte, minister [1849–53].
                Birdhopecraig House, Otterburn, Newcastle upon
                Tyne.

3.18   English Presbyterian, Falstone (557.4)

Name   Falstone Presbyterian Church.
Erected   Before 1800. [1735, new building 1807, restored 1876.]
Building   [Separate and entire. Exclusively used for worship.]
Sittings   [None free.] Other 400. Total [400].
Attendance 30 March   Morning 340 + 39 SS. Total 379.
Average attendance   Morning 300 + 46 SS. Total 346.
Remarks   For six Sabbaths in the year public worship is not held
                in the Falstone Presbyterian Church.
Dated   31 March 1851.
Signed   Donald MacNaughton Stuart, minister [1849–59].
                Falstone, Northumberland.
[Donald MacNaughton Stuart (1819–1894) was the first minister
of Knox Church, Dunedin, New Zealand, 1860–94. From 1871 he
was also the vice-chancellor of the nearby Otago University, and
chancellor from 1879. In 1872 he was awarded a DD from the
University of St Andrews.]

3.19   English Presbyterian, Keilder (557.5)
Name   Tynehead Presbyterian Church.
Erected   Before 1800. [Built 1709, new chapel 1874.]
Building   [Separate and entire. Exclusively used for worship.]
Sittings   [None free.] Other 150. Total [150].
Attendance 30 March   [Not given.]
Average attendance   Morning 120 + 22 SS. Total 142.
Remarks   Regular service is only held in this chapel twelve
                times in the year. The Sabbath school also is only
                taught on the days of public worship there.
Dated   31 March 1851.
Signed   Donald MacNaughton Stuart, minister [1849–59].
                Falstone, Northumberland.

3.20   English Presbyterian, Wark (557.15)
Name   Presbyterian Chapel. [Chapel House.]
Erected   About 1848. [Rebuilt 1875.]
Building   Separate building. Exclusively as [a] place of worship.
Sittings   Free 144 (sittings promiscuous). Total [144].
Attendance 30 March   [Morning, afternoon and evening no services
                were held.]
Average attendance   Morning, afternoon and evening for last three
                months average attendance 60. Total [60].
Remarks   NB. No settled minister at present. The congregations
                of Wark and [Beggar] Bog [Housesteads Chapel (**7.25**)]
                are the joint charge of the same minister who officiates
                alternately. The distance between places being nine
                miles.
Dated   31 March 1851.
Signed   William Armstrong, member of Wark Cong[regation]
                (surgeon).
                Wark, Hexham, Northumberland.
Minister   [Thomas Johnstone 1838–51.]

3.21   Wesleyan Methodist, Wark (557.16)
Name   Wark Wesleyan Chapel.
Erected   Year 1835. [Rebuilt 1880 to seat 174.]
Building   Chapel with a dwelling house adjoining. [Not
                exclusively used for worship.]
Sittings   Free 50. Other 72 lets. Total [122]. Standing room 30
                people.
Attendance 30 March   Morning [9] SS (4 m[ale], 5 f[emale]). Total 9.

	Afternoon 20 + 11 SS (5 m[ale], 6 f[emale]). Total [31].
Average attendance	Morning [16] SS (9m[ale], 7 f[emale]). Total 16. Afternoon 30 + SS ditto. Total 32 (*sic*).
Dated	31 March 1851.
Signed	Joseph Lowes, member on [*sic*] society [agricultural labourer]. [The Square], Wark, County of Northumberland.

3.22   Primitive Methodist, Little Bavington (557.20)

Name	Little Bavington Chapel.
Erected	1829.
Building	[Separate and entire. Exclusively used for worship.]
Sittings	Free 200. Total [200].
Attendance 30 March	Morning 35 SS. Total 35. Evening 38. Total 38.
Average attendance	Morning 40 SS. Total 40. Evening 60. Total 60.
Dated	30 March 1851.
Signed	John Henderson, chapel steward [master tailor]. Little Bavington, Capheaton, Newcastle upon Tyne.

3.23   Roman Catholic, Bellingham (557.13)

Name	St Oswald's.
Erected	1839. [Opencd 26 June 1839.]
Building	[Separate and entire. Exclusively used for worship.]
Sittings	[Not given.]
Attendance 30 March	Morning 34 + 20 SS. Total 54. Afternoon 16 + 20 SS. Total 36.
Average attendance	Morning 60 + 15 SS. Total 75.
Remarks	Those who can afford it are expected to pay a small sum quarterly for their sitting.
Dated	31 March 1851.
Signed	Nicholas Brown, Roman Catholic priest [1838–51]. St Oswald's, Bellingham, via Hexham.

4. Berwick District (HO 129/561)
33 places of worship

4.1   Church of England, St Anne, Ancroft (561.6)
Population 1851: 1,883 (parochial chapelry)

Name   Ancroft. Church of an ancient chapelry.
Consecrated Before 1800. [Restored 1836, enlarged 1870.]
Endowment   [£131.]
Sittings   Free 181. Other 119. Total 300.
Attendance 30 March   Morning 170 + 85 SS. Total 255.
                        Afternoon 20 + 25 SS. Total 45.
Average attendance   [Not given.]
Dated   31 March 1851.
Signed   William Hewitt, minister [1827–60].
               Ancroft Parsonage, Berwick upon Tweed.
{1857   Attendance 200. 46 communicants.}   {B 13.}

4.2   Church of England, Holy Trinity, Berwick upon Tweed
(561.16)
Population 1851: 10,067 (parish and 227 in the barracks)

Name   Trinity Church, a vicarage.
Consecrated Before 1800. [Foundation stone laid, 26 April 1650,
               opened June 1652, consecrated 1662. Small chancel
               added and church re-opened 26 August 1855. Restored
               and enlarged at a cost of £3,000, £250 of which from
               the Dean and Chapter.]
Endowment   Land £76. OPE £180. By the [...] of the titles belonging
               to the Dean and Chapter of Durham. Fees £16. [Total
               £289.]
Sittings   Free 350. Other 900. Total 1,250.
Attendance 30 March   Morning 750 + 20 SS. Total 770.
                        Afternoon 500 + 20 SS. Total 520.
Average attendance   Morning 800 + 20 SS. Total 820.
                        Afternoon 550 + 20 SS. Total 570.
Remarks   The Dean and Chapt[er] of Durham possess all the
               tithes rectorial and vicarial, and the Easter offerings,
               permanent endowment £5 for HerMajesty's Exchequer.
Dated   31 March 1851.
Signed   Joseph Barnes, vicar [1805–53].
               Berwick upon Tweed.

{1857   Attendance 1,400. 250 communicants.}   {B 197.}
[Other parish churches erected during the Commonwealth period included St Matthew, Dendron, Barrow in Furness (1642), Staunton Harold Chapel, Leicestershire (1653), St Matthias, Poplar (1654) and St Ninian, Ninebanks, Cumbria (1659).]

4.3 Church of England, St Helen, Cornhill on Tweed (561.33)
Population 1851: 973 (chapelry)

Name   Perpetual curacy of Cornhill.
Consecrated Before 1800. [Rebuilt 1752, enlarged 1840, restored 1866.]
Endowment OPE [...]dation by Dean and Chapter of Durham. Fees [ditto]. Easter offerings commuted. [Total £240.]
Sittings   Free 145. Other 101. Total 246.
Attendance 30 March   Morning about 165 + 36 SS. Total 201.
            Afternoon about 65 + 36 SS. Total 101.
Average attendance   [Not given.]
Remarks   Several of the usual congregation were absent.
Dated   31 March 1851.
Signed   Samuel Arnot Fyler, perpetual curate [1834–80]. Cornhill, near Coldstream.
{1857   Attendance 160. 25 communicants.}   {B 8.}

4.4 Church of England, St Mary the Virgin, Holy Island (561.3)
Population 1851: 908 (parish)

Name   The church is an ancient parish church built before the year 1145 and dedicated to St Mary.
Consecrated [Restored 1860, at a cost of about £1,200.]
Endowment [£183.]
Sittings   Free 110. Other 84. Total 194.
Attendance 30 March   Morning 66 + 35 SS. Total 101.
            Afternoon 15 + 47 SS. Total 62.
Average attendance   Morning 100 + 43 SS. Total 143.
            Afternoon 30 + 50 SS. Total 80.
Dated   31 March 1851.
Signed   Anthony Watson, incumbent [1822–67]. Holy Island, Berwick upon Tweed.
{1857   Attendance 80. 16 communicants.}   {B 24.}

4.5   Church of England summary (561.7)
[Summary form]
[Includes the four churches of Ancroft, Holy Island, Kyloe and Scremerston.]

Erected   Ancroft 600 years ago, Holy Island unknown, Kyloe
                also unknown, Scremerston 1843.

Sittings   Free 657. Other 396. Total 1,053.

Usual attendance   Morning 385 + 360 SS. Total [745].
                Afternoon 155 (SS within the above).
                Evening none.

Remarks   [The] majority of the inhabitants in this district
                are dissenters, which makes ample room [for]
                episcopalians in these churches.

Signed   John Anderson, registrar.
                John Morrell, informant.

{1857   Attendance 130. 55 communicants.}

4.6   St Nicholas, Kyloe (561.7a)
[See **4.5.**]

Name   [St Nicholas, which was rebuilt in 1792, replacing an
                earlier building. A chancel was added in 1861–62, and
                the building was restored in 1868.]

Endowment   [£138.]

Incumbent   [Robert Smith 1829–51.]

                                                        {B 10.}

4.7   Church of England, St Cuthbert, Norham (561.29)
Population 1851: 1,033 (township)

Name   St Cuthbert's, Norham. The ancient parish church.

Consecrated (Built about 1160AD. Enlarged 1845.) Said to have
                been erected by Hugh Pudsey, Bishop of Durham
                [Crossed out]. [Restored 1837–46, 1852, 1883.]

Endowment   Tithe £460. Glebe £40. OPE £67. Held under lease of
                Dean and Chapter of Durham. Fees £10.

Sittings   Free 70. Other 380. Total 450.

Attendance 30 March   Morning 200 + 38 SS. Total 238.
                Evening 160. Total 160.

Average attendance   Morning 300 + 50 SS. Total 350*.
                Evening 160. Total 160.

Remarks   The services of the Ch[urch] of England are performed
                on Sundays in other parts of the parish for the

accommodation of those who live at a distance from the parish church which is not centrally situated. At Duddo chapel of ease. Usual number of attendants. Morning 65. Shoreswood schoolroom. Usual number of attendants. Evening 50. Horncastle schoolroom. Usual number of attendants. Evening 40. Total 155. *The two numbers 350 + 155 give a total of 505 usual attendants on the services of the church in Norham.

Dated	31 March 1851.
Signed	William Stephen Gilly DD, vicar [1831–55].
	Norham vicarage, near Berwick upon Tweed.
{1857	Attendance 350. 50 communicants.} {B 34.}

['William Stephen Gilly (1789–1855)', *ODNB*, vol. 2, p. 305. He was the Perpetual Curate of St Margaret's, Durham, 1827–31, and from 1853 a residentiary canon of Durham cathedral. In 1823 he first visited the Waldenses, a small persecuted church in northern Italy and subsequently published works on them.]

4.8   Church of England, St James the Great, Duddo (561.32)
Population 1851: 286 (township)

Name	Chapel of ease to the parish church of Norham.
Consecrated	Licensed [17 July] 1832 [but] not consecrated as chapel of ease to parish church. [Subsequently consecrated 22 June 1866, and replaced by All Saints, consecrated 9 November 1880.]
Erected	Cost of erection met by subscription. Dr [William Stephen] Gilly, vicar of the parish. [£50 from the Dean and Chapter of Durham.] Private £314 10s 4d. Total cost £314 10s 4d.
Endowment	No endowment at present but will have an endowment of £50 a year from the Dean and Chapter of Durham in 1857.
Sittings	All free. Total 150.
Attendance 30 March	Morning 35 + 30 SS. Total 65.
Average attendance	[Not given.]
Dated	31 March 1851.
Signed	Henry Harrison, officiating minister, stipendiary curate of Norham [1851–54].

Duddo, near Berwick upon Tweed.
Incumbent [William Stephen Gilly 1831–55.]
{1857 Attendance 30. 15 communicants.}

4.9 Church of England Schoolroom, Horncastle (561.29a)
Average attendance Evening 40. Total [40].
Incumbent [William Stephen Gilly 1831–55.]

4.10 Church of England Schoolroom, Shoreswood (561.34)
Population 1851: 428 (township)

[Summary form]
Name Schoolroom used for divine service Sunday afternoon.
Sittings Free 70. Total 70.
Usual attendance Afternoon 40 + 30 SS. Total [70].
Dated 29 December 1851.
Signed Jos[eph] Scott, registrar.
Henry Harrison, curate [1851–54].
Norham.
Incumbent [William Stephen Gilly 1831–55.]
{1857 Attendance 50. – communicants.}

4.11 Church of England, St Peter Scremerston (561.5)
Population 1851: (A township within the parish of Ancroft)

Name St Peter's consolidated chapelry of Scremerston.
Consecrated [23 August] 1843, as an additional church. [As chapel
of ease to Ancroft. District created 3 September 1844
out of the parishes of Ancroft and Tweedmouth.]
Erected By subscription. Total cost unknown.
Endowment OPE Payments by [the Dean and] Chapter of Durham
and Ecclesiastical Commissioners. [With £75 from the
Bishop of Durham. Total £120.]
Sittings Free 280. Other 70. Total 350.
Attendance 30 March Morning 57 + 71 SS. Total 126.
Afternoon 22 + 29 SS. Total 51.
Average attendance Morning 75 + 60 SS. Total 135.
Afternoon 35 + 40 SS. Total 75.
Dated 4 April 1851.
Signed Hugh Evans, perpetual curate [1850–95].
Scremerston, n[ea]r Berwick upon Tweed.
{1857 Attendance 123. 37 communicants.}

4.12   Church of England, St Bartholomew, Tweedmouth (561.11)
Population 1851: 5,714 (parish) 3,054 (township)

Name   Tweedmouth Church, an ancient parish church.
Consecrated   Before 1800. [Rebuilt 1780, enlarged 1841, restored
             1866, 1903–06.]
Endowment   Land £59. Tithe £4. Fees £6. Other £81.
Sittings   Free 168. Obtained by an addition to the church in the
             year 1841.
             Other 132. Total 300.
Attendance 30 March   Morning 150 + 75 SS. Total 225.
                    Afternoon 110 + 75 SS. Total 185.
Average attendance   [Not given.]
Dated   31 March 1851
Signed   John Leach, perpetual curate [1827–64].
             Tweedmouth, Berwick upon Tweed.
{1857   Attendance 250. 60 communicants.}   {B 156.}
[In December 1995 the dedication was changed to St Bartholomew
and St Boisil.]

4.13   Church of Scotland, High Street, Berwick upon Tweed
(561.24)
Name   High Meeting [House].
Erected   1724.
Building   [Separate and entire. Exclusively used for worship.]
Sittings   [None free.] Other 798. Total [798].
Attendance 30 March   Morning 436. Total [436].
Average attendance   [Not given.]
Dated   31 March 1851.
Signed   James Aitchison Miller, minister of the gospel [1844–
             74].
             Berwick upon Tweed.

4.14   Church of Scotland, Tweedmouth (561.12)
Name   Scotch Church.
Erected   Before 1800. [1783.]
Building   [Separate and entire. Exclusively used for worship.]
Sittings   [Not given.]
Attendance 30 March   Morning 700. Total [700].
                    Afternoon 400 to 500. Total [400–500].
Average attendance   Morning 700 + about 80 SS. Total [780].

Afternoon 400 to 500 + about 80 SS.
Total [480–580].
Dated   31 March 1851.
Signed   David Drummond, minister [1848–52].
Tweedmouth.

4.15   United Presbyterian, Chapel Street, Berwick upon Tweed
(561.27)
Name   United Presbyterian Church. [Middle Meeting or
Chapel Street Church.]
Erected   1756.
Building   [Separate and entire. Exclusively used for worship.]
Sittings   [None free.] Other 900. Total [900].
Attendance 30 March   Morning 550. Total 550.
Afternoon 600. Total 600.
Evening 80 SS. Total 80.
Average attendance   [Not given.]
Dated   31 March 1851.
Signed   William Ritchie, minister [1835–59].
Berwick upon Tweed.
[In 1835 some of the congregation formed Zion Chapel (**4.18**) and in
1917 united with the Church Street Church (**4.17**).]

4.16   United Presbyterian, Golden Square, Berwick upon Tweed
(561.19)
Name   Golden Square Chapel. [The Session Church.]
Erected   Before 1800. [Congregation formed 1769, chapel
erected 1771, enlarged 1796.]
Building   [Separate and entire. Exclusively used for worship.]
Sittings   [None free.] Other 850. Total [850].
Attendance 30 March   Morning 800 and upwards [SS] not separate.
Total 800.
Afternoon 850 to 900. Total 850–900.
Average attendance   Morning 800. Total 800.
Afternoon 850 to 900. Total 850–900.
Remarks   There is occasional service in the evening at other
times and always once a quarter for the dispensation
of the Lord's Supper. The attendance is generally
upward of 800 on each occasion.
Dated   31 March 1851.
Signed   John Cairns, minister [1845–76].
Berwick upon Tweed.

[From 1867 Dr John Cairns (1818–1892) was also the Professor of Apologetics in the United Presbyterian Theological Hall, Edinburgh. In 1876 he became the full-time associate Professor of Dogmatics and Apologetics, and Principal 1879–91. 'The personal influence of this highly erudite, cultured and saintly man, especially among United Presbyterians, was immense in his own lifetime.' N.M. De S. Cameron, *Dictionary of Scottish Church History and Theology* (Edinburgh, 1993), p. 117.

When he was at Berwick upon Tweed 'People have said that they would walk miles to hear John Cairns say, "Let us pray". His prayer lasted for 15–20 minutes, and the sermon 50 minutes. A.R. MacEwen, *Life and Letters of John Cairns* (London, 1898), p. 322.

The new church in Wallace Green, opened on 19 June 1859, had 970 sittings and cost £5,705.]

4.17   United Presbyterian, Church Street, Berwick upon Tweed
(561.26)

Name   United Presbyterian Church. [Church Street Church.]
Erected   1812.
Building   Separate and entire. Exclusively [used for worship].
Sittings   Free 30. Other 470. Total [500].
Attendance 30 March   Morning 350. Total 350.
                        Afternoon 420. Total 420.
                        Evening 125 SS. Total 125.
Average attendance   Morning 400. Total 400.
                        Afternoon 450. Total 450.
                        Evening 125 SS. Total 125.
Dated   31 March 1851.
Signed   John Peden, minister [1842–59].
                Berwick upon Tweed.
[In 1917 united with the Presbyterian Church, Chapel Street Church (**4.15**).]

4.18   United Presbyterian, Bankhill, Berwick upon Tweed
(561.18)

Name   Zion Chapel.
Erected   In the year 1835. [Opened 26 February 1836.]
Building   [Separate and entire. Exclusively used for worship.]
Sittings   Free 365. Other 165. Total [530].
                Standing room. The aisles of the chapel 360 square feet.
Attendance 30 March   Morning 132. Total [132].
                        Afternoon 175. Total [175].

Evening 192 + 36 SS. Total [228].

Average attendance   Morning and afternoon 180 + 40 SS (average number at each [service]). Total [220].

Remarks   The Sunday scholars do not meet for public worship in a distinctive capacity. They are instructed during the interval between afternoon and evening service, but almost all meet for public worship in this chapel. The chapel is fully fitted up.

Dated   31 March 1851.

Signed   Manners Patterson, elder and manager [rope and sail maker].

Quay Walls, Berwick upon Tweed.

Minister   [Hugh Dunlop 1848–51.]

[The chapel closed in 1853 and the building was sold to the Low Meeting House, Hide Hill.]

4.19   **United Presbyterian, Norham** (561.30)

Name   Old Dissenting Meeting House.

Erected   Before 1800. [1753.]

Building   [Separate and entire. Exclusively used for worship.]

Sittings   Free (see remarks). Other 400. Total [400].

Attendance 30 March   Morning and afternoon 155. Morning and afternoon services held without intermission between services. Total [155].

Average attendance   [Not given.]

Remarks   No sittings are set apart expressly by the name of 'free sittings', but as is commonly the case with voluntary churches, individuals wishing to attend ordinances, but unable to pay seat rents, are supplied with sittings gratuitously. There are several such cases in connection with the chapel.

Dated   31 March 1851.

Signed   James T. Anderson, minister.

Norham by Berwick [upon Tweed].

[In 1845 the two Presbyterian churches in Norham divided and were reunited in 1897.]

4.20   **United Presbyterian, Spittal** (561.14)

Name   Spittal Church or Chapel.

Erected   Before 1800. Existed, I believe as a place of worship since 1745.

[Meeting house built 1752. St Paul's church opened 1878.]

Building [Separate and entire. Exclusively used for worship.]
Sittings The chapel is seated for 730 and seats are let as applications come forward. Total [730].
Attendance 30 March Morning 600. Total 600.
                       Afternoon 600. Total 600.
                       Evening no service.
Average attendance [Not given.]
Remarks In reference to attendance, I have stated it in round numbers, and I may state also that it is not our custom to have the Sabbath school class there as such, though of course some are present with their parents.
Dated 31 March 1851.
Signed William Porteous, junior minister (or colleague and successor) [rope maker].
          Spittal, Berwick upon Tweed.

4.21   English Presbyterian, Ancroft Moor (561.9)

Name Ancroft Moor.
Erected 1845. [Inscription: 'Ancroft English Presbyterian Church erected for the Rev. W. Ryder, 1845']
Building [Separate and entire. Exclusively used for worship.]
Sittings [None free.] Other 360. Total [360].
Attendance 30 March Morning 160 + 20 SS. Total 180.
                       Afternoon 130. Total 130.
Average attendance [Not given.]
Remarks There are no 'free sittings' allocated, but parties unable to pay for sittings can have them 'free' on making application.
Dated 31 March 1851.
Signed William Ryder, minister.
          Horncliff, Berwick upon Tweed.

4.22   English Presbyterian, Norham (561.31)

Name English Presbyterian Church.
Erected 1845.
Building [Separate and entire. Exclusively used for worship.]
Sittings Free (see remarks). Other 600 [Crossed out 623 with difficulty [and] 527 with ease].
Attendance 30 March Morning 334. Total 334.   {The few SS sit
                       Afternoon 323. Total 323. {with their parents.

Average attendance	Morning about 400. Total 400. {Most remain
	Afternoon [390]. Total 390. {for both
	services.
Remarks	There is no particular part of the church set aside
	as free sittings. The poorer members of the church
	who cannot afford to pay for seats retain the seats
	they occupied when they could pay for them. To
	accommodate the people, the majority of whom come
	from a considerable distance, there is no interval
	between our services. We have two sermons in
	summer, and during the winter months we have but
	one.
Dated	31 March 1851.
Signed	James Stewart, minister.
	Norham, near Berwick upon Tweed.

[In 1845 the two Presbyterian churches in Norham divided and were reunited in 1897.]

4.23   English Presbyterian, Tweedmouth (561.10)

[On a Church of England form]

Name	English Presbyterian Church. [Scobie's Chapel.]
Erected	Opened for public worship in 1848. In consequence
	of the disruption in the Church of Scotland [in 1843].
	Erected by private subscription. Total cost £1,000.
Endowment	Pew rents £50. Other £50.
Sittings	[None free.] Other 360. Total 360.
Attendance 30 March	Morning 95 +12 SS. Total 107.
	Afternoon 99 + 9 SS. Total 108.
Average attendance	Morning 110 + 10 SS. Total 120.
	Afternoon 116 + 8 SS. Total 124.
Remarks	There are no free sittings, but poor persons are
	sometimes allowed to occupy a seat in any part of the
	church without paying for it.
Dated	31 March 1851.
Signed	Robert McClelland, minister.
	Tweedmouth, Berwick upon Tweed.

4.24   Independent [Congregational], Castlegate, Berwick upon Tweed (561.17)

Name	Independent Chapel.
Erected	Opened 18 December 1849 [closed 1859].

Building   A separate and entire building. Exclusively [used for worship].
Sittings   [None free.] Other 400. Total [400].
Attendance 30 March   Morning 60 + 15 SS. Total 75.
Afternoon no service.
Evening 300. Total 300.
Average attendance   [Not given.]
Remarks   The great difference between the morning and evening attendance is owing to the recent commencement of the church.
Dated   31 March 1851.
Signed   William Duncan Knowles, minister [1848–52]. Berwick upon Tweed.

4.25   Baptist, Walkergate Lane, Berwick upon Tweed (561.22)
Name   Baptist Chapel.
Erected   1811. [Enlarged 1832. Moved to Independent Chapel, Castlegate and opened 24 July 1859.]
Building   [Separate and entire. Exclusively used for worship.]
Sittings   All free sittings. No standing room. 1,200 square feet.
Attendance 30 March   Morning 150. Total [150].
Afternoon 250. Total [250].
Evening 160. Total [160].
Average attendance   [Not given.]
Dated   31 March 1851.
Signed   Alexander Kirkwood, minister [1809–55]. Berwick upon Tweed.
[The numbers grew from a membership of 14 in 1809 to 127 in 1850, then reduced to 85 when the rest emigrated to the USA. Alexander Kirkwood preached at Ford Forge (**6.22**), and from 1809–43 he taught at the Lancasterian School, Berwick upon Tweed.]

4.26   Wesleyan Methodist, Walkergate Lane, Berwick upon Tweed (561.20)
Name   Wesleyan Chapel.
Erected   Before 1800. [1797, altered 1825, rebuilt 1878.]
Building   [Separate and entire. Exclusively used for worship.]
Sittings   Free 300. Other 80. Total [380].
Attendance 30 March   Morning 76 + 44 SS. Total 120.
Evening 111. Total 111.
Average attendance   Morning 116 + 45 SS. Total 161.
Evening 130. Total 130.

Remarks   The average number of this congregation is affected by
Her Majesty's troops that may be stationed here.
Dated   31 March 1851.
Signed   Lancelot Railton, minister [1850–52].
Berwick upon Tweed.

4.27   Primitive Methodist, Ancroft (561.2)

Name   Primitive Methodist Chapel.
Erected   In the year 1816.
Building   [Separate and entire. Exclusively used for worship.]
Sittings   Free 74. Total [74].
Attendance 30 March   Morning 50. Total [50]. [No SS.]
                       Afternoon 26. Total [26].
Average attendance   [Not given.]
Remarks   A day school was in connection with this chapel until
about the year 1845.
Dated   30 March 1851.
Signed   George Craith, steward.
Ancroft, South Moor by Berwick upon Tweed.

4.28   Primitive Methodist, College Place, Berwick upon Tweed (561.25)

Name   College Place Chapel.
Erected   In 1829. [Opened 18 February 1830, cost £630].
Building   Separate [and entire]. Exclusively [used for worship].
Sittings   Free 190. Other 310. Total [500]. Standing room 150.
Attendance 30 March   Morning 37 + 25 SS. Total 62.
                       Afternoon 88 + 10 SS. Total 98.
                       Evening 58 + 13 SS. Total 71.
Average attendance   Morning 350 (*sic*). Total [350].
Remarks   *W. Fulton will give any additional information when
applied to.
Dated   30 March 1851.
Signed   *Rev. William Fulton, minister.
Chapel House, College Place, Berwick upon Tweed.

4.29   Primitive Methodist, Holy Island (561.4)

Name   None.
Erected   Before 1800.
Building   [Separate and entire. Exclusively used for worship.]
Sittings   Free 100. Total [100].
Attendance 30 March   Evening 82 + 14 SS. Total 96.

Average attendance   [Not given.]
Dated   31 March 1851.
Signed   William Fulton, minister.
Chapel House, Berwick upon Tweed.

4.30 Primitive Methodist, Back Street, Spittal (561.15)

Name   None.
Erected   Before 1800.
Building   [Separate and entire. Exclusively used for worship.]
Sittings   Free 60. Total [60]. Standing room 40.
Attendance 30 March   Evening 48. Total [48].
Average attendance   [Not given.]
Remarks   *W. Fulton is the superintendent of the circuit and will communicate all needful information when applied for.
Dated   30 March 1851.
Signed   Adam Paxton, local preacher [commercial traveller].
*Rev William Fulton, Chapel House, Berwick upon Tweed.
[The first camp meeting, held in Spittal on 27 June 1830, attracted 4,000 people.]

4.31 Primitive Methodist, Church Square, Tweedmouth (561.13)

Name   None.
Erected   Before 1800.
Building   A room devoted solely for religious worship.
[Exclusively used for worship.]
Sittings   Free 30. Total [30]. Standing room 30.
Attendance 30 March   Evening 50. Total [50].
Average attendance   [Not given.]
Remarks   *W. Fulton, who is the superintendent of the circuit will give you any additional information if needed, when applied to.
Dated   30 March 1851.
Signed   Robert Lisle, lay preacher.
*Rev W[illiam] Fulton, Chapel House, Berwick upon Tweed.

4.32 Non-denominational, Chapel Street, Berwick upon Tweed (561.21)

Name   Town Mission Station. (For all denominations.)
Erected   About the year 1841.

Building   [Not separate and entire or exclusively used for
              worship.]
Sittings   Free 60. Total [60].
Attendance 30 March   Evening 43. Total [43].
Average attendance   Evening 48. Total [48].
Remarks   The Town Mission of Berwick upon Tweed is
              supported exclusively by Golden Square United
              Presbyterian congregation (**4.16**). The Station Room
              is hired from a private person, where the missionary
              holds Sabbath evening meetings for the benefit of
              those desolate persons who go nowhere else to
              worship God in public.
Dated   31 March 1851.
Signed   George Sudden, town missionary.
              Berwick upon Tweed.

**4.33   Roman Catholic, Ravensdowne Street, Berwick upon
Tweed** (561.23)
Name   St Mary and St Cuthbert.
Erected   [Opened 25 June] 1829. [Restored 1886.]
Building   A separate and entire building. Exclusively [used for
              worship].
Sittings   All free. Other 15.
Attendance 30 March   Morning 200. Total 200.
              Afternoon 60 + 20 SS. Total 80.
Average attendance   [Not given.]
Dated   31 March 1851.
Signed   Anthony MacDermott, Catholic priest [1848–55].
              Ravensdowne [Street], Berwick upon Tweed.

4.34   Roman Catholic, Haggerston Castle, Haggerston (561.8)
Name   St Mary and St Cuthbert.
Erected   Unknown. [Church opened 23 April 1861.]
Building   [Separate and entire. Exclusively used for worship.]
Sittings   Free 130. Other 10. Total [140]. All free sittings.
Attendance 30 March   [Not given.]
Average attendance   Morning 120. Total 120.
              Afternoon 30. Total 30.
Dated   31 March 1851.
Signed   Charles Petre Eyre, domestic chaplain [1850–56].
              Haggerston Castle, Berwick upon Tweed.
['Charles Eyre (1817–1902)', *ODNB*, vol. 18, pp. 841–842. In 1868 he

became the vicar-general of Hexham and Newcastle. In the following year he was consecrated bishop of the titular Roman Catholic see of Anazarbus and apostolic delegate of the Western District of Scotland, and from 1878–1902 the Archbishop of Glasgow.]

5. Castle Ward District (HO 129/554)
40 places of worship

5.1   Church of England, St Andrew, Bolam (554.19)
Population 1851: 634 (parish) 86 (township and 14 at Bolam vicarage)

Name   Bolam Church, dedicated to St Andrew.
Consecrated   Unknown. Very old. [Restored 1882]
Erected   Unknown.
Endowment   Land £180. Tithe £72 10s. Glebe £24. Fees £2 10s.
Sittings   Free 20. Other 170. Total 190.
Attendance 30 March   Morning 32 SS. Total [32].
Average attendance   [Not given.]
Remarks   The church being situated close to the northern
                    boundary of the parish with but a very small
                    population near it. The attendance at church is as
                    variable as the weather, so that though [the] church is
                    sometimes pretty full; the above is merely an average
                    congregation for 12 months. Aft[ernoon] service in a
                    schoolroom at Belsay. Attendance for 80.
Dated   31 March 1851.
Signed   Septimus Stanley Meggison, vicar [1817–79].
                    Bolam, Newcastle upon Tyne.
{1857   Attendance 120. 30 communicants.}   {B 12.}
['Bolam church is one of the most interesting in the deanery, but it needs a thorough restoration. So much so, that it would not be advisable to do anything at all until at least the whole of the nave and aisle could be restored.' R.C. Coxe, *A Cursory Survey of the Churches and Church Buildings within the Archdeaconry of Lindisfarne* (London, 1860), pp. 21–22.]

5.2   Church of England Schoolroom, Belsay (554.20)
Population 1851: 330 (township)

Name   Belsay Schoolroom.
Licensed   1840.
Erected   Sir Charles [M. L.] Monck Bart, having recently built
              the schoolhouse, has offered the use of it for divine
              service. The vicar consented to perform it there on
              Sunday afternoons, for doing which he obtained the
              bishop's license.
Sittings   Free 85. Total [85].
Attendance 30 March   Afternoon 50. Total [50].
Average attendance   Afternoon 70. Total [70].
Remarks   The schoolhouse is the property of Sir C[harles M. L.]
              Monck Bart, granted by him for the use of the parish,
              and as the church is inconveniently situated to the
              north, the inhabitants of Belsay township and others
              in the neighbourhood resort to it. The vicar's services
              are gratuitous.
Dated   31 March 1851.
Signed   Septimus Stanley Meggison, vicar of Bolam [1817–79].
              Bolam Vicarage, Newcastle upon Tyne.
{1857   Pretty full attendance.}

5.3   Church of England, St Matthew, Dinnington (554.5)
Population 1851: 668 (parish) 263 (township)

Name   St Matthew, Dinnington. New district church.
Consecrated [23 October] 1835 [by the Bishop of Carlisle] as an
              additional church. [As a chapel of ease to Ponteland,
              created as a separate parish (from the parishes of
              Dinnington and Gosforth) on 27 October 1835 (58
              Geo. III c.45.) Replaced by a new church consecrated 6
              December 1886.]
Erected   By [private] subscription.
Endowment   Land £20. Tithe £58. OPE £75. Fees £2.
Sittings   Free 150. Other 150. Total 300.
Attendance 30 March   Morning 150 + 72 SS. Total 222.
                        Afternoon 70 + 60 SS. Total [130].
Average attendance   [Not given.]
Dated   [Not given.]
Signed   John Mayne St Clere Raymond [1847–57].

Vicarage, Dinnington, Newcastle upon Tyne.
{1857   Attendance 120. 40 communicants.}   {B 28.}

5.4 Church of England, St Nicholas, Church Road, Gosforth (554.11)

Population 1851: 2,319 (parish) 246 (South Gosforth township) 123 (North Gosforth township)

Name	St Nicholas, commonly called Gosforth Church, being the ancient church of the chapelry of Gosforth, attached to the vicarage of Newcastle on Tyne (**10.1**).
Consecrated	Before 1800. [District created 30 January 1868.]
Erected	[Rebuilt 1798–99, enlarged 1818–20, restored 1884, enlarged 1913.]
Endowment	(By the vicar of Newcastle.)
Sittings	Free 150. Other 350. Total 500.
Attendance 30 March	Morning 200 + 43 SS. Total 243.
Average attendance	Morning about 200 + about 50 SS. Total [about] 250.
Remarks	The number of Sunday scholars is no criterion of the state of the school, which is very well attended on weekdays, but very thinly on Sundays. There is [an] afternoon service at Kenton in this parish.
Dated	30 March 1851.
Signed	Evelyn Boothby, curate [1848–51]. Gosforth, Newcastle upon Tyne.
Incumbent	[Richard Charles Coxe 1841–53.]

{B 71.}

[Richard Coxe was the Archdeacon of Lindisfarne and vicar of Eglingham 1853–65 (**10.1**).]

5.5 Church of England Schoolroom, Kenton (554.10)

Population 1851: 549 (township)

Name	[Kenton] licensed [National] schoolroom in the parish of Gosforth.
Licensed	[In 1844] as an additional place of worship for people at a distance from the church.
Erected	Private subscription.
Endowment	(Gosforth.)
Sittings	Free 100. Total 100.
Attendance 30 March	Afternoon 61 + 27 SS. Total 88.

Average attendance   Afternoon about 65 + 25 SS. Total 90.

Remarks   This room is situated about 2½ [miles] from the church, and the same remark is applicable to the Sunday school as was made with reference to that of Gosforth (**5.4**).

Dated   30 March 1851.

Signed   Evelyn Boothby, curate [1848–51].
Gosforth, Newcastle upon Tyne.

Incumbent   [Richard Charles Coxe 1841–53.]

{1857   Attendance 80.}

5.6   Church of England, St Philip and St James, Heddon on the Wall (554.38)
Population 1851: 813 (parish) 345 (township)

Name   St Philip and St James. Ancient parish church. [Later St Andrew.]

Consecrated Before 1800.

Endowment Tithe £200. Glebe £42 10s.

Sittings   All free. Total 500.

Attendance 30 March   Morning 154 + 53 SS. Total 207.
Afternoon 20 SS. Total 20.
Evening 90 + 20 SS. Total 110.

Average attendance   Morning 130 + 60 SS. Total 190.
Afternoon 80 SS. Total 80.
Evening 70 + 30 SS. Total 100.

Dated   31 March 1851.

Signed   Michael Heron Maxwell, vicar of Heddon on the Wall [1850–73].
Heddon Vicarage, Gateshead.

{1857   Attendance 300. 45 communicants.}   {B 19.}

5.7   Church of England, St Bartholomew, Kirkheaton (554.28 and 554.1a)
Population 1851: 153 (township)

[Summary form]

Name   Kirkheaton Chapel.

Erected   [Rebuilt 1753, restored 1866–67.]

Endowment [£60.]

Sittings   Free 100. The clergyman's pew contains about eight sittings.
Total 108.

[Letter to Horace Mann Esq.]
Sittings   Free 100. Appropriated 8. Total 108.
Sir,
All the sittings in Kirkheaton Chapel belong to the several farmers and their families in the chapelry, and the clergyman's pew which I have mentioned above, but none of the sittings are let. Your letter for Kirkheaton duly arrived but having got misplaced I have made the return on this page, which I hope will answer, but if it should not, if you will send me another one and I will fill it up.
I am, sir, your obedient servant,
[Rev.] Humphrey Brown [perpetual curate 1815–60].
Kirkheaton, 2 September 1852.

{B 12.}

[The former incumbent was Humphrey Brown (senior) 1770–1815. He was succeeded by his son, Humphrey Brown (junior) 1815–60, who was also the incumbent of St Aidan, Thockrington (**3.11**). Horace Mann was the Assistant Commissioner of the Religious Census.]

[Summary form (**5.9**)]
(The Rev. Humphrey Brown informs me that he has given you the information you require respecting the chapel at Kirkheaton.
30 September 1852.
George Crow, registrar.)

5.8 Church of England, Holy Trinity, Matfen (554.27)
Population 1851: 412 (West Matfen township) 164 (East Matfen township)

Name   Trinity Church. District chapelry of Matfen.
Consecrated   [17] September 1844. In lieu of the old dilapidated church of Ryal.
[District created 25 February 1846 out of the parish of Stamfordham.]
Erected   By Sir Edward Blackett Baronet at his sole charge. [Rebuilt 1879.]
Endowment   Land £30. Tithe £86. Fees £2.
Sittings   Free 200. Other 30. Total 230.
Attendance 30 March   Morning 149. Total [149].
Afternoon 60. Total [60].
Average attendance   [Not given.]
Dated   31 March 1851

Signed   John Smith Priestman, perpetual curate [1846–61].
               Matfen, Gateshead.
{1857   Attendance 300. 40 communicants.}   {B 16.}

5.9 Church of England summary (554.1)
[Summary form]
I wrote to the Rev. John Reed, vicar of Newburn respecting the
information you want about Newburn, Dalton and Sugley, but I
received no answer.
30 September 1852.
George Crow, registrar.

5.10 Church of England, St Michael and All Saints, Newburn (554.1c)
Population 1851: 4,316 (parish) 938 (township)

Name   St Michael and All Saints.
Endowment   [£230.]
Incumbent   [John Reed 1832–84.]
{1857   Attendance 400. 40 communicants.}   {B 122.}

5.11 Church of England, Holy Trinity, Dalton (554.32 and 554.1b)
Population 1851: 113 (township)

Name   Dalton Church.
Consecration [9 October 1837 as a chapel of ease to Newburn.]
Sittings   [Free 180. Other 20. Total 200.]
Attendance 30 March   [Not given.]
Average attendance   [Not given.]
Remarks   Regret that I can furnish no return.
Dated   30 March 1851.
Signed   Edward David Cree, curate [1849–52].
               Newburn, Newcastle upon Tyne.
Incumbent   [John Reed 1832–84.]

5.12 Church of England, Holy Saviour, Sugley (554.1d)
Name   Holy Saviour.
Consecrated 10 October 1837 [as a chapel of ease to Newburn.
               Parish created 1887].
Incumbent   [John Reed 1832–84.]

5.13   Church of England, St Mary the Virgin, Ponteland (554.8)
Population 1851: 1,137 (parish) 495 (township)

Name   St Mary. An ancient church.
Consecrated   Unknown. [Restored 1810, 1861, 1880.]
Endowment   Land 143 acres. Tithe (commuted). £296 4s. Fees £4 10s.
                Easter offerings and other sources (commuted with
                tithe).
Sittings   [None free.] Other 457. Total 457.
Attendance 30 March   Morning 198 + 40 SS. Total 238.
                Afternoon 40 + 20 SS. Total 60.
Average attendance   Morning 200 + 40 SS. Total 240.
                Afternoon 50 + 20 SS. Total 70.
Remarks   The sittings are all appropriated, pews are exclusive of
                a gallery for the Sunday scholars.
Dated   30 March 1851.
Signed   James Robson, curate of Ponteland [1841–60].
                Ponteland Vicarage, Newcastle upon Tyne.
Incumbent   [John Lightfoot 1823–63.]
{1857   Attendance 110. 34 communicants.}   {B 29.}

5.14   Church of England, St Mary the Virgin, Stamfordham
(554.29)
Population 1851: 1,781 (parish) 448 (township)

Name   St Mary's. Ancient parish church.
Consecrated   About 700 years ago. [Rebuilt 1847–48.]
Endowment   [£574.]
Sittings   Free 100 (children's seats 90). Other 220. Total 320.
Attendance 30 March   Morning 133 + 68 SS. Total 201.
                Afternoon 62 + 62 SS. Total 124.
Average attendance   Morning 175 + 75 SS. Total 250.
                Afternoon 180 + 70 SS. Total 250.
Dated   31 March 1851.
Signed   John Frederic Bigge, vicar of Stamfordham [1847–85].
                Stamfordham, Newcastle upon Tyne.
{1857   Attendance 200. 33 communicants.}   {B 22.}

5.15   Church of England, St Mary the Virgin, Stannington (554.3)
Population 1851: 1,000 (parish) 396 (South Quarter) 361 (North East
Quarter) 243 (North West Quarter)

Name   St Mary's, Stannington, an ancient church.
Consecration Before 1800. [New church consecrated 31 October
               1871.]
Endowment   Tithe and glebe £355. Fees £6.10s.
Sittings   Free 52. Other 242. Total 294.
Attendance 30 March   Morning 61 + 49 SS. Total 110.
                        Afternoon 16 + 64 SS. Total 80.
Average attendance   [Not given.]
Dated   31 March 1851
Signed   Henry King Collinson, minister [1845–67].
               Stannington, Morpeth, Northumberland.
{1857   Attendance 150. 30 communicants.}   {B 26.}
[Henry King Collinson was the eldest son of John Collinson, rector
of Gateshead 1810–39. Henry Collinson 'was much addicted to the
bottle, a disgrace to his high calling'. DUL, ASC, Huddleston Clergy
Index. However, John Collinson actively supported the temperance
cause.]

5.16   Church of England, St Barnabas, Thorny Ford (554.17)
Population 1851: 46 (township)

[Summary form]
Name   Thorny Ford.
Erected   1845.
Sittings   Free 120. Total 120.
Attendance 30 March   Afternoon 60 + 20 SS. Total 80.
Average attendance   [Not given.]
Dated   [Not given.]
Signed   Ralph Brown, enumerator [teacher and auctioneer].
               Ponteland.
Incumbent   [Francis Richard Grey, rector of Morpeth 1842–90.]
[Francis Grey's brother John Grey was the rector of Houghton-le-
Spring 1847–95 (**19.2**). They were the sons of the second Earl Grey.
St. Barnabus was a chapel of ease to St Mary the Virgin, Morpeth
(**9.12**) and later as 'Kirkley Chapel' closed *c*.1970.]

5.17   Church of England, St Mary Magdalene, Whalton (554.18)
Population 1851: 461 (parish) 287 (township)

Name   Whalton Church.
Consecrated Before 1800. [Repaired 1783, restored 1908.]
Endowment   Tithe £700. Glebe £125.
Sittings   Total 227.
Attendance 30 March   Morning 66 + 7 SS. Total 73.
                              Afternoon 58 + 10 SS. Total 68.
Average attendance   Morning 90 + 14 SS. Total 104.
                              Afternoon 80 + 12 SS. Total 92.
Dated   31 March 1851.
Signed   John Elphinstone Elliot, rector [1843–80].
                   Whalton, near Morpeth.
{1857   Attendance varies greatly.}   {B 9.}

5.18   United Presbyterian, Matfen (554.30)
Name   Matfen Preaching Station.
Erected   Before 1820.
Building   [Separate and entire. Exclusively used for worship.]
Sittings   Free 17. Other 20. Total [37].
Attendance 30 March   [Not given.]
Average attendance   Afternoon 27. Total 27.
Remarks   The services in this place of worship are only once in
                   the month.
Dated   31 March 1851.
Signed   William Fisken, minister [1847–84].
                   Stamfordham, Newcastle upon Tyne.

5.19   United Presbyterian, Stamfordham (554.31)
Name   Stamfordham United Presbyterian Church.
Erected   Before 1750. [1742. New chapel opened 29 November
                   1863.]
Building   Separate [and entire]. Exclusively [used for worship].
Sittings   Free 96. Other 90. Total [186].
Attendance 30 March   Morning 50 + 7 SS. Total 57.
                              Evening 31 + 6 SS. Total 37.
Average attendance   [Not given.]
Remarks   By free sittings, I understand none not paid for.
                   Other sittings these paid for.
Dated   31 March 1851.
Signed   William Fisken, minister [1847–84].
                   Stamfordham, Newcastle upon Tyne.

5.20 Wesleyan Methodist, Bulman Village [Gosforth] (554.21)
[Summary form]
Name   Gosforth Methodist Chapel.
Sittings   Free 140. Other 20. Total [160].
Usual attendance 30 March   [Not given.]
Dated   20 September 1852.
Signed   James Spragger.

5.21 Wesleyan Methodist, Harlow Hill (554.40)
Name   None.
Erected   Before 1800.
Building   [Not separate and entire or exclusively used for worship.]
Sittings   Free 40. Total [40].
Attendance 30 March   [Not given.]
Average attendance   Evening 30. Total [30].
Remarks   No preaching on 31 [March 18]51.
Dated   31 March 1851.
Signed   William Hirst, Wesleyan minister [1850–51]. Hexham, Northumberland.
[William Hirst was also a minister in Hexham (**8.62**).]

5.22 Wesleyan Methodist, Stamfordham (554.24)
Name   None.
Erected   About 1820.
Building   [Separate and entire. Exclusively used for worship.]
Sittings   Free 100. Total [100].
Attendance 30 March   Afternoon 70. Total 70.
Average attendance   Afternoon 45. Total 45.
Dated   31 March 1851.
Signed   William Hirst, Wesleyan minister [1850–51]. Hexham, Northumberland.

5.23 Wesleyan Methodist, Kenton (554.13)
Name   Kenton Wesleyan Chapel.
Erected   Before 1800.
Building   Entire building. [Exclusively] used for [a] place of worship and Sunday school.
Sittings   Free 100. Other 12. Total [112].
Attendance 30 March   Morning 33 + 17 SS. Total 50.
                      Afternoon (school).
                      Evening 41 + 26 SS. Total 67.

Average attendance   Morning 33 + 25 SS. Total 58.
Afternoon (school).
Evening 45 + 25 SS. Total 70.
Dated   30 March 1851.
Signed   Thomas Buckham, society steward [coal miner].
Corving House, Bulman Village [Gosforth].

5.24   Wesleyan Methodist, Milburn Grange (554.7)
Name   Milburn Grange Wesleyan Chapel.
Erected   Before 1800.
Building   [Separate and entire. Exclusively used for worship.]
Sittings   Free 100. Total [100].
Attendance 30 March   Morning 63 + 23 SS. Total 86.
Afternoon none.
Evening none.
Average attendance   [Not given.]
Remarks   This place of worship was formerly a cottage, was
opened as a place of public worship on 16 October
1846, and has since been occupied as preaching and
Sunday school room.
Dated   31 March 1851.
Signed   Thomas Scott, manager [cartwright and joiner].
Kirkley Westgate, Ponteland, Newcastle upon Tyne.

5.25   Wesleyan Methodist, Newburn (554.33)
Name   Wesleyan Chapel.
Erected   1832. [Inscription '1839 Wesleyan Centenary Chapel'.]
Building   [Separate and] entire. Exclusively are (*sic*) place of
worship and S[unday] school.
Sittings   Free 200. Other 56. Total [256].
Attendance 30 March   Morning none.
Afternoon 100. Total [100].
Evening 50. Total [50].
Average attendance   Morning 130 + 100 SS. Total [230].
Dated   29 March 1851.
Signed   James Taylor, steward and trustee (grocer).
Newburn.

5.26   Wesleyan Methodist, Ponteland (554.9)
Name   Wesleyan Chapple (*sic*).
Erected   [April] 1841. [Rebuilt 1908.]
Building   [Separate and entire. Exclusively used for worship.]

Sittings   Free 70. Other 50. Total [120].
Attendance 30 March   Afternoon 14. Total [14].
                        Evening 14. Total [14].
Average attendance   [Not given.]
Dated   30 March 1851.
Signed   Michael Chipson, leader [brick and tile manufacturer].
                Ponteland, Northumberland.

5.27   Wesleyan Methodist, Rudchester (554.39)

Name   Preaching House.
Erected   Time unknown.
Building   [A] dwelling house [not exclusively used for worship].
Sittings   Free 40. Total [40]. Standing room 20.
Attendance 30 March   Afternoon 30. Total 30.
Average attendance   Morning [20]. Total 20.
Dated   25 March 1851.
Signed   John Stephenson, elder [farmer].
                Rudchester, near Newcastle upon Tyne.

5.28   Wesleyan Methodist, Stamfordham (554.25)

Name   Wesleyan Chapel.
Erected   1840.
Building   Separate [and entire. Exclusively used for worship.]
Sittings   Free 104. Other 56. Total [160].
Attendance 30 March   Evening 85. Total [85].
Average attendance   Morning 100. Total [100].
Dated   31 March 1851.
Signed   George Forster, chapel steward [bailiff].
                Matfen, Newcastle upon Tyne, Northumberland.

5.29   Wesleyan Methodist, Stannington (554.4)

Name   Wesleyan Chapel.
Erected   Unknown.
Building   Adjoining houses. Used for a place of worship and
                Sunday school exclusively.
Sittings   All free sittings.
Attendance 30 March   Morning 40 + 40 SS. Total 80.
Average attendance   [Not given.]
Dated   31 March 1851.
Signed   John Brown, Sunday school teacher [agent].
                Netherton, Morpeth.

5.30   Wesleyan Methodist, Sugley (554.1e)
[Summary form]
Sittings   Free 220. Others 80. Total 300.
Dated   30 September 1852.
Signed   George Crow, registrar.

5.31   Wesleyan Methodist, Throckley (554.37)
Name   Throckley Chapel.
Erected   Before 1800.
Building   [Separate and entire. Exclusively used for worship.]
Sittings   All free 120. Total [120].
Attendance 30 March   Morning 30 SS. Total 30.
                              Afternoon 60. Total 60.
Average attendance   Morning 35 SS. Total 35.
                              Afternoon 70. Total 70.
Dated   [Not given.]
Signed   [Not given.]

5.32   Wesleyan Methodist, Walbottle (554.34)
Name   Walbottle Wesleyan Chapel.
Erected   1837.
Building   [Separate and entire. Exclusively used for worship.]
Sittings   Free 200. Other 62. Total [262].
Attendance 30 March   Morning 62. Total 62.
                              Evening 50. Total 50.
Average attendance   Morning 70. Total 70.
Dated   30 March 1851.
Signed   Aaron W. Chicken, steward [under-viewer].
                  Walbottle, Northumberland.

5.33   Primitive Methodist, Bulman Village, [Gosforth] (554.15)
[Shared building with Wesleyan Reformers (**5.38**)]
Name   Primitive Methodist Meeting House.
Erected   1830.
Building   [Separate and entire. Exclusively used for worship.]
Sittings   Free 70. Total [70].
Attendance 30 March   Afternoon [used by Wesleyan Reformers].
                              Evening 50. Total [50].
Average attendance   [Not given.]
Dated   31 March 1851.
Signed   John Bolam, steward [coal miner].
                  Bulman Village, near Newcastle upon Tyne.

5.34   Primitive Methodist, Ingoe (554.26)
Name   Primitive Methodist Chapel.
Erected   1848.
Building   Separate and entire building. Exclusively [used] for
                worship and Sabbath school.
Sittings   Free 100. Other 48. Total [148].
Attendance 30 March   Afternoon 60 + 22 SS. Total 82.
Average attendance   Morning 80 + 40 SS. Total 120.
Dated   31 March 1851.
Signed   John Harrison, managing trustee [farmer].
                Ingoe, near Matfen, Newcastle upon Tyne.

5.35   Primitive Methodist, Walbottle Colliery (554.36)
Name   Primitive Methodist Chapel.
Erected   One thousand, eight hundred and thirty-six [1836].
Building   [Separate and entire. Exclusively used for worship.]
Sittings   Free 225. Other 25. Total [250]. Standing room 150.
Attendance 30 March   Morning none.
                Afternoon 260. Total [260].
                Evening 275. Total [275].
Average attendance   Afternoon 200 + 74 SS. Total 274.
                Evening 250. Total 250.
Dated   30 March 1851.
Signed   Edward Laws, steward [schoolmaster of the colliery
                school].
                Walbottle.

5.36   Wesleyan Reformers, Coxlodge (554.12)
Name   Fawdon Chapel.
Erected   1819.
Building   Ann [*sic*] entire building. [Exclusively] for worship.
                Sunday and every day a school.
Sittings   Free 170. Other 18. Total [188].
Attendance 30 March   Afternoon 30. Total [30].
                Evening 30. Total [30].
Average attendance   [Not given.]
Dated   30 March 1851.
Signed   Edward Harle, class leader and society steward [coal
                miner].
                Coxlodge Colliery.

5.37 Wesleyan Reformers, Gosforth (554.14)

Name   Dwelling House.
Erected   About 1800.
Building   [Not separate and entire.] (This place is a private
              dwelling house.)
Sittings   [Not given.]
Attendance 30 March   Evening 32 + 24 SS. Total 56.
Average attendance   [Not given.]
Dated   30 March 1851.
Signed   James Hays, steward [coal miner].
              Cause End, Newcastle upon Tyne.

5.38 Wesleyan Reformers, Bulman Village, [Gosforth] (554.16)
[Shared with Primitive Methodists (**5.33**)]

Name   Primitive Methodist Preaching Room.
Erected   1830.
Building   [Not separate and entire but exclusively used for
              worship.]
Sittings   Free 70. Other 40. Total [110].
Attendance 30 March   Afternoon 36 + 14 SS. Total 50.
                        Evening [Used by Primitive Methodists.]
Average attendance   [Not given.]
Dated   30 March 1851.
Signed   James Hays, steward.
              Cause End, near Newcastle upon Tyne.

5.39 Wesleyan Reformers Schoolroom, Ponteland (554.6)

Name   Mr Brown's Schoolroom.
Erected   Before 1800. Rebuilt in the year 1822.
Building   [Separate and entire but not exclusively used for
              worship.]
Sittings   Free 150. Total [150].
Attendance 30 March   Afternoon 50. Total [50].
                        Evening 60 + 10 SS. [Total 70.] Total [for the
                        day] 120.
Average attendance   Afternoon 50 + 10 SS. Total 60.
                        Evening 40 + 10 SS. Total 50.
Dated   31 March 1851.
Signed   James Stobert, leader and steward [miller].
              Ponteland Mill, Northumberland.

5.40   Wesleyan Reformers, Walbottle (554.35)

Name   None.
Erected   [Not given.]
Building   [Separate and entire but not exclusively used for
              worship.]
Sittings   Free [not given]. Other [not given]. Standing room 100.
Attendance 30 March   Morning 60 + [45 SS]. Total 105.
                        Evening 90. Total [90].
Average attendance   Morning 50. Total [50].
Dated   31 March 1851.
Signed   Isaac Maddison, steward [coal miner].
              Walbottle, Newcastle upon Tyne.

5.41   Roman Catholic, Cheeseburn Grange Hall, Stamfordham
        (554.23)

Name   Grange Chapel.
Erected   Before 1800. [1775.]
Building   [Separate and entire.] Used for a place of worship.
Sittings   Free 170. Total [170].
Attendance 30 March   Morning 170. Total [170].
                        Evening 50. Total [50].
Average attendance   Morning SS none.
                        Evening 180. Total [180].
Dated   31 March 1851.
Signed   Thomas Gillett, Catholic minister [1850–55].
              Hexham, Northumberland.

6. Glendale District (HO 129/562)
26 places of worship

6.1   Church of England, St Paul, Branxton (562.3)
Population 1851: 284 (township)

Name   St Paul's. Rebuilt in 1849. Style early Norman. Ancient
              vicarage. The arch dividing the chancel from the nave
              has been preserved in the present building and is
              supposed to be nearly 800 years old. Distinct parish.
Consecrated Before 1800.
Erected   The present building [erected] by subscription. Private
              £420. Total cost £420.

Endowment Land £75. Tithe £100. OPE £60. Fees £1. Easter
offerings £3.
Other £11. Total £250.
Sittings   Free 77. Other 14. Total 91.
Attendance 30 March Morning 50. Total 50.
Afternoon 55. Total 55.
Average attendance   Morning 50. Total 50.
Afternoon 65. Total 65.
Dated   4 April 1851.
Signed   Robert Jones, minister [1834–70].
Branxton, near Coldstream, Northumberland.
{1857   Attendance 70. 33 communicants.}   {B 4.}

6.2   Church of England, St Cuthbert, Carham (562.2)
Population 1851: 1,362 (parish)

Name   St Cuthbert's Church, Carham. An ancient church.
Consecrated Unknown when consecrated, before 1800. [Rebuilt
1790, restored and enlarged 1862–64.]
Erected   Not known, but long before 1800.
Endowment   Tithe £248. Glebe £12. Fees £2.5s.
Sittings   [None free.] Other 120. Total 120.
Attendance 30 March Morning 37. Total 37.
Afternoon 13. Total 13.
Average attendance   Morning 55 (12 months). Total 55.
Afternoon 20 (9 months). Total 20.
Remarks   The sittings are all appropriated to the different
landed proprietors of the parish and their tenants,
who are principally dissenters, and therefore do not
occupy them; so that there is always ample room for
the few inhabitants belonging [to] our own church
who attend divine service. Some of the dissenters and
also the Scotch Church attend the church service.

[On separate sheet]
During the months of November, December and first
part of January, morning service is only performed in
this church in consequence of the principal [members]
of the congregation [living] at a distance from their
[place] of worship, some of them coming from the
adjacent [church] in Scotland who belong to our
church. The inhabitants of this parish are primarily

seceeders from the Church of Scotland or Burghers, or belonging to the Free Kirk. Several of them belong to the established Church of Scotland. Those belonging to the Church of England are comparatively few in number. Thirty only. F. T.

Dated   31 March 1851.
Signed   Francis Thompson LLB, incumbent [1844–65].
             Carham, near Coldstream
{1857   Attendance 50. 20 communicants.}   {B 10.}
[Francis Thompson had previously served as the curate of Carham 1843–44.]

6.3   Church of England, Holy Cross, Chatton (562.24)
Population 1851: 1,765 (parish)

Name   The parish church, dedicated to the Holy Cross.
Consecrated Before 1800. [Rebuilt 1763, enlarged 1846.]
Endowment Tithe £543 2s. Glebe £25. Fees £3. Easter offerings
             (commuted).
Sittings   Free 300. Other 130. Total 430.
Attendance 30 March Morning 133 + 79 SS. Total 212.
                       Afternoon 20 + 77 SS. Total 97.
Average attendance   Morning 200 + 70 SS. Total 270.
                       Afternoon 50 + 55 SS. Total 105.
Dated   [...] March 1851.
Signed   Matthew Burrell, minister [1844–69].
             Chatton, near Belford, Northumberland.
{1857   Attendance 150. 33 communicants.}   {B 24.}

6.4   Church of England, St Peter, Chillingham (562.26)
Population 1851: 380 (parish) 158 (Chillingham township);
107 (Hebburn township); 115 (Newton township)

Name   St Peter's ancient parish church.
Consecrated Before 1800. [Restored 1829–39.]
Endowment Tithe £368 18s. Dues £2.
Sittings   Free 40. Sunday school 50. Other 60. Total 150.
Attendance 30 March Morning 48 + 40 SS. Total 88.
                       Afternoon 15 + 30 SS. Total 45.
Average attendance   Average number a little greater than what I
                       have stated.
Remarks   The population of my small parish is scattered. Out of

five hamlets, only one is situated near to the church,
wh[ich] accounts for the small attendance in the
afternoon.

Dated   31 March 1851.
Signed   William Dodd, vicar [1849–66].
          Chillingham, near Belford, Northumberland.
{1857   Attendance 50. 24 communicants.}   {B 2.}
[William Dodd was the third son of John Dodd, the vicar of St
Nicholas', Newcastle 1826–40. William Dodd was the curate
of Whickham 1829–34; then his father appointed him to be the
incumbent of St Andrew's, Newcastle, 1834–49, where he became
'the recognised leader of Puseyism in Newcastle'.
J.A. Venn, *Alumni Cantabrigienses*, part II, vol. 2 (Cambridge, 1944),
p. 312. He died in Nice in 1866. His brother Henry Alison Dodd was
appointed by their father as the incumbent of St John's, Newcastle,
1826–34.]

6.5 Church of England, St Mary and St Michael, Doddington
(562.16)
Population 1851: 825 (parish) 397 (township)

Name   Doddington Church. Church of the ancient parochial
          chapelry of Doddington.
Consecrated [Not given.] [Enlarged 1838, restored 1893.]
Endowment   [Not given.] [£180.]
Sittings   Free 150. Other 60. Total 210.
Attendance 30 March   Morning 90 + 91 SS. Total 181.
                      Afternoon 26 + 61 SS. Total 87.
Average attendance   [Not given.]
Remarks   The 210 sittings are for adults without crowding.
          Including children a crowded congregation may
          amount to 300.
Dated   30 March 1851.
Signed   William Procter [senior], minister [1834–77].
          Doddington, near Wooler.
{1857   Attendance 100. 19 communicants.}   {B 5.}
[William Procter was also the lecturer at Berwick upon Tweed 1824–
76. His son William Procter was the curate of Doddington 1865–67
and again 1870–74. Aislabie Procter, the eighth son of William Procter,
was the vicar of Alwinton (**11.2**).]

6.6   Church of England, St Michael and All Angels, Ford (562.6)
Population 1851: 2,322 (parish)

Name   Ancient parish church.
Consecrated   [Not given.] [Enlarged and restored 1853.]
Endowment   [Not given.] OPE (rent charge). [£625.]
Sittings   Free 210. Other 200. Total 410.
Attendance 30 March   Morning 300 + 50 SS. Total [350].
                        Afternoon 50. Total [50].
Average attendance   Morning 300 + 50 SS. Total [350].
                        Afternoon 50. Total [50].
Dated   31 March 1851.
Signed   Thomas Knight, rector [1819–72].
                        Ford, by Coldstream.

{B 24.}

6.7   Church of England Schoolroom, Etal (562.7)
[Summary form]
Name   There is no church in Etal. There is afternoon service
                        in a schoolroom by permission of the Bishop of
                        Durham. [The church of the Blessed Virgin Mary was
                        consecrated 30 April 1859.]
Licensed   (Licensed.)
Sittings   [Not given.]
Usual attendance   Afternoon 20 + 20 SS. Total [40].
Dated   [Not given.]
Signed   Thomas Knight, rector of Ford [1819–72].

6.8   Church of England, St Michael, Ilderton (562.22)
Population 1851: 641 (parish) 145 (township)

Name   Ilderton Church. Ancient parish church.
Consecrated   Before 1800. [Rebuilt in the late 18th century, restored
                        1851, 1879.]
Endowment   Tithe *£120. Glebe 50 acres. Other sources (*sic*) Queen
                        Anne's Bounty £10 12s 2d.
Sittings   Free 72. Other 72. Total 144.
Attendance 30 March   Morning 45 + 31 SS. Total 76.
Average attendance   [Not given.]
Remarks   *The tithes have just been commuted. The
                        congregation varies very much, for when the landlords
                        are resident and not in London, it is nearly double.

Dated   31 March 1851.
Signed   Henry Parker, rector [1840–71].
             Ilderton Rectory, Belford.
{1857   Attendance 120. 30 communicants.}   {B 3.}

6.9   Church of England, St Michael and All Angels, Ingram
(562.28)
Population 1851: 198 (parish) 70 (township)

Name   St Michael's parish church (ancient).
Consecrated Before 1800. [Restored 1877–79.]
Endowment   Tithe £380. Glebe £95.
Sittings   [None free.] Other 112. Total 112.
Attendance 30 March   Morning 20. Total 20.
Average attendance   Morning 28. Total 28.
Remarks   Ingram is a parish at the foot of the Cheviots.
                       Composed chiefly of Presbyterians.
Dated   31 March 1851.
Signed   John Hicks, rector [1850–52].
                       High Hidgeley, Whittingham, Northumberland.
{1857   Attendance 40. 15 communicants.}   {B 6.}

6.10   Church of England, St Gregory the Great, Kirknewton
(562.4)
Population 1851: 1,732 (parish) 186 (Akeld township) 49 (Selby's
Forest township)

Name   St Gregory's Church. An ancient parish church.
Consecrated Before 1800. [Rebuilt 1856–60.]
Endowment   Tithe £490. Glebe (house, garden and small
                       [holding?]). Fees £3.
                       Dues £1. Easter offerings £1.
Sittings   Free 160. Other 16. Total 176.
Attendance 30 March   Morning 65 + 24 SS. Total 89.
                                    Afternoon 16. Total 16.
Average attendance   Morning 90 + 30 SS. Total 120.
                                    Afternoon 16 + 10 SS. Total 26.
Remarks   [From memory] the church is frequently [generally?]
                       full. The number of the congregation on the 30 March
                       was below the average from the [number?] that of the
                       […].
Dated   31 March 1851.

Signed   Christopher Robinson, vicar [1827–55].
             Kirknewton, Wooler.
{1857   Attendance 40. 12 communicants.}   {B 7.}
['At Kirknewton the church is very truly reported as being ruinous,
disgraceful and dangerous: the worst in the deanery of Bamburgh.'
R.C. Coxe, *A Cursory Survey of the Churches and Church Buildings
within the Archdeaconry of Lindisfarne* (London, 1860), p. 16.]

6.11   Church of England, St John the Baptist, Lowick (562.11)
Population 1851: 1,941 (parish)

[Summary form]
Name   No name that I can discover except 'Lowick Church'.
Erected   Rebuilt in 1794. [New chancel consecrated 1 June
                1887.]
Endowment   [Not given.] [£150.]
Sittings   [None free.] Other *200. Total [200].
Usual attendance   Morning about 60. [No SS.] Total [60].
                       Afternoon about 20. [No SS.] Total [20].
Remarks   *I believe the seats are all appropriated, that is they
                are all appropriated to the respective properties of the
                parish, each property having sittings according to its
                size etc.
Dated   [Not given.]
Signed   John Craig, registrar.
                Having applied twice to the present incumbent for
                the necessary information, who refuses to give any, I
                have given the above on the best authority that I could
                obtain and believe it to be correct. J. C.
Incumbent   [George Jenkinson 1829–73.]
{1857   Attendance 100. 30 communicants.}   {B 16.}
[From 1850 to 1852 George Jenkinson was suspended from the living
due to drunkenness. Clergy Discipline 1846–56, DUL, ASC, DDR/
EJ/CLD/2. Inscription: 'This chapell (*sic*) rebuilt An. Dom. 1794. Rev
George Goodwill, minister. Will. Smith. Thos. Hill. Geo. Hall. Jos.
Sample. Churchwardens. Henry Penny Selby Morton, Archit.']

6.12   Church of England, St Mary, Church Street, Wooler (562.23)
Population 1851: 1,911 (parish)

Name	St Mary's church, an old parish church.
Consecrated	Before 1800. [Built 1764–6, enlarged 1826 and 1835, restored 1873, new chancel consecrated 9 October 1913.]
Endowment	Land £110 (rent per annum). Tithe £404. Glebe house. OPE (no other). Pew rents [none]. Fees £2 7s (average). Easter offerings £1 10s. Other [none].
Sittings	Free 433. Other 367. Total 800.
Attendance 30 March	Morning 200 + 57 SS. Total [257].
	Afternoon 90 + 63 SS. Total [153].
Average attendance	Morning 300 + 70 SS. Total [370].
	Afternoon 150 + 70 SS. Total [220].
Remarks	In answering [the questions on the endowment] these amounts represent the gross value, and to obtain a fair estimate the usual rates, cesses, and ecclesiastical dues, ought to be deducted.
Dated	31 March 1851.
Signed	Alexander Mitchell, churchwarden.
	Ramsay Lane, Wooler.
Incumbent	[John Samuel Green 1843–80.]

{B 21.}

6.13   Church of Scotland, Lowick (562.12)

Name	Bethel Chapel.
Erected	1821. [Replaced a chapel erected in 1743, restored 1878.]
Building	[Separate and entire. Exclusively used for worship.]
Sittings	Free 298 (unlet). Other 442. Total [740].
Attendance 30 March	Morning 420. Total 420.
	Afternoon 34 SS. Total 34.
Average attendance	Morning 370. Total 370.
	Afternoon 35 SS. Total 35.
	Evening 350. Total 350.
Remarks	The congregation meeting in this chapel was founded about the year 1661, and the present chapel erected in 1821 is the third, which since 1661 has been occupied by this same body of Scottish Presbyterians. NB. The evening service in this chapel is only very occasional.
Dated	31 March 1851.

Signed   William Hownam, minister.
Lowick, Northumberland.
[The congregation divided in 1847 and formed the English Presbyterian church in Lowick (**6.20**).]

6.14   United Presbyterian, Chatton (562.25)

Name   [None.]
Erected   1850. [Foundation stone April 1849 and church opened December 1850.]
Building   Separate [and entire]. Exclusively [used for worship].
Sittings   [None free.] Other 500. Total [500].
Attendance 30 March   Morning 200. Total [200].
                              Evening 130. Total [130].
Average attendance   [Not given.]
Remarks   The church is just being erected and not yet any name given to it.
[The congregation had previously met in a cottage and from March 1850 in the Mason's Arms.]
Dated   31 March 1851.
Signed   William Jobson, elder [boot and shoemaker].
Chatton by Belford, Northumberland.
Minister   [David Young October 1851–90.]

6.15   United Presbyterian, Tower Hill, Wooler (562.20)

Name   United Presbyterian Church. [Tower Hill Church.]
Erected   About 1770 or 1771. [Replaced by a church erected in 1868.]
Building   Separate and entire. Exclusively [used for worship].
Sittings   [None free.] Other 400. Total [400].
Standing room. Nothing of this kind.
Attendance 30 March   Morning 196 + 49 SS. Total 245.
Average attendance   Morning 180 + 53 SS. Total [233].
Dated   [Not given.]
Signed   James Robertson (sen[ior] minister) [1802–55].
or Rev. Peter Whyte (colleague) [1848–55; minister 1855–80].
Wooler, Northumberland.
[In 1903 united with Cheviot Street Church (**6.16**).]

6.16   United Presbyterian, Cheviot Street, Wooler (562.17)

Name   Relief Chapel. [Cheviot Street Church.]
Erected   1775. [Altered 1900.]

Building   [Separate and entire. Exclusively used for worship]
except for a Sunday school.
Sittings   Free 30. Other 1,000. Total [1,030].
Attendance 30 March   Morning 614. Total [614].
Average attendance   Morning 800 + 104 SS. Total 904.
Dated   30 March 1851.
Signed   James L. Muirhead, minister [1833–97].
Wooler, Northumberland.
[In April 1952 the congregations of the Cheviot Street Church and the
West Church (**6.21**) were united.]

6.17   English Presbyterian, Branton (562.27)
Name   Branton Presbyterian Church in connection with the
English Synod.
Erected   Before 1800. [Chapel erected 1764, replaced 1781.]
Building   [Separate and entire. Exclusively used for worship.]
Sittings   [None free.] Other 700. Total [700].
Attendance 30 March   Morning 461 [including SS]. Total [461].
Afternoon no service.
Evening no service.
Average attendance   Morning 600 + 252 SS. Total 852.
Dated   31 March 1851.
Signed   James Blythe, minister [1853–91].
Powburn Cottage, Alnwick, Northumberland.

6.18   English Presbyterian, Crookham (562.8)
Name   Presbyterian Church.
Erected   Before 1800. [1745.]
Building   [Separate and entire. Exclusively used for worship.]
Sittings   [None free.] Other 996. Total [996].
Attendance 30 March   Morning 600 + 100 SS. Total 700.
Evening 200. Total 200.
Average attendance   Morning about 500 + 100 SS. Total 600.
Evening about 150. Total 150.
Remarks   Members of the congregation in indigent
circumstances are not called upon to pay pew rents, or
in any way to support ordinances.
Dated   31 March 1851.
Signed   Alexander Cromer, minister [1847–51].
Crookham Manse by Coldstream.

6.19   English Presbyterian, Etal (562.10)
Name   Etal Chapel.
Erected   Rebuilt 1800. [Erected *c.*1703, rebuilt 1806.]
Building   [Separate and] entire building. Exclusively [used for worship].
Sittings   [None free.] Other 650. Total [650].
Attendance 30 March   Morning 300. Total [300].
Average attendance   [Not given.]
Dated   28 March 1851.
Signed   David Aitken, minister of Etal [1789–1851]. Coldstream.

6.20   English Presbyterian, Lowick (562.14)
Name   English Presbyterian Church. (Presbyterian Church in England of the same principles as the Free Church in Scotland.)
Erected   1848. [Later permanent chapel 1862.]
Building   A separate and entire [wooden] building. Used also at present as a day school during the week.
Sittings   [None free.] Other 330. Total [330]. Standing room 330 (*sic*).
Attendance 30 March   Morning 140 + 14 SS. Total 154.
                       Evening 49 + 7 SS. Total 56.
Average attendance   Morning 180 + 20 SS. Total 200.
                       Evening 50 + 10 SS. Total 60.
Remarks   There are none of the sittings specially marked out as 'free sittings', but provision is made that sittings should be given *gratis* to any who may be unable to pay for them.
Dated   31 March 1851.
Signed   John Fraser, minister [1848–74]. Lowick, Berwick on Tweed.

6.21   English Presbyterian, High Street, Wooler (562.18)
Name   West Chapel.
Erected   [Opened October] 1818. [Cost £1,350.]
Building   [Separate and entire. Exclusively used for worship.]
Sittings   [None free.] Other 650. Total [650].
Attendance 30 March   Morning 244. Total [244].
                       Evening 190. Total [190].
Average attendance   Morning 230. Total [230].
                       Evening 150. Total [150].

Remarks   The congregation of this chapel is drawn from the
surrounding parishes, as well as from Wooler, some of
the people coming six miles or even further.
Dated   31 March 1851.
Signed   James Alexander Hine, minister [1844–84].
Wooler.
[In April 1952 the congregations of the West Chapel and the Cheviot
Street Church (**6.16**) were united.]

6.22   Baptist, Ford Forge, Ford (562.9)
Name   Baptist Chapel.
Erected   1843.
Building   Separate [and entire. Exclusively used for worship]
except for Sunday school.
Sittings   All free. Standing room 16 feet by 22 feet.
Attendance 30 March   Morning 65. Total [65].
Evening 70. Total [70].
Average attendance   Morning 65 + 35 SS. Total 100.
Evening 70. Total [70].
Remarks   The chaple (*sic*) or place of worship is built the back
part of the dwelling house. The extent of building, 22
feet by 16 feet.
Dated   31 March 1851.
Signed   Thomas Black, minister [toolmaker].
[Ford Forge] by Coldstream.

6.23   Baptist, Church Street, Wooler (562.21)
Name   A room for public worship knowen (*sic*) by the name
of the Baptist Meeting Room.
Erected   [Not given.]
Building   [Not separate and entire or exclusively used for
worship.] (Part of a workshop, crossed out.)
Sittings   Free 60.
Attendance 30 March   Morning 20. Total [20].
Average attendance   [Not given.]
Dated   31 March 1851.
Signed   James Halliday, elder [weaver].
Millvale, Wooler, Northumberland.

6.24   Primitive Methodist, Lowick (562.13)
Name   Primitive Methodist Chapel.
Erected   About the year 1821. [Jubilee Chapel opened 7 October
                1860.]
Building   [Separate and entire. Exclusively used for worship.]
Sittings   Free 20. Other 120. Total [140].
Attendance 30 March   Morning 90 + 33 SS. Total 123.
                        Evening 88 + 33 SS. Total 121.
Average attendance   [Not given.]
Dated   31 March 1851.
Signed   William Alderson, minister.
                11 Walkergate Lane, Berwick upon Tweed.

6.25   Primitive Methodist, Milfield (562.5)
Name   None.
Erected   See 'Remarks'. [Chapel opened 1856, renovated 1876.]
Building   [Not separate and entire or exclusively used for
                worship.]
Sittings   Free 150. Total [150].
Attendance 30 March   Morning 101. Total 101.
                        Evening 80. Total 80.
Average attendance   [Not given.]
Remarks   The building was erected for a day school, and the
                time of its erection will be stated on the day school
                return. But it has been used as a place of public
                worship for above 20 years by the Primitive Methodist
                Connexion. It will seat about 150 persons. All the
                sittings are free.
Dated   31 March 1851.
Signed   William Alderson, minister.
                11 Walkergate Lane, Berwick upon Tweed.

6.26   Roman Catholic, Wooler (562.19)
Name   St Ninian's Chapel.
Erected   Before 1800. [Chapel opened 1797. St Ninian's Church
                opened 24 June 1856.]
Building   [Not separate and entire but exclusively used for
                worship.]
Sittings   Free 35. Other 50. Total [85]. Standing room [for] about
                20.
Attendance 30 March   Morning 63. Total [63].
                        Afternoon 18 SS. Total [18].

Evening 48. Total [48].

Average attendance   Morning about 80. Total [80].
Afternoon 30 SS. Total [30].
Evening between 80 and 90. Total [80–90].

Remarks   [The] chapel is small and inconvenient.

Dated   31 March 1851.

Signed   Edward Consett, missionary priest [1850–52].
St Ninian's, Wooler, Northumberland.

7. Haltwhistle District (HO 129/556)
26 places of worship

7.1 Church of England, St Cuthbert, Beltingham (556.19)
Population 1851: (A township within the parish of Haltwhistle 5,378)

Name   Beltingham Chapel. Chapel of ease. No district assigned nor cure of souls.

Consecrated   Before 1800. [Restored 1812, 1884.]
As a chapel of ease to the mother church of Haltwhistle, being about five miles distant there from.

Erected   Not known. Total cost not known.

Endowment   OPE £75 10s. [From] Ecc[lesiastical] Comm[issioners] £4. Fees 10s.

Sittings   Free 10. Other 180. Total 190.

Attendance 30 March   Afternoon 30 + 24 SS. Total 54.

Average attendance   Morning 40 + 20 SS. Total 60.

Dated   31 March 1851.

Signed   James Ord Clark, incumbent [1845–81].
Beltingham, Bardon Mill.

{B 32.}

7.2 Church of England, St Cuthbert, Greenhead (556.26)
Population 1851: (A township within the parish of Haltwhistle 5,378)

Name   Chapel of Greenhead, chapel of ease.

Consecrated   About the year 1828 [11 September 1828], as a chapel of ease to the mother church of Haltwhistle, being

three miles distant with a large population. [Restored
and enlarged 1900–01.]

Erected   By subscription with a grant from the Society for
Promoting the Enlargement and Rebuilding of
Churches and Chapels.

Endowment OPE £47 19s. Pew rents £2 10s. Fees £1.

Sittings   Free 182. Other 120. Total 302.

Attendance 30 March   Morning 26 + 84 SS. Total 110.

Average attendance   Morning 30 + 80 SS. Total 110.

Dated   31 March 1851.

Signed   James Ord Clark, incumbent [1845–81].
Haltwhistle, Northumberland.

7.3   Church of England, Featherstone Castle Chapel, Haltwhistle
(556.20 and 556.2)
Population 1851: 314 (township)

Name   Featherstone Castle Chapel. Licensed by the bishop of
the diocese. [A] private chapel built and endowed by
the late Lord Wallace.

Consecrated About the end of 1845 or the beginning of 1846.
Licensed by the Bishop of Durham, being endowed by
the will of the late Lord Wallace, with a sum of money
to his trustees.

Erected   [By] the late Lord Wallace of Featherstone Castle.

Sittings   Total 100. The public are admitted free, but the
chapel being altogether a private one, they are
[inappropriate?].

Attendance 30 March   Morning 15 + 15 SS. Total [30].
Afternoon 40. Total [40].

Average attendance   Morning 30 + 35 SS. Total [65].
Afternoon 60. Total [60].

Remarks   The chaplaincy being at this moment vacant, and
only supplied from Sunday to Sunday has caused the
present reduction of attendance both of congregation
and school.

Dated   31 March 1851.

Signed   James Hope Wallace, Justice of the Peace, Co[unty]
Northumberland.
Featherstone Castle, Haltwhistle.

[Summary form (556.2)]
Name   Featherstone Castle chapel 'was opened for divine
                service in Jan[uar]y 1846.
Sittings   Free 200. Total [200].
Usual attendance   Morning 40. Total [40].
                Afternoon 100. Total [100].
Signed   John Clark [agent].

7.4   Church of England, Holy Paraclete, Kirkhaugh (556.6)
Population 1851: 285 (parish)

Name   Kirkhaugh. Ancient parish church.
Consecrated   Before 1800. [Rebuilt 1869.]
Endowment   Tithe £80. Glebe £12. OPE £565 15s 5d. ([...]
                Parliamentary Fund.)
                Fees 12s. Easter offerings £1.
Sittings   Free 160. Total 160.
Attendance 30 March   Morning 20. Total 20.
Average attendance   Morning 30 to 40. Total [30–40].
Dated   30 March 1851.
Signed   Octavius James, rector [1846–89].
                Kirkhaugh, Alstone (*sic*), Cumberland.
{1857   Attendance 25. 15 communicants.}   {B 8.}
[Octavius James designed the new church. He was 'somewhat
eccentric in his habits, he was burned to death in his bed ... he
slept in his study'. J.A. Venn, *Alumni Cantabrigienses*, part II, vol. 3
(Cambridge, 1947), p. 548.]

7.5   Church of England, St Jude, Knarsdale (556.8)
Population 1851: 917 (parish)

Name   Knarsdale Parish Church.
Consecrated   Before 1800. [Rebuilt 1833, enlarged 1891–92, 1906.]
Erected   By rate and subscription. Total cost £300.
Endowment   Land. Tithe (rent charge). Easter offerings. [£135.]
Sittings   All free [300]. Total 300.
Attendance 30 March   Morning 30. Total [30].   ⎱ No
                Afternoon 40. Total [40].   ⎰ SS
Average attendance   [Not given.]
Remarks   As the church was rebuilt on the old site in 1833, and
                the old one before 1800, a new consecration was not
                necessary.

Dated   31 March 1851.
Signed   Thomas Bewsher, rector [1824–53].
            [Knarsdale] rectory, Alston, Cumberland.
{1857   Attendance 90. 5 communicants.}   {B 19.}
[Previously Thomas Bewsher had been the headmaster of Penrith
Grammar School, 1812–24. From 1969 Knarsdale parish church has
been dedicated to St Jude.]

7.6   Church of England, St Mary and St Patrick, Lambley (556.9)
Population 1851: 365 (parish) [Includes the hamlet of Asholme]

Name   Parish Church of Lambley.
Consecrated Before 1800. [Rebuilt and consecrated on 4 June 1886.]
Endowment Tithe and glebe (rent charge).
Sittings   All free. Total [sittings] not known at present as the
            church is under repair. [100 written over.]
Attendance 30 March   [Not given.]
Average attendance   [Not given.] Church under repair.
Remarks   This is as accurate a return as I can make.
Dated   25 March 1851.
Signed   Thomas Bewsher, curate [1824–53].
            [Knarsdale Rectory], Alston, Cumberland.

7.7   Church of England, St John, Whitfield (556.1)
Population 1851: 340 (parish)

Name   Whitfield Church.
Consecrated Before 1800. [Rebuilt 1813. New church dedicated to
            Holy Trinity consecrated 11 September 1860.]
Endowment Tithe £240. Glebe £66. Fees £1 10s.
Sittings   Free 70. Other 110. Total 180.
Attendance 30 March   Morning 31 + 16 SS. Total 47.
Average attendance   Morning 47 + 8 SS. Total 55.
Dated   7 April 1851.
Signed   Thomas Hobbes Scott, rector [1822–60].
            Whitfield Rectory, near Haydon Bridge,
            Northumberland.
{1857   Attendance 80. 14 communicants.}   {B 9.}
[Thomas Hobbes Scott (1783–1860) was the Secretary to the
Commission of Inquiry into the affairs of New South Wales, and in
that capacity was in Australia 1819–21. He was ordained in 1821 and
the following year became the rector of Whitfield. In April 1824 he was

appointed Archdeacon of New South Wales and resigned in October 1829, returning to Whitfield in 1831 (S. Judd and K. Cable, *Sydney Anglicans* (Sydney, 2000), pp. 8–10). During Scott's absence the curate in charge was Anthony Hedley, 1824–31. With a stipend of £200 a year, a glebe of 40 acres, and 'with a house, garden and churchyard, all taxes paid and repairs of every kind set up. It is indeed quite the bishopric of curacies.' Letter from Anthony Hedley to his friend the historian John Hodgson, 23 February 1824, in J. Raine, *A Memoir of the Rev John Hodgson* (London, 1858), vol. 1, p. 27.]

7.8   Church of Scotland, Haltwhistle (556.25)

Name   Established Church of Scotland.
Erected   1762. [Rebuilt 1899.]
Building   A separate and entire building. It is used exclusively as a place of worship.
Sittings   There are 12 sittings free to all [...]. No free space or standing room.
Attendance 30 March   Morning 20. Total [20]. [No SS.]
               17 [having] attended on 30 March 1851.
Average attendance   Morning 20. Total [20]. [No SS.]
Dated   31 March 1851.
Signed   James Stevenson [minister 1812–62].
               Haltwhistle, Northumberland.

7.9   Wesleyan Methodist, Gilsland (556.22)

Name   Ebenezer Chapel.
Erected   1827.
Building   [Separate and entire. Exclusively used for worship.]
Sittings   Free 100. Other none. Total [100].
Attendance 30 March   Morning 24. Total 24.
               Afternoon 37. Total 37.
Average attendance   Morning 30. Total 30.
Dated   31 March 1851.
Signed   William Tweedale, leader and local preacher (boot and shoe man).
               Gilsland.

7.10   Wesleyan Methodist Schoolroom, Blenkinsopp, Haltwhistle (556.27b)

[Shared with Primitive Methodists (**7.20**)]
Name   Blenkinsopp Schoolroom.
Erected   1839.

Building   Separate [and entire. Used for worship and] as a day
and Sunday school.
Sittings   All free. Fitted up for schoolroom. Standing room all
free.
Attendance [The attendance figures refer to the Primitive
Methodists (**7.20**).]

7.11   Wesleyan Methodist, Birch Tree, Haltwhistle (556.14)
Name   None.
Erected   Before 1800.
Building   [Not separate and entire or exclusively used for
worship.]
              [In another hand] Dwelling house.
Sittings   [Not given.]
Attendance 30 March   Afternoon 40. Total 40.
Average attendance   Afternoon 40. Total 40.
Dated   31 March 1851.
Signed   William Shaw, Wesleyan minister [1849–51].
Alston, Cumberland.

7.12   Wesleyan Methodist, Garbutt Hill, Coanwood, Haltwhistle
(556.13)
Name   None.
Erected   Before 1800.
Building   [Not separate and entire or exclusively used for
worship.] Room (in another hand).
Sittings   [Not given.]
Attendance 30 March   Afternoon 40. Total 40.
                        Evening 20. Total 20.
Average attendance   Afternoon 40. Total 40.
                        Evening 20. Total 20.
Dated   31 March 1851.
Signed   William Shaw, Wesleyan minister [1849–51].
Alston, Cumberland.

7.13   Wesleyan Methodist, Bellister Park, Haltwhistle (556.21 and
556.4)
Name   Park Chapel.
Erected   1850.
Building   [Separate and entire. Exclusively used for worship.]
Sittings   Free 150. Total [150].
Attendance 30 March   Morning 60. Total 60.

Evening 110. Total 110.
Average attendance   [Not given.]
Dated   31 March 1851.
Signed   William Shaw, Wesleyan minister [1849–51].
Alston, Cumberland.

[Summary form (556.4)]
Name   Park Chapel.
Erected   1851.
Building   Chapel and schoolroom. [Exclusively used for
worship] except this day school.
Sittings   Free 120. Total [120].
Usual attendance   Morning 30. Total [30]. [No SS.]
Afternoon 50. Total [50].
Evening 50. Total [50].
Dated   [Not given.]
Signed   Cuthbert Oliver, informant [store man].
Haltwhistle, North[umberlan]d.

7.14   Wesleyan Methodist, Haltwhistle (556.23)
Name   Wesleyan Methodist Chapel.
Erected   1843.
Building   [Separate and entire. Exclusively used for worship.]
Sittings   Free 100. Other 121. Total [221].
Attendance 30 March   Afternoon 80 + 10 SS. Total 90.
Evening 100 + 10 SS. Total 110.
Average attendance   Afternoon 80 + 10 SS. Total 90.
Evening 100 + 10 SS. Total 110.
Remarks   A day and Sunday school are taught under the chapel.
Dated   31 March 1851.
Signed   Thomas Ballingall, [Wesleyan] minister [1850–51].
Alston, Cumberland.
[Thomas Ballingall was also responsible for chapels in the Alston
area (**25.6–12**).]

7.15   Wesleyan Methodist, Kirkhaugh (556.7)
Name   None.
Erected   About 1800.
Building   [Not separate and entire or exclusively used for
worship.]
Sittings   [Not given.]
Attendance 30 March   Evening 30. Total 30.

Average attendance   Evening 30. Total 30.
Dated   31 March 1851.
Signed   Thomas Ballingall, Wesleyan minister [1850–51].
               Alston, Cumberland.

7.16   Wesleyan Methodist, Slaggyford (556.5)

Name   Wesleyan Methodist Chapel.
Erected   1810.
Building   [Separate and entire.] A day school is taught in it.
Sittings   Free 60. Total [60].
Attendance 30 March   Afternoon 30 + 6 SS. Total 36.
Average attendance   Afternoon 30 + 6 SS. Total 36.
Dated   31 March 1851.
Signed   Thomas Ballingall, [Wesleyan] minister [1850–51].
               Alston, Cumberland.

7.17   Wesleyan Methodist, Henshaw (556.17)

Name   Wesleyan Methodist Chapel.
Erected   In the year 1840. [New adjacent chapel 1897.]
Building   [Separate and entire. Exclusively used for worship.]
Sittings   Free 86. Other 64. Total [150].
Attendance 30 March   Evening 58. Total [58].
Average attendance   Afternoon 90. Total [90].
Dated   31 March 1851.
Signed   William Cook, steward [master carpenter].
               [Tow House, Henshaw.]

7.18   Wesleyan Methodist, Lane Head, Lambley (556.10)

Name   Lane Head.
Erected   Since 1800.
Building   [Not separate and entire or exclusively used for
               worship.]
Sittings   Free 60. Total [60].
Attendance 30 March   Evening 50. Total 50.
Average attendance   [Not given.]
Dated   31 March 1851.
Signed   William Oliver, local preacher [farmer].
               Garbut Hill, near Haltwhistle.

7.19   Primitive Methodist, Crowburn (556.16)

Name   None.
Erected   [Not given.]

Building   [Not separate and entire but exclusively used for
             worship.]
Sittings   Free 60. Total [60].
Attendance 30 March   Afternoon 40. Total [40].
Average attendance   Afternoon 50. Total [50].
Dated   31 March 1851.
Signed   Thomas Greenfield, minister.
             Haltwhistle, Northumberland.

7.20   Primitive Methodist Schoolroom, Blenkinsopp, Haltwhistle
(556.27a)
[Shared with Wesleyan Methodists (**7.10**)]
Name   Blenkinsopp Schoolroom.
Erected   1839.
Building   Separate [and entire. Used for worship and] as a day
             and Sunday school.
Sittings   All free. Fitted up for schoolroom. Standing room all
             free.
Attendance 30 March   Evening 50. Total 50.
Average attendance   Evening 40. Total 40.
Dated   31 March 1851.
Signed   Thomas Greenfield, minister.
             Haltwhistle, Northumberland.

7.21   Primitive Methodist, Mill Lane, Haltwhistle (556.24)
Name   Low Chapel. [Mill Lane Chapel.]
Erected   In the year 1828.
Building   [Separate and entire. Exclusively used for worship.]
Sittings   Free 50. Other 75. Total [125].
Attendance 30 March   Afternoon 60. Total [60].
                        Evening 120. Total [120].
Average attendance   [Not given.]
Dated   31 March 1851.
Signed   Thomas Greenfield, minister.
             Haltwhistle, Northumberland.

7.22   Primitive Methodist, Harper Town, Lambley (556.12)
Name   Harper Town.
Erected   Since 1820.
Building   [Not separate and entire or exclusively used for
             worship.] A dwelling house.
Sittings   Free 50. Total [50].

Attendance 30 March   Afternoon 20. Total 20.
                         Evening 15. Total 15.
Average attendance   [Not given.]
Remarks   Evening [service] held once a month by Mr [Thomas]
               Greenfield, minister.
Dated   31 March 1851.
Signed   Isaac Brown, local preacher [shop keeper].
               Lane Head, Haltwhistle, North[umberlan]d.

7.23   Primitive Methodist, Lane Head, Lambley (556.11)

Name   Lane Head.
Erected   Before 1800.
Building   [Not separate and entire or exclusively used for
               worship.] A dwelling house.
Sittings   Free 40. Total [40].
Attendance 30 March   Evening 30. Total 30.
Average attendance   Morning and afternoon 40. Total 40.
Dated   31 March 1851.
Signed   Isaac Brown, local preacher [shop keeper].
               Lane Head, Haltwhistle, North[umberlan]d.

7.24   Primitive Methodist, Henshaw (556.3)

[Summary form]
Name   Henshaw Primitive Methodist Chapel.
Erected   1836.
Building   A Separate and entire building. Exclusively as a place
               of worship.
Sittings   Free 80. Other 46. Total [126].
Usual attendance   Afternoon 90. Total 90.
                       Evening 100. Total 100.
Dated   [Not given.]
Signed   Rev. Edward Barrass, informant.
               Haltwhistle, Northumberland.

7.25   [Non-denominational] Free Church, Beggar Bog [Housesteads] (556.18)

Name   Housesteads Chapel. [Free Church]
Erected   1840.
Building   Entire building separate. Exclusively for a place of
               worship.
Sittings   [None free.] Other 104. Total [104]. Standing room
               none.

Attendance 30 March   Morning 47. Total [47]. [No SS.]
Average attendance   Morning 70. Total 70. [No SS.]
Dated   31 March 1851.
Signed   Thomas Errington, trustee [farmer].
               Sewingshields, Haydon Bridge, Hexham.
Minister   [Thomas Johnstone 1838–51.]
[The minister of the Presbyterian church at Wark (**3.20**) also officiated
at Beggar Bog.]

7.26   Society of Friends [Quakers], Coanwood, Haltwhistle
(556.15)
Name   [Not given.]
Erected   Before 1800. [1760, closed c.1960.]
Building   [Separate and entire. Exclusively used for worship.]
Sittings   Total 100.
               Floor area 18 x 38 = 684 sq. ft. No gallery.
Attendance 30 March   Morning 12. Total [12].
Remarks   A division in the Meeting House is occasionally used
               as a schoolroom.
Dated   31st day of 3rd month (March) 1851.
Signed   Robert Wigham [farmer].
               Hargill House, Haltwhistle.

8. Hexham District (HO 129/555)
98 places of worship

8.1   Church of England, St Mary, Allendale Town (555.51)
Population 1851: 6,383 (parish)

Name   Allendale Parish Church. Ancient church. [From 1874
               St Cuthbert.]
Consecrated Before 1800. [Rebuilt 1807, 1874.]
Endowment   Land £18. Tithe £98 [commuted]. Glebe £34. Other £30.
               Fees about £10.
Sittings   Free 240. Total 240.
Attendance 30 March   Morning 100 + 40 SS. Total 140.
                        Afternoon 25 + 30 SS. Total [55].
Average attendance   Morning 140 + 40 SS. Total 180.
                        Afternoon 30. Total [30].
Dated   10 April 1851.

Signed   John Rawes, incumbent [1843–52].
          Haydon Bridge, Allendale.
{1857   Attendance 150. 30 communicants.}   {B 63.}

8.2   Church of England, Allenheads Chapel, Allenheads (555.52)
[Summary form]
Name   Allenheads Chapel. [Chapel of ease to St Mary,
          Allendale Town.]
Erected   1701, rebuilt 1826.
Endowment [£50.]
Sittings   Free 250. Other 20. Total [270].
Attendance 30 March   [Not given.]
Average attendance   Morning 70 + 80 SS. Total [150].
                  Afternoon 80 + 80 SS. Total [160].
Dated   [Not given.]
Signed   George Dickinson, registrar.
Incumbent [Constantine O'Donel 1851–78.]
[Constantine O'Donel was also the incumbent of St Peter in the
Forest 1851–71.]

8.3   Church of England, St Peter, Allenheads (555.83)
[Summary form]
Name   St Peter's. [Chapel of ease to St Mary, Allendale
          Town.]
Erected   I can find no record whatever to say when St Peter's
          was built, but it must have been considerably above
          100 years ago. It was rebuilt in the year 1825.
Endowment [£120.]
Sittings   Free 300. Total 300.
Usual attendance   Morning 50 + 12 SS. Total [62].
                  Afternoon 60 + 12 SS. Total [72].
                  Evening nil.
Dated   [Not given.]
Signed   George Dickinson, registrar.
Incumbent [Constantine O'Donel 1851–78.]
                                          {B 49.}

8.4   Church of England, West Allen Chapel, Carrshield (555.53)
Name   West Allen Chapel in the high district of West Allen in
          the parish [of] Allendale. [Chapel of ease to Allendale.]
Consecrated In the year 1822. [23 September 1825.] The chapel was
          consecrated as an additional chapel.

Erected   The chapel was built by Mrs [Diana] Beaumont, lady of the manor of Hexham and by a parliamentary grant [of] £200.
Endowment   Other £100.
Sittings   Free 381. Other 40. Total 421.
Attendance 30 March   Morning 50 + 84 SS. Total 134.
Average attendance   [Not given.]
Dated   31 March 1851.
Signed   Joseph Reed, perpetual curate [1843–67].
[Coalcleugh], Haydon Bridge, Northumberland.

8.5   Church of England, St John of Beverley, St John Lee (555.85)
Population 1851: 2,073 (parish)

Name   St John Lee Church.
Consecrated Before 1800. [Rebuilt 1650, 1818, enlarged 1841, restored 1885–86.]
Endowment   OPE £265 ([residence] included in the parish of St Oswald Lee). Easter offerings about [the amount not given].
Sittings   Free 48. Other 326. Total 406 (*sic*). [Total 374.]
Attendance 30 March   Morning 132 + 60 SS. Total 192.
Average attendance   [Not given.]
Dated   31 March 1851.
Signed   Charles Lee, minister [1815–62].
Brinton, Hexham.
{1857   Attendance 280. 80 communicants. Total for St John Lee, Bingfield and Heavenfield.}   {B 43.}
[Charles Lee was also the lecturer at St Andrew, Hexham, 1824–62.]

8.6   Church of England, St Mary, Bingfield (555.89)
Population 1851: 125 (township)

Name   [St] Mary in Bingfield. Chapel of ease to St John Lee church.
Consecrated Before 1800. [Restored 1875.]
Endowment   OPE included in St John Lee.
Sittings   Free 18. Other 128. Total 146.
Attendance 30 March   [Not given.]
Average attendance   No service at Bingfield Chapel on the 30th inst.
Dated   30 March 1851.

Signed   Charles Lee, minister [1815–62].
           Brinton, Hexham.

8.7   Church of England, St Oswald Lee, Heavenfield (555.88)

Name   St Oswald's Chapel.
Consecrated   [Not given.] [1737, restored 1887.]
Endowment   OPE included in St John Lee.
Sittings   Free 40. Other 190. Total 230.
Attendance 30 March   Morning 62 + 30 SS. Total 92.
Average attendance   [Not given.]
Dated   30 March 1851.
Signed   Charles Lee, minister [1815–62].
           Brinton, Hexham.

8.8   Church of England, St Andrew, Bywell (555.29)
Population 1851: 480 (parish) 46 (township)

Name   St Andrew's Parish Church.
Consecrated   Not known. Before 1800. [Restored 1830, 1850, 1871.]
Erected   Not known.
Endowment   Land £50. Tithe £100 4s. Glebe £1. Fees trifling.
Sittings   Free 30 (*for children). Other 120. Total 150.
Attendance 30 March   Morning 75 + 55 SS. Total 130.
Average attendance   [Not given.]
Remarks   It should be remarked that the parish only numbers
           about 500 in all, that the greater part of these live
           in the out-townships, and that the church is three
           miles from the mass of the population. In sum[me]r
           the congregations are very good indeed; and there
           are *no free sittings, except two or three forms for
           the children, that is, all the pews in the ch[urc]h are
           appropriated to the different families in the parish and
           their servants.
           [Footnote] Return for Broomhaugh School house.
Dated   31 March 1851.
Signed   Joseph Jacques, vicar [1844–66].
           Riding Mill, near Gateshead.
{1857   100. 40 communicants.}   {B 5.}

8.9   Church of England, Schoolroom, Broomhaugh (555.31)
Population 1851: 134 (township)

Name	Village Schoolroom. [In the parish of St Andrew, Bywell.]
Licensed	Licensed about 15 years ago by [the] late Bishop of Durham. Licensed for divine worship to accommodate two townships adjoining each other, situated nearly three miles from [the] parish church, and containing the principal part of the population.
Erected	It was erected originally for a school only, and divine service is held there by permission of the trustees, under license from the late bishop with the consent of the present [bishop]. Total cost about £150.
Endowment	The service is entirely gratuitous.
Sittings	Free 100 with crowding. Total 100.
Attendance 30 March:	Afternoon about 87. Total 87.
Average attendance:	Morning From 60 to 70. Total 60–70. Afternoon 100. Total 100.
Remarks	The service is alternately here and at Bywell. When it is at the church in the morning, it is in this schoolhouse in the afternoon, and vice versa, so that there are usually two services in the parish every Sunday.
Dated	31 March 1851.
Signed	Joseph Jacques, vicar [1844–66]. Riding Mill, near Gateshead.

8.10   Church of England, St Peter, Bywell (555.26)
Population 1851: 1,674 (parish) 130 (township)

Name	St Peter's in Bywell (parish church).
Consecrated	Before 1800. [Restored 1849.]
Endowment	Glebe £21 10s. OPE £130. Fees £3 5s.
Sittings	Free 80. Other 292. Total 372.
Attendance 30 March	Morning 46. Total [46]. Afternoon 50 + 27 SS. Total 77.
Average attendance	[Not given.]
Dated	31 March 1851.
Signed	Richard Twigg, curate [1850–52]. Bywell, Gateshead.

Incumbent   [Brereton Edward Dwarris 1845–1901.]
{1857   Attendance 150. 25 communicants.}   {B 20.}

8.11   Church of England, St Giles, Chollerton (555.90)
Population 1851: 1,151 (parish) 157 (township)

Name   Ancient parish church of the parish of Chollerton,
             dedicated to St Giles.
Consecrated Before 1800. [Rebuilt 1769, restored 1893.]
Erected   The church having existed before the Conquest and
             appeared to have been consecrated at the period of its
             erection.
Endowment   Tithe £364 19s 11d. Glebe £8. Fees £5.
Sittings   Free 100. Other 160. Total 260.
Attendance 30 March   Morning 102 + 10 SS. Total 112.
Average attendance   [Not given.]
Remarks   I presume what is meant, is the net aggregate annual
             value of the living, which is as above, as near as I can
             estimate.
Dated   31 March 1851.
Signed   Christopher Bird [senior] minister [1821–67].
             Hexham, Northumberland.
{1857   Attendance 140. 45 communicants.}   {B 23.}
[Christopher Bird (1778–1867) was also the incumbent of Warden
with Newbrough and Haydon Bridge (**8.21–23**). On his death he was
succeeded at Chollerton by his son, Christopher Bird (1816–1896).]

8.12   Church of England, St Andrew, Corbridge (555.34)
Population 1851: 2,163 (parish) 1,363 (township)

Name   The ancient parish church of Corbridge. [AD 675.]
Consecrated Before 1800. [Restored 1850.]
Endowment   [£482.]
Sittings   Free about 400. Other about 100. Total 500.
Attendance 30 March   [Not given.]
Average attendance   [Not given.]
Dated   31 March 1851.
Signed   Henry Gipps, vicar [1829–53].
             Corbridge, Northumberland.
{1857   Attendance 230. 40 communicants.}   {B 44.}
[Henry Gipps was the examining chaplain to the Bishop of Carlisle
(Hugh Percy) 1827–56; canon residentiary of Carlisle cathedral 1845–

77; vicar of Crosthwaite 1855–77. At Corbridge he was succeeded by his son, Frederick Gipps 1853–73.]

8.13   Church of England, St Oswald, St Cuthbert and King Alfwald, Halton (555.38)
Population 1851: 48 (township)

Name   The ancient chapel of the ancient chapelry of Halton.
Consecrated   Before 1800. [Rebuilt 1706, restored 1880.]
Endowment   [Not given.]
Sittings   Total about 200.
Attendance 30 March   [Not given.]
Average attendance   [Not given.]
Dated   31 March 1851.
Signed   Henry Gipps, vicar of Corbridge [1829–53].
    Corbridge, Northumberland.
{1857   Attendance 'depends on the weather sometimes full, often empty'.}

8.14   Church of England, St Andrew, Market Place, Hexham (555.40)
Population 1851: 6,537 (parish) 5,231 (township)

Name   St Andrew's, Hexham, now the parish church, but anciently the abbey church. [Rectory created 14 December 1866.]
Consecrated   Before 1800. [Restored 1858–60, 1869–70, nave consecrated 8 August 1908.]
Endowment   Land £60. OPE £13 6s 8d. Fees £15. Other £48.
Sittings   Free 100. Other 580. Total 680.
Attendance 30 March   Morning 440 + 112 SS. Total 552.
    Afternoon 143 + 124 SS. Total 267.
    Evening 282. Total 282.
Average attendance   [Not given.]
Dated   31 March 1851.
Signed   Joseph Hudson, minister [1845–66].
    Hexham, Northumberland.
{1857   Attendance 600. 100 communicants.}   {B 158.}

8.15   Church of England, St Peter, Humshaugh (555.94)
Population 1851: 446 (township)

Name   Humshaugh Chapel. District chapelry. Built under
               local Act of Parliament [of 1811 (51 Geo. III c.194)] for
               division of parish of Simonburn.
Consecrated [11] August 1818 [by the Bishop of Oxford] on the
               division of Simonburn parish into parochial districts.
               [Became a separate vicarage in 1832.]
Erected   [By the] Governors of Greenwich Hospital. Private
               £4,000.
               Total cost £4,000.
Endowment [£120. See **8.19**.]
Sittings   Free 118. Other 144. Total 262.
Attendance 30 March   Morning 113 + 28 SS. Total 141.
                         Afternoon 30 + 10 SS. Total 40.
Average attendance   Morning 120 + 30 SS. Total 150.
                         Afternoon 16 + 15 SS. Total 31.
Remarks   Income of this chapelry paid by the rector of
               Simonburn out of tithes. Fixed amount £120 per
               annum.
Dated   30 March 1851.
Signed   William Blamire Young, curate [1844–54].
               Hexham, Northumberland.
Incumbent [Edward Brice 1832–68.]

{B 19.}

8.16   Church of England, St Mark, Ninebanks (555.54)
Population 1851: [Not given]

Name   Ninebanks Chapel, the church of a district and
               separate distinct chapelry created under an Act of
               Parliament passed in the first year of the [reign] of
               His Majesty, King George the First. [Parish created
               3 May 1844.]
Consecrated [Before] 1800. [Consecrated 4 July 1764 by the
               Archbishop of York as a chapel of ease to St Mary,
               Allendale Town. Rebuilt 1813, enlarged 1846, restored
               1871.]
Endowment Land £100. Glebe £10. OPE £22 17s 4d. Fees £5.
               Other £10 (exchange). Total £147 17s 4d.
Sittings   Free 113. Other 32. Total 145.

Attendance 30 March   Morning 40 + 9 SS. Total 49.
Average attendance   [Not given.]
Remarks   There is no afternoon service.
Dated   31 March 1851.
Signed   Jonathan Scurr, incumbent [1837–89].
                   Ninebanks Parsonage, Haydon Bridge.
{1857   Attendance 60. 18 communicants.}   {B 2.}
[Until December 1836 Ninebanks was in Hexhamshire (part of the
diocese of York) and was then transferred to the diocese of Durham.]

8.17   Church of England, St Mary the Virgin, Ovingham (555.8)
Population 1851: 3,962 (parish) 330 (township)

Name   St Mary's Church, Ovingham.
Consecrated   Before 1800. [Restored and enlarged 1855–57.]
Endowment   Glebe £44. OPE [Queen Anne Boun[ty] fund £14. Fees
                £14. Other £41 (lay rector); £40 14s 8d (parl[ia]m[entar]
                y grant).
Sittings   [None free.] Other about 500. Total 500.
Attendance 30 March   Morning 150. Total [150].
                        Afternoon no service.
Average attendance   Afternoon 35. Total [35].
Dated   30 March 1851.
Signed   George Richard Bigge, minister [1850–69].
                   Ovingham, Newcastle on Tyne.
{1857   Attendance 320. 50 communicants.}   {B 72.}

8.18   Church of England, St George, Mickley (555.10)
Population 1851: 566 (township)

Name   Mickley Chapel, chapel of ease to Ovingham church.
                [Parish created 1866.]
Consecrated   July 1825. Consecrated as an additional chapel, 25
                July 1825. [Consecrated 31 August 1824 by the Bishop
                of Oxford. Replaced by a new church consecrated 30
                November 1886.]
Erected   By Parliamentary grant and private benefaction of
                William B. Wrightson MP.*
Endowment   OPE Royal [i.e. Queen Anne] Bounty Fund, £52.
Sittings   Free 100. Other 20. Total 120.
Attendance 30 March   Afternoon 75. Total [75].
Average attendance   [Not given.]

Remarks   *Unable to give the amount of the cost of building the chapel.

Dated   [Not given.]

Signed   George Richard Bigge, minister [1850–69].
              Ovingham, Newcastle on Tyne.

{B none.}

8.19   Church of England, St Mungo, Simonburn (555.93) [Earlier St Simon]
Population 1851: 1,080 (parish) 495 (township)

Name   Simonburn. Ancient parish church.

Consecrated Before 1800. [Alterations 1763, restored 1863–64, 1875–77.]

Endowment   Tithe £540. Glebe £80. Fees £1.

Sittings   Free 40. Other 270. Total 310.

Attendance 30 March   Morning 115 + 60 SS. Total 275.
                        Evening 60. Total 60.

Average attendance   Morning 140 + 60 SS. Total 200.
                        Evening 60. Total 60.

Remarks   The stipend of the perpetual curate of Humshaugh (£120 per annum) is paid out of the living of Simonburn.

Dated   31 March 1851.

Signed   Meyrick Beebee, rector [1841–73].
              Simonburn Rectory, Hexham, Northumberland.

{B 16.}

[Under an Act of Parliament of 1811 (51 Geo. III c.194) the huge parish of Simonburn was subdivided, and four new churches were erected and consecrated in August 1818 – Greystead, Humshaugh, Thorneyburn and Wark (**3.7**; **8.15**; **3.12**; **3.13**). Falstone, a chapel of ease to Simonburn, was consecrated in September 1825 (**3.6**).

The governors of Greenwich Hospital were the patrons of Simonburn, Greystead, Humshaugh, Thorneyburn, Wark and Falstone together with Alston and Bellingham. In October 1951 the patronage was transferred to the Bishop of Newcastle.]

8.20   Church of England, St Mary the Virgin, Slaley (555.33)
Population 1851: 581 (parish)

Name   No name. An ancient parish church.

Consecrated [Rebuilt, but not] consecrated [on 4 November] 1832,

in lieu of an old, previously existing one. [Restored
and reopened 14 December 1907.]

Erected   [The foundation stone was laid on 25 May 1832.]
Endowment Land £40. Tithe £6 13s. OPE £24. Fees £2. Dues 6s 6d
(or rent charge on land). Other £3 (rent of a house).
Sittings   Free 6. Other [not given]. Total [not given]. [500.]
Attendance 30 March   Morning 143. Total 143.
                                     Evening [60]. Total 60.
Average attendance   [Not given.]
Remarks   Being inducted to this living in 1850, I am not in
possession of the necessary documents to supply the
required information.
Dated   31 March 1851.
Signed   Blythe Hurst, perpetual curate [1850–54].
Slaley, Northumberland.

{B 15.}

[Blythe Hurst had previously been a blacksmith and Wesleyan
Methodist local preacher. He became a distinguished linguist, and
in 1863 was awarded a PhD from the University of Rostock.
On 29 September 1831 a licence was granted to hold services in a
schoolroom while the church was being rebuilt.]

8.21   Church of England, St Michael the Archangel, Warden
(555.96)
Population 1851: 646 (township)

Name   The church at Warden is dedicated to St Michael
the Archangel, [and] is the ancient parish church of
Warden. [Built by St Wilfrid AD 704.]
Consecrated [Not given.] [Nave 1765, chancel rebuilt 1889.]
*Endowment Tithe £500. Glebe £45. OPE house and garden. Fees £3.
Sittings   Free 20. Other 180. Total 200.
Attendance 30 March   Morning [76]. Total 76.
Average attendance   Morning [80]. Total 80.
Remarks   *There is no separate endowment for this church as
distinct from the rest of the parish. The tithes of which
have been commuted.
Dated   30 March 1851.
Signed   Christopher Bird, junior, curate [1839–55].
Warden, near Hexham, Northumberland.
Incumbent   [Christopher Bird, senior 1827–67.]

[A plan in the church dated 1868 indicates that the 'present' sittings were 179 and that the new seating would be 56 in the nave, 48 in the transcepts and 24 for the choir = 128 sittings.]

{B 5.}

8.22 Church of England, St Peter, Newbrough (555.98)
Population 1851: 551 (parochial chapelry)

Name Newbrough Chapel. An ancient chapelry [of Warden].
Consecrated [Not given.] [Rebuilt 1732, restored 1795 and fell into disrepair. New church opened 15 May 1866.]
Endowment Fees £1.
Sittings [None free.] Other 100. Total 100.
(Exclusive of forms in open seats for the scholars.)
Attendance 30 March Afternoon 60 + 29 SS. Total 89.
Average attendance [Not given.]
Remarks This chapelry has no endowment as distinct from the rest of the parish.
Dated 30 March 1851.
Signed Christopher Bird, junior, curate [1839–55].
Warden, near Hexham.
Incumbent [Christopher Bird (senior) 1827–67.]

{B 13.}

8.23 Church of England, St Cuthbert, Haydon Bridge (555.57)
Population 1851: 2,085 (parochial chapelry)

Name St Cuthbert's Chapel, Haydon Bridge, ancient chapelry of the parish of Warden, chapel of ease.
Consecrated [Before] 1800. [20 July 1797. The new church replaced a ruinous building. Restored 1898.]
Endowment No endowment distinct from the mother church. Fees £3 3s.
Sittings Free 18 (the Sunday school boys are seated in the chancel). Other 345. Total 363.
Attendance 30 March Morning 90 + 148 SS. Total 238.
Afternoon 90 + 78 SS. Total 168.
Average attendance Morning 150 + 190 SS. Total 340.
Afternoon 130 + 110 SS. Total 240.
Dated 31 March 1851.
Signed George Richmond, curate [and lecturer 1834–64].
Haydon Bridge.

Incumbent   [Christopher Bird (senior) 1827–67.]

{B 42.}

[An Act for taking down the chapel of the chapelry of Haydon, in the parish of Warden, in the county of Northumberland, and for building a new chapel, in a convenient situation, within the said chapelry, 35 Geo. III, c.47, 1795. George Richmond was also the headmaster of Haydon Bridge Grammar School 1834–64.]

8.24   Church of England, St Helen, Whitley Chapel (555.50)

Name   Whitley or Hexhamshire Chapel, dedicated to St Helen.
Consecrated In the year 1764 [6 July]. Had been from time immemorial used as a chapel [in the 17th century by the Quakers] and was consecrated at the request of the surrounding inhabitants by the Arch[bisho]p of York [as a chapel of ease to St Andrew, Hexham] and had a district assigned.
Endowment Land £6. Glebe £8. Other £2. Fees £2. Other £98.
Sittings   Free 188. Other 62. Total 250.
Attendance 30 March   Morning 61. Total [61].
              Afternoon 87. Total [87].
Average attendance   Morning 70. Total 70.
              Afternoon, not usual.
Dated   31 March 1851.
Signed   William Sisson, perpetual curate [1841–1906].
              Whitley, Hexham.
{1857   Attendance 60. 10 communicants.}
[Until December 1836 Whitley Chapel was in Hexhamshire (part of the diocese of York), and was then transferred to the diocese of Durham.]

8.25   Church of England Schoolroom, Lilswood (555.48)
Name   Lilswood Schoolhouse.
Licensed   1843.
Erected   The High Quarter being very remote from Whitley Chapel, the schoolhouse at Lilswood (three miles from Whitley chapel) was licensed for divine service.
Sittings   Free 60. Total 60.
Attendance 30 March   [Not given.]
Average attendance   Afternoon 50 SS. Total 50.

Dated	31 March 1851.
Signed	William Sisson, perpetual curate of Whitley Chapel [1841–1906 and minister of the above-named school house].
	Whitley, Hexham.
{1857	Attendance 40.}

8.26   Church of England, St Philip and St James, Whittonstall
(555.18)

Population 1851: 198 (Whittonstall township) 174 (Newlands township)

Name	Whittonstall Church. The parish of Whittonstall comprises two townships, Whittonstall and Newlands, and was an ancient parochial chapelry in the parish of Bywell, St Peter's. [The] book of rates for the repairs of the parish church of Whittonstall and parochial purposes existed as far back as 1743. The present structure was built in the year 1832 upon the site of the [old] church dedicated to St Philip and St James, augmented by Queen Anne's Bounty in 1773 or [177]4.
Consecrated	[Not given.] [New chancel 1896.]
Erected	Built at the expense of the Dean and the Chapter of Durham, the patrons and [by] the Commissioners of the Greenwich Hospital, the owners of the whole parish; and perhaps some private donations, but the amount of the last I have no means of ascertaining. [Total cost] not known.
Endowment	Land £40. Tithe £120 (augmentation by the Chapter […]). Glebe £14. OPE £4. Fees very seldom received.
Sittings	Free about 200. Total 200.
Attendance 30 March	Morning 12. Total [12].
	Afternoon 28. Total [28].
Average attendance	Morning total about 25 to 30.
	Afternoon total about 40 to 50. (During summer)
	Evening total about 60.
Remarks	The attendance at church depends very much upon the state of the weather, as the parishioners are spread over an area of about ten square miles and of course attend other churches which happen to be nearer than their own parish church. In the summer season I

have an evening service at Newlands, where there is generally a congregation from 60 to 80. But few attend both morning and evening or afternoon. They may be considered as distinct congregations composed of different individuals.

Dated   31 March 1851.
Signed   Richard Marshall, perpetual curate [1837–72].
Whittonstall by Gateshead.

{1857   Attendance 40. 12 communicants.}   {B 15.}

[In 1818 the church was described as 'a perfect hovel', and by 1830 only the chancel was in use (the chancel arch having been bricked up). The building was then demolished and rebuilt in 1832. A chancel was added in 1896 (J.L. Low, 'Whittonstall Church', *Arch. Ael.*, new series, xi (1896), p. 180).

Richard Marshall 'who held the living for thirty-six years and died in 1872, was highly respected by his congregation, and by all the neighbourhood. He had been the physician, the lawyer and the peacemaker, as well as the Christian pastor in his little domain. He was a man of extensive information, and had some skill in astronomy. He built an observatory in his garden, and placed in it a transit instrument. The observatory still remains in place, and may be seen in the ordinance map of the district' (G. Neasham, *The History and Biography of West Durham* (Durham, 1881), p. 113). Marshall's successor John Low Low, the vicar 1872–88, was the author of *Diocesan Histories. Durham* (London, 1881).]

8.27   United Presbyterian, Gilligate, Hexham (555.47)

Name   None.
Erected   Before 1800 [opened in 1717, enlarged in 1806].
Building   [Separate and entire. Exclusively used for worship.]
Sittings   [None] free. Other 250. Total [250].
Attendance 30 March   Morning 73. Total [73].
                              Afternoon 80. Total [80].
Average attendance   [Not given.]
Dated   31 March 1851.
Signed   James Turnbull, elder [retired innkeeper].
2 Orchard Place, [Hexham].

[The United Presbyterian Church split off from the Scotch Church in 1830, and these two Presbyterian congregations were reunited in 1883.]

8.28   English Presbyterian, Hencotes Street, Hexham (555.44)

Name   Scotch Church.
Erected   1825. [Opened 8 July 1825 and a division took place in
              the congregation in 1831.]
Building   [Separate and entire. Exclusively used for worship.]
Sittings   About 500. Total [500].
Attendance 30 March   Morning 192. Total [192].
                        Afternoon 180. Total [180].
Average attendance   [Not given.]
Remarks   I have given accurately the number in attendance
              at the two services yesterday. It was just about an
              average attendance. There are about 120 families, or
              above 500 souls in connexion with this church.
Dated   31 March 1851.
Signed   Joseph Gordon, minister [1843–55].
              [Market Street], Hexham.

8.29   Independent [Congregational], Acomb (555.86b)
[Shared with Wesleyan Methodists (**8.55**)]
Remarks   The Independent congregation [occupy the chapel]
              every fortnight Sunday night at six o'clock, and one
              Sunday in six weeks at two o'clock in the afternoon.

8.30   Independent [Congregational] Haydon Bridge (555.78)
Name   Zion Chapel.
Erected   In the year 1816. [Foundation stone of the new chapel
              laid 29 June 1863].
Building   [Separate and entire. Exclusively used for worship.]
Sittings   Free 75. Other 75. Total [150].
Attendance 30 March   Morning 55. Total [55].
                        Afternoon 40 SS. Total [40].
                        Evening 70. Total [70].
Average attendance   Morning 80. Total [80].
                        Afternoon 50 SS. Total [50].
                        Evening 100. Total [100].
Remarks   The chapel will seat about 150, but if we take into
              consideration the amount of standing room, the chapel
              will accommodate upwards of 200. This number has
              often been present.
Dated   31 March 1851.
Signed   James Smith, minister [1836–51].
              Haydon Bridge, Northumberland.

8.31   Independent [Congregational] Broadgate, Hexham (555.41)
Name   Ebenezer Chapel.
Erected   1789. [The congregation was established in 1786. In
              1869 it moved to a new chapel seating 360 and cost
              £3,800.]
Building   Separate [and entire]. Exclusively as a place of
              worship.
Sittings   Free 162 [?]. Total [162?].
Attendance 30 March   Morning 130 + 20 SS. Total 150.
                        Evening 123. Total [123].
Average attendance   Morning 127 + 20 SS. Total 147.
Dated   30 March 1851.
Signed   Thomas Spratt, minister.
              Commercial Place, Hexham.
[Stone inscription: 'Ebenezer, hitherto hath the Lord helped us.
1 Sam. 7:12. Anno. Domini 1790.'
In his younger years Joseph Parker (1830–1902) had been a member
of the congregation. After various pastorates, he was the minister
of the City Temple, London 1876–1902. 'Joseph Parker (1830–1902)',
ODNB, 2003, vol. 42, pp. 699–701.]

8.32   Independent [Congregational], Horsley (555.3)
Name   Independent Chapel.
Erected   Before 1800. [Enlarged 1729, rebuilt 1890.]
Building   [Separate and entire. Exclusively used for worship.]
Sittings   Free 250. Other 50. Total [300].
Attendance 30 March   Morning 45 + 48 SS. Total 93.
                        Evening 23. Total 23.
Average attendance   Morning 60 + 45 SS. Total 105.
                        Evening 25. Total 25.
Dated   31 March 1851.
Signed   John Raine, minister [1832–59].
              Horsley on Tyne, Newcastle on Tyne.

8.33   Baptist, Broomhaugh (555.28)
Name   Broomhaugh Chapel.
Erected   1842. [Inscription 'Baptist Jubilee Chapel, built AD
              1842'.]
Building   [Separate and entire. Exclusively used for worship.]
Sittings   Free 160. Other none. Total [160]. Standing room none.
Attendance 30 March   Evening 35. Total 35.
Average attendance   Evening 45. Total 45.

Dated   31 March 1851.
Signed   William McLean, minister.
             Riding Mill Station, Newcastle and Carlisle Railway.

8.34   Baptist, Broomley, Bywell (555.22)
Name   Broomley Chapel.
Erected   In 1835.
Building   [Separate and entire. Exclusively used for worship.]
Sittings   Free 130. Total [130].
Attendance 30 March   Morning 34. Total 34.
                        Afternoon 47. Total 47.
Average attendance   [Not given.]
Dated   31 March 1851.
Signed   William McLean, minister.
             Riding Mill Station, Newcastle and Carlisle Railway.
[From the 17th century the Baptists of the area met for worship in the homes of the members. When the chapel was demolished in 1905, the stone was used in the construction of Stocksfield Baptist Church.]

8.35   Baptist, Bywell (555.25)
Name   None.
Erected   [Not given.]
Building   [Not given.]
Sittings   [Not given.]
Attendance 30 March   Evening 40. Total [40].
Average attendance   [Not given.]
Remarks   A dwelling house, where service is done once a month
             on the Sunday evening.
Dated   31 March 1851.
Signed   William Richardson [farmer].
             High Fotherley, Riding Mill.

8.36   Baptist, Shotley Field (555.15)
Name   Baptist Chaple (*sic*).
Erected   1836.
Building   [Separate and entire. Exclusively used for worship.]
Sittings   Free 76. Other 66. Total [142].
Attendance 30 March   Afternoon 35. Total [35].
Average attendance   Morning 30 + 30 SS. Total [60].
Dated   30 March 1851.
Signed   Ebenezer Le Fevre, pastor [1850–52].
             Shotley Bridge.

[Ebenezer Le Fevre was also the pastor of Shotley Bridge (**16.30**) and Rowley (**16.31**).]

8.37   Wesleyan Methodist, Allendale Town (555.58)
Name   Wesleyan Chapel.
Erected   1778.
Building   [Separate and entire. Exclusively used for worship.]
Sittings   Free 130. Other 76. Total [206].
Attendance 30 March   Morning 68 SS. Total 68.
               Afternoon 68. Total 68.
               Evening 93. Total 93.
Average attendance   Afternoon 70. Total 70.
               Evening 110. Total 110.
Dated   31 March 1851.
Signed   George Ellidge, superintendent minister [1850–51].
               Allendale Town, Northumberland.

8.38   Wesleyan Methodist, Allendale (555.68)
Name   None.
Erected   Before 1800.
Building   [Not separate and entire or exclusively used for
               worship.]
Sittings   Free 35. Total [35].
Attendance 30 March   Afternoon 25. Total 25.
Average attendance   Afternoon 25. Total 25.
Dated   2 April 1851.
Signed   George Ellidge, superintendent minister [1850–51].
               Allendale, Northumberland.

8.39   Wesleyan Methodist, Allendale (555.69)
Name   None.
Erected   Before 1800.
Building   [Not separate and entire or exclusively used for
               worship.]
Sittings   Free 35. Total [35].
Attendance 30 March   Morning 12. Total 12.
               Afternoon 14. Total 14.
               Evening 30. Total 30.
Average attendance   Morning 12. Total 12.
               Evening 30. Total 30.
Dated   2 April 1851.
Signed   George Ellidge, superintendent minister [1850–51].
               Allendale, Northumberland.

8.40   Wesleyan Methodist, Holly Close, Allendale (555.64)
Name   None.
Erected   Before 1820.
Building   [Not separate and entire or exclusively used for
              worship.]
Sittings   Free 25. Total [25].
Attendance 30 March   Afternoon 20. Total 20.
Average attendance   Afternoon 15. Total 15.
Dated   2 April 1851.
Signed   George Ellidge, superintendent minister [1850–51].
              Allendale, Northumberland.

8.41   Wesleyan Methodist, High House, Allendale (555.77)
Name   High House Chapel.
Erected   1829. [Enlarged 1859.]
Building   [Separate and entire. Exclusively used for worship]
              except day school.
Sittings   Free 110. Total [110].
Attendance 30 March   Morning 60. Total 60.
                         Afternoon 100. Total 100.
Average attendance   Morning 60. Total 60.
                         Afternoon 100. Total 100.
Dated   31 March 1851.
Signed   George Ellidge, superintendent minister [1850–51].
              Allendale, Northumberland.

8.42   Wesleyan Methodist, Limestone Brae, Allendale (555.71)
Name   Limestone Brae Chapel.
Erected   1827. [Rebuilt 1847.]
Building   [Separate and entire. Exclusively used for worship.]
Sittings   Free 200. Other 72. Total [272].
Attendance 30 March   Afternoon 112. Total 112.
                         Evening 78. Total 78.
Average attendance   Afternoon 112. Total 112.
                         Evening 78. Total 78.
Remarks   About thirty of the congregation would be Sunday
              school scholars, but the distinction was not made in
              the return to me.
Dated   31 March 1851.
Signed   George Ellidge, superintendent minister [1850–51].
              Allendale Town, Northumberland.

8.43   Wesleyan Methodist, Allenheads (555.56)
Name   Allenheads Chapel.
Erected   1834. [Enlarged 1859.]
Building   [Separate and entire. Exclusively used for worship.]
Sittings   Free 110. Other 135. Total [245].
Attendance 30 March   Afternoon 108 + 42 SS. Total 150.
                        Evening 86. Total 86.
Average attendance   Afternoon 120 + 40 SS. Total 160.
                        Evening 90. Total 90.
Dated   5 April 1851.
Signed   George Ellidge, superintendent minister [1850–51].
                Allendale, Northumberland.

8.44   Wesleyan Methodist, Catton (555.60)
Name   Catton Chapel.
Erected   1840.
Building   [Separate and entire. Exclusively used for worship.]
Sittings   Free 45. Other 15. Total [60].
Attendance 30 March   Afternoon 30. Total 30.
Average attendance   Afternoon 35. Total 35.
                        Evening 30. Total 30.
Dated   2 April 1851.
Signed   George Ellidge, superintendent minister [1850–51].
                Allendale, Northumberland.

8.45   Wesleyan Methodist, Keenley (555.63)
Name   Wesleyan Chapel.
Erected   1752. [Rebuilt in 1874.]
Building   [Separate and entire. Exclusively used for worship.]
Sittings   Free 78. Other 60. Total [138].
Attendance 30 March   Afternoon 40 + 23 SS. Total 63.
Average attendance   Afternoon 25 + 15 SS. Total 40.
Remarks   This chapel is situate amidst a very scattered
                population and stands in the place of one in which
                some think [John] Wesley himself preached, others say
                he preached in a neighbouring barn.
Dated   31 March 1851.
Signed   George Ellidge, superintendent minister [1850–51].
                Allendale Town, Northumberland.

8.46   Wesleyan Methodist, Langley Mills (555.81)
Name   Langley Chapel.
Erected   1849.
Building   [Separate and entire. Exclusively used for worship.]
Sittings   Free 100. Other 58. Total [158].
Attendance 30 March   Afternoon [6]. Total 6.
                Evening 80. Total 80.
Average attendance   Morning 8 + 24 SS. Total 32.
                Afternoon 60. Total 60.
                Evening 80. Total 80.
Dated   31 March 1851.
Signed   George Ellidge, superintendent minister [1850–51].
                Allendale, Northumberland.

8.47   Wesleyan Methodist, Hesleywell, West Allendale (555.73)
Name   Hesleywell Chapel.
Erected   1828.
Building   [Separate and entire. Exclusively used for worship]
                except for a Sunday and day school.
Sittings   Free 150. Total [150].
Attendance 30 March   Morning 63. Total 63.
                Evening 96. Total 96.
Average attendance   Morning 50 + 15 SS. Total 65.
                Evening [96]. Total 96.
Dated   31 March 1851.
Signed   George Ellidge, superintendent minister [1850–51].
                Allendale, Northumberland.

8.48   Wesleyan Methodist, West Allen (555.72)
Name   None.
Erected   About 1810.
Building   [Not separate and entire or exclusively used for
                worship.]
Sittings   Free 45. Total [45].
Attendance 30 March   Evening 23. Total 23.
Average attendance   Evening 33. Total 33.
Remarks   Sickness prevailing in the neighbourhood is assigned
                as the reason why the congregation on the 30 [March]
                was below the average.
Dated   5 April 1851.
Signed   George Ellidge, superintendent minister [1850–51].
                Allendale Town, Northumberland.

8.49   Wesleyan Methodist, Barrasford (555.91)
Name   Barrasford Chapel.
Erected   Ab[ou]t 1836.
Building   Separate building. Used for a place of worship only.
Sittings   Free 70. Other 30. Total [100]. Standing room 20.
Attendance 30 March   Afternoon 60. Total 60.
                        Evening 30. Total 30.
Average attendance   Morning 60. Total 60.
Dated   23 March 1851.
Signed   Joseph Whitehead, Wesleyan minister [1850–51].
               Hexham, Northumberland.

8.50   Wesleyan Methodist, Gilligate, Hexham (555.46)
Name   Hexham Wesleyan Chapel.
Erected   [1789.] 1839.
Building   [Separate and entire. Exclusively used for worship.]
Sittings   Free 150. Other 550. Total [700]. Standing room 200.
Attendance 30 March   Morning 200. Total 200.
                        Evening 300. Total 300.
Average attendance   Morning 200. Total 200.
                        Evening 300. Total 300.
Dated   31 March 1851.
Signed   Joseph Whitehead, minister [1850–51].
               Hexham, Northumberland.

8.51   Wesleyan Methodist, Horsley (555.5)
Name   Preaching House.
Erected   [Not given.]
Building   Used for a dwelling house, as well as for preaching.
               [Not exclusively used for worship a] dwelling house
               [belonging to a Mr Archibold in which John Wesley is
               said to have preached].
Sittings   Free 80. Total [80]. Standing room 20.
Attendance 30 March   Afternoon 70. Total 70.
Average attendance   [Not given.]
Dated   25 March 1851.
Signed   Joseph Whitehead, minister [1850–51].
               Hexham, Northumberland.

8.52   Wesleyan Methodist Schoolroom, Humshaugh (555.95)
Name   Humshaugh Day School.
Erected   Since 1800. [Chapel erected 1862, enlarged 1879.]

Building   Separate building. Used for a day school as well as for
              preaching.
Sittings   Free 100. Total [100]. Standing room 30.
Attendance 30 March   Morning 50 SS. Total 50.
                        Evening 60. Total 60.
Average attendance   Evening 60. Total 60.
Dated   23 March 1851.
Signed   Joseph Whitehead, Wesleyan minister [1850–51].
              Hexham, Northumberland.

8.53   Wesleyan Methodist, Ovington (555.9)
Name   Preaching Room.
Erected   Cannot tell when.
Building   Partly a dwelling house. [Not exclusively used for
              worship.]
Sittings   All free 50. Total [50]. Standing room 12.
Attendance 30 March   Afternoon 50 + 12 SS. Total 62.
                        Evening 50. Total 50.
Average attendance   [Not given.]
Dated   31 March 1851.
Signed   Joseph Whitehead, minister [1850–51].
              Hexham, Northumberland.

8.54   Wesleyan Methodist, Wall (555.87)
Name   Preaching Room.
Erected   Used for preaching two years [1849].
Building   Separate building. Used also as a day school.
Sittings   Free 60. Total [60]. Standing room 10.
Attendance 30 March   Afternoon 52. Total [52].
Average attendance   Morning 60. Total [60].
Dated   31 March 1851.
Signed   Joseph Whitehead, minister [1850–51].
              Hexham, Northumberland.

8.55   Wesleyan Methodist, Acomb (555.86a)
[Shared with Independents (**8.29**)]
Name   Wesleyan Methodist Chapel.
Erected   Burnt down in 1806 and erected for a chapel 1831. One
              room above it, [a] dwelling house.
Building   [Not separate and entire but exclusively used for
              worship.]
Sittings   Free 55. Other 49. Total [104]. No standing room.

Attendance 30 March   Afternoon 26. Total 26.
Average attendance   [Not given.]
Remarks   The Wesleyan Methodists occupy the chapel every
Sunday afternoon at two o'clock, and the Independent
congregation every fortnight Sunday night at six
o'clock, and one Sunday in six weeks at two o'clock in
the afternoon.
Dated   31 March 1851.
Signed   John Hutchinson, manager (tailer) (*sic*).
Acomb near Hexham.

8.56   Wesleyan Methodist, Broomhaugh (555.30)
Name   [Not given.]
Erected   [Not given.]
Building   [Not given.]
Sittings   [Not given.]
Attendance 30 March   [Not given.]
Average attendance   Morning 20. Total [20].
Remarks   The service is held in part of a dwelling house
fortnightly on Sunday afternoons.
Dated   31 March 1851.
Signed   James Richardson [grocer].
Broomhaugh, Northumberland.

8.57   Wesleyan Methodist, Bywell (555.27)
Name   [None.]
Erected   [Not given.]
Building   [Not separate and entire or exclusively used for
worship.]
Sittings   [Not given.]
Attendance 30 March   Evening 53. Total [53].
Average attendance   [Not given.]
Dated   31 March 1851.
Signed   John Hunter, Wesleyan local preacher.
Hinnishill by Blanchland.

8.58   Wesleyan Methodist, Bywell (555.19)
Name   Wesleyan Methodist Chapel.
Erected   1844.
Building   Separate and entire. Exclusively as a place of worship
(except sc[hool]).
Sittings   Free 100. Other 26. Total [126]. Standing room 30.

Attendance 30 March   Evening 40 + 10 SS. Total 50.
Average attendance   Evening 40 + 10 SS. Total 50.
Dated   31 March 1851.
Signed   Richard Oley, steward [grocer and shoemaker].
   Whittonstall, Northumberland.

8.59 Wesleyan Methodist, Corbridge (555.37)
Name   Wesleyan Methodist Chapel.
Erected   About the year 1815.
Building   [Separate and entire. Exclusively used for worship.]
Sittings   Free 100. Other 100. Total [200]. Standing room 30.
Attendance 30 March   Afternoon 113 + 20 SS. Total 133.
   Evening 55 + 20 SS. Total 75.
Average attendance   Morning and afternoon 170 + 80 SS.
   Total 250.
Dated   30 March 1851.
Signed   Robert Forster, leader and local preacher
   [watchmaker].
   Corbridge, Northumberland.

8.60 Wesleyan Methodist, Haydon Bridge (555.79)
Name   Methodist Chapel.
Erected   In the year 1818. [New chapel opened 10 June 1874.]
Building   [Separate and entire. Exclusively used for worship.]
Sittings   Free 200. Other 60. Total [260].
Attendance 30 March   Morning 45. Total [45].
   Evening 120. Total [120].
Average attendance   [Not given.]
Remarks   The chapel will seat about 200 but if we take into
   consideration the space or standing room, the chapel
   will accommodate upwards of 300. This number has
   frequently been present.
Dated   31 March 1851.
Signed   William Smith, chapel steward [iron founder].
   Haydon Bridge, Northumberland.

8.61 Wesleyan Methodist, Hedley on the Hill (555.12)
Name   Wesleyan Methodist Chapel.
Erected   1837.
Building   Separate and entire. Used exclusively as a place of
   worship.
Sittings   Free 70. Other 25. Total [95]. Standing room 30.

Attendance 30 March   Afternoon 55 + 25 SS. Total 80.
Average attendance   [Not given.]
Dated   31 March 1851.
Signed   Richard Dodd, society steward.
               Hedley, Northumberland.

8.62   Wesleyan Methodist, Hexham (555.42)
Name   Fine Chambers.
Erected   About 1820. [1789, then 1839 at Abbey Gate.]
Building   [Separate and entire. Exclusively used for worship.]
Sittings   Free 100. Other 70. Total [170].
Attendance 30 March   Afternoon 24. Total [24].
Average attendance   Afternoon 35 + 24 SS. Total 59.
Dated   22 March 1851.
Signed   William Hirst, Wesleyan minister [1850–51].
               Hexham, Northumberland.
[William Hirst was also the minister of Harlow Hill (**5.21**) and
Stamfordham (**5.22**).]

8.63   Wesleyan Methodist Schoolroom, Newbrough (555.99)
Name   Schoolroom.
Erected   1823.
Building   [Separate and entire.] Not exclusively a place of
               worship.
Sittings   All free 80. Total [80]. Standing room none.
Attendance 30 March   Morning none.
               Afternoon none.
               Evening 62. Total 62.
Average attendance   Morning none.
               Afternoon none.
               Evening 50. Total 50.
Remarks   Used as a Wesleyan chapel every Sunday evening
               and Friday evening by leave from Capt. Gustavus H.
               Coulson.
Dated   31 March 1851.
Signed   Thomas Forrester, steward (farmer).
               Newbrough, Hexham.

8.64   Wesleyan Methodist, Newlands (555.20)
Name   Wesleyan Methodist Chapel.
Erected   About 1800.
Building   The Wesleyan Chapel, a separate and entire building.

Used as a place of worship exclusively (except sch[ool]).

Sittings	Free all 100 sittings. Total [100]. Standing room 50.
Attendance 30 March	Morning 26 + 24 SS. Total 50.
Average attendance	Morning 25 + 30 SS. Total 55.
Dated	30 March 1851.
Signed	John Lowes, local preacher (blacksmith).
	Newlands.

### 8.65	Wesleyan Methodist, Mickley (555.13)

Name	None.
Erected	Before 1800. [New chapel erected 1855.]
Building	A dwelling house. No school.
Sittings	All free. Other none.
Attendance 30 March	Morning 35. Total [35].
	Evening 36. Total [36].
Average attendance	Morning 35. Total [35].
	Evening 40. Total [40].
Remarks	There is worship held in this house every Sunday, in the morning or one in the evening, on the alternate Sunday. The number in the evening is the exact number that attended on 30 March 1851.
Dated	30 March 1851.
Signed	John Philipson (shoemaker).
	Mickley, Northumberland.

### 8.66	Wesleyan Methodist, South Road, Prudhoe (555.11)

Name	Wesleyan Chapel.
Erected	Before 1800. [1757, 1794. New chapel opened September 1871, and the previous chapel re-named the Wesley Hall.]
Building	[Separate and entire. Exclusively used for worship.]
Sittings	Free 261. Other 39. Total [300]. Standing room 50.
Attendance 30 March	Morning 150. Total [150].
	Evening 60. Total [60].
Average attendance	[Not given.]
Dated	31 March 1851.
Signed	Michael Hall, steward [boot and shoemaker and post master].
	Prudhoe, Newcastle, Northumberland.

8.67   Wesleyan Methodist, East Ridley (555.21)
Name   None. Dwelling house [rubbed out].
Erected   [Not given.]
Building   [Not given.]
Sittings   [Not given.]
Attendance 30 March   Evening 40. Total [40].
Average attendance   [Not given.]
Dated   30 March 1851.
Signed   William Ridley Pigg.

8.68   Wesleyan Methodist, Shotley Bridge (555.16)
Name   None.
Erected   1843.
Building   A back room occasionally used for other purposes.
               [Not exclusively used for worship.]
Sittings   Free 70. Other none. Total [70]. Standing room 12.
Attendance 30 March   Evening 58. Total 58.
Average attendance   [Not given.]
Remarks   Our congregation would be more numerous, could
               they be more comfortably seated. But owing to the
               whole of the property in the parish belonging to the
               trustees of the late Lord Crewe, we are unable to
               procure a larger place of worship.
Dated   31 March 1851.
Signed   William Bell for John Lee, society steward.
               Blanchland, Gateshead on Tyne, Northumberland.

8.69   Wesleyan Methodist, Shotley Bridge (555.24)
Name   None.
Erected   [Not given.]
Building   [Not exclusively used for worship.]
Sittings   [Not given.] Standing room 50.
Attendance 30 March   Afternoon 19. Total [19].
Average attendance   Afternoon 35. Total [35].
Dated   30 March 1851.
Signed   Henry Brown, local preacher.
               Green Street, Shotley Bridge, Durham.

8.70   Wesleyan Methodist, Slaley (555.35)
Name   Slaley.
Erected   1842. [Opened 6 November 1842. New chapel opened
               5 April 1901, and cost of £850.]

Building   [Separate and entire, but not exclusively used for
              worship.]
Sittings   Free 100. Other 40. Total [140].
Attendance 30 March   [Not given.]
Average attendance   Afternoon 25. Total 25.
Dated   30 March 1851.
Signed   Thomas Jameson, steward [blacksmith].
              Slaley, Hexham.

8.71   Wesleyan Methodist, Warden (555.97)

Name   Hardhaugh.
Erected   1820.
Building   [Not separate and entire or exclusively used for
              worship.]
              Dwelling house [cottage crossed out].
Sittings   All free.
Attendance 30 March   Afternoon 35. Total [35].
Average attendance   Morning 35. Total 35.
Dated   31 March 1851.
Signed   Thomas Stirling, steward [paper maker].
              Warden, n[ea]r Hexham, Northumberland.

8.72   Wesleyan Methodist, Welton (555.2)

Name   None.
Erected   1848.
Building   [Not separate and entire or exclusively used for
              worship.]
Sittings   [Not given.]
Attendance 30 March   Afternoon 30. Total 30.
Average attendance   Afternoon 30. Total [30].
Remarks   I have public worship performed in my hamlet every
              Sabbath afternoon by local preachers of the Wesleyan
              Methodist denomination. George Brown, farmer, [of
              Great] Whittington], preached here on Sunday, 30 inst.
              Henderson Pearson, Welton.
Dated   30 March 1851.
Signed   Henderson Pearson.
[For George Brown see **8.73**.]

8.73   Wesleyan Methodist, Great Whittington (555.39)

Name   Wesleyan Chapel.
Erected   1835.

Building   [Separate and entire. Exclusively used for worship.]
Sittings   Free 100. Other 56. Total [156].
Attendance 30 March   Evening 45. Total [45].
Average attendance   Afternoon 70. Total [70].
Dated   31 March 1851.
Signed   George Brown, class leader [farmer].
         Great Whittington, near Matfen, Northumberland.

8.74   Wesleyan Methodist, Wylam (555.6)
Name   Wylam Chapel.
Erected   Before 1840. [1834, new chapel opened 29 April 1876.]
Building   Separate building. Used for nothing but religious
         services, except Sunday school.
Sittings   Free 100. Other 44. Total [144].
Attendance 30 March   Morning 50 + 30 SS. Total 80.
         Evening 140. Total 140.
Average attendance   [Not given.]
Dated   31 March 1851.
Signed   John Moore, elder [colliery agent].
         Wylam, Newcastle, Northumberland.

8.75   Primitive Methodist, Allendale Town (555.59)
Name   Primitive Methodist Chapel.
Erected   1835. [New adjacent chapel opened 1878.]
Building   [Separate and entire. Not exclusively used for
         worship.] A day school taught in it.
Sittings   Free 80. Other 80. Total [160].
Attendance 30 March   Morning 30 + 40 SS. Total 70.
         Afternoon 50 SS. Total 50.
         Evening 100. Total 100.
Average attendance   Morning 30 + 48 SS. Total 78.
         Afternoon 48 SS. Total 48.
         Evening 100. Total 100.
Remarks   The divine service at which the scholars are returned
         as attending is distinct from the general congregational
         service. When the latter commences the scholars retire
         home.
Dated   31 March 1851.
Signed   Thomas Southern, one of the ministers.
         Allendale Town, Northumberland.

8.76   Primitive Methodist, Allenheads (555.65)
Name   Primitive Methodist Chapel.
Erected   1841. [Replaced 1849.]
Building   [Separate and entire. Exclusively used for worship.]
Sittings   Free 100. Other 180. Total [280].
Attendance 30 March   Morning 60 SS. Total 60.
                           Afternoon 80 + 60 SS. Total 140.
                           Evening 170. Total 170.
Average attendance   Morning 80 SS. Total 80.
                           Afternoon 80 + 80 SS. Total 160.
                           Evening 160. Total 160.
Remarks   The divine service at which the scholars are returned
                as attending is distinct from the general congregational
                service. When it commences they retire home. There is
                divine service for the school at the times returned.
Dated   31 March 1851.
Signed   Thomas Southern, one of the ministers.
                Allendale Town, Northumberland.

8.77   Primitive Methodist, Appletree Shield (555.74)
Name   Primitive Methodist Chapel.
Erected   1829.
Building   [Separate and entire. Exclusively used for worship.]
Sittings   Free 80. Total [80].
Attendance 30 March   Morning 20 SS. Total 20.
                           Afternoon 40 + 20 SS. Total 60.
Average attendance   Morning 20 SS. Total 20.
                           Afternoon 35 + 20 SS. Total 55.
Remarks   The divine service at which the scholars are returned
                as attending is [a] service distinct for them. When the
                general congregational service begins they then retire
                home.
Dated   31 March 1851.
Signed   Thomas Southern, one of the ministers.
                Allendale Town, Northumberland.

8.78   Primitive Methodist, Corry Hill (555.76)
Name   Primitive Methodist Chapel.
Erected   1844.
Building   [Separate and entire. Exclusively used for worship.]
Sittings   Free 58. Other 76. Total [134].
Attendance 30 March   Morning 30 SS. Total 30.

Afternoon 49 + 30 SS. Total 79.
Evening 105. Total 105.

Average attendance   Morning 30 SS. Total 30.
Afternoon 60 + 30 SS. Total 90.
Evening 100. Total 100.

Remarks   The scholars returned as attending divine service
are not present at the general congregational service.
There being divine service for the school at the
time of day returned, apart from the congregational
service, and the scholars retiring home when the latter
commences.

Dated   30 March 1851.
Signed   Thomas Southern, one of the ministers.
Allendale Town, Northumberland

8.79   Primitive Methodist Schoolroom, Keenley (555.62)

Name   Schoolhouse.
Erected   1849.
Building   [Separate and entire. Not exclusively used for
worship.] A day school taught in it.
Sittings   Free 40. Other 40. Total [80].
Attendance 30 March   Evening 60. Total 60.
Average attendance   Morning 20. Total 20. (Morning service once a
fortnight.)
Evening 56. Total 56.
Dated   31 March 1851.
Signed   Thomas Southern, one of the ministers.
Allendale Town, Northumberland.

8.80   Primitive Methodist, Sinderhope (555.67)

Name   Primitive Methodist Chapel.
Erected   1829. [Rebuilt 1861, and cost £500.]
Building   [Separate and entire. Exclusively used for worship.]
Sittings   Free 40. Other 35. Total [75].
Attendance 30 March   Morning 40 SS. Total 40.
Afternoon 65. Total 65.
Evening 50. Total 50.
Average attendance   [Not given.]
Remarks   The morning service is for the school only.
Dated   30 March 1851.
Signed   Thomas Southern, one of the ministers.
Allendale Town, Northumberland.

8.81   Primitive Methodist, Swinhope (555.66)
Name   Primitive Methodist Chapel.
Erected   1845.
Building   [Separate and entire. Exclusively used for worship.]
Sittings   Free 84. Other 84. Total [168].
Attendance 30 March   Morning 20 SS. Total 20.
                        Afternoon 80 + 29 SS. Total 109.
                        Evening 65. Total 65.
Average attendance   Morning 40 SS. Total [40].
                        Afternoon 60 + 44 SS. Total 104.
                        Evening 65. Total 65.
Remarks   There is divine service for the scholars apart from the
             general congregational service, for this the return of
             scholars is made. When the congregational service
             commences they retire home.
Dated   31 March 1851.
Signed   Thomas Southern, one of the ministers.
             Allendale Town, Northumberland.

8.82   Primitive Methodist, Whitley Shield (555.70)
Name   None.
Erected   Not known. [Inscription 1857.]
Building   [Not separate and entire or exclusively used for worship.]
Sittings   Free 50. Total [50].
Attendance 30 March   Evening 40 SS. Total 40.
Average attendance   [Not given.]
Dated   31 March 1851.
Signed   Thomas Southern, one of the ministers.
             Allendale Town, Northumberland

8.83   Primitive Methodist, Wooley (555.55)
Name   None.
Erected   Not known.
Building   [Not separate and entire or exclusively used for
             worship.]
Sittings   Free 35. Total [35].
Attendance 30 March   [Not given.]
Average attendance   Afternoon 20. Total 20.
Remarks   Divine service held once a fortnight.
Dated   31 March 1851.
Signed   Thomas Southern, one of the ministers.
             Allendale Town, Northumberland

8.84   Primitive Methodist, Blanchland (555.17)

Name   None.
Erected   Before 1800.
Building   [Not separate and entire or exclusively used for worship.]
Sittings   Free 60. Total [60]. Standing room 20 square yards.
Attendance 30 March   Evening 50. Total 50.
Average attendance   [Not given.]
Dated   30 March 1851.
Remarks   Simon Hodgson's family occupies the house where we preach in etc.
Dated   30 March 1851.
Signed   Charles Harrowby, minister.
                Priest Popple, Hexham.
[Charles Harrowby was also the minister of Muggleswick (**16.79**).]

8.85   Primitive Methodist, Catton Lane Foot (555.61)

Name   Primitive Methodist Chapel.
Erected   About the year 1825. [New chapel opened opposite 1882.]
Building   [Separate and entire. Exclusively used for worship.]
Sittings   Free 100. Other 32. Total [132].
Attendance 30 March   Afternoon 40 + 20 SS. Total 60.
                Evening 50 + 20 SS. Total 70.
Average attendance   Afternoon 50. Total [50].
                Evening 70. Total [70].
Remarks   The chapel is used for a day school.
Dated   31 March 1851.
Signed   Joseph Parker, chapel steward [lead ore smelter].
                Law Mill Cottage, Allendale, Northumberland.

8.86   Primitive Methodist, Corbridge (555.36)

Name   Primitive Methodist Preaching Room.
Erected   1850. [Foundation stone of new chapel laid 28 August 1867, cost £330.]
Building   [Separate and entire.] Exclusive for worship.
Sittings   Free 90. Total [90].
Attendance 30 March   Morning 45. Total [45].
                Evening 50. Total [50].
Average attendance   [Not given.]
Dated   31 March 1851.
Signed   William Wood, steward.
                Corbridge.

8.87   Primitive Methodist, Dye House (555.49)
Name   Primitive Methodist Chapel.
Erected   1832. [New chapel 1862.]
Building   [Separate and entire. Exclusively used for worship.]
Sittings   Free 80. Other 36. Total [116].
Attendance 30 March   Morning 24. Total [24].
                Afternoon 25 SS. Total [25].
                Evening 30. Total [30].
Average attendance   Morning 40 (for early service). Total [40].
                Afternoon 45 SS. Total [45].
Dated   30 March 1851.
Signed   Thomas Simpson, steward.
                Black Hall Mill, Hexhamshire, Northumberland.

8.88   Primitive Methodist, Haydon Bridge (555.82)
Name   Primitive Methodist Chapel.
Erected   1847. [New chapel 1863.]
Building   Separate [and entire]. Exclusively for worship.
Sittings   Free 48. Other 48. Total [96].
Attendance 30 March   Morning 26. Total [26].
                Evening 19. Total [19].
Average attendance   [Not given.]
Dated   31 March 1851.
Signed   William Stubbs, chapel steward.
                Haydon Bridge.

8.89   Primitive Methodist, Bull Bank, Hexham (555.45)
Name   Bull Bank Chapel.
Erected   1830. [From 1827 in Battle Hill then Bull Bank. New
                chapel 1863.]
Building   [Separate and] entire. Exclusively except for Sunday
                school.
Sittings   Free 180. Other 120. Total [300].
Attendance 30 March   Afternoon 50 + 20 SS. Total 70.
                Evening 60. Total 60.
Average attendance   [Not given.]
Dated   31 March 1851.
Signed   William Lister, minister.
                Bull Bank, Hexham, Northumberland.
[In 1863 replaced by Hebbron Memorial Chapel in memory of Henry
Hebbron, a Primitive Methodist local preacher.]

8.90   Primitive Methodist, Horsley (555.4)

Name	None.
Erected	1849.
Building	[Not separate and entire or exclusively used for worship.]
Sittings	Free room.

Attendance 30 March   Morning 10. Total 10.
Afternoon 50. Total 50.
Evening 40. Total 40.

Average attendance	[Not given.]
Dated	31 March 1851.
Signed	James Potts, steward.
	Horsley, Tyne Side, Northumberland.

8.91   Primitive Methodist, Newbrough (555.100)

Name	Newbrough.
Erected	Built in 1846.
Building	[Not separate and entire or exclusively used for worship. A] dwelling house.
Sittings	[Not given.]

Attendance 30 March   Morning 20. Total 20.
Average attendance   Morning 30. Total [30].

Dated	31 March 1851.
Signed	John Pearson, steward [agricultural labourer].
	Newbrough, Hexham, Northumberland.

8.92   Primitive Methodist (Ranters), Shotley Bridge (555.14)

Name	None.
Erected	[Opened 22 October 1843.]
Building	[Not separate and entire or exclusively used for worship.]
Sittings	Free room.

Attendance 30 March   Morning 50. Total [50].

Average attendance	[Not given.]
Dated	[Not given.]
Signed	[Not given.]

8.93   Primitive Methodist, Langley, Smith Mills (555.80)

Name	None.
Erected	Before 1800.
Building	[Not separate and entire or exclusively used for worship.]

Sittings   All free. Other none. *Standing room.
Attendance 30 March   Afternoon 70. Total 70.
Average attendance   Afternoon 100. Total 100.
                        **Evening.
Remarks   *The space available for public worship is about 30
             feet by 20 feet. Moveable benches are used for sittings,
             and of course are all free.
             **The meetings are held on a Sunday afternoon and
             evening alternately. The evening congregation being
             generally larger.
Dated   30 March 1851.
Signed   James Weir, leader and local preacher [separator of
            silver and lead].
            Langley, South Mills, Haydon Bridge,
            North[umberlan]d.

8.94   Primitive Methodist, Wylam (555.7)

Name   Dwelling House.
Erected   1850.
Building   [Not separate and entire or exclusively used for
              worship.]
Sittings   All free. Standing room 50.
Attendance 30 March   Morning (no service).
                         Afternoon (no service).
Average attendance   [Not given.]
Remarks   The Primitive Methodists met first in Wylam in the
             year 1850 in a cottage. There are ten members, they
             have service once every Sabbath, in the evening. There
             are generally from 20 to 30 tickets [for members]. Two
             itinerant preachers supply Wylam, one local preacher
             every Sabbath.
Dated   30 March 1851.
Signed   George Dixon, steward [coal miner].
            Wylam, Ovingham, Northumberland.

8.95   Society of Friends (Quakers), Wooley (555.75)

Name   Wooley, Burnfoot, Allendale.
Erected   Before 1800. [Built 1688, rebuilt 1733, 1868.]
Building   [Separate and entire. Exclusively used for worship.]
Sittings   Free 300. Total [300].
              Floor area 30 by 24 = 720. Galleries 4 by 24 = 96 [and]
              11 by 24 = 264. Total 1,080 [square feet].

Attendance 30 March   Morning 9. Total [9].
                        Afternoon none held.
                        Evening none held
Dated   The seventh day of the fourth month 1851 [7 April
               1851].
Signed   William Wilson [boot and shoemaker].
               Allendale Town.

8.96   Roman Catholic, Hencotes, Hexham (555.43)

Name   St Mary's.
Erected   About 1830. [Opened 22 September 1830.] In lieu of
               two smaller chapels [opened in 1751 and 1796].
Building   Separate [and entire]. Exclusively [used for worship].
Sittings   Free 200. Other 186. Total 386.
Attendance 30 March   Morning 364 + 77 SS. Total 364 (*sic*) [441].
                        Afternoon 190 + 70 SS. Total 190 (*sic*) [260].
Average attendance   Morning 400 + 77 SS. Total 400 (*sic*) [477].
                        Afternoon about 190 + 77 SS. Total 77 (*sic*) [267].
Remarks   The dimensions of St Mary's R[oman] Cath[olic]
               Chapel, Hexham, are 70 by 40 feet; gallery 24 by 40
               ditto. Standing room 2,020 square feet. Free sittings
               200. Other sittings 186.
Dated   31 March 1851.
Signed   Rev. Michael Singleton, Roman Cath[olic] priest [and
               the architect of the building].
               St Mary's, Hexham, Northumberland.

8.97   Roman Catholic, Minsteracres Hall, Minsteracres (555.23)

Name   Roman Catholic Chapel.
Erected   [Not given.] [Chapel opened 22 June 1834, new church
               opened 24 August 1854, to seat 200.]
Building   Domestic chapel, not a separate building. [Exclusively
               used for worship.]
Sittings   All free sittings.
Attendance 30 March   Morning 60. Total [60].
                        Afternoon 20. Total [20].
                        Evening 4. Total [4].
Average attendance   [Not given.]
Dated   31 March 1851.
Signed   John Singleton Rogerson, Roman Catholic priest and
               private chaplain [1842–53].
               Minsteracres, by Newcastle on Tyne.

8.98   Roman Catholic, Swinburne Castle Chapel, Swinburne
(555.92)

Name   Swinburne Catholic Chapel.
Erected   1842. [Opened 28 September 1841.]
Building   [Separate and entire.] Excl[usively used for worship].
Sittings   Free 80. Other 20. total [100].
Attendance 30 March   Morning 50. Total [50].
Average attendance   Morning 120. Total [120].
Remarks   Whole number that ever attends.
Dated   31 March 1851.
Signed   Peter Allanson, Catholic priest [1831–75].   }   [In a
    Swinburne Hermitage, near Hexham.   different
    hand.]

9. Morpeth District (HO 129/558)
36 places of worship

9.1   Church of England, St Cuthbert, Bedlington (558.2b)
Population 1851: 5,101 (parish)

Name   St Cuthbert. Ancient parish church.
Consecrated   [Chancel rebuilt 1736, enlarged 1818, north aisle 1912.]
Endowment   Land £8. Tithe £208. Glebe £230. Fees £17.
    Easter offerings not collected.
Sittings   Free 150. Other 550. Total 700.
Attendance 30 March   Morning 400 + 60 SS. Total 460.
    Evening 350. Total 350.
Average attendance   [Not given.]
Remarks   The evening is the average congregation for the last
    nine months.
Dated   31 March 1851.
Signed   Robert Taylor, curate of Bedlington [1850–60].
    Bedlington, Morpeth.
Incumbent   [Edward Chaloner Ogle 1835–54.]
{1857   Attendance 300. 40 communicants.}   {B 172.}

9.2   Church of England, St Andrew, Bothal (558.21b)
Population 1851: 946 (parish) 269 (township)

[Summary form]
Name   St Andrew's, Bothal.

Erected	I think not less than 300 years ago. [Restored 1857, 1887.]
Endowment	[£1,307.]
Sittings	350 in all. Total 350.
Usual attendance	Morning 70 + 20 SS. Total [90]. [Average] number about 70. Afternoon generally once a month. Evening none.
Dated	[Not given.]
Signed	Robert Soulsby, registrar.
Incumbent	[Henry Hopwood 1845–59.]
{1857	Attendance 50. – communicants.} {B 29.}

[By the late 18th century the ancient parish church of Sheepwash was in ruins.]

9.3   Church of England, St Cuthbert, Hebburn (558.20b)
Population 1851: 117 (township)

[Summary form]

Name	Hebburn in the parish of Bothal.
Erected	Rebuilt about fifty-four years ago. The date of the original building unknown.
Sittings	[None free.] Other 240. Total 240.
Usual attendance	(On 30 March 1851.) Morning 73. Total [73]. No Sunday school within the chapelry.
Dated	[Not given.]
Signed	Simpson Brown Maughan, curate [1836–42].
Incumbent	[Henry Hopwood 1845–59.]
{1857	Attendance 70. 9 communicants.}

9.4   Church of England, Holy Trinity, Cambo (558.4a)
Population 1851: 106 (township)

Name	[Holy] Trinity Church, a district parish under the provision of 16 Sect. 59th George III [c.134], separate from the parish of Hartburn, Northumberland [parish created 23 May 1844].
Consecrated	17 August 1843. As an additional church. There was a chapel at Cambo township which was suffered to fall into disuse and decay after the reign of Queen Elizabeth. There were likewise three other chapels in the district at Cramlington, Hartington and Shaftoe.

[Holy Trinity restored 1884.]

Erected   Sir John Trevelyan Bart., gave the land for [the] site,
the sum of £500 towards the building, likewise £600
towards [the] endowment.
From Ecclesiastical Commissioners £175. Private £1,075
3s 4d. Total cost £1,250 3s 4d.

Endowment   Tithe £43 12s 6d. OPE £33 19s 7d. Fees £1 6s.
Other £11 13s.

Sittings   Free 256. Other 26. Total 282.

Attendance 30 March   Morning 43 + 77 SS. Total 120.
Afternoon 78 + 53 SS. 131.

Average attendance   Morning 60 + 75 SS. Total 135.
Afternoon 100 + 60 SS. Total 160.

Remarks   From the above mentioned income the incumbent
has to provide himself with a house. There are many
Presbyterians in the parish, but few other dissenters.
There are not any Roman Catholics excepting some
Irish who are temporarily employed in draining.

Dated   31 March 1851.

Signed   John Wilkinson, perpetual curate [1846–55].
Cambo, Morpeth, Northumberland.

{B 10.}

[Before the church was opened a schoolroom at Cambo was licensed
for worship on 26 March 1841.]

9.5   Church of England, St Bartholomew, Cresswell (558.17b)
Population 1851: 251 (township)

Name   Cresswell Church, belonging to a district formed
under 1 & 2 Will. IV c.38.

Consecrated   [22 October] 1836, as the church of a newly formed
parish [created on 19 November 1836 out of the parish
of Woodhorn].

Erected   Believed to be at the cost of A[ddison] J[ohn] Baker-
Cresswell Esq., the patron of the church.

Endowment   [£100.]

Sittings   Free about 84. Other about 89. Total 173, exclusive of
gallery for school children.

Attendance 30 March   Morning about 90 + 50 SS. Total 140.
Afternoon about 85 + 50 SS. Total 135.

Average attendance   [Not given.]

Remarks   The number above stated are believed to be rather

	below the average attendance during last three months.	
Dated	31 March 1851.	
Signed	John Ewbank Leefe, incumbent [1849–82].	
	Cresswell Parsonage, Morpeth.	
{1857	Attendance 100. 20 communicants.}	{B 15.}

9.6 Church of England, St Andrew, Hartburn (558.5a)

Population 1851: 1,506 (parish) 40 (township)

Name   Hartburn Parish Church.
Consecrated   Built and consecrated probably about AD 1150.
           [Restored 1890.]
Endowment   Tithe £670, of which £40 charged to Netherwitton.
           Glebe £100.
           Fees £8.
Sittings   [None free.] Other 260 + 30 children's seats. Total 290.
Attendance 30 March   Morning 92 + 26 SS. Total 118.
                         Afternoon 27 + 12 SS. Total 39.
Average attendance   [Not given.]
Dated   30 March 1851.
Signed   Richard Croft, vicar [1845–56].
           Hartburn, Morpeth.
{1857   Attendance 50. 17 communicants.}   {B 18.}
[The previous vicar of Hartburn, 1833–45, was the distinguished antiquarian John Hodgson (1779–1845), *ODNB*, vol. 27, pp. 494–495. He contributed to the *Gentleman's Magazine* and was the author of the five-volume *History of Northumberland* (published 1820–40). 'John Hodgson's enthusiasm for records publication, particularly his proposal of 1819 for a journal of historical records, foreshadowed the establishment in 1834 of the Surtees Society, of which he was a founder member.' C.R.J. Currie and C.P Lewis (eds.), *A Guide to English County Histories* (Stroud, 1994), p. 310.]

9.7 Church of England, St Helen, Longhorsley (558.9a)

Population 1851: 995 (parish) 43 (township)

Name   Parish church dedicated to St Helen.
Consecrated   Before 1800. [Rebuilt 1783.]
Endowment   Land rent charge. Tithe (as commuted) £315 18s. Glebe
           (including house and garden) £81. Total £396 18s.
Sittings   [None free.] Other 292. Total 292.

Attendance 30 March   Morning 125 + 35 SS. Total 160.
Average attendance   [Not given.]
Remarks   The church being situated in the fields at the extremity
               of the parish, there is no afternoon service in it, but
               evening service in the schoolroom in the village
               instead.
Dated   31 March 1851.
Signed   Robert Green, vicar [1824–77].
               Longhorsley, Morpeth.
{1857   Attendance 100. 50 communicants.}   {B 27.}
['The church at Longhorsley is in a very bad taste, but very good
condition. The situation of it too exceedingly inconvenient, as it
stands quite by itself, at some distance from the village. A removal
would be very advantageous, and is very much desired by the vicar.'
R.C. Coxe, *A Cursory Survey of the Churches and Church Buildings
within the Archdeaconry of Lindisfarne* (London, 1860), p. 23.]

9.8   Church of England, Schoolroom, Longhorsley (558.10a)
Name   A schoolroom in the village of Longhorsley in
               which evening service is held on account of the very
               inconvenient situation of the parish church, by leave
               of the bishop.
Erected   [Not given.]
Sittings   Free about 150. Total 150.
Attendance 30 March   Evening 100. Total 100.
Average attendance   [Not given.]
Dated   31 March 1851.
Signed   Robert Green, visitor and trustee [vicar of Longhorsley
               1824–77].
               Longhorsley, Morpeth.
{1857   Attendance 100.}
[In 1966 the parish church was closed and the schoolroom became
the parish church.]

9.9   Church of England, St John the Baptist, Meldon (558.12a)
Population 1851: 144 (parish)

Name   St John's, Meldon. A church of ancient foundation.
Consecrated Before 1800. [Repaired 1733, restored 1849.]
Endowment   [£322.]
Sittings   [80.]
Attendance 30 March   Morning [55]. Total 55 .

Average attendance   Morning from 40 to 50. Total from 40–50.
Remarks   Church sufficiently large to contain the whole
                 population.
Dated   31 March 1851.
Signed   Pierce Galliard Smith, minister [–1860].
                 Meldon Cottage, Morpeth.
Incumbent   [James Raine 1822–58.]
{1857   Attendance 80. 16 communicants.}   {B 6.}
['James Raine (1791–1858)', *ODNB*, vol. 45, pp. 817–818. He was a
noted 'antiquary and topographer', the incumbent of St-Mary-the-
Less, Durham, 1828–58 (**16.7**) and the librarian to the Dean and
Chapter 1816–58. He was the first secretary of the Surtees Society
and between 1835 and 1858 edited seventeen volumes. During
Raine's incumbency at Meldon there were legal problems. 'Litigation
with the landowners, the Greenwich Hospital Commissioners, over
the Meldon rectory tithes until 1846, when the case was decided in
Raine's favour' (*ODNB*, p. 817).
On leaving Meldon in 1860 the curate, Pierce Smith (1826–1908)
moved to Sydney, Australia.]

9.10   Church of England, St Mary Magdalene, Mitford (558.11a)
Population 1851: 700 (parish) 217 (township)

Name   Mitford Church. An ancient parish church. Church –
                 Norman architecture; chancel, Gothic. A vicarage.
Consecrated   Before 1800. [Restored and enlarged 1874–77;
                 rededicated as St Mary Magdalene, 18 October 1881;
                 restoration completed 1883.]
Endowment   Land £41. OPE £47. Fees £2. Other £10.
Sittings   Free 52. Other 250. Total 302.
Attendance 30 March   Morning 130 + 34 SS. Total 164.
                 Afternoon 55 + 30 SS. Total 85.
Average attendance   Morning 150 + 30 SS. Total 180.
                 Afternoon 45 + 20 SS. Total 65.
Remarks   In summer the congregation exceeds the average
                 number stated and in winter frequently falls below it.
Dated   31 March 1851.
Signed   Ralph Errington, vicar [1844–53].
                 Mitford, Morpeth, Northumberland.
{1857   Attendance 180. 30 communicants.}   {B 13.}

9.11   Church of England, Holy Trinity, Widdrington (558.18b)
Population 1851: 429 (parochial chapelry that includes the hamlets
of Dunridge and Linton)

Name   Widdrington Chapel severed from Woodhorn Church
in the year 1767. Now a perpetual curacy.
Consecrated Before 1800. [Restored 1875.]
Endowment Land £42 10s. OPE £22 15s. Fees £2.
Sittings   Free 20. Other 150. Total 170.
Attendance 30 March Morning 70 + 8 SS. Total 78.
Average attendance   Morning 50 or 60 + 10 SS. Total [60–70].
Remarks   All the above details, except [sittings and attendance]
are given by the incumbent, the Rev. R[alph]
Errington.
Dated   31 March 1851.
Signed   Alfred William Hobson, sub-curate [1849–51].
Widdrington, near Morpeth.
Incumbent [Ralph Errington 1828–53.]
{1857   Attendance 60. 14 communicants.}
[Alfred Hobson was a librarian at the University of Cambridge 1859–
64.]

9.12   Church of England, St Mary the Virgin, Kirkhill, Morpeth
(558.3a)
Population 1851: 5,020 (parish) 4,102 (township) 171 (Morpeth
Castle)

[Summary form]
Name   St Mary's Church.
Erected   About 500 years ago. [Enlarged 1843, restored 1865–66.]
Endowment [£1,611.]
Sittings   All free. Total 531.
Usual attendance   Morning from 170* to 200 [no SS]. Total
[170–200].
Remarks   *The number attending on Sunday, 14 Dec. 1851 was
171.
Dated   [Not given.]
Signed   William Richard Watson, registrar.
Incumbent [Francis Richard Grey, rector 1842–90.]
{1857   Attendance 180. 30 communicants.}   {B 95.}
[Francis Grey's brother John Grey was the rector of Houghton-le-
Spring 1847–95 (**19.2**). They were the sons of the second Earl Grey.

Attached to St Mary the Virgin was a chapel of ease, St Barnabas, Thorny Ford (**5.16**).]

9.13   Church of England, St James the Great, Newgate Street, Morpeth (558.2a)

[Summary form]
Name   St James Church.
Erected   [Consecrated 15 October] 1846. [Total cost £5,435.
              Parliamentary grant £400.]
Sittings   Free 913. Total 913.
Usual attendance   Morning 173 + 133 SS. Total [306].
              Afternoon 95 + 149 SS. Total [244].
              Evening 380 (no scholars). Total [380].
Remarks   As the attendance at each of the three services on
              Sunday, 14 Dec. [1851] instant, was an average
              attendance, I have given above the actual numbers
              attending on that day.
Dated   [Not given.]
Signed   William Richard Watson, registrar.
Incumbent   [Francis Richard Grey 1842–90.]

9.14   Church of England, St John the Baptist, Ulgham (558.19b)
Population 1851: 329 (parochial chapelry)

Name   St John's, Ulgham.
Erected   Cannot ascertain when erected. [Rebuilt between 1862
              and 1863. Became a separate parish in 1875.]
Endowment Tithe amounting to £320 per annum.
Sittings   Free 24 (4 pews). Other 120 (20 pews).
              Total 144 (estimating them to hold six persons).
Attendance 30 March   30 to 60. Total [30–60]. [For SS] see school
              return.
Remarks   The congregation varies here exceedingly. Sometimes
              not twenty present. Some say not even ten.
Dated   [Not given.]
Signed   Robert Soulsby, registrar.
Incumbent   [Francis Richard Grey 1842–90.]
{1857   Attendance 100. 20 communicants.}   {B 8.}

9.15 Church of England, St Giles, Netherwitton (558.7a)
Population 1851: 303 (township)

Name	Netherwitton Parochial Chapel. It is the church of an ancient chapelry [of Hartburn] and was made a separate benefice in 1834 by agreement with the governors of Queen Anne's Bounty.
Consecrated	There is no record of the consecration. [The nave was rebuilt in the 18th century, restored 1881, 1886.]
Endowment	Tithe £105. Glebe £1. OPE £53. Fees £1. Easter offerings £2 10s. Total £161 10s.
Sittings	Free 50. Other 110. Total 160.
Attendance 30 March	Morning 90 + 15 SS. Total 105.
Average attendance	Morning 90 + 20 SS. Total 110.
Remarks	Glebe. This £1 is a prescript rent and there is about ⅛ of an acre forming the site of the parsonage house and garden.
Dated	31 March 1851.
Signed	Richard Wearing, minister [1834–57]. Netherwitton, Morpeth, Northumberland.
{1857	Attendance 100. 25 communicants.} {B 9.}

[Richard Wearing had previously been the curate of Netherwitton 1829–34.]

9.16 Church of England, St Mary the Virgin, Woodhorn (558.13b)
Population 1851: 1,598 (parish) 131 (township)

Name	Woodhorn Church. An ancient parish church lately rebuilt.
Consecrated	Before 1800.
Erected	Rebuilt by the landowners [1842–43].
Endowment	Tithe £500. Glebe 90 acres. Fees £7.
Sittings	All free. Total from 3[00] to 400.
Attendance 30 March	Morning 150 + 25 SS. Total [175].
Average attendance	[Not given.]
Dated	31 March 1851.
Signed	Thomas Richard Shipperdson, vicar [1842–65]. Morpeth, Northumberland.
{1857	Attendance 140. 24 communicants.} {B 9.}

9.17 Church of England, St Bartholomew, Newbiggin by the Sea (558.14b)
Population 1851: 717 (parochial chapelry)

Name	Newbiggin Church. An ancient chapel lately rebuilt.
Consecrated	Before 1800. [Restored 1845–46, 1898.]
Erected	Built from money raised on land belonging [to] the church.
Endowment	Tithe £18. OPE one house, value £6. Fees £3.
Sittings	Free all in body of church. Other [in the] gallery. Total 300.

Attendance 30 March   Afternoon about 100. Total [100].

Average attendance   [Not given.]

Dated   [Not given.]

Signed   Thomas Richard Shipperdson, vicar [1842–65]. Morpeth, Northumberland.

{1857   Attendance 190. 30 communicants.}   {B 17.}

9.18 United Presbyterian, Bedlington (558.10b)

Name	United Presbyterian Chapel.
Erected	1845.
Building	Separate and entire. Exclusively a place of worship.
Sittings	Free seated for 300. Total [300].

Attendance 30 March   Morning 144 + 60 SS. Total 204.
Evening 73. Total 73.

Average attendance   Morning 180 + 88 SS. Total 268.

Dated   30 March 1851.

Signed   Ebenezer George Dall, minister. Bedlington, Morpeth.

9.19 United Presbyterian, North Middleton (558.6a)

Name	Presbyterian Chapel of North Middleton.
Erected	1820.
Building	[Separate and entire. Exclusively used for worship.]
Sittings	Free 200. Other 100. Total [300].

Attendance 30 March   Morning 86. Total [86].

Average attendance   Morning 100. Total [100].

Dated   30 March 1851.

Signed   James Robertson, minister. North Middleton, by Morpeth.

[The congregation was formed in 1803 by those who left the Presbyterian church at Great Bavington (3.16).]

9.20   United Presbyterian, Sleekburn (558.9b)

Name   Preaching station of the United Presbyterian Church,
              Bedlington.

Erected   [Not given.]

Building   Used as a dwelling house at other times. [Not
              exclusively used for worship. A] Sabbath school.

Sittings   Free 40. Total [40].

Attendance 30 March   Evening 30. Total 30.

Average attendance   [Not given.]

Dated   30 March 1851.

Signed   James Temple, elder [coal miner].
              Bedlington Colliery, [West Sleekburn].

9.21   English Presbyterian, Cottingwood Lane, Morpeth (558.14a)

Name   Presbyterian Church or Chapel.

Erected   Before 1800. [1721. Replaced by St George's
              Presbyterian Church, Bridge Street opened on 12 April
              1860.]

Building   Separate [and entire]. Exclusively [a place of worship]
              except for a Sunday school.

Sittings   Free 50. Other 650. Total [700].

Attendance 30 March   Morning 600. Total 600.
                        Evening 480. Total 480.

Average attendance   [Not given.]

Remarks   The Sunday scholars are included in the general
              congregation. There is no separation from the church
              appropriated to them and only a portion of them can
              be accommodated.

Dated   31 March 1851.

Signed   James Anderson, minister [1843–82].
              Morpeth.

[John Horsley (1685–1732), the minister of the church, was a leading
antiquary and author of *Britannia Romana* (1732). Alexander Hutton
Drysdale, the minister of the church from 1882, was the author of the
History of the Presbyterians in England: their Rise, Decline and Revival
(London, 1889).]

9.22   English Presbyterian, West Thirston (558.16b)

Name   Presbyterian Chapel.

Erected   1819. [Foundation stone laid 7 September 1819.]

Building   [Separate and entire. Exclusively used for worship.]

Sittings   Free 145. Other 175. Total [320].

Attendance 30 March   Morning 120 + 40 SS. Total [160].
Evening 30. Total [30].
Average attendance   Morning between 120 and 200 + from 30 to
40 SS.
Total [150–240].
Dated   31 March 1851.
Signed   Alexander Hoy, minister [1828–].
Felton, Northumberland.

9.23   English Presbyterian, Widdrington (558.4b)
Name   Widdrington Presbyterian Church.
Erected   Before 1800. [1765, new church 1894]
Building   Separate and entire. Exclusively as a place of worship,
except for S[unday] s[chool].
Sittings   Free 176. Other 124. Total [300].
Attendance 30 March   [Not given.]
Average attendance   Morning from 50 to 90 in winter; from 90
to 140 in summer. Total [50–90 (winter) and
90–140 (summer)].
Remarks   I return no answer for 30 March not having been
at home. The answer to [attendance] applies to my
general congregation. Sunday scholars [are] from 30 to
40 on an average.
Dated   31 March 1851.
Signed   Matthew Edwards, minister [1844–92].
Widdrington, Co[unty]. Northumberland.

9.24   Independent [Congregational], King Street, Morpeth
(558.16a)
Name   The Independent Chapel.
Erected   In the year 1829. [Opened 20 September 1829; closed
in 1899 and replaced by a Congregational chapel in
Dacre Street opened in 1898.]
Building   [Separate and entire. Exclusively used for worship.]
Sittings   All free 700. Total [700]. Standing room 300 persons
more than the seats for 700, which space may be used
in an emergency.
Attendance 30 March   Morning 150 + 80 SS. Total 230.
Evening 201. Total 201.
Average attendance   Morning 300 + between 80 and 100 SS.
Total [380–400].
Remarks   The chapel is entirely filled with pews. It will seat

seven hundred people. As, however, the usual
congregation is not more than three hundred, there is
plenty of free room for casual hearers.

Dated   31 March 1851.
Signed   William Ayre, minister [1848–72].
Newminster Buildings, Morpeth.

9.25   Baptist, Bedlington (558.6b)
Name   Christian Meeting House.
Erected   1841.
Building   Not [separate and entire and also] used also as a day
school.
Sittings   Free 50. Other none. Total [50]. Standing room 20.
Attendance 30 March   Morning 37 + 10 SS. Total 47.
Afternoon 24. Total 24.
Evening 38. Total 38.
Average attendance   Morning 12 + 20 SS. Total 32.
Afternoon 18. Total 18.
Evening 20. Total 20.
Dated   31 March 1851.
Signed   William Dickinson and Samuel Briggs, preacher and
president [both were grocer and draper].
Bedlington.

9.26   Wesleyan Methodist, Bedlington (558.11b)
Name   Wesleyan Chapel.
Erected   1828.
Building   [Separate and entire. Exclusively used for worship.]
Sittings   Free 86. Other 94. Total [180].
Attendance 30 March   Afternoon 73 + 12 SS. Total 85.
Evening 100 + 20 SS. Total 120.
Average attendance   [Not given.]
Remarks   The chapel contains 123 square yards available for
worship.
Dated   31 March 1851.
Signed   John Elam, minister [1849–50].
Bedlington near Morpeth, Northumberland.
[John Elam was also the minister of Ballast Hills, Blyth (**12.25**).]

9.27   Wesleyan Methodist, Bedlington Colliery (558.8b)
Name   Wesleyan Methodist.
Erected   Nine years. [1842.]

Building   A dwelling house [not exclusively used for worship].
Sittings   All free. Other none.
Attendance 30 March   Afternoon 60. Total [60].
Average attendance   Morning 60. SS none. Total 60.
Remarks   For a few years a Sabbath school was held in an
empty dwelling house, where seventy children were
taught. But for want of a more convenient place, it had
to be abandoned.
Dated   30 March 1851.
Signed   Robert Dobson, class leader [grocer].
Bedlington, near Morpeth.

9.28   Wesleyan Methodist, Broomfield (558.22b)
Name   None.
Erected   1850.
Building   [Separate and] entire building. [Exclusively used for] a
place of worship.
Sittings   Free 33. Total [33].
Attendance 30 March   Morning 34. Total [34].
Evening 33. Total [33].
Average attendance   [Not given.]
Dated   31 March 1851.
Signed   John Russell, clerk.
Broomhill near Acklington, Northumberland.

9.29   Wesleyan Methodist, Manchester Lane, Morpeth (558.15a)
Name   Wesleyan Chapel.
Erected   Before 1800. [Rebuilt 1823, demolished 1883, new
chapel opened 1 April 1884.]
Building   [Separate and entire. Exclusively used for worship.]
Sittings   Free 180. Other 70. Total [250].
Attendance 30 March   Afternoon 105. Total [105].
Evening 81. Total [81].
Average attendance   Afternoon 100 + 50 SS. Total [150].
Dated   [30] March 1851.
Signed   John Gustard, chapel steward (hosier).
[Newgate Street], Morpeth.
[In 1809 the chapel was purchased from the Countess of Huntingdon's
Connexion.]

9.30   Wesleyan Methodist, Netherton (558.3b)

Name	None.
Erected	[Not given.]
Building	[Neither separate and entire or exclusively used for worship.]
	(Dwelling house.)
Sittings	[Not given.]
Attendance 30 March	Morning 35. Total 35.
	Evening 50. Total 50.
Average attendance	Morning 35. Total 35.
	Evening 45. Total 45.
Dated	31 March 1851.
Signed	William Lee, leader (overman).
	Netherton, near Morpeth.

9.31   Wesleyan Methodist, Newbiggin by the Sea (558.15b)

Name	Wesleyan Methodist Chapel.
Erected	1844.
Building	[Separate and] entire. Both [exclusively used for worship].
Sittings	Free 150. Other 50. Total [200]. Standing room 50.
Attendance 30 March	Morning 63 SS. Total 63.
	Afternoon 59. Total 59.
	Evening 120. Total 120.
Average attendance	Morning 63 SS. Total 63.
	Afternoon 59. Total 59.
	Evening 120. Total 120.
Dated	[Not given.]
Signed	Hunter Jefferson, class leader [fisherman].
	Newbiggin.

9.32   Primitive Methodist, Bedlington (558.7b)

Name	None.
Erected	[Not given.]
Building	[Not given.] (Dwelling house.)
Sittings	[Not given.]
Attendance 30 March	Evening 20. Total [20].
Average attendance	Evening 18. Total [18].
Remarks	We have preaching on the Wednesday evenings once a fortnight, in the dwelling houses of Mr Thomas Elliot and Mr John Norns.
Dated	[Not given.]

Signed   Joshua Morris, local preacher [coal miner].
             No. 12, Sleekburn Colliery, near Bedlington.

9.33   Primitive Methodist, Chapel Row, Bedlington (558.12b)

Name   Primitive Methodist Chapel.
Erected   1828. [New chapel 1893.]
Building   Sep[arate] and entire. [Exclusively used for worship.]
Sittings   Free 64. Other 172. Total [236]. Standing room none.
Attendance 30 March   No service as we are making an alteration to
             our chapel at present.
Average attendance   Morning 119 SS. Total 119.
             Afternoon 80. Total 80.
             Evening 140. Total 140.
Dated   31 March 1851.
Signed   George Richardson, steward [and Sunday school
             superintendent].
             No. 40, Bedlington Colliery.

9.34   Roman Catholic, Longhorsley (558.8a)

Name   St Thomas [of Canterbury].
Erected   1841. [Opened 16 November 1841.]
Building   [Separate and entire. Exclusively used for worship.]
Sittings   Free 100 (all free). Other none. Total [100]. No standing
             room.
Attendance 30 March   Morning 56. Total [56].
             Afternoon 13. Total [13].
             Evening 30. Total [30].
Average attendance   Morning 90. [No] SS. Total [90].
Remarks   Sometimes we have considerably above 100 at chapel,
             and sometimes about 100. But perhaps taking one
             time with another we may call the average about 90 or
             between 90 and 100.
Dated   31 March 1851.
Signed   James Hubbersty, Roman Catholic priest [1848–53].
             Longhorsley, Morpeth, Northumberland.
[James Hubbersty also served at Witton Shields and Amble.]

9.35   Roman Catholic, Oldgate Street, Morpeth (558.13a)

Name   St Robert's, Catholic Church.
Erected   1849. [Opened 1 August 1850 and cost £2,300.]
Building   [Separate and entire. Exclusively used for worship.]
Sittings   Free 200. Total [200]. Standing room 200.

Attendance 30 March   Morning 200 + 50 SS. Total [250].
                        Afternoon 150. Total [150].
Average attendance   [Not given.]
Remarks   At present sittings for 200 and space for 200 more.
Dated   30 March 1851.
Signed   George Augustine Lowe [OSB], Catholic priest [1836–
               69].
               Morpeth.

9.36   Latter-day Saints [Mormons], Bedlington (558.5b)
Name   Baptist Chapel (*sic*).
Erected   1839.
Building   An exclusive building [also used] for a day school.
Sittings   All free.
Attendance 30 March   Morning 21 + 35 SS. Total 56.
                        Evening 38 + 20 SS. Total 58.
Average attendance   [Not given.]
Dated   31 March 1851.
Signed   Alfred Sharp, bishop [schoolmaster and Baptist bishop
               (Mormon priest)].
               Bedlington, near Morpeth.
[In the Religious Census of 1851 Alfred Sharp called himself a
'bishop', and in the Civil Census of the same year he is described as
a 'Baptist bishop (Mormon priest'.]

10. Newcastle upon Tyne District (HO 129/552)
52 places of worship
Population 1851: 89,156 (district) 87,784 (township)

10.1   Church of England, St Nicholas, Mosley Street (552.36)
Population 1851: 6,586 (parish)

Name   St Nicholas. Ancient parish church.
Consecrated Before 1800. [Restored 1785–98, 1871–77.]
Endowment   Ground rent £21. Tithe about £350. Glebe £40. Fees
               about £100. Dues about £30. Total about £541. See
               below.
Sittings   Free 650. Other 926. Total 1,576.
Attendance 30 March   [Not given.]
Average attendance   Morning 1,000 + 510 SS. Total 1,510.

Afternoon 400 + 510 SS. Total 910.
Evening 1,500 (SS excused). Total 1,500.
A free service.

Remarks	Net income deducting salary of two curates, collection taxes and rates about £226.
Dated	30 March 1851.
Signed	Richard Charles Coxe, vicar [1841–53]. Vicarage, Newcastle on Tyne.
{1857	Attendance 1,700. 137 communicants. Twice a week a divinity lecture is held in the vestry.} {B 122.}

[St Nicholas, Newcastle, had two chapels of ease at Cramlington Chapel (12.2) and St Nicholas, Gosforth (5.4) and became the Anglican cathedral on 3 August 1882.
'Richard Charles Coxe (1800–1865)', *ODNB*, vol. 13, pp. 877–878. A high-churchman, he was the Archdeacon of Lindisfarne and vicar of Eglingham 1853–65 (1.4).]

10.2   Church of England, St John the Baptist, Westgate Road
(552.26)
Population 1851: 31,146 (parish)

Name	St John's church or parochial chapel.
Consecrated	Before 1800. [Restored 1848, 1862, 1875–77.]
Endowment	Permanent endowment £130. [No] pew rents to clergyman. Fees and dues £131. No Easter offerings to incumbent. Other £44.
Sittings	Free 150 + 400 school children. Other 1,150. Total 1,700.
Attendance 30 March	Morning between 1,000 & 1,100 + about 290 SS. Total 1,390. Afternoon about 300 + about 200 SS. Total 500. Evening between 500 and 600. Total 500 or 600.
Average attendance	[Not given.]
Dated	31 March 1851.
Signed	Henry Wildey Wright MA, incumbent [1835–73]. St John's, Newcastle on Tyne.
{1857	Attendance 800. 80 communicants.} {B 609.}

[The Evangelical Henry Wright was responsible for the erection of St Paul's chapel of ease (10.4).]

10.3   Church of England, St James, Benwell Lane, Benwell
(552.1)
Population 1851: 1,272 (township)

Name	St James (Benwell). The name given at consecration. The church of a district created on the 2 November 1842, by the [Order] in Council, under the 16th section of the 59 Geo. III c.134 and named 'The chapelry of St James, Benwell' [in the parish of St John].
Consecrated	Church consecrated 8 October 1832 by the Bishop of Bristol for the Bishop of Durham, as a chapel of ease to St John's, Newcastle on Tyne, in which parish it was situated. [The parish was created on 29 July 1856, and the church enlarged 1864, 1894–95, 1902–03.]
Erection	Erection promoted by the Rev. Henry Dodd, then perp[etua]l curate of the parish of St John, Newcastle on Tyne.
	Bishop of Durham £100. Lord Crewe's Trustees £100. Diocesan Ch[urch] Building Society £50. Incorporated Church Building Society £250. Church Commissioners £250. Private benefaction £918 14s 5d.
	Total cost £1,668 14s 5d.
Endowment	In March 1843 [endowed] by the Ecclesiastical Commissioners for England with £126 per annum: to put the average of the rents so as to average the income to £150 per annum. Fees go to the incumbent of St John and the vicar of Newcastle until St John's be vacated [by] the present incumbent when […] will fall to the perpetual curate of […]. They amount to about […] per annum.
Sittings	Free about 250. Other about 210. Total 560.
Attendance 30 March	Morning 311 + 86 SS. Total 397.
	Afternoon 211 + 73 SS. Total 284.
Average attendance	The return for 30 March [is] about an average for the past twelve months.
Remarks	The church was estimated by the architect [John Dobson] to contain 400 free sittings and 232 other sittings: but the pews calculated by him to hold six each only hold five comfortably, and such of them as are let, are let only for five sittings each. Since the church was endowed there has been a small increase

in attendance at worship, and the average increase of about £20 in pew rents.

The general congregation both [morning] and afternoon included 131 children [from the] workhouse of the Newcastle on Tyne which is situated in the township of Elswick and chapelry of St James, Benwell.

(A chaplain is sadly wanted at the Newcastle on Tyne workhouse.)

Dated   31 March 1851.

Signed   William Maughan, perpetual curate [1843–70].
Benwell Parsonage, St James, Benwell, Newcastle on Tyne.

{1857   Attendance 500. 28 communicants. More room is required.}   {B 44.}

[On 9 June 1830 a schoolroom was licensed for worship until the chapel of ease was opened.

John Dodd was the vicar of St Nicholas' 1826–40, and as patron he appointed his sons to two Newcastle churches: Henry Alison Dodd as the incumbent of St John's 1826–34, and William Dodd as the incumbent of St Andrew's 1834–49. While he was in Newcastle William Dodd was the leading supporter of Tractarianism in the town, and after leaving St Andrew's he became the vicar of Chillingham (**6.4**).

There was correspondence about the need for a chaplain to the union workhouse in the *Newcastle Journal*, 9 October, 20 and 27 November 1841.

In 1860 William Maughan conducted his own very detailed 'analysis of the population of the townships of Benwell and Elswick including the workhouse population in the parish of St James', Benwell'. It listed each family and gave their religious background. Tyne and Wear Archives, DX 678/1.]

10.4   Church of England, St Paul, Westgate Road (552.5)

Name   The proprietary chapel of St Paul, Westgate, Newcastle upon Tyne [opened as a chapel of ease in the parish of St John].

Consecrated Built and consecrated in [31 August] 1841 at the request of the proprietors.

Erected   By shares and private benefaction. Shares £3,500. Private benefaction £600. Total £4,100.

Endowment No endowment. Pew rents and parochial fees etc. go
to a general fund   as interest for the money invested.
Sittings Free 20. Other 608. Total 628.
Attendance 30 March Morning 411 + 89 SS. Total 500.
Afternoon no service.
Evening 350. Total 350.
Average attendance Morning 460 + 90 SS. Total 550.
Afternoon no service.
Evening 380. Total 380.
Remarks The chapel of St Paul is very near to the eastern
boundary of my district of St Paul, High Elswick.
Allowing no church of my own, I am allowed the
free use of it without remuneration or stipend for the
benefit of my parishioners.
Dated 31 March 1851.
Signed Robert Shepherd, officiating minister [1848–55].
5 Elswick Lane, Newcastle on Tyne.
[The chapel of ease and 'beadle's house' was sold by auction in
November 1854 and was bought by the Congregationalists for £1,700,
and in March 1855 it re-opened as the St Paul's Congregational
Church. Involved with the purchase was Robert Hood Haggie
(**12.78**). In 1931 the building became a centre for the unemployed,
from 1934–60 the Gem cinema and was demolished in 1967.]

10.5   Church of England Schoolroom, High Elswick (552.4)
Population 1851: 3,559 (township)

Name The district of St Paul, High Elswick, Newcastle on
Tyne, and without church and chapel [in the parish of
St John].
Licensed Formed under Peel's Act in 1846 [6 & 7 Vic. c.37,
1843)]. Schoolroom licensed in 1846 is also allowed the
payment of the chapel of St Paul. [District created 21
April 1846.]
Endowment By the Ecclesiastical Commissioners, £130 per annum.
Sittings Free 120. Total 120.
Attendance 30 March [Not given.]
Average attendance Afternoon 30 + 80 SS. Total 110.
Remarks With the sanction of the bishop, I have the free use
without remuneration or stipend of the proprietary
chapel of St Paul for the benefit of my parishioners.

Dated   31 March 1851.
Signed   Robert Shepherd, perpetual curate [1848–76].
              5 Elswick Lane, Newcastle on Tyne.
{1857. The room in the [former Barber Surgeons' Hall] could accommodate 340 people. There was an attendance of 320 and with 30 communicants. 'No church at present'.}
[From 1841 services were held in the nearby chapel of ease (St Paul's Chapel) situated in St John's parish and located very near to the district (**10.4**). In 1855 the services were discontinued in the schoolroom and transferred to the former Barber Surgeons' Hall which was licensed for worship in September 1855. St Paul's church, High Elswick was consecrated on 30 September 1859.]

10.6   Church of England, All Saints, Pilgrim Street (552.49)
Population 1851: 26,117 (parish)

[Summary form]
Name   All Saints church.
Erected   [Not given.] [The church was rebuilt and consecrated
              on 17 November 1789. The building completed 21
              October 1796. Cost £27,000. Altered 1904.]
Endowment   [£300.]
Sittings   Free 362. Other 1,340. Total 1,702.
Usual attendance   Morning 660. Total [600].
                        Afternoon no service.
                        Evening 500. Total [500].
Dated   27 July 1852.
Signed   Matthew Renwick [registrar].
              [15 Stepney Terrace.]
Incumbent   [Ryce Wellington Lloyd Jones 1847–53.]
{1857   Attendance 600. 50 communicants.}   {B 797.}
[An Act for pulling down and rebuilding the church of All Saints, in the Town of Newcastle upon Tyne, and for enlarging the churchyard, and making convenient avenues and passages thereto, 24 Geo. III c.117, 24 January 1786. The only two elliptical churches are All Saint's, Newcastle (1789) and St Andrew's, Dublin (1807). From 1851 to 1853 Ryce Jones was suspended from his duties due to drunkenness. Clergy Discipline 1846–56, DUL, ASC, DDR/EJ/CLD/2.]

10.7   Church of England, St Ann, New [later City] Road
(552.50)
[Summary form]
Name   St Ann's church.
Erected   [Not given.] [Consecrated 8 September 1768. Restored
            1873. [Chapel of ease to All Saints, district created 10
            December 1842.]
Endowment [£150.]
Sittings   Free 75. Other 427. Total 502.
Usual attendance   Morning 550. Total [550].
                        Evening 250. Total [250].
Dated   28 July 1852.
Signed   Matthew Renwick [registrar].
            [15 Stepney Terrace.]
Incumbent   [George Heriot 1842–69.]
{1857   Attendance 500. 36 communicants.}   {B 71.}
[The New Road, which was opened in 1776, was renamed as City
Road in 1882.]

10.8   Church of England, Byker Church, [later Headlam Street]
(552.50a)
Population 1851: 7,040 (township)

[Summary form]
Name   Byker Church.
Licensed   [17 June 1845 as chapel of ease to All Saints. District
            created 3 June 1844.]
Sittings   Free 350. Other 100. Total 450.
Usual attendance   [Not given.]
{1857   Average attendance 150.}   {B none.}

Sir
The Rev Mr Green told me that he had answered all these
questions twice before and therefore refused to give any further
information respecting Byker Chapel, but requests me to inform
you that they were going to build a new one containing 450
sittings, 350 of which will be free.

'This building is situated in the village of Byker, and was built by
the Wesleyan Methodists about 50 years ago. The inside size is
36 feet 6 in[ches] by 30 feet from north to south, it is entered by
a porch 6 feet square, and contains on the ground floor five pews
with 80 feet of sittings, and sixteen forms with 213 feet of sittings.

A staircase of 23 steps against the east wall leads to a gallery with three front pews, containing 40 feet of seats; 226 feet of seats in five forms. Total sittings 372. [The pulpit is fixed against the south wall, and the clerk's seat in front. The front gallery is 12 feet 7in from the south wall, and the east gallery 12 feet; total height 20 feet. Ministers, same as in Brunswick Chapel.]' Extracted from Oliver's *Plan of Newcastle*. [T. Oliver, *Reference to a Plan of the Borough of Newcastle upon Tyne and parts of the Borough of Gateshead* (Newcastle, 1844), p. 26.]

Dated	10 August 1852.
Signed	John Findley [registrar.]
	[1 Sumner Street.]
Incumbent	[Thomas Robinson Green, vicar 1844–71 and chaplain of the Trinity House Chapel, Newcastle upon Tyne.]

[A former Wesleyan Methodist chapel in what became Headlam Street was licensed for Anglican worship in 1844. St Michael, Byker (a chapel of ease to All Saints) was consecrated 11 March 1862 and cost £2,500. In 1936 a north aisle was built of the stone taken from the demolished St Peter's, Newcastle (**10.11**) and consecrated on 8 March 1937.]

10.9   Church of England, St Andrew, Newgate Street (552.11)
Population 1851: 15,202 (parish and 441 soldiers in the barracks)

Name	St Andrews. Perpetual curacy. Separate parish within the ancient vicarage of Newcastle on Tyne.
Consecrated	Before 1800. [Restored 1840, 1866.]
Endowment	Parliamentary grant and fees £250.
Sittings	Free 150. Other 900. Total 1,050.
Attendance 30 March	Morning 800 + 320 SS. Total 1,120.
	Afternoon 200 + 300 SS. Total 500.
	Evening 900. Total 900.
Average attendance	Morning 800 + 320 SS. Total 1,120.
	Afternoon 200 + 300 SS. Total 500.
	Evening 900. Total 900.
Remarks	All the sittings are free during the evening service. Part of the children sit on forms in the chancel.
Dated	31 March 1851.
Signed	Richard Buckeridge, perpetual curate [1849–57].
	St Andrew's Vestry, Newcastle on Tyne.

{B 410.}

10.10   Church of England, St Thomas' Chapel, Barras Bridge (552.9)

Name   St Thomas' Chapel [in the parish of St Andrew].

Consecrated 18 [19] October 1830. Consecrated [by the Bishop of Carlisle] in lieu of a small ancient chapel in the town of Newcastle on Tyne.

Erected   Erected at the sole expense of the Master and Brethren of the Hospital of [St] Mary Magdalene, Newcastle on Tyne. Total cost £7,500.

Endowment   [Land] and houses in Newcastle on Tyne. [£700.] Pew rents £250.

Sittings   Free 200. Other 1,300. Total 1,500 (exclusive of children).

Attendance 30 March   Morning 958 + 314 SS. Total 1,272.
                        Afternoon 305 + 318 SS. Total 623.
                        Evening 441. Total 441.

Average attendance   Morning 1,100 + 300 SS. Total 1,400.
                        Afternoon 300 + 300 SS. Total 600.
                        Evening 500. Total 500.

Remarks   This chapel has no district attached to it. It is extra-parochial and extra-diocesan. Built by Act of Parliament, 7 & 8 Geo. IV [c.72]. 1826–27. All the sittings are let.

Dated   31 March 1851.

Signed   Richard Clayton MA of Oxford, chaplain [1836–56]. [16 Northumberland Street], Newcastle on Tyne.

[Richard Clayton (1802–1856) was the chaplain of St Thomas' Chapel 1836–56 and Master of St Mary Magdalene Hospital 1826–56, and became the leading Anglican Evangelical in Newcastle upon Tyne. His successor was not an Evangelical, so members of the congregation raised funds and erected Jesmond Church (known as the Clayton Memorial Church) which was consecrated on 14 January 1861. A. Munden, *A Light in a Dark Place. Jesmond Parish Church, Newcastle upon Tyne* (Newcastle, 2006). Those who assembled at St Thomas' Chapel were described as 'the wealthiest congregation in the town'. Church of England Record Centre, St Paul's church, High Elswick, 10133, letter from the Rev Robert Shepherd to the Church Building Commission, 10 December 1856.]

10.11   Church of England, St Peter, Oxford Street (552.22)
[Summary form]

Name   St Peter's church [in the parish of St Andrew].

Erected   1844. [Consecrated 23 February 1843. Total cost £5,858;
             Parliamentary grant of £700.Parish created 4 March
             1844.]
Endowment   [£150.]
Sittings   Free 300. Other 300. Chancel 100. Total 700.
Usual attendance   Morning on the average 250 persons.
             Total [250].
             Evening on the average 400 persons.
             Total [400].
             No [Sunday] school attached.
Dated   [Not given]
Signed   Thomas Doubleday, registrar.
             16 Ridley Place, Newcastle upon Tyne.
Incumbent   [Charles Alfred Raines, vicar 1844–92.]
{1857   Attendance 500. 60 communicants.}   {B 35.}
[After St Peter's church closed in 1936 it was demolished. Some of
the stone was used to construct the north aisle of St Michael, Byker
(**10.8**).]

10.12   Church of Scotland, Blackett Street (552.23)
[Summary form]
Name   Scotch Church.
Erected   [Not given.] [Founded 1743, chapel opened 17 May
             1822 and cost £1,350, rebuilt 1858.]
Building   Separate building. Exclusively [used] as a chapel.
Sittings   Free 500 persons may sit. Total [500].
Attendance 30 March   Morning 250. Total [250].
             Evening 300. Total [300].
Average attendance   [Not given.]
Dated   [Not given.]
Signed   Thomas Doubleday [registrar].
             [16] Ridley Place, Newcastle.
[In 1902 the congregation moved to College Road, Barras Bridge, and
in 1933 united with Trinity Presbyterian Church (**10.18**).]

10.13   Church of Scotland, Argyle Street (552.41)
Name   Caledonian Church. [Argyle Street Chapel.]
Erected   1842. [Opened 5 August 1842. Cost £1,303.]
Building   [Separate and] entire building, exclusively as a place
             of worship.
Sittings   Free no particular number. Other lets for nearly 1,000.
             Total [nearly 1,000].

Attendance 30 March   Morning 300 + between 70 to 80 SS.
Total [370–380].
Evening 500. Total [500].
Average attendance   [Not given.]
Dated   30 March 1851.
Signed   Andrew Broom, minister [1845–62].
8 Wesley Street, [Shieldfield, Newcastle upon Tyne].
[In 1843 some of the congregation left to form what became Trinity Presbyterian Church, New Bridge Street (**10.18**).]

10.14   [United Presbyterian], High Bridge (552.16)
Name   High Bridge Presbyterian Church.
Now unconnected: about to be joined to the United Presbyterian denomination.
Erected   Before 1800. [1766.]
Building   [Separate and entire. Exclusively used for worship.]
Sittings   [585.] Total [585]. Standing room none.
Attendance 30 March   Morning 250. Total [250].
Afternoon between 200 to 250. Total [200–250].
Evening 250 to 300. Total [250–300].
Average attendance   General congregation 300 + 100 SS.
Total [400].
Remarks   C. S. Parsons is not a regular ordained minister; but a licensed preacher of the gospel.
Dated   31 March 1851.
Signed   Charles S. Parsons, preacher of the gospel.
19 Villa Place, Newcastle on Tyne.

10.15   United Presbyterian, Clavering Place (552.28)
Name   Clavering Place Chapel.
Erected   [Opened 21 March] 1813. Rebuilt in 1822 [after a fire and opened on 25 December 1822. Cost £1,221.]
Building   [Separate and entire. Exclusively used for worship.]
Sittings   700 sittings. Total [700].
Attendance 30 March   [Not given.]
Average attendance   Morning and afternoon [550]. Total 550.
Dated   31 March 1851.
Signed   James Pringle, senior minister [1804–66].
John Clark Houston, junior minister.
Newcastle on Tyne.

[In 1847 some members of the congregation joined the Scotch Church (**10.12**) and in 1852 a larger group formed Erskine Chapel. In 1872 the Clavering Place congregation moved to Westmorland Road.]

10.16   United Presbyterian, Carliol Street (552.12)

Name   Carliol Street Chapel.
Erected   1822. [Opened 25 December 1823. Cost £1,430.]
Building   [Separate and entire. Exclusively used for worship.]
Sittings   About 500 sittings in all. Free sittings for all who are
              unable to pay. Total [500].
Attendance 30 March   [Not given.]
Average attendance   Morning about 300 + about 70 SS. Total 420
              (*sic*) [370].
Dated   31 March 1851.
Signed   George Bell, minister [1834–76].
              3 Brandling Place, Newcastle on Tyne.

[In 1872 the congregation moved to Barras Bridge and the chapel was opened 30 April 1873 and cost £5,000. In September 1888 the congregation transferred to a new chapel in Burdon Terrace, Jesmond.]

10.17   English Presbyterian, Pudding Chare, Groat Market (552.30)

Name   Groat Market Chapel.
Erected   Before 1800, about 1698. [Built 1715. In 1853 moved to
              Berwick Street and renamed John Knox Chapel.]
Building   [Separate and entire. Exclusively used for worship.]
Sittings   [None free.] Other 450. Total [450].
Attendance 30 March   Morning 294. Total 294.
              Afternoon 130 SS. Total [130].
              Evening 234. Total 234.
Average attendance   [Not given.]
Dated   31 March 1851.
Signed   W. R. Richardson, elder and session clerk.
              23 Blandford Street, Newcastle on Tyne.

10.18   English Presbyterian, New Bridge Street (552.14)

Name   Trinity Presbyterian Church of England.
Erected   1847. [Opened 3 October 1847. Cost £3,000.]
Building   Separate and entire. Exclusively [used for worship].
Sittings   Free 260. Other 860. Total [1,120].
Attendance 30 March   Afternoon 350 + 60 SS. Total 350 (*sic*) [410].

Evening 314. Total [314].
Average attendance   Afternoon 350 + 50 SS. Total 400.
Dated   31 March 1851.
Signed   Thomas Duncan, minister.
                 7 Lovaine Crescent, Newcastle upon Tyne.
[In 1933 united with the Scotch Church (**10.12**).]

10.19   Independent [Congregational], Westgate Road (552.29)
Name   Zion Chapel. [Westgate Street Chapel.]
Erected   Before 1800.
Building   [Separate and entire. Exclusively used for worship.]
Sittings   [None free.] Other 450. Total [450].
Attendance 30 March   Morning 293 + 56 SS. Total 349.
                 Evening 240. Total 240.
Average attendance   [Not given.]
Remarks   Though no seats are what are usually termed 'free
                 sittings', yet provision is made for poor persons who
                 cannot pay seat rent by them being allowed to occupy
                 pews free of charge. The seat rents being voluntary on
                 the part of all who attend the services conducted in
                 this chapel.
                 The congregation occupying Zion Chapel are engaged
                 in erecting a chapel of larger dimensions (to seat 800)
                 in the same parish, [St John's in Clayton Street West]
                 which will be ready for their use in two months from
                 this time. [Subsequently this congregation moved to
                 Beech Grove, and in 1855 Alexander Reid became the
                 minister of St Paul's Congregational Church (**10.4**)
                 until 1880.]
                 This congregation are mere tenants of this chapel
                 (which is private property) their former place of
                 worship [Postern Chapel, opened 1 January 1797]
                 (which they had occupied for upward of fifty years)
                 having been pulled down by the York, Newcastle and
                 Berwick Railway, to whom it was sold, upwards of
                 four years ago.
Dated   2 April 1851.
Signed   Alexander Reid, minister [1830–54].
                 [5] Westgate Hill [Terrace], Newcastle on Tyne.
[Before 1808 the chapel had been occupied by Roman Catholics,
then by Wesleyan Methodists, Presbyterians and finally, from 15

September 1821, by Independents. Until 1810 Postern Chapel was served by ministers of the Countess of Huntingdon's Connexion.]

10.20   Independent [Congregational], Blackett Street (552.19)

Name	St James' Chapel.
Erected	Built 1826 [and opened 31 August] by the [Scotch] Presbyterians (in lieu of an old chapel they previously had in Silver Street, parish of All Saints, from before 1800, but now a dwelling house) and transferred to the Independents in 1831. [Cost £2,320.]
Building	[Separate and entire. Exclusively used for worship.]
Sittings	Free 86. Other 500. Total [586].
Attendance 30 March	Morning 315 + 162 SS. Total 477.
	Afternoon 222 SS. Total [222].
	Evening 278. Total 278.
Average attendance	[Not given.]
Remarks	The gross number in attendance on 30 March was about 450, exclusive of Sunday scholars.
Dated	31 March 1851.
Signed	James Guinness Rogers, minister [1845–51]. 30 Westmorland Terrace, Newcastle on Tyne.

[On 5 October 1859 an enlarged chapel seating 800 was opened on the same site, and was sold to the YMCA. On 12 February 1884 the new St James' Chapel was opened in Bath Road; it had cost about £18,000, seated over 1,000 people and was regarded as 'a nonconformist cathedral'. 'St James's was an influential church. The foundations for that influence had been laid in the 1840s, but the rapidest growth had been after the church [was] rebuilt in the 1880s … [James Guinness Rogers] became a leading protagonist for nonconformity in the city.' J.C.G. Binfield, 'The Building of a Town Centre Church: St James's Congregational Church, Newcastle upon Tyne', *Northern History*, xviii (1982), pp. 159, 162, 163.]

10.21   Baptist, Tuthill Stairs, Bewick Street (552.37)

Name	Baptist Chapel.
Erected	AD 1798, but other chapels have existed there from about the year 1652. [Opened 19 February 1798, gallery 1820. On 31 August 1853 the congregation moved into a new chapel in Bewick Street.]
Building	A separate and entire building with vestry attached and rooms underneath. Exclusively as a place of worship.

Sittings   All free 600. Other 120 (vestry). Total [720].
Standing room only in the aisles.
Attendance 30 March   Morning 271 + 86 SS. Total 357.
Afternoon no service.
Evening 267. Total 267.
Average attendance   Morning 400. Total [400].
Remarks   All the sittings are free, but voluntary offerings are received from those who choose to give. Owing to sickness and the weather the attendance on the 30 March was below the average.
PS. If these returns were not sufficiently clear, I shall be most happy to give any further information I may possess.
Dated   1 April 1851.
Signed   Thomas Pottinger, minister [1849–59].
[3] Summerhill Terrace, Newcastle upon Tyne.
[During the ten-year ministry of Thomas Pottinger, the membership increased from 251 to 347.]

10.22   Baptist, Westgate Road (552.33)
Name   [House] Carpenters' Hall.
Erected   1811.
Building   Not separate [and entire]. Used also for the meetings of the House Carpenters' Society.
Sittings   Free 70. Other 30. Total [100].
Attendance 30 March   Morning 35. Total [35].
Afternoon 40. Total [40].
Evening 35. Total [35].
Average attendance   Morning 50. Total [50].
Dated   31 March 1851.
Signed   Joseph Bailey, Baptist minister [bookseller].
49 West Clayton Street, Newcastle on Tyne, Northumberland.

10.23   Particular Baptist, New Court, Westgate Road (552.31)
Name   New Court Chapel.
Erected   1818. [Opened 22 September 1819.]
Building   A separate and entire building. Used exclusively as a place of worship.
Sittings   Free 400. Other 200. Total [600].
Attendance 30 March   Morning 250 + 201 SS. Total [451].
Afternoon 201 SS. Total [201].

Evening 300. Total [300].
Average attendance   [Not given.]
Dated   30 March 1851.
Signed   John Fenwick, deacon [solicitor].
11 Ellison Place, Newcastle upon Tyne.
[The first wedding conducted in a nonconformist place of worship took place in New Court Chapel on 18 December 1837.]

10.24   Particular Baptist, Brandling Village, Jesmond
(552.58)
Name   Brandling Place Chapel.
Erected   1827.
Building   [Separate and entire. Exclusively used for worship.]
Sittings   Free 165. Total [165]. Standing room 13.
Attendance 30 March   Evening 96. Total [96].
Average attendance   [Not given.]
Remarks   Originally in the use of Wesleyan Methodists, then of the Established Church, now of the Baptists.
Dated   30 March 1851.
Signed   Richard Burdon Sanderson, junior, minister [son of a landed proprietor farming 233 acres, employing four labourers].
West Jesmond, Newcastle upon Tyne.
[Richard Burdon Sanderson, who was the mayor of Newcastle 1870–71, died in a railway accident in 1876. From 1863–97 the former chapel was used as the laundry of the Brandling Place Home for Fallen Women.]

10.25   Particular Baptist, Marlborough Crescent (552.8)
Name   Providence Chapel.
Erected   1835.
Building   [Separate and entire. Exclusively used for worship.]
[Opened 23 September 1835. Cost £800. Replaced by a new chapel in Osborne Road, Jesmond, opened on 19 December 1887.]
Sittings   Free 313. Total [313].
Attendance 30 March   Morning 73 + 112 SS. Total 185.
Afternoon and evening no service.
Average attendance   [Not given.]
Dated   30 March 1851.
Signed   Richard Burdon Sanderson [junior], minister.
West Jesmond, Newcastle upon Tyne.

10.26   Scottish Baptist, New Bridge Street (552.40)
Name   New Bridge Chapel.
Erected   In the year 1839–40.
Building   [Separate and entire. Exclusively used for worship.]
Sittings   Free 250. Total [250].
Attendance 30 March   Morning 44. Total 44.
                        Evening 42. Total 42.
Average attendance   [Not given.]
Remarks   The pastor of the church presently here having
              lately resigned through the infirmities of old age, the
              pastoral office is vacant and his place is supplied by
              two temporary presidents, viz., George Rea, deacon
              [baker] and Charles Campbell, deacon.
Dated   31 March 1851.
Signed   Charles Campbell, president *(pro tempore)* [lace man's
              clerk].
              12 Leazes Crescent, Newcastle upon Tyne.
[Separated from the New Court Chapel (**10.23**) in 1824.]

10.27   Wesleyan Methodist, Ropery Road, St Anthony's (552.46)
Name   St Anthony's Chapel.
Erected   1789.
Building   An entire building. Used exclusively for a place of
              worship, except for a Sunday school.
Sittings   Free 100. Other 114. Total [214]. Standing room none.
Attendance 30 March   Afternoon 52 + 12 SS. Total [64].
                        Evening 43 + 6 SS. Total 49.
Average attendance   [Not given.]
Dated   30 March 1851.
Signed   William Todd, steward [grocer].
              St Anthony's, near Newcastle upon Tyne.

10.28   Wesleyan Methodist, New [later City] Road (552.47)
Name   New Road Chapel.
Erected   1812. [Opened on 10 October 1813. Cost £4,700.]
Building   [Separate and entire. Exclusively used for worship.]
Sittings   Free 360. Other 440. Total [800].
Attendance 30 March   Morning 156 + 110 SS. Total 266.
                        Evening 260. Total 260.
Average attendance   [Not given.]
Dated   30 March 1851.

Signed   William Andrews, minister [1848–51].
10 Ridley Villas, Newcastle on Tyne.
[Between 1808 and 1813 the congregation met in a chapel in Westgate Road.]

10.29   Wesleyan Methodist, Brunswick Place, Northumberland Street (552.15)
Name   Brunswick Place Chapel.
Erected   1820. [Inscription 'Methodist Chapel 1820'. Opened 23 February 1821. Cost £6,726.]
Building   [Separate and entire. Exclusively used for worship.]
Sittings   Free 270. Other 1,130. Total [1,400].
Attendance 30 March   Morning 591 + 57 SS. Total 648.
Afternoon none.
Evening 446. Total 446.
Average attendance   Morning 700 + 120 SS. Total 820.
Evening 800. Total [800].
Dated   31 March 1851.
Signed   Robert Gillespie, steward [gentleman].
20 Brandling Place, Newcastle upon Tyne.
Minister   [William Burt 1849–51.]
[The nearby Orphan House, Northumberland Street, opened in 1743. The final service was held there on 10 September 1856, and the building was demolished in 1857.]

10.30   Wesleyan Methodist, Blenheim Street (552.35)
Name   Blenheim Street Chapel.
Erected   The year of our Lord 1838. [Opened 26 October 1838. Cost £3,800.]
Building   [Separate and entire. Exclusively used for worship.]
Sittings   Free 200. Other 518. Total [718].
Attendance 30 March   Morning 236 + 120 SS. Total 356.
Evening 436 + 30 SS. Total 466.
Average attendance   [Not given.]
Remarks   Sunday school room underneath chapel to contain 300 scholars, also rooms for chapel keeper.
Dated   30 March 1851.
Signed   George Marshall, chapel steward [agent].
41 Westmorland Terrace, Newcastle on Tyne.

10.31　Wesleyan Methodist, St Lawrence (552.51)

Name　　　　Centenary Chapel.
Erected　　　1839. [Foundation stone laid 5 March 1840.]
Building　　　Separate [and entire]. Used for public worship, day
　　　　　　　school [and] Sunday school.
Sittings　　　Free 120. Other 360. Total [480].
Attendance 30 March　Afternoon 53 + 22 SS. Total 75.
　　　　　　　　　　　Evening 24 + 12 SS. Total 36.
Average attendance　　Afternoon 50 + 25 SS. Total 75.
　　　　　　　　　　　Evening 40 + 20 SS. Total 60.
Dated　　　　30 March 1851.
Signed　　　 Joseph Greener, steward [cart-proprietor].
　　　　　　　St Lawrence, Newcastle.

10.32　Methodist New Connexion, St Peter's Quay (552.54)

Name　　　　Bethlehem [Chapel].
Erected　　　1827.
Building　　　[Separate and] entire. Both [a] chapel and school etc.
Sittings　　　Free 220. Other 182. Total [402]. Standing room 60.
Attendance 30 March　Morning 147 SS. Total [147].
　　　　　　　　　　　Afternoon 85. Total 85.
　　　　　　　　　　　Evening 80. Total 80.
Average attendance　　Morning from 80 to 90 + 104 SS. Total 147
　　　　　　　　　　　(*sic*) [184–194].
Dated　　　　30 March 1851.
Signed　　　 Adam Brown, chapel steward [waterman].
　　　　　　　Dent's Hole, near Newcastle upon Tyne.
[Replaced by the Brown Memorial Chapel, opened on 12 September
1883, and erected in memory of Adam Brown.]

10.33　Methodist New Connexion, Jesmond Vale (552.57)

Name　　　　None.
Erected　　　1830.
Building　　　[Not separate and entire or exclusively used for
　　　　　　　worship.]
Sittings　　　Free 60. Total [60].
Attendance 30 March　Morning 10 + 50 SS. Total 60.
Average attendance　　[Not given.]
Dated　　　　30 March 1851.
Signed　　　 George Wright, manager [coal miner, furnace men].
　　　　　　　William Pitt [Cottages], near Longbenton.

10.34   Methodist New Connexion, Scotswood (552.3)

Name	Scotswood Chapel.
Erected	1835.
Building	[Separate and entire. Exclusively used for worship.]
Sittings	Free 64. Other 84. Total [148]. Standing room '40 feet' (*sic*).

Attendance 30 March   Afternoon 69 + 20 SS. Total 89.

Evening 95 + 12 SS. Total 107.

Average attendance   Afternoon 100 + 20 SS. Total 120.

Evening 118 + 12 SS. Total 130.

Remarks	Prospect of improvement.
Dated	31 March 1851.
Signed	Edward Hodgson, chapel steward [gardener]. Scotswood, Newcastle on Tyne.

10.35   Methodist New Connexion, Hood Street (552.20)

Name	Salem Chapel. [Hood Street Chapel.]
Erected	[1 May] 1836 site entirely new. [Cost £3,700.]
Building	[Separate and entire. Exclusively used for worship.] Sunday school below.
Sittings	Free 400. Other 600. Total [1,000]. Standing room none, except the aisles on occasion.

Attendance 30 March   [Not given.]

Average attendance   Morning 150 + 60 SS. Total 210.

Evening 200. Total 200.

Remarks	We think that this return – if required at all – ought to have been obligatory on all parties without exception.
Dated	31 March 1851.
Signed	Thomas Boycott, minister. 57 Percy Street, Newcastle upon Tyne.

[Ten years before being expelled from the Methodist New Connexion in 1841, Joseph Barker (1806–1875) had been the minister of Salem chapel. While 'his forcible and attractive preaching excited much attention, and drew large audiences' his unorthodox teaching divided many Methodist congregations, and 4,348 members left the Connexion. J.T. Barker, *The Life of Joseph Barker* (London, 1880), p. 132.]

10.36   Primitive Methodist, Byker Hill (552.53)

Name	Chapel.
Erected	Before 1800.

Building   No[t separate and entire. Used also for a] Sunday and
day class.
Sittings   Free 150. Total [150].
Attendance 30 March Afternoon 56. Total [56].
Evening 40. Total [40].
Average attendance   [Not given.]
Dated   30 March 1851.
Signed   Thomas Gibson, pastor [butcher].
Byker High Hill.

10.37   Primitive Methodist, Nelson Street (552.18)
Name   Nelson Street Chapel.
Erected   [7 October] 1838. [Cost £2,950. After it closed on 4
October 1899 the Central Primitive Methodist Church
was opened in Northumberland Road.]
Building   [Separate and entire. Exclusively used for worship.]
Sittings   Free 500. Other 611. Total 1,111.
Attendance 30 March Morning 243 + 147 SS. Total 390.
Afternoon 120 + 144 SS. Total 264.
Evening 336. Total 336.
Average attendance   Morning 250 + 141 SS. Total 391.
Afternoon 100 + 176 SS. Total 276.
Evening 350. Total 350.
Dated   31 March 1851.
Signed   Andrew Whey, chapel steward.
72.73 and 74 (*sic*).
[From 1826 to 1838 the congregation worshipped at a chapel in Silver
Street, previously occupied by the Independents. The foundation
stone of the Nelson Street Chapel was laid on 21 November 1837
by William Clowes, one of the founders of Primitive Methodism. In
1842 the first Primitive Methodist camp meeting in Newcastle was
held on the Town Moor. Primitive Methodist conferences were held
in Newcastle in 1842, 1859, 1876 and 1903.]

10.38   Primitive Methodist, Bird's Nest, Byker (552.56)
Name   Bird's Nest Primitive Methodist [Chapel].
Erected   In the year 1839.
Building   An entire building. [Exclusively used for worship.]
Sittings   Free 96. Other 16. Total [112].
Attendance 30 March Morning 53 SS. Total 53.
Afternoon 50. Total 50.
Evening 60. Total 60.

Average attendance   [Not given.]
Dated   30 March 1851.
Signed   William Bolton, leader (or elder) [labourer].
          West House, near Dent's Hole, Newcastle.
['Dent's Hole was once one of the prettiest spots on Tyneside.' R.J. Charleton, *A History of Newcastle on Tyne* (Newcastle, n.d.), p. 368.]

10.39   Primitive Methodist, Ballast Hills, Byker (552.52)
Name   Ballast Hills Primitive Methodist Chapel. [Ouseburn
          Chapel.]
Erected   1841. [Cost £550. Gallery 1853.]
Building   [Separate and entire. Exclusively used for worship.]
Sittings   Free 320. Other 130. Total [450].
Attendance 30 March   Morning 146 + 270 SS. Total 416.
          Afternoon 313 SS. Total 313.
          Evening 306. Total [306].
Average attendance   Morning 150 + 250 SS. Total 400.
          Afternoon 320 SS. Total 320.
          Evening 300. Total 300.
Remarks   No schedule has been furnished to the Sunday school
          which is taught in the chapel. We therefore add that
          it was begun in 1829 and […] had on the books 450
          scholars and 40 gratuitous teachers. Nothing is paid
          by any of the scholars. R. Cook.
Dated   30 March 1851.
Signed   Ralph Cook, leader and steward [butcher].
          [East] Ballast Hills, Newcastle on Tyne.
[Ballast Hills became one of the largest nonconformist burial grounds outside London.]

10.40   Wesleyan Reformers, Benwell (552.7)
Name   [Not given.]
Erected   [18]22.
Building   Dwelling house [in another hand].
Sittings   [Not given.]
Attendance 30 March   Evening 50. Total [50].
Average attendance   [Not given.]
Dated   31 March 1851.
Signed   John Johnson [butcher].

10.41   Wesleyan Reformers, Grey Street (552.17)
Name   Victoria Room. [Victoria Assembly Rooms.]
Erected   A public building rented only. [Used by the Reformers
                from December 1850.]
Building   [Separate and entire. Exclusively used as a place of
                worship] excepting when let or granted for public
                meetings.
Sittings   Free 450. Total [450]. Standing room 100.
Attendance 30 March   Morning 300 + 110 SS. Total 410.
                        Evening 480. Total 480.
Average attendance   Morning 300 + 110 SS. Total 410.
                        Evening 500. Total 500.
Dated   31 March 1851.
Signed   John Benson, steward [grocer].
                6 Grainger Street, Newcastle on Tyne.
[John Benson (1818–1866) had been very active within Wesleyan
Methodism before he joined the Wesleyan Reformers. He was a total
abstainer and a town councillor for the St Andrew ward (South)
1856–66. On 22 February 1852 the congregation moved to the Old
Coach House, New Bridge Street, and then to a new chapel in
Prudhoe Street opened on 17 September 1862. The chapel had 800
sittings and cost £3,500).]

10.42   Wesleyan Reformers, Gibson Street (552.42)
Name   Gibson Street Chapel [or Zion Chapel].
Erected   1835. [Cost £1,835.]
Building   [Separate and entire. Exclusively used for worship.]
Sittings   Free 45. Others none. Total [45]. Standing room none.
Attendance 30 March   Morning 220. Total [220].
                        Evening 300. Total [300].
Average attendance   Morning 300 + 120 SS. Total 420.
Dated   31 March 1851.
Signed   Thomas Kirkup, chapel steward [draper].
                8 Buxton Street, Newcastle, Tyne.

10.43   Non-denominational, *'Christian', Monk Street (552.32)
Name   The Smith's Hall.
Erected   Before 1800.
Building   [Separate and entire but not exclusively used for
                worship.]
Sittings   Free 150. Total [150].
Attendance 30 March   Morning 8. Total [8].

Afternoon 36. Total [36].
Evening 33. Total [33].
Average attendance   [Not given.]
Remarks   *This society acknowledges no other name but
'Christian'.
Dated   30 March 1851.
Signed   Joseph Moffitt, elder [clerk].
Cramer Dykes, [High Street], Gateshead.

10.44   Non-denominational, Ancrum Street, Spital Tongues
(552.24)
[On a Church of England form]
Name   Spital Tongues Chapel and Schoolroom.
Consecrated Never.
Erected   [1845. Replaced by the Benson Memorial Church in
1867.]
Sittings   Free 100. Total 100.
Attendance 30 March   Evening 30 + 20 SS. Total 50.
Average attendance   Evening 30 + 20 SS. Total 50.
Dated   30 March 1851
Signed   Nicholas Scott, class leader [cabinet maker].
3 Saville Court, Newcastle.

10.45   Non-denominational Union of Evangelical Christians for
the Sailors, Bethel Quay (552.45)
Name   Sailors' Bethel.
Erected   Part of an old building.
Building   As part of [a] building. Exclusively for preaching the
gospel.
Sittings   All free (all formed or seated).
Attendance 30 March   Morning no service.
Afternoon 30. Total [30].
Evening 24. Total [24].
Average attendance   [Not given.]
Remarks   We have much need of a better Sailors' Chapel. Many
sailors attend various chapels in the town in which I
rejoice.
Dated   31 March 1851.
Signed   Joseph Cowell, sailors' missionary [builder].
16 Carlton Street, Shieldfield, Newcastle upon Tyne.
[The Sailors' Bethel, Horatio Street, was opened on 12 April 1877.]

10.46   Society of Friends [Quakers], Pilgrim Street (552.43, and 552.44)

Name	Friends Meeting House.
Erected	Before 1800. Rebuilt in 1805. [Erected 1698, enlarged 1813.]
Building	Primarily so, but meetings for pious or benevolent purposes are sometimes permitted.
Sittings	Ground floor 360 (area 1,914 [square] feet). Galleries 152 (area 493 [square] feet). Total 512 (area 2,407 [square] feet).

Attendance 30 March   Morning 207. Total [207].

Afternoon 112. Total [112].

Remarks	I have also made a return forwarded to London on a form specially provided for the Society of Friends.
Dated	30 of 3rd month 1851.
Signed	Robert Wilson [cheesemonger, and provision merchant] (specially appointed by the monthly meeting of people). 8 Ravensworth Terrace, Newcastle on Tyne.

10.47   Roman Catholic, St Andrew, Pilgrim Street (552.13)

Name	St Andrew's Catholic Chapel.
Erected	About the year 1801. [Opened 11 February 1798, enlarged 1808, 1826.]
Building	[Separate and entire. Exclusively used for worship.]
Sittings	Free 210. Other 634. Total [844]. Standing room 200.

Attendance 30 March   Morning 1,389 + 300 SS. Total 1,689.

Evening 604. Total 604.

Average attendance	[Not given.]
Remarks	There are 10,000 Roman Catholics in Newcastle: 6,000 of whom are served by one Roman Catholic priest attached to this chapel. About 1,000 labourers having families in Ireland attend this chapel. Two services [are held] in the morning.
Dated	30 March 1851.
Signed	Joseph Cullen, Roman Catholic priest [1847–51]. 73 Pilgrim Street, Newcastle on Tyne.

[In 1852 the estimated number of Roman Catholics in the area was 8,500.]

10.48   Roman Catholic, St Mary, Clayton Street West (552.38)
Name   St Mary's Church.
Erected   [21 August] 1844. [Became the Roman Catholic
              Cathedral on 21 August 1860.]
Building   [Separate and entire. Exclusively used for worship.]
Sittings   Free 200. Other 700. Total [900]. Standing room 500.
Attendance 30 March   Morning 1,500 + 200 SS. Total 1,700.
              Afternoon 400 + 500 SS. Total 900.
Average attendance   [Not given.]
Remarks   13 Forth Bank Baptist missing (*sic*). [In another hand.]
Dated   31 March 1851.
Signed   Joseph Humble, clergyman.
              St Mary's, Catholic Church, Newcastle on Tyne.
[When a mission was held in January 1846, 1,800 Roman Catholics
received communion, and 49 were admitted into the church (B.W.
Kelly, *Historical Notes on English Catholic Missions* (London, 1907), p.
288). In 1852 the estimated number of Roman Catholics in the area
was 6,500.]

10.49   Synagogue, Temple Street (552.6 duplicate return 552.34)
Name   Synagogue.
Erected   September 1838. [Foundation stone laid 11 July and
              the building opened for worship on 19 September.
              Cost £360.]
Building   Separate and entire. Exclusively for [a] place of
              worship.
Sittings   Free 74. Other 30. Total [104].
Attendance 29 March   [Not given.]
Average attendance   Morning 50. Total 2,400 (*sic*).
Remarks   28 March. No service.
              25 [March] Saturday morning 44. 29th 44. Total [44].
Dated   30 March 1851.
Signed   Isaac Abraham Jacques, president [medicine vender].
              19 Carliol Street, Newcastle on Tyne.
              Joseph Carr, secretary [Jewish rabbi].
[Before 1838 there was only a small Jewish community in Newcastle
and they met in various hired rooms and even in a public house.
After the congregation divided another congregation was established
in Charlotte Square in 1867, but the two were reunited when a new
synagogue was opened for worship in Albion Street on 25 August
1880. It cost £5,222 and had 300–400 seats for men on the ground floor
and 200–300 seats for women in the gallery. *Proceedings of the Town*

Council of the Borough of Newcastle upon Tyne for 1879–80 (Newcastle, 1880), pp. xlix–liii.]

10.50   Unitarian, Hanover Square (552.27)

Name   Hanover Square Chapel. [Unitarian Christian.]
Erected   In the year 1720. [Opened 26 March 1727, enlarged
               1810. Moved in 1854 to New Bridge Street as the
               Church of the Divine Unity.]
Building   [Separate and entire. Exclusively used for worship.]
Sittings   Free 107. Other 815. Total [922]. Standing room [in]
               aisles.
Attendance 30 March   Morning 205 + 116 SS. Total 321.
                        Evening 118. Total 118.
Average attendance   Morning 350 + 110 SS. Total 460.
                        Evening 460. Total [460].
Dated   30 March 1851.
Signed   George Harris, minister [1845–59].
               [2] Woodbine Place, Gateshead, Tyne.
[The Rev. William Turner (1761–1859), the minister of the chapel 1782–1841, became one of the leading nonconformists in Newcastle and in 1793 a founding member of the Literary and Philosophical Society. S. Harbottle, *The Reverend William Turner. Dissent and Reform in Georgian Newcastle upon Tyne* (Newcastle, 1997). On 21 January 1940 the congregation moved to Oxford Street, the site of St Peter's church (**10.11**).]

10.51   Unitarian, Glass House Street, Byker (552.55)

Name   [14] Glass House Street. [St Peter's.]
Erected   [Not given.]
Building   [Occupies] two rooms. [Exclusively used for worship
               and] Sunday school.
Sittings   Free 150. Total [150].
Attendance 30 March   Morning 60 + 50 SS. Total [110].
Average attendance   [Not given.]
Dated   31 March 1851.
Signed   Robert Heppell, treasurer [shipwright].
               St Peter's, William Street, [Newcastle upon Tyne].

10.52   Swedenborgian, New Jerusalem Temple, Percy Street
(552.21)
Name   New Jerusalem Temple. [New Church.]
Erected   1822. [Opened on 16 February 1823. Cost £1,221.]
Building   [Separate and] entire. [Exclusively used for worship.]
Sittings   Free 350. Other 50. Total [400]. Standing room none.
Attendance 30 March   Morning 70. Total [70].
                        Afternoon none.
                        Evening 70. Total [70].
Average attendance   [Not given.]
Dated   [Not given.]
Signed   John Giliott, secretary and treasurer.
                Northumberland and Durham District Bank,
                Newcastle on Tyne.

11. Rothbury District (HO 129/563)
14 places of worship

11.1   Church of England, St Mary, Alnham (563.2) [Later
St Michael and All Angels]
Population 1851: 291 (parish) 132 (township)

Name   St Mary's (it is believed). Ancient parish church.
Consecrated   About the 13th century. [Restored 1870–71.]
Endowment   Tithe £154 7s 11d. Glebe £16. OPE £13. Fees 10s.
                Total £183 17s 11d.
Sittings   [None free.] Other 97. Total [97].
Attendance 30 March   Morning 61 [including SS]. Total 61.
Average attendance   Morning 62 [including SS]. Total 62.
Dated   31 March 1851.
Signed   George Selby Thompson MA, vicar [1848–65].
                [The Tower], Alnham, Alnwick.
{1857   Attendance 50. 22 communicants.}   {B 5.}
[The church of Alnham 'is in a most dilapidated and disgraceful
state. It is in a worse state than any church I ever saw; but the walls
being strong, and the oaken beams of the roof quite sound, it might
be restored. No doubt at considerable cost.' R.C. Coxe, *A Cursory
Survey of the Church Buildings within the Archdeaconry of Lindisfarne*
(London, 1860), pp. 25–26.]

11.2   Church of England, St Michael and All Angels, Alwinton
(563.16)
Population 1851: 853 (parish) 77 (township)

Name   St Michael's church. It is an ancient parish church
               and united with Holystone into one cure on account
               of the poverty of the two parishes which were
               originally impoverished by Holystone nunnery, their
               endowments were restored to them.
Consecrated Before 1800. [Restored 1851–52.]
Endowment   [£100.]
Sittings   Free 14. Other 140. Total [154].
Attendance 30 March   [Not given.]
Average attendance   [Not given.]
Remarks   Nearly every seat in this church is appropriated to
               some particular house, but as the occupants of some
               of the houses do not attend church, their seats are
               practically free. An attempt is now making by a better
               arrangement greatly to increase the number of free
               sittings.
               (I certify my belief) as far as I am [able] to [answer
               questions stated].
Dated   25 March 1851.
Signed   Aislabie Procter, vicar or incumbent minister [1833–
               77].
               Alwinton, Morpeth, Northumberland.
{1857   Attendance 150. 30 communicants.}   {B 12.}
[Aislabie Procter was the eighth son of William Procter, the incumbent
of Doddington (**6.5**).]

11.3   Church of England, St Mary the Virgin, Holystone (563.13)
Population 1851: 436 (parish) 135 (township)

Name   St Mary's church or chapel. It is an ancient parish
               church or ancient chapelry, as it is commonly called,
               and united with Alwinton parish into one cure on
               account of the poverty of the two benefices or parishes
               wh[ich] were originally impoverished for Holystone
               nunnery when endowments were restored to them.
Consecrated Before 1800. [Restored 1848–49.]
Endowment   [Not given.]
Sittings   Free 86. Other 80. Total [166].

Attendance 30 March   [Not given.]
Average attendance   [Not given.]
Remarks   In the number of sittings the calculation is five to
each seat, but they can and often do contain six
people each, and in fact the church can seat about 200
generally well.
(I certify my belief) as far as I am [able] to answer
[questions stated].
Dated   25 March 1851.
Signed   Aislabie Proctor, incumbent minister [1833–77].
Alwinton, Morpeth, Northumberland.

11.4   Church of England, St Cuthbert, Elsdon (563.12)
Population 1851: 1,643 (parish) 313 (township)

Name   St Cuthbert's. Ancient parish church.
Consecrated Before 1800. [Restored 1837, 1877.]
Endowment   Tithe £800 (rent charges). Glebe 63 ac[res].
Sittings   [None free.] Other 400. Total [400].
Attendance 30 March   Morning 130 + 60 SS. Total 190.
                        Evening 30. Total 30.
Average attendance   Morning 170 + 60 SS. Total 230.
                        Evening 30. Total 30.
Dated   31 March 1851.
Signed   Percy Gilpin, rector [1842–54].
Elsdon, Newcastle upon Tyne.
                                                    {B 13.}
[Elsdon had two chapels of ease, St Francis, Byrness (**3.3**) and Holy
Trinity, Horsley (**3.4**).]

11.5   Church of England, St Lawrence, Longframlington (563.9)
[Later St Mary the Virgin]
Population 1851: 549 (township)

Name   St Lawrence, an ancient chapel of ease in the parish of
[St Michael and All Angels], Felton (**1.8**).
Consecrated Before 1800. [Rebuilt 1849, restored 1882, 1896.]
Endowment   OPE [Not given].
Sittings   [None free.] Other 188. Total 188.
Attendance 30 March   Morning 135 + 40 SS. Total 175.
                        Afternoon no service.
Average attendance   Morning 130 + 40 SS. Total 170.

Afternoon no service.

Dated   4 April 1851.
Signed   Thomas Ilderton, vicar [1850–71].
Felton, North[umberlan]d.
[Thomas Ilderton was also responsible for Felton (**1.8**).]

11.6   Church of England, All Saints, Rothbury (563.8)
Population 1851: 2,545 (parish) 895 (township)

Name   All Saints. An ancient, recently restored, parish church.
Consecrated   Before 1800. [Rebuilt 1863.]
Endowment   Land £80. Tithe £1,500. Glebe £75. Fees £5.
Sittings   Free 150. Other 370. Total 520.
Attendance 30 March   Morning 243 + 56 SS. Total 299.
Afternoon 213 + 49 SS. Total 262.
Average attendance   Morning 200 + 55 SS. Total 255.
Afternoon 100 + 45 SS. Total 145.
Remarks   The falling off in the afternoon congregation may be accounted for by there being no sermon. The public catechising increases it during Lent.
Dated   31 March 1851.
Signed   Nicholas Frees Young Kemble, curate [1849–52].
Rothbury, Morpeth, Northumberland.
Incumbent   [Charles George Venables Vernon Harcourt, rector 1822–70.]

{B 16.}

[Charles Harcourt was the son of Edward Venables Vernon Harcourt (1757–1847) the Archbishop of York 1808–47.]

11.7   Church of England, St Bartholomew, Whittingham (563.4)
Population 1851: 1,905 (parish) 726 (township)

Name   Parish church dedicated to St Bartholomew.
Consecrated   Before 1800. [Rebuilt and enlarged 1840, Chancel 1871.]
Endowment   Land, tithe and glebe rated at house, garden etc.
Land £35 10s. Tithe £556 3s.
Glebe £137 10s 6d. OPE none. Fees £2 17s. Easter offerings £2 15s. Other none.
Sittings   Free 166. Other 339. Total 505.
Attendance 30 March   Morning 211 + 45 SS. Total 256.
Evening 59 + 28 SS. Total 87.

Average attendance   Morning 200 + 75 SS. Total 275.
Evening 70 + 40 SS. Total 110.
Remarks   Our Sunday school is held only from May till
November, owing to the distances which are great. The
children's number for 30 March is given, representing
such children present as attend the Sunday school.
Dated   30 March 1851.
Signed   Robert William Goodenough, vicar [1835–80].
Whittingham, Alnwick.

{B 15.}

11.8   English Presbyterian, Harbottle (563.14)
Name   Harbottle Presbyterian Church.
Erected   The present church in 1756. But there was a former
one in this place. [From 1713.] [New church opened 12
July 1855.]
Building   Separate and entire, for public worship and used for
the Sabbath school.
Sittings   Free 12 (others if needed). Other 440. [Total] 450 or 460
for sitting.
Attendance 30 March   Morning 240. Total 240.
Average attendance   Morning 250 to 300 (summer). 150 (winter).
Total [150–300].
Dated   31 March 1851.
Signed   Samuel Cathcart [DD], minister [1846–70].
Harbottle Manse, Rothbury, Northumberland.
[During the ministry of Samuel Cathcart the congregation increased
from 189 to 240. In 1870 he became an assistant secretary of the
Religious Tract Society.]

11.9   English Presbyterian, Thropton (563.7)
Name   Presbyterian Church.
Erected   Anno. 1799. [Rebuilt 1863.]
Building   Separate and entire. [Exclusively used for worship.]
Sittings   Free. There are sometime about 80 sittings
unappropriated to which free access is given.
Other, between 220 and 230 sittings let. Total [300–310].
Attendance 30 March   Morning 190 + 23 SS. Total 213.
Average attendance   [Not given.]
Remarks   Only one service during the winter months, the
congregation living widely scattered. The attendance at
the ev[enin]g service in summer, considerable less than
that indicated in the preceding column.

Dated   31 March 1851.
Signed   David Stevenson Furgus AM, minister [1849–88].
Thropton Manse, Rothbury, Northumberland.

11.10   English Presbyterian, Longframlington (563.10)
Name   Presbyterian Church of England.
Erected   Before 1800. [1739, rebuilt 1854.]
Building   [Separate and entire. Exclusively used for worship.]
Sittings   Free 176. Other 104. Total [280].
Attendance 30 March   Morning 60 + 25 SS. Total 85.
Evening 30. Total 30.
Average attendance   Morning 130 + 35 SS. Total 165.
Evening 40. Total 40.
Dated   31 March 1851.
Signed   John Gillespie, minister.
Longframlington, Northumberland.

11.11   Independent [Congregational], Rothbury (563.5)
Name   Rothbury Independent Chapel.
Erected   1842. [Established 1835, new church opened 1863,
enlarged 1908.]
Building   [Separate and entire. Exclusively used for worship.]
Sittings   [None free.] Other 250. Total [250].
Attendance 30 March   Morning 90 + 10 SS. Total 100.
Evening 30. Total 30.
Average attendance   [Not given.]
Dated   31 March 1851.
Signed   Alfred Scales, minister [1848–51].
Rothbury, Northumberland.

11.12   Roman Catholic, Biddlestone Hall, Biddlestone (563.15)
Name   Biddlestone Roman Catholic Chapel.
Erected   Date unknown, but very ancient.
Building   Separate building used exclusively as a place of
worship.
Sittings   [All] free sittings.
Attendance 30 March   Morning 120. Total 120.
Afternoon 20. Total 20.
Average attendance   [Not given.]
Dated   31 March 1851.
Signed   Thomas Hogget, Roman Catholic priest [1841–86].
Biddlestone, Rothbury, Northumberland.

11.13   Roman Catholic, Thropton Hall, Thropton (563.6)

Name   Catholic Chapel of All Saints.
Erected   Before 1800. [Enlarged 1842.]
Building   Separate building. [Exclusively used for worship.]
Sittings   Free about 40. Other 66. Total [106]. Standing room
                18'6" by 7' 6".
Attendance 30 March   Morning about 70 to 80. Total [70–80].
                        Afternoon about 20 to 25. Total [20–25].
Average attendance   [Not given.]
Dated   30 March 1851.
Signed   George Joshua Austin Corless DD, Catholic priest.
                Dean [1839–52].
                Thropton Hall, Rothbury.

['Thropton remained a Catholic centre: by 1767 a church had been built there, and it continued to expand into the 19th century.' J.A. Hilton, 'Catholicism in Elizabethan Northumberland', *Northern History*, xiii (1977), p. 55.]

11.14   Roman Catholic, Callaly Castle, Whittingham (563.3)

[Summary form]
Name   Callaly Castle Chapel.
Erected   About 1750. [Closed 1877 when the castle passed to
                a non-Roman Catholic family. St Mary (Our Lady
                Immaculate), Whittingham was opened 11 September
                1881.]
Building   A separate building. Used exclusively as a place of
                worship.
Sittings   Free 120. Total [120].
Usual attendance   Morning 35. Total [35].
Dated   [Not given.]
Signed   John Hopper, registrar.
                Rothbury, Northumberland.
                (Thomas Ord, priest) [1840–650].

[In the previous century there were more Roman Catholics in the area. In the 1780s there was a congregation of nearly 300, many of whom were illiterate. J. Bossy, *The English Catholic Community 1570–1850* (London, 1975), p. 276 note 63.]

12. Tynemouth District (HO 129/553)
83 places of worship

12.1   Church of England, Blyth Chapel [later St Cuthbert], Blyth
(553.73)
Population 1851: 2,060 (township) 524 Newsham (lordship)

Name   Blyth Chapel. A private chapel, the property of Sir
                Matthew White Ridley Bart [of Blagdon, afterwards
                Viscount Ridley].
Consecrated   [Not given.] [Erected 1751. Replaced by St Cuthbert's
                church, consecrated 5 November 1885.]
Endowment   Pew rents £6. Fees £15.
Sittings   Free 84. Other 116. Total 200.
Attendance 30 March   Morning 66 + 50 SS. Total [116].
                        Evening 133. Total [133].
Average attendance   [Not given.]
Remarks   Blyth Chapel was erected in the year 1751 by Matthew
                Ridley Esq. Fees for baptisms and burials belong to
                the Rev. H[enry] Warkman, minister of the parish of
                Earsdon [(**12.3**)]. The stipend of the minister etc. is
                supplied by Sir Matt[hew] White Ridley, Bart.
Dated   31 March 1851.
Signed   Robert Greenwood, minister [1814–59].
                [Link House], Blyth, North Shields.

{B 15.}

12.2   Church of England, Cramlington Chapel, Cramlington
(553.83)
Population 1851: 3,367 (chapelry)

Name   Cramlington Chapel, ancient chapel of ease to St
                Nicholas, Newcastle upon Tyne (**10.1**).
Consecrated   [Not given. Replaced by St Nicholas' church,
                consecrated 12 May 1868.]
Endowment   Land £60. Glebe and rent charge. OPE £5. Fees £10.
Sittings   Free 20. Other 100. Total 120.
Attendance 30 March   Morning 80 + 20 SS. Total [100].
                        Afternoon 80 + 20 SS. Total [100].
Average attendance   Morning 100 + 20 SS. Total [120].
                        Afternoon 100 + 20 SS. Total [120].
Remarks   Return to the best of my belief.

Dated   31 March 1851.
Signed   Robert Greenwood, perpetual curate [1839–59].
             [Link House], Blyth, North Shields.
{1857   Attendance 120. 20 communicants.}   {B 39.}
[Robert Greenwood had previously been the curate of Cramlington
1829–39.]

12.3   Church of England, St Alban, Earsdon (553.63)
Population 1851: 10,982 (parish) 551 (township)

Name   St Alban's Parish Church, Earsdon.
Consecrated Before 1800. The church rebuilt in consequence of the
               decay of the old one. [Consecrated 12 October 1837,
               restored 1889.]
Erected   Private subscription. The Incorporated Society for
               Building, Enlarging and Repairing of Churches. [Total
               cost] not known [£2,200].
Endowment   Land £20. Fees not known. Dues, yes. Easter offerings,
               yes.
Sittings   Free 200. Other 400. Total 600.
Attendance 30 March   Morning 70 [no SS]. Total 70.
               Afternoon no service.
               Evening no service.
Average attendance   Morning 40 [no SS]. Total 40.
               Afternoon none.
               Evening none.
Remarks   The above is as accurate an account as I can give as
               the clergyman refused to fill it up.
Dated   6 April 1851.
Signed   Gavin Watson, enumerator.
               Earsdon, Newcastle on Tyne.
Incumbent   [Henry Warkman 1811–57.]
                                                        {B 98.}

12.4   Church of England, Seaton Delaval Hall Chapel [later Our Lady], Seaton Delaval (553.70)
Population 1851: 2,726 (township).

Name   Private chapel of Lord Hastings.
Consecrated Unknown.
Erected   Supposed by the late Delaval family.
Endowment   OPE £40 yearly.

Sittings   Free 40. Total 40.
Attendance 30 March   Afternoon 30. Total [30].
Average attendance   Afternoon 60. Total [60].
Remarks   Service held on Sunday afternoons, and the incumbent
         [of Earsdon] is paid [£40 a year] by Lord Hastings.
Dated   31 March 1851.
Signed   Andrew Davie, jun[ior], enumerator,
         Lysdon, near North Shields.
{1857   Attendance 60.}
[In 1720 Seaton Delaval Hall was rebuilt by Sir John Vanbrugh, and
partially destroyed by fire in 1752 and 1822. By the 18th century
the chapel was a chapel of ease to Earsdon, and it became a parish
church in 1891.]

12.5   Church of England, St Mary the Virgin, Horton Grange
         (553.81)
Population 1851: 4,449 (parish) 210 (township)

Name   Chapel of Horton, an ancient chapelry.
Consecrated Before 1800. [Rebuilt 1827, restored 1864, 1902–3.]
Endowment Land £60. Tithe £2 10s. OPE £81. Fees £15.
Sittings   [None free.] Other 220. Total 220.
Attendance 30 March   Morning 68. Total 68.
Average attendance   [Not given.]
Remarks   The chapel was rebuilt in 1827 at a cost of £463 3s. £34
         3s 3d of which was raised by subscriptions and £120
         by parochial rate.
Dated   30 March 1851.
Signed   N. A. Ireton, perpetual curate.
         Bedlington, Horton, Northumberland.
Incumbent [Nathaniel Atkinson 1847–55.]
{1857   Attendance 80. 24 communicants.}   {B 53.}

12.6   Church of England, St Bartholomew, Longbenton (553.50)
Population 1851: 9,205 (parish) 2,238 (township)

[Summary form]
Name   Longbenton Church.
Consecrated [Not given. St Andrew's church was replaced by
         St Bartholomew, consecrated by the Bishop of

Peterborough on 2 November 1791. Repaired 1842,
restored 1855 and enlarged 1873–75.]
Endowment   [£353.]
Sittings   Free 105. Other 335. Total 440.
Usual attendance   Morning 160 (including SS). Total [160].
Afternoon 80 (including SS). Total [80].
Dated   6 August 1852.
Signed   William Nesbit.
Incumbent   [John Besly 1830–68.]
{1857   Attendance 150. 40 communicants.}   {B 49.}

12.7   Church of England, Christ Church, Preston Lane, North Shields (553.24)
Population 1851: 30,524 (Tynemouth parish) 14,493 (Tynemouth township) 8,882 (North Shields township)

[Summary form]
Name   Christ's Church.
Erected   [Consecrated 5 July] 1668. [Rebuilt 1792–93, restored and enlarged 1868–69.]
Endowment   [£298.]
Sittings   Free 65 (in aisles only). Other 2,000. Total 2,000
(exclusive of 60 or 70 sittings in aisles).
Usual attendance   Morning 1,500. Total [1,500].
Afternoon say about 700. Total [about 700].
Evening 1,500. Total [1,500].
Remarks   [Of the] three churches in the parish of Tynemouth
only Christ's Church, Trinity Church and St Saviour's
are under the pastorate [of] a vicar (the Rev.
Christ[opher] Reed) assisted by three curates.
In my return sent to you on the 24 April last I made
memoranda on all the church schedules [with], the
effect that Mr Reed (the vicar) refused to make returns
for any of the above churches.
W[illia]m Harrison.
Dated   [Not given.]
Signed   William Harrison, registrar.
[Dockwray Square, North Shields.]
Incumbent   [Christopher Reed 1830–68.]
{1857   Attendance 1,700. 70 communicants. There is much
need of more churches.}
{B 495.}

[Christ Church was built to serve the townships of Tynemouth, North Shields, Preston, Chirton, Whitley, Murton and Cullercoats.]

12.8   Church of England, Holy Trinity, Collingwood Street, North Shields (553.25)

[Summary form]

Name	Trinity Church.
Erected	1832. [Consecrated 21 October 1836. Total cost £3,594, with a Parliamentary grant of £2,276. Parish created 16 April 1861.]
Sittings	Free 500. Other 700. Total 1,200.
Usual attendance	Morning 250. Total [250].
	Afternoon 70. Total [70].
Remarks	100 National [school] scholars.
Dated	[Not given.]
Signed	William Harrison, registrar.
	[Dockwray Square, North Shields.]
Incumbent	[Christopher Reed 1830–68.]
{1857	Attendance 270. 25 communicants.}

12.9   Church of England, Holy Saviour, Whitley Road, Tynemouth (553.26)

Population 1851: 14,493 (township of Tynemouth) 157 (soldiers in barracks)

[Summary form]

Name	St Saviour's.
Erected	1840. [Consecrated 11 August 1841, restored and enlarged 1882–84. Parish created 16 April 1861.]
Sittings	Free 400. Other 300. Total 700.
Usual attendance	Morning full.
Dated	[Not given.]
Signed	William Harrison, registrar.
	[Dockwray Square, North Shields.]
Incumbent	[Christopher Reed 1830–68.]
{1857	'There is much need of more churches. Population 33,000'.}

12.10   Church of England, Holy Trinity, Seghill (553.60)

Population 1851: 1,869 (township)

Name	Holy Trinity Church, Seghill, the parish church of

a new parish under 6 & 7 Vic. c.37 [Peel's District Churches Act].

Consecrated	[21 July] 1849, as an additional church. [Parish created on 23 June 1846 out of part of Earsdon.]
Erected	Parliamentary grant £200. Private contributions and grants from Church Building Societies £1,470 (nearly). [Parliamentary grant £200.] Total cost £1,670.
Endowment	[Ecclesiastical] Commissioners £150. Pew rents £12 (or nearly so). Fees £10 (or nearly so).
Sittings	Free 426. Other 104. Total 530.
Attendance 30 March	Morning 103 + 44 SS. Total 147. Evening 53 + 33 SS. Total 86.
Average attendance	Morning 200 + 36 SS. Total 236. Evening 100 + 20 SS. Total 120.
Remarks	I have stated the average attendance as accurately as I could, but have no accurate means of knowing it.
Dated	2 April 1851.
Signed	Thomas Henry Bunbury, perpetual curate [1846–55]. Backworth, Newcastle on Tyne.
{1857	Attendance 150. 24 communicants.} {B 54.}

12.11   Church of England, Christ Church, Church Street, Walker (553.52)
Population 1851: 3,963 (township and included the hamlet of Little Benton)

Name	Christ Church. A new church built under provisions of 6 & 7 Vic. c.37 (Sir Rob[er]t Peel's Act).
Consecrated	The church was consecrated [on] 22 [23] August 1848. [Enlarged 1871.] Consecrated for a new parish church for all ecclesiastical purposes [created 17 April 1846 out of the parish of Longbenton].
Erected	[By] private benefaction [and] subscription £1,450. Total cost £1,450.
Endowment	OPE £150 (endowed by the Ecclesiastical Commissioners). Dues £15 2s 6d.
Sittings	Free 420. Total 420.
Attendance 30 March	Morning 180 + 130 SS. Total 310. Afternoon 100 + 80 SS. Total 180.
Average attendance	[Not given.]
Dated	31 March 1851.

Signed   Christopher Thompson, minister [1846–81].
Walker Parsonage, Newcastle on Tyne.
{1857   Attendance 350. 30 communicants.}   {B 167.}
[From 6 July 1846 the congregation met in a schoolroom at the Iron
and Alkali Works until the church was opened in 1848.]

12.12   Church of England, St Peter, Wallsend (553.1)
Population 1851: 5,721 (parish) 2,161 (township)

[Summary form]
Name   St Peter's, Wallsend.
Erected   [Consecrated 27 April] 1809 [by the Bishop of St
David's. Restored and enlarged 1892.]
Endowment [Not given.] [£289.]
Sittings   Free 220. Other 210. Total 430.
Usual attendance   250 + 35 SS. Total [285].
Afternoon 160. Total [160].
No [evening] service except during Lent.
Dated   [Not given.]
Signed   Wardle Shaw [cartwright].
Incumbent [John Armstrong 1830–71.]
{1857   Attendance 700. 70 communicants.}   {B 74.}
[Marriages that had previously been conducted in a schoolroom were
illegal, but the Act of 1807 legalised them and provided for a new
church to replace a small ruinous building. 'An Act for taking down
the present church, and providing a new church and churchyard in
the parish of Wallsend, in the County of Northumberland' (47 Geo.
III 8 August 1807).]

12.13   United Presbyterian, Waterloo Place, Blyth (553.79)
Name   United Presbyterian Church.
Erected   [Not given.] [Opened 1828, moved to Bridge Street in
1864.]
Building   Separate and entire building. Exclusively for a place of
worship except for a Sunday school.
Sittings   Free 10. Other 390. Total [400]. Standing room 100.
Attendance 30 March   Morning 200 + 150 SS. Total 350.
Evening 300. Total 300.
Average attendance   [Not given.]
Dated   31 March 1851.
Signed   Daniel Carmichael, minister [1829–60].
Waterloo, Blyth.

12.14   United Presbyterian, Norfolk Street, North Shields
(553.31)
Name   United Presbyterian Church.
Erected   About 1811. [1812. From 1821 the congregation met
                in a former Unitarian chapel in Norfolk Street, and in
                December 1857 moved to Northumberland Square,
                where the new building cost £1,800.]
Building   [Separate and entire. Exclusively used for worship.]
Sittings   Free 40. Other 366. Total [406].
Attendance 30 March   Morning 253. Total 253.
                        Afternoon 358. Total 358.
Average attendance   [Not given.]
Dated   31 March 1851.
Signed   Henry Erskine Fraser MA, minister [1845–56].
                79 Bedford St[reet], North Shields.
[In 1855 the afternoon service was replaced by an evening service.]

**12.15   United Presbyterian, Walker Iron Works, Chapel Street,
Walker** (553.51)
Name   United Presbyterian Church.
Erected   February 1838. [Rebuilt 1866.]
Building   A separate and entire building. Exclusively for a place
                of worship.
Sittings   Free 107. Other 100. Total [207].
Attendance 30 March   Morning 80 + 45 SS. Total [125].
                        Evening 92. Total [92].
Average attendance   [Not given.]
Remarks   This place of worship [Zion Chapel] was transferred
                from the New Connexion Methodists in June 1842.
Dated   30 March 1851.
Signed   James Watson AM, minister [1849–51].
                St Anthony's by Newcastle on Tyne.

12.16   United Presbyterian, High Street West, Wallsend (553.5)
Name   United Presbyterian Church.
Erected   1820. [Opened 1823. Moved to Border Road in 1866.]
Building   [Separate and entire. Exclusively used for worship.]
Sittings   [None free.] Other 260. Total [260].
Attendance 30 March   Morning 94 + 50 SS. Total 144.
                        Afternoon 86 + 30 SS. Total 116.
Average attendance   [Not given.]
Remarks   The number of sittings provided in the chapel is about

260. No particular part of the chapel is set apart for
free sittings, but any person who is not able to pay for
a sitting is provided with a free sitting.

Dated   31 March 1851.

Signed   Daniel Wilson, minister [1846–77].
Wallsend, near Newcastle.

12.17   English Presbyterian, Church Street, Blyth (553.75)

Name   Ebenezer Chapel.

Erected   1814. [New church in Waterloo Road opened 6 June
1876.]

Building   [Separate and entire. Exclusively used for worship.]

Sittings   [None free.] Other 250. Total [250]

Attendance 30 March   Morning 120 + 30 SS. Total 150.
Evening 250 + 15 SS. Total 265.

Average attendance   Morning 180 + 30 SS. Total 210.
Evening 250 + 20 SS. Total 270.

Remarks   No settled minister at present. The former minister [W.
Oscar Johnson 1845–51] having lately gone to America.

Dated   31 March 1851.

Signed   John Newman, elder (baker).
Blyth, Northumberland.

12.18   English Presbyterian, Howard Street, North Shields
(553.30)

Name   Scotch Church.

Erected   1811. [In 1817 some of the congregation formed St
Andrew's Chapel (**12.20**).]

Building   Separate [and entire]. Exclusively [used for worship].

Sittings   Free 100. Other 700. Total [800].

Attendance 30 March   Morning 600 + 60 SS. Total 660.

Average attendance   Morning 560 + 55 SS. Total 615.

Remarks   The stated minister of this congregation is at present
from home.

Dated   30 March 1851.

Signed   George Hall, elder [grocer and tea-dealer].
2 Newcastle Street, No[rth] Shields.

Minister   [George John Clark Duncan 1844–51.]

[The Trust Deed stipulated that the minister had to be of the Church
of Scotland.]

12.19   Independent [Congregational], Row Road, Howdon Pans
(553.13)

Name   Howdon Pans, Independent Chapel.
Erected   1835. [Opened 8 June 1835.]
Building   [Separate and entire. Exclusively used for worship.]
Sittings   [None free.] Other 350. Total [350].
Attendance 30 March   Morning 189 + 20 SS. Total 209.
                        Evening 138. Total 138.
Average attendance   Morning 170 + 30 SS. Total 200.
                        Evening 200. Total 200.
Remarks   Bible class on the Sabbath afternoon, twenty in
                attendance. The Lord's Supper administered every
                month on the first Sabbath in the afternoon. Forty-two
                communicants. Preaching every Tuesday night,
                attendance from twenty to fifty. Children's Testament
                Class for an hour on the Tuesday night for an hour,
                forty-five in attendance.
Dated   31 March 1851.
Signed   William Stead, minister, [1849–83].
                Willington, Newcastle on Tyne.

[On 17 November 1891 the Stead Memorial Church was opened
in memory of William Stead. He was the father of the newspaper
editor and spiritualist William Thomas Stead who lost his life on the
RMS *Titanic*. 'William Thomas Stead (1849–1912)', *ODNB*, vol. 52,
pp. 331–332.]

**12.20   Independent [Congregational], Camden Street, North
Shields** (553.29)

Name   St Andrew's Chapel.
Erected   1817.
Building   [Separate and entire. Exclusively used for worship.]
Sittings   Free 270. Other 715. Total [985].
Attendance 30 March   Morning 505 + 45 SS. Total 505 (*sic*) [550].
                        Evening 416. Total 416 (the ordinary
                        congregation).
Average attendance   [Not given.]
Remarks   As the Sabbath school is held in a separate building,
                very few of the children ordinarily attend public
                worship in the chapel.
Dated   30 March 1851.
Signed   Archibald Jack, minister [1834–67].
                [3] Lovaine Terrace, Bor[ough] of Tynemouth.

12.21   Independent [Congregational], Ropery Bank, North Shields (553.19)

Name   Bethel Chapel. [Ropery Bank Chapel.]
Erected   Before 1800.
Building   [Separate and entire. Exclusively used for worship.]
Sittings   Free 60. Other 240. Total [300]. Standing room 20.
Attendance 30 March   Morning 71 +30 SS. Total 101.
                Evening 93 + 25 SS. Total 118.
Average attendance   Morning 74 + 25 SS. Total 99.
                Evening 97 + 30 SS. Total 127.
Dated   31 March 1851.
Signed   Michael Henderson, minister [1844–67].
                81 Howard Street, North Shields.

12.22   Welsh Independent, Losh Street, Walker (553.54)

Name   Welsh Chapel.
Erected   1847. [In Zion Chapel, Chapel Street 1866–88.]
Building   A long room adjoining this house. [Exclusively used
                for worship.]
Sittings   Free 180. Other none. Total [180].
Attendance 30 March   Morning 78 SS. Total [78].
                Afternoon 84. Total 84
                Evening 105. Total 105.
Average attendance   Evening 100 + 70 SS. Total [170].
Dated   30 March 1851.
Signed   Michael Henderson, minister [1844–67].
                81 Howard Street, North Shields.

12.23   Baptist, Howard Street, North Shields (553.21)

Name   Baptist Chapel.
Erected   In 1846 in lieu of a chapel in Stephenson St[reet
                1799–1846], erected before 1800.
Building   [Separate and entire. Exclusively used for worship.]
Sittings   Free 100. Other 590. Total [690].
Attendance 30 March   Morning 220. Total 220.
                Evening 260. Total 260.
Average attendance   Morning 200. Total 200.
                Evening 280. Total 280.
Remarks   The […] profession of the great bulk of the
                people occasions great fluctuations in the Sabbath
                congregation.
Dated   31 March 1851.

Signed   John Donald Carrick, minister [1839–66].
17 Walker Place, Walker, North Shields.

12.24   Wesleyan Methodist, Benton Square (553.39 and 553.48)
Name   Benton Square Chapel.
Erected   1819.
Building   A separate building. Used only as a place of worship
and school.
Sittings   Free 160. Other 40. Total [200].
Attendance 30 March   [Not given.]
Average attendance   Morning 20. Total [20].
    Afternoon 40. Total [40].
    Evening 20. Total [20].
Dated   [Not given.]
Signed   George Brown, chapel steward [nail maker].
Waggoner's Row, Longbenton, Newcastle on Tyne.

(553.48)
Name   1st Benton Square Chapel.
2nd and a house at Waggoner's Row.
Erected   1st in 1816.
2nd first used in 1819.
Building   1st [Separate and entire. Exclusively used for worship.]
2nd [Not separate and entire or exclusively used for
worship.]
Sittings   1st Free 160. Other 40. Total [200]. 1st standing room 40
places.
2nd Free 50. Total [50].
Attendance 30 March   1st Morning 45. Total [45].
    2nd Afternoon 40. Total [40].
    1st Evening 3[0]. Total [30].
Average attendance   1st Morning 50 + 70 SS. Total 120.
    2nd Afternoon 30. Total 30.
    1st Evening 20 + 20 SS. Total 40.
Remarks   The upper part [of the estimated attendance] has not
been filled as the attendance is not truly represented
on account of the existing division in the Wesleyan
body.
Dated   31 March 1851.
Signed   George Brown, chapel steward [nail maker].
Waggoner's Row, Longbenton, Newcastle on Tyne.

12.25   Wesleyan Methodist, Ballast Hills, Blyth (553.74)
Name   Wesleyan Chapel.
Erected   1815. [Removed to Blyth Bridge 1867.]
Building   [Separate and entire. Exclusively used for worship.]
Sittings   Free 185. Other 315. Total [500].
Attendance 30 March   Morning 300 + 110 SS. Total 410.
                                   Afternoon 22. Total 22.
                                   Evening 400. Total 400.
Average attendance   Morning 350 + 120 SS. Total 470.
                                   Afternoon 40. Total 40.
                                   Evening 450 + 30 SS. Total 480.
Remarks   On 30 March the congregation was below the average
                     on account of a Sunday school anniversary at another
                     chapel [the Methodist New Connexion] in the town.
Dated   31 March 1851.
Signed   John Elam, minister [1849–50].
                     Bedlington, near Morpeth, Northumberland.
[John Elam was also the minister of Bedlington (**9.26**).]

12.26   Wesleyan Methodist, Buddle Street, Carville (553.7)
Name   [Not given. Carville Chapel.]
Erected   [Not given. Opened 12 January 1812. New chapel
                     opened on 16 May 1906.]
Building   [Not separate and entire or exclusively used for
                     worship.]
Sittings   Free 50. Total [50].
Attendance 30 March   Afternoon 15. Total [15].
                                   Evening 24. Total [24].
Average attendance   [Not given.]
Dated   31 March 1851.
Signed   John Scott, steward [joiner at colliery].
                     Wallsend, n[ea]r, Newcastle Tyne.

12.27   Wesleyan Methodist, Chirton (553.16)
Name   None.
Erected   1820.
Building   [Not separate and entire or exclusively used for
                     worship.]
Sittings   Free 100. Other 40. Total [140].
Attendance 30 March   Afternoon 50 + 20 SS. Total 70.
                                   Evening 49 + 15 SS. Total 64.
Average attendance   Afternoon 54 + 20 SS. Total 74.

Evening 56 + 14 SS. Total 70.

Dated   31 March 1851.
Signed   Charles Turnbull, chapel steward (draper) [linen and wool].
            Chirton.

12.28   Wesleyan Methodist, East Cramlington Colliery (553.84)

Name   Wesleyan Chapel.
Erected   1833.
Building [Separate and entire. Also used as a] day school.
Sittings Free 216. Other 27. Total [243].
Attendance 30 March   Morning 62 + 139. Total [201].
            Evening 66. Total [66].
Average attendance   [Not given.]
Dated   31 March 1851.
Signed   Edward Shield, society steward [mason].
            East Cramlington.

12.29   Wesleyan Methodist, West Cramlington Colliery (553.85)

Name   None.
Erected   In the year 1849.
Building [Separate and entire. Exclusively used for worship.]
Sittings Free 114. Other 56. Total [170].
Attendance 30 March   Morning 106 SS. Total 106.
            Afternoon 104. Total 104.
            Evening 103. Total 103.
Average attendance   [Not given.]
Dated   31 March 1851.
Signed   Thomas P. Edgar, steward [grocer and flour-dealer].
            West Cramlington, Newcastle on Tyne.

12.30   Wesleyan Methodist, Earsdon (553.67)

Name   Wesleyan Centenary Chapel.
Erected   1839.
Building [Separate and entire. Exclusively used for worship.]
Sittings Free 160. Other 350. Total [510].
Attendance 30 March   Morning 100. Total 100.
            Afternoon 63 SS. Total 63.
            Evening 110. Total 110.
Average attendance   Morning 250. Total 250.
            Afternoon 110 SS. Total 110.
            Evening 300. Total 300.

Dated   31 March 1851.
Signed   William Laidman, steward to the trustees.
            Hartley, near North Shields.

12.31   Wesleyan Methodist, Hazlerigg (553.40)
Name   Wesleyan Methodist Chapel.
Erected   In the year 1830. [Enlarged 1862.]
Building [Separate and entire. Exclusively used for worship.]
Sittings Free 80. Other 50. Total [130].
Attendance 30 March Morning 56 SS. Total 56.
            Afternoon 50 + 30 SS. Total 80.
            Evening 50 + 20 SS. Total 70.
Average attendance   Morning 60 SS. Total 60.
            Afternoon 50 + 30 SS. Total 80.
            Evening 50 + 20 SS. Total 70.
Dated   31 March 1851.
Signed   Edward Davidson, steward [collector of poor rates].
            Hazlerigg, near Newcastle upon Tyne.

12.32   Wesleyan Methodist, West Holywell Colliery (553.65)
Name   Holywell Chapel.
Erected   Year 1829.
Building [Separate and entire. Exclusively used for worship.]
Sittings Free 70. Other 50. Total [120].
Attendance 30 March Afternoon 34. Total 34.
            Evening 64. Total 64.
Average attendance   Afternoon 50 + 10 SS. Total 60.
            Evening 70. Total 70.
Dated   31 March 1851.
Signed   John Hedley, steward [cashier].
            [West] Holywell Colliery, Earsdon, Newcastle on Tyne.

12.33   Wesleyan Methodist, Chapel Street, Howdon Pans (553.15)
Name   Wesleyan Chapel.
Erected   In 1805. [Building sold to the Salvation Army in 1887.]
Building [Separate and entire. Exclusively used for worship.]
Sittings Free 130. Other 200. Total [330].
Attendance 30 March Morning 130 + 54 SS. Total 184.
            Afternoon 59 SS. Total 59.
            Evening 160. Total 160.
Average attendance   [Not given.]
Dated   31 March 1851.

Signed   Joseph Salkeld, trustee [sail maker].
             [Chapel Street], Howdon, near Newcastle on Tyne.

12.34   Wesleyan Methodist, West Moor, Killingworth (553.43)

Name   West Moor, Wesleyan Methodist Chapel.
Erected   1815.
Building   [Separate and entire. Exclusively used for worship.]
Sittings   Free 130. Other 130. Total [260].
Attendance 30 March   Morning 66 SS. Total 66.
                       Afternoon 50. Total 50.
                       Evening 70. Total 70.
Average attendance   [Not given.]
Dated   30 March 1851.
Signed   George Gray, steward, minor (*sic*) [coal miner].
             West Moor Colliery, West Moor.

12.35   Wesleyan Methodist, Killingworth (553.45)

Name   Wesleyan Methodist Chapel.
Erected   1834.
Building   [Separate and entire. Exclusively used for worship.]
Sittings   Free 100. Other 50. Total [150].
Attendance 30 March   Morning 30. Total [30].
                       Evening 30. Total [30].
Average attendance   [Not given.]
Dated   30 March 1851.
Signed   Henry Jefferson, Wesleyan local preacher [commercial
             agent].
             60 Eldon Street, Newcastle on Tyne.

12.36   Wesleyan Methodist, Longbenton (553.46)

Name   Gosforth Wesleyan Chapel.
Erected   1841.
Building   [Separate and entire. Used for worship and] also a day
             school.
Sittings   Free 100. Other 40. Total [140]. Standing room 20.
Attendance 30 March   Afternoon 31 + 38 SS. Total 69.
                       Evening 81 + 6 SS. Total 87.
Average attendance   [Not given.]
Dated   30 March 1851.
Signed   Joseph Hays, steward [coal miner, overman].
             Gosforth, near Newcastle on Tyne.

12.37   Wesleyan Methodist, Monkseaton (553.36)
Name   Wesleyan Chapel.
Erected   1843.
Building   [Separate and entire. Exclusively used for worship.]
Sittings   Free 170. Other 30. Total [200].
Attendance 30 March   Evening 38 + 17 SS. Total 55.
Average attendance   [Not given.]
Dated   30 March 1851.
Signed   Robert Bell, steward (grocer).
              Monkseaton, No[rth] Shields.

12.38   Wesleyan Methodist, New York (553.22)
Name   New York Chapel.
Erected   11 January 1823.
Building   [Separate and] entire building. Place of worship and
              Sunday school.
Sittings   Free 89. Other 60. Total [149]. Standing room 20 or 30.
Attendance 30 March   Morning 100. Total 100.
                       Afternoon 70 SS. Total 70.
                       Evening 145. Total 145.
Average attendance   [Not given.]
Remarks   The number of hearers cannot be ascertained for any
              specified number of months, but they will be about
              100 in the morning, from that up to 200 in the evening.
              The Sabbath scholars fluctuate between 50 and 100.
Dated   30 March 1851.
Signed   John Hunter, chapel steward [collier's agent].
              [3 Quality Row], Backworth, Newcastle upon Tyne.

12.39   Wesleyan Methodist, Howard Street, North Shields
(553.20)
Name   Howard Street, Wesleyan Chapel.
Erected   1808. [Moved to Tynemouth Road in 1889.]
Building   [Separate and entire. Exclusively used for worship.]
Sittings   Free 300. Other 1,200. Total [1,500].
Attendance 30 March   Morning 600 + 126 SS. Total 726.
                       Evening 800. Total 800.
Average attendance   Morning 800 + 150 SS. Total 950.
                       Evening 1,000. Total 1,000.
Dated   31 March 1851.
Signed   Robert Leake, minister [1850–51].
              Howard Street, North Shields.

12.40   Wesleyan Methodist, Seaton Delaval (553.62)

Name   Wesleyan Methodist Chapel.
Erected   1845.
Building   A separate and entire building. A place of worship
                exclusively.
Sittings   Free 140. Other 120. Total [260].
Attendance 30 March   Afternoon 202. Total [202].
                        Evening 141. Total [141].
Average attendance   [Not given.]
Dated   31 March 1851.
Signed   Robert Patterson, chapel steward [engine man].
                [Double Row], Seaton Delaval, near North Shields.

12.41   Wesleyan Methodist Schoolroom, Seatonburn (553.41)

Name   Seatonburn Village School.
Erected   August 1833.
Building   [Separate and entire. Used for worship and] also as
                day school.
Sittings   Free about 300. Other none. Total [300].
Attendance 30 March   Afternoon 53 + 25 SS. Total 78.
                        Evening 67 + 15 SS. Total 82.
Average attendance   Afternoon 100 + 35 SS. Total 135.
                        Evening 130. Total 130.
Remarks   The building is lent to the Wesleyans by the Rev.
                R[alph] H[enry] Brandling and Rev. Rich[ard] Clayton
                of the Church of England.
Dated   30 March 1851.
Signed   Henry Elliot, local preacher.
                Walter Thompson, class leader.

[Richard Clayton, the Master of St Mary Magdalene Hospital and
chaplain of St Thomas' Chapel, Newcastle upon Tyne (**10.10**). Ralph
Henry Brandling of Gosforth House. Following his death in 1836 his
library of over 1,000 books, portraits and prints was sold by auction
over the course of nine days.]

12.42   Wesleyan Methodist, Walker (553.55)

Name   Walker Chapel.
Erected   1839. [Opened 1 January 1840, replaced 12 September
                1872.]
Building   An entire building. Part used for a day school.
Sittings   Free 250. Other 108. Total [358].
Attendance 30 March   Morning 40 + 52 SS. Total 92.

Afternoon Sunday school.
Evening 117. Total 117.
Average attendance   Morning and afternoon 130 + 60 SS. Total 190.
Dated   31 March 1851.
Signed   Cuth[ber]t Hunter, trustee [brick and tile
             manufacturer].
             Walker Cottage, near Newcastle upon Tyne.

12.43   Wesleyan Methodist, Wallsend (553.8)
Name   Wesleyan Methodist Chapel.
Erected   1820.
Building   [Separate and entire. Exclusively used for worship and
             a] day school.
Sittings   Free 250. Other 48. Total [298].
Attendance 30 March   Morning 88 SS. Total [88].
             Afternoon 50 + 34 SS. Total [84].
             Evening 40 + 20 SS. Total [60].
Average attendance   [Not given.]
Dated   31 March 1851.
Signed   Edward Horsley, manager [agent to Whitley Colliery].
             Willington, Newcastle upon Tyne.

12.44   Wesleyan Methodist, Whitley (553.37b)
[Summary form]
No service has been performed here since the beginning of March
1850.
31 August 1852.
William Harrison [registrar.]
[Dockwray Square, North Shields.]

12.45   Wesleyan Methodist, Willington (553.9)
Name   Willington [Gardens, a] dwelling house.
Erected   Commenced to be used as a place of worship in 1837.
Building   [Separate and entire. Exclusively used for worship. In
             another hand, no.]
Sittings   Free 110. Total [110].
Attendance 30 March   Afternoon 73 (children and adults). Total [73].
             Evening 64 (children and adults). Total [64].
Average attendance   Afternoon 90. Total [90].
Dated   31 March 1851.
Signed   Frederick Watson, steward.
             Willington Colliery, N[ew]castle, Northumberland.

12.46 Methodist New Connexion, Cowpen (553.77)

Name Zion Chapel.

Erected In the year 1818. [In 1866 a new chapel was opened in Waterloo Road, and a year later a group of seceders opened an independent chapel in Stanley Street, Blyth.]

Building A separate and entire building. Exclusively as a place of worship.

Sittings Free 150. Other 400. Total [550]. Standing room 100 persons.

Attendance 30 March Morning 130 + 80 SS. Total 210.

Evening 300 + 30 SS. Total 330.

Average attendance [Not given.]

Dated 31 March 1851.

Signed John Charlton Alder, chapel steward [boot and shoe manufacturer].

[Market Place], Blyth, Northumberland.

12.47 Methodist New Connexion, Hartley (553.68)

Name New Connexion Chapel.

Erected 1838.

Building An entire building. Exclusively as a place of worship and a Sunday school.

Sittings Free 42. Other 66. Total [108]. Standing room 30 persons.

Attendance 30 March Afternoon 30 + 30 SS. Total 60.

Evening 50 + 12 SS. Total 62.

Average attendance Afternoon 40 + 22 SS. Total 62.

Evening 60 + 8 SS. Total 68.

Remarks I here have given you, as far as I can, a correct statement as our attendance is very fluctuating.

Dated 30 March 1851.

Signed Mark Hedby, chapel steward.

Seaton Sluice, near North Shields, Northumberland.

12.48 Methodist New Connexion, West Moor, Killingworth (553.58)

Name New Chaple (*sic*).

Erected 1822.

Building Separate [and entire. Used for] publick (*sic*) worship and Sunday school.

Sittings Free 100. Other 88. Total [188].

Attendance 30 March Morning 110 SS. Total [110].
                       Afternoon 50. Total [50].
                       Evening 50. Total [50].
Average attendance   Morning 100 + 110 SS. Total [210].
Dated   31 March 1851.
Signed   Thomas Ridley [retired coal miner].
               William Horton, steward.

12.49   Methodist New Connexion, Milburn Place, South Street, North Shields (553.18)

Name   Milburn Place Chaple (*sic*).
Erected   About the year 1790. [1786.]
Building   [Separate and entire] with dwelling rooms underneath
               the chapel. Exclusively for worship on Sundays,
               Wednesdays and Fridays.
Sittings   Free 150 (all with comfortable seats). Other 450.
               Total [600].
Attendance 30 March Morning 300 + 80 SS. Total 380.
                       Afternoon, a class meeting [for fellowship
                       and pastoral care].
                       Evening 350 + 40 SS. Total 390.
Average attendance   Morning 300 + 80 SS. Total 380 [during
                       winter months].
                       Evening 350 + 40 SS. Total 390 [during winter
                       months].
Remarks   Soon after the chaple (*sic*) was built, John Wesley
               agreed to send preachers to preach in the said chaple
               (*sic*) if the trustees would turn or sign it over to
               the Wesleyan Conference, to wich (*sic*) the trustees
               objected, and about the year 1800 [Alexander] Kilham,
               the first Wesleyan Reformer, sent a supply of preachers
               and it has continued a New Connexion Methodist
               Society till [today].
Dated   31 March 1851.
Signed   Benjamin Pearson, member and trustee [steamboat
               proprietor].
               Milburn Place, North Shields, Northumberland.

[On 11 April 1789 John Wesley wrote to three of the preachers in the Newcastle circuit about the situation at the chapel and ordered them to communicate with Edward Coates. 'Will you, or will you not, settle the house at Milburn Place, North Shields, on the Methodist Plan? If he will not do it within another week, I further require that none of you preach in that house, unless you will renounce all connection with your affectionate brother, John Wesley. I am at a point I will be trifled with no longer.' L. Tyerman, *The Life and Times of the Rev John Wesley MA* (London, 1890), vol. 3, p. 573.]

12.50   Methodist New Connexion, Linskill Street, North Shields (553.34)

Name   Salem Chapel.
Erected   Erected in 1836 in lieu of the 'Low Chapel' occupied since 1815.
Building   Separate and entire. Exclusively used as a place of worship, except as a Sunday school.
Sittings   Free 150. Other 500. Total [650].
Attendance 30 March   Morning 160 + 60 SS. Total [220].
                Afternoon 70 SS. Total [70].
                Evening 200. Total [200].
Average attendance   [Not given.]
Dated   3 April 1851.
Signed   John Beasley, minister.
                12 West Percy Street, North Shields.

12.51   Methodist New Connexion, Wallsend (553.6)

Name   None.
Erected   1830. [1835.]
Building   Separate building. A place of worship and day school. No Sunday school.
Sittings   All free sittings.
Attendance 30 March   Morning no service.
                Afternoon 35. Total [35].
                Evening 25. Total [25].
Average attendance   [Not given.]
Dated   31 March 1851.
Signed   Edward Moore, grocer [local preacher].
                Wallsend, near Newcastle on Tyne.

[In 1841 the congregation was much affected by the schism instigated by Joseph Barker (**10.35**).]

12.52   Methodist New Connexion, Whitley (553.37c)

[Summary form]
Primitive Methodist Chapel was many months, previous to July 1851, altogether closed, was opened twelve months since, by the

'Methodist New Connexion' Reformers. Service afternoon and evening. Sittings all free. Congregation averaging 30.
31 August 1852.
William Harrison, [registrar].
[Dockwray Square, North Shields.]

12.53   Primitive Methodist, Benton Square (553.49)
Name   Primitive Methodist Chapel.
Erected   1833. [Rebuilt and enlarged 1904.]
Building   [Separate and entire. Exclusively used for worship.]
Sittings   Free 200. Other 28. Total [228]. Standing room none.
Attendance 30 March   Morning 90 SS. Total [90].
                        Afternoon 80. Total [80].
                        Evening 56. Total [56].
Average attendance   [Not given.]
Dated   30 March 1851.
Signed   Ralph Dawson, chapel steward [coal miner, hewer].
              Benton Square, near Killingworth, Newcastle on Tyne.
[In July 1823 thousands of people attended a camp meeting at Scaffold Hill, near Benton Square, and 20 people professed conversion. Ralph Dawson and his two brothers Thomas and Matthew were well-known Primitive Methodists. 'Benton Square has thus exercised an enormous influence over a large number of societies and circuits' (W.M. Patterson, *Northern Primitive Methodism* (London, 1909), p. 344). Inscription: 'Benton Square Methodist Chapel stood on this site. Built by the miners in 1833. Used continuously until it closed in Nov(ember) 1977.']

12.54   Primitive Methodist, York Street, Cowpen Quay, Blyth (553.78)
Name   None.
Erected   1850. And opened for divine worship 5 May [18]50.
Building   It is a building of two stories. We occupy the lower part and above us are two rooms. [Not exclusively used for worship] we have a week day school as well as a Sabbath school.
Sittings   Free 72. Other 32. Total [104]. [On] special occasions thirty may be seen standing.
Attendance 30 March   Morning 76 SS (these are there at 9 o'clock in am). Total 76.
                        Afternoon 70. Total [70].
                        Evening 90. Total [90].

Average attendance   Morning 60 SS. Total 60.
Afternoon 30. Total [30].
Evening 100. Total 90 (*sic*). Total [100].
Remarks   The reason we assign for our attendance not being
so good today as it regularly is, so owing to a special
service which was held in the Methodist New
Connexion chapel.
Dated   31 March 1851.
Signed   William Gleghorn, local preacher and leader [draper
and grocer].
Cowpen Quay, Blyth.

12.55   Primitive Methodist, West Cramlington Colliery (553.86)
Name   Primitive Methodist Chapel.
Erected   1850.
Building   [Separate and entire. Exclusively used for worship.]
Sittings   Free 148. Other 52. Total [200]. Standing room none.
Attendance 30 March   Morning 58 + 14 SS. Total 72.
Afternoon 92 SS. Total 92.
Evening 130 + 30 SS. Total 160.
Average attendance   [Not given.]
Dated   31 March 1851.
Signed   Christopher Stoddart, chapel steward.
West Cramlington Colliery, Northumberland.
['West Cramlington was the centre of the most vigorous, intelligent
and spiritual societies I ever beheld.' W.M. Patterson, *Northern
Primitive Methodism* (London, 1909), p. 348.]

12.56   Primitive Methodist, Earsdon (553.64)
Name   Earsdon Primitive Methodist Chapel.
Erected   1834. [Rebuilt 1886.]
Building   [Separate and entire. Exclusively used for worship.]
Sittings   Free 100. Other 72. Total [172].
Attendance 30 March   Morning 84 SS. Total [84].
Afternoon 50. Total [50].
Evening 96. Total [96].
Average attendance   Morning 74 SS. Total [74].
Afternoon 50. Total [50].
Evening 90. Total [90].
Dated   31 March 1851.
Signed   Edward Dunn, chapel steward [boot and shoe maker].
Earsdon, Newcastle upon Tyne.

12.57 Primitive Methodist, Hartley (553.69)

Name Primitive Methodist Chapel.
Erected 1825. [New chapel 1885.]
Building Separate and entire. Exclusive[ly used for worship].
Sittings Free 150. Other 20. Total [170]. Standing room 30.
Attendance 30 March Morning [Sunday] school.
Afternoon 65 SS. Total 73 (*sic*) [65].
Evening 80 SS. Total [80].
Average attendance [Not given.]
Dated 30 March 1851.
Signed John Dawson, class leader [coal miner].
Hartley.

[In the Hartley Pit disaster of January 1862, 204 men and boys were killed. A prayer meeting was held by those trapped underground, four of whom were Primitive Methodists. By the tragedy 407 were left destitute and a relief fund raised £82,000 for the weekly support of the bereaved families. A monument to the deceased miners was erected in Earsdon churchyard.]

12.58 Primitive Methodist, Killingworth Colliery (553.44)

Name Primitive Methodist Chapel.
Erected 1838.
Building Separate building. Exclusively a place of worship.
Sittings Free 166. Other 50. Total [216].
Attendance 30 March Morning 150. Total [150].
Afternoon 80. Total [80].
Average attendance [Not given.]
Dated 28 March 1851.
Signed J. Boral, James Cossar [coal miner].
George Orton [coal miner], manager of Killingworth Colliery.

12.59 Primitive Methodist, Longbenton (553.47)

Name An inhabited private dwelling house.
Erected Established four months.
Building A private house. Only a place of worship.
Sittings All free. Standing room for 76.
Attendance 30 March Morning 50. Total [50].
Evening 70. Total [70].
Average attendance [Not given.]
Dated 30 March 1851.

Signed   John Gray, manager and householder [coal miner, hewer].
Gosforth Row, Longbenton.

12.60   Primitive Methodist, Union Street, North Shields (553.35)

[Summary sheet]

Name   Primitive Methodist Connexion Chapel.
Erected   Purchased by the Connexion [from the Wesleyan Methodists] in 1825 [and moved to Saville Street in 1861].
Building   [Separate and entire.] Exclusively [used for worship].
Sittings   Free 200. Other 250. Total [450].
Attendance 30 March   Morning no service. 100 SS. Total 100.
                Afternoon 200 + 100 SS. Total 300.
                Evening 350. Total 350.
Average attendance   [Not given.]
Dated   [Not given.]
Signed   For Thomas Smith [steamboat owner]. [... ...]
[On top of the page: The Rev. Thomas Smith, Primitive Methodist minister, 27 Nile Street.]

12.61   Primitive Methodist, Seaton Delaval (553.71)

Name   Primitive Methodist Chapel.
Erected   1845.
Building   Separate and entire. [Exclusively used for worship and] a day school also.
Sittings   Free 185. Other 165. Total [350].
Attendance 30 March   Afternoon 250. Total 250.
                Evening 350. Total 350.
Average attendance   Afternoon 250. Total 250.
                Evening 350. Total 350.
Dated   30 March 1851.
Signed   William Robinson, chapel steward [coal miner].
                128 Delaval Colliery.
[In 1849 there were 150 members at Seaton Delaval. In 1859, when the colliers were on strike, nine men from Seaton Delaval were arrested and eight spent two months in the County Gaol at Morpeth. Of the men, all were teetotallers and six were Primitive Methodists (two of whom were local preachers).]

12.62   Primitive Methodist, Seghill (553.61)
Name   Primitive Methodist Chapel.
Erected   1838. [New chapel 1891.]
Building   [Separate and entire. Exclusively used for worship.]
Sittings   Free 122. Other 78. Total [200]. Standing room none.
Attendance 30 March   Morning 130. Total 130.
                         Afternoon 88 SS. Total 88.
                         Evening 120. Total 120.
Average attendance   [Not given.]
Dated   31 March 1851.
Signed   Thomas Harrison, steward [coal miner].
              Seghill, Northumberland.

12.63   Primitive Methodist, Walker (553.53)
Name   None.
Erected   [June] 1850.
Building   [Separate and entire. Exclusively used for worship.]
Sittings   Free 50. Other none. Total [50].
Attendance 30 March   Morning 18 + 12 SS. Total 30.
                         Evening 20 + 7 SS. Total 27.
Average attendance   Morning 20. Total 20.
                        Evening 40. Total 40.
Remarks   The place occupied as a chapel, was erected for a
              stable about 1830, and converted into a chapel, June
              1850. The school in connexion (*sic*) with the above
              chapel was commenced in February last.
Dated   31 March 1851.
Signed   Thomas Scott, leader and local preacher [engine man].
              124 Chapel Street, Walker, Newcastle upon Tyne.
['What Thomas Scott and his family did for Primitive Methodism
in Walker cannot be computed.' W.M. Patterson, *Northern Primitive
Methodism* (London, 1909), p. 324.]

12.64   Primitive Methodist, Portugal Place, Wallsend (553.4)
Name   Primitive Methodist Chaple (*sic*).
Erected   1829. [Rebuilt 1871.]
Building   A separate and entire building. For both [worship and
              Sunday school].
Sittings   Free 70. Other 70. Total [140]. Standing room 60.
Attendance 30 March   Morning 94. Total [94].
                         Afternoon 38*. Total [38].
                         Evening 58*. Total [58].

Average attendance   [Not given.]
Remarks   *This number is from two branch societies held in two dwelling houses.
Dated   30 March 1851.
Signed   William Daglish, class leader [linseed oil press man]. Walker Oil Mill, near Newcastle on Tyne, Northumberland.

12.65   Primitive Methodist, East Terrace, Willington Quay (553.12)

Name   Primitive Methodist Chapel.
Erected   In the year of our Lord 1844. [New chapel opened 17 April 1881.]
Building   [Separate and] entire. [Exclusively used for worship.]
Sittings   Free 100. Other 136. Total [236].
Attendance 30 March   Morning 133 SS. Total 133.
                  Afternoon 150. Total 150.
                  Evening 160. Total 160.
Average attendance   [Not given.]
Dated   31 March 1851.
Signed   Joseph Salkeld, steward [ballast assessor]. Willington Quay.

12.66   Wesleyan Reformers Schoolroom, Bigges Main (553.57)

Name   Wesleyan Chapel Reformers.
Erected   1821.
Building   [Separate and] entire. [Exclusively used for worship.]
Sittings   Free 200. Other 54. Total [254].
Attendance 30 March   Morning 70 + 138 SS. Total 208.
                  Evening 70 + 20 SS. Total 90.
Average attendance   Morning 65 + 140 SS. Total 205.
                  Evening 65 + 20 SS. Total 85.
Dated   31 March 1851.
Signed   John Laws, steward [under-viewer]. Bigges Main, Newcastle Tyne.

12.67   Wesleyan Reformers, Earsdon (553.82)

Name   None.
Erected   [Not given.]
Building   [Not separate and entire or exclusively used for worship.]
Sittings   [Not given.]

Attendance 30 March   Afternoon 76. Total [76].
                     Evening 89. Total [89].
Average attendance   Afternoon 70. Total [70].
                     Evening 80. Total [80].
Remarks   The services are held in a dwelling house.
Dated   30 March 1851.
Signed   John Thompson, manager.
              West Holywell Colliery, n[ea]r Earsdon, Newcastle
              upon Tyne.

12.68   Wesleyan Reformers, Longbenton (553.42)
Name   Wesleyan Chapel.
Erected   1811.
Building   [Separate and entire. Exclusively used for worship.]
Sittings   Free 150. Total [150]. Standing room 50.
Attendance 30 March   Morning 15 + 13 SS. Total 28.
                     Evening 45 + 46 SS. Total 91.
Average attendance   Morning 20 + 15 SS. Total 35.
                     Evening 60 + 30 SS. Total 90.
Remarks   This chapel is the private property of a gentleman
              who allows the gratuitous use of the place for public
              worship and Sabbath school, and considering the
              smallness of the population, and that there is two
              other places for worship, we consider we have
              generally a fair proportionate share of hearers to the
              present population.
Dated   31 March 1851.
Signed   Thomas Everate, steward.
              Byker Hill, n[ea]r Newcastle on Tyne.

12.69   Wesleyan Reformers, Norfolk Street, North Shields
(553.32)
Name   Temperance Hall.
Erected   [Not given. From 1850 then moved to Howard Street
              in 1857.]
Building   [Not separate and entire or exclusively used for
              worship.]
Sittings   Free 450. Total [450].
Attendance 30 March   Morning 350 + 70 SS. Total [420].
                     Afternoon 110 SS. Total [110].
                     Evening 450. Total 450.
Average attendance   Evening 500. Total [500].

Remarks   The Temperance Hall was opened as a place of
worship about three months ago. The tyranny of
Wesleyan ministers is [increasing?]. Good men from
the Society was the occasion of its being opened.
Religious services conducted chiefly by local
preachers.
Dated   31 March 1851.
Signed   Jos. Green, Sunday school sup[erintenden]t.
53 Church Road, North Shields.

12.70   Wesleyan Reformers, Percy Main (553.17)

Name   Percy Main Chapel.
Erected   About 1813.
Building   [Separate and entire. Exclusively used for worship.]
Sittings   Free 20. Other 30. Total [50].
Attendance 30 March   Afternoon 42. Total [42].
Evening 44. Total [44].
Average attendance   [Not given.]
Dated   30 March 1851.
Signed   Joseph Read, steward.
Percy Main.

12.71   Wesleyan Reformers Schoolroom, Seaton Sluice (553.66)

Name   Schoolroom.
Erected   Before 1800.
Building   [Not separate and entire or exclusively used for
worship.]
Sittings   Free 250. Other none. Total [250].
Attendance 30 March   Morning 200. Total 200.
Afternoon 40. Total 40.
Evening 300. Total [300].
Average attendance   [Not given.]
Dated   31 March 1851.
Signed   Robert Gray, leader.
Seaton Sluice, North Shields.

12.72   Wesleyan Reformers, Walker (553.56)

Name   None. A room [crossed out].
Erected   23 October 1837.
Building   [Not separate and entire but exclusively used for
worship.]
Sittings   All free. Total 80.

Attendance 30 March   Morning 29. Total 29.
                        Evening 56. Total 56.
Average attendance   [Not given.]
Dated   31 March 1851.
Signed   John Woodifield, steward.
               Walker, n[ea]r Newcastle on Tyne.

12.73   Wesleyan Reformers, Wallsend (553.3)
Name   Wesleyan Reform Chapel.
Erected   [12 January] 1812. [New chapel erected 1870.]
Building   [Separate and] entire. [Exclusively] used for both.
Sittings   Free 250. Other 150. Total [400].
Attendance 30 March   Afternoon 120. Total [120].
                        Evening 160. Total [160].
Average attendance   Morning 140 + 180 SS. Total [320].
Dated   30 March 1851.
Signed   John Reay, trustee [under-viewer and cashier].
               Wallsend, Northumberland.
[In 1850, John Reay, his wife and about 100 other people became
members of the Wesleyan Reformers. Under them the numbers
increased to 400 members and with 500 in the Sunday school. W.R.
Sunman, *The History of Free Methodism in and about Newcastle upon
Tyne* (Newcastle, 1902), pp. 50–57.]

12.74   Wesleyan Reformers, Wallsend (553.2)
Name   Temperance Hall.
Erected   1840.
Building   [Not separate and entire or exclusively used for
               worship.]
Sittings   All free. Total [200]. Standing room all free.
Attendance 30 March   Morning 46. Total 46.
                        Evening 20. Total 20.
Average attendance   Morning 40. Total 40.
                        Evening 20. Total 20.
Remarks   This hall seats about 200 persons and is occupied by
               this denomination mornings and evenings only.
Dated   31 March 1851.
Signed   Robert Plues, steward [grocer and] (confectioner).
               Howdon, near Newcastle – Tyne.

12.75   Wesleyan Reformers, Walker Place, Westheath (553.37a)
[Summary form]
Walker Place Methodist meeting is a 'Reformed' Methodist Chapel.
It is called the 'Branch Society of Wesleyan Methodists'. Service
is performed in the evenings (Sunday) only. The congregation
averages 50. Sittings all free. A morning and afternoon Sunday
school under the direction of Robert Swift is held in the chapel. The
scholars (children) average about 35.
31 August 1852.
William Harrison [registrar].
[Dockwray Square, North Shields.]

12.76   Wesleyan Reformers, Willington Quay (553.11)
Name   Willington Quay Methodist.
Erected   1840. [Rebuilt 1866.]
Building   A separate and entire building. Used as a school.
              Morning for worship afternoon and night.
Sittings   Free 96. Other 36. Total [132].
Attendance 30 March   Morning 83 SS. Total [83].
                        Afternoon 45. Total [45].
                        Evening 50. Total [50].
Average attendance   [Not given.]
Dated   30 March 1851.
Signed   John Richardson, chapel steward [cashier].
              Willington Quay, near Newcastle on Tyne,
              Northumberland.

**12.77   Non-denominational, 'Primitive Christians or Disciples of
Christ', Brunton Street, Howdon** (553.14)
Name   Temperance Hall.
Erected   1840.
Building   [Not separate and entire or exclusively used for
              worship.]
Sittings   All free. Total [200]. Standing room all free.
Attendance 30 March   Afternoon 15. [SS] none. Total [15].
Average attendance   Afternoon 15. Total [15].
Remarks   This place of worship, the Temp[eranc]e Hall, will seat
              about 200 persons, and is used by this denomination
              only on Sabbath afternoons.
Dated   31 March 1851.
Signed   William Ramshaw, deacon (coal trimmer).
              Howdon, near Newcastle – Tyne.

12.78   Non-denominational, 'Unsectarian. Supplied by various denominations, Evangelical', Willington Ropery, Willington Quay (553.10)

Name   Home Mission Chapel.
Erected   1845.
Building   Separate and entire. Used for British School for girls.
Sittings   Free 150. Total [150].
Attendance 30 March   Afternoon 40 SS. Total 40.
                        Evening 45. Total [45].
Average attendance   [Not given.]
Remarks   This building erected by Robert Hood Haggie
               gratuitously for the education of the poor children at
               23 per week (*sic*) and for preaching the gospel on the
               Sabbath evenings free of charge. Day scholars 100 on
               books, 70 to 80 in attendance.
Dated   30 March 1851.
Signed   Robert Hood Haggie, deacon or elder [rope
               manufacturer].
               Willington Villa, n[ea]r Newcastle on Tyne.
[Robert Haggie, a Congregationalist, was a member of the St Paul's
Congregational Church (**10.4**).]

12.79   Society of Friends [Quakers], Stephenson Street, North Shields (553.33)

Name   Stephenson Street, North Shields.
Erected   About 1800. [Erected 1801, enlarged 1849.]
Building   [Separate and entire. Exclusively used for worship]
               except being occasionally lent for benevolent objects
               without any charge.
Sittings   Estimate of persons seated, 400. Total [400].
               Floor area 1,995 [square] feet. No gallery. Total 1,995
               [square] feet.
Attendance 30 March   Morning 78. Total [78].
                        Afternoon no meeting.
                        Evening 85. Total [85].
Remarks   The space listed for meetings for worship on ordinary
               occasions is only 1,190 [square] feet, being divided
               from the remainder by movable shutters.
Dated   31 (3rd month) 1851.
Signed   John R. Trotter [general agent and provision
               merchant].
               [Dockway Square], North Shields.

12.80   Roman Catholic, Cowpen (553.80)

Name   St Cuthbert's.
Erected   1840. [Opened 1842, enlarged 1860.]
Building   [Separate and entire. Exclusively used for worship.]
Sittings   Free 105 (including 45 for children). Other 95. Total
                [200]. Standing room 30.
Attendance 30 March   Morning 180 + 40 SS. Total 220.
                         Afternoon about 60 + 35 SS. Total 95.
Average attendance   [Not given.]
Remarks   There are in this congregation about 400 Catholics,
                including children. About 100 are from four to six
                miles from Cowpen, the rest are within three miles.
Dated   30 March 1851.
Signed   James Wilfrid Burchall, Catholic priest [1845–66].
                Cowpen, Morpeth, Northumberland.

12.81   Roman Catholic, Bedford Street, North Shields (553.27)

Name   St Cuthbert's Catholic Church.
Erected   1824. [Opened 14 June 1821.]
Building   [Separate and entire. Exclusively used for worship.]
Sittings   Free 166 (unlet). Other 334 (let). Total [500]. Standing
                room 100.
Attendance 30 March   Morning 200 (two services) + 168 SS.
                         Total [368].
                         Evening 550. Total [550].
Average attendance   [Not given.]
Dated   31 March 1851.
Signed   Thomas Richard Gillow, Roman Catholic priest
                [1821–57].
                [St Cuthbert's Terrace, Bedford Street] North Shields,
                Northumberland.
[Roman Catholics living in South Shields crossed the River Tyne in
small sculler boats to attend worship in North Shields until the ferry
commenced in 1829.]

12.82   Synagogue, Church Road, North Shields (553.28)

Name   Jewish Synagogue.
Erected   1846.
Building   [Not separate and entire] one room let off. [Exclusively
                used for worship.]
Sittings   Free 6. Other 24. Total [30]. Standing room 6 (as
                above).

Attendance 29 March   Morning 20. Total [20].   (On the average.)
                        Afternoon 15 to 18. Total [15–18]. (On the average.)
                        Evening 15 to 20. Total [15–20].   (On the average.)
Average attendance   Morning 18. Total 18.   (On the average.)
Dated   31 March 1851.
Signed   Samuel Lotinga, president [ship and insurance broker].
               6 Toll Square, North Shields.

12.83   Latter-day Saints [Mormons], Earsdon (553.76)
Name   None.
Erected   1850.
Building   [Not separate and entire or exclusively used for
               worship.]
Sittings   All free. Standing room 200.
Attendance 30 March   Morning 20. SS none. Total [20].
                        Afternoon 30. Total [30].
                        Evening 50. Total [50].
Average attendance   180 per month for two months since opening.
                        Total 360.
Remarks   Our preaching place was used as a stable until last
               year when it was fit (*sic*) up for a day school, which it
               continues as such to the present. Our seats are all free
               and no Sunday school.
Dated   30 March 1851.
Signed   John Hair, elder [coal miner.]
               6 Cowpen Quay, Blyth, Northumberland.

Summary of All Places of Worship
in Northumberland

475 places of worship

1. Alnwick District (HO 129/559)   **31 places of worship**

Church of England churches	13
Presbyterian	
United churches	3
English churches	2
Independent chapels	2
Methodist	
Wesleyan chapels	6
Wesleyan schoolroom	1
New Connexion chapel	2
Roman Catholic church	1
Unitarian chapel	1

2. Belford District (HO 129/560)   **13 places of worship**

Church of England churches	6
Presbyterian	
Church of Scotland church	1
United churches	2
English churches	3
Roman Catholic church	1

3. Bellingham District (HO 129/557)   **23 places of worship**

Church of England churches	12
Church of England schoolroom	1
Presbyterian	
United churches	2
English churches	5
Methodist	
Wesleyan chapel	1
Primitive chapel	1
Roman Catholic church	1

4. Berwick District (HO 129/561)   **33 places of worship**

Church of England churches	9
Church of England schoolrooms	2

Presbyterian
    Church of Scotland churches   2
    United churches   6
    English churches   3
Independent chapel   1
Baptist chapel   1
Methodist
    Wesleyan chapel   1
    Primitive chapels   5
Non-denominational chapel   1
Roman Catholic churches   2

5. Castle Ward District (HO 129/554)   **40 places of worship**
Church of England churches   14
Church of England schoolrooms 2
Presbyterian
    United churches   2
Methodist
    Wesleyan chapels   13
    Primitive chapels   3   (1 shared with Wesleyan Reformers)
    Reformers chapels   4   (1 shared with Primitive Methodists)
    Reformers schoolroom   1
Roman Catholic church   1

6. Glendale District (HO 129/562)   **26 places of worship**
Church of England churches   11
Church of England schoolroom   1
Presbyterian
    Church of Scotland church   1
    United churches   3
    English churches   5
Baptist chapels   2
Methodist
    Primitive chapels   2
Roman Catholic church   1

7. Haltwhistle District (HO 129/556)   **26 places of worship**
Church of England churches   7
Presbyterian
    Church of Scotland church   1

Methodist
Wesleyan chapels	9	
Wesleyan schoolroom	1	(1 shared with Primitive Methodists]
Primitive chapels	5	
Primitive schoolroom	1	(1 shared with Wesleyan Methodists)
Non-denominational chapel	1	
Society of Friends meeting house	1	

8. Hexham District (HO 129/555)   **98 places of worship**

Church of England churches	24	
Church of England schoolrooms	2	
Presbyterian		
United church	1	
English church	1	
Independent chapels	4	(1 shared with Wesleyan Methodists)
Baptist chapels	4	
Methodist		
Wesleyan chapels	36	(1 shared with Independents)
Wesleyan schoolrooms	2	
Primitive chapels	19	
Primitive schoolroom	1	
Society of Friends meeting house	1	
Roman Catholic churches	3	

9. Morpeth District (HO 129/558)   **36 places of worship**

Church of England churches	16
Church of England schoolroom	1
Presbyterian	
United churches	3
English churches	3
Independent chapel	1
Baptist chapels	1
Methodist	
Wesleyan chapels	6
Primitive chapels	2
Roman Catholic churches	2
Latter-day Saints (Mormons)	1

10. Newcastle upon Tyne District
(HO 129/552)
           52 places of worship

Church of England churches	10
Church of England schoolroom	1
Presbyterian	
Church of Scotland churches	2
United churches	3
English churches	2
Independent chapels	2
Baptist	
General chapels	2
Particular chapels	3
Scottish chapel	1
Methodist	
Wesleyan chapels	5
New Connexion chapels	4
Primitive chapels	4
Reformers chapels	3
Non-denominational chapels	3
Society of Friends meeting house	1
Roman Catholic churches	2
Synagogue	1
Unitarian chapels	2
Swedenborgian chapel	1

11. Rothbury District (HO 129/563)
           14 places of worship

Church of England churches	7
Presbyterian	
English churches	3
Independent chapel	1
Roman Catholic churches	3

12. Tynemouth District (HO 129/553)
           83 places of worship

Church of England churches	12
Presbyterian	
United churches	4
English churches	2
Independent chapels	3
Welsh chapel	1
Baptist chapel	1
Methodist	
Wesleyan chapels	21

Wesleyan schoolroom 1
New Connexion chapels 7
Primitive chapels 13
Reformers chapels 9
Reformers schoolrooms 2
Non-denominational chapels 2
Society of Friends meeting house 1
Roman Catholic churches 2
Synagogue 1
Latter-day Saints (Mormons) 1

Total Summary	**475**
Church of England churches	141
Church of England schoolrooms	10
Presbyterian	
Church of Scotland churches	7
United churches	29
English churches	29
Independent chapels	15
Baptist	
General chapels	11
Particular chapels	3
Scottish chapel	1
Methodist	
Wesleyan chapels	98
Wesleyan schoolrooms	5
New Connexion chapels	13
Primitive chapels	54
Primitive schoolrooms	2
Reformers chapels	16
Reformers schoolrooms	3
Non-denominational	7
Society of Friends meeting houses	4
Roman Catholic churches	19
Synagogues	2
Unitarian chapels	3
Swedenborgian chapel	1
Latter-day Saints (Mormons)	2

Numerical Strength	**475**
Methodist	191
Church of England	151
Presbyterian	65
Roman Catholic	19
Baptist	15
Independent	15
Non-denominational	7
Society of Friends (Quakers)	4
Unitarian	3
Synagogues	2
Latter-day Saints (Mormons)	2
Swedenborgian	1

Places of Worship not listed in the Religious Census

This is an incomplete list. County and town directories may indicate the existence of a church or chapel but rarely give the date when the building was opened, and whether or not it was in use in March 1851.

Church of England
St Paul, Alnwick (consecrated 16 October 1846). {B52.}
St Mary, Blanchland. {B 14.}
Corenside schoolroom (1846). {1857 attendance 110.}
St Mary, Dilston Hall Chapel.
Ford, schoolroom (from 1839). {1857 attendance 50.}
Ford, schoolroom (from 1845). {1857 attendance 30.}
Holy Cross, Haltwhistle. {B 110.}
Hexham schoolroom. {1857 attendance 50.}
Kirkheath, Hexham.
Howdon Panns, room (from 1847).
Longbenton, two schoolrooms (1845).
Monkseaton room (from 1840).
Newcastle Goal (145 inmates in 1851).
Trinity House Chapel, Newcastle.
Newton Hall, room (from 1849).
St Paul, North Sunderland (consecrated 14 January 1834).
Holy Trinity, Old Berwick.
St John, Snods End, Shotley (consecrated 30 August 1837). {B 15.}

Presbyterian
Alnwick, Lisburn Street (1840).
Berwick upon Tweed, Low Meeting House (1719).
Felton (1820).
Haltwhistle (1744).
Moss Kennell, Haydon Bridge (1841).
Ponteland.
Seaton Deleval (1845).
Thornyford (1730–1853).

Baptist
Forth Bank, Newcastle.

Methodist

Wesleyan Methodist
Featherstone (1850).
Ireshopeburn.
Knaresdale.
Matfen (1840).

Primitive Methodist
Consett, Trafalgar Street (1848).
Cullercoats.
Eyemouth, Berwick upon Tweed (1835).
Great Whittington Schoolroom.
Matfen (1848).
Percy Main (1829, rebuilt 1867).
Mickley.

Wesleyan Reformers
Byker Hill.
Carville.
Corbridge.
Fawdon.
Hazlerigg.
Haydon Bridge.
Kenton.
Langley Mills (1849).
Lemington.
Newburn.
Paradise.
Spital Tongues.
West Moor.
Wideopen.

Sandemanian
Bethel Chapel, Forster Street, Newcastle (1757).
Wooler (1798).

Roman Catholic
St Mary, Bailiffgate, Alnwick (8 August 1836).

Latter-day Saints (Mormons)
Blyth.

THE
RELIGIOUS CENSUS
OF 1851

COUNTY DURHAM

13. Auckland District (HO 129/542)

61 places of worship

13.1 Church of England, St Andrew, South Church, Auckland
(542.13)
Population 1851: 22,628 (parish) 1,329 (township)

Name	St Andrew, Auckland. Ancient parish church.
Consecrated	Before 1800.
Endowment	Land £45. Tithe £46. Glebe (house). OPE £348. Fees £36. Easter offerings £5. Other £30 [an annual payment from the Lord Crewe Charity]. Total £510.
Sittings	Total 900.*
Attendance 30 March	[Not given.]
Average attendance	[Not given.]
Remarks	*As the space is at present divided. There are sittings I should think for about 900, but the area of the church is capable of accommodating considerably more as to the particulars mentioned.
Dated	31 March 1851.
Signed	George Edward Green, incumbent [1848–63]. Parsonage, Bishop Auckland, Durham.
{1857	St Andrew and St Anne attendance 150. 20 communicants.} {B 220.}

13.2 Church of England, St Anne, Market Place, Bishop Auckland (542.6)
Population 1851: 5,112 (township)

Name	St Anne's Chapel. Chapel of ease to the parish church of St Andrew, Auckland.
Consecrated	[22 February] 1848. [Restored 1869.] In lieu of a smaller one previously existing [opened 1782 and demolished in 1847].
Erected	By private benefaction and subscriptions, aided by grants from Church Building Societies. Private £2,638 [£325 from the Bishop of Durham]. Total cost £2,638.
Endowment	Land £60. Total £60.
Sittings	Free 444. Other 277. Total 721.
Attendance 30 March	[Not given.]
Average attendance	[Not given.]

Remarks   All fees payable to the parish church of St Andrew,
              Auckland.
Dated   31 March 1851.
Signed   George Edward Green, incumbent [1848–63].
              Parsonage, Bishop Auckland, Durham.

**13.3   Church of England, St Helen, Manor Road, Bishop
Auckland** (542.28)
Population 1851: 789 (township)

Name   St Helen, Auckland in the county of Durham. Ancient
              chapelry.
Consecrated Not known. Before 1800. [Restored 1866.]
Erected   Not known.
Endowment   Tithe £12. Glebe £180. Fees £16. Easter offerings £5.
              Other £80 [included £10 a year from the Lord Crewe
              Charity].
Sittings   Free 40. Other 500. Total 540.
Attendance 30 March   [Not given.]
Average attendance   Morning 350 + 80 or 100 SS. Total 450.
              Afternoon 90 + 80 SS. Total 170.
Dated   31 March 1851.
Signed   Matthew Chester, perpetual curate [1822–71].
              St Helen, Auckland, Darlington.
{1857   Attendance 150. 30 communicants.}   {B 130.}

13.4   Church of England, Bolam Chapel, Gainford (542.41)
Population 1851: 125 (township)

Name   A chapel not named.
Consecrated Licensed by Dr [William] Van Mildert, Bishop of
              Durham.
Erected   By the vicar of Gainford, in which parish Bolam is
              situate.
              No parliamentary grant. No rate. Total cost chiefly
              by the vicar of Gainford. (Assisted by Trinity College,
              Cambridge [the patron] and the late Bishop of
              Durham. The cost was about £400.)
Endowment   No endowment whatever.
Sittings   Free 50. Other 50. Total 100.
Attendance 30 March   Morning 39 + 11 SS. Total 50.
Average attendance   Morning 25 + 10 SS. Total 35.

Dated   31 March 1851.
Signed   George Macfarlan, vicar of the parish of Gainford
               [1824–62].
               Gainford, near Darlington.

{B 29.}

[George Macfarlan was the vicar of Gainford (**23.2**).]

13.5   Church of England, St Peter, Byers Green (542.39)
Population 1851: 1,025 (township)

[Summary form]
Name   Byers Green Church.
Erected   [Consecrated 10 July 1845. Restored 1873–90. District
               created on 8 August 1845 out of the parish of St
               Andrew, Auckland.]
Endowment   [£180.]
Sittings   Free 212. Other 71. Total 283.
Usual attendance   Morning average about 94. [Total 94.]
                        Afternoon average about 94. [Total 94.]
Dated   17 July 1852.
Signed   Ralph Joplin [registrar].
Incumbent   [James Watson Hick 1845–75.]
{1857   Attendance 100. 20 communicants.}   {B 68.}
[James Hick was also the organising secretary for the Durham branch
of the Society for the Propagation of the Gospel.]

13.6   Church of England, St James, Coundon (542.19)
Population 1851: 1,073 (township)

Name   St James. District parish of Coundon, made under the
               provisions of an Act passed in 58th of George III [c.45]
               for building churches in populous places.
Consecrated 30 July 1841 [13 July]. As an additional church to part
               of St Andrew, Auckland, including the townships of
               Coundon, Westerton and Windlestone, then made a
               separate district [created 2 February 1842. Rebuilt and
               consecrated 8 July 1873.]
Erected   By the Lord Bishop of Durham [by] his private
               benefaction [of] £850. From the Diocesan Church
               Building Society, £50.
               Total cost £900.

Endowment Land £160. Tithe (commuted £58) £56. Glebe £6. Fees £5. Easter offerings £1. Total £230.

Sittings Free 221. Other 84. Total 305.

Attendance 30 March Morning 58 + 79 SS. Total 137.
Afternoon 33 + 40 SS. Total 73.

Average attendance Morning 50 + 100 SS. Total 150.
Afternoon 40 (adults) + 60 SS. Total 120 (*sic*) [100].

Remarks General congregation 75 in the summer; 35 in the winter. Colliery not at work. Many coal-miners have left at least 30 houses unoccupied.

Dated 31 March 1851.

Signed Charles Duberly, incumbent of Coundon [1844–56]. Coundon Parsonage, B[isho]p Auckland.

{1857 Attendance 50. 8 communicants.}   {B 47.}

13.7 Church of England, St Catherine, Crook (542.56)
Population 1851: 2,764 (township)

Name Crook, St Catherine P[erpetual] C[uracy]. (Brancepeth.) District chapelry, 1 & 2 Will. IV c.38.

Consecrated 1842 [12 September 1843]. Additional church in the parish of Brancepeth. [Enlarged 1878, 1885. District created 13 January 1845.]

Erected By private benefactions and other sources. Grants and other sources £500. By the rector of Brancepeth £280. Total cost £780.

Endowment Tithe £66. OPE £60 (ecclesiastical grant). Fees £5.

Sittings Free 406. Total 406.

Attendance 30 March [Not given.]

Average attendance Morning 200 (summer), 150 (winter) + 50 to 60 SS. Total [200–260].
Afternoon 50 (winter) + 60 SS. Total [100–110].
Evening 150 (summer). Total [150].

Remarks The population chiefly pitmen who are chiefly Ranters.

Dated 5 April 1851.

Signed William Sandford, perpetual curacy (*sic*) [1850–72]. Crook, Darlington.

{1857 Attendance 200. 25 communicants.}

13.8   Church of England, St John the Evangelist, Escomb (542.35)
Population 1851: 1,293 (chapelry)

Name   Escomb Church. Ancient church or chapel of an
          ancient chapelry.
Consecrated   Before 1800. [Restored 1880.]
Endowment   Answered in yearly return to my diocesan [bishop].
          [£220.]
Sittings   Free 71. Other 35. Total 106.
Attendance 30 March   Morning 35 + 26 SS. Total 51.
          Afternoon 30 + 30 SS. Total 60.
Average attendance   Morning 30 + 45 SS. Total 75.
          Afternoon 50 + 30 SS. Total 80.
          Evening no service.
Remarks   The greater part of the population living at a
          considerable distance from the church, the number
          varies very greatly.
Dated   31 March 1851.
Signed   Henry Arthur Atkinson, perpetual curate [1848–67].
          Escomb, Bishop Auckland.
{1857   Attendance 90. 15 communicants. 'A new church and
          burial ground are much needed'.}   {B 34.}
[A new church dedicated to St John the Baptist was consecrated on
15 September 1863 and demolished in 1971.]

13.9   Church of England, St Cuthbert, Etherley (542.43)
Population 1851: 961 (township)

Name   Etherley Chapel, commonly known as Etherley
          Church, having a new parochial district or chapelry.
Consecrated   24 Nov[ember] 1832 [by the Bishop of Bristol]. As
          an additional church [in the parish of St Andrew,
          Auckland. Restored 1867, 1901.]
Erected   Chiefly at the expense of the late Bishop [William] Van
          Mildert [and the Church Building Society]. Total cost
          about £750.
Endowment   OPE declined. [£220.]
Sittings   Free 154. Other 106. Total 260.
Attendance 30 March   Morning 70 + 40 SS. Total 110.
          Evening 65. Total 65.
Average attendance   Morning 75 + 45 SS. Total 120.
          Evening 70. Total 70.

Remarks   An account of the endowment of the chapel is in the
possession of the government as published in the
London Gazette of 14 July 1837.
Dated   30 March 1851.
Signed   George Watson, perpetual curate [1833–65].
Etherley Parsonage, Bishop Auckland.
{1857   Attendance 80. 24 communicants.}   {B 21.}

13.10   Church of England, St James, Hamsterley (542.51)
Population 1851: 532 (township)

Name   Dedicated to St James. Hamsterley Church, an ancient
chapelry under St Andrew, Auckland.
Consecrated   Before 1800. [Restored 1883–84.]
Endowment   [£96. Included £10 a year from the Lord Crewe
Charity.]
Sittings   Free 12. Other 300. Total 312.
Attendance 30 March   Morning 53 + 10 SS. Total 63.
Average attendance   [Not given.]
Remarks   The Sunday schoolroom is a mile from the church. In
the winter season I have no duty at the church in the
afternoons, and am always engaged in the schoolroom
with the Sunday scholars which is generally well
attended.
Dated   10 April 1851.
Signed   James George Milner, incumbent [1825–85].
Hamsterley, n[ea]r Bishop Auckland.
{1857   Attendance 80. 30 communicants.}   {B 16.}
[John Milner was also the incumbent of St John, Bellerby, Yorkshire
1829–82.]

13.11   Church of England, St Paul, Hunwick (542.5)
Population 1851: 486 (township of Hunwick and Helmington)

Name   St Paul's, Hunwick. District chapelry to the parish of
St Andrew, Auckland.
Consecrated   [15 July] 1845. Consecrated as an additional chapel to
the parish of St Andrew, Auckland. [Enlarged 1854 and
restored 1886–87. District created 8 August 1845.]
Erected   By subscription and grants from Church Building
Societies.*

[Total cost about £700.]

Endowment Land £55. OPE £50. Fees £2. Total £107.

Sittings Free 119. Other 42. Total 161.

Attendance 30 March [Not given.]

Average attendance [Not given.]

Remarks *The cost of the chapel I am unable to state, except it was built some years before my incumbency; and the papers are not in my possession as to the particulars mentioned.

Dated 31 March 1851.

Signed George Edward Green, incumbent of St Andrew, Auckland [1848–63].
Parsonage, Bishop Auckland, Durham.
This return filled up by me in the absence of the incumbent [James Richards 1851–81]. Witness my hand, 31 March 1851. John (*sic*) Green.

{1857 Attendance 140. 16 communicants.}   {B 32.}

13.12 Church of England, St John the Evangelist, Lynesack

(542.50)

Population 1851: 787 (township of Lynesack and Softley)

Name St John the Evangelist, Lynesack. District chapelry. [58] George III 16th section [c.45].

Consecrated 17 October 1848. As an additional church [in the parish of St Andrew, Auckland. District created 19 June 1850.]

Erected By the inhabitants, with the aid of the different societies and individuals. Total cost £758.

Endowment [Not given.]

Sittings Free 166. Other 84. Total 250.

Attendance 30 March Morning 70. Total [70].
Afternoon 50. Total [50].

Average attendance Morning 150. Total [150].
Afternoon 150. Total [150].

Remarks With respect to the [endowment] query: the endowment is not settled to the best of my belief.

Dated 31 March 1851.

Signed James Evans Jones, perpetual curate [1848–55]. Lynesack Parsonage, n[ea]r Barnard Castle.

{1857 Attendance 80. 12 communicants.}   {B 23.}

13.13   Church of England, St John, Shildon (542.22)
Population 1851: 2,144 (township)

Name	St John's church, Shildon.
Consecrated	AD 1834. [Opened by licence 20 June, consecrated 9 September. Rebuilt and enlarged 1881–82. District created 21 June 1837 out of the parish of St Andrew, Auckland.]
Erected	By subscription from the then Bishop of Durham [William Van Mildert]; the Incorporated Church Building Society, and from private individuals. Total cost believed to have been about £1,700.
Endowment	OPE £225 (subtract from income of £225, £33 per an.). Fees £6.
Sittings	Free 400. Other 300. Total 700.
Attendance 30 March	Morning 400 + 90 SS. Total 490. Afternoon 70 SS. Total 70. Evening 250. Total 250.
Average attendance	Morning 350 + 90 SS. Total 440. Afternoon 70 SS. Total 70. Evening 300. Total 300.
Dated	[Not given.]
Signed	James Manisty, incumbent [1834–62]. Shildon Parsonage, Darlington.
{1857	Attendance 450. 60 communicants.} {B 90.}

13.14   Church of England, St Mary the Virgin, Middridge (542.31)
Population 1851: 300 (township)

Name	Middridge licensed chapel. A chapel of ease to Shildon church.
Consecrated	Before 1800. This hamlet being at considerable distance from the parish church.
Erected	By Bishop [Shute] Barrington and others.
Endowment	No endowment. No fees.
Sittings	Free 150. Total 150.
Attendance 30 March	Afternoon 79 + 32 SS. Total 111.
Average attendance	Afternoon 100 + 36 SS. Total 136.
Dated	31 March 1851.
Signed	James Manisty, incumbent of Shildon and chapel of Middridge [1834–63].

Shildon Parsonage, Darlington.

13.15   Church of England, St Philip and St James, Witton-le-Wear (542.60)
Population 1851: 918 (parochial chapelry)

Name   Parish church of Witton-le-Wear.
Consecrated   Before 1800. [Restored 1830. Restored and enlarged
                and consecrated 18 October 1902.]
Endowment   Land £36. Tithe £14. Glebe £9. OPE £30 [included £10 a
                year from the Lord Crewe Charity]. Total £96.
                Fees about £7.
Sittings   Free 20. Other 320. Total 340.
Attendance 30 March   Morning 109 + 52 SS. Total 161.
Average attendance   Morning 130 + 60 SS. Total 190.
Dated   31 March 1851.
Signed   Laurence Lawson Brown, incumbent [1846–60].
                The Parsonage, Witton-le-Wear, Darlington.
{1857   Attendance 160. 22 communicants.}   {B 71.}

13.16   Church of England Schoolroom, Fir Tree, Witton-le-Wear
(542.54)
Name   Fir Tree schoolroom used during the week as a school,
                and on Sundays for divine service and a Sunday
                school.
Licensed   Licensed February 1840. Being in a populous part of
                the parish far from the church.
Erected   By G[eorge]. H. Wilkinson Esquire of Harperley
                Park and some of neighbouring farmers. By private
                benefaction and subscription.
Sittings   Free 100. Total 100.
Attendance 30 March   Afternoon 27 + 34 SS. Total 61.
Average attendance   Afternoon 50 + 40 SS. Total 90.
Dated   31 March 1851.
Signed   Laurence Lawson Brown, incumbent [1846–60].
                The Parsonage, Witton-le-Wear, Darlington.
{1857   Attendance 90.}

13.17   Independent [Congregational], Greatgates, Bishop Auckland (542.11)

Name	Bethesda.
Erected	1828 [1829].
Building	[Separate and entire. Exclusively used for worship. Later occupied by the Salvation Army. Replaced by a new chapel in Victoria Street, opened in 1876.]
Sittings	Free 50. Other 150. Total 200. Standing room 50.

Attendance 30 March   Morning 50 + 11 SS. Total 61.
　　　　　　　　　　　 Evening 60 + 11 SS. Total 71.
Average attendance　　 Morning 80 + 20 SS. Total 100.
　　　　　　　　　　　 Evening 80 + 30 SS. Total 110.

Dated	30 March 1851.
Signed	Thomas Thornton, managing member [clerk to Board of Health and deputy coroner].
	[South Terrace], Bishop Auckland.

13.18   Baptist, Hamsterley (542.53)

Name	Baptist Chapel.
Erected	Before 1800 viz. 1777.*
Building	[Separate and entire. Exclusively used for worship.]
Sittings	Free 50. Other 150. Total [200].

Attendance 30 March   Morning 130 + 29 SS. Total 159.
　　　　　　　　　　　 Afternoon 100 + 24 SS. Total 124.
　　　　　　　　　　　 Evening 60. Total 60.
Average attendance　　 Morning 120 + 30 SS. Total 150.
　　　　　　　　　　　 Afternoon 100 + 24 SS. Total 124.
　　　　　　　　　　　 Evening 50. Total 50.

Remarks	*This chapel was erected in the place of an old one which was built about 200 years ago. [Erected 1715, replaced 1774. In 1790 a theological library of 400–500 books was opened.]
Dated	31 March 1851.
Signed	Thomas Cardwell, minister.
	Hamsterley, near B[isho]p Auckland.

[Thomas Cardwell was also the minister of Wolsingham (**24.11**).]

13.19   Baptist Schoolroom, Witton-le-Wear (542.61)

Name	Witton-le-Wear.
Erected	1808.
Building	Schoolroom licensed for public worship. School [not exclusively used for worship].

Sittings   Free 200. Total [200].
Attendance 30 March   [Not given.]
Average attendance   Morning 168. Total [168].
Remarks   A neighbouring Baptist minister preaches in the
               aforesaid schoolroom once a fortnight.
Dated   31 March 1851.
Signed   Thomas Jopling, deacon (grocer and draper).
               Witton-le-Wear, Durham.

13.20   Wesleyan Methodist, South Church, Auckland (542.18)
Name   Wesleyan Chapel.
Erected   1835 [cost £350] and enlarged 1851.
Building   [Separate and entire. Exclusively used for worship.]
Sittings   Free 100. Other 70. Total [170]. Standing room 60.
Attendance 30 March   Afternoon 65 + 10 SS. Total 75.
                        Evening 64 + 23 SS. Total 87.
Average attendance   Afternoon 60 + 15 SS. Total 75.
                        Evening 70 + 20 SS. Total 90.
Dated   30 March 1851.
Signed   William Russell, steward.
               South Church, [Auckland].

**13.21   Wesleyan Methodist, Back Bondgate Street, Bishop
Auckland** (542.8)
Name   Wesleyan Chapel.
Erected   About the year 1810 [Opened 1804 (and cost £534
               and enlarged 1811] and enlarged 1842. [Opened
               1 November 1842. Rebuilt and enlarged, and opened
               24 July 1866.]
Building   [Separate and entire. Exclusively used for worship.]
Sittings   Free 160. Other 338. Total 498. Standing room 200.
Attendance 30 March   Morning 170 + 35 SS. Total 205.
                        Evening 210 + 15 SS. Total 225.
Average attendance   Morning 200 + 40 SS. Total 240.
                        Evening 250 to 400 + 30 SS. Total 330 (*sic*)
                        [280–430].
Remarks   The congregation on Sunday, 30 March, was smaller
               than usual, owing to many of the regular hearers
               suffering from influenza and not being able to attend.
Dated   31 March 1851.
Signed   Robert Cooke, minister [1849–51].
               Bishop Auckland, Durham.

13.22   Wesleyan Methodist, Bolam, Gainford (542.42)
Name   None.
Erected   [Not given.]
Building   [Not separate and entire.] Exclusively for a place of
             worship and Sunday school.
Sittings   [Not given.]
Attendance 30 March   Afternoon 46. Total [46].
Average attendance   [Not given.]
Dated   30 March 1851.
Signed   Robert Marley, manager (farmer) [local preacher].
             Bolam.

13.23   Wesleyan Methodist, Bowdon Close (542.33)
Name   None.
Erected   [Not given.]
Building   [Not separate and entire or exclusively used for
             worship.]
Sittings   [Not given.]
Attendance 30 March   Morning 45 + 55 SS. Total 100.
Average attendance   [Not given.]
Dated   31 March 1851.
Signed   Robert Copeland, society steward [coal miner].
             Bowdon Close Colliery, Durham.

13.24   Wesleyan Methodist, Byers Green (542.4)
Name   Dwelling House, Wesleyan Methodist.
Erected   About 1850. [Enlarged 1862.]
Building   [Not separate and entire.] The upper room of a cottage
             house. [Not exclusively used for worship.]
Sittings   Free 90. Total [90]. Standing room 40.
Attendance 30 March   Evening 100 + 12 SS. Total 112.
Average attendance   Morning 100 + 12 SS. Total 112.
Dated   30 March 1851.
Signed   Thomas Stoves, society steward [local preacher. Engine
             man in colliery.]
             [Colliery House], Byers Green, Durham.

13.25   Wesleyan Methodist, Crook and Billy Row (542.58)
Name   Wesleyan Chapel.
Erected   1844. [Opened 22 November 1844, and a new chapel in
             Hope Street opened 23 November 1862.]
Building   [Separate and entire. Exclusively used for worship.]

Sittings   Free 100 (space available 24 feet by 88). Other 100.
Total [200].
Attendance 30 March   Morning 63 + 72 SS. Total 135.
Afternoon 74 SS. Total 74.
Evening 139. Total 139.
Average attendance   [Not given.]
Dated   31 March 1851.
Signed   George Lax, steward (shoemaker).
Crook, Durham.
[Before the chapel was opened in 1844, the Wesleyan Methodists met in various locations. First in a room, then the village school (until ejected by the rector of Brancepeth), then in a granary, then a house and for thirteen years in a kitchen.]

13.26   Wesleyan Methodist, Escomb (542.36)
Name   Escomb Wesleyan Chapel.
Erected   1841. [Cost £67.]
Building   [Separate and entire. Exclusively used for worship.]
Sittings   Free 120. Total [120].
Attendance 30 March   Evening 56. Total [56].
Average attendance   Evening 50. Total [50].
Dated   30 March 1851.
Signed   John Raine, steward [coal miner].
Escomb, near Bishop Auckland, Durham.

13.27   Wesleyan Methodist, Evenwood (542.45)
[Simplified form]
Name   Oaks Wesleyan Chapel.
Erected   1837. [Cost £180.] [Foundation stone of a new chapel laid 18 April 1876.]
Building   Separate and entire building, used exclusively as a place of worship.
Sittings   Free 80. Other 120. Total [200].
Usual attendance   Morning 40 SS. Total 40.
Afternoon 40 SS. Total 40.
Evening 30. Total 30.
Dated   [Not given.]
Signed   L. P. Booth.
Evenwood, Bishop Auckland.

13.28　Wesleyan Methodist, Hamsterley (542.52)

Name　　Wesleyan Methodist Chapple (*sic*).
Erected　　Since 1800. [1812, cost £350. Closed 1854 and sold for £30.]
Building　　[Separate and entire. Exclusively used for worship.]
Sittings　　Free 100. Other 50. Total [150]. Standing room none.
Attendance 30 March　　Afternoon 55. Total [55].
Average attendance　　[SS] none.
Dated　　31 March 1851.
Signed　　William Stephenson [house-carpenter].
　　　　　　Hamsterley, Bishop Auckland.

13.29　Wesleyan Methodist, Hunwick Colliery (542.2)

Name　　Joiner's Shop.
Erected　　1849.
Building　　[Not given.]
Sittings　　[Not given.]
Attendance 30 March　　Morning 23 + 33 SS. Total 56.
Average attendance　　Afternoon 37 + 33 SS. Total 70.
Dated　　30 March 1851.
Signed　　William Peel, class leader, steward, etc.
　　　　　　Hunwick Colliery, B[ishop] Auckland, Durham.

13.30　Wesleyan Methodist, Merrington (542.1)

Name　　Wesleyan Chapel.
Erected　　1841. [New chapel 1861.]
Building　　[Separate and entire. Exclusively used for worship.]
Sittings　　[Not given.]
Attendance 30 March　　Afternoon 55. Total [55].
　　　　　　　　　　　　Evening 48. Total [48].
Average attendance　　Afternoon 60 + 96 SS. Total 156.
Dated　　31 March 1851.
Signed　　William Sedgwick, society steward [shoemaker].
　　　　　　Merrington, Durham.

13.31　Wesleyan Methodist, North Beechburn (542.55)

Name　　None.
Erected　　Dec[ember] 1849.
Building　　[Not separate and entire or exclusively used for worship.]
Sittings　　Free – yes.
Attendance 30 March　　Afternoon 30 + 10 SS. Total 40.

Average attendance   Afternoon 30 + 10 SS. Total 40.
Dated   31 March 1851.
Signed   Thomas Hedley, manager [quarry owner].
               Howden, near Crook, Durham.

13.32   Wesleyan Methodist, Shildon (542.24)
Name   Wesleyan Chapel.
Erected   1830. [1829 (cost £341) enlarged 1859 and 1866. New
              chapel opened 8 June 1878.]
Building   [Separate and entire. Exclusively used for worship.]
Sittings   Free 110. Other 140. Total [250].
Attendance 30 March   Afternoon 99 + 40 SS. Total 139.
                        Evening 67 + 31 SS. Total 98.
Average attendance   Afternoon 120 + 45 SS. Total 165.
                        Evening 120 + 40 SS. Total 160.
Remarks   The congregation yesterday were considerably below
              an average.
Dated   31 March 1851.
Signed   Jacob Goundry, steward [collicry agent].
              Shildon, n[ea]r B[isho]p Auckland.

13.33   Wesleyan Methodist, New Shildon (542.26)
Name   New Shildon Wesleyan Methodist Chapel.
Erected   1832. [Cost £450. Enlarged 1871.]
Building   [Separate and entire. Exclusively used for worship.]
Sittings   Free 250. Other 126. Total [376]. Standing room none.
Attendance 30 March   Morning 100 + 70 SS. Total 170.
                        Evening 150. Total 150.
Average attendance   [Not given.]
Dated   31 March 1851.
Signed   Richard Pickering, chapel steward [railway agent].
              [Thickley Place, East Thickley], New Shildon, near
              Darlington.

13.34   Wesleyan Methodist, Quarry Heads, Toft Hill (542.47)
Name   Wesleyan Chapel. [Toft Hill Chapel.]
Erected   1829. [Cost £240. New chapel erected a mile away in
              1861.]
Building   [Separate and entire. Exclusively used for worship.]
Sittings   Free 80. Other 72. Total [152].
Attendance 30 March   Afternoon 47 + 10 SS. Total 57.
                        Evening 27 + 12 SS. Total 39.

Average attendance   Afternoon 68 + 20 SS. Total 88.
Evening 55 + 15 SS. Total 70.
Dated   31 March 1851.
Signed   David Fawell, chapel steward [cartwright].
Toft Hill, Durham.

13.35   Wesleyan Methodist, West Auckland (542.44)
Name   Wesleyan Chapel.
Erected   Chapel erected 1827 [opened 2 October, and cost £209.
Wesleyan Methodist] Society formed before 1800.
Building   [Separate and entire. Exclusively used for worship.]
Sittings   Free 80. Other 116. Total [196].
Attendance 30 March   Morning 45 + 55 SS. Total 100.
Afternoon no service.
Evening [120]. Total 120.
Average attendance   Morning 60 + 60 SS. Total 120.
Evening 140. Total 140.
Dated   31 March 1851.
Signed   Thomas Price Robinson, chapel steward [proprietor of
houses].
West Auckland, Durham.

13.36   Wesleyan Methodist, Witton Park (542.37)
Name   Wesleyan Chapel.
Erected   October 1847. [Adjacent new chapel opened in 1861.]
Building   [Separate and entire. Exclusively used for worship.]
Sittings   Free 70. Other 90. Total [160]. Standing room 30.
Attendance 30 March   Afternoon 67 + 36 SS. Total 103.
Evening 46 + 32 SS. Total 78.
Average attendance   Afternoon 60 + 30 SS. Total 90.
Evening 50 + 20 SS. Total 70.
Remarks   In consequence of a rainy day the congregation was
decreased.
Dated   30 March 1851.
Signed   Joseph E. Brentnall, society steward [grocer].
Witton Park, Durham.

13.37   Primitive Methodist Schoolroom, South Church, Auckland
(542.16)
Name   Schoolroom.
Erected   Before 1800.

Building   [Not separate and entire or exclusively used for
              worship.]
Sittings   Free 60. Total [60].
Attendance 30 March   Evening 30 + 67 SS. Total 97.
Average attendance   [Not given.]
Dated   5 April 1851.
Signed   William Jacques, society steward, Fielding Bridge.
            Burns House, near West Auckland.

13.38   Primitive Methodist, South Church, Auckland (542.14)
Name   West Pitts Chapel.
Erected   About the year 1825.
Building   [Separate and entire. Exclusively used for worship.]
Sittings   Free 30. Other 60. Total [90].
Attendance 30 March   Morning 40. Total [40].
Average attendance   [Not given.]
Dated   30 March 1851.
Signed   Stephen Smith, steward.
            Lang Head.

13.39   Primitive Methodist, South Church, Auckland (542.17)
Name   Primitive Methodist Chapel.
Erected   February 1836.
Building   Entire building [separate]. Exclusively a place of
              worship.
Sittings   Free 130. Other 96. Total [226].
Attendance 30 March   Morning 39 SS. Total [39].
                         Afternoon 70. Total [70].
                         Evening 80. Total [80].
Average attendance   Afternoon 80. Total [80].
                         Evening 90. Total [90].
Dated   31 March 1851.
Signed   William Race, steward [forge man].
            South Church Forge, n[ea]r Bishop Auckland, Durham.

13.40   Primitive Methodist, South Church, Auckland (542.15)
Name   Primitive Methodist Chapel.
Erected   In the year 1844.
Building   [Separate and entire. Exclusively used for worship]
              excepted for a Sunday school.
Sittings   Free 54. Other 132. Total [186].
Attendance 30 March   Afternoon 56 + 23 SS. Total 79.

Evening 44 + 21 SS. Total 65.
Average attendance   Afternoon 80 + 30 SS. Total 110.
Evening 35 + 15 SS. Total 50.
Dated   30 March 1851.
Signed   William Simpson, manager for steward [coal miner].
Care of Matthew Dowson, South Side, near Staindrop,
Durham.

13.41   Primitive Methodist, Auckland (542.29)
Name   Primitive Methodist Chapel.
Erected   1849.
Building   [Separate and entire. Exclusively used for worship.]
Sittings   Free 38. Other 28. Total [66].
Attendance 30 March   Afternoon 32. Total 32.
Evening 58. Total 58.
Average attendance   Afternoon 32. Total 32.
Evening 58. Total 58.
Dated   31 March 1851.
Signed   Roger Paley, manager.
St Helen's, Auckland, Durham.

13.42   Primitive Methodist, Newgate Street, Bishop Auckland (542.7)
Name   Primitive Methodist Chapel.
Erected   1842.
Building   [Separate and entire. Exclusively used for worship.]
Sittings   Free 90. Other 71. Total [161].
Attendance 30 March   Afternoon 100 + 45 SS. Total 145.
Evening 120. Total 120.
Average attendance   [Not given.]
Remarks   This congregation is a part of the Wolsingham circuit
where our ministers reside. The Sabbath services are
partly conducted by local preachers and partly by
the itinerant ministers. The latter are supported by
the voluntary contributions of the members of [the]
Society and the former by their own labour.
Dated   30 March 1851.
Signed   William Eckersall, local preacher [draper].
Newgate Street, Bishop Auckland.

13.43   Primitive Methodist, Bowdon Close (542.34)
Name   None.
Erected   [Not given.]
Building   [Separate and entire] dwelling house. [Not exclusively used for worship.]
Sittings   [Not given.]
Attendance 30 March   Evening 50. Total 50.
Average attendance   [Not given.]
Dated   31 March 1851.
Signed   Ralph Reddy, locale (*sic*) preacher.
                Crook, Darlington.

13.44   Primitive Methodist, Byers Green (542.3)
Name   Primitive Methodist. (Held in the upper room of a cottage house [in another hand].)
Erected   1850.
Building   [Separate and entire. Exclusively used for worship.] Not separate and entire. The upper room only [in another hand].
Sittings   Free 120. Other 30. Total 150. Standing room 40.
Attendance 30 March   Afternoon 66 SS. Total 66.
                Evening 76 SS. Total 76.
Average attendance   Afternoon 40. Total [40].
Dated   30 March 1851.
Signed   Isaac Alderson, steward [coke drawer].
                Byers Green, near Bishop Auckland.

13.45   Primitive Methodist Schoolroom, Coundon Grange (542.20)
Name   None
Erected   Occupied two years. [1849.]
Building   [Separate and entire, but not exclusively used for worship.]
Sittings   Free 70. Total [70].
Attendance 30 March   Afternoon 30 + 20 SS. Total 50.
                Evening 35 + 15 SS. Total 50.
Average attendance   [Not given.]
Remarks   A day school teached (*sic*) in our place of worship.
Dated   30 March 1851.
Signed   John Vipond, local preacher [grocer and coal miner].
                Coundon, near Bishop Auckland, Durham.

13.46   Primitive Methodist, Crook and Billy Row (542.57)

Name   Chapel Street Chapel, Crook.
Erected   1847. [From 1844 met in a cottage.]
Building   [Separate and] entire building. Exclusively [used for
                worship] except for Sunday school.
Sittings   Free 100. Other 100. Total [200]. Standing room none.
Attendance 30 March   Afternoon 132. Total [132]. } Total 290.
                        Evening 158. Total [158].   }
Average attendance   Afternoon 180. Total [180]. } Total 360.
                        Evening 180. Total [180].   }
Remarks   We intend enlarging the present chapel to hold as
                many more, and to have a school separate from the
                chapel.
Dated   30 March 1851.
Signed   James Wilson, steward (grocer) [and draper and
                druggist].
                Crook, Durham.

13.47   Primitive Methodist, Evenwood and Barony (542.49)

Name   Wind Mill Preaching Room.
Erected   About the year 1831.
Building   [Separate and entire. Exclusively used for worship.]
Sittings   Free 60. Total [60].
Attendance 30 March   Afternoon 40. Total [40].
                        Evening 12. Total [12].
Average attendance   Morning 40. Total [40].
Remarks   The morning service being once a fortnight. The
                evening service being a prayer meeting. The building
                was erected about the year 1831 for a dwelling house,
                but was converted into a preaching room about the
                year 1840.
Dated   30 March 1851.
Signed   William Vasey, local preacher and class leader [farm
                labourer].
                Cox House, [Evenwood and Barony].

13.48   Primitive Methodist, Evenwood and Barony (542.46)

Name   Primitive Methodist Chapel.
Erected   1837.
Building   [Separate and entire. Exclusively used for worship.]
Sittings   Free 94. Other 105. Total [199]. Standing room 60.
Attendance 30 March   Morning 95 SS. Total 95.

Afternoon 120. Total 120.
Evening 120. Total 120.
Average attendance   Morning 95 SS. Total 95.
Afternoon 120. Total 120.
Evening 120. Total 120.
Remarks   This is about the average number of our congregation.
Dated   31 March 1851.
Signed   Thomas Wakers, class leader and steward (colliery agent).
Evenwood, West Auckland, Durham.

13.49   Primitive Methodist, Middridge (542.32)
Name   Primitive Methodist Chapel.
Erected   Set up in 1836. [£200 given by Mrs Burton to erect the chapel.]
Building   [Separate and entire. Exclusively used for worship.]
Sittings   Free 70. Other 36. Total 106. Standing room 36.
Attendance 30 March   Morning 53 + 49 SS. Total 102.
Afternoon 49 SS. Total 49.
Evening 72. Total 72.
Average attendance   Morning 50 + 49 SS. Total 99.
Afternoon 49 SS. Total 49.
Evening 75. Total 75.
Dated   31 March 1851.
Signed   Joseph Graham, steward [joiner].
Middridge near Shildon, Durham.

13.50   Primitive Methodist Schoolroom, Roddymoor, Crook
(542.59)
Name   Primitive Methodist Preaching Station [in] Pease's West School.
Erected   1849.
Building   [Not separate and entire or exclusively used for worship.]
Sittings   Free 50. Total [50]. Standing room 30 [and] 80. [Total] 110.
Attendance 30 March   Evening 40. Total [40].
Average attendance   Morning 70 SS. Total 70.
Evening 50. Total 50.
Remarks   This meeting is held in the day schoolroom on Sabbath evenings, only by permission of Joseph Pease Esq. and partners, but is the only place of meeting

at Roddymoor, and is attended by the work people
alone.
Dated   31 March 1851.
Signed   James Lawton, resident instead of steward
             [schoolmaster].
             Pease's West School (or Roddymoor).
[Many local people were employed at Pease's West Collieries.]

13.51   Primitive Methodist, Shildon (542.23)

Name   Primitive Methodist Chapel.
Erected   In the year 1835. [Opened 11 May 1834.]
Building   [Separate and entire. Exclusively used for worship.]
Sittings   Free 125. Other 151. Total [276]. Standing room 50.
Attendance 30 March   Morning 65 SS. Total 65.
             Afternoon 130. Total 130.
             Evening 182. Total 182.
Average attendance   Morning 74 SS. Total 74.
             Afternoon 120. Total 120.
             Evening 190. Total 190.
Dated   31 March 1851.
Signed   David Pickering, chapel steward ([black] smith).
             Shildon, Near Darlington, Durham.

13.52   Primitive Methodist, East Thickley (542.21)

Name   Primitive Methodist Chapple (*sic*).
Erected   1838.
Building   [Separate and entire. Exclusively used for worship.]
Sittings   Free 20. Other 84. Total [104]. Standing room 30.
Attendance 30 March   Morning 26 SS. Total 26.
             Afternoon 38 + 50 SS. [Total 88.]
             Evening 90. Total 90.
Average attendance   [Not given.]
Dated   30 March 1851.
Signed   John Maddison, steward [boiler-smith].
             [Railway Cottages], New Shildon, Darlington,
             Durham.

13.53   Primitive Methodist, Toft Hill (542.48)

Name   Primitive Methodist Chapel.
Erected   October 1829.
Building   [Separate and entire. Exclusively used for worship.]
Sittings   Free 158. Other 92. Total [250]. Standing room 50.

Attendance 30 March   Afternoon 150 + 25 SS. Total 170 (*sic*) [175].
                         Evening 157 + 30 SS. Total 187.
Average attendance   Afternoon 156 + 25 SS. Total 181.
                         Evening 166 + 30 SS. Total 196.
Dated   30 March 1851.
Signed   Ralph Burn, steward [factory labourer].
                 Toft Hill, near B[isho]p Auckland, Durham.

13.54   Primitive Methodist, Witton-le-Wear (542.62)
Name   Primitive Methodist. [Rehoboth Primitive Methodist
                 Chapel.]
Erected   5 May 1850.
Building   [Separate and] entire building. [Exclusively used as a]
                 place of worship.
Sittings   Free 83. Other 76. Total [159]. Standing room 50.
Attendance 30 March   Afternoon 97. Total [97].
                         Evening 122. Total [122].
Average attendance   Morning 58 SS. Total [58].
Dated   30 March 1851.
Signed   James Anderson, trustee [colliery overman].
                 Witton-le-Wear, near Darlington.

13.55   Primitive Methodist, Witton Park (542.38)
Name   Witton Park.
Erected   1847. [Enlarged 1862.]
Building   [Separate and entire. Exclusively used for worship.]
Sittings   Free 160. Other 140. Total [300]. Standing room 50.
Attendance 30 March   Morning 90 + 60 SS. Total 150.
                         Afternoon 80 + 66 SS. Total 146.
                         Evening 70. Total 70.
Average attendance   Morning 100 + 70 SS. Total 170.
Dated   30 March 1851.
Signed   John Dent, steward [stock-taker in iron works].
                 Witton Park, near Darlington.

**13.56   Wesleyan Methodist Association, South Road, Bishop
Auckland** (542.12)
Name   South Road Chapel.
Erected   In 1844. [Opened 21 July 1844, cost £400.]
Building   [Separate and] entire. Exclusively for worship and
                 Sunday school.
Sittings   Free 100. Other 300. Total [400].
                 Standing room none particular except the isles (*sic*).

Attendance 30 March   Morning – school.
                          Afternoon 58. Total [58].
                          Evening 54. Total [54].
Average attendance   Morning 100 + 51 SS. Total [151].
Dated   31 March 1851.
Signed   Joseph Dawson, chapel steward.
                 Addolade (*sic*) [Adelaide] Street, Bishop Auckland.
[The United Methodist Free Church was formed in 1857. A new chapel for this denomination was opened in Bishop Auckland on 10 May 1870.]

13.57   Wesleyan Methodist Association, Shildon (542.25)
Name   Wesleyan Methodist Association Chapel.
Erected   1837.
Building   [Separate and entire. Exclusively used for worship.]
Sittings   Free 75. Other 75. Total [150].
Attendance 30 March   Morning 25. Total [25].
                          Afternoon 25. Total [25].
Average attendance   Morning 25. Total [25].
                          Afternoon 25. Total [25].
Remarks   This place of worship was well attended for years, but owing to schism in the church the chapel has nearly been deserted.
Dated   31 March 1851.
Signed   John Robinson, manager [agricultural labourer].
                 Chapel Row, Shildon, N[ea]r Darlington.

13.58   Wesleyan Methodist Association, Chapel Street, West Auckland (542.30)
Name   Bethel Chapel.
Erected   1837.
Building   Separate [and entire. Exclusively used for worship.]
Sittings   Free 154. Other 116. Total [270].
Attendance 30 March   Morning 28 + 70 SS. Total 98.
                          Afternoon no service. 90 SS. Total 90.
                          Evening 70. Total 70.
Average attendance   Morning 36 + 80 SS. Total 116.
                          Afternoon no service. 86 SS. Total 86.
                          Evening 100. Total 100.
Dated   31 March 1851.
Signed   Thomas Ayer, trustee and manager.
                 West Auckland, Durham.

13.59   Society of Friends [Quakers], Newgate Street, Bishop Auckland (542.10)

Name	[Not given.]
Erected	Before 1800. [Erected 1686. New meeting house opened 1840.]
Building	[Separate and entire. Exclusively used for worship.]
Sittings	Floor area 1,041 square feet. [To seat] 174.
	Gallery 514 square feet. [To seat] 116.
	Total 1,555 square feet. [To seat] 290.
Attendance 30 March	Morning 37. Total [37].
	Afternoon 10. Total [10].
Dated	Eleventh day of fourth month 1851.
Signed	John Beaumont Pease [woollen merchant].
	Of Darlington monthly meeting.
	North Lodge, Darlington.

[John Beaumont Pease (1803–1873) was also involved with several other Quaker meeting houses (**13.60, 21.63, 21.92, 23.30** and **23.56**). His second son, John William Pease (1836–1901) the Newcastle banker and partner of Hodgkin, Barrett, Pease and Spencer, gave Benwell Tower, Benwell, Newcastle upon Tyne, to be the residence of the Bishop of Newcastle.]

13.60   Society of Friends [Quakers], New Shildon (542.27)

Name	[Not given.]
Erected	1842. [New meeting house opened 1862.]
Building	[Not separate and entire but exclusively used for worship.]
Sittings	Floor area 398 square feet (no gallery). Total 398. [To seat] 60.
Attendance 30 March	Afternoon 13. Total [13].
Remarks	A meeting for worship only held in the afternoons of 1st days [i.e. Sundays]. The attendance in the morning being at the Friends' meeting at Bishop Auckland.
Dated	Eleventh day of fourth month 1851.
Signed	John Beaumont Pease [woollen merchant]
	Of Darlington monthly meeting.
	North Lodge, Darlington.

13.61   Roman Catholic, Bishop Auckland (542.9)

Name   St Wilfrid's Catholic Church.
Erected   [22] July 1845. [Cost about £1,000. Opened 13 October
              1846 and enlarged 1857.]
Building   [Separate and entire. Exclusively used for worship.]
Sittings   [None free.] Other 240. Total [240]. Standing room
              about 60.
Attendance 30 March   [Not given.]
Average attendance   Morning 240. Total [240].
Remarks   If it be desired to know how many persons are able
              and do attend from time to time during the year, the
              stating of the average number of persons attending
              on a Sunday will not be satisfactory as many persons
              from distance of residence or other causes are impeded
              and only come to church on the Sunday occasionally.
              The number of persons so able will not be less than
              900.
Dated   30 March 1851.
Signed   John Smith, Catholic priest.
              Bishop Auckland, Durham.

[In 1842 support was canvassed for a new mission at Bishop
Auckland. 'In consequence of the numerous coal mines opened in
this neighbourhood, and the establishment of several public works,
the influx of population has been very great, and many of the new
residents are [Roman] Catholics.' All of the 400 Roman Catholics
in the area were labourers. Quoted in J. Bossy, *The English Catholic
Community 1570–1850* (London, 1975), p. 321. In 1852 the estimated
number of Roman Catholics in the area was 750.]

14.   Chester le Street District (HO 129/548)
36 places of worship

14.1   Church of England, St John the Evangelist, Birtley (548.18)
Population 1851: 1,833 (township)

Name   St John's Church. A chapelry district under the
              provisions of the Church Building Acts, 58th George III
              (chapter not known) [c.45].
Consecrated 9 August 1849. It was consecrated, as stated above, as

	[a] district church in the parish of Chester-le-Street. [Enlarged 1887–89. District created 8 January 1850.]
Erected	By grants from Her Majesty's Commissioners for building churches [£200]; the Incorporated Society for Building and Enlarging Churches [£50]; the Diocesan Church Building Society [£40]; and by subscriptions. No grant or rate. Private £1,800. Total cost £1,800.
Endowment	No endowment at present from any source.
Sittings	All free. Total 359. [Free 324. Other 35. Total 359.]

Attendance 30 March   Morning 150. Total 150.
                         Evening 250. Total 250.
Average attendance   Morning 150. Total 150.
                         Evening 250. Total 250.

Remarks	Under the head of endowment, I have to remark that the case of the chapelry district of Birtley is on the books of the Ecclesiastical Commissioners for future consideration.
Dated	31 March 1851.
Signed	Francis William Bewsher, perpetual curate [1850–1881]. Birtley House, Gateshead.

{B 55.}

14.2 Church of England, St Cuthbert, Chester-le-Street (548.10)
Population 1851: 18,119 (parish) 2,580 (township)

Name	Church of St Cuthbert. Parish Church.
Consecrated	Before 1800. [Restored 1862.]
Endowment	Land £29. Tithe £447. OPE £12. Dues £42. Easter offerings £5. Other £5.
Sittings	Free 220. Other 650. Total 870.

Attendance 30 March   Morning about 400 + 110 SS. Total 510.
                        Evening about 300. Total [300].
Average attendance   Morning about 600 or 700 + 110 SS. Total 810.
                        Evening about 600. Total 600.

Dated	31 March 1851.
Signed	Edward C. Williams MA, curate. Chester-le-Street.
Incumbent	[Thomas Hyde Ripley 1828–65.]
{1857	Attendance 475. 25 communicants. Much room lost by the inconvenient shape of the pews.} {B 187.}

14.3   Church of England Schoolroom, Great Lumley (548.6)
Population 1851: 1,730 (township)

Name   A licensed [National] schoolroom.
Licensed   January 1849, as a chapel of ease to Chester-le-Street.
Sittings   [Not given.]
Attendance 30 March   Morning 47 + 45 SS. Total 92.
Afternoon 45 + 33 SS. Total 78.
Average attendance   [Not given.]
Dated   30 March 1851.
Signed   Joseph Price De Pledge, off[iciatin]g minister [1850–65].
Chester-le-Street.
[Christ Church, Great Lumley, was consecrated on 12 July 1861.]

14.4   Church of England, St Andrew, Lamesley (548.20)
Population 1851: 1,914 (chapelry)

Name   Lamesley Church. Church of an ancient chapelry.
Consecrated   Before 1800. [Rebuilt 1758, enlarged 1821, restored 1884.]
Endowment   Tithe £21. OPE £9–£12. Fees £12. Other £14.
[Total] £138 12s.
Sittings   Free 120. Other 302. Total 422.
Attendance 30 March   Morning 201 + 94 SS. Total 295.
Afternoon 78. Total 78.
Evening 114. Total 114.
Average attendance   Evening 130. Total 130.
Remarks   The great mass of the population live 2½ miles from the church at Eighton Banks. The evening service is therefore held in a schoolroom at that place during six months in the year. There is no afternoon service in summer.
The average attendance at church in the evenings during the summer months is 220, rather larger than that in the afternoon and that in the evenings during winter.
Dated   30 March 1851.
Signed   Robert Hopper Williamson, perpetual curate [1847–65].
Lamesley Parsonage, Gateshead.
{B 110.}
[Robert Hopper Williamson (1813–1891) succeeded his father, also called Robert Hopper Williamson (1784–1865), as the rector of Hurworth 1865–75 (**15.12**).]

14.5   Church of England Schoolroom, Eighton Banks, Lamesley
(548.20a)

Attendance   Evening service held during six months of the year.
[See **14.4.**]

Incumbent   [Robert Hopper Williamson, perpetual curate 1847–65.]

{1857   Attendance 250. 43 communicants.}

[St Thomas, Eighton Banks, was consecrated by the Bishop of Exeter on 6 September 1854.]

14.6   Church of England, Holy Trinity, Pelton (548.11)
Population 1851: 1,207 (township)

Name   Trinity Church, Pelton, district parish chapelry.

Consecrated   24 October 1842, a new church for a district attached.
[Created 3 April 1843 out of the parish of Chester-le-Street.]

Erected   By a committee of subscribers. Private £2,000.
[Parliamentary grant of £300.] Total about £2,000.

Endowment   OPE £145. Pew rents average £5.
Fees and dues average £15. Other 15s.

Sittings   Free 267. Other 183. Total 450.

Attendance 30 March   [Not given.]

Average attendance   Morning 250 + 65 SS. Total 315.
Afternoon 150 + 15 SS. Total 165.

Remarks   The return as to cost and income are as near as I can give them, being from home, from bad health and not having the papers before me. The [actual attendance on 30 March] will be afterward certified and supplied.

Dated   29 March 1851.

Signed   Henry Barrett, perpetual curate [1842–71].
Pelton Parsonage, Fence Houses, Durham.

{1857   Attendance 200. 22 communicants.}   {B 95.}

14.7   Church of England, Holy Trinity, Usworth (548.28)
Population 1851: 2,051 (township)

Name   Usworth chapelry, Trinity Chapel. District chapel [of Washington].

Consecrated   1835. [Erected 1831, opened by licence 8 April 1832, consecrated by the Bishop of St David's, 5 March 1835.
Enlarged 1904–06.]

Erected   By Rev. Henry Perceval [rector of Washington 1826–37]. Generally by private subscription and a grant from the Church Building Society. Total cost £882.

Endowment Tithe £145. Glebe £30. OPE Q[ueen] Anne's Bounty £21 6s. Fees £3.

Sittings   Free 410. Other 23. Total 433.

Attendance 30 March   Morning 50 + 39 SS. Total 89.
Afternoon 45 + 22 SS. Total 67.

Average attendance   Morning 55 + 40 SS. Total 95.
Afternoon 36 + 28 SS. Total 64.
Evening none.

Remarks   Two Methodist chapels in the parish (**14.24** and **14.25**), a pit population; the clergyman's house three miles from [the] chapel; number of scholars in week days 140.

Dated   31 March 1851.

Signed   Richard Collinson, incumbent [1847–53].
North Biddick Hall, Washington, Gateshead, Durham.

{1857   Attendance 100. 24 communicants.}   {B 35.}

[Richard Collinson had previously been the curate of Usworth 1835–46.]

14.8   Church of England, St Michael and All Angels, Witton Gilbert (548.14a)

Population 1851: 1,758 (parochial chapelry)

[Summary form]

Name   Witton Gilbert Church.

Erected   [Not given c.1170. Restored and enlarged 1859–60.]

Endowment [£303.]

Sittings   Free 125. Total 125.

Dated   1 September 1852.

Signed   William Crowdace, registrar.

Incumbent [Cuthbert John Carr perpetual curate of Witton Gilbert and Kimblesworth 1848–88.]

{1857   Attendance 120. 35 communicants.}   {B 38.}

[The parishes of Witton Gilbert and Kimblesworth were united in 1593.]

14.9   Church of England Schoolroom, Sacriston (548.14b)

[Summary form]

Name   Sacriston p[arochial] c[hapel]. [In use since 1843.]

Sittings   Free 90. Total 90.
Dated   1 September 1852.
Signed   William Crowdace, registrar.
Incumbent   [Cuthbert John Carr 1848–88.]
{1857   Attendance 50.}
[St Peter, Sacriston, was consecrated on 2 August 1866 and enlarged in 1888 and 1898.]

14.10   Church of England, Holy Trinity, Washington (548.31)
Population 1851: 1,224 (township)

Name   Parish Church.
Consecrated 1832. [Church demolished April 1832 and after rebuilding it was re-opened in the spring of 1833. It was enlarged and re-opened 22 May 1883, and replaced by a new church consecrated on 1 November 1902.]
Erected   By private subscriptions, a parochial rate, expense of the materials of the old parish church and a grant from the Diocesan Church Building Society. The Rev. H[enry] Perceval, a former rector, caused it to be built. Diocesan Church Building Society £75. Parochial rate £25. Private £996 6s 5d (NB. the Rev. H[enry] Perceval gave of this £468 12s 11d). Total cost £1,096 6s 5d.
Endowment   OPE Coal under glebe. [£900.]
Sittings   Free 256. Other 149. Total 405.
Attendance 30 March   Morning 87 + 46 SS. Total 133.
                        Afternoon 45 + 34 SS. Total 79.
Average attendance   Morning 70 + 45 SS. Total 115.
                        Afternoon 25 + 30 SS. Total 55.
Dated   30 March 1851.
Signed   Lewis William Denman, rector [1847–61].
               Washington, Gateshead.
{1857   Attendance 150. 20 communicants.}   {B 57.}
[Henry Perceval, rector of Washington 1826–37, was the third son of Spencer Perceval (1762–1812), the Prime Minister assassinated on 11 May 1812. Lewis William Denman was the youngest son of the Lord Chief Justice, the first Lord Denman (1779–1854).]

14.11   Independent [Congregational], Low Chare, Chester-le-Street (548.2)
Name   Bethel Chapel.
Erected   1814. [Rebuilt 1861.]

Building   [Separate and entire. Exclusively used for worship.]
Sittings   Free 50. Other 300. Total [350].
Attendance 30 March   Morning 85 + 20 SS. Total 105.
          Evening 142. Total 142.
Average attendance   Morning 120 + 30 SS. Total 150.
          Evening 180. Total 180.
Remarks   The attendance on the 30 March was not equal to
          the average, the influenza being very prevalent.
          Many normally attend in the morning and not in the
          evening, and [... ...] the average attendance is not
          more than 200–300 of the persons who compose the
          congregation worshipping in this chapel. Some of the
          Sunday scholars return home after the school.
Dated   31 March 1851.
Signed   Charles Pedley, minister [1849–57].
          Chester-le-Street.
[On leaving Bethel Chapel, Charles Pedley (1827–1872) moved to
Canada and served at St John's, Newfoundland, 1857–63, and then
at two churches in Ontario 1864–66 and 1866–72.]

14.12   Wesleyan Methodist, Birtley (548.19)
Name   None.
Erected   1830. [Opened 1832, new chapel in Durham Road
          opened 10 March 1883.]
Building   [Separate and entire. Exclusively used for worship.]
Sittings   Free 80. Other 80. Total [160].
Attendance 30 March   Afternoon 80. Total [80].
          Evening 100. Total [100].
Average attendance   Morning [Not given]. Total 190.
Dated   31 March 1851.
Signed   Joseph Emerson, steward [tailor].
          Birtley, near Gateshead.

14.13   Wesleyan Methodist, Low Chare, Chester-le-Street (548.1)
Name   Wesleyan Chapel.
Erected   1807. [Replaced by a new chapel in Station Road
          opened in 1880.]
Building   [Separate and entire. Exclusively used for worship.]
Sittings   Free 184. Other 116. Total [300].
Attendance 30 March   Morning 78 + 22 SS. Total 100.
          Evening 100 + 10 SS. Total 110.
Average attendance   Morning 98 + 22 SS. Total 120.

Evening 140 + 10 SS. Total 150.
Dated   31 March 1851.
Signed   Richard Dalkin, leader (saddler).
            Chester-le-Street.

14.14   Wesleyan Methodist, Chester-le-Street (548.5)
Name   Chartershaugh Chapel.
Erected   Old 1793; new 1845.
Building   [Separate and] entire. [Used exclusively for worship
            and] Sunday school.
Sittings   Free 72. Other 104. Total [176].
Attendance 30 March   Morning 95. Total [95].
            Evening 100. Total [100].
Average attendance   Morning 85 SS. Total [85].
Dated   31 March 1851.
Signed   Benjamin Robinson Falfield, steward.
            Fence House Station, Chester-le-Street, Durham.

14.15   Wesleyan Methodist, Edmondsley (548.3)
Name   Edmondsley Wesleyan Chapel.
Erected   1842.
Building   [Separate and entire but not exclusively used for
            worship.]
Sittings   Free 150. Other 32. Total [182].
Attendance 30 March   Morning 35 + 38 SS. Total 73.
            Evening 50. Total 50.
Average attendance   Morning 50 + 80 SS. Total 130.
            Evening 95. Total 95.
Dated   31 March 1851.
Signed   William [Ivan?] Moon Lynas, steward [schoolmaster].
            Edmondsley [Edge], near Sacriston, Durham.

14.16   Wesleyan Methodist, Eighton Banks, Lamesley (548.22)
Name   Chapel.
Erected   Before 1800.
Building   [Separate and entire. Exclusively used for worship.]
Sittings   Free 108. Other 72. Total [180].
Attendance 30 March   Afternoon 114 + 15 SS. Total 129.
            Evening 47 + 13 SS. Total 60.
Average attendance   Afternoon 80 + 20 SS. Total 100.
            Evening 40 + 10 SS. Total 50.
Dated   30 March 1851.

Signed   Robert Chisholm, society steward.
Black Fell Colliery, near Gateshead, Durham.

14.17   Wesleyan Methodist, Great Lumley (548.9)

Name   Lumley Wesleyan Methodist.
Erected   Before 1800. [1796, enlarged 1821. New chapel opened 1906.]
Building   [Separate and entire. Exclusively used for worship.]
Sittings   Free 150. Other 190. Total [340].
Attendance 30 March   Morning 66 SS. Total 66.
Afternoon 83. Total 83.
Evening 90. Total 90.
Average attendance   [Not given.]
Dated   31 March 1851.
Signed   Thomas Bradford, society steward (tailor) [and draper].
Great Lumley, Durham.

14.18   Wesleyan Methodist, Harraton, Birtley (548.25)

Name   Brown's Buildings Preaching House.
Erected   Been a preaching house since 1843.
Building   [Separate and entire.] Day school and Sunday school. [Exclusively used for worship.]
Sittings   All [free].
Attendance 30 March   Afternoon 36. Total [36].
Average attendance   Morning 50 + 50 SS. Total [100].
Dated   30 March 1851.
Signed   John Ritson, leader [coal miner].
Brown's Buildings.

14.19   Wesleyan Methodist, Kimblesworth (548.26)

Name   Kimblesworth Wesleyan Chapel.
Erected   Before 1800.
Building   (Part of a building.) [Not separate and entire or exclusively used for worship.]
Sittings   Free 60. Other 66. Total [126].
Attendance 30 March   Afternoon 30 + 20 SS. Total 50
Evening 41 + 21 SS. Total 62.
Average attendance   Afternoon 45 + 20 SS. Total 65.
Evening 90 + 20 SS. Total 110.
Dated   30 March 1851.
Signed   Samuel Forster, chapel steward [coal miner].
Kimblesworth, n[ea]r Gateshead.

14.20   Wesleyan Methodist, Pelton (548.13)
Name   Chapel.
Erected   Before 1800.
Building   [Separate and entire. Exclusively used for worship.]
Sittings   Free 50. Other 24. Total [74]. Standing room none.
Attendance 30 March   Afternoon 30. Total 30.
Average attendance   Morning 40. Total 40.
Dated   31 March 1851.
Signed   Philip Kirkup, class leader [butcher].
              Pelton, Chester-le-Street, Durham

14.21   Wesleyan Methodist, Pelton Fell (548.12)
Name   Pelton Fell Wesleyan Methodist Chapel.
Erected   1838.
Building   [Separate and entire but not exclusively used for
              worship.]
Sittings   Free 130. Other 30. Total [160]. Standing room none.
Attendance 30 March   Morning 70 + 54 SS. Total 124.
              Afternoon 132 + 22 SS. Total 154.
              Evening 124 + 43 SS. Total 167.
Average attendance   Morning and afternoon 110 + 55 SS. Total 165.
Dated   30 March 1851.
Signed   Martin Greaves Morgan, steward.
              Pelton Colliery, n[ea]r Chester-le-Street.

14.22   Wesleyan Methodist, Rupells Houses (548.4b)
[Shared with Primitive Methodists (**14.33**)]
Name   Rupells Houses.
Erected   [Not given.]
Building   [Not separate and entire or exclusively used for
              worship.]
Sittings   Free 90. Total [90].
Attendance 30 March   Morning 76. Total [76]. [Primitive Methodist.]
              Afternoon 53. Total [53]. [Wesleyan
              Methodist.]
Average attendance   Morning 60. Total [60]. [Primitive Methodist.]
              Afternoon 70. Total [70]. [Wesleyan
              Methodist.]
Remarks   The higher nos. refer to the Primitive Methodists, and
              the afternoon services to the Wesleyans.
Dated   30 March 1851.
Signed   Jonathan Hall [schoolmaster].

Thomas Oliver, [Primitive Methodist] minister.
Pitt Hill, [Urpeth], near Chester-le-Street.

14.23   Wesleyan Methodist, Sacriston (548.17)
Name   Wesleyan Chapel.
Erected   1840.
Building   [Separate and entire. Exclusively used for worship.]
Sittings   Free 80. Other 70. Total [150]. Standing room none.
Attendance 30 March   Morning 36 + 55 SS. Total 91.
                        Evening 36 + 17 SS. Total 53.
Average attendance   [Not given.]
Remarks   A Sunday school in the afternoons, but temporarily
               closed on Sunday afternoon, 30 March 1851.
Dated   30 March 1851.
Signed   George Marshall, steward (blacksmith).
               Sacriston, Durham.

14.24   Wesleyan Methodist, Usworth (548.21)
Name   Usworth Methodist Chapel.
Erected   24 July 1805.
Building   A separate and entire building. Used exclusively as a
               place of worship and Sunday school.
Sittings   Free 200. Other 119. Total [319].
Attendance 30 March   Morning 38 + 44 SS. Total 82.
                        Evening 70. Total 70.
Average attendance   Afternoon 150. Total [150].
                        Evening 150. Total [150].
Remarks   The time of service changed recently from 2 o'clock to
               10½ in the morning; this, together with removals, has
               caused a decrease in the attendance.
Dated   31 March 1851.
Signed   Samuel Southern, chapel steward [chemist and grocer].
               Usworth, Gateshead.

14.25   Wesleyan Methodist Schoolroom, Usworth Colliery
(548.29a)
[Shared with Primitive Methodists (**14.34**)]
Name   Usworth Colliery Schoolroom.
Erected   1850.
Building   [Separate and entire. Exclusively used for worship.]
Sittings   Free 100. Other none. Total [100].
Attendance 30 March   Morning 50 [no SS]. Total 50.

Afternoon 50 [no SS]. Total 50.
Evening 50. Total 50.
Average attendance   Morning 50 [no SS]. Total 50.
Afternoon 50 [no SS]. Total 50.
Evening 50. Total 50.
Dated   31 March 1851.
Signed   Joseph Cook, steward (viewer) [colliery agent].
Usworth Colliery, Durham.

14.26   Wesleyan Methodist, Wapping (548.8)
Name   Wapping.
Erected   Cottage in lieu of a chapel erected since 1800.
Building   [Separate and entire. Exclusively used for worship.]
Sittings   All 100 free. Total [100].
Attendance 30 March   Afternoon 40 + 20 SS. Total 60.
Average attendance   Afternoon 50 + 20 SS. Total 70.
Dated   31 March 1851.
Signed   Harrison Fenwick, class leader [coal miner].
Wapping, Fence Houses.

14.27   Wesleyan Methodist, Washington Row (548.27b)
[Shared with Primitive Methodists (**14.35**)]

14.28   Wesleyan Methodist, Sacriston Lane, Witton Gilbert
(548.16)
Name   Methodist Chapel.
Erected   In the year 1825.
Building   [Separate and entire. Exclusively used for worship.]
Sittings   Free 76. Other 114. Total [190]. Standing room none.
Attendance 30 March   Afternoon 56 + 25 SS. Total 81.
Evening 46 + 10 SS. Total 56.
Average attendance   Afternoon 110 + 35 SS. Total 145.
Evening 96 + 15 SS. Total 111.
Remarks   [In another hand, 15 and 16 missing, Witton Gilbert
Church and Sacriston. (But see **14.8** and **14.9**).]
Dated   31 March 1851.
Signed   John Barker, steward [grocer and postmaster].
Witton Gilbert, Durham.

14.29   Methodist New Connexion, Great Lumley (548.7)
Name   Zoar.
Erected   1821.

Building   [Separate and entire. Exclusively used for worship.]
Sittings   Free 110. Other 86. Total [196].
Attendance 30 March   No service.
Average attendance   Morning 150. Total [150].
                        Afternoon 200. Total [200].
Dated   31 March 1851.
Signed   Peter Hall, steward [coal miner].
               Great Lumley, near Fence Houses.

14.30   Methodist New Connexion, Sunniside (548.24)
Name   Methodist New Connexion Chapel.
Erected   1840.
Building   [Separate and entire. Exclusively used for worship.]
Sittings   Free 114. Other 36. Total [150].
Attendance 30 March   Afternoon 57. Total [57].
                        Evening 80. Total [80].
Average attendance   [Not given.]
Dated   30 March 1851.
Signed   William Cocker, minister.
               18 Jackson St[reet], Gateshead.
[William Cocker was also a minister in Gateshead (**18.42** and **18.43**).]

14.31   Primitive Methodist, Edon Row, Chester-le-Street (548.15)
Name   Edon Row.
Erected   [Not given.]
Building   [Not separate and entire or exclusively used for
               worship.]
Sittings   [Not given.]
Attendance 30 March   Afternoon 44. Total [44].
Average attendance   Afternoon 40. Total [40].
Dated   30 March 1851.
Signed   John Hey.
               Robert Hepplewhite.
               [Pitt Hill, Urpeth], Chester-le-Street.

14.32   Primitive Methodist, Eighton Banks, Lamesley (548.23)
Name   Chapel.
Erected   About 1823.
Building   Separate and entire. [Exclusively used for worship.]
Sittings   Free 100. Other 100. Total [200].
Attendance 30 March   Morning 40. Total [40].
                        Evening 40. Total [40].

Average attendance   Morning 40. Total [40].
Dated   31 March 1851.
Signed   Abner Lucas, local preacher [fire-brick maker].
               Eighton Banks, n[ea]r Gateshead.

14.33   Primitive Methodist, Rupells Houses (548.4a)
[Shared with Wesleyan Methodists (**14.22**)]

14.34   Primitive Methodist Schoolroom, Usworth Colliery
(548.29b)
[Shared with Wesleyan Methodists (**14.25**)]
[A Primitive Methodist chapel was erected at Usworth in 1885.]

14.35   Primitive Methodist, Washington Row (548.27a)
[Shared with the Wesleyan Methodists (**14.27**)]
Name   Washington Row Chaple (*sic*).
Erected   Rebuilt in 1848. [New chapel opened 1866.]
Building   [Separate and] entire building. [Exclusively used for
               worship.]
Sittings   Free 138. Other 22. Total [160].
Attendance 30 March   Afternoon (Sunday school).
                         Evening 36 + 20 SS. Total 56.
Average attendance   Morning 80 + 40 SS. Total 120.
Remarks   NB. This chapel is held by the Wesleyan Methodists
               and the Primitive Methodists.
Dated   [Not given.]
Signed   Peter Horn, society steward [coal miner].
               Washington Row, Durham.

14.36   Wesleyan Methodist Association, Washington Staiths
           (548.30)
Name   None.
Erected   [Not given.]
Building   [Not separate and entire but exclusively used for
               worship.]
Sittings   Free 80. Other none. Total [80].
Attendance 30 March   Morning 64 SS. Total [64].
                         Afternoon 57. Total [57].
                         Evening 80. Total [80].
Average attendance   Morning 60 SS. Total [60].
                         Afternoon 50. Total [50].
                         Evening 70. Total [70].

Dated   30 March 1851.
Signed   William Banks, steward [cordwainer].
             Washington Staiths, Durham.

15. Darlington District (HO 129/540)
38 places of worship (and 10 in Yorkshire)

15.1 Church of England, St Mary the Virgin, Aycliffe (540.44)
Population 1851: 812 (township)

Name   Aycliffe Church dedicated to St Mary the Virgin. An
             ancient parish church, the church of a distinct parish.
Consecrated Before 1800. [Restored 1881–82.]
Endowment [£246.]
Sittings   Free 95 (for adults), 60 (for children). Other 308.
             Total 463.
Attendance 30 March Morning 204 + 84 SS. Total 288.
                       Afternoon 77 + 60 SS. Total 137.
Average attendance   [Not given.]
Dated   31 March 1851.
Signed   John Davie Eade, vicar [1835–80].
             Aycliffe vicarage, near Darlington.
{1857   Attendance 300 [in] summer. 200 [in] winter. 70
            communicants [at] great feasts. 32 communicants
            commonly.}   {B 54.}
[From 1875 Charles John Aylmer Eade was his father's curate, and
on his death in 1880 succeeded him and remained as the incumbent
until his death in 1926.]

15.2 Church of England, St Edwin, Coniscliffe (540.31)
Population 1851: 451 (parish)

Name   Name given at consecration. It is the ancient parish
             church.
Consecrated Consecrated.
Endowment Tithe £184 (commuted). Glebe £70. OPE none. Pew
             rents none. Fees £2 or £3. Dues none. Other, cannot
             tell. May be none.
Sittings   Free 120. Other 184. Total 304.
Attendance 30 March Morning 45 SS. Total 45.

Afternoon 26 SS. Total 26.

Average attendance   Morning 120. Total 120.
Afternoon 50. Total 50.
Evening 75. Total 75. (In summer the service
time is changed to evening.)

Remarks   A large proportion of the parishioners are Roman
Catholics. It is only during the last twelve months that
I have established a late afternoon service. There was
no congregation before.

Dated   30 March 1851.

Signed   Henry Algernon Baumgartner, minister i.e. vicar
[1849–58].
Coniscliffe vicarage, near Darlington.

{1857   Attendance 70. 12 communicants.}   {B 14.}

15.3   Church of England, St Cuthbert, Darlington (540.22)
Population 1851: 12,453 (parish) 11,582 (township)

[Summary form]

Name   St Cuthbert's.

Erected   Nearly 700 years ago. [Restored 1862–65, re-opened 14
December 1865.]

Endowment   [£680.]

Sittings   Free 100. Other 1,100. Total 1,200.

Usual attendance   Morning 400 to 500 + 120 SS. Total [520–620].
Afternoon no service.
Evening 600 to 700 + 120 SS. Total [720–820].

Dated   [Not given.]

Signed   John Tweddle, registrar.

Incumbent   [Alexander James Howell 1846–60.]

{1857   Attendance 1,000. 300 communicants.}   {B 309.}

[From 1856–58 Alexander Howell was suspended from the living
due to drunkenness.]

15.4   Church of England, Holy Trinity, Darlington (540.23)
Population 1851: 3,779 (district)

Name   Holy Trinity Church. A distinct parish [created 3 April
1843].

Consecrated   6 December 1838, as an additional church. [Restored
1883, 1890 and chancel enlarged 1900.]
(The district consists of part of the township of

Darlington and the township of Cockerton Newton.
[Situated] between the town of Darlington and the
village of Cockerton.)

Erected   Private benefactors, the Incorporated Society for
Building Churches, the Diocesan Society [and] a
bazaar. Private £3,500. Total cost £3,500.

Endowment Land £21 (last charge). OPE £89 12s 6d [included £10
a year from the Lord Crewe Charity]. Pew rents £45.
Fees £25.
Other   £180 12s 6d
         £100 (curate)
         £280 12s 6d [total].

Sittings   Free 570. Other 410. Total 980.

Attendance 30 March Morning 650 + 235 SS. Total 895 [885].
Afternoon 300. Total 300.
Evening 200 (in a village National school).
Total 200.

Average attendance   [Not given.]

Remarks   The scholars are not taken to church in the afternoon,
but are instructed in the schoolroom.

Dated   31 March 1851.

Signed   Thomas Webb Minton, incumbent [1847–65].
Darlington, County of Durham.

{1857   Attendance 500. 45 communicants.}   {B 136.}

15.5   Church of England Schoolroom, Cockerton (540.35)
Population 1851: 537 (township)

[Summary form]

Name   A [National] schoolroom.

Opened   1826.

Sittings   Free 200. Other none. Total 200.

Usual attendance   Morning none.
Afternoon none.
Evening about 200 + 40 SS. Total [240].

Remarks   NB. This place is only open for public worship during
the winter half-year; and the number will be returned
from Trinity Church by the Rev. Mr [Thomas Webb]
Minton for the morning and afternoon attendance at
that church, but if he has made a return of the evening
attendance, the 200 will be included in his return.

Dated   [Not given.]

Signed   Thomas Broader [teacher].
Incumbent [Thomas Webb Minton 1847–65.]
{1857   A licensed schoolroom to hold 400.}
[The National School was opened in 1825 and endowed with £5 yearly from the Trustees of the Lord Crewe Charity. St Mary, Cockerton was consecrated on 9 November 1901.]

15.6   Church of England, St John the Evangelist, Neasham Road, Darlington (540.21)

[Summary form]
Name   St John's Church. [The Railway Man's Church.]
Erected   1849. [Cost about £4,000. A Parliamentary grant of £150. Foundation stone laid 10 September 1847, and the building consecrated on 16 July 1853. Parish created 4 July 1845.]
Endowment   [£130.]
Sittings   Free 420. Other 250. Total 670.
Attendance Morning 150 + 75 SS. Total [225].
              Evening 400. Total [400].
Dated   [Not given.]
Signed   George Brown, incumbent [1845–56].
{1857   Attendance 150. 30 communicants.}

15.7   Church of England, St Mary the Virgin, Denton (540.38)
Population 1851: 121 (township)

Name   The old church or chapel of Denton was dedicated to St Mary. The present chapel of Denton was erected on the old site in 1810, opened in 1811, and enlarged in 1836. It is a chapel of ease or a perpetual chapelry [of Gainford (**23.2**)].
Consecrated [Not given.] [New church opened 22 October 1891.]
Erected   By private benefaction and subscription. Private £357. Total cost £357.
Endowment   Land £14. Glebe and parsonage house £14. OPE £50. Fees £2.
Sittings   Free 90. Other 220. Total 310.
Attendance 30 March   Morning 40 + 20 SS. Total 60.
              Afternoon 8 + 34 SS. Total 42.
Average attendance   Morning 38 + 20 SS. Total 58.
              Afternoon 10 + 30 SS. Total 40.

Dated   31 March 1851.
Signed   John Birkbeck, incumbent [1836–84].
              Denton, Darlington.
{1857   Attendance 50. 16 communicants.}   {B 12.}
[Following his ordination John Birkbeck was the curate of Denton 1824–25.]

15.8   Church of England, St John the Baptist, Low Dinsdale
(540.14)
Population 1851: 157 (parish)

Name   Dinsdale Church. Dedicated to St John, and an ancient
              parish church.
Consecrated Before 1800. [Restored 1875–76.]
Endowment   Land, tithe, glebe £224.
Sittings   [None free.] Other 120. Total 120.
Attendance 30 March   Morning 58 + 29 SS. Total 87.
                        Afternoon 38. Total [38].
Average attendance   [Not given.]
Remarks   Only prayers in afternoon and a voluntary attendance
              of Sunday scholars.
Dated   31 March 1851.
Signed   John William Smith, curate [1850–59].
              Dinsdale, Darlington.
Incumbent   [William Smoult Temple 1835–59.]
{1857   Attendance 60. 25 communicants.}   {B 8.}
[In 1859 John Smith became the incumbent and remained in post until his death in 1897.]

15.9   Church of England, St Andrew, Haughton-le-Skerne
(540.48)
Population 1851: 1,403 (parish) 474 (township)

Name   Before 1800. [Restored and enlarged 1895.]
Endowment   [Not given. £1,279.]
Sittings   Free 100 (for school children only). Other 300. Total
              400.
Attendance 30 March   Morning 225. Total 225.
                        Afternoon 130. Total 130.
Average attendance   Morning 240 + 80 SS. Total 320.
                        Afternoon 175. Total 175.
Dated   30 March 1851.

Signed   Thomas Dalton, curate [1847–52].
             Haughton rectory, Darlington.
Incumbent [Bulkeley Bandinel 1822–61.]
{1857   Attendance 250. 40 communicants.}   {B 23.}
[Bulkeley Bandinel was also the librarian of the Bodleian Library,
Oxford, 1813–60. His successor at Haughton-le-Skerne, Edward
Cheese 1861–82, was the son-in-law of the Bishop of Durham, Henry
Montagu Villiers. His appointment to one of the wealthiest livings
in the diocese evoked criticism from those who were opposed to
the Evangelical bishop. A.F. Munden, 'The First Palmerston Bishop:
Henry Montagu Villiers, Bishop of Carlisle 1856–60 and Bishop of
Durham 1860–61', *Northern History*, xxvi (1990), pp. 186–206.]

15.10   Church of England, St Andrew, Sadberge (540.50)
Population 1851: 371 (township)

Name   Sadberge Chapel attached to the parish of Haughton-
             le-Skerne.
Consecrated [30] September 1831 [by the Bishop of Chester].
Erected   Built by the rector of Haughton by subscription.
             His own subscription about £200. Bishop of Durham
             £100. Church Building Society £120. Sir William
             Perryman £70. Carriage of materials £100 from Bishop
             of Durham. [Also] private subscriptions. [Total cost]
             £770.
Endowment Land a small farm. Tithe £228 (commuted). Glebe I
             don't know what the glebe rents are. The land is poor
             and the farm very small. Pew rents £1.
Sittings   Free 190. Other 164. Total 354.
Attendance 30 March   Morning 67 + 48 SS. Total 115.
             Afternoon no service. Minister's serious
             illness.
Average attendance   [Not given.]
Remarks   Last Sunday was probably about an average
             attendance. Slightly above our winter and below our
             summer attendance.
Dated   4 April 1851.
Signed   David Piper, stipendiary curate [1828–56, then
             incumbent of the new district 1856–61].
             Sadberge, Darlington.
Incumbent [Bulkeley Bandinel 1822–61.]

{1857   Attendance 70. 12 communicants.}   {B 10.}

15.11   Church of England, St Michael the Archangel, Heighington (540.40)
Population 1851: 1,294 (parish) 685 (township)

Name   St Michael's church, Heighington, [an] ancient church.
Consecrated Before 1800. [Enlarged 1876.]
Endowment   Tithe £322 (rent charge). OPE £5 10s. Fees £6.
             Easter offerings £1 10s. Other £10. Total £345.
Sittings   Free 80. Other 320. Total 400.
Attendance 30 March   Morning 211 + 84 SS. Total 295.
                       Afternoon 88 + 79 SS. Total 167.
Average attendance   Morning 211 + 84 SS. Total 295.
                       Afternoon 88 + 79 SS. Total 167.
Remarks   Instalment and interest to the governors of Queen
             Anne's Bounty. Reserved bank rates. Agency. Income
             to so amount to £80, which reduces the income to
             £265 and this is suffering a gradual reduction from the
             recession.
Dated   30 March 1851.
Signed   Wilson Beckett, vicar [1836–68].
             Heighington, Darlington.
{1857   Attendance 300. 25 communicants.}

15.12   Church of England, All Saints, Hurworth (540.16)
Population 1851: 1.154 (township)

Name   Ancient parish church dedicated to All Saints.
Consecrated Unknown. Centuries ago. [Rebuilt and enlarged
             and re-opened 27 May 1832, at cost of £1,965 16s 4d.
             Restored 1871.]
Endowment   Tithe gross commuted rent charge, rates etc. being
             high £550. Glebe £200 (estimated value). Surplice [fees]
             average £6.
Sittings   Free 406. Other 429. Total 835.
Attendance 30 March   Morning 253 + 87 SS. Total 340.
                       Afternoon 136 + 60 SS. Total 196.
Average attendance   [Not given.]
Remarks   The rates and leases are high which greatly reduce
             the net produce of the tithes. The second service is in

the afternoon in winter and evening in summer. The congregation on 30 March would be about the average of the preceding year.

Dated   31 March 1851.
Signed   Robert Hopper Williamson, rector [1832–65].
             Hurworth Rectory, Darlington.
{1857   Attendance 350. 56 communicants.}   {B 40.}
[Robert Hopper Williamson (1784–1865) was succeeded by his son, also called Robert Hopper Williamson (1813–1891) who had previously been the incumbent of Lamesley 1847–65 (**14.4**).]

15.13 Church of England, St George, Middleton St George
(540.15 and 540.14a)
Population 1851: 332 (township)

Name   Middleton St George. St George, the name given on its consecration. It is an ancient parish church. (The church is placed centrally.)
Consecrated Before 1800. [Chancel rebuilt 1805, church enlarged 1822.]
Endowment   Tithe £75. Glebe £11. OPE £6 19s. Fees £1.
Sittings   Free 20. Other 120. Total 140.
Attendance 30 March   Morning SS none.
             Afternoon 69. SS none. Total 69.
Average attendance   Morning 40. SS none. Total [40].
             Afternoon 40. SS none. Total [40].
Dated   31 March 1851.
Signed   Henry Graves, rector [1837–65].
             Yarm, Yorkshire.
{1857   Attendance 50. 8 communicants.}   {B 6.}
[Henry Graves was also the minister of All Saints, High Worsall (**21.74**). According to the 1851 Civil Census, Middleton St George was 'much resorted to as a watering place' and consequently during the summer months the population was increased.]

(540.14a)
Yarm,
4 April 1851.
Sir,
Althou[gh] rector of the parish of Middleton St George, Co. of Durham, I reside in the town of Yarm, and as no one has called for the Return, prepared some days ago, wishing to render my best

assistance to your inquiries. I take the liberty of forwarding the enclosed form thro[ugh] your medium to the Registrar General, and remain yours obediently, Henry Graves.

15.14   Church of England, All Saints, Girsby, Sockburn (540.13)
Population 1851: 218 (parish) 43 (township)

Name   All Saints. Ancient parish church.
Consecrated   [25 September 1838] in lieu of an old one.
Erected   By private benefactors, [namely] Rev. G. S. Faber BD [the patron and Master of Sherburn Hospital (**16.25**) and patron of Sockburn, and] H. C. Blackett Esq. [of Sockburn Hall].
Endowment   Tithe £115. Glebe £3. OPE £33. Pew rents 10s. Other £40.
Sittings   Free 16. Other 90. Total 106.
Attendance 30 March   Afternoon 63 + 27 SS. Total 90.
Average attendance   [Not given.]
Dated   1 April 1851.
Signed   William Henry Elliot, minister [1847–70].
    Worsall Hall, Yarm, [Yorkshire].
{1857   Attendance 30. 8 communicants.}   {B 4.}
[The ruinous Sockburn parish church was replaced by All Saints', Girsby.]

15.15   Independent [Congregational] Union Street, Darlington
(540.30]
Name   Bethel Chapel.
Erected   About 1812. [Enlarged 1822, replaced by the Congregational
    Bicentenary Memorial Chapel, opened 24 August 1862.]
Building   [Separate and entire. Exclusively used for worship.]
Sittings   Free 120. Other 320. Total [440].
Attendance 30 March   Morning 217 + 109 SS. Total 326.
    Evening 218. Total [218].
Average attendance   [Not given.]
Dated   31 March 1851.
Signed   Robert Macbeth, minister [1851–53].
    Darlington.
[Under the Act of Uniformity of 1662 upwards of 2,000 ministers

(who were not prepared to submit to episcopal ordination) were ejected from their livings, university appointments and schools. A.G. Matthews, *Calamy Revised* (Oxford, 1934).]

15.16   Baptist, Upper Archer Street, Darlington (540.26)

Name   Archer Street Chapel.
Erected   1847. [Opened 12 August 1847 and cost £800. Sold in May 1870 for £670. New chapel opened in Grange Road, 8 June 1871.]
Building   [Separate and entire. Exclusively used for worship.]
Sittings   Free 300. Other 51. Total [351].
Attendance 30 March   Morning 50. Total 50.
Afternoon 44 SS. Total 44.
Evening 60. Total 60.
Average attendance   Morning 50. Total 50.
Afternoon 44 SS. Total 44.
Evening 70. Total 70.
Remarks   I do not approve of seat rents, and hope all the seats will soon be free. We have no Sunday school in the morning. Several of the children attend (say 20) but not as a school, therefore I have not put down the attendance of Sunday scholars at the morning service.
Dated   31 March 1851.
Signed   James Fyfe, minister [1849–51].
[Upper] Archer Street, Darlington, Durham.

15.17   Wesleyan Methodist, Aycliffe (540.47)

Name   Wesleyan Methodist.
Erected   1829.
Building   Separate and entire building. Exclusively as a place of worship.
Sittings   Free 79. Other 56. Total [135].
Attendance 30 March   Afternoon 31. Total [31].
Evening 80. Total [80].
Average attendance   [Not given.]
Dated   31 March 1851.
Signed   Jonathan Gill, chapel steward [miller].
Aycliffe, near Darlington, Durham.

15.18   Wesleyan Methodist, Cockerton (540.37)
Name   Wesleyan Chapel.
Erected   1823. [Cost £102. New chapel opened 30 November
              1875 and cost £1,550.]
Building   [Separate and entire. Exclusively used for worship.]
Sittings   Free 100. Other 18. Total [118].
Attendance 30 March Morning no service 45 SS. Total [45].
Average attendance   Morning 40 + 40 SS. Total 80.
Dated   31 March 1851.
Signed   Joseph Waugh [former lead miner].
              [Cockerton Hall.]

15.19   Wesleyan Methodist, Bondgate, Darlington (540.25)
Name   Bondgate Wesleyan Methodist Chapel.
Erected   Before 1800. [1777–78, enlarged 1786, 'Methodist
              Chapel 1812' cost £4,000, opened 4 July 1813.]
Building   [Separate and entire. Exclusively used for worship.]
Sittings   Free 630. Other 640. Total [1,270].
Attendance 30 March Morning 514 + 135 SS. Total 649.
                       Evening 707. Total 707.
Average attendance   [Not given.]
Dated   30 March 1851.
Signed   George Jackson, superintendent minister [1849–51].
              Wesley Place, Darlington, Durham.
[George Jackson was also the minister at Stapleton (**15.46**).]

15.20   Wesleyan Methodist, Park Street, Darlington (540.28)
Name   Park Street Wesleyan Chapel.
Erected   In 1831. [Opened 27 August 1831, closed 1854.]
Building   [Separate and entire. Exclusively used for worship.]
Sittings   Free 152. Total [152].
Attendance 30 March [No services.]
Average attendance   Afternoon 20 + 93 SS. Total 113.
Dated   31 March 1851.
Signed   George Jackson, superintendent minister [1849–51].
              Wesley Place, Darlington, Durham.

15.21   Wesleyan Methodist, Sadberge (540.51)
Name   Wesleyan Preaching Room.
Erected   Occupied since 1825.
Building   [Not separate and entire.] Part of a house. [Exclusively
              used for worship.]

Sittings   Free 38. Other 56. Total [94].
Attendance 30 March   Evening 71. Total [71].
Average attendance   [Not given.]
Dated   31 March 1851.
Signed   George Jackson, superintendent minister [1849–51].
Wesley Place, Darlington, Durham.

15.22   Wesleyan Methodist, Haughton-le-Skerne (540.49)
Name   Haughton Wesleyan Chapel.
Erected   1825. [Cost £325. Restored 1887.]
Building   [Separate and entire but not exclusively used for
worship.] Also a day school (dames).
Sittings   Free 60. Other 32. Total [92].
Attendance 30 March   Afternoon 23. Total [23].
Evening 48. Total [48].
Average attendance   [Not given.]
Dated   31 March 1851.
Signed   Christopher Boddy, member [cartwright].
Haughton-le-Skerne, Darlington.

15.23   Wesleyan Methodist, Heighington (540.41)
Name   Wesleyan Chapel.
Erected   1815.
Building   [Separate and entire. Exclusively used for worship.]
Sittings   Free 120. Other 30. Total [150].
Attendance 30 March   Evening 100. Total [100].
Average attendance   Morning 100. Total [100].
Dated   30 March 1851.
Signed   Thomas Gibson, chapel steward [rail labourer].
Heighington, Durham.

15.24   Wesleyan Methodist, High Coniscliffe (540.32)
Name   Wesleyan Methodist Chapel.
Erected   1826. [Opened 14 March 1827.]
Building   [Separate and entire. Exclusively used for a] place of
worship.
Sittings   Free 74. Other 44. Total [118].
Attendance 30 March   Evening 14. Total [14].
Average attendance   Evening 25. Total [25].
Dated   31 March 1851.
Signed   William Pomfret, chapel steward [retired shoemaker].
High Coniscliffe, Darlington, Durham.

15.25   Wesleyan Methodist, Hurworth (540.17)

Name   Wesleyan Methodist Chapel.
Erected   In 1827. [Cost £748.]
Building   A separate and entire building. [Exclusively used for
                worship.]
Sittings   Free 170. Other 90. Total [260].
Attendance 30 March   Morning 76 + 33 SS. Total 109.
                         Evening 96 + 12 SS. Total 108.
Average attendance   Morning 80 + 30 SS. Total 110.
                         Evening 95 + 20 SS. Total 115.
Dated   31 March 1851.
Signed   George James, trustee and steward [proprietor of land
                and houses].
                Hurworth upon Tees, Durham.

15.26   Wesleyan Methodist, Hurworth Place (540.19)

Name   None.
Erected   1834.
Building   [Not separate and entire but exclusively used for
                worship.] (No school.)
Sittings   Free 80 (or all). Total [80]. Standing room none.
Attendance 30 March   Afternoon 24, SS none. Total 24.
Average attendance   [Not given.]
Dated   31 March 1851.
Signed   William Pulse, proprietor [grocer].
                Hurworth Place, Croft near Darlington (County)
                Durham.

15.27   Wesleyan Methodist Schoolroom, Piecebridge (540.33)

Name   Chapel and schoolroom.
Erected   1828.
Building   [Separate and entire but not exclusively used for
                worship.]
Sittings   Free 40. Other 15. Total [55]. Standing room 12.
Attendance 30 March   Morning 28 SS. Total 28.
                         Evening 30. Total 30.
Average attendance   Morning 26 SS. Total 26.
                         Evening 25. Total 25.
Remarks   None.
Dated   31 March 1851.
Signed   William Wilson, steward and leader [blacksmith].

Piecebridge near Darlington, Durham.

15.28   Wesleyan Methodist, Redworth, Heighington (540.43)
Name   Wesleyan Chappel (*sic*).
Erected   1834.
Building   [Separate and entire.] For a place of worship and
              Sunday school.
Sittings   Free 80. Total [80].
Attendance 30 March   Morning 30 SS. Total [30].
                        Afternoon 30 + 30 SS. Total [60].
Average attendance   Morning 30 + 30 SS. Total [60].
Dated   30 March 1851.
Signed   Thomas Singleton, leader [shoemaker.]
              Redworth, Durham.

15.29   Wesleyan Methodist, Summerhouse (540.39)
Name   None.
Erected   About 1821.
Building   [Separate and entire. Exclusively used for worship.]
Sittings   Free 36. Other 14. Total [50].
Attendance 30 March   Evening 30. Total 30.
Average attendance   [Not given.]
Dated   31 March 1851.
Signed   John Greenwell, manager [grocer].
              Summerhouse, Darlington, Durham.

15.30   Primitive Methodist, Aycliffe (540.45)
Name   None.
Erected   [Not given.]
Building   [Separate and entire. Exclusively used for worship.]
Sittings   Free 60. Total [60].
Attendance 30 March   Evening 50. Total [50].
Average attendance   Evening 60. Total [60].
Dated   31 March 1851.
Signed   William Walker Garvey, assisting manager.
              Great Aycliffe, Durham.

15.31   Primitive Methodist, Queen Street, Darlington (540.27)
Name   Primitive Methodist Chapel.
Erected   In the year 1821. [Foundation stone laid 16 October
              1821, chapel opened 3 March 1822.]
Building   [Separate and entire. Exclusively used for worship.]

Sittings   Free 130. Other 340. Total [470]. Standing room 150.
Attendance 30 March   Morning 65 + 99 SS. Total 164.
                Afternoon 116 SS. Total 116.
                Evening 146. Total 146.
Average attendance   Morning 80 + 102 SS. Total 182.
                Evening 165. Total 165.
Dated   30 March 1851.
Signed   Lancelot Booth, steward [joiner].
            42 Northgate, Darlington, Durham.

15.32   Primitive Methodist, Redworth, Heighington (540.42)
Name   Primitive Methodist Meeting House.
Erected   1837.
Building   [Separate and entire. Exclusively used for worship.]
Sittings   Free 72. Other 8. Total [80].
Attendance 30 March   Afternoon 29. Total 29.
Average attendance   Afternoon 30. Total 30.
                Evening 20. Total 20.
Dated   30 March 1851.
Signed   James Anderson, steward [stone cutter].
            Redworth, near Darlington, Durham.

15.33   Primitive Methodist, Hurworth (540.18)
Name   Primitive Methodist Chapel.
Erected   In AD 1836.
Building   [Separate and entire. Exclusively used for worship.]
Sittings   Free 55. Other 55. Total [110].
Attendance 30 March   Afternoon 21. Total 21.
                Evening 42. Total 42.
Average attendance   Afternoon 30. Total 30.
                Evening 30. Total 30.
Dated   31 March 1851.
Signed   Ralph Fenwick, minister.
            Chapel Row, Shildon, Durham.

15.34   Wesleyan Methodist Association, Blackwell (540.20)
Name   None.
Erected   [Not given.]
Building   [Not separate and entire or exclusively used for
            worship.]
Sittings   Free 60. Total [60].
Attendance 30 March   Afternoon 31. Total [31].

Average attendance   [Not given.]
Dated   31 March 1851.
Signed   Henry Tarrant, minister.
     [5] Prebend Row, Darlington.
[Henry Tarrant was also the minister of Croft (**15.48**).]

15.35   Wesleyan Methodist Association, Paradise Row, Darlington (540.29)
Name   Paradise Chapel.
Erected   In the year 1840. [Opened 28 May 1841. Cost £2,700.]
Building   Yes, a separate and entire building.
     Yes, exclusively a place of worship.
Sittings   Free 266. Other 438. Total [704]. Standing room 150.
Attendance 30 March   Morning 300 + 230 SS. Total 530.
     Evening 400. Total 400.
Average attendance   Morning 450 + 250 SS. Total 700.
Dated   31 March 1851.
Signed   Henry Tarrant, minister.
     [5] Prebend Row, Darlington.

15.36   Wesleyan Methodist Association, Cockerton (540.36)
Name   None.
Erected   Before 1800, but not used for religious services till 1835.
Building   [Not separate and entire but exclusively used for worship.]
Sittings   Free 60. Total [60].
Attendance 30 March   Evening 24. Total [24]. [No SS.]
Average attendance   Evening 30. Total [30]. [No SS.]
Dated   31 March 1851.
Signed   Francis Lodge, class leader [gardener].
     Cockerton, near Darlington, Durham.

15.37   Wesleyan Methodist Association, Brafferton (540.46)
Name   Wesleyan Association Chapel.
Erected   About the year 18 [crossed out].
Building   [Separate and entire. Exclusively used for worship.]
Sittings   Free 80. Total [80].
Attendance 30 March   Evening 46. Total [46].
Average attendance   Morning 60. Total [60].
Remarks   This place of worship was built and used for a

dwelling house, but is now let to this body and used
only for a place of worship. They have rented it for
one year.
Dated   31 March 1851.
Signed   John Dea, leader.
             Coatham, near Darlington.

15.38   Roman Catholic, Paradise Row, Darlington (540.24)
Name   St Augustine's Cath[olic] Chapel.
Erected   Before 1800. [1783. Foundation stone laid 12 September
             1825, opened 29 May 1827. Enlarged 1874, 1899.]
Building   A separate and entire building, used exclusively as a
             place of worship.
Sittings   Free about 100. Total [100]. [Had seats for 500.]
Attendance 30 March   Morning 350. Total [350].
                        Evening 400. Total [400].
Average attendance   [Not given.]
Dated   31 March 1851.
Signed   +William Hogarth, Catholic bishop officiating at
             the above named place of worship [1823–50].
             [Paradise Row], Darlington.
['William Hogarth (1786–1866)', *ODNB*, vol. 27, pp. 555–556. Hogarth
was the vicar-apostolic of the Northern district 1848–50, and Bishop
of Hexham 1850–66 (renamed Hexham and Newcastle in 1861). His
congregation at Darlington rose from 200 (in 1824) to 3,000 (in 1866).
In 1852 the estimated number of Roman Catholics in the area was
1,150.]

16. Durham District (HO 129/545)
90 places of worship

16.1   Church of England, St Cuthbert, Benfieldside (545.18)
Population 1851: 2,475 (township)

Name   St Cuthbert. New parish under 6 & 7 Vic. ch.37,
              (Sir R[obert] Peel's Act [1843]). [Created 3 September
              1847 out of the parish of Medomsley.]
Consecrated 18 September 1850, as an additional church. [Enlarged
              1881–86.]
              [The deed of consecration has 12 September 1850.]

Erected   Church Commissioners grant £200. Private benefaction
              £2,400. Parochial rate nothing. Total cost £2,600.
Endowment   OPE £150. Pew rents £16. Fees £10.
Sittings   Free 279. Other 126. Total 405.
Attendance 30 March   Morning 150 + 95 SS. Total 245.
              Afternoon 130 + 104 SS. Total 234.
Average attendance   [Not given.]
Remarks   The amount of pew rents, though assigned by the
              Church Commissioners to the incumbent, are obliged
              to be appropriated by him to match the necessary
              expenses connected with the church owing to the
              difficulty of collecting a church rate.
Dated   31 March 1851.
Signed   Frederick Brewster Thompson, incumbent [1847–1881].
              Shotley Bridge, Gateshead.
{1857   Attendance 250. 21 communicants.}   {B 88.}

16.2   Church of England, St Brandon, Brancepeth (545.46)
Population 1851: 6,441 (parish) 470 (township)

Name   Brancepeth Church.
Consecrated Before 1800.
Endowment   [£811.]
Sittings   Total 450.
Attendance 30 March   Morning 173 + 43 SS. Total 216.
              Afternoon 36 + 20 SS. Total 56.
Average attendance   Morning 250. Total [250].
              Afternoon 60. Total [60].
Remarks   Congregation depends on weather, being some
              distance from many parts of the parish. Better
              therefore in summer than in winter.
Dated   31 March 1851.
Signed   John Duncombe Shafto, minister [1840–54].
              Brancepeth Rectory, Durham.
{1857   Attendance 200. 30 communicants.}   {B 53.}
[John Shafto was succeeded by his brother Arthur Duncombe Shafto
1854–1900.]

16.3   Church of England Schoolroom, Brandon (545.49)
Population   1851 525 (township of Brandon and Byshottles)

Name   Brandon Schoolroom.
Licensed   [Not given.]
Sittings   Free 50 Total 50.
Attendance 30 March   Evening 47 + 18 SS. Total 65.
Average attendance   Evening 45 + 35 SS. Total 80.
Remarks   Only an evening service during winter.
Dated   31 March 1851.
Signed   Charles Henry Ford, curate of Brancepeth [1846–54].
              Brandon, Durham.
Incumbent   [John Duncombe Shafto 1840–54.]
[St John the Evangelist was consecrated on 31 December 1862.
Enlarged 1905.]

16.4   Church of England, St Thomas, Collierley [Dipton] (545.10)
Population 1851: 576 (township)

Name   St Thomas' District Church.
Consecrated 4 August 1841. Consecrated as an additional church.
              [District created 24 September 1842 out of the parish of
              Lanchester.]
Erected   Church Building Society, London £150. Church
              Building Society, Durham £50. Bishop [Shute]
              Barrington's Fund £50. Private subscriptions £473 19s
              1½. Total £723 19s 1½d.
Endowment   Eccles[iastical] Commissioners £135 annually. From the
              Bishop of Durham's reserved common rents £15 per
              annum. Fees £5. Making altogether £155 per annum.
Sittings   All free. Total 300.
Attendance 30 March   Morning 63 + 41 SS. Total 104.
                        Afternoon 87 + 23 SS. Total 100.
Average attendance   Morning 40 + 60 SS. Total 110 (*sic*). [100]
                        Afternoon 50 + 50 SS. Total 100.
Remarks   This district consists chiefly of pitmen, very few of
              whom, I believe, attend church, and those who go
              to any place of worship go to the Wesleyan chapels.
              There are a great number too of Romanists here. I
              have collected the above as well as I could, but I have
              been here a very short time and know but little about
              the district.

Dated   30 March 1851.
Signed   Charles Langley Maltby MA, minister [1850–54].
               Dipton, n[ea]r Gateshead, Durham.
{1857   Attendance 150. 24 communicants.}   {B 55.}
[Charles Maltby (1816–1858) was the second son of the Rev. John Ince
Maltby, the rector of Shelton, Nottinghamshire, 1814–63.]

16.5   Church of England, St Bartholomew, Croxdale (545.50)
Population 1851: 438 (township)

Name   St Bartholomew, Croxdale. The church of a
               consolidated chapelry district. [Also called Sunderland
               Bridge Church.]
Consecrated 24 September 1846. Consecrated in lieu of the old
               chapel at Croxdale. [Enlarged 1876.]
Endowment   Land £41 10s. Tithe £204. Glebe house. *OPE £245 10s.
               Fees 10s. Other 10s.
Sittings   Free 140. Other 42. Total 182.
Attendance 30 March   Morning 60 + 25 SS. Total 85.
               Afternoon 30 + 10 SS. Total 40.
Average attendance   Morning 100 + 33 SS. Total 133.
               Afternoon 50 + 20 SS. Total 70.
Remarks   *The glebe house was built in the year 1845–6, and
               the sum of £495 1s 10d was borrowed for the purpose
               of the governors of Queen Anne's Bounty, to which
               amount the living is mortgaged.
Dated   31 March 1851.
Signed   Henry Chaytor, minister [1841–73].
               Croxdale parsonage, Durham.
{1857   Attendance 120. 25 communicants.}   {B 25.}

[Additional sheets between 545.49 and 545.50 (**16.3** and **16.5**)]
Before the year 1843 the chapelry of Croxdale consisted only of the
single township of Sunderland Bridge; but on the 10th day of June
1843, by an Order of Her Majesty in Council, the township of Hett,
together with the detached part of the township of Ferryhill, in the
parish of Merrington, was annexed to it under the 6th Section of the
59th of Geo. III c.134, and constituted a consolidated chapelry district.
Soon after that time, the old chapel of Croxdale being found too small
and in a dilapidated state, and also inconveniently situate for the
great majority of the inhabitants of the district, it was determined to
erect a new church on a larger scale, and in a more eligible situation,

which was finally effected in the year 1845–46, by which means an increase of accommodation was provided.

The provision of church room previously to the rebuilding was for 96 persons, including 26 free seats, whereas the present provision for 182 persons and 140 of the seats are free and unappropriated forever.

16.6 Church of England, St Mary-le-Bow, North Bailey, Durham (545.59)
Population 1851: 269 (parish)

[Summary form]
Name   St Mary-le-Bow.
Erected   Supposed to be [AD] 995 as a resting place for the body of St Cuthbert. [Rebuilt 1685, restored 1875.]
Endowment   [£111.] [£10 a year from the Lord Crewe Charity.]
Sittings   Free 14. Other 266. Total 280.
Usual attendance   Morning 120 + 30 SS. Total [150].
                      Afternoon 25 + 15 SS. Total [40].
                      Evening no service.
Dated   [Not given.]
Informant   John Day, registrar.
            [180 Gilesgate, Durham.]
Incumbent   [William Clarke King 1843–55.]
{1857   Attendance 130. 22 communicants.}   {B 7.}
[The parish was united with St Mary-the-Less on 14 May 1912.]

16.7 Church of England, St Mary-the-Less, South Bailey, Durham (545.58)
Population 1851: 104 (parish)

[Summary form]
Name   St Mary-the-Less.
Erected   Previous to 1500 and this church has been rebuilt in 1847.
Endowment   [£119.]
Sittings   Free 12. Other 100. Total 112.
Usual attendance   Morning 36 [No SS]. Total [36].
                      Afternoon 12 [No SS]. Total [12].
                      Evening no service.
Dated   [Not given.]
Informant   John Day, registrar.
            [180 Gilesgate, Durham.]

Incumbent [James Raine 1828–58.]
{1857   Attendance 70. 35 communicants.}   {B 2.}
[James Raine was also the librarian to the Dean and Chapter of Durham 1816–58, and the rector of St John the Baptist, Meldon, 1822–58 (**9.9**). The parish was united with St Mary-the-Bow on 14 May 1912. From 1919 St Mary-the-less became the chapel of St John's College.]

16.8 Church of England, St Oswald, Crossgate, Durham (545.54)
Population 1851: 10,868 (parish)

Name   St Oswald. Ancient parish church.
Consecrated Before 1800. [Restored 1834, 1864, 1883.]
Endowment   Tithe £191. Glebe £4 4s. Other £170. Fees £14. Easter
             offerings £6.
Sittings   Free 60. Other 782. Total 842.
Attendance 30 March   Morning 335 + 79 SS. Total 414.
             Afternoon 40 + 68 SS. Total 108.
             Evening 364. Total 364.
Average attendance   [Not given.]
Dated   31 March 1851.
Signed   Edward Sneyd, minister [1848–62].
{1857   Attendance 460. 75 communicants.}   {B 97.}
[Edward Sneyd's successor was John Bacchus Dykes (1823–1876), *ODNB*, vol. 17, pp. 449–500. He was the precentor of Durham Cathedral 1849–62 and minister at St Oswald's 1862–75; he composed nearly 300 hymns. His grandfather was the Evangelical Thomas Dykes, vicar of St John, Hull, 1791–1847.]

16.9 Church of England, St Margaret of Antioch, Crossgate, Durham (545.53)
[Summary form]
Name   Chapel of St Margaret.
Erected   About the year 1165. [Restored and enlarged 1880.]
Sittings   Free 150. Other 350. Total 500.
Usual attendance   Morning 250 + 35 SS. Total [285].
             Afternoon no service.
             Evening 250 + 35 SS. Total [285].
Informant   Received information from parish clerk.
             Thomas Clamp, registrar.
Incumbent   [John Cundill 1842–89.]
                                                          {B 129.}

[John Cundill's son James John Cundill was the curate of Billingham (**21.1**).]

16.10   Church of England, St Giles, Gilesgate, Durham (545.65)
Population 1851: 5,423 (parish)

Name   St Giles' Church. An ancient parish church.
Consecrated   Before 1800. [Restored 1828, restored and enlarged
                1873–74, completed 1876.]
Endowment   Tithe £42. Glebe £63. OPE £54. Fees £24. Easter
                offerings £3. Other £7.
Sittings   Free 100. Other 170. Total 270.
Attendance 30 March   Morning 140 + 80 SS. Total 220.
                        Afternoon 60 + 85 SS. Total 145.
Average attendance   Morning 140 + 70 SS. Total 210.
                        Afternoon 70 + 70 SS. Total 140.
Remarks   I make this return, trusting that no part of the
                information contained in it, will ever be made known,
                except for the purpose of aiding and extending the
                usefulness of the Church of England.
Dated   31 March 1851.
Signed   Francis Thompson, perpetual curate [1841–72].
                [The] Parsonage, St Giles', Durham.
{1857   Attendance 150. 20 communicants. A north aisle
                would be a desirable addition.}
                                                          {B 202.}
['I am miserably poor and my parishioners are in the same plight'
(Letter from Francis Thompson to the Ecclesiastical Commissioners,
26 December 1848).]

16.11   Church of England, St Nicholas, Market Place, Durham
(545.61)
Population 1851: 3,031 (parish)

Name   St Nicholas, Durham, ancient parish church.
Consecrated   Before 1800. [After rebuilding, reopened 21 December
                1858.]
Endowment   Land £30. OPE £20. Fees £2. Easter offerings £5.
Sittings   Free 150. Other 350. Total 500.
Attendance 30 March   Morning 150 + 350 SS. Total 500.
                        Afternoon 30 + 300 SS. Total 330.

	Evening 400. Total 400.
Average attendance	Morning 120 + 300 SS. Total 420.
	Afternoon 20 + 280 SS. Total 300.
	Evening 350. Total 350.
Dated	[Not given.]
Signed	Edward Davison, perpetual curate [1821–56].
	Church Street, Durham.

{1857   Attendance 500. 60 communicants. The new town hall was licensed for worship during the rebuilding of the church.}

{B 54.}

16.12   Church of England, Durham County Gaol Chapel (545.60)

Name	The Chapel of Durham County Gaol and House of Correction.
Licensed	New chapel opened 2 June 1843.
Erected	By the County Magistrates in Quarter Sessions.
	Total cost about £400 (county rate).
Sittings	Free 312. Total 312.
Attendance 30 March	Morning 216. Total 216.
	Afternoon 202. Total 202.
Average attendance	Morning 250. Total 250.
	Afternoon 250. Total 250.
Remarks	No endowment. Chaplain's salary £220 per annum.
Dated	31 March 1851.
Signed	George Hans Hamilton, chaplain [1848–54].
	County Gaol and House of Correction, Durham.

[The prison was erected between 1809 and 1811 and cost £140,000. According to the 1851 Civil Census there were 245 inmates in Durham Gaol. George Hans Hamilton was subsequently the Archdeacon of Lindisfarne and vicar of Eglingham 1865–82, and Archdeacon of Northumberland 1882–1905. He was a founder member of the Durham Protestant Alliance.]

16.13   Church of England, St Ebba, Ebchester (545.15)
Population 1851: 610 (township)

Name	St Ebba, a small and ancient structure.
Consecrated	[Not given.] [Restored 1876–77.]
Endowment	Land £90. Other £60.
Sittings	Free 130. Total 130.
Attendance 30 March	Morning 65 + 12 SS. Total 77.

Afternoon 12 + 25 SS. Total 37.

Average attendance   [Not given.]

Remarks   Owing to their age ye Sunday scholars are only req[uire]d to attend prayers in ye afternoons.

Dated   31 March 1851.

Signed   George Stubbs, minister [1838–72].
                    Ebchester, Gateshead.

{1857   Attendance 140. 15 communicants.}   {B15.}

16.14   Church of England, St Michael and All Angels, Esh (545.37)

Population 1851: 642 (township)

Name   Esh Church.

Consecrated   Before 1800. [Rebuilt 1770, restored and enlarged 1850.]

Endowment   Land £95. Glebe £15 (20 acres). OPE Ecclesiastical Commissioners £100. Fees £1.

Sittings   Free 63. Other 68. Total 131.

Attendance 30 March   Morning 36 + 20 SS. Total 56.
                                    Afternoon 32 + 24 SS. Total 56.

Average attendance   [Not given.]

Remarks   The church was almost completely rebuilt in 1850, at an expense exceeding £800 by voluntary contributions. The greater part of the land in the parish belongs to Roman Catholics. Tithe even for the glebe land is paid by the incumbent to a Roman Catholic layman.

Dated   31 March 1851.

Signed   Temple Chevallier, perpetual curate [1835–69].
                    Parsonage, Esh, near Durham.

{1857   Attendance 50. 20 communicants.}   {B 8.}

[Temple Chevallier was also Professor of Mathematics 1835–71 and Professor of Astronomy 1841–71 of the University of Durham.]

16.15   Church of England, All Saints, Lanchester (545.34)

Population 1851: 15,814 (parish) 752 (township)

Name   Lanchester Church. An ancient parish church.

Consecrated   Before 1800.

Endowment   Land £70. Tithe £16 10s. Glebe £6. OPE £150 [included £10 a year from the Lord Crewe Charity].
                       Fees £28. Other £270 10s.

Sittings   Free 42. Other 315. Total 357.
Attendance 30 March   Morning 111 + 85 SS. Total 196.
                     Evening 94. Total 94.
Average attendance   Morning 113 + 83 SS. Total 196.
                     Evening 121. Total 121.
Remarks   To ascertain the attendants (*sic*) at divine worship
              in Lanchester parish in the Church of England, see
              Leadgate School, Castleside School, [and] Holmside
              School returns (**16.16, 16.17**).
Dated   31 March 1851.
Signed   John Faithful Fanshaw, perpetual curate of Lanchester
              [1842–56].
              N[ea]r Durham City.
{1857   Attendance 90. 25 communicants.}   {B 103.}

16.16   Church of England Schoolroom, Castleside (545.25)
Name   Castleside Schoolroom.
License   Opened [1850] by license and leave of the Bishop for
              divine worship.
Sittings   [Not given.]
Attendance 30 March   Morning 56. Total 56.
Average attendance   Morning 70. Total 70 (five months all the time
                     it has been opened).
Remarks   This schoolroom is opened for divine worship in a
              district six miles from Lanchester parish church and
              has 700 or 800 people near it.
              For endowment, see Lanchester (**16.15**).
Dated   31 March 1851.
Signed   John Faithful Fanshaw, perpetual curate of Lanchester
              [1842–56].
              Near Durham City.

16.17   Church of England Schoolroom, Holmside (545.33)
Name   Holmside Schoolroom.
License   Opened [1847, enlarged 1877] by license and leave of
              the Bishop for divine worship.
Sittings   [Not given.] {1857 has 60 sittings.}
Attendance 30 March   Afternoon 26. Total 26.
Average attendance   Afternoon 43. Total 43.
Remarks   This schoolroom is opened for divine worship in a
              district with 1,000 people, 3½ miles from the parish
              church of Lanchester.

For endowment, see Lanchester (**16.14**).

Dated 31 March 1851.

Signed John Faithful Fanshaw, perpetual curate of Lanchester [1842–56]. Near Durham City.

[St John the Evangelist, Holmside, was consecrated on 13 January 1870.]

16.18 Church of England Schoolroom, Leadgate (545.29)

Name Leadgate Schoolroom.

License Opened by license and leave of the Bishop for divine worship.

Sittings [Not given.] {1857 has 100 sittings.}

Attendance 30 March Evening 86 + 36 SS. Total 122.

Average attendance Evening 80 + 38 SS. Total 118.

Remarks This schoolroom is opened for divine worship in a district 3½ miles from the parish church of Lanchester with three or four thousand people near it. For endowment, see Lanchester (**16.14**).

Dated 31 March 1851.

Signed John Faithful Fanshaw, perpetual curate of Lanchester [1842–56].
N[ea]r Durham City.

[St Ives, Leadgate, was consecrated on 12 September 1867.]

16.19 Church of England, St Mary Magdalene, Medomsley (545.13)

Population 1851: 840 (township)

Name A parochial chapel dedicated to St Mary Magdalene. Built during the transition from the Norman to the Early English, and has escaped mutilation; tho[ugh] in a dilapidated state.

Consecrated [Not given. Restored 1877–78, re-opened 29 May 1878.]

Endowment Land £54 14s. OPE £203 9s. Fees £5.

Sittings Fee and other 300. Total 300.

Attendance 30 March Morning 28 + 10 SS. Total 38.

Average attendance Morning 100. Total 100.

Remarks This chapelry consists of three townships until last year when a new district was formed under Peel's Act [6 and 7 Vic. c.37], and two townships assigned to it. The chapel is now connected with the township of

Medomsley. The chapel is in an exposed situation and except in fine weather not well attended.

Dated	31 March 1851.
Signed	Edward James Midgley BA, perpetual curate [1838–74].
	Medomsley by Gateshead.
{1857	Attendance 60. 15 communicants.} {B 28.}

[The two townships were Medomsley and Conside-cum-Knitsley (where the population of the township was 2,777).]

16.20   Church of England, All Saints, Muggleswick (545.41)
Population 1851: 688 (parochial chapelry)

[Summary form]

Name	Muggleswick.
Erected	[Not given. Rebuilt 1829, 1868–69.]
Endowment	[£93.]
Sittings	Total 140.
Usual attendance	Morning 25. Total [25].
Dated	[Not given.]
Informant	J[ohn] D[ay, registrar].
	[180 Gilesgate, Durham.]
Incumbent	[Samuel Kennedy 1837–51.]
{1857	Attendance 20. 8 communicants.} {B 13.}

[From 1803–17 Samuel Kennedy was the Independent minister of a chapel in Stockton-upon-Tees. In 1820 he was ordained into the Church of England ministry and served as a curate at Ryton and then Falstone. In 1990 Muggleswick was transferred to the diocese of Newcastle.]

16.21   Church of England, St Lawrence, Pittington (545.79)
Population 1851: 2,530 (township)

Name	St Lawrence, commonly known by the name 'Pittington Church'. It is an ancient parish church.
Consecrated	Before 1800. [Restored and enlarged 1846–47, 1905.]
Endowment	Tithe £600. Fees £11 10s. [£10 a year from the Lord Crewe Charity.]
Sittings	Free 286. Other 136. Total 422.
Attendance 30 March	Morning 190 + 50 SS. Total 240.
Average attendance	Morning 200 + 50 SS. Total 250.

Dated   5 April 1851.
Signed   Thomas Nicholson Wannop, curate [1849–55].
             Sherburn, near Durham.
Incumbent [James Miller 1822–54.]
{1857   Attendance 120. 30 communicants.}   {B 77.}

16.22   Church of England Schoolroom, Sherburn (545.76)
[On a Nonconformist form]
Name   Sherburn Schoolhouse.
Erected   [1804. Rebuilt] 1848.
Building   Separate building [but not exclusively used for
             worship].
Sittings   Free 130. Total [130].
Attendance 30 March   See remarks.
Average attendance   Afternoon 75 + 45 SS. Total 120.
Remarks   Service is performed in this schoolroom only on every
             alternate Sunday. On Sunday 30 March there will be
             no service.
Dated   27 March 1851.
Signed   Thomas Nicholson Wannop, curate [1849–55].
             Sherburn, near Durham.
Incumbent [James Miller 1822–54.]
[St Mary, Sherburn, was consecrated on 28 May 1872.]

16.23   Church of England, St Cuthbert, Shadforth (545.84 and
545.83)
Population 1851: 1,348 (township)

Name   St Cuthbert's. District chapelry assigned under 16th
             Section, 59th of George III c.134. [District created 8
             May 1841 out of the parish of Pittington.]
Consecrated 5 August 1839. As an additional church. [Chancel
             rebuilt 1889–91 and nave in 1917.]
Erected   Through the efforts of the Dean and Chapter of
             Durham [who contributed £100]. Private £1,000. Total
             cost about £1,000.
Endowment With corn tithe, glebe and surplice fees. [£250.]
             What is the difference between land and glebe?
Sittings   Free 350. Other 155. Total 505.
Attendance 30 March   [Not given.]
Average attendance   [Not given.]

Remarks	I do not think that the replies concerning the endowment and to the attendance should be sent thro[ugh] local officers; if the Registrar General wishes this for the benefit of the country and will apply direct to myself for them I can have no objection to give whatever information he requires.
Dated	31 March 1851.
Signed	Richard George Leaton Blenkinsopp, incumbent [1839–76].
	Shadforth Parsonage, Durham.
{1857	Attendance – . 50 communicants.} {B 106.}

[Summary form (545.83)]

Name	St Cuthbert's, Shadforth.
Erected	1839.
Sittings	Free 350. Other 150. Total 500.
Usual attendance	Morning about 200 + about 60 SS.
	Total [about 260].
	Afternoon from 50 to 150 + about 70 SS.
	Total [about 120–220].
	Evening no service.
Remarks	Very difficult to say, sometimes the numbers are very large, and at others much smaller owing to the distance of the church from the population. Perhaps this is as near correct as possible.
Dated	[Not given.]
Informant	Richard George Leaton Blenkinsopp, incumbent [1839–76].
	[Shadforth Parsonage, Durham.]

16.24   Church of England, St Cuthbert, Satley (545.40)
Population 1851: 287 (chapelry)

[Summary form]

Name	Satley.
Erected	Unknown. The present church rebuilt about fifty years ago, [c.1825. Restored 1870].
Endowment	[£114.]
Sittings	Free 46. Other 94. Total 140.
Usual attendance	Morning about 60 + 30 SS. Total [90].
	Afternoon 40 to 55 + about 20 SS.
	Total [60–75].

Dated   [Not given.]
Informant   Joseph Thompson, incumbent [1835–67].
{1857   Attendance 80. 25 communicants.}   {B 24.}

16.25   Church of England, Sherburn Hospital Chapel, Sherburn
(545.75)
Population 1851: 34 (inhabitants in nineteen houses)

Name   A private extra-parochial chapel belonging to the
                Master and Brethren of Sherburn Hospital.
Consecrated Supposed in AD 1181. The anti-chapel was built by
                Hugh Pudsey, Bishop of Durham, the founder. The
                choir was added, it is supposed, about AD 1400.
                [The Master's House built 1832; new aisle to chapel
                consecrated, 26 March 1861. Chapel entirely restored
                in 1868.]
Erected   By the founder, Hugh Pudsey, long before the year
                1800.
Endowment No endowment to the chapel, it being a private one
                belonging to the Master and Brethren of the Hospital.
Sittings   No seats are appropriated except the stalls of the
                Master and Brethren. It will hold about 100 persons.
                Total [100].
Attendance 30 March   Morning 84. Total [84].
                Afternoon 42. Total [42].
Average attendance   Morning about 60 or 70. Total [60–70].
                Afternoon about 40 or 50. Total [40–50].
Remarks   I should suppose, that in the summer months the
                average number of attendants may be 90; in the
                winter, 60; thus making the yearly average about 75.
                In the afternoon, there is little difference in average of
                summer and winter.
                As the chapel, belonging to Sherburn Hospital, is
                neither a parish church, nor a chapel of ease within
                a parish, I doubt whether a paper should have been
                sent here more than to any college in Oxford or
                Cambridge.
Dated   31 March 1851.
Signed   George Stanley Faber BD, Master of Sherburn Hospital
                [1832–54].
                Sherburn House, Durham.
[George Stanley Faber (1773–1854), a learned Evangelical and

prolific author, was the uncle of the Tractarian Frederick William Faber (1814–1863). In 1851 George Faber appointed the Evangelical Edward Prest as chaplain to assist him in his duties, and on his death Prest succeeded him as the Master. From 1861 Prest was the rector of Gateshead and from 1863 to 1882 the Archdeacon of Durham. He named his second son Stanley Faber Prest (1858–1931).

In the early 1830s it was suggested that Sherburn Hospital could become the location for the University of Durham.]

16.26   Church of England, St Mary the Virgin, Shincliffe (545.71)
Population 1851: 1,175 (township)

[Summary form]
Name   St Mary, Shincliffe.
Consecrated   [23 September 1826.] Rebuilt and enlarged 1850
                [consecrated 5 August 1851. District created 13 July
                1831 out of the parish of St Oswald's, Durham.]
Endowment   [£380.]
Sittings   Free 249. Other 108. Total 357.
Usual attendance   Morning 150 + 110 SS. Total [260].
                Afternoon 50 + 35 SS. Total [85].
                Evening no service.
Dated   [Not given.]
Signed   Isaac Todd, incumbent [1826–72].

{B 45.}

16.27   Church of England Schoolroom, Shincliffe (545.72)
Name   [National] Parochial School, new Shincliffe.
Erected   1842.
Sittings   Free 140. Total 140.
Average attendance   Afternoon 20 + 75 SS. Total [95].
Dated   [Not given.]
Signed   Isaac Todd, incumbent [1826–72].
{1857   Attendance 40. [Building] used for 12 years.}

16.28   Church of England, St Margaret of Antioch, Tanfield
(545.1)
Population 1851: 3.480 (parish)

Name   St Margaret's church or chapel, an ancient chapelry,
                and a distinct and separate parish.

Consecrated   Before 1800. [Reopened 1750, restored 1749, 1853, 1878.]
Endowment   By land, tithe, glebe, funds, fees, yes. [£133.]
Sittings   Free 26. Other 60. Total 86.
Attendance 30 March   [Not given.]
Average attendance   [Not given.]
Remarks   I can give no account of the congregation as to number, sometimes large, sometimes small, according to weather and other circumstances.
Dated   31 March 1851.
Signed   William Simpson, in[cumben]t curate [1824–57]. Tanfield, Fence Houses, County Durham.
{1857   Attendance 180. 15 communicants.}   {B 77.}

16.29   Independent [Congregational] Claypath, Durham (545.63)
Name   Claypath Chapel.
Erected   Before 1800. [1751, altered 1848. Larger chapel opened 1 September 1886.]
Building   [Separate and entire. Exclusively used for worship.]
Sittings   Fee [none]. Other 400. Total [400].
Attendance 30 March   Morning 165 + 50 SS. Total 215.
   Evening 205. Total 205.
Average attendance   [Not given.]
Dated   30 March 1851.
Signed   Samuel Goodall, minister [1841–81]. Durham.

16.30   Baptist, Rowley, Muggleswick (545.44)
Name   Baptist Chapel.
Erected   1700. [Original chapel 1652, subsequent chapel 1717. Rebuilt 1823, reopened on 25 February 1824, enlarged 1864.]
Building   [Separate and] entire building. Exclusively [used for worship].
Sittings   All free 150. Total [150].
Attendance 30 March   Morning 45 + 29 SS. Total 74.
   Afternoon 23 SS. Total 23.
Average attendance   [Not given.]
Dated   30 March 1851.
Signed   Ebenezer Le Fevre, pastor [1850–52]. Wood St[reet], Shotley Bridge.
[Ebenezer Le Fevre was also pastor of Shotley Field (**8.36**).]

16.31   Baptist, Shotley Bridge (545.20)

Name   None.
Erected   Before 1800. [New chapel opened 1851.]
Building   [Not separate and entire or exclusively used for
                worship.]
Sittings   Room [in another hand].
Attendance 30 March   Evening 50 + 8 SS. Total 58.
Average attendance   Evening 40 + 10 SS. Total 50.
Dated   30 March 1851.
Signed   Ebenezer Le Fevre, pastor [1850–52].
                Shotley Bridge, Durham.

16.32   Wesleyan Methodist, Blackhill, Benfieldside (545.24)
[Summary form]
Name   Benfieldside, Blackhill, Wesleyan Methodist.
Erected   [Not given.] [1849. New chapel opened 3 May 1872.]
Building   [Not given.]
Sittings   Free 120. Other 70. Total 190.

Crookhall, Wesleyan Church. (See **16.49**).
There is not a chapel at Crookhall that I am aware of. There are
meetings held in some of the houses. Consequently they will all be
free seats.
Dated   10 September 1852.
Signed   W. W. Thompson, registrar.

16.33   Wesleyan Methodist, Brancepeth (545.47)
Name   Worship in a dwelling house.
Erected   Before (*sic*).
Building   [Not separate and entire or exclusively used for
                worship.]
Sittings   [Not given.]
Attendance 30 March   [Not given.]
Average attendance   Morning 15. Total [15].
Dated   31 March 1851.
Signed   William Bell, shoemaker and postmaster.
                [Brancepeth.]

16.34   Wesleyan Methodist, Burnopfield (545.3)
Name   Wesleyan Methodist Chapel.
Erected   1775. [Rebuilt 1880.]
Building   [Separate and entire. Exclusively used for worship.]

Sittings   Free 175. Other 114. Total [289].
Attendance 30 March   Afternoon 74 + 34 SS. Total 108.
     Evening 25 + 12 SS. Total 37.
Average attendance   [Not given.]
Dated   30 March 1851.
Signed   George Todd, steward (teacher) [also grocer and
     postmaster].
     Burnopfield, Gateshead.

['I preached to a lovely congregation at Burnopfield, on "Rejoice in
the Lord, O ye righteous." I have found nothing like it, since I left
London, such was "The overwhelming power of grace divine."' (7
June 1788) *The Journal of the Rev. J. Wesley* (Dent edition, 1906), vol.
4, p. 434.]

16.35   Wesleyan Methodist, New Cassop (545.86)
Name   Chapel.
Erected   1843 [cost £200].
Building   Separate building. [Exclusively used for worship] and
     day school.
Sittings   Free 180. Other 72. Total [252].
Attendance 30 March   Morning 48. Total 48.
     Afternoon 93 SS. Total [93].
     Evening 54. Total 54.
Average attendance   Morning 60. Total 60.
     Afternoon 95 SS. Total 95.
     Evening 70. Total 70.
Dated   31 March 1851.
Signed   Matthias Stokoe, steward [grocer and draper].
     Cassop Colliery (Ferryhill) [crossed out], Durham.

16.36   Wesleyan Methodist, Collierly Dykes, [Dipton] (545.9)
Name   Wesleyan Methodist Chapel.
Erected   Before 1800. [1792. Replaced by a new chapel in Front
     Street, Dipton, 1876, restored 1894.]
Building   [Separate and entire. Exclusively used for worship.]
Sittings   Free 204. Other 40. Total [244].
Attendance 30 March   Morning 78. Total [78].
Average attendance   Morning 60. Total [60].
     Afternoon 30 SS. Total [30].
Remarks   It is usual to discontinue this school during three
     months in winter. It is in the midst of a scattered
     population. I have given the average attendance of the

scholars for the twelve months previous to December last.

Dated	31 March 1851.
Signed	William Urwin, steward (grocer).
	Collierly Dykes, near Gateshead on Tyne.

16.37 Wesleyan Methodist, Front Street, Consett (545.27)

Name	Wesleyan Methodist Chapel.
Erected	In the year 1849. [Replaced by new chapel opened on 17 April 1872.]
Building	[Separate and entire. Exclusively used for worship.]
Sittings	Free 188. Other 132. Total [320].
Attendance 30 March	Morning 89 + 81 SS. Total 170.
	Evening 189. Total 189.
Average attendance	[Not given.]
Dated	31 March 1851.
Signed	John Dickinson, trustee and steward [fire-brick manufacturer].
	Consett Cottage, Shotley Bridge.

16.38 Wesleyan Methodist, Causey Row (545.5)

Name	None.
Erected	[Not given.]
Building	[Separate and entire.] Exclusively [used for worship].
Sittings	Free 100. Total [100].
Attendance 30 March	Morning 20. Total [20].
Average attendance	[Not given.]
Dated	31 March 1851.
Signed	Edward Drummond, steward [farmer].
	[Beckley Hill, Tanfield.]

16.39 Wesleyan Methodist Schoolroom, Coxhoe (545.89)

Name	Wesleyan Chapel and Schoolroom.
Erected	1840.
Building	[Separate and entire.] The schoolroom is occasionally used for religious worship. [Exclusively used for worship.]
Sittings	Free 150. Other 150. Total [300]. Standing room 100.
Attendance 30 March	Morning 41 + 61 SS. Total 102.
	Evening 51 + 31 SS. Total 82.
Average attendance	Morning 65 + 70 SS. Total 135.
	Evening 70 + 30 SS. Total 100.

Dated   5 April 1851.
Signed   James Newton, steward [grocer, draper and
             shopkeeper].
             Coxhoe, n[ea]r Durham.

16.40   Wesleyan Methodist, Old Elvet, Durham (545.55)

[Summary form]
Name   Wesleyan Methodist Chapel.
Erected   1808. [Opened 13 November 1808. Cost £1,000.]
Building   Separate and entire. Exclusively as a place of worship.
Sittings   Free 188. Other 424. Total [612].
Usual attendance   Morning 150 + 70 SS. Total 220.
                       Evening 250. Total 250.
Dated   [Not given.]
Informant John Wilson [Wesleyan minister.]
             Old Elvet, Durham.

16.41   Wesleyan Methodist, Gilesgate, Durham (545.66)

Name   Wesleyan Methodist Chaple (*sic*).
Erected   1843.
Building   [Separate and entire. Exclusively used for worship.]
Sittings   Free 70. Other non (*sic*). Total [70]. Standing room non
             (*sic*).
Attendance 30 March Morning 31 SS. Total [31].
                       Afternoon 32 + 19 SS. Total [51].
                       Evening 30. Total [30].
Average attendance   [Not given.]
Dated   30 March 1851.
Signed   Robert Oswald, manager [boot and shoemaker].
             [9 and] 10 New Elvet, Durham.

16.42   Wesleyan Methodist, St Giles Grange, Durham (545.69)

Name   Wesleyan Methodist Chapel. [Grange Chapel.]
Erected   1835. [Cost £150. Rebuilt 1845, cost £110.]
Building   [Separate and entire. Exclusively used for worship.]
Sittings   Free 112. Other 130. Total [242]. Standing room none.
Attendance 30 March Morning 130 SS. Total 130.
                       Afternoon 126. Total 126.
                       Evening 128. Total 128.
Average attendance   Morning 130 SS. Total 130.
                       Afternoon 138. Total 138.
                       Evening 130. Total 130.

Dated   31 March 1851.
Signed   William Burgess, steward [bookseller and stationer].
Broomside, near Durham.

16.43   Wesleyan Methodist, St Oswalds, Durham (545.73)

Name   Wesleyan Chapel.
Erected   1808.
Building   [Separate and entire.] Used exclusively as a place of worship.
Sittings   Free 194. Other 606. Total [800].
Attendance 30 March   Morning 200 + 60 SS. Total 260.
Evening 225. Total 225.
Average attendance   [Not given.]
Dated   30 March 1851.
Signed   Henry Fenwick, steward of the trustees [cheese-monger and bacon-factor].
21 Elvet Bridge, Durham.

16.44   Wesleyan Methodist, Ebchester (545.17)

Name   Wesleyan Chapel.
Erected   1842.
Building   [Separate and entire. Exclusively used for worship.]
Sittings   Free 200. Other 20. Total [220].
Attendance 30 March   Evening 40. Total [40].
Average attendance   [Not given.]
Dated   [Not given.]
Signed   [Not given.]

16.45   Wesleyan Methodist, Hallgarth (545.85)

Name   Wesleyan Methodist Chapel.
Erected   In the year of our Lord, 1833.
Building   A separate and entire building. It is used exclusively as a place of worship.
Sittings   Free 70. Other 36. Total [106].
Attendance 30 March   Evening 36. Total [36].
Average attendance   Evening 50. Total [50].
Remarks   The above building was erected in the year of our Lord, 1833 by the Independents, but having no regular society it was shut up for some time, and has been rented by the Wesleyan Methodists since the year 1847.
Dated   30 March 1851.

Signed   John Roantree, steward [grocer].
Shadforth, Durham.

16.46   Wesleyan Methodist Schoolroom, Hallgarth (545.77)

Name   It is called the Wesleyan Methodist Chapel by way
of distinction because the Ranters [i.e. Primitive
Methodists] have a similar place (**16.80**). (Wesleyan
Methodist as founded by the late Rev. John Wesley.)
Erected   It was erected in the year of our Lord, 1834.
Building   It is a separate and entire building. A day school is
taught in it through the week, and a Sunday school in
the Sunday aforenoon, and public worship, afternoon
and evening.
Sittings   The sittings are all free.
Attendance 30 March   Afternoon 75 + 19 SS. Total 94.
Evening 80 + 48 SS. Total 128.
Average attendance   [Not given.]
Remarks   The above building was erected in the year of our
Lord, 1834 by Mr Thomas Crawford sen[ior], one of
the Earl of Durham's agents, and the use of it offered
to the Wesleyan Methodists on condition that they
should teach a Sunday school in it one part of the
Sunday, for the benefit of the children belonging to the
Earl of Durham's workmen.
Dated   30 March 1851.
Signed   William Sigmour, class leader and local preacher.
Sherburn Hill, near Durham.

16.47   Wesleyan Methodist Schoolroom, Littletown, Hallgarth
(545.80)
Name   Littletown Preaching Room
Erected   1837.
Building   [Separate and entire but not exclusively used for
worship.]
Sittings   Free 200. Total [200]. Standing room none.
Attendance 30 March   Morning 82 + 30 SS. Total 112.
Evening 100 + 20 SS. Total 120.
Average attendance   Morning 120 + 30 SS. Total 150
Evening 120 + 30 SS. Total 150.
Remarks   The place of worship at Littletown is a preaching
room on Sundays and a schoolroom on the weekdays.

The weather being unfavourable on the 30 March our
congregation was thin.
Dated   31 March 1851.
Signed   George Johnson jun[ior], steward [coal miner].
Littletown, Durham.

16.48   Wesleyan Methodist Schoolroom, East Hetton Colliery
(545.90)
[Shared with Primitive Methodists (**16.76**)]
Name   Schoolroom built for the use of the inhabitants'
children by the owners of East Hetton Colliery.
Erected   About the year 1839 or [18]40.
Building   One half occupied by the Primitives and female
day schools [for the district?]. Occupied for a day
and night school, Sabbath school and the average
attendance is 120 taught by the Methodist and the
service is afternoon and night average.
Sittings   All free sittings.
Attendance 30 March   Morning Sabbath school average 120.
Total [120].
Afternoon religious service 70. Total [70].
Evening religious service [not given].
Average attendance   Morning 70 or upward + 120 SS. Total 190.
Dated   30 March 1851.
Signed   Robert Embleton, class leader [grocer and draper].
East Hetton, No. 170.

16.49   Wesleyan Methodist, Iveston (545.32)
Name   Wesleyan Methodist Chapel.
Erected   1837.
Building   [Separate and] entire building [not exclusively used
for worship].
Sittings   Free 60. Other 30. Total [90].
Attendance 30 March   Afternoon 28. Total 28.
Evening 36. Total 36.
Average attendance   [Not given.]
Remarks   [In another hand. No Crookhall, Wesleyan missing
(**16.32**).]
Dated   30 March 1851.
Signed   Jonathan Stokoe, trustee [labourer].
Iveston, Durham.

16.50   Wesleyan Methodist, Kip Hill (545.6)
Name   None.
Erected   Before 1800.
Building   [Not separate and entire but exclusively used for
                worship.]
Sittings   Free 78. Total [78].
Attendance 30 March   Afternoon 67. Total 67.
Average attendance   [Not given.]
Remarks   This place of worship is an upper room in a house, the
                under part of which is used for a dwelling.
Dated   30 March 1851.
Signed   Thomas M'Cullagh, minister [1849–51].
                Shotley Bridge, Co[unty] of Durham.

16.51   Wesleyan Methodist Schoolroom, Kyo (545.12)
Name   A. Mackey's Day School.
Erected   In 1838.
Building   A separate building. Used as a day and Sunday
                school.
Sittings   Free all 100. Other none. Total [100].
Attendance 30 March   Evening 100 + 20 SS. Total 120.
Average attendance   Afternoon 100 + 20 SS. Total 120.
Dated   31 March 1851.
Signed   John Ward Cowey, steward [grocer].
                Anfield Plain by Lanchester, Durham.

16.52   Wesleyan Methodist, Lanchester (545.36)
Name   Wesleyan Methodist Chapel.
Erected   1819.
Building   [Separate and entire. Exclusively used for worship.]
Sittings   Free 50. Other 56. Total [106].
Attendance 30 March   Afternoon 50 [including SS]. Total [50].
Average attendance   [Not given.]
Dated   31 March 1851.
Signed   Joseph James, chapel steward.
                Lanchester, Durham.

16.53   Wesleyan Methodist, Leadgate (545.31)
Name   Wesleyan Methodist Chapel.
Erected   1847.
Building   A separate and entire building [given by the Leadgate
                Iron and Brass Foundry]. Used exclusively as a place of
                worship and Sunday school.

Sittings   Free 190. Other 85. Total [275]. Standing room none.
Attendance 30 March   Morning 48 + 40 SS. Total 88.
                 Afternoon no service except Sunday School.
                 Evening 37 + 7 SS. Total 44.
Average attendance   Morning 60 + 30 SS. Total 90.
                 Evening 60 + 30 SS. Total 90.
Dated   30 March 1851.
Signed   John Davison, society steward [shopkeeper].
              Leadgate, Shotley Bridge, Durham.

16.54   Wesleyan Methodist, Lintz Green (545.2)
Name   None.
Erected   In the year 1848.
Building   [Separate and entire but not exclusively used for
              worship.]
Sittings   Free 50. Total [50]. Standing room 60.
Attendance 30 March   Afternoon no service.
Average attendance   Morning 40. Total 40.
Dated   [Not given.]
Signed   Thomas Burn, manager [miller].
              Burnopfield.

16.55   Wesleyan Methodist, Medomsley (545.14)
Name   None.
Erected   1842.
Building   Not separate [and entire]. Place of worship, day and
              Sabbath school.
Sittings   All free 150. Total [150].
Attendance 30 March   Morning 56 SS. Total 56.
                 Afternoon 60 + 23 SS. Total 83.
                 Evening 40. Total 40.
Average attendance   Morning 54 SS. Total 54.
                 Afternoon 60 + 23 SS. Total 83.
Dated   30 March 1851.
Signed   Jacob Dent, local preacher and leader [grocer and
              draper].
              Medomsley, Gateshead, Durham.

16.56   Wesleyan Methodist, Castleside, Muggleswick (545.43)
Name   Watergate Chaple (*sic*).
Erected   1807.
Building   [Separate and entire. Exclusively used for worship.]

Sittings   Free 150. Other 62. Total 212. Standing room 60.
Attendance 30 March   Afternoon 57 + 46 SS. Total 103.
                        Evening 43 + 6 SS. Total 49.
Average attendance   Afternoon 85 + 50 SS. Total 135.
                        Evening 50 + 8 SS. Total 58.
Dated   30 March 1851.
Signed   John Rand, chaple (*sic*) steward.
               Castleside.

16.57   Wesleyan Methodist, Pittington (545.82)
Name   Wesleyan Methodist Chapel.
Erected   1830.
Building   [Separate and entire. Exclusively used for worship.]
Sittings   Free 104. Other 108. Total [212].
Attendance 30 March   Afternoon 146. Total [146].
                        Evening 100. Total [100].
Average attendance   [Not given.]
Dated   30 March 1851.
Signed   James Corby, society steward (colliery viewer).
               Pittington, Durham.

16.58   Wesleyan Methodist, Sherburn (545.78)
Name   [Not given.]
Erected   [Not given.]
Building   [Not given whether separate and entire. Not
               exclusively used for worship.] It is a dwelling house.
Sittings   Free 80. Total [80].
Attendance 30 March   Afternoon 30 + 20 SS. Total [50].
                        Evening 35 + 12 SS. Total [47].
Average attendance   Afternoon 40 + 20 SS. Total [60].
                        Evening 60 + 10 SS. Total [70].
Dated   31 March 1851.
Signed   John Young, leader [corn miller].
               Sherburn East Mill.

16.59   Wesleyan Methodist, Shincliffe Colliery (545.74)
Name   Wesleyan Chapel.
Erected   1838.
Building   [Separate and entire. Exclusively used for] public
               worship and Sunday school.
Sittings   Free 100. Other 50. Total [150]. Standing room 40.
Attendance 30 March   Morning 85 + 20 SS. Total [105].

Evening 95 + 25 SS. Total [120].

Average attendance   Morning 40 + 30 SS. Total [70].

Evening 70 + 35 SS. Total [105].

Dated   31 March 1851.

Signed   Nicholas Dixon, chapel steward (pitman).

Shincliffe Colliery, Durham.

16.60 Wesleyan Methodist, Wood Street, Shotley Bridge (545.21)

Name   Wesleyan Methodist Chapel.

Erected   In the year 1810 and rebuilt and enlarged in 1837.
[New chapel 1855.]

Building   Separate and entire building. Exclusively as a place of worship (except for a Sunday School).

Sittings   Free 180. Other 156. Total [336].
Room for about 60 persons to stand.

Attendance 30 March   Morning 50 + 50 SS. Total 100.

Afternoon no service

Evening 220. Total [220].

Average attendance   Morning and afternoon 300 + 56 SS.
Total 356.

Dated   31 March 1851.

Signed   Peter Wilkinson, Wesleyan minister [1849–51].
Holly Cottage, Shotley Bridge.

16.61 Wesleyan Methodist, Tantobie (545.7)

Name   Wesleyan.

Erected   1832.

Building   [Separate and entire. Exclusively used for worship.]

Sittings   Free 140. Other 49. Total [189].

Attendance 30 March   Afternoon 60. Total [60].

Evening 170. Total [170].

Average attendance   [Not given.]

Dated   [Not given.]

Signed   Copied from information sent by the minister, John Watson, by R. King.

16.62 Methodist New Connexion, Brancepeth (545.48)

Name   Methodist New Connexion Chapel.

Erected   1845.

Building   [Separate and entire. Exclusively used for worship.]

Sittings   Free 80. Other 60. Total [140]. Standing room 30.

Attendance 30 March   Morning no service 90 SS. Total 90.

Afternoon 110 + 40 SS. Total 150.
Evening 120 + 30 SS. Total 150.
Average attendance   [Not given.]
Dated   1 April 1851.
Signed   Joseph Love, trustee [colliery owner].
Willington House, Durham

16.63   Methodist New Connexion, Old Elvet, Durham (545.57)
Name   New Connexion Chapel.
Erected   Opened in 1846.
Building   Two rooms in, but separated from, a dwelling house
[15 Old Elvet. Exclusively used for worship.]
Sittings   Free 28. Other 29. Total [57]. Standing room 70.
Attendance 30 March   Morning 60 + 56 SS. Total [116].
Evening 75. Total [75].
Average attendance   Morning 50 + 50 SS. Total [100].
Evening 75. Total [75].
Dated   30 March 1851.
Signed   John Ward, steward and manager [solicitor].
54 Old Elvet, [Durham].

16.64   Methodist New Connexion, St Giles, Durham (545.68)
Name   Methodist New Connexion Chapel.
Erected   In the year of our Lord, 1838.
Building   [Separate and entire. Exclusively used for worship.]
Sittings   Free 100. Other 50. Total [150].
Attendance 30 March   Morning 90 SS. Total [90].
Afternoon 50. Total [50].
Evening 40. Total [40].
Average attendance   [Not given.]
Dated   30 March 1851.
Signed   Joshua Staker, steward (miner).
New Durham in the County of Durham.

16.65   Primitive Methodist, Anfield Plain (545.11)
Name   Primitive Methodist Chapel.
Erected   1839 [when two cottages were made into one.
Enlarged 1867, and replaced by a new chapel opened
on 21 October 1896.]
Building   [Separate and entire. Exclusively used for worship.]
Sittings   Free 114. Other 36. Total [150].
Attendance 30 March   Morning 21 + 44 SS. Total 65.

Evening 28 + 3 SS. Total 31.
Average attendance   Morning 30 + 40 SS. Total 70.
Evening 60. Total 60.
Dated   30 March 1851.
Signed   Isaac Newton, secretary [coke burner].
Kyo [Laws, Anfield Plain].

16.66   Primitive Methodist, Blackhill, Benfieldside (545.23)
Name   Primitive Methodist Chapel.
Erected   1842.
Building   [Separate and entire. Exclusively used for worship.]
Sittings   Free 112. Other 34. Total [146]. Standing room 20.
Attendance 30 March   Morning 38 + 5 SS. Total 43.
Afternoon 38 + 19 SS. Total 57.
Evening 260 + 10 SS. Total 270.
Average attendance   Morning 30 + 10 SS. Total 40.
Afternoon 50 + 14 SS. Total 64.
Evening 100 + 20 SS. Total 120.
Dated   30 March 1851.
Signed   Thomas Carrick, minister [in 1851].
Bible Passage, Gateshead, Durham.

16.67   Primitive Methodist, Berry Edge (545.28)
Name   Primitive Methodist Chapel.
Erected   1848.
Building   Separate and entire. Exclusively for a place of worship
except for a Sunday school.
Sittings   Free 140. Other 90. Total [230]. Standing room 70.
Attendance 30 March   Afternoon 100 [including SS]. Total [100].
Evening 150 + 30 SS. Total [180].
Average attendance   Afternoon 150 + 40 SS. Total 190.
Evening 160 + 30 SS. Total 190.
Dated   30 March 1851.
Signed   Thomas Carrick, minister [in 1851].
Shotley Bridge, Gateshead, Durham.

16.68   Primitive Methodist, Ebchester (545.16)
Name   Primitive Methodist Chapel.
Erected   In 1848.
Building   [Separate and entire. Exclusively used for worship.]
Sittings   Free 100. Other none. Total [100].
Attendance 30 March   Morning 10. Total 10.

Afternoon 15. Total [15].
Average attendance   Morning 12. Total 12.
Afternoon 20. Total 20.
Dated   30 March 1851.
Signed   Thomas Carrick, minister [in 1851].
Shotley Bridge, Gateshead, Durham.

16.69   Primitive Methodist, New Cassop (545.87)
Name   Primitive Methodist Chapel.
Erected   1842. [Cost £150.]
Building   [Separate and entire but not exclusively used for worship.]
Sittings   Free 100. Other 120. Total [220].
Attendance 30 March   Afternoon 120 + 30 SS. Total 150.
Evening 100 + 40 SS. Total 140.
Average attendance   Afternoon 150 + 40 SS. Total 190.
Evening 160 + 45 SS. Total 205.
Dated   30 March 1851.
Signed   Henry Phillipps, minister.
2 Leazes Place, Durham.

16.70   Primitive Methodist, Castleside (545.26)
Name   Primitive Methodist chapel.
Erected   In 1843.
Building   Separate [and entire] building. [Exclusively used for worship] except for Sunday School.
Sittings   Free 70. Other 30. Total [100].
Attendance 30 March   Morning [Not given.] Total 66.
Afternoon 32. Total 32.
Evening 66. Total 66.
Average attendance   [Not given.]
Dated   31 March 1851.
Signed   Anthony Male, steward.
Castleside, Durham.

16.71   Primitive Methodist, Causey Row (545.4)
Name   Causey Row Chapel.
Erected   In 1843. [New chapel 1866.]
Building   [Separate and entire but not exclusively used for worship.]
Sittings   Free 100. Other none. Total [100].
Attendance 30 March   Afternoon 46. Total 46.

Average attendance   Afternoon 50. Total 50.
                         Evening 60. Total 60.
Dated   30 March 1851.
Signed   Samuel Gibson, chapel steward [wagon builder].
                 Causey Row, near Tanfield.

16.72   Primitive Methodist, Coxhoe (545.88)
Name   Chapel.
Erected   1839.
Building   Separate and entire building. Place of worship, Sunday
                 school and day school.
Sittings   Free 180. Other 120. Total [300].
Attendance 30 March   Afternoon 150. Total [150].
                        Evening 170. Total [170].
Average attendance   [Not given.]
Dated   31 March 1851.
Signed   Thomas Hay, manager.
                 Coxhoe, Durham.

16.73   Primitive Methodist, Silver Street Lane, Durham (545.64)
Name   Primitive Methodist Chapel.
Erected   1826. [New chapel in Silver Street opened 19 May
                 1861.]
Building   [Separate and entire. Exclusively used for worship.]
Sittings   Free 100. Other 120. Total [220]. Standing room none.
Attendance 30 March   Afternoon 175. Total [175].
                        Evening 187. Total [187].
Average attendance   [Not given.]
Dated   30 March 1851.
Signed   Peter Kemble, Primitive Methodist minister.
                 Crossgate, Durham.

16.74   Primitive Methodist, Gilesgate Moor, Durham (545.67)
Name   Primitive Methodist Chapel.
Erected   1838.
Building   [Separate and entire but not exclusively used for
                 worship.]
Sittings   All free. Standing room none.
Attendance 30 March   Morning 200 [includes SS]. Total [200].
                        Afternoon none.
                        Evening 250 + 70 SS. Total 320.
Average attendance   [Not given.]

Dated　　　[Not given.]
Signed　　Thomas Shapley, steward [shopkeeper].
　　　　　　Dragon Villa, near New Durham.

16.75　Primitive Methodist, St Giles, Durham (545.70)
Name　　　Primitive Methodist Chapel.
Erected　　1839.
Building　　[Separate and entire. Exclusively used for worship]
　　　　　　with day school.
Sittings　　Free 184. Other 82. Total [266].
Attendance 30 March　Morning 120. Total [120].
　　　　　　　　　　　Afternoon 120 SS. Total [120].
　　　　　　　　　　　Evening 200. Total [200].
Average attendance　　Morning 1,320. Total 1,320 (*sic*).　　　[crossed
　　　　　　　　　　　Afternoon 1,872 SS. Total 1,872 (*sic*).}　out.]
　　　　　　　　　　　Evening 1,320. Total 1,320 (*sic*).
Dated　　　30 March 1851.
Signed　　George Lee, trustee.
　　　　　　Gilesgate Moor, Durham.

16.76　Primitive Methodist Schoolroom, East Hetton Colliery
(545.91)
[Shared with Wesleyan Methodists (**16.48**)]
Name　　　East Hetton Colliery schoolroom for the female sex.
Erected　　In May 1840.
Building　　Adjoined by the school for the male sex. [Exclusively
　　　　　　used for worship and] for a day school.
Sittings　　Free 150. Total [150].
Attendance 30 March　Morning 80 + 163 SS. Total [243].
　　　　　　　　　　　Evening 150. Total [150].
Average attendance　　Morning 80 + 160 SS. Total [240].
　　　　　　　　　　　Evening 150. Total [150].
Dated　　　31 March 1851.
Signed　　James Scott, chapel steward [coal miner].
　　　　　　No. 17, East Hetton, Durham.

16.77　Primitive Methodist, Huntley Grange, Lanchester (545.35)
Name　　　Knitsley Grange.
Erected　　1842.
Building　　[Separate and] entire. [Exclusively used for worship.]
Sittings　　Free 42. Other 28. Total [70].
Attendance 30 March　Afternoon 12. Total [12].

Average attendance   Afternoon 16. Total [16].
Dated   31 March 1851.
Signed   John Dobson, in charge [farmer].
                 Knitsley Grange, Lanchester, Durham.

16.78   Primitive Methodist Schoolroom, Leadgate (545.30)
Name   Derwent Ironwork Co[mpany] School.
Erected   1846 [and provided by the Leadgate Iron and Brass
                 Foundry].
Building   [Separate and entire. Exclusively used for worship
                 and] also day school.
Sittings   Free 250. Total [250].
Attendance 30 March   Afternoon 79 SS. Total [79].
                        Evening 141 SS. Total [141].
Average attendance   Afternoon 100 + 50 SS. Total 150.
                        Evening 200 [including SS]. Total 200.
Dated   31 March 1851.
Signed   John Dorith for Jonathan Wright, chaple (*sic*) steward.
                 Leadgate, No 166.

16.79   Primitive Methodist, Muggleswick (545.42)
Name   None.
Erected   [Not given.]
Building   [Not separate and entire or exclusively used for
                 worship.]
Sittings   Free 60. Total [60]. Standing room 25 square yards.
Attendance 30 March   Afternoon 50. Total [50].
Average attendance   [Not given.]
Dated   30 March 1851.
Signed   Charles Harrowby, minister.
                 Priest Pople (*sic*), Hexham.
[Charles Harrowby was also the minister of Blanchland (**8.84**).]

16.80   Primitive Methodist, Hallgarth (545.81)
Name   Primitive Methodist Chapel.
Erected   1842.
Building   [Separate and entire. Exclusively used for worship.]
Sittings   Free 72. Other 94. Total [166].
Attendance 30 March   Morning 100. Total [100].
                        Afternoon 127 SS. Total 127.
                        Evening 160. Total [160].
Average attendance   [Not given.]

Dated   30 March 1851.
Signed   Joseph Watson, steward (coal miner).
             Near Pittington, Durham.
[See Wesleyan Methodist, Hallgarth (**16.46**).]

16.81   Primitive Methodist, Shotley Bridge (545.22)
Name   Primitive Methodist.
Erected   1825. [A new chapel in Wood Street was opened in
             1852.]
Building   [Separate and entire. Exclusively used for worship.]
Sittings   Free 120. Total [120].
Attendance 30 March   Afternoon 100. Total [100].
Average attendance   Afternoon 100. Total [100].
                          Evening 100. Total [100].
Dated   31 March 1851.
Signed   John Brodie, circuit steward [tailor and draper].
             Shotley Bridge.

16.82   Primitive Methodist, Tanfield (545.8)
Name   Primitive Methodist Chapel.
Erected   1834.
Building   [Separate and entire but not exclusively used for
             worship.]
Sittings   Free 132. Other 28. Total [160]. Standing room 50.
Attendance 30 March   Morning no service [crossed out].
                        Afternoon 64 + 20 SS. Total 84.
                        Evening 100 + 15 SS. Total 115.
Average attendance   Morning no service.
                        Afternoon 100 [including SS]. Total 100.
                        Evening 150 [including SS]. Total 150.
Dated   31 March 1851.
Signed   Mathew Smaile, steward.
             Flint Hill, near Tanfield, Durham.

16.83   Primitive Methodist Schoolroom, Waskerley (545.45)
Name   School Room.
Erected   1836.
Building   Separate [and entire but not exclusively used for
             worship].
Sittings   All free.
Attendance 30 March   Morning 20 SS. Total [20].
Average attendance   Morning 30. Total [30].

Dated   31 March 1851.
Signed   Joseph Petty [joiner].
              [Waskerley.]

16.84   Society of Friends [Quakers], Claypath, Durham (545.62)

Name   [Not given.]
Erected   Before 1800. [Erected 1692, enlarged 1716 and closed
              1859.]
Building   [Separate and entire. Exclusively used for worship.]
Sittings   Free 225. Total [225].
              [Ground floor] 1,323 [square feet]. No gallery. Total
              1,323 [square feet].
Attendance 30 March   Morning 11. Total [11].
                        Afternoon 9. Total [9].
Dated   31 day of 3rd month [1851].
Signed   Joseph Holmes [grocer].
              19 Elvet Bridge, Durham.

16.85   Society of Friends [Quakers] Snows Green, Shotley Bridge (545.19)

Name   [Not given.]
Erected   In the year 1843 instead of one erected before 1800.
              [1790.]
Building   [Separate and entire. Exclusively used for worship.]
Sittings   [Free] 150. Total 150.
              Ground floor area 910 [square feet]. No gallery. Total
              910 [square feet].
Attendance 30 March   Morning 54. Total [54].
                        Afternoon 40. Total [40].
Dated   2nd day of 4th month 1851.
Signed   Jonathan Richardson [banker].
              [Shotley Park], Shotley Bridge.
[Jonathan Richardson (1802–1871) developed Shotley Spa, built the
Springfield Hotel and the Quaker Meeting House. His brothers were
partners who developed the Derwent Iron Company.]

16.86   Roman Catholic, High Brooms, Leadgate (545.52)

[On a Church of England form]
Name   Catholic Chapel (St Cuthbert's), Brooms.
Consecrated Sometime before 1800 [1794]. By private subscription.
              [Opened 1802 and became the vestry of the new
              church when it was opened on 25 October 1869.]

Sittings   Total 240.
Attendance 30 March   [Not given.]
Average attendance   Morning 2,000 (*sic*). Total [2,000].
Remarks   The total number of sittings in this chapel is 240, while that of the congregation amounts to 2,000 souls. The living is [...] on demand from the voluntary offerings of the faithful. [...] of this [... ... ...] does not apply to us as far as it applies to this chapel.
Dated   17 April 1851.
Signed   Francis Kearney, clergyman [1849–90].
          Brooms, Gateshead.
[In 1852 the estimated number of Roman Catholics in the area was 1,930.]

16.87   Roman Catholic, Croxdale Hall (545.51)
Name   Croxdale Catholic Chapel [St Herbert].
Erected   1808 [by William Thomas Salvin].
Building   Attached to the house. Exclusively for worship.
Sittings   Free length 16 yards. Broad 8 yards. Total [200].
Attendance 30 March   Morning 130. Total [130].
                Afternoon 30. Total [30].
Average attendance   Morning 130. Total [130].
Dated   31 March 1851.
Signed   Thomas Smith, [Roman Catholic priest 1808–53].
          Croxdale [Hall] near Durham.
[In 1852 the estimated number of Roman Catholics in the area was 280.]

16.88   Roman Catholic, Old Elvet, Durham (545.56)
Name   St Cuthbert's Chapel.
Erected   1827. [Opened 31 May 1827.]
Building   [Separate and entire. Exclusively used for worship.]
Sittings   Free 150. Other 280. Total [430]. Standing room 150.
Attendance 30 March   Morning 470 + 110 SS. Total 580.
                Evening 450 + 100 SS. Total 550.
Average attendance   [Not given.]
Remarks   According to a census lately taken by Roman Catholics belonging to the congregation of Durham, the number is 1,220. The chapel being too small to contain them many do not come to chapel on Sundays.
Dated   30 March 1851.

Signed   William Fletcher [DD], Roman Catholic priest [1840–
56].
Old Elvet, Durham.
[In 1852 the estimated number of Roman Catholics in the area was
1,307.]

16.89   Roman Catholic, Esh Laude (545.38)
Name   St Michael's.
Erected   Before 1800. [1799.]
Building   [Separate and] entire. [Exclusively used for worship.]
Sittings   Free 50. Other 224. Total [274].
Attendance 30 March   Morning 208 + 73 SS. Total [281].
                        Afternoon 140 + 67 SS. Total [207].
Average attendance   [Not given.]
Dated   30 March 1851.
Signed   William Thompson, clergyman [1841–80].
Esh Laude, Durham.
[In 1852 the estimated number of Roman Catholics in the area was
530.]

16.90   Roman Catholic, Ushaw College (545.39)
Name   St Cuthbert's College Chapel.
Erected   1808. [The college opened on 19 July 1808. The
buildings cost £6,245. The chapel was consecrated on
27 September 1848.]
Building   [Separate and entire. Exclusively used for worship.]
Sittings   Free [none]. Other 150. Total [150]. Standing room
100.
Attendance 30 March   Morning 190. Total 190.
                        Afternoon 160. Total 160.
Average attendance   [Not given.]
Remarks   The numbers [attending] include our own
community and casual attendants. We have no
regular congregation from without as we perform no
parochial duty, and those who do attend, attend only
on sufferance, the chapel being erected solely for the
private use of the inmates of the college.
Dated   31 March 1851.
Signed   Michael Gibson, priest [vice-president and Professor of
Moral Divinity].
[Charles Newsham DD, president 1837–63.]
St Cuthbert's College, Ushaw, Durham.

[From 1794 the college was located at Crook Hall, then at Ushaw College. Between 1794 and 1894 upwards of 800 priests had been trained at the college.]

17. Easington District (HO 129/546)
32 places of worship (and 1 in East Yorkshire)

17.1   Church of England, St James, Castle Eden (546.8)
Population 1851: 491 (parish)

Name   St James. An antient (*sic*) parish church.
Consecrated Before 1800. [Rebuilt 1762.]
Endowment   Land £35. Tithe £12 5s. Glebe none (no house). OPE £77.
              Fees 15s. Other £10 [from the Lord Crewe Charity].
              Total £135.
Sittings   Free 440. Other none. Total 440.
Attendance 30 March   Morning 202 + 53 SS. Total 255.
              Afternoon 118 + 42 SS. Total 160.
              (The gross of the two congregations above (415) contained 334 individuals.)
Average attendance   About the same as on 30 March.
Remarks   The church which had been in ruins for centuries was rebuilt in 1762 by R[owland] Burdon Esq., the patron. The permanent endowment of £77 has been added since 1830 by R. Burdon Esq. and the Dean and Chapter of Durham.
Dated   31 March 1851.
Signed   Henry Baker Tristram MA, perpetual curate [1849–60]. Castle Eden, near Ferryhill.
{1857   Attendance 150. 30 communicants.}   {B 18.}
[Henry Baker Tristram (1822–1906) was a biblical writer and ornithologist, a founding member of the British Ornithologists Union. He visited the Holy Land in 1858, 1863, 1872 and 1881 and wrote numerous books on his travels. He also visited Norway and Japan. Tristram was the vicar of Greatham 1860–73, a canon of Durham cathedral from 1873 and a leading Freemason. His father, Henry Baker Tristram, had been the vicar of Eglingham 1821–37 (**1.4**).]

17.2   Church of England, St Andrew, Dalton-le-Dale (546.27)
Population 1851: 5,125 (parish) 83 (township)

[Summary form]
Name   [Not given.]
Erected   About 500 years ago. [Enlarged 1907.]
Endowment   [£201.]
Sittings   Free 50. Other 150. Total 200.
Usual attendance   Morning 50 + 20 SS. Total [70].
                          Afternoon 20 SS. Total [20].
Informant   R. Richardson, registrar.
              [Dalton-le-Dale.]
              The vicar refused to fill up a return.
Incumbent   [James Humphrey Brown 1832–67.]
[1857   Attendance 90. 14 communicants.}   {B 69.}
[Holy Trinity, East Murton, was consecrated on 1 June 1877.]

17.3   Church of England, St Mary the Virgin, Easington (546.17)
Population 1851: 7,062 (parish) 916 (township)

Name   St Mary. Easington parish church.
Consecrated Ancient church. [Restored 1852–53.]
Erected   Anciently endowed.
Endowment   Glebe and tithe. [Total £1,311.]
Sittings   Free 120. Other 400. Total 520.
Attendance 30 March   Morning 120 + 60 SS. Total 180.
                        Afternoon 77 + 30 SS. Total 107.
Average attendance   [Not given.]
Dated   31 March 1851.
Signed   Henry George Liddell, rector [1832–72].
              Rectory Mill, Durham.
{1857   Attendance 180. 18 communicants.}   {B 69.}
[Until 1832 the Archdeaconry of Durham was annexed to Easington, and then to Ryton (**18.10**).
William Wren Liddell, the son of the rector, was the curate of Easington 1855–61.]

17.4   Church of England, Holy Trinity, South Hetton (546.23)

Name   Trinity Chapel, South Hetton. Chapel of ease to
              Easington church.
Consecrated In 1838 [11 October] as an additional church for the

use of the colliery population of South Hetton, and was before settled on the [...].

Erected   By subscriptions with the aid of the Church Building Society.

Endowment [Not given.]

Sittings   Free 250. Other 150. Total 400.

Attendance 30 March Morning 110 + 76 SS. Total 186.
                       Evening 105 + 70 SS. Total 175.

Average attendance   Morning 100 + 80 SS. Total 180.
                       Evening 100 + 80 SS. Total 180.

Remarks   There is an afternoon service at Haswell Colliery in the schoolroom in the same parish. The church has a burial ground attached to it. Marriages are performed at Easington. The church would be better attended but for the number of Methodists.

Dated   29 March 1851.

Signed   Humphrey Fitzroy Woolrych, curate of South Hetton [1851–54].
              South Hetton, Fence Houses, Durham.

Incumbent   [Henry George Liddell 1832–72.]

{1857   Attendance 50. 16 communicants.}

17.5   Church of England, St Peter, Monkhesleden (546.14)
Population 1851: 2,709 (parish) 1,495 (township)

Name   An old church dedicated to St Peter.
              The church dates back to 1578 AD.

Consecrated It cannot be ascertained, the register goes back to 1578. Before 1800.

Endowment   Land £2. Tithe £298. Glebe £1. Fees £4. Easter offerings £2.

Sittings   Free 200. Total [200].

Attendance 30 March Morning 75. Total [75].

Average attendance   Morning 100. Total [100].

Remarks   There are no free sittings. All of the pews are free but appropriated to various houses. The net income that I receive is £130.

Dated   30 March 1851.

Signed   William Hayes, vicar [1806–59].
              Monkhesleden, Ferryhill, Durham.

{B 41.}

17.6   Church of England Schoolroom, Hutton Henry (546.11)
Name   Chapel of ease.
Licensed   1843. Licensed as an additional chapel.
Erected   Two cottages connected into a school and afterwards
                licensed for divine service. Benefaction of the vicar
                £25.
Sittings   Free 120. Total [120].
Attendance 30 March   Afternoon 45. Total [45].
Average attendance   Afternoon 80. Total [80].
Dated   30 March 1851.
Signed   Disney Legard Alexander, curate of Hesledon [1832–54].
                Ferryhill, Durham.
Incumbent   [William Hayes, vicar [1806–59].
{1857   Attendance 40.}
[St Paul, Haswell, was consecrated on 1 July 1867.]

17.7   Church of England, St Helen, Kelloe (546.1)
Population 1851: 149 (township)

Name   Consecrated to St Helen. An ancient parish church.
Consecrated   Before 1800. [Chancel rebuilt 1854.]
Endowment   Land say £150. Tithe £80. Fees £20.
                Other £480 deducting outgoings.
Sittings   Free 125. Other 125. Total 250.
Attendance 30 March   Morning 120 + 28 SS. Total 148.
                Afternoon 14 + 12 SS. Total 26.
Average attendance   Morning 125 + 40 SS. Total 165.
                Afternoon 25 + 45 SS. Total 70.
Remarks   The principal part of the income of the living arises
                from way-leaves and a small coal [fund?] – both very
                variable. The above is approximately [true?].
Dated   29 March 1851.
Signed   Robert Birkett, minister [1814–51].
                Kelloe, Ferryhill.
{1857   Attendance 180. 24 communicants. The church is much
                too small and not centrally situated.}   {B 260.}

17.8   Church of England, St Mary the Virgin, Seaham (546.32)
Population 1851: 929 (parish) 729 (township)

Name   Saint Mary's. An ancient parish church.

Consecrated   Before 1800.
Endowment   Tithe £360. Glebe £300. Fees £1.
Sittings   Free and other 100. Total 100.
Attendance 30 March   Morning 51. Total 51.
Average attendance   [Not given.]
Dated   [Not given.]
Signed   Robert Houghton Baxter, vicar [1850–59].
               Fence Houses, Seaham, Durham.
{1857   Attendance 30. – communicants.}   {B 11.}

17.9   Church of England, St John the Evangelist, Seaham Harbour (546.31)
Population 1851: 3,538 (township)

Name   St John's Church. The church of a district chapelry.
Consecrated [21 October] 1841 as an additional church. [Enlarged
              1860–61. District created 23 August 1843 out of the
              parish of Dalton-le-Dale.]
Erected   By subscription, aided by a grant from the Church
              Building Society (£300). Private £1,218 [of which £150
              from the Dean and Chapter of Durham]. Total cost
              £1,518.
Endowment   Tithe £90. OPE £100.
Sittings   Free 280. Other 200. Total 480.
Attendance 30 March   Morning 138 + 90 SS. Total 228.
                        Evening 152 + 24 SS. Total 176.
Average attendance   Morning 150 + 120 SS. Total 270.
                        Evening 250 + 50 SS. Total 300.
Remarks   The attendance on the 30 March 1851 was considerably
              below the average especially in the evening. The
              average returned fairly represent the usual attendance.
              The morning and evening congregations are nearly
              distinct. The Sunday school children are not required
              to attend in the evening. The school is at present
              thinner by the prevalence of measles.
Dated   31 March 1851.
Signed   Angus Bethune, perpetual curate [1845–59].
              Seaham, Durham.
{1857   Attendance 430. 35 communicants.}   {B 139.}
[Angus Bethune, who was the vicar of Seaham 1859–1908, was
succeeded at Seaham Harbour by George Howard Wilkinson (1833–
1907), *ODNB*, vol. 58, pp. 1002–1003. He was the incumbent 1860–63,

vicar of Bishop Auckland 1863–68, vicar of St Peter, Great Windmill Street, London, 1867–70, vicar of St Peter, Eaton Square, 1870–83, Bishop of Truro 1883–91, Bishop of St Andrews, Dunkeld and Dunblane 1893–1904, and primus of the Scottish Episcopal Church 1904–07. His biography outlines his ministry at Seaham Harbour and Bishop Auckland. A.J. Mason, *Memoir of George Howard Wilkinson* (London, 1909), vol. 1, pp. 45–203.]

17.10   Church of England, St Bartholomew, Thornley [Kelloe] (546.2)
Population 1851: 2,740 (township)

Name	Thornley District Church, St Bartholomew. District assigned under the 16th section, 59th Geo. III c.134. [District created 31 January 1844 out of the parish of Kelloe.]
Consecrated	[8] August 1843 as an additional church.
Erected	By private subscription. Total cost £950.
Endowment	Tithe £9 15s. OPE From Ecclesiastical Commissioners £134. [£250.] Fees (say) £12. Total £155 15s.
Sittings	Free 500. Total 500.
Attendance 30 March	Morning 149 + 60 SS. Total 209. Afternoon 60 SS. *Total [60]. Evening 102. Total 102.
Average attendance	No means of correctly answering this.
Remarks	* There is no service in the afternoon at church, but the Sunday scholars attend school for 1½ hours.
Dated	31 March 1851.
Signed	William Ashley Shute, incumbent [1844–62]. Thornley, Ferryhill, Durham.
{1857	Attendance 160. 30 communicants.}

17.11   Church of England, Holy Trinity, Wingate Grange (546.9)
Population 1851: 2,436 (township)

Name	Holy Trinity. Consolidated chapelry district. About 1841. 6 Section of an Act 59 Geo. III. [c.134].
Consecrated	About 1841 [22 October 1841]. An additional church. [District created 3 June 1842 out of the parish of Castle Eden.]

Erected   Private subscriptions and by a grant from the
Ecclesiastical Comm[issioners]. Private about £1,600.
Total cost £1,600.

Endowment Land £1. Tithe £12 5s. OPE £139. Pew rents about £6.
Fees £15. Total £173 5s.

Sittings   Free 225. Other 225. Total 450.

Attendance 30 March   Morning 100 + 90 SS. Total 190.
Afternoon (children in school).
Evening 70. Total 70.

Average attendance   [Not given.]

Remarks   The expenses attending the cleaning of the church
etc. rest on the incumbent. It is impossible for me
to say what is the average attendance at my church.
My people are mostly fishermen and are constantly
moving from one place to another. They are a class
of people most constantly ignorant and have been
sadly neglected at the church. The greater part of them
cannot be persuaded to attend my place of worship.
E. V. Boydell.

Dated   31 March 1851.

Signed   Edward Neville Valentine Boydell, incumbent
[1842–84].
Wingate Parsonage, Ferryhill, Durham.

{1857   Attendance 200. 30 communicants.}   {B 75.}

17.12   Wesleyan Methodist, Easington (546.19)

Name   Wesleyan Methodist Chapel.

Erected   Open[e]d for divine worship, 27 July 1815.

Building   [Separate and entire. Exclusively used for worship.]

Sittings   Free 48. Other 57. Total [105].

Attendance 30 March   Morning [no SS].
Afternoon 33. Total [33].
Evening no service.

Average attendance   [Not given.]

Dated   31 March 1851.

Signed   William Miller, leader and chapel steward (boot and
shoemaker).
Easington, Durham.

17.13   Wesleyan Methodist, Haswell Colliery (546.25)
[Simplified form]
Name   Wesleyan Methodist Chapel.
Erected   1847.
Building   [Separate and entire. Exclusively used for worship.]
Sittings   Free 120. Other 100. Total [220].
Usual attendance   Morning 130 SS. Total 130.
                          Afternoon 150. Total 150.
                          Evening 100. Total 100.
Dated   [Not given.]
Informant   R. Richardson (on enquiry) [registrar].
              Dalton-le-Dale.

17.14   Wesleyan Methodist, South Hetton (546.20)
Name   Wesleyan Methodist Chapel.
Erected   1836.
Building   [Separate and entire. Exclusively used for worship.]
Sittings   Free 200. Other 156. Total [356].
Attendance 30 March   Morning 73 + 16 SS. Total 89.
                          Evening 89 + 12 SS. Total 101.
Average attendance   [Not given.]
Dated   31 March 1851.
Signed   Matthew Elliott, steward [grocer and draper].
              South Hetton, Durham.

17.15   Wesleyan Methodist, Monkchester Colliery (546.15)
[Simplified form]
Name   Wesleyan Methodist Meeting Room.
Erected   A room.
Building   A room [crossed out]. [Exclusively used for worship.]
Sittings   Free 50. Total [50].
Usual attendance   Morning 30. Total 30.
                          Afternoon 30 SS. Total 30.
                          Evening 40. Total 40.
Dated   [Not given.]
Informant   R. Richardson (on enquiry) [registrar].
              Dalton-le-Dale.

17.16   Wesleyan Methodist, East Murton Colliery (546.28)
Name   Wesleyan Chapel.
Erected   1846.

Building   [Separate and entire but not exclusively used for worship.] A day school taught in it.

Sittings   Free 100. Other 72 (paid). Total [172]. Standing room none.

Attendance 30 March   Afternoon 70 + 56 SS. Total 126.
Evening 70 + 74 SS. Total 144.

Average attendance   [Not given.]

Remarks   Hansard the case stands. This through the day. General congregation 140, Sabbath scholars 130.

Dated   30 March 1851.

Signed   Richard Platts, steward [coal miner].
East Murton Colliery, near Hetton, County Durham.

17.17   Wesleyan Methodist, Tempest Place, Seaham Harbour (546.29)

Name   Wesleyan Chapel.

Erected   1833. [Foundation stone laid 26 March 1833. Cost £300.]

Building   Separate and entire building. [Exclusively used for worship.]

Sittings   Free 66. Other 180. Total [246]. Standing room none.

Attendance 30 March   Morning 80 + 20 SS. Total 100.
Evening 200 + 15 SS. Total 215.

Average attendance   [Not given.]

Dated   31 March 1851.

Signed   James Foggin, chapel steward [tailor].
[North] Rail Street, Seaham.

17.18   Wesleyan Methodist Schoolroom, Shotton Colliery (546.21)

Name   Shotton Colliery Schoolroom and preaching d[itt]o for the Wesleyan Methodists.

Erected   1845.

Building   [Separate and] entire building. Day school and Sunday school.

Sittings   250 all free. Total [250].
Standing room 38½ [ft.] long by 20ft. broad.

Attendance 30 March   Morning 130 SS. Total 130.
Afternoon 200 [including SS]. Total [200].
Evening 300 [including SS]. Total [300].

Average attendance   Morning 250 (including the scholars) + 123 SS. Total 373.

Dated   31 March 1851.
Signed   Andrew Hogg, class leader and superintendent.
Shotton Colliery, Durham.

17.19   Wesleyan Methodist, Thornley (546.4)

Name   Wesleyan Chapel.
Erected   1839.
Building   [Separate and entire but not exclusively used for worship.]
Sittings   Free 150. Other 94. Total [244].
Attendance 30 March   Afternoon 160. Total [160].
                        Evening 139. Total [139].
Average attendance   Afternoon 120 + 60 SS. Total 180.
                        Evening 120 + 50 SS. Total 170.
Remarks   A private school (not connected with the Wesleyans) is kept in the chapel on weekdays.
Dated   31 March 1851.
Signed   James Raine, trustee and steward (grocer and draper).
Thornley Colliery, Durham.

17.20   Wesleyan Methodist, Wingate Colliery (546.7)

[Simplified form]
Name   Wesleyan Methodist Chapel.
Erected   1845.
Building   [Separate and entire.] Also for a day school.
Sittings   Free 150. Other 50. Total [200].
Usual attendance Morning 50 SS. Total 50.
                   Afternoon 100. Total 100.
                   Evening 60. Total 60.
Dated   [Not given.]
Informant   R. Richardson (on enquiry) [registrar].
Dalton-le-Dale.

17.21   Wesleyan Methodist, Wingate Grange Colliery (546.6)

Name   Wingate Wesleyan Methodist Chapel.
Erected   In the year 1842.
Building   [Separate and] entire building. [Exclusively used as] a place of worship.
Sittings   Free 186. Other 24. Total [210]. Standing room none.
Attendance 30 March   Afternoon 56 + 13 SS. Total 69.
                        Evening 83. Total 83.
Average attendance   Afternoon 66 + 20 SS. Total 86.

Evening 74 + 17 SS. Total 91.

Dated   30 March 1851.
Signed   John Curry, chapel steward [coal miner].
             Wingate Grange Colliery.

17.22   Primitive Methodist, Castle Eden Colliery (546.10)

Name   Primitive Methodist Chapel.
Erected   In the year of our Lord 1842.
Building   [Separate and] entire building. A place of worship and Sunday school.
Sittings   Free – a single box containing a dozen.
             Other – four pues (*sic*) contain six each.
             Standing room 25 ft. by 18 ft.
Attendance 30 March   Morning 99. Total 311 (*sic*) [99].
             Afternoon 111. Total [111].
             Evening 90. Total [90].
Average attendance   Afternoon 80. Total [80].
Dated   31 March 1851.
Signed   Joseph Innes [farmer].
             Andrew Thoubburn, chapel steward.
             Castle Eden Colliery.

17.23   Primitive Methodist, Haswell Lane (546.24)

Name   Primitive Methodist Chapel.
Erected   1839.
Building   [Separate and entire. Exclusively used for worship.]
Sittings   Free 178. Other 92. Total [270].
Attendance 30 March   Morning 253 SS. Total [253].
             Afternoon 210. Total [210].
             Evening 260. Total [260].
Average attendance   Morning 235 + 270 SS. Total [505].
Dated   30 March 1851.
Signed   Henry Tarbit, leader or elder [joiner].
             Haswell, Durham.

17.24   Primitive Methodist, South Hetton (546.13)

Name   Primitive Methodist Chapel.
Erected   1850.
Building   Not separate [and entire. A] place of worship and Sabbath school only.
Sittings   Free 184. Other 116. Total [300]. Standing room 30.
Attendance 30 March   Morning 245 SS. Total 245.

Afternoon 330 [including SS]. Total 330.
Evening 330 [including SS]. Total 330.
Average attendance   [Not given.]
Remarks   We the teachers of this Sunday school would be much
obliged to your honourable house too (*sic*) assist us
with a few books for the Sabbath school, South Hetton
Sabbath school.
Dated   30 March 1851.
Signed   Thomas Richardson, leader [farmer].
South Hetton.

17.25   Primitive Methodist, Monkchester Colliery (546.16)
[Simplified form]
Name   Primitive Methodist Meeting Room.
Erected   [Not given.]
Building   A room in a dwelling house. [Not exclusively used for
worship a] dwelling house.
Sittings   Free 30. Total [30].
Usual attendance   Afternoon 20. Total 20.
Evening 20. Total 20.
Dated   [Not given.]
Informant   R. Richardson (on enquiry) [registrar].
Dalton-le-Dale.

17.26   Primitive Methodist, Murton Colliery (546.26)
Name   Primitive Methodist Chapel.
Erected   1850.
Building   An entire building. Exclusively [used for worship]
except for Sunday school.
Sittings   Free 110. Other 102. Total [212]. Standing room 40.
Attendance 30 March   Morning 96. Total 96.
Afternoon 180 SS. Total 180.
Evening 200. Total 200.
Average attendance   Morning 96. Total 96.
Afternoon 180 SS. Total 180.
Evening 200. Total 200.
Dated   30 March 1851.
Signed   Henry Hebbon, minister.
William Taylor.
Murton Colliery, Durham.

17.27   Primitive Methodist, Tempest Place, Seaham Harbour (546.33)

Name   Primitive Methodist Chapel.
Erected   1850. [Opened for worship, 4 October 1846.]
Building   [Separate and entire.] Chapel and Sabbath school.
Sittings   Free 120. Other 180. Total [300].
Attendance 30 March   Morning 126 SS. Total 126.
          Afternoon 130. Total 130.
          Evening 213. Total 213.
Average attendance   Morning 140 SS. Total 140.
          Afternoon 130. Total 130.
          Evening 213. Total 213.
Dated   30 March 1851.
Signed   Henry Hebbon, minister.
          Robert Stamp.
          Seaham Harbour, County of Durham.

17.28   Primitive Methodist Schoolroom, Shotton Colliery (546.22)

Name   Girls' Schoolroom.
Erected   1845.
Building   [Separate and entire.] Day and Sabbath school
          likewise.
Sittings   Free 170. Other none. Total [170].
Attendance 30 March   Afternoon 100 + 54 SS. Total 154.
          Evening 115 + 50 SS. Total 165.
Average attendance   Afternoon (about) 100 + 56 SS. Total [156].
          Evening (about) 114 + 48 SS. Total 162.
Remarks   Superficial area 530 ft. Built 1845 for a Girls'
          Schoolroom by the owners of the colliery.
Dated   31 March 1851.
Signed   John Wall, steward [coal miner].
          131, Shotton Colliery.

17.29   Primitive Methodist, Thornley (546.5)

Name   Primitive Methodist Chapel.
Erected   1836.
Building   [Separate and] entire building. [Exclusively used for
          worship.]
Sittings   Free 222. Other 78. Total [300].
Attendance 30 March   Morning 120. Total 120.
          Afternoon 141 SS. Total 141.
          Evening 132. Total 132.

Average attendance　　Morning 130. Total 130.
　　　　　　　　　　　Afternoon 160 SS. Total 160.
　　　　　　　　　　　Evening 180. Total 180.
Remarks　　There is a weekday school and a dwelling house
　　　　　　under the Primitive Methodist Chapel, Thornley.
Dated　　31 March 1851.
Signed　　Thomas Atkinson, steward and trustee [coal miner].
　　　　　Thornley Colliery via Ferryhill, Durham.

17.30　Wesleyan Methodist Association, Dawdon (546.30)
Name　　Wesleyan Association Tabernacle.
Erected　　1839.
Building　　[Separate and entire. Exclusively used for worship.]
Sittings　　Free 118. Other 130. Total [248]. Standing room none.
Attendance 30 March　　Morning 73 SS. Total [73].
　　　　　　　　　　　Afternoon 65. Total [65].
　　　　　　　　　　　Evening 98. Total [98].
Average attendance　　Morning 90 SS. Total [90].
　　　　　　　　　　　Afternoon 86. Total [86].
　　　　　　　　　　　Evening 100. Total [100].
Dated　　31 March 1851.
Signed　　John Storey, local preacher [grocer and tea dealer].
　　　　　5 Railway St[ree]t, Seaham Harbour, Durham.

17.31　Roman Catholic, Hutton House, Castle Eden (546.12)
Name　　St Peter and St Paul.
Erected　　1825.
Building　　Separate [and entire. Exclusively used for worship.]
Sittings　　Free 50. Other 50 (never counted them).
　　　　　Standing room (never counted them).
Attendance 30 March　　Morning 70 SS. Total [70].　} Total
　　　　　　　　　　　Afternoon 80 SS. Total [80].　}　150
Average attendance　　Afternoon 80 SS. Total [80].
Dated　　31 March 1851.
Signed　　Thomas Augustine Slater, Catholic clergyman [1825–].
　　　　　Hutton House, Castle Eden, Co. Durham.
[In 1852 the estimated number of Roman Catholics in the area was
211.]

17.32　Roman Catholic, New Thornley (546.3)
Name　　St Godric's Chapel.
Erected　　Erected in ... purchased by Catholics in 1850.

Building   [Separate and entire. Exclusively used for worship.]
Sittings   Free about 250. Total [250].
               (I have called all free sittings as there is access to
               all without payment, but payment is expected of all
               competent.
Attendance 30 March   [Not given.]
Average attendance   Morning about 200 + about 50 SS. Total 250.
                        Evening about 120 + 30 SS. Total 150.
Remarks   Though virtually parish priests, we are only
               administrators until certain hierarchical arrangements
               are completed.
Dated   30 March 1851.
Signed   Robert Suffield, administrator.
               St Godric's, New Thornley, Ferryhill.
[Robert Suffield was also a priest at Sedgefield (**21.65**). In 1852 the
estimated number of Roman Catholics in the area was 130.]

18. Gateshead District (HO 129/551)
65 places of worship

18.1   Church of England, St Mary, Gateshead (551.17)
Population 1851: 24,805 (parish of Gateshead and Gateshead Fell)

Name   Parish Church. St Mary's, Gateshead.
Consecrated [Not given. Repaired and re-pewed 1838–39 and
               reopened in January 1839; and reopened after fire in
               September 1855; restored 1874–75 and reopened in
               November 1875.]
Endowment   Land £35. Tithe £620 8s 2d. Fees £160. Easter
               offerings £8.
               Other £240.
Sittings   Total about 1,350.
Attendance 30 March   Morning 700 + 300 SS. Total 1,000.
                        Evening about the same. Total [1,000].
Average attendance   The preceding is a fair average.
Remarks   NB. Three sources of income in [... ...] pay from
               [...]. This number is a fair average. Easter offerings if
               properly administered would amount to more than
               £100 per annum. More than one third of the above

goes to the payment of curates, poor rates and other charges.

Dated   31 March 1851.

Signed   John Davies, minister [1840–61].
[Rector of Gateshead and master of King James' Hospital.]
St Mary's, Gateshead.

{1857   Attendance -. 150 communicants in the whole parish.}
{B 511.}

[In September 1856 John Davies recorded that throughout his parish 'there are nine regular public services – eight Sunday and one weekday – besides a weekly gratuitous lecture at the workhouse, and one or two cottages and schoolroom lectures'. During the previous fifteen years there had been a District Visiting Society (run by about thirty ladies) and for the last three years a lay Scripture Reader had been employed. J. Davies, *A sermon occasioned by the re-opening of St Mary's, Gateshead* (Gateshead, 1855), pp. 15, 16.]

18.2   Church of England, St Edmund's Chapel, High Street, Gateshead (551.18)

Name   St Edmund's Chapel, belonging to King James' Chapel.

Consecrated   1811. [7 August 1810, as a chapel of ease. Reseated 1871.]

Erected   Rebuilt by subscription. I have no means of knowing the cost.

Endowment   [Not given.]

Sittings   Total 400 all free.

Attendance 30 March   Afternoon 100. Total [100]. No Sunday school.

Average attendance   [Not given.] Only afternoon service.

Remarks   The above is a free chapel. The chaplain appointed by the rector of the parish, subject to the bishop's approval, and paid out of the [King James'] Hospital funds.

Dated   31 March 1851.

Signed   John Davies, rector of Gateshead [1840–61].

[King James' Hospital was re-founded on 4 January 1610. The statutes were framed on 7 October 1811, and the following year almshouses were erected near to St Edmund's Chapel. The rector of Gateshead was also the master of the King James' Hospital.]

18.3   Church of England, Holy Trinity, High Street, Gateshead
(551.16)

Name   Trinity Chapel at present a chapel of ease belonging to
              the parish of Gateshead. [St Edmund's Chapel formed
              the south aisle.]

Consecrated 1836. [Restored and re-opened for worship 15 October
               1837, enlarged 1894.]

Erected   An old ruined chapel restored. I have no means of
               [providing] all the sources of contributions.

Endowment   Pew rents about £30. No endowment of any kind.

Sittings   Total about 300 half free.

Attendance 30 March   [Not given.]

Average attendance   [Not given. 150 + 50 SS.] Total [200].

Remarks   I understand the average attendance is considered
               to be about 150 general congregation and about 50
               Sunday school children. 200 total.
               NB. Application has been repeatedly been made to the
               Ecclesiastical Commissioners to have an endowment
               and a district attached to the above chapel, but petition
               without support. J. D.

Dated   31 March 1851.

Signed   John Davies, rector of Gateshead [1840–61].

18.4   Church of England, St Cuthbert, Bensham, Gateshead
(551.14)

Name   St Cuthbert's, at present a chapel of ease belonging to
              the parish of St Mary's, Gateshead.

Consecrated 1848. [16 March 1848, enlarged 1875.]

Erected   By subscription and grants from various societies,
               and £200 from Church Commissioners. [£200 from
               the Church Building Society. £140 from the Diocesan
               Church Building Society. £105 from Rev. John Davies.
               £300 from Cuthbert Ellison of Hebburn Hall and Lord
               of the Manor of Gateshead.] Total cost £2,000 or nearly.

Endowment   Pew rents about £50. No endowment of any kind.

Sittings   Total 550 (about half free). [Free 284. Other 274.
               Total 558.]

Attendance 30 March   [Not given.]

Average attendance   [Not given. 220 + 80 SS. Total 300.]

Remarks   Average congregation about 300, including Sunday
               school children about 80 in number.

NB. I give the above as what I understand is a fair approximation, but I do not pledge myself to the absolute accuracy.

Dated   31 March 1851.

Signed   John Davies, rector of Gateshead [1840–61].

18.5 Church of England Schoolroom, Friar's Goose, Gateshead (551.15)

Name   Friar's Goose licensed schoolroom.

Licensed   1849.

Sittings   Total 100 all free.

Attendance 30 March   Morning 20 + 60 SS. Total 80.

Average attendance   Only morning service.

Remarks   The above is a schoolroom attached to one of the large manufactories, where the chaplain of King James' Hospital has been licensed by the bishop to perform prayer.

NB. The above schoolroom is on the premises of King James' Hospital and is […].

Dated   [Not given.]

Signed   John Davies, rector of Gateshead [1840–61].

[In 1827 the Quaker Anthony Graham established a chemical works at Friar's Goose on five acres of land owned by the Master and Brethren of the King James' Hospital for an annual rental of £300. F.W.D. Manders, *A History of Gateshead* (Gateshead, 1975), pp. 74–76.]

18.6 Church of England, St John the Evangelist, Sour Milk Hill, Gateshead Fell (551.20)

Name   St John's. Built under the authority of a local Act of Parliament.
49 Geo. III (1809).

Consecrated   30 August 1825 [by the Bishop of Oxford], as an additional church with a district attached to it, which was henceforth to become a separate and distinct parish. [Restored 1885.]

Erected   By parochial rate and subscriptions. Rate £1,000. Private £1,980. Total cost £2,980.

Endowment   Tithe £95. OPE £100. Fees, dues and Easter offerings £30.

Sittings   Free 500. Other 515. Total 1,015.

Attendance 30 March   Morning 290 + 213 SS. Total 503.
Afternoon 284 + 235 SS. Total 519.

Average attendance   [Not given.]
Dated   30 March 1851.
Signed   William Atkinson, minister [1838–70].
    Rectory, [Sheriff Hill], Gateshead Fell.
{1857   Attendance 1,000. 80 communicants.}   {B 103.}
[An Act for building a church on Gateshead Fell, in the parish of Gateshead, in the County of Durham; and for making Gateshead Fell aforesaid a distinct rectory and parish. 49 Geo. III (1809). When the foundation stone was laid by the rector of Gateshead, the Rev. John Collinson, on 13 May 1824, 'on the conclusion of the ceremony, a salute of nine guns was fired by a temporary battery, which was answered by nine cheers from the polulace'. J. Sykes, *Local Records and Historical Register* (Newcastle, 1866), vol. 2, p. 174.]

18.7   Church of England Schoolroom, Wreckenton, Gateshead Fell (551.19)
Name   Wreckenton National school. A chapel of ease [to St John, Gateshead Fell].
Licensed   1842, as an additional place of worship.
Erected   By subscription. Private £360. Total cost £360.
Sittings   Free 180. Total 180.
Attendance 30 March   Evening 162. Total 162.
Average attendance   [Not given.]
Dated   30 March 1851.
Signed   William Atkinson, minister [1838–70].
    Rectory, [Sheriff Hill], Gateshead Fell.

18.8   Church of England, St Mary, Heworth (551.1)
Population 1851: 8,869 (chapelry)

Name   Heworth Church, an ancient church.
Consecrated   [6 August] 1822 [by the Bishop of Oxford], in lieu of a smaller church which was pulled down. [Cost £2,200.]
Endowment   Tithe £120. Glebe house. Fees £40. Dues £6 6s 8d. Easter offerings £6. Other £22. Total £194 6s 8d.
Sittings   Free 687. Other 294. Total 981.
Attendance 30 March   [Not given.]
Average attendance   Average con[gregation] about 200.
Dated   26 March 1851.
Signed   Matthew Plummer, [curate 1831–34, vicar 1834–79]. Heworth, near Gateshead.
{1857   Attendance 250. 50 communicants.}   {B 73.}

[Over a two-year period, 1850–52, Matthew Plummer was involved in a mild controversy at his church. Anonymous complainants accused him of locking the galleries and preventing people occupying 300 seats. But in his defence he maintained that this was 'to prevent idle boys from throwing orange-peel and nut-shells, and from spitting upon the congregation who sat below'. Then after two unsympathetic churchwardens were appointed they too railed against Plummer (whom they described as 'an obstinate and wary man') over the removal of the pulpit and reading desk; the restoration of a stone altar; the provision of two candles on the communion table and placing chairs behind the communion rails; the repositioning of the royal arms and the way in which the services were conducted. Plummer referred to his opponents as 'a set of brawling agitators … [who were] allowed to annoy a peaceable and respectable congregation … [and who made Plummer and his curates] to be held up to public indignation as abettors of popery'. M. Plummer, *A Letter to the Lord Bishop of Durham in reference to the late proceedings in the Parish of Heworth* (Newcastle, 185?), pp. 4, 15, 16.]

18.9 Church of England, St Alban, Windy Nook, Heworth
(551.2)
Population 1851: 2,288 (township)

[Summary form]

Name	St Alban's.
Erected	8 to 9 years ago [consecrated 25 August 1842]. £200 from the Dean and Chapter of Durham and £200 from a Parliamentary grant. Total cost £777. [District chapelry created 24 February 1843 out of the parish of Jarrow.]
Sittings	Free 300. Total 300.
Usual attendance	Morning 14 + 50 SS. Total [64].
	Afternoon 14 + 50 SS. Total [64].
	Evening none.
Dated	[Not given.]
Signed	Thomas Snowdon, churchwarden [miller and farmer].
Incumbent	[Edward Hussey Adamson 1843–98.]
{1857	Attendance 80. 12 communicants.} {B 16.}

18.10   Church of England, Holy Cross, Ryton (551.48)
Population 1851: 2,757 (parish) 739 (township)

[Summary form]
Name   Holy Cross, the parish church of Ryton.
Erected   In 12th century.
Endowment   [£956.]
Sittings   Free 139. Other 329. Total 468 + 40 are free. Total 508.
Usual attendance   Morning in fair weather 400 + 70 SS.
                 Total [470].
                 Afternoon half filled 200 + 60 SS. Total [260].
Dated   [Not given.]
Informant   Charles Thorp, rector [1807–62].
{1857   Attendance 250. 30 communicants.}   {B 47.}
[Robert Thorp (1736–1812) and Charles Thorp (1783–1862), *ODNB*,
vol. 54, pp. 662–663. Robert Thorp was the rector of Gateshead
1781–95, the Archdeacon of Northumberland 1792–1812 and rector
of Ryton 1795–1807; he was succeeded at Ryton by his son Charles
Thorp. The latter was also the Archdeacon of Durham 1831–62
and the first Warden and Master of University College, Durham,
1833–62, and was responsible for the erection of St John, Greenside
(consecrated 18 September 1857) and for the creation of the parishes
of Winlaton and Blaydon.]

18.11   Church of England, St Paul, Winlaton (551.47)
Population 1851: 6,085 (parish) 5,627 (township)

Name   St Paul's Parish Church, Winlaton.
Consecrated In [9 September] 1828. A new parish church for a
                 parish formed out of the parish of Ryton [created
                 6 November 1832].
Erected   By the rector of Ryton [Charles Thorp]. Parliamentary
                 grant one half [£1,531]. Rate nil. Total cost [£2,281].
Endowment   [£265.]
Sittings   Free 401. Other 400. Total 801.
Attendance 30 March   Morning 350 + 80 SS. Total 430.
                 Afternoon 300 + 50 SS. Total 350.
Average attendance   Morning 400 + 100 SS. Total 500.
                 Afternoon 350 + 80 SS. Total 430.
Dated   31 March 1851.
Signed   Henry Wardell, rector [1833–84].
                 Winlaton, n[ea]r Newcastle on Tyne.

{1857   Attendance 400. 30 communicants.}   {B. 84.}
[Henry Wardell had previously been the curate of Ryton 1824–33.]

18.12   Church of England, St John the Evangelist, Chopwell
(551.60)
Population 1851: 458 (township)

Name   St John's, Chopwell.
Consecrated   Licensed 1842 by the Bishop of Durham [as a chapel
                of ease to Winlaton. Replaced by a new church
                consecrated on 7 December 1915.]
Erected   [By] Robert Thorp Esq. Private entirely.
Endowment   [Not given.]
Sittings   Free 100. Total 100.
Attendance 30 March   [Not given.]
Average attendance   Afternoon 90. Total [90].
Remarks   This is a private chapel.
Dated   31 March 1851.
Signed   Henry Wardell, rector of Winlaton [1833–84].
                Winlaton, near Newcastle on Tyne.
{1857   Attendance 80.}

18.13   Church of England Schoolroom, Barlow, Winlaton (551.49)
[Summary form]
Name   Barlow School.
Sittings   Free 100. Total [100].
Usual attendance   12. Total [12].
Congregation There is no regular service in this room at the [present]
                but oftener than [say?] in the year none […].
Dated   30 March 1851.
Signed   George Allison, schoolmaster.
                [Barlow.]
Informant   Thomas Hall, [registrar].
                [Winlaton.]
Incumbent   [Henry Wardell 1833–84.]

18.14   Church of England, St Cuthbert, Stella [Blaydon] (551.46)
Population 1851: 2,479 (parish) 565 (township)

Name   St Cuthbert's, Stella. New church under Sir R[obert]
                Peel's Act, 1843. [6 and 7 Vic. c.37].
Consecrated   [25 August] September 1845. As an additional church.

[District created on 8 August 1845 from the parishes of Ryton and Winlaton. Church enlarged 1862, restored 1882.]

Erected   [By] private benefactions and subscriptions. Private £700. Total £700.

Endowment OPE £150. Fees £4.

Sittings   Free 178. Other 154. Total 332.

Attendance 30 March   Morning 96 + 127 SS. Total 223.
                         Evening 125. Total 125.

Average attendance   [Not given.]

Remarks   Evening lectures in the parochial schoolroom, Blaydon, every Wednesday, and in the schoolroom, Derwent Haugh, every Thursday evenings.

Dated   31 March 1851.

Signed   William Brown, incumbent [1845–77].
            Blaydon parish, Newcastle upon Tyne.

{1857   Attendance 250. 35 communicants.}   {B 64.}

[Though the parish is Stella, the church is situated in Blaydon.]

18.15   Church of England, St Mary the Virgin, Whickham
(551.38)
Population 1851: 5,565 (parish) 910 (township)

[Summary form]

Name   Whickham Church.

Erected   [Not given. Restored and enlarged 1862 to seat 549, and cost £2,875.]

Endowment [£663.]

Sittings   Free seats 10. Others 490. Total 500.

Usual attendance   Morning 220. Total [220].
                      Afternoon 190. Total [190].
                      Evening no service.

Remarks   [In another hand] Sunday scholars 120. Included in the above 220 and 190.

Dated   17 July 1852.

Signed   William Oswald, [registrar].
            [Whickham.]

Incumbent   [Henry Byne Carr 1846–96.]

{1857   Attendance 350. 30 communicants. A great need of free sittings.}   {B 171.}

[Henry Byne Carr (1812–1898) was responsible for the erection of Christ Church, Dunston (consecrated 26 April 1876); St Cuthbert,

Marley Hill (consecrated 15 November 1877); and Holy Saviour, Swalwell (consecrated 17 February 1894).]

18.16   United Presbyterian, Swalwell, Whickham (551.40)
Name   Ebenezer Chapel.
Erected   1750.
Building   [Separate and entire. Exclusively used for worship.]
Sittings   Free [none]. Other 350. Total [350].
Attendance 30 March   Afternoon 80 + 30 SS. Total 110.
                         Evening 40 + 10 SS. Total 50.
Average attendance   Morning 45 + 35 SS. Total 80.
Dated   31 March 1851.
Signed   Thomas Cheesman, elder.
                Whickham, near Gateshead.
Minister   [William Rattray 1831–51.]
[William Rattray died on 6 January 1851 but no successor was appointed until 1858.]

18.17   English Presbyterian, Melbourne Street, Gateshead (551.22)
Name   Presbyterian Church.
Erected   Before 1800.
Building   [Separate and entire. Exclusively used for worship.]
Sittings   Free [none]. Other about 600. Total [600].
Attendance 30 March   Afternoon 250 + 40 SS. Total 290.
                         Evening 100. Total 100.
Average attendance   [Not given.]
Dated   31 March 1851.
Signed   Thomas Knox Anderson, minister [1844–58].
                [Borough Field], Gateshead, Durham.

18.18   Independent [Congregational], Heworth (551.8)
Name   Zion Chapel.
Erected   1835.
Building   [Separate and entire.] Exclusively as a place of worship.
Sittings   Free 50. Other 236. Total [286]. Standing room 114.
Attendance 30 March   Morning 55 + 60 SS. Total 115.
                         Afternoon 75 + 50 SS. Total 125.
                         Evening 50 + 20 SS. Total 70.
Average attendance   [Not given.]
Dated   31 March 1851.

Signed   James Wood, minister [1849–53].
                High Felling, n[ea]r Gateshead, Durham.

18.19   Independent [Congregational], Ryton (551.64)
Name   Congregational Chapel.
Erected   1833.
Building   [Separate and entire. Exclusively used for worship.]
Sittings   Free 90. Total [90].
Attendance 30 March   Evening 50. Total 50.
Average attendance   [Not given.]
Remarks   Ryton is the place and parish also.
Dated   31 March 1851.
Signed   David Walters, pastor [1850–52].
                Whitehouse, Ryton.

18.20   Independent [Congregational], Crawcrook (551.62)
Name   Congregational Chapel, Crawcrook.
Erected   1837. [Opened 24 October 1837. New chapel opened
                13 December 1861.]
Building   [Separate and entire. Exclusively used for worship.]
Sittings   Free 200. Total [200].
Attendance 30 March   Morning 150 +80 SS. Total 230.
Average attendance   [Not given.]
Remarks   Ryton is the parish. Crawcrook is the place.
Dated   31 March 1851.
Signed   David Walters, pastor.
                Whitehouse, Ryton.
[In 1856 it was proposed to erect a new chapel between Ryton and
Crawcrook, and then for Crawcrook Chapel to become a school. W.
Whellan, *History of the County Palatine of Durham* (London, 1856),
p. 911.]

18.21   Independent [Congregational], Winlaton (551.57)
Name   Providence Chapel.
Erected   1832. [Opened 5 December 1832.]
Building   [Separate and entire. Exclusively used for worship.]
Sittings   Free 200. Other none. Total [200].
Attendance 30 March   Afternoon 40 + 50 SS. Total 90.
                        Evening 55 + 30 SS. Total 85.
Average attendance   [Not given.]
Dated   31 March 1851.
Signed   David Wilson, minister.
                Winlaton.

18.22   Independent [Congregational], Barlow, Winlaton (551.54)

Name   [Providence] Independent Chapel.
Erected   Don't know.
Building   [Separate and entire. Exclusively used for worship.]
Sittings   Free 80. Total [80].
Attendance 30 March   Morning 33. Total 33.
                           Evening 37. Total 37.
Average attendance   [Not given.]
Dated   31 March 1851.
Signed   David Wilson, minister.
                Winlaton.

18.23   Baptist, Blaydon (551.51)

[Simplified form]
Name   Blaydon Baptist Meeting Room.
Erected   Used as a dwelling house up to 1830.
Building   [Not separate and entire or exclusively used for
                worship.] Used for a library and reading room.
Sittings   18 feet square. All free sittings.
Usual attendance   No Sabbath service. Week-nights 35. Total 35.
Dated   [Not given.]
Signed   Thomas Emerson [agent for W. B. Lead Company].

18.24   Wesleyan Methodist, Low Bensham (551.24)

Name   None
Erected   [Not given.]
Building   [Not separate and entire. Exclusively used] for both
                [worship and Sunday school.]
Sittings   Free 100. Total [100].
Attendance 30 March   Morning 25 SS. Total [25].
                           Afternoon 41 + 25 SS. Total [66].
                           Evening 37. Total [37].
Average attendance   Morning 20. Total [20].
Dated   [Not given.]
Signed   Thomas Watson, class leader [cast-iron moulder].
                [Low Team], Team Iron Works.

18.25   Wesleyan Methodist, Black Hall Mill, Chopwell (551.61)

Name   Upper Room.
Erected   [Not given.]
Building   No part occupied for any other purpose. Exclusively
                [used] as a place of worship.

Sittings   Free 80. Total [80]. Standing room 120.
Attendance 30 March   Afternoon 30. Total [30].
Average attendance   Morning 35. Total [35].
Dated   31 March 1851.
Signed   Robert Jewitt, steward [farmer].
Chopwell Hall, Durham.

18.26   Wesleyan Methodist, High Street, Gateshead (551.26)
Name   Wesleyan Methodist Chapel.
Erected   1813. [1815.]
Building   [Separate and] entire building. [Exclusively used for worship.]
Sittings   Free 188. Other 562. Total [750].
Attendance 30 March   Morning 214 +123 SS. Total 337.
Afternoon 24. Total 24.
Evening 351. Total 351.
Average attendance   [Not given.]
Dated   30 March 1851.
Joseph Kimpster, steward [grocer].
21 Claremont Place, Gateshead.

18.27   Wesleyan Methodist, Pipewellgate, Gateshead (551.25)
Name   Pipewellgate Chapel.
Erected   1832.
Building   Separate [and entire building. Exclusively used as a] chapel and Sunday school.
Sittings   Free 180. Other 20. Total [200].
Attendance 30 March   Evening 31. Total 31.
Average attendance   [Not given.]
Dated   29 March 1851.
Signed   James Hugill, steward [labourer].
Chapel Yard, Pipewellgate, Gateshead.

18.28   Wesleyan Methodist, Gateshead Fell (551.29)
Name   Wesleyan Chapel.
Erected   1800.
Building   Separate [and entire. Exclusively used for] worship and school.
Sittings   Free 200. Other 178. Total [378]. Standing room none.
Attendance 30 March   Afternoon 104 + 61 SS. Total 165.
Evening 100 + 30 SS. Total 130.

Average attendance   Afternoon 180 + 60 SS. Total 240.
                        Evening 150 + 25 SS. Total 175.
Dated   31 March 1851.
Signed   John N. Pattison, trustee and steward (joiner).
                Gateshead Fell.

18.29   Wesleyan Methodist, Sheriff Hill, Gateshead Fell (551.34)
Name   Sheriff Hill Wesleyan Chapel.
Erected   Before 1820.
Building   [Separate and entire. Exclusively used for worship].
Sittings   Free 130. Other 50. Total [180].
Attendance 30 March   Morning 40 + 30 SS. Total 70.
                        Evening 50 + 10 SS. Total 60.
Average attendance   [Not given.]
Dated   31 March 1851.
Signed   George Patterson, chapel steward [earthenware
                manufacturer].
                Sheriff Hill Pottery, near Gateshead.

18.30   Wesleyan Methodist, Felling Shore, Heworth (551.13)
Name   None.
Erected   1819.
Building   [Separate and entire. Exclusively used for worship.]
Sittings   Free 175. Other 75. Total [250].
Attendance 30 March   Afternoon 66 + 25 SS. Total 91.
                        Evening 84. Total 84.
Average attendance   Morning 70 + 30 SS. Total 100.
Dated   30 March 1851.
Signed   William Bell, steward.
                Heworth Lane.

18.31   Wesleyan Methodist, Heworth (551.7)
Name   Wesleyan Methodist Chapel.
Erected   1829.
Building   [Separate and entire. Exclusively used for worship.]
Sittings   Free 140. Other 140. Total [280].
Attendance 30 March   Afternoon 200. Total 200.
                        Evening 220. Total 220.
Average attendance   [Not given.]
Dated   31 March 1851.

Signed   William Haswell, society steward [coal miner].
Low Felling.

18.32   Wesleyan Methodist, Bill Quay, Heworth (551.12)
Name   Bill Quay Chapel.
Erected   1839.
Building   [Separate and entire. Exclusively used for worship.]
Sittings   Free 200. Other 56. Total [256]. Standing room none.
Attendance 30 March   Morning 200 + 50 SS. Total 250.
Afternoon no service.
Evening 230 + 20 SS. Total 250.
Average attendance   Morning 170 + 25 SS. Total 195.
Dated   30 March 1851.
Signed   George Alexander, class leader [bottle maker].
Bill Quay, Durham.

18.33   Wesleyan Methodist, Ryton (551.63)
Name   Wesleyan Methodist Chapel.
Erected   1848.
Building   A separate and entire building. Exclusively [used] for worship.
Sittings   Free 160 sittings. Total [160].
Attendance 30 March   Evening [150]. Total 150.
Average attendance   [Not given.]
Dated   31 March 1851.
Signed   William Green.
Crawcrook.

18.34   Wesleyan Methodist, Swalwell, Whickham (551.39)
Name   Swalwell Wesleyan Methodist Chapel.
Erected   1824. [1817.]
Building   [Separate and entire. Exclusively used for worship.]
Sittings   Free 135. Other 200. Total [335].
Attendance 30 March   Morning 113 SS. Total 113.
Afternoon 90 + 20 SS. Total 110.
Evening 200 + 30 SS. Total 230.
Average attendance   [Not given.]
Remarks   [In another hand] No list of any of Whickham district.
Dated   31 March 1851.
Signed   Edward Lawson, chapel steward (joiner).
Swalwell.

18.35   Wesleyan Methodist, West End, Whickham (551.42)

Name   None. [In another hand] Wesleyan Methodist Chapel.
Erected   Before 1800. [1790. Replaced by new chapel opened
                 2 April 1869.]
Building   [Not separate and entire but exclusively used for
                 worship.]
Sittings   Free 100. Total [100].
Attendance 30 March   Evening 80. Total 80.
Average attendance   [Not given.]
Dated   30 March 1851.
Signed   Thomas Faldon, steward [labourer].
                 Whickham, Durham.

18.36   Wesleyan Methodist Schoolroom, Marley Hill, Whickham
(551.44)

Name   Marley Hill Wesleyan Methodist Chapel.
Erected   1843.
Building   [Separate and entire but not exclusively used for
                 worship.] Occupied during the week for a day school.
Sittings   Free 180. Other 44. Total [224]. Standing room none.
Attendance 30 March   Afternoon 34 + 85 SS. Total 119.
                        Evening 60 + 43 SS. Total 123.
Average attendance   Afternoon 59 + 94 SS. Total 153.
                        Evening 75 + 87 SS. Total 162.
Dated   31 March 1851.
Signed   William Kent, schoolmaster.
                 Marley Hill, near Whickham, Durham.

18.37   Wesleyan Methodist, Winlaton (551.55)

Name   [None.]
Erected   Before 1800.
Building   Part of a building. Warehouse underneath.
Sittings   250. Total [250].
Attendance 30 March   Morning and afternoon Sunday school
                        [Not given].
                        Evening 40. Total [40].
Average attendance   [Not given.]
Dated   31 March 1851.
Signed   William [Kyle?], chapel steward.
                 Winlaton.

18.38   Wesleyan Methodist, Winlaton (551.50)

Name	Wesleyan Methodist Chapel.
Erected	1813.
Building	[Separate and] entire. Exclusively [used for worship] except Sunday school.
Sittings	Free 130. Other 50. Total [180]. Standing room 30.

Attendance 30 March   Morning 150 + 30 SS. Total 180.

Evening 130. + 30 SS. Total 160.

Average attendance   Morning 100 + 30 SS. Total 130.

Evening 130 + 30 SS. Total 160.

Dated	30 March 1851.
Signed	Thomas March, steward (builder). Blaydon [Bank].

18.39   Wesleyan Methodist, Black Toad, Wrekenton (551.32)

Name	Wesleyan Chapel.
Erected	1832.
Building	[Separate and entire. Exclusively used for worship.]
Sittings	Free 280. Other 70. [Total 350.] Standing room. Properly speaking there is no standing room but the isles (*sic*) or passages in the chapel.

Attendance 30 March   Morning 66 + 43 SS. Total 109.

Afternoon 43 SS. Total [43].

Evening 55. Total [55].

Average attendance   Morning 70 + 60 SS. Total 130.

Afternoon 60 SS. Total [60].

Evening 70. Total [70].

Remarks	The hours of public worship, half past ten in the morning, and six o'clock in the evening. We have a Sunday school in the chapel. The school goes in at nine o'clock in the morning, and continues till a quarter past ten; and goes in at two o'clock in the afternoon and continues till four o'clock.
Dated	30 March 1851.
Signed	William Allison, chapel steward [butcher]. Wrekenton, near Gateshead, Durham.

18.40   Methodist New Connexion, Derwent Haugh, Winlaton (551.59)

Name	None.
Erected	Before 1800.

Building   [Not separate and entire but exclusively used for
worship.]
Sittings   Free 70. Total [70].
Attendance 30 March   Afternoon 18 + 16 SS. Total 34.
                        Evening 17 + 14 SS. Total 31.
Average attendance   Afternoon 35 + 20 SS. Total 55.
                        Evening 35 + 20 SS. Total 55.
Remarks   The numbers attending worship vary much,
sometimes the place [is] full. This day attendance very
small from some unknown cause.
Dated   30 March 1851.
Signed   Thomas E. Hawks, leader [coal staith agent].
                Derwent Haugh by Gateshead.

18.41   Methodist New Connexion, Dunston (551.36)
Name   Providence Chapel.
Erected   1838.
Building   [Separate and] entire building. Exclusively as a place
of worship and Sunday school.
Sittings   Free 80. Other 46. Total [126].
Attendance 30 March   Afternoon 40 + 36 SS. Total 76.
                        Evening 70 + 6 SS. Total 76.
Average attendance   Afternoon 50 + 36 SS. Total 86.
                        Evening 70 + 18 SS. Total 88.
Remarks   The congregation in the afternoon was far below the
average of adults. The Sunday scholars attend the
afternoon service but few at the night service.
Dated   30 March 1851.
Signed   John Blenkinsop, chapel steward.
                Dunston near Gateshead, Durham.

**18.42   Methodist New Connexion, Melbourne Street, Gateshead
(551.21)**
Name   Bethesda.
Erected   1836. [Opened 1 April 1836. Cost £3,300.]
Building   [Separate and entire. Exclusively used for worship.]
Sittings   Free 200. Other 1,100. Total [1,300]. Standing room nil.
Attendance 30 March   Morning 500 + 200 SS. Total [700].
                        Evening 700. Total [700].
Average attendance   [Not given.]

Dated   31 March 1851.
Signed   William Cocker, minister.
             18 Jackson Street, Gateshead.
[William Cocker was also the minister of Sunniside (**14.30**). William
Booth, the founder of the Salvation Army, was the minister of
Bethesda 1858–61. 'William Booth (1829–1912)', *ODNB*, vol. 6, pp.
635–636. On 29 February 1896 a new chapel was opened in Whitehall
Road.]

18.43   Methodist New Connexion, Teams, Gateshead (551.23)
Name   Ebenezer.
Erected   1850.
Building   [Separate and entire. Exclusively used for worship.]
Sittings   Free 80. Other 60. Total [140].
Attendance 30 March   Morning 90 + 40 SS. Total [130].
                        Evening 120. Total [120].
Average attendance   [Not given.]
Dated   7 April 1851.
Signed   William Cocker, minister.
             18 Jackson Street, Gateshead.

**18.44   Methodist New Connexion Schoolroom, Sheriff Hill,
Gateshead Fell** (551.35)
Name   Zion Chapel.
Erected   1836. [Opened 7 February.]
Building   [Separate] an entire building [used for worship and]
             Sunday and day school.
Sittings   Free 135. Other 75. Total [210].
Attendance 30 March   Morning 30 + 35 SS. Total 65.
                        Afternoon 40 SS. Total 40.
                        Evening 65. Total 65.
Average attendance   [Not given.]
Dated   31 March 1851.
Signed   John Edward, chapel steward [grocer and tailor].
             Sheriff Hill, Gateshead.

18.45   Methodist New Connexion, Felling Shore, Heworth
(551.10)
Name   Methodist New Connexion Chaple (*sic*).
Erected   1820. [Rebuilt 1836.]
Building   Separate [and entire. Exclusively used for worship.]

Sittings   Free 90. Other 50. Total [140]. Standing room 50.
Attendance 30 March   Morning 40 + 80 SS. Total 120.
                        Afternoon 80 SS. Total [80].
                        Evening 80 + 20 SS. Total 100.
Average attendance   Morning 120. Total [120].
Remarks   The Felling Shore New Connexion Chapel was
               formerly an Independent chaple (*sic*.) and was rebuilt
               about the year 1836 by the above society.
Dated   30 March 1851.
Signed   Robert Rennison, chaple (*sic*) steward [shipwright].
               Felling Shore, near Gateshead.

18.46   Methodist New Connexion, High Felling, Heworth (551.5)
Name   Methodist New Connexion Chapel.
Erected   Before 1800.
Building   [Separate and entire. Exclusively used for worship.]
Sittings   Free 150. Other 120. Total [270].
Attendance 30 March   Afternoon 60 + 20 SS. Total 80.
                        Evening 50 + 15 SS. Total 65.
Average attendance   Afternoon 50 + 20 SS. Total 70.
Dated   31 March 1851.
Signed   Ralph Porter, society steward (builder [and cabinet
               maker].
               High Felling.

18.47   Methodist New Connexion, Low Fell, Gateshead (551.30)
Name   [None.]
Erected   Since 1800.
Building   [Separate and entire. Exclusively used for worship.]
Sittings   Free 100. Other 50. Total [150]. Standing room 60.
Attendance 30 March   Morning 10 + 23 SS. Total 33.
                        Evening 45 + 18 SS. Total 63.
Average attendance   [Not given.]
Dated   30 March 1851.
Signed   John Saul, society steward [mason].
               Low Fell, Gateshead.

18.48   Methodist New Connexion, Windy Nook, Heworth (551.4)
Name   Windy Nook Methodist New Connexion Chapel.
Erected   AD 1836.
Building   [Separate and entire. Exclusively used for worship.]

Sittings   Free 120. Other 30. Total [150]. Standing room none.
Attendance 30 March   Morning school.
Afternoon 47 + 30 SS. Total 77.
                    Evening 61 + 51 SS. Total 112.
Average attendance   Morning, school.
                    Afternoon 90 + 30 SS. Total 120.
                    Evening 100 + 30 SS. Total 130.
Dated   30 March 1851.
Signed   Percival Dixon, society steward [collier, coal hewer].
                    Windy Nook.

18.49   Methodist New Connexion, Winlaton (551.58)
Name   Zion Chapel.
Erected   1830.
Building   [Separate and] entire. [Exclusively used for worship]
                    except
                    Sunday school.
Sittings   Free 250. Total [250].
Attendance 30 March   Morning Sunday school.
                    Afternoon 50 + 20 SS. Total 70.
                    Evening 74 + 6 SS. Total 80.
Average attendance   Morning 52 SS. Total 52.
                    Afternoon 58 + 23 SS. Total 81.
                    Evening 76 + 25 SS. Total 101.
Remarks   From a combination of circumstances our congregation
                    and school have been reduced in number.
Dated   30 March 1851.
Signed   Joseph Snaith, society steward (schoolmaster).
                    Winlaton.

18.50   Primitive Methodist, Blaydon (551.52)
Name   Primitive Methodist Chapel.
Erected   Fitted up 16 years ago. [1835.]
Building   [Separate and] entire. [Exclusively used for worship.]
                    A day school and Sabbath d[itt]o. taught.
Sittings   Free 180. Total [180].
Attendance 30 March   Morning 62 SS. Total [62].
                    Afternoon 100 + 60 SS. Total [160].
                    Evening 120. Total [120].
Average attendance   Morning 70 SS. Total [70].
                    Afternoon 160 + 70 SS. Total [230].
                    Evening 160. Total [160].

Dated   31 March 1851.
Signed   Bartholomew Stokoe [skinner].
               Blaydon, near Newcastle upon Tyne.

18.51   Primitive Methodist, Dunston (551.41)
[On a Church of England form]
Name   Primitive Methodist Chapel
Erected   [Not given.]
Building   [Not given.]
Sittings   Free 140. Total 140.
Attendance 30 March   Morning 40 SS. Total 40.
                        Afternoon 60. Total [60].
                        Evening 100. Total [100].
Average attendance   [Not given.]
Dated   31 March 1851.
Signed   John Thompson, chapel steward (schoolmaster).
               Gateshead, Durham.

18.52   Primitive Methodist, Carr Hill, Heworth (551.3)
Name   Primitive Methodist Meeting House.
Erected   1844.
Building   [Separate and entire. Exclusively used for worship.]
Sittings   Free 100. Total [100].
Attendance 30 March   Afternoon 67 + 37 SS. Total 104.
                        Evening 55 + 12 SS. Total 67.
Average attendance   Morning 67 + 30 SS. Total 97.
Dated   30 March 1851.
Signed   Joseph Proud, leader (grocer etc.) [provisions dealer
               and draper].
               Carr Hill, n[ea]r Gateshead, Durham.

18.53   Primitive Methodist, Heworth Lane, Heworth Shore
(551.11)
Name   Primitive Methodist Chapel.
Erected   1833.
Building   [Separate and entire. Exclusively used for worship]
               also as a day school.
Sittings   Free 120. Other 64. Total [184].
Attendance 30 March   Afternoon 70 + 30 SS. Total 100.
                        Evening 121. Total 121.
Average attendance   Afternoon 30 + 20 SS. Total 50.
                        Evening 100. Total 100.

Dated   30 March 1851.
Signed   Thomas Lowes, trustee and leader [paper maker].
     Felling Shore, near Gateshead.

18.54   Primitive Methodist, High Street, High Felling, Heworth (551.6)
Name   None.
Erected   1833. [New chapel opened 1896.]
Building   [Separate and entire. Exclusively used for worship.]
Sittings   Free 100. Other 60. Total [160].
Attendance 30 March   Morning 80 + 12 SS. Total 92.
     Evening 64. Total 64.
Average attendance   Morning and afternoon 70 + 10 SS. Total 80.
Dated   31 March 1851.
Signed   William Charlton, class leader [shopkeeper].
     High Felling, near Gateshead, Durham County.

18.55   Primitive Methodist, Swalwell, Whickham (551.45)
Name   Primitive Methodist Chaple (*sic*).
Erected   1849.
Building   [Separate and entire. Exclusively used for worship.]
Sittings   Free 110. Other 24. Total [134].
Attendance 30 March   Afternoon 50. Total [50].
     Evening 100. Total [100].
Average attendance   [Not given.]
Dated   30 March 1851.
Signed   Surtess Newton, elder [firebrick burner].
     Swalwell.

18.56   Primitive Methodist, Swinburn, Gateshead (551.27)
Name   Swinburn Place Chaple (*sic*).
Erected   In the year 1841.
Building   [Not separate and entire but] connected. Exclusively as
     a place of worship.
Sittings   Free 32. Other 26. Total [58].
Attendance 30 March   Morning no service.
     Afternoon 60 + 89 SS. Total [149].
     Evening 70. Total [70].
Average attendance   [Not given.]
Dated   30 March 1851.
Signed   Michael Hymers, chapel stewerd (*sic*).
     8 William Street, Gateshead.

['In 1825 Isaac Thompson declared that "Gateshead was a place much noted for hardness": hardness of heart, that is, to the gospel.' W.M. Patterson, *Northern Primitive Methodism* (London, 1909), p. 326.]

18.57   Primitive Methodist, Whickham (551.43)
Name   Primitive Methodist Chapel.
Erected   1843. [New chapel 1871.]
Building   [Separate and] entire. [Exclusively used for worship.]
Sittings   Free 150. Other 32. Total [182].
Attendance 30 March   Afternoon 40. Total [40].
                Evening 50. Total [50].
Average attendance   [Not given.]
Dated   30 March 1851.
Signed   Thomas Newton, manager [farmer].
                [Mount House, Whickham.]

18.58   Primitive Methodist, Winlaton (551.56)
Name   Salem Chapel.
Erected   1850.
Building   Separate and entire. [Exclusively used for worship.]
Sittings   Free 300. Other 42. Total [342].
Attendance 30 March   Morning 75 + 95 SS. Total 170.
                Evening 238. Total 238.
Average attendance   Morning 80 + 100 SS. Total 180.
                Evening 280. Total 280.
Remarks   On special occasions our congregations doth vary from 350 to 400 or upwards.
Dated   30 March 1851.
Signed   John Bunyan, steward.
                Winlaton, Durham.

18.59   Primitive Methodist, Winlaton (551.53)
Name   Bedlem.
Erected   [Not given.]
Building   Part of a dwelling house. [A] place of worship and school.
Sittings   Free 80. Other none. Total [80]. Standing [room] none.
Attendance 30 March   Afternoon 40 + 8 SS. Total 48.
Average attendance   Afternoon 40 + 10 SS. Total 50.
Dated   31 March 1851.
Signed   Johnson Scott, leader [tile cutter].
                Winlaton Mill, Gateshead, Durham.

18.60   Primitive Methodist, Wrekenton (551.31)

Name   None.
Erected   1838.
Building   No[t separate and entire]. There are two rooms
                underneath the chapel occupied. [Exclusively used for
                worship.]
Sittings   Free 100. Other 30. Total [130].
Attendance 30 March   Morning none.
                         Afternoon 16. Total [16].
                         Evening 12. Total [12].
Average attendance   [Not given.]
Dated   30 March 1851.
Signed   John Grieveson, steward [tailor].
                Wrekenton, Gateshead.

18.61   Primitive Methodist, Ship Lane, Wrekenton (551.33)

Name   Ship Lane Chapel.
Erected   1820.
Building   [Separate and entire. Exclusively used for worship.]
                Both Sunday school and day school.
Sittings   Free 80. Other 34. Total [114].
Attendance 30 March   Morning 29 SS. Total [29].
                         Afternoon 75. Total [75].
Average attendance   [Not given.]
Dated   31 March 1851.
Signed   William Hunter, local preacher (grocer) [provision
                dealer].
                Wrekenton, near Gateshead, Durham.

18.62   Wesleyan Reformers, Greenside (551.37)

Name   Wesleyan Reform Chapel.
Erected   1781.
Building   [Separate and] entire. [Exclusively used for worship.]
Sittings   Free 302. Other 48. Total [350].
Attendance 30 March   Afternoon 200. Total [200].
Average attendance   Morning 200 + 60 SS. Total 260.
Dated   31 March 1851.
Signed   James Spencer, steward and trustee (merchant tailor)
                [and draper].
                Greenside, Ryton, Durham.

18.63   Roman Catholic, Felling Shore, Heworth (551.9)

Name   St Patrick's Cath[olic] Chapel.

Erected   1841. [Opened 25 January 1842. Enlarged 1853.
             Replaced by a new church opened on 17 March 1895
             and the former building became an engine shed for
             Felling Colliery.]

Building   [Separate and entire. Exclusively used for worship.]

Sittings   Free 250. Total [250]. Standing room 50.

Attendance 30 March   Morning 400 + 80 SS. Total 480.
             Afternoon 150 SS. Total 150.
             Evening 400. Total 400.

Average attendance   Morning 400–500 + 150 SS. Total [550–650].

Dated   29 March 1851.

Signed   John Kelly, Catholic priest [1848–79].
             High Felling, n[ea]r Gateshead.

[In March 1860 John Kelly (1802–1883) was imprisoned for 40 hours
in Durham Gaol for not revealing the secrets of the confessional,
and on being released he was warmly welcomed by members of his
congregation. In 1852 the estimated number of Roman Catholics in
the area was 1,106.]

18.64   Roman Catholic, Hillgate, Gateshead (551.28)

Name   Temporary chapel of Our Lady and St Wilfrid,
             Hillgate.

Erected   Used for two months. Top flat of a bond warehouse
             now empty.

Building   [Separate and entire] i.e. consisting of five flats all
             unoccupied, but   also used as a boys' day school. [Not
             exclusively used for worship.]

Sittings   All free seats for 300. No charge obtained for seats on
             entrance. Total [300]. Standing room about 400.

Attendance 30 March   Morning 380 + 120 SS (actual). Total 500.
             Afternoon 80 + 120 SS (approximate). Total 200.

Average attendance   Morning 500 + 120 SS. Total 620. At first there
             were no seats. The Mass or Morning Service
             is the only obligatory service in the Cath[olic]
             ch[urch].

Remarks   The Catholic parochial district is co-extensive as to
             boundaries with those of the township. Number of
             Catholic parishioners 3,000, of whom the great portion
             are either Irish or born of I[rish] parents.

Dated   30 March 1851.
Signed   Frederick Betham, rector [1850–54].
            [13 Catherine Terrace], Gateshead.
[The temporary chapel in Hillgate replaced a chapel burnt down
in 1850. In October 1854 the chapel was destroyed by the fire and
huge explosion that rocked Gateshead and Newcastle. The Roman
Catholic congregation then moved to the Queen's Head Inn, Bottle
Bank, until St Joseph's church was opened on 5 July 1859. In 1852 the
estimated number of Roman Catholics in the area was 1,948.]

18.65   Roman Catholic, Stella (551.65)
Name   Church of St Mary and St Thomas Aquinas.
Erected   1831. [Opened 12 October 1832, enlarged 1849.]
Building   [Separate and entire. Exclusively used for worship.]
Sittings   Free 100. Other 225. Total [325]. Standing room 100.
Attendance 30 March   Morning 234 + 84 SS. Total 318.
                       Afternoon 40 + 84 SS. Total 124.
Average attendance   Morning 230 + 80 SS. Total 310.
                       Afternoon 50 + 80 SS. Total 130.
Dated   30 March 1851.
Signed   Ralph Platt, priest [canon of Hexham 1847–57].
            Stella, near Newcastle upon Tyne.
[In the late 18th century Stella had one of the largest Roman Catholic
congregations in the north-east. In the 1780s there were 334 Roman
Catholics in the parish of Ryton (which included Stella). In 1852 the
estimated number of Roman Catholics in the area was 800.]

19. Houghton-le-Spring District (HO 129/547)
37 places of worship

**19.1   Church of England, Holy Trinity, [later St Nicholas],
Hetton-le-Hole** (547.28)
Population 1851: 5,664 (township)

Name   Hetton-le-Hole. Parish church, not dedicated to any
            saint.
Consecrated [15] November 1832 [by the Bishop of Bristol] as a
            chapel of ease to Houghton-le-Spring. [District created
            15 May 1838. The church was replaced by a new

church (dedicated to St Nicholas) consecrated on 29
April 1901.]

Erected   By the Rev. Edward South Thurlow, rector of
Houghton-le-Spring Church Building Society [£650]
and private benefactions [that included £50 from the
Dean and Chapter of Durham]. Total cost £1,450.

Endowment Tithe (commuted) rent charge £321 18s 2d. Fees
variable. Easter offerings fluctuating.

Sittings   Free 365. Other 135. Total 500.

Attendance 30 March Morning 260 + 65 SS. Total 325.
Evening 280. Total 280.

Average attendance   Morning 350 + 40 SS. Total 470 (*sic*) [390].
Evening 380. Total 380.

Remarks   Hetton Church, as stated above, was originally erected
as a chapel of ease to Houghton-le-Spring. [In 1847] on
the death of Rev. E[dward South] Thurlow the parish
was divided and Hetton became a rectory endowed
with tithes etc. etc. etc.

Dated   31 March 1851.

Signed   John Scymeour Nichol, rector [1847–77].
Hetton Rectory, Fence Houses, Durham.

{1857   Attendance 400. 60 communicants.}   {B 178.}

[John Nichol had previously been the curate of Hetton-le-Hole 1832–
47.]

**19.2   Church of England, St Michael and All Angels, Houghton-
le-Spring** (547.19)

Population 1851: 20,284 (parish) 4,075 (township)

[Summary form]

Name   St Michael's Church, Houghton-le-Spring.

Erected   Supposed to be in the 12th century. [Restored and
enlarged 1857–58.]

Endowment [£2,157, of which £400 paid to curates.]

Sittings   Total more than 1,000. About a thousand. It would
be difficult to say which are free and which are
appropriated.

Usual attendance   Morning I suppose about 500 including the
schools.
About 100 SS. Total [500].

> Afternoon 150 [including] same (about 100) SS. Total 150.
> Evening about 500. [SS] do not attend in the evening. Total [500].

Remarks   It is obvious that some attending may be more and sometimes fewer. The above numbers are conjectural as I am not in the habit of counting the congregation. I do not go to church for that purpose.

Dated   [Not dated.]

Signed   John Grey, rector of Houghton-le-Spring [1847–95]. [Fence Houses, Durham.]

{1857   Attendance 400. 15 communicants.}   {B 188.}

[During the ministry of the wealthy and well-connected pluralist Edward South Thurlow, 1789–1847 (who was the nephew of the Bishop of Durham, Thomas Thurlow and also of the Lord Chancellor, Edward Thurlow) three churches were erected – West Rainton (1825), Hetton-le-Hole (1832) and Herrington (1840). On 15 May 1838 three districts were created – Hetton-le-Hole, Penshaw and West Rainton. In 1832 Thurlow's total income was £4,700.

John Grey's brother Francis Richard Grey was the rector of Morpeth 1842–90 (**9.12**). They were the sons of the second Earl Grey.]

19.3   Church of England, St Cuthbert, Herrington (547.4)
Population 1851: 218 (township)

Name   St Cuthbert, chapel of ease [to Houghton-le-Spring].

Consecrated   8 September 1840, as an additional church.

Erected   By the Rev. E[ward South] Thurlow, late rector of Houghton-le-Spring, at his sole cost.

Endowment   [Not given.]

Sittings   Free 200. Total 200.

Attendance 30 March   Morning 100 + 15 SS. Total 115.

Average attendance   [Not given.]

Remarks   Rather below the average summer attendance.

Dated   [Not given.]

Signed   [Not given.]

Incumbent   [John Grey 1847–95.] [Fence Houses, Durham.]

{1857   Attendance 140. 25 communicants.}

19.4   Church of England, St Matthew, Newbottle (547.12)
Population 1851: 2,067 (township)

[Summary form]
Name   St Matthew's Church.
Erected   1849–50. [Consecrated 7 August 1851. Replaced by
            church dedicated to St Michael and All Angels, 1 June
            1886.]
Endowment   [Not given.]
Sittings   All free. Other none. Total 250.
            The church was […] built to hold but 280 has been
            present at divine service, so for support it may hold
            250 without undue crowding. On any day it might
            hold 250.
Usual attendance   About 200.
            Morning once a month 200. Total [200].
            Afternoon about 200. Total [200].
            Evening none.
Dated   [Not dated.]
Signed   John Grey, rector of Houghton-le-Spring [1847–95].
            [Fence Houses, Durham.]

19.5   Church of England, All Saints, Penshaw (547.6)
Population 1851: 2,120 (township)

Name   Penshaw Rectory. At its erection it was, I believe
            a chapel of ease to Houghton-le-Spring, and so
            remained till about five years ago. I know not what
            name was given to it.
Consecrated Before 1800 (26 October 1746 by the Bishop of
            Gloucester). [Restored and enlarged 1876–77. District
            created 15 May 1838 (as a chapel of ease to Houghton-
            le-Spring, I believe).] [crossed out].
Endowment   Land and tithe, 58 acres at Barnard Castle of the parish
            of Penshaw. Glebe lands, 11 yards by 39 [yards] only.
            OPE I know not of any. Pew rents, nil. Fees, from
            Oct[ober] 1850 to 31 March 1851, £7 10s 9d. Dues, nil
            that I know of. Easter offerings, I know not of any.
            Other, I know not of any.
Sittings   Total about 300*
Attendance 30 March   From 12 October to 30 March 1851:
            Morning about 200. Total 200.

	Afternoon about 50. Total 50.
Average attendance	Morning sometimes upwards of 200. Total 200. Afternoon sometimes 120. Total 120.
Remarks	*By taking down a partition, which I insisted [?] upon doing, this space will be ⅓ larger. By a different arrangement many more may be accommodated. I have had the living only a few months. The church has been badly attended, but I hope to have it much better soon. NoSunday school.
Dated	31 March 1851.
Signed	James Waters, rector [1850–67]. Rectory, Penshaw, Fence Houses, Durham.
{1857	Attendance 100. 20 communicants. Music played by harmonium.} {B 91.}

19.6   Church of England, St Mary, West Rainton (547.36)
Population 1851: 942 (township)

Name	West Rainton Parish Church. Built under the provisions of the 16th section of the 58th Geo. III c.45.
Consecrated	29 August 1825 [by the Bishop of Oxford], as an additional church. [District created 15 May 1838 out of the parish of Houghton-le-Spring. Replaced by new church consecrated on 21 April 1864.]
Erected	By Parliamentary grant (£550); private benefaction [£300 from the Dean and Chapter of Durham] and subscription (£727 5s). Total cost £1,277 5s.
Endowment	Tithe £305. Fees £6. Easter offerings £8.
Sittings	Free 375. Other 225. Total 600.
Attendance 30 March	Morning 510 + 120 SS. Total [630]. Evening 369. Total [369].
Average attendance	Morning 470 + 130 SS. Total [600]. Evening 360 + 20 SS. Total [380].
Remarks	Morning service chiefly attended by persons from a distance, and that in the evening by those who are nearer. Owing to the inclemency of the weather, the prevalence of an […] especially […] children, the congregations have lately been much smaller than previous.
Dated	30 March 1851.

Signed   Joseph Tiffin, rector [1847–58].
                West Rainton, Durham.
{1857   Attendance 300. 40 communicants.}   {B 182.}
[Joseph Tiffin had previously been the curate of West Rainton 1825–38.]

19.7   United Presbyterian, Newbottle Lane, Houghton-le-Spring (547.26)

Name   Presbyterian Chapel.
Erected   1824. [Foundation stone laid 27 December 1824.]
Building   Separate [and entire]. Exclusively [used for worship].
Sittings   None free. Other 220. Total [220]. Standing room none.
Attendance 30 March   Morning 150. Total [150].
                        Evening 70. Total [70].
Average attendance   Morning as above. Total [150].
                        Evening as above. Total [70].
Dated   31 March 1851.
Signed   Anderson Drysdale, minister [1847–55].
                Newbottle Lane, Houghton-le-Spring, Durham.

19.8   Independent [Congregational], Easington Lane (547.29)

[Simplified form]
Name   Bethel Chapel.
Erected   1832. [Enlarged 1842.]
Building   [Separate and entire. Exclusively used for worship.]
Sittings   Free 50. Other 120. Total [170].
Usual attendance   Morning 50 SS. Total 50.
                     Afternoon 60. Total 60.
                     Evening 50. Total 50.
Dated   [Not given.]
Signed   Christopher Storey [grocer and flour dealer].
                Lane Ends, Hetton-le-Hole.
Minister   [John Fogg 1850–57.]

19.9   Baptist Schoolroom, Sunderland Street, Houghton-le-Spring (547.23)

Name   Mr [George] Bee's Schoolroom.
Erected   About the year 1816.
Building   A room [not exclusively used for worship].
Sittings   Free 200. Other none. Total [200].
Attendance 30 March   Morning 10. Total [10].
                        Afternoon 14. Total [14].

Average attendance   Morning 14. SS none. Total [14].
Dated   31 March 1851.
Signed   William Earle, deacon (draper).
               [Quay], Houghton-le-Spring.

19.10   Wesleyan Methodist, Cox Green (547.5)

Name   Wesleyan Chapel.
Erected   1820.
Building   [Separate and entire. Exclusively used for worship.]
Sittings   Free 80. Other 50. Total [130].
Attendance 30 March   Afternoon 32. Total [32].
                         Evening 60. Total [60].
Average attendance   Morning 40 + 15 SS. Total 55.
Remarks   Free sittings 70. Other sittings 75.
Dated   31 March 1851.
Signed   Richard Atkinson, leader and steward [farmer].
               Fence Houses, Cox Green, Durham.

19.11   Wesleyan Methodist, Easington Lane (547.31)

Name   None.
Erected   1827.
Building   [Separate and entire. Exclusively used for worship.]
Sittings   Free 160. Other 150. Total [310].
Attendance 30 March   Afternoon 196. Total [196].
                         Evening 143. Total [143].
Average attendance   [Not given.]
Dated   31 March 1851.
Signed   Samuel Lucas, minister [1849–51].
               Houghton-le-Spring, Durham.

19.12   Wesleyan Methodist, Houghton-le-Spring (547.21)

Name   None.
Erected   1837. [Cost £900.]
Building   [Separate and entire. Exclusively used for worship.]
Sittings   Free 220. Other 250. Total [470].
Attendance 30 March   Morning 117. Total 117.
                         Evening 229. Total 239.
Average attendance   [Not given.]
Date   31 March 1851.
Signed   Samuel Lucas, minister [1849–51].
               Houghton-le-Spring, Durham.

19.13   Wesleyan Methodist, Philadelphia Row, Newbottle
(547.18)
Name   None.
Erected   1824.
Building   [Separate and entire. Exclusively used for worship.]
Sittings   Free 120. Other 64. Total [184].
Attendance 30 March   Morning 62 + 6 SS. Total 68.
                        Evening 51 + 15 SS. Total 66.
Average attendance   [Not given.]
Dated   31 March 1851.
Signed   Samuel Lucas, minister [1849–51].
                  Houghton-le-Spring, Durham.

19.14   Wesleyan Methodist Schoolroom, Shiney Row (547.11)
Name   None.
Erected   1805.
Building   [Separate and entire but not exclusively used for
                  worship. Also] used as a Methodist day school.
Sittings   Free 90. Total [90].
Attendance 30 March   Afternoon 62. Total [62].
                        Evening 36. Total [36].
Average attendance   [Not given.]
Dated   31 March 1851.
Signed   Samuel Lucas, minister [1849–51].
                  Houghton-le-Spring, Durham.

19.15   Wesleyan Methodist, East Herrington (547.2)
Name   Wesleyan Methodist Chappell (*sic*).
Erected   In the year 1839. [Cost £250.]
Building   [Separate and entire. Exclusively used for worship.]
Sittings   Free 260. Other 34. Total [294].
Attendance 30 March   Afternoon 21. Total [21].
                        Evening 53. Total [53].
Average attendance   Afternoon 20. Total [20].
                        Evening 50. Total [50].
Dated   31 March 1851.
Signed   Barnabas Rutter, trustee [farmer].
                  East Herrington, Durham.

19.16   Wesleyan Methodist, Front Street, Hetton-le-Hole (547.33)

Name   Hetton Wesleyan Methodist Chapel.
Erected   1824. [In 1858 a new chapel was opened in Union
                Street.]
Building   [Separate and entire. Exclusively used for worship]
                and a Sunday school.
Sittings   Free 186. Other 210. Total [396]. Standing room – no
                space set apart for this purpose, but isles (*sic*) where
                210 may stand in cases of emergency.
Attendance 30 March   Morning 131 + 81 SS. Total 212.
                Afternoon 28 (teachers) + 136 SS. Total 136
                (*sic*). [164.]
                Evening 156 + 55 SS. Total 211.
Average attendance   Morning 145 + 90 SS. Total 235.
                Afternoon 27 + 132 SS. Total 159.
                Evening 174 + 66 SS. Total 240.
Dated   30 March 1851.
Signed   George Cockburn, society steward [clerk, Hetton
                Colliery].
                Hetton Colliery Office, Fence Houses, Durham.

19.17   Wesleyan Methodist, Colliery Row, Houghton-le-Spring
(547.25)

Name   Wesleyan Chapel.
Erected   The year of our Lord 1820. [Consisted of two cottages
                made into a chapel. A new chapel was opened in 1872.]
Building   [Separate and entire. Exclusively used for worship.]
Sittings   Free 170. Other 80. Total [250]. Standing room none.
Attendance 30 March   Morning 111 + 20 SS. Total 131.
                Evening 80 + 35 SS. Total 115.
Average attendance   [Not given.]
Remarks   The number here stated will be about an average
                number of attendants.
Date   31 March 1851.
Name   Thomas Colling, steward [coal miner and
                schoolmaster].
                Colliery Row, Fence Houses, Durham.

19.18   Wesleyan Methodist, Newbottle (547.13)
Name   None.
Erected   Before 1800. [1786.]
Building   [Separate and entire. Exclusively used for worship.]
Sittings   Free 120. Other 140. Total [260].
Attendance 30 March   Morning 57. Total 57.
                        Evening 100. Total 100.
Average attendance   Morning 90 + 20 SS. Total 110.
                        Evening 150 + 20 SS. Total 170.
Remarks   The number in attendance considerably less on this
               day by reason of the Primitive Methodist school
               anniversary. (See **19.29**, **19.30**.)
Dated   30 March 1851.
Signed   Daniel Stokoe, steward [grocer].
               Newbottle, Durham.

19.19   Wesleyan Methodist, Offerton (547.8)
Name   None.
Erected   1832.
Building   [Separate and entire. Exclusively used for worship.]
Sittings   Free 100. Other none. Total [100].
Attendance 30 March   Morning 37 SS. Total [37].
                        Afternoon 50. Total [50].
                        Evening 50. Total [50].
Average attendance   Morning and afternoon 56 + 37 SS. Total 87.
Dated   31 March 1851.
Signed   John Plues, minister.
               Derwent Iron Works, Sunderland, Durham.

19.20   Wesleyan Methodist, Penshaw (547.9)
Name   Wesleyan Methodist Chaple (*sic*).
Erected   [1778.]
Building   [Separate and] entire building. A place of worship and
               Sunday school.
Sittings   Free 150. Total [150].
Attendance 30 March   Morning [42 SS] scholars. Total 42.
Average attendance   Morning 15 SS. Total [15].
                        Afternoon 64 SS. Total [64].
Dated   30 March 1851.
Signed   W[illia]m Caisley, superintendent.
               Penshaw, via Fence Houses.

19.21   Wesleyan Methodist, East Rainton (547.35)
Name   Wesleyan Methodist Chapel.
Erected   1827.
Building   A separate and entire building. Used exclusively as a
              place of worship.
Sittings   Free 100. Other 50. Total [150].
Attendance 30 March   Afternoon 60. Total [60].
                        Evening 54. Total [54].
Average attendance   [Not given.]
Dated   19 April 1851.
Signed   George Hodgson, chapel steward [lime maker].

19.22   Wesleyan Methodist, West Rainton (547.37)
Name   Ebenezer.
Erected   1822.
Building   [Separate and entire. Exclusively used for worship.]
Sittings   Free 120. Other 138. Total [258].
Attendance 30 March   Morning 152 + 10 SS. Total [162].
Average attendance   [Not given.]
Dated   31 March 1851.
Signed   Joseph Thomas Proud, steward [boot and]
              (shoemaker).
              Middle Rainton, Durham.

19.23   Wesleyan Methodist, Moorsley, West Rainton (547.38)
Name   Wesleyan Methodist Chapel.
Erected   1837.
Building   There is a tenement below it. [Not exclusively used for
              worship. Used] also as a day school.
Sittings   Free 200. Other none. Total [200].
Attendance 30 March   Afternoon 174. Total [174].
                        Evening 174. Total [174].
Average attendance   Morning 170 (each Sunday) + 120 SS (each
                        Sunday). Total 290.
Dated   31 March 1851.
Signed   [William] Hedley Curry, foreman [overman].
              Moorsley, Fence Houses, Durham.

19.24   Methodist New Connexion, Philadelphia Row, Newbottle
(547.15)
Name   Methodist New Connexion.
Erected   Before 1810.

Building   [Not separate and entire. A] place of worship and
Sunday school.
Sittings   [Not given.] Standing room 10 yards by 6 [yards] all
free.
Attendance 30 March   Morning 40 + 12 SS. Total [52].
Evening 40 + 12 SS. Total 52.
Average attendance   51 (over past two months).
Dated   30 March 1851.
Signed   Jhon (*sic*) White, local preacher [coal miner].

19.25   Primitive Methodist, Easington Lane (547.30)
Name   Primitive Methodist Chapel.
Erected   1830. [Rebuilt and enlarged in 1853. Cost £400.]
Building   [Separate and entire. Exclusively used for worship.]
Sittings   Free 111. Other 88. Total [199].
Attendance 30 March   Morning 160. Total 160.
Afternoon 155 SS. Total 155.
Evening 190. Total 190.
Average attendance   Morning 185. Total 185.
Afternoon 155 SS. Total 155.
Remarks   The difference between the year 1824 and 1830 is by
reason of having a room previous to having the chapel
built.
Dated   30 March 1851.
Signed   John Robson, steward [cabinet maker].
Easington Lane, Durham

19.26   Primitive Methodist, Middle Herrington (547.3)
Name   None.
Erected   [Not given.]
Building   [Not separate and entire or exclusively used for
worship.]
Sittings   Free 50. Other none. Total [50]. Standing room none.
Attendance 30 March   Morning 17. Total 17.
Evening 37. Total 37.
Average attendance   [Not given.]
Dated   30 March 1851.
Signed   John Hobson, class leader [wagon-way labourer].
Middel (*sic*) Herrington Hall, Durham.

19.27   Primitive Methodist, Hetton-le-Hole (547.32)

Name   Primitive Methodist Chapel.
Erected   In the year of our Lord 1824. [New chapel opened
                22 May 1858 to seat 750 and with a school to
                accommodate 600 children.]
Building   A separate and entire building. Exclusively a place of
                worship except for a Sunday school.
Sittings   Free 60. Other 260. Total [320].
Attendance 30 March   Morning 271 SS. Total 271.
                Afternoon 225. Total 225.
                Evening 270. Total 270.
Average attendance   Morning 240 SS. Total 240.
                Afternoon 230. Total 230.
                Evening 250. Total 250.
Dated   [Not given.]
Signed   Abraham William Errington, chapel steward [coal
                miner].
                [John Street], Hetton-le-Hole, Durham, by Fence
                Houses.

19.28   Primitive Methodist, Houghton-le-Spring (547.22)

Name   None.
Erected   [Not given. New chapel opened September 1855.]
Building   [Not given.]
Sittings   Free 50. Total [50].
Attendance 30 March   Morning 30. Total 30.
                Evening 40. Total 40.
Average attendance   [Not given.]
Dated   30 March 1851.
Signed   Joseph Dixon, leader and local preacher.
                Sunderland Street, Houghton-le-Spring.

19.29   Primitive Methodist, Newbottle (547.14)

Name   Primitive Methodas (*sic*) Chaple (*sic*).
Erected   8 December 1850.
Building   Separate [and entire. Exclusively used for worship.]
Sittings   Free 140. Other 116. Total [256]. Standing room none.
Attendance 30 March   Morning 220. Total [220].
                Afternoon 250. Total [250].
                Evening 259. Total [259].
Average attendance   Morning and afternoon 170 + 25 SS.
                Total [195].

Remarks   On the 30 March we have their particular [Sunday
         school anniversary] services.
Dated   30 March 1851.
Signed   Luke Elliott, manager [coal miner].
         Newbottle, Fence Houses.

19.30   Primitive Methodist, Philadelphia Row, Newbottle
(547.17)
Name   Primitive Methodist Preaching Room.
Erected   Before the year of our Lord 1800.
Building   [Not separate and entire. Exclusively used for worship.]
Sittings   Free 60. Other 20. Total [80]. Standing room 20.
Attendance 30 March   Morning 34. Total 34.
                 Afternoon 20. Total [20].
                 Evening 30. Total [30].
Average attendance   Morning 36. Total [36].
                 Afternoon 70. Total [70].
                 Evening 70. Total [70].
Remarks   The reason why our congregations has been so
         small today, 30 March, our people, viz the Primitive
         Methodists, have had their Sunday school anniversary
         at Newbottle (**19.29**). The children have been repeating
         their pieces.
Dated   30 March 1851.
Signed   (I remain your humble servant) [Crossed out].
         Jonathan Blakelock, superintendent of the school [coal
         miner].
         Philadelphia, Fence Houses.

19.31   Primitive Methodist, Middle Rainton (547.34)
Name   Primitive Methodist Chapel.
Erected   1831.
Building   [Separate and entire. Exclusively used for worship.]
Sittings   Free 101. Other 149. Total [250]. Standing room
         90 sup[plementary] feet.
Attendance 30 March   Morning 157 SS. Total 157.
                 Afternoon 150. Total 150.
                 Evening 200. Total 200.
Average attendance   [Not given.]
Dated   30 March 1851.
Signed   John Gargett, steward (joiner).
         Middle Rainton.

19.32   Wesleyan Methodist Association, Houghton-le-Spring (547.20)

Name	Tabernacle.
Erected	1836.
Building	[Separate and] entire. Exclusively for worship and Sunday school.
Sittings	Free 60. Other 200. Total [260].
Attendance 30 March	Afternoon 40 + 20 SS. Total 60.
	Evening 74 + 12 SS. Total 86.
Average attendance	Afternoon 185 + 20 SS. Total 205.
	Evening 203 + 27 SS. Total 230.
	The total number of attendants and scholars in the afternoon and evening 435.
Dated	30 March 1851.
Signed	Thomas Walker, superintendent.
	Rainton Bridge, C[ounty] Durham.

19.33   Wesleyan Methodist Association, Colliery Row, Houghton-le-Spring (547.27)

Name	Tabernacle.
Erected	1839.
Building	[Separate and entire. Exclusively used for worship.]
Sittings	Free 146. Other 74. Total [220].
Attendance 30 March	Afternoon 75. Total [75].
	Evening 70. Total [70].
Average attendance	Afternoon 50. Total [50].
	Evening 60. Total [60].
Dated	30 May 1851.
Signed	George Robinson, minister.
	1 D'Arcy Street, Sunderland.

19.34   Wesleyan Methodist Association, Philadelphia Row, Newbottle (547.16)

Name	Tabernacle, Philledelpha (*sic*).
Erected	1836.
Building	[Separate and entire. Exclusively used for worship.]
Sittings	Free 136. Other 87. Total [223].
Attendance 30 March	Morning 23 + 19 SS. Total 42.
	Evening 25 + 7 SS. Total 32.
Average attendance	Morning 43 + 18 SS. Total 61.
Remarks	Out of 87 rented sittings, only 33 are taken.
Dated	30 March 1851.

Signed   John Taylor, society steward.
Succes (*sic*) Row, near Fence Houses, C[oun]ty Durham.

19.35   Wesleyan Methodist Association, near Penshaw (547.7)
Name   Wesleyan Methodist Association.
Erected   [Not given.]
Building   [Separate and entire. Exclusively used for worship.]
Sittings   Free 100. Total [100]. Standing room none.
Attendance 30 March   Morning 30 SS. Total 30.
                         Afternoon 50. Total [50].
                         Evening 40. Total 70 (*sic*).
Average attendance   70 [no details].
Dated   31 March 1851.
Signed   John Drummond, superintendent [sailor].
               Near Penshaw, via Fence House (*sic*).

19.36   Wesleyan Methodist Association, Fence Row, Penshaw
(547.10)
Name   Wesleyan Association Chapell (*sic*).
Erected   1805.
Building   [Separate and] entire building. Not used for any other
               purpose.
Sittings   Free 428. Other 112. Total [540].
Attendance 30 March   Afternoon 150 + 50 SS. Total 200.
                         Evening 130 + 20 SS. Total 150.
Average attendance   [Not given.]
Dated   30 March 1851.
Signed   James Smarthwaite, steward [grocer].
               Penshaw Colliery, Durham.

19.37   Roman Catholic, Houghton-le-Spring (547.24)
Name   St Michael's.
Erected   1837. [Opened 9 November 1837.]
Building   [Separate and entire. Exclusively used for worship.]
Sittings   Free 135. Other 155. Total [290].
               Standing room about 2 feet per head. [Total] 222.
Attendance 30 March   Morning 340 + 54 SS. Total 394.
                         Afternoon 120 + 52 SS. Total 172.
Average attendance   [Not given.]
Dated   31 March 1851.
Signed   Arsenius Watson, priest [1845–57].

[Presbytery, Durham Road], Houghton-le-Spring.
['When Catholicity first reared its head at Houghton-le-Spring, the place was described as a locality of "all pervading bigotry".' B.W. Kelly, *Historical Notes on English Catholic Missions* (London, 1907), p. 220. In 1852 the estimated number of Roman Catholics in the area was 830.]

20. South Shields District (HO 129/550)
49 places of worship

20.1   Church of England, St Nicholas, West Boldon (550.2)
Population 1851: 1,108 (parish)

Name   Ancient parish church dedicated to St Nicholas.
Consecrated   Consecrated from time immemorial.
Endowment   Annual value returned £653 chiefly from tithe and glebe.
Sittings   Free 137 (including 60 for children). Other 194. Total 331.
Attendance 23 March   Morning 120 + 33 SS. Total 153. (A wet day.)
Average attendance   Morning 160 + 40 SS. Total 200.
Dated   24 March 1851.
Signed   John Collinson, rector of Boldon [1840–57]. Boldon Rectory, Gateshead.
{1857   Attendance 140. 27 communicants [in the] whole parish.}   {B 28.}
[John Collinson had previously been the rector of Gateshead 1810–39. His eldest son, Henry King Collinson, was the incumbent of Stannington (**5.15**).]

20.2   Church of England, St George, East Boldon (550.1)
Name   The parochial chapel at East Boldon.
Consecrated   Licensed in February 1845, as a chapel of ease to the church at West Boldon. [Consecrated on 7 February 1845, replaced by new church consecrated on 8 December 1923.]
Erected   By dissenters, and bought by the late rector of Boldon, Rev. N[athaniel] J[ohn] Hollingsworth [1829–39] for the use of the established church. The present bishop

of Durham [Edward Maltby] purchased it for £300
from Mr Hollingworth's executors and licensed it.
Endowment No endowment. Pew rents £1 18s (per annum).
Sittings   Free 35. Rented 19. Other 67. Total 121.
Attendance 23 March Afternoon 30 + 10 SS. Total 40.
Average attendance   Afternoon 40 + 20 SS. Total 60.
Dated   24 March 1851.
Signed   John Collinson, rector of Boldon [1840–57].
              Boldon Rectory, Gateshead.

20.3 Church of England, St Paul, Jarrow (550.36)
Population 1851: 42,448 (parish)

[Summary form]
Name   Jarrow P[arish] Ch[urch].
Erected   [Dedicated 23 April 685. Rebuilt 1783, enlarged 1866.]
Endowment [£200.]
Sittings   Free 100. Other 220. Total 320.
Dated   26 August 1852.
Informant Richard Rees [registrar].
Incumbent [John Mason-Mason 1849–60.]
{1857   Attendance 200. 30 communicants.}   {B 108.}
[John Mason-Mason had been the curate of Jarrow 1844–49.]

20.4 Church of England, Monkton Chapel, Jarrow (550.42)
[Summary form]
Name   Monkton Chapel.
Erected   A room used about seven years. [Licensed 11 May
             1841.]
Sittings   Free about 100. Total 100.
Usual attendance   Morning nil.
                      Afternoon about 50. Total [about 50].
                      [No Sunday school.]
                      Evening nil.
Dated   [Not given.]
Informant William W. Brook, enumerator.
[Previously the room, situated two miles from the parish church,
had been used by dissenters, and then acquired by Henry Major of
Simonside Hall. DUL, ASC, DDE/EA/CH/D/1–2, letter dated 14
April 1841.]

20.5   Church of England, St Hilda, Market Place, South Shields
(550.37)
Population 1851: 28,974 (township) 10,263 (district)

[Summary form]

Name	St Hilda.
Erected	About 1600. [Rebuilt 1782, enlarged 1784. Rebuilt and enlarged (at a cost of £6,860) and consecrated 30 July 1819 by the Bishop of Oxford. Restored 1866. The parish was created on 30 June 1845.]
Endowment	[£460.]
Sittings	Free 130. Other 1,400. Total 1,530.
Usual attendance	Morning 200. Total [200].
	Afternoon 150. Total [150].
	Evening 400. Total [400].
Dated	[Not given.]
Informant	R[ichard] Rees, registrar.
	From enquiry of E. Romsey, sexton.
Incumbent	[James Carr 1831–62.]

{1857   Attendance 1,000. 60 communicants.}   {B 434.}
['An Act for defraying the expenses incurred in taking down and rebuilding and enlarging the chapel of St Hilda etc', 19 May 1819. James Carr was commended for his ministry during the outbreaks of cholera in 1832, 1834, 1848, 1849 and 1853. After leaving South Shields he was the Master of Sherburn Hospital 1862–74.]

20.6   Church of England, St Thomas, Fowler Street, Westoe
(550.13 and 550.14a)
[Summary form]

Name	Westoe Church.
Erected	[Built by subscription. Dean and Chapter £1,000. Lord Crewe's Trustees £500. National School society £200. Total cost £2,600.
Consecrated	29 July 1818. [Chapel of ease to St Hilda, South Shields. Parish created on 27 August 1864. Replaced by a new church consecrated on 11 October 1877.]
Endowment	[£220.]
Sittings	Free 400. Other 600. Total 1,000.
Usual attendance	Morning 480. Total [480].
	Afternoon no public service. [Sunday] school 250. Total [250].

Evening 380 (exclusive of children, belonging
to [Sunday] school). Total [380].

Dated	16 July 1852.
Signed	E[van] Hunter [registrar].
	[12 Sackville Street, South Shields.]
Incumbent	[William Coward 1829–53.]
{1857	Attendance 800. 30 communicants.}

(550.14a) [Summary form]

Sittings	Free 600. Other 500. Total 1,100.
Dated	25 August 1852.
Signed	E[van] Hunter, registrar.
	[12 Sackville Street, South Shields.]

20.7   Church of England, Harton Chapel, Westoe Lane, Harton
(550.9)
Population 1851: 770 (township)

[Summary form]

Name	Harton Chapel. [Chapel of ease to St Thomas, Westoe.]
Erected	1836. [Opened 6 November 1836. Parish created 27 August 1864.]
Sittings	Free 136. Other 144. Total 280.
Usual attendance	Morning 16 SS. Total [16].
	Afternoon 200 + 16 SS. [Total 216.]
Dated	[Not dated.]
Signed	William Coward (informant). [Curate of Westoe 1829–53.]

[St Peter, Harton, was consecrated on 15 August 1867.]

**20.8   Church of England, St Stephen, Mile End Road, South
Shields** (550.15)
Population 1851: 6,287 (district)

[Summary form]

Name	St Stephen's, district church.
Erected	[Consecrated 13 October] 1846. Total cost £2,500 (included £500 from the Dean and Chapter of Durham). Restored 1896. Parish created on 12 August 1848 out of the parish of St Hilda's, South Shields, and became a rectory on 5 July 1866.]
Endowment	[£200.]

Sittings   Free 500. Other 300. Total 800.
Usual attendance   Morning about 150 + from 50 to 60 SS.
                        Total [200–210].
                        Afternoon about 200. Total [200].
                        Evening about 400. Total [400]
Sir,
The above is the best information I can procure. The incumbent, Mr Brasher, objected to supply it.
I am, sir, your obedient servant, E[van] Hunter, registrar.
Incumbent   [Samuel Benton Brasher 1848–68.]
{1857   Attendance 150. 18 communicants.}   {B 101.}

20.9   Church of England, Holy Trinity, Commercial Road, South Shields (550.16)
Population 1851: 9,625 (township)

Name   Holy Trinity Church, South Shields. It is the church
                 of a district chapelry [created out of the parish of St
                 Hilda, South Shields on 12 August 1848].
Consecrated   18 September 1834 [by the Archbishop of York] as
                 an additional church. Restored and enlarged, and
                 reopened 6 August 1879].
Erected   By the incumbent of South Shields encouraged by the
                 Dean and Chapter of Durham and others. Grant by
                 the Church Building Societies £600. Private £1,800.
                 Total cost about £2,400.
Endowment   Tithe, yes. Pew rents, yes. Fees, yes. Easter offerings,
                 yes.
Sittings   Free 800. Other 400. Total 1,200.
Attendance 30 March   [Not given.]
Average attendance   Morning about 400 + 220 SS. Total 620.
                         Afternoon 270 SS. Total 270.
                         Evening about 800. Total 800.
Remarks   The church is not opened for divine service in the
                 afternoon, but the children assemble in the schoolroom
                 immediately contagious.
Dated   31 March 1851.
Signed   Thomas Dixon, incumbent [1834–72].
                 [Frederick Street], South Shields.
{1857   Attendance 900. 50 communicants. The population is
           13,000 and should have two churches.}   {B 274.}

[In 1833 the Dean and Chapter of Durham gave £1,089 towards the cost of the new church; and in the following year a further £1,061; with a similar amount each year from 1835 to 1838.]

20.10   Church of England, Templetown Chapel, South Shields
(550.18)

Name	Templetown Chapel. It was formerly a Ranters' chapel.
Licensed	With the sanction of the Bishop of Durham, I established a Sabbath day service and Sunday school in it, about two and a half years ago, connected with Trinity Church.
Erected	By the Ranters [i.e. Primitive Methodists].
Endowment	No endowment nor any income from it.
Sittings	Free about 100. Total about 100.

Attendance 30 March   [Not given.]

Average attendance   Morning 25 + 20 SS. Total 45.

Remarks	With the Bishop of Durham's sanction, I took possession of this chapel to do good to the colliery population.
Dated	31 March 1851.
Signed	Thomas Dixon, incumbent of Holy Trinity [1834–72]. [Frederick Street], South Shields.

20.11   Church of England, Academy Hill Chapel, Chapel Hill, South Shields (550.17)

Name	Academy Hill Chapel occupied by Chartists, Socialists and Barkerites, before I got possession of it and established in it the service of the Church of England.
Licensed	About two years ago. Opened with the sanction of the Bishop of Durham for a Sabbath day service and Sunday and week-day school in connection with Trinity Church.
Erected	By dissenters and was always a dissenting chapel till I took possession of it.
Endowment	No endowment or income whatever from it.
Sittings	Free about 300. Total about 300.

Attendance 30 March   [Not given.]

Average attendance   Morning 50 SS. Total 50.
                         Afternoon 80 + 50 SS. Total 130.

Remarks	This chapel was for many years the resort of itinerant orators and leaders of mischievous sects, religious

and political, who did much mischief in the poor
neighbourhood where it is.

Dated   31 March 1851.

Signed   Thomas Dixon, incumbent of Holy Trinity [1834–72].
[Frederick Street], South Shields.

[The Barkerites were the followers of the radical Methodist Joseph
Barker (**10.35**). J.T. Barker, *The Life of Joseph Barker* (London, 1880).]

20.12   Whitburn Parish Church [St Andrew], Whitburn
(550.6)
Population 1851: 1,203 (parish)

Name   Whitburn Parish Church, an ancient building,
affording accommodation equal to the population.

Consecrated [Restored 1860.]

Endowment   Land tithe and glebe [200 acres] (rent charges) both
reducing in value. [£1,113.]

Sittings   Free 41. Other 368. Total 409.
[Each sitting calculated] at 18ins for each.

Attendance 30 March   Morning 186 + 49 SS (counted). Total 235.
Afternoon 75 + 20 SS. Total 95.

Average attendance   Morning 170 + 45 SS. Total 215.
Afternoon 70 + 20 SS. Total 90.

Remarks   There are not any data from which to form an average.
The numbers   inserted result from occasional counting
loosely. The state of the weather has a considerable
effect as the parish extends three and four miles from
the church. The attendance is considered very good.

Dated   30 March 1851.

Signed   Thomas Baker MA, rector [1810–66].
Whitburn, Sunderland.

{1857   Attendance 150. 60 communicants. More sittings for
the poor desirable.}   {B 28.}

20.13   United Presbyterian, Heugh Street, South Shields (550.28)
Name   Heugh Street Church.

Erected   Before 1800. [1779. Rebuilt and enlarged 1817. New
church opened in Ingham Street in 1858.]

Building   [Separate and entire. Exclusively used for worship.]

Sittings   None free. Other 250. Total [250].

Attendance 30 March   Morning 130 + 50 SS. Total 180.
Afternoon 60 SS. Total 60.

	Evening 180 + 20 SS. Total 200.
Average attendance	Morning and afternoon 160 + 20 SS. Total 180.
Dated	30 March 1851.
Signed	Joseph L. Thompson, elder [sail-maker and ship-owner]. Palatine Street, So[uth] Shields.
Minister	[Thomas McCreath 1835–64.]

20.14   United Presbyterian, East Street, South Shields (550.39)

Name	United Presbyterian Congregation.
Erected	Uncertain. First erected by the Wesleyan body; in our possession [in 1808] more than forty years. [Replaced by St Paul's Presbyterian Church, opened on 16 February 1880.]
Building	An entire building. Used as a place of worship and for a Sunday school exclusively.
Sittings	Free 50. Other 400. Total [450]. Standing room about 20.
Attendance 30 March	Morning 120 + 35 SS. Total 155. Afternoon 116 + 48 SS. Total 164. Evening 150 + 30 SS. Total 180.
Average attendance	Morning 137 + 75 SS. Total 212. Afternoon – cannot say.
Remarks	We have occasionally more by the attendance of strangers, but I have stated the general and average attendance.
Dated	31 March 1851.
Signed	Henry Lawson, minister [1830–68]. 2 Catherine Street, [South Shields].

[The first wedding conducted in a nonconformist place of worship took place in the East Street Presbyterian church on 31 July 1837.]

20.15   English Presbyterian, Saville Street, South Shields (550.25)

Name	St John's Presbyterian Church. (English Presbyterian church. Holding the Westminster [Confession] standards.)
Erected	Before 1800. [1718. Replaced by new chapels in 1834, 1842 and 1877.]
Building	[Separate and entire. Exclusively used for worship.]
Sittings	About 100. Other about 460. Total [about 560].
Attendance 30 March	Morning 260. Total [260]. Evening 280. Total [280].

Average attendance   [Not given.]
Remarks   The congregation about the average size. The Sunday
school meets in the school house at 2.00pm.
Dated   30 March 1851.
Signed   John Storie, minister [1847–58].
[Wellington Terrace], South Shields.

20.16   English Presbyterian, Frederick Street, South Shields
(550.31)
Name   Laygate Presbyterian Church.
Erected   Opened [8] August 1849. [Cost £2,000.]
Building   Separate and entire. Exclusively [used for worship]
except as above.
Sittings   Free 336 (free let). Other 200 lets. Total [536].
Attendance 30 March   Morning 139 + 28 SS. Total 167.
Afternoon 122 + 23 SS. Total 145.
Average attendance   Morning 150 + 30 SS. Total 180.
Afternoon 150 + 30 SS. Total 180.
Remarks   Built in the Early English style from plan by [John]
Dobson Esq. of Newcastle, architect. Opened by James
Bamuld DD of Regent Square, London. About seven
hundred and sixty persons present at opening. First
minister Rev. William Traill. Removed September 1850
to Manchester. Pulpit now vacant. Not settled minister
since.
[PS]. Of the Sunday scholars, [204 in another hand]
part meet between the forenoon and afternoon services
in the vestry and part in the day school. At [the] same
hour, about 30 only attend the church; many of them
belong to different denominations.
Dated   31 March 1851.
Signed   James Stevenson, elder [senior partner in the Jarrow
Chemical Company].
Laygate House, South Shields.
[The first minister, William Traill 1849–50, was followed by W.G.
Allen 1851–56.]

20.17   Independent [Congregational], East Boldon (550.5)
Name   Independent Chapel.
Erected   Nil. [Opened 1829.]
Building   A hired house. [Exclusively used for worship.]

Sittings   All free sittings 80. Total [80].
Attendance 30 March   Morning 35 SS. Total 35.
                        Afternoon 21. Total 21.
                        Evening 41. Total 41.
Average attendance   Morning 30 SS. Total 30.
                        Afternoon 30. Total 30.
                        Evening 50. Total 50.
Dated   [Not given.]
Signed   George Nicholson, maneger (*sic*).
                East Boldon.

20.18   Independent [Congregational], Jarrow (550.44)
Name   Salem Chapel.
Erected   1844.
Building   Separate and entire. Exclusively [used for worship].
Sittings   Free 20. Other 80. Total [100].
Attendance 30 March   Afternoon 40 + 15 SS. Total 55.
                        Evening 50 + 10 SS. Total 60.
Average attendance   [Not given.]
Dated   31 March 1851.
Signed   James Sanderson, manager [agent].
                Jarrow, near South Shields.

20.19   Independent [Congregational], Wallis Street, South Shields (550.23)
Name   Congregational Chapel.
Erected   1824 [opened 5 April 1825] enlarged 1850. [Replaced
                by a new chapel in James Mather Street opened
                9 December 1884. Cost £1,000.]
Building   [Separate and] entire. [Exclusively used for worship.]
Sittings   [None fee.] Other 900. Total [900].
Attendance 30 March   Morning 271 + 81 SS. Total 352.
                        Afternoon (occasional).
                        Evening 301 + 40 SS. Total 341.
Average attendance   [Not given.]
Remarks   The evening of Sabbath the 30 March, an average by
                at least 100, the cause uncertain. Always service in
                the chapel on the afternoons of the first and second
                Sabbaths of each month. Occasional at other times.
Dated   31 March 1851.

Signed   David Moir, minister [1844–52].
             4 Laygate Terrace, South Shields.

20.20   Baptist, Barrington Street, South Shields (550.22)
Name   Baptist Chapel.
Erected   1821. [Foundation stone laid 25 April 1821. Cost £900.
             The chapel was closed on 3 April 1881 and replaced
             by a new chapel that opened in Westoe Road on
             5 April 1881.]
Building   [Separate and entire. Exclusively used for worship.]
Sittings   None free. Other 420. Total [420].
Attendance 30 March   Morning 195 + 29 SS. Total 224.
                        Evening 276. Total 276.
Average attendance   [Not given.]
Remarks   The congregation on Sabbath evening 30 March was
             below the average.
Dated   31 March 1851.
Signed   Richard Bottomley Lancaster, minister [1848–58].
             Westoe Terrace, South Shields.

20.21   Particular Baptist, Mile End Road, South Shields
            (550.26)
Name   Particular Baptists Meeting House.
Erected   1836.
Building   [Separate and entire. Exclusively used for worship.]
Sittings   Free 70. Other none. Total [70].
Attendance 30 March   Morning 40. Total 40.   No
                        Afternoon 40. Total 40.   ⎫ Sunday
                        Evening 40. Total 40.   ⎬ school
Average attendance   Morning 45 to 50. Total 50.
                        Afternoon 45 to 50. Total 50.
                        Evening 45 to 50. Total 50.
Remarks   This place is open for public worship three times
             every Lord's Day and on the Thursday evenings in
             each week. The sittings are all free, a plate stands at
             the door to receive what any person may think proper
             to give, out of which expenses are paid and what is
             over is given to the poor. The minister is a blacksmith.
             He receives no pay nor desires any, preaching morning
             and evening
Dated   31 March 1851.
Signed   George Lawson, minister [blacksmith].

Mile End Road, South Shields.
[George Lawson (1833–1891) eventually became the principal chain-
and anchor-smith in the area and also a ship-owner.]

20.22 Wesleyan Methodist, West Boldon (550.3)

Name	Wesleyan Methodist Chapel.
Erected	About the year 1801.
Building	Separate and entire building. [Exclusively used for worship.]
Sittings	Free 40. Other about 150. Total [190].
Attendance 30 March	[Not given.]
Average attendance	Morning no service.
	Afternoon 30. Total [30].
	Evening 40. Total [40].
Dated	30 March 1851.
Signed	John Edward Merriman, steward [blacksmith].
	West Boldon.

20.23 Wesleyan Methodist, Cleadon (550.8)

Name	Wesleyan Methodist preaching room.
Erected	Before 1800.
Building	[Separate and entire. Exclusively used for worship.]
Sittings	Free 70. Other none. Total [70].
Attendance 30 March	Afternoon 45. Total 45.
	Evening 21. Total 21.
Average attendance	Afternoon 60. Total 60.
	Evening 40. Total 40.
Dated	31 March 1851.
Signed	Thomas Burdon, leader [farmer].
	Cleadon, Sunderland.

20.24 Wesleyan Methodist, Harton (550.10)

Name	Harton Wesleyan Chapel.
Erected	Before 1800. [New chapel opened 7 April 1882.]
Building	[Separate and entire. Exclusively used for worship.]
Sittings	Free 110. Total [110].
Attendance 30 March	Evening 56. Total [56].
Average attendance	Morning 56 + 33 SS. Total 89.
Dated	31 March 1851.
Signed	James Urwin, steward [grocer and flour-dealer].
	Harton Groin, near South Shields, Durham.

20.25   Wesleyan Methodist Schoolroom, Harton Colliery (550.11)
Name   Wesleyan Preaching Room.
Erected   1846. [From 1848 met in an upstairs room in Isaac's
              Court. Chapel opened 1863. Replaced by a chapel
              opened on 7 April 1882.]
Building   [Not separate and entire or exclusively used for
              worship.]
Sittings   Free 70. Total [70].
Attendance 30 March   Afternoon 41 + 11 SS. Total 52.
                        Evening 47 + 15 SS. Total 62.
Average attendance   [Not given.]
Remarks   There is a day school in the room during the week.
Dated   31 March 1851.
Signed   Fenwick Todd, steward [shopkeeper].
              Harton Colliery, near So[uth] Shields, Durham.

20.26   Wesleyan Methodist, Hebburn (550.46)
Name   Hebburn Wesleyan Methodist Chapel.
Erected   1806.
Building   [Separate and entire. Not exclusively used for
              worship.*]
Sittings   Free 200. Other 88. Total [288].
Attendance 30 March   Afternoon 66 + 20 SS. Total 86.
                        Evening 64 + 40 SS. Total 104.
Average attendance   Afternoon 100 + 20 SS. Total 120.
                        Evening 100 + 40 SS. Total 140.
Remarks   *Part of this chapel is used for a day school.
Dated   30 March 1851.
Signed   Ralph Jameson, steward [coal engineer].
              Hebburn Colliery, Gateshead.

20.27   Wesleyan Methodist, Hedworth (550.48)
Name   None.
Erected   About the year 1815.
Building   [Not separate and entire, but exclusively used for
              worship.]
Sittings   Free 60. Total [60].
Attendance 30 March   Evening 17 + 20 SS. Total 37.
Average attendance   Evening 30 + 20 SS. Total 50.
Dated   31 March 1851.
Signed   Robert Gregory, leader [proprietor of houses].
              Hedworth Vale, near Jarrow.

20.28   Wesleyan Methodist, Jarrow (550.41)
Name   Wesleyan Chapel.
Erected   1806.
Building   [Separate and entire. Exclusively used for worship.]
Sittings   Free 152. Other 98. Total [250].
Attendance 30 March   Morning no service.
                        Afternoon 70 + 65 SS. Total 135.
                        Evening 120 + 60 SS. Total 180.
Average attendance   Morning no service
                        Afternoon 60 + 30 SS. Total 90.
                        Evening 170 + 30 SS. Total 200.
Dated   30 March 1851.
Signed   Leonard Dobson, society steward (blacksmith).
              Jarrow Coll[ier]y.

20.29   Wesleyan Methodist, Jarrow (550.49)
Name   Wesleyan.
Erected   Beforc 1847.
Building   Separate building. Place of worship and Sunday
              school.
Sittings   Free 50. Total [50]. Standing room 70.
Attendance 30 March   Morning 20 SS. Total 20.
                        Evening 42. Total 42.
Average attendance   Morning 30 SS. Total 30.
                        Evening 34. Total 34.
Remarks   [In another hand – 14 Jarrow Chapel missing.]
Dated   30 March 1851.
Signed   Joseph Swinburne, steward [farmer].
              Monkton, [Jarrow.]

20.30   Wesleyan Methodist, East Jarrow (550.34)
Name   Wesleyan Preaching Room.
Erected   The present room open[e]d for divine service, [29]
              Aug[us]t 1849.
Building   The room as a preaching room, the upper flat as a
              dwelling house. [Exclusively used for worship.]
Sittings   All free. Other d[itt]o.
Attendance 30 March   Morning 28 + 47 SS. Total 75.
                        Afternoon 38 SS. Total [38].
                        Evening 68. Total [68].
Average attendance   Morning and afternoon 50 to 60 + 50 SS.
                        Total [100–110].

Remarks   There are no other Sunday school or place of worship
at East Jarrow, but previous to opening this room,
service has been conducted in several dwelling houses
since 1843.
Dated   30 March 1851.
Signed   Joseph Reed, society steward [temperance hotelier].
11 Dean Street, South Shields.

20.31   Wesleyan Methodist, Wellington Street, South Shields
(550.40 and 550.14b)
Name   Wellington Street.
Erected   Before 1800.
Building   [Separate and entire. Exclusively used for worship.]
Sittings   Free 100. Other 350. Total 450.
Attendance 30 March   Morning 25 + 50 SS. Total [75].
Afternoon none.
Evening 52 + 35 SS. Total [87].
Average attendance   Morning 90 [? ink smudged] + 80 SS.
Total [170].
Evening 160 + 60 SS. Total [220].
Remarks   The reduction in the number of the congregation is
owing to a temporary separation.
Dated   31 March 1851.
Signed   William Chambers, minister [1850–51].
Chapter Row, [South Shields].

(550.14b) [Summary form]
Sittings   Free 76. Other 256. Total 332.
Dated   25 August 1852.
Signed   E[van] Hunter, registrar.
[12 Sackville Street, South Shields.]
(This chapel is in the registration district of So[uth] Shields. E. H.)

20.32   Wesleyan Methodist, Chapter Row, South Shields (550.38)
Name   Chapter Row.
Erected   1808. [Opened 21 February 1809. Cost £3,800,
restored 1865.]
Building   [Separate and entire. Exclusively used for worship.]
Sittings   Free 120. Other 1,000. Total [1,200].
Attendance 30 March   Morning 220. Total [220].
Evening 350. Total [350].
Average attendance   Morning and afternoon 480. Total [480].
Evening 900. Total [900].

Remarks   The reduction in the number of the congregation is
              owing to a temporary separation.
Dated   31 March 1851.
Signed   John Walters, minister [1849–51].
              Chapter Row, South Shields.

20.33   Wesleyan Methodist, Templetown, South Shields (550.33)
Name   Templetown.
Erected   1829.
Building   [Separate and entire. Exclusively used for worship.]
Sittings   Free 182. Other 100. Total [282].
Attendance 30 March   Afternoon 97 + 15 SS. Total 112.
                        Evening 81 + 26 SS. Total 107.
Average attendance   [Not given.]
Dated   31 March 1851.
Signed   Henry Martin, society steward.
              Cornwallis Square, South Shields.

20.34   Wesleyan Methodist, Westoe (550.24)
Name   Seamen's Hall (Wesleyan Branch Society).
Erected   [Not given.]
Building   [Not given.] [Used for] general purposes.
Sittings   Free 600. Total [600].
Attendance 30 March   Morning 300. Total [300].
                        Afternoon none.
                        Evening 340. Total [340].
Average attendance   [Not given.]
Dated   1 April 1851.
Signed   Stephenson Fletcher, society steward [grocer and tea
              dealer].
              73 King Street, South Shields.

20.35   Wesleyan Methodist, Whitburn (550.7)
Name   Wesleyan Methodist Chapel.
Erected   1806.
Building   [Separate and entire. Exclusively used for worship.]
Sittings   Free 100. Other 100. Total [200]. Standing room 30.
Attendance 30 March   Evening 150. Total [150].
Average attendance   [Not given.]
Dated   31 March 1851.
Signed   John Henderson, leader [farmer].
              Moor Lane, Cleadon, near Sunderland.

20.36   Methodist New Connexion, Johnson's Hill, West Holborn
(550.28a)
Name   West Holborn Chapel.
Erected   Probably 80 or a 100 years since for Lady
                Huntingdon's Connexion. Rebuilt by the Methodist
                New Connexion in 1814.
Building   [Separate and entire. Exclusively used for worship.]
Sittings   Free 100. Other 400. Total [500]. Standing room none.
Attendance 30 March   Morning 65 + 80 SS. Total [145].
                        Afternoon 180 + 86 SS. Total [266].
                        Evening 230. Total [230].
Average attendance   Morning 76 + 85 SS. Total [161].
                        Afternoon 225 + 85 SS. Total [310].
                        Evening 300. Total [300].
Remarks   A M[ethodist] New Connexion was founded in 1797.
                Congregation less at present than it has been for some
                time past. There being many sailors in it, it is always
                best in the winter months.
                Children of the Sabbath school attend the chapel on
                the first Sabbath morning of each month, and every
                Sabbath in the afternoon. Some of the older scholars
                also come in the evening.
Dated   30 March 1851.
Signed   Alexander McLustridge, first minister.
                41 Green Street, S[outh] Shields.
[From 1867 the building was occupied by Bristol Brethren (**20.47**).
New Zion Chapel opened 10 March 1859.]

20.37   Methodist New Connexion, Jarrow (550.45)
Name   Methodist New Connexion.
Erected   1840.
Building   [Separate and entire but not exclusively used for
                worship.]
Sittings   About 100. Other about 100. Total [about 200].
Attendance 30 March   [Not given.]
Average attendance   [Not given.]
Dated   30 March 1851.
Signed   James Dixon, trustee [block and mast-maker].
                Dunkirk Place, Jarrow.

20.38   Methodist New Connexion, Johnson Street, South Shields
(550.14c)
[Summary form]
Erected   [1785. Rebuilt 1814.]
Sittings   Free 100. Other 350. Total 450.
Dated   25 August 1852.
Signed   E[van] Hunter, registrar.
              [12 Sackville Street, South Shields.]

20.39   Primitive Methodist, Harton Colliery (550.35 and 550.12)
Name   Fauld Chapel, Harton Colliery.
Erected   1849.
Building   Separate and entire. Exclusively as a place of worship.
Sittings   Free 140. Total [140]. Standing room 40.
Attendance 30 March   Morning 40. Total [40].
                        Afternoon 112 SS. Total [112].
                        Evening 90. Total [90].
Average attendance   Morning 60 + 100 SS. Total 160.
Remarks   [In another hand. Missing: 35 Wellington Street,
              Wesleyans (**20.31**). 36 New Methodist, Johnson Street
              (**20.38**).]
Dated   31 March 1851.
Signed   Moses Supton, minister.
              5 East Catherine Street, South Shields.

(550.12)
Name   Primitive Methodist Chapel.
Erected   In 1848. [Rebuilt 1869.]
Building   [Separate and entire. Exclusively used for worship.]
Sittings   Free 140. Other none. Total [140]. Standing room none.
Attendance 30 March   Morning 35. Total [35].
                        Evening 60. Total [60].
Average attendance   [Not given.]
Remarks   In the winter evenings the chapel is generally
              crowded. The Sunday school is held in the afternoon.
Dated   6 April 1851.
Signed   Thomas Robson, chapel steward [coal miner].
              Harton Colliery.

20.40   Primitive Methodist, Hebburn Colliery (550.47)
Name   Primitive Methodist.
Erected   1848.

Building   Separate [and entire]. Exclusively as a place of worship.
Sittings   Free 177. Other 48. Total [225]. Standing room 50.
Attendance 30 March   Morning 180. Total 180.
                         Afternoon 209 SS. Total 209.
                         Evening 240. Total 240.
Average attendance   [Not given.]
Remarks   A Sabbath school meets in the afternoon.
Dated   30 March 1851.
Signed   Moses Supton, minister.
             5 East Catherine Street, South Shields, Durham.
[The first Primitive Methodist class meeting was held in 1823.]

20.41   Primitive Methodist, Cornwallis Street, South Shields
(550.21)
Name   Glebe.
Erected   1823. [Opened 24 August 1823. Cost £1,000, built mostly by the members. Inscription 'Hitherto the Lord hath helped us' (1 Samuel 7:12). Rebuilt 1865 and known as the Glebe Church.]
Building   Separate and entire. Exclusively as a place of worship.
Sittings   Free 300. Other 600. Total [900]. Standing room 150.
Attendance 30 March   Morning 150 + 230 SS. Total [380].
                         Afternoon 500. Total [500].
                         Evening 850. Total [850].
Average attendance   [Not given.]
Dated   31 March 1851.
Signed   Moses Supton, minister.
             5 East Catherine Street, South Shields.

20.42   Primitive Methodist, Templetown, South Shields (550.32)
Name   Templetown Chapel.
Erected   1840. [New chapel opened on 24 December 1859 in Corstorphine Town.]
Building   Separate and entire. Exclusively as a place of worship.
Sittings   Free 160. Other 160. Total [320]. Standing room 80.
Attendance 30 March   Morning 150. Total [150].
                         Afternoon 115 SS. Total [115].
                         Evening 300. Total [300].
Average attendance   [Not given.]
Dated   31 March 1851.

Signed   Moses Supton, minister.
            5 East Catherine Street, South Shields.

20.43 Primitive Methodist Schoolroom, Jarrow Colliery (550.43)

Name   Long Road Chapel, Jarrow Colliery.
Erected   1849.
Building   [Separate and] entire. Exclusively [used for worship].
                [In another hand, No.]
Sittings   Free 150. Total [150]. Standing room 30.
Attendance 30 March   Morning 58. Total 58.
                        Afternoon nil.
                        Evening 100. Total 100.
Average attendance   [Not given.]
Remarks   [Also] a week day school.
Dated   30 March 1851.
Signed   Thomas Tinkler, steward [coal miner].
                [High Row], Jarrow, Durham.

[In 1822 when the first Primitive Methodist preachers arrived in Jarrow it was described as 'an insignificant colliery village'. After a strike of Jarrow pitmen in 1832 seven were convicted and transported to Botany Bay (five of whom claimed connection with the Primitive Methodists). After the pit closed in 1852 the chapel was forced to close. W.M. Patterson, *Northern Primitive Methodism* (London, 1909), pp. 236–237.]

20.44 Wesleyan Methodist Association, Albion Street, South Shields (550.27)

Name   Albion Street Preaching Room.
Erected   [Not given.]
Building   Part of a house. [Not exclusively used for worship.]
Sittings   Free 130. Other 0. Total [130].
Attendance 30 March   Evening 26 + 3 SS. Total 29.
Average attendance   Evening about 70 + about 12 SS. Total 80
                        (*sic*) [82].
Remarks   This is the smallest attendance by a great deal, and
                is owing to the influence of certain individuals who
                have been 'whipping in' for their congregation. The
                congregation on [average?] has ranged during the five
                months from 120 to 60 odd.
Dated   30 March 1851.
Signed   Thomas L. Ainsley, manager.
                16 Saville Street.

20.45   Wesleyan Methodist Association, Salem Street, Westoe (550.20)

Name   Salem Chapel.

Erected   1824. [Enlarged and re-opened 2 September 1850.]

Building   [Separate and entire. Exclusively used for worship.]

Sittings   Free 300. Other 450. Total [750].

Attendance 30 March   Morning 200 + 100 SS. Total 300.

Afternoon 250 + 120 SS. Total 370.

Evening 560. Total 560.

Average attendance   [Not given.]

Remarks   This chapel was built by the [Particular] Baptists, and its present occupiers purchased it in the year 1836. Since that time it has been altered, so that it will now accommodate 350 persons more than it originally did.

Dated   31 March 1851.

Signed   John Martin, minister.

14 Winchester Street, South Shields.

20.46   Wesleyan Reformers, West Boldon (550.4)

Name   Wesleyan (Reform) Chapel.

Erected   [Not given.]

Building   A separate [and entire building]. Only [used] as a place of worship.

Sittings   Free 75. Other 0. Total [75].

Attendance 30 March   Evening [70]. Total 70.

Average attendance   [Not given.]

Remarks   This place has been opened on account of the disturbance theit (*sic*) is in the Methodist Connexion.

Dated   31 March 1851.

Signed   James Cruickshank, lockel (*sic*) preacher (bleacher).

Neir (*sic*) West Boldon.

20.47   Non-denominational, Ebenezer Christian Missionary Society, West Holborn (550.29)

Name   Ebenezer Mission Chapel, commonly known as Old Station Chapel.

Erected   Don't know. It was formerly the Railway Station.

Building   [Separate and entire.] A Sunday school is held in the chapel and also an evening school for adults.

Sittings   Free 210. Other 30. Total [240].

Attendance 30 March   Morning 25 + 64 SS. Total 89.

Afternoon 74 + 70 SS. Total 144.

Evening 150. Total 150.

Average attendance   Morning 25 + 60 SS. Total 85.

Afternoon 70 + 70 SS. Total 140.

Evening 200. Total 200.

Remarks   Although there are thirty sittings which are paid for, still the payment is optional, and the congregation can occupy any seats which they may choose.

Dated   31 March 1851.

Signed   Joseph D. Richardson, minister [1842–58].

54 Green Street, South Shields, Durham.

[This congregation was associated with the Bristol Brethren. On 30 September 1855 Ebenezer Chapel opened in Cambridge Street, and in 1867 it transferred to the former Countess of Huntingdon's chapel in Johnson's Hill (**20.36**). A new chapel was erected in Laygate Lane and opened on 19 July 1871.]

20.48   Roman Catholic, Cuthbert Street, Westoe (550.19)

[Simplified form]

Name   St Bede's Catholic Chapel.

Erected   Came into possession in 1849. [Opened 4 December 1849. New church in Westoe Lane opened on 22 August 1876.]

Building   [Separate and entire. Exclusively used for worship.]

Sittings   Free 270. Other 100. Total [370].

Usual attendance   Morning 370 + 60 SS. Total 430.

Afternoon 60 + 50 SS. Total 110.

Dated   [Not given.]

Signed   Richard Singleton, [Roman Catholic priest 1849–52].

Cuthbert Street, South Shields.

[Opened as Durham Hall, the building was previously occupied by the Bristol Brethren. In 1852 the estimated number of Roman Catholics in the area was 1,200.]

20.49   Latter-day Saints [Mormons], Windmill Hill, Westoe (550.30)

Name   None.

Erected   Since 1850.

Building   Mere room or part of a building. Exclusively for a place of worship.

Sittings   All free. (8 x 6 = 48). No standing room. Qualified to hold fifty persons.

Attendance 30 March   Morning 11. Total 11.

Afternoon 23. Total 23.
Evening 41. Total 41.

Average attendance   Morning 12. Total 12.
Afternoon 25. Total 25.
Evening 35. Total 35.

Dated   30 March 1851.
Signed   John Shewan, deacon.
No 1, Windmill Hill, [South Shields].

21. Stockton District (HO 129/541)
68 places of worship (and 26 in Yorkshire)

21.1   Church of England, St Cuthbert, Billingham (541.48)
Population 1851: 723 (township)

Name   Billingham Church; dedicated to St Cuthbert; of great
antiquity.
Consecrated   Before 1800. [Rebuilt 1846–47; restored and enlarged
1864–65, restored 1882–83.]
Endowment   Land £129 2s. Tithe £140 11s. Fees £5.
Sittings   In consequence of no pew book having been kept, it
is impossible to state the proportion of free and other
sittings. A considerable number are free, and but few
can be proved to be appropriated.
Total about 340.
Attendance 30 March   Morning 80 + 20 SS. Total 100.
Afternoon 14 + 22 SS. Total 36.
Average attendance   [Not given.]
Remarks   I really am unable to state the average number of
attendants, having no data on the […] upon which I
could rely. The attendance of Sunday scholars is less
on the present Sunday than usual, in consequence of
many being absent through illness.
It may be right to state that the major part of the
parishioners reside at a considerable distance from
the parish church, which is imperfectly warmed; this
causes the congregation to fluctuate, it being larger in
warm and fine weather, than at other seasons.
Dated   30 March 1851.
Signed   James John Cundill, curate of the parish [1842–53].

Billingham, Stockton-on-Tees.

Incumbent   [Thomas Ebdon 1831–52.]

{1857   Attendance 170. 27 communicants.}

[James Cundill's father, also called John Cundill, was the incumbent of St Margaret of Antioch, Durham (**16.9**).]

21.2   Church of England, St Michael, Bishop Middleham (541.93)

Population 1851: 1,719 (parish) 446 (township)

Name   Bishop Middleham Church.

Consecrated   Not known. [Restored 1843–46, 1905–06.]

Endowment   Tithe £149 15s by commutation. Glebe £44. Fees £4 10s.
                Easter offerings 10s.

Sittings   Free about 50 besides that for scholars. Other about
                500. Total [about 550].

Attendance 30 March   Morning believed to be 130. Total [130].
                Evening believed to be about 45. Total [45].

Average attendance   Morning supposed 80 SS. Total [80].
                Afternoon 40 SS. Total [40].

Dated   31 March 1851.

Signed   Thomas Henry Yorke, vicar [1813–68].
                Bishop Middleham, Ferryhill Station.
                For information not supplied above, see Surtees',
                History of Durham.

{1857   Attendance 50. 25 communicants.}   {B 57.}

[R. Surtees, *The History and Antiquities of the County Palatine of Durham* (London, 1823), vol. 3, pp. 1–24. Thomas Yorke was also the rector of St Cuthbert, Peasholme Green, York, 1818–59, where the Religious Census return recorded 'The rector who knows and manages the temporalities is non-resident, he living at Bishop Middleham in the County of Durham.' J. Wolffe (ed.), *Yorkshire Returns of the 1851 Census of Religious Worship* (York, 2000), vol. 1, p. 6.]

21.3   Church of England Schoolroom, Cornforth (541.94)

Population 1851: 1,040 (township)

Name   Cornforth Chapel.

Licensed   Used as a schoolroom and licensed [22 May 1840] by
                the Bishop of Durham for church services owing to
                the distance of the Cornforth people from the parish
                church of Bishop Middleham.

Erected   By subscription of Rev. T[homas] H[enry] Yorke, Mrs
               Surtees and others.
Endowment None.
Sittings   All free.
Attendance 30 March Evening about 25 + about 20 SS. Total 45.
Average attendance   Evening about 30 + about 15 SS. Total 40
               (*sic*) [45].
Dated   31 March 1851.
Signed   Andrew Robert Fausset, curate of Bishop Middleham
               [1847–58].
               Bishop Middleham, Ferryhill Station.
               Attested by me T[homas] H[enry] Yorke, vicar of
               Bishop Middleham.

[Holy Trinity, Cornforth, was consecrated on 21 September 1868.
Andrew Faussett succeeded Thomas Yorke as the rector of St
Cuthbert, Peasholme Green, York, 1859–1909.]

21.4   Church of England, St Peter, Bishopton (541.90)
Population 1851: 365 (township)

[Summary form]
Name   Bishopton.
Erected   About 1100. [Rebuilt and enlarged 1846–47 at the sole
               expense of the incumbent, Thomas Burton Holgate and
               his three sisters.]
Endowment [£165.]
Sittings   Free 100. Other 200. Total 300.
Usual attendance   Morning 140 + 55 SS. Total 195.
               Afternoon 45 + 50 SS. Total 95.
Dated   [Not given.]
Informant   Thomas Burton Holgate, vicar [1838–57].
               [The Vicarage, Bishopton.]
{1857   Attendance 180. 38 communicants.}   {B 11.}

21.5   Church of England, St John the Baptist, Egglescliffe (541.6)
Population 1851: 701 (parish) 493 (township)

Name   Egglescliffe Church dedicated to St John the Baptist.
               Ancient parish church.
Consecrated About AD 1400. The church was originally Norman
               and was restored or rebuilt early in the 14th century.
               [Restored 1864.]

Endowment Tithe £475 (rent charge). Glebe £285. [Total] £760.
Sittings   Free 40. Other 220. Total 260.
Attendance 30 March Morning 170 + 68 SS. Total 238.
                Afternoon 140 + 68 SS. Total 208.
Average attendance   Morning 180 + 70 SS. Total 250.
                Afternoon 120 + 70 SS. Total 190.
Remarks   £760 is the net income (rates only deducted) but £100
                per ann[um] for curate, and £80 for mortgage. Queen
                Anne's Bounty sh[ould] also be added which [...] to
                make net £580.
Dated   31 March 1851.
Signed   Henry Joseph Maltby, rector [1843–63].
                Egglescliffe, Yarm.
{1857   Attendance 250. 26 communicants.}   {B 20.}
[Henry Maltby (1814–1863), the fifth son of Edward Maltby, the
Bishop of Durham 1836–56, was also one of his seven chaplains.]

21.6   Church of England, St John, Elton (541.3)
Population 1851: 84 (parish)

Name   Elton Church.
Consecrated Before 1800.
Erected   Rebuilt in 1841 by the present incumbent. [Re-opened
                27 December 1841.] The Bishop of Durham [Edward
                Maltby] contributing £25. The Rev G[eorge] S[tanley]
                Faber £20. Miss H. Griffiths £10, and the incumbent
                the remainder. The total expense £500. Private £55.
                Total £500.
Endowment Tithe £155. Glebe £50.
Sittings   Free 25. Other 75. Total 100.
Attendance 30 March Morning 35. Total [35].
                Afternoon 12. Total [12].
Average attendance   Morning 35. Total [35].
                Afternoon 10. Total [10].
Dated   [Not given.]
Signed   Albany Wade, rector of Elton [1840–52].
                Stockton-on-Tees.
{1857   Attendance 35. 12 communicants.}   {B 3.}

21.7   Church of England, St Peter, Elwick Hall (541.75)
Population 1851: 187 (parish)

Name   Parish church dedicated to St Peter.
Consecrated Before 1800. [Repaired 1887, 1895.]
Endowment   Tithe £260. Glebe £205. Fees about £1.
Sittings   [None free.] Other 160. Total 160.
Attendance 30 March   Morning 106 + 30 SS. Total 136.
                      Afternoon 67 + 28 SS. Total 95.
Average attendance   [Not given.]
Dated   31 March 1851.
Signed   James Allan Park, minister [1828–71].
              Elwick Hall, Castle Eden, by Ferryhill.
{1857   Attendance 124. 55 communicants.}   {B 6.}

21.8   Church of England, St Luke the Evangelist, Ferryhill
(541.96)
Population 1851: 958 (township)

Name   Church of St Luke. District Chapelry [in the parish
              of Kirk Merrington. District created 15 July 1843.
              Replaced by a new church opened 20 September 1853.]
Consecrated 19 October 1829. Consecrated as an additional church.
Erected   By private benefaction or subscription. Private £700 [of
              which £175 from the Dean and Chapter of Durham].
              Total cost £700.
Endowment   Tithe £272.
Sittings   Free 256. Other 96. Total 352.
Attendance 30 March   Morning 84 + 52 SS. Total 136.
                      Afternoon 54 + 50 SS. Total 104.
Average attendance   [Not given.]
Dated   31 March 1851.
Signed   David Bruce, minister [1845–64].
              Parsonage, Ferryhill.
{1857   Attendance 110. 9 communicants.}   {B 53.}

21.9   Church of England, St John the Baptist, Greatham (541.54)
Population 1851: 651 (township)

Name   Parish Church, ancient.
Consecrated Before 1800. [Rebuilt 1792–93, enlarged 1855.]

Endowment Land £113 12s 6d. Tithe £57 5s. Glebe (house and
garden). Fees £2.
Sittings Free 31 + 20 (gallery singers). Benches for Sunday
school. Other 249. Total 300.
Attendance 30 March Morning 140 + 65 SS. Total 205.
Afternoon none.
Evening 118 + 48 SS. Total 166.
Average attendance Many of Sunday scholars to (*sic*) young
to attend regularly were prevented on the
30th by scarlatina.
Dated 3 April 1851.
Signed John Brewster, vicar [1818–60].
Greatham, Stockton-on-Tees.
{1857 Attendance 200. 60 communicants.} {B 23.}
[John Brewster's father (also called John Brewster) had previously
been the vicar of Greatham 1790–1818. John Brewster (junior) was
the curate to his father 1815–18, and from 1822 he was also the vicar
of Laughton with Wildsworth, near Gainsborough.]

21.10 Church of England, Holy Trinity, Grindon (541.5)
Population 1851: 267 (township)

Name Trinity Church, Grindon.
Consecrated 9 Nov[embe]r 1849 [6 November 1849]. In lieu of a
previously existing church.
Erected By private benefactions [Marquis and Marchioness of
Londonderry, Bishop of Durham £50, Diocesan Society
£50, Incorporated Church Building Society £40], also
produce of a bazaar, aided by donations, from the
church societies amounting to £120 and £40 of a rate.
Rate £40. Private £871. Total cost £911.
Endowment Land £20. Tithe £99. Glebe 13 acres. OPE £10 from
Lord Crewe's Trustees. Fees £1 5s. Other – the patron
gives me £60 per an[nu]m.
Sittings Free 120. Other 55. Total 175.
Attendance 30 March Morning 60 + 20 SS. Total 80.
Afternoon 22 + 13 SS. Total 35.
Average attendance This day I think about a summer and winter
average.
Dated 31 March 1851.
Signed William Cassidi, vicar [1841–82].
Grindon, Stockton-on-Tees.

{1857   Attendance 75. 22 communicants.}   {B 17.}
[Holy Trinity, the parish church of Grindon and situated at Thorpe
Thewles, was replaced by St James, Thorpe Thewles, consecrated on
17 May 1887.]

21.11   Church of England, St Mary Magdalene, Hart (541.74)
Population 1851: 920 (parish) 297 (township)

Name   An ancient parish church, dedicated to St Mary
                Magdalene.
Consecrated   [Not given.] [Chancel restored 1806; church restored
                1884–85, 1889–91, 1898.]
Endowment   Tithe £160. Glebe £80. Fees £3.*
Sittings   Free 25. Other 225. Total 250.
Attendance 30 March   Morning 116 + 20 SS. Total 136.
                Afternoon 40 + 15 SS. Total 55.
Average attendance   Morning 85 + 15 SS. Total 100.
                Afternoon 40 + 10 SS. Total 50.
Remarks   *Above I have stated the gross am[ount] of my income
                from the living of Hart, but out of that I have to
                pay £20 for collecting tithes and rates and £20 to the
                Gov[ernors] of Queen Anne's Bounty, which being
                deducted leaves the net income = £203.
Dated   31 March 1851.
Signed   William Gorst Harrison, vicar [1845–72].
                Hart, Hartlepool.
{1857   Attendance 100. 20 communicants.}   {B 20.}

21.12   Church of England, St Hilda, Hartlepool (541.64)
Population 1851: 9,503 (parish)

Name   St Hilda's, an old parish church.
Consecrated   [Rebuilt 1724, restored 1838, 1851–52, reseated 1866–67,
                restored 1869–70, 1893.]
Endowment   Land £70. Tithe £15. Other £10 (from Lord Crewe's
                Charity).   Fees £60. Easter offerings £10.
Sittings   Free 300. Other 212. Total 512 (the schools not
                included).
Attendance 30 March   Morning 450 + 346 SS. Total 796.
                Evening 506. Total 506.
Average attendance   Morning 400. Total 400.
                Evening 500. Total 500.

At church morning:

Boys' parish school   160. [In Prissick Street.]

Girls' parish school   100. [In Prissick Street]

Ragged Sunday school 66. [In Northgate
                              Street]

Crooks Free school   20. [In Crossgate.]

Total   346.

Dated   31 March 1851.

Signed   Robert Taylor, perpetual curate [1834–67].

           Hartlepool.

{1857   Attendance 600. 50 communicants.}   {B 232.}

[The Crooks School, Crossgate, was endowed from the estate of John Crooks (by his will of 1 September 1742). The Ragged School was opened in 1848.]

21.13   Church of England, St Mary, Long Newton (541.2)

Population 1851: 325 (parish)

Name   St Mary's in 1807. An ancient parish church, partly
           rebuilt.

Consecrated Before 1800. [Rebuilt 1806 and 1856–57.]

Endowment Tithe [commuted 1836] £602 15s 6d. Glebe £20. Easter
           offerings £1 16s 0½d.

Sittings   Free 50. Other 130. Total 180.

Attendance 30 March Morning 82 + 26 SS. Total 108.
                        Afternoon 53 + 20 SS. Total 73.

Average attendance   [Not given.]

Remarks   The amount returned for tithe corresponds with the
           receipts for 1850; £612 6s 4d being the original rent
           charge for which the tithes were commuted.

Dated   31 March 1851.

Signed   Thomas Hart Dyke, rector [1832–66].

           Long Newton, Darlington.

{1857   Attendance 80. 40 communicants.}   {B 9.}

[Thomas Dyke was also the rector of the family living of Lullingstone, Kent, 1828–66.]

21.14   Church of England, St Mary the Virgin, Norton (541.46)
Population 1851: 1,725 (parish)

[Summary form]
Name   Norton P[arish] C[hurch].
Erected   [Not given.] [Enlarged 1823, restored 1876, 1879 and
               1889.]
Endowment [£378.]
Sittings   Free 370. Other 730. Total 1,100.
Dated   24 August 1852.
Signed   Richard Langdale [registrar].
               [Workhouse, Stockton.]
Incumbent   [Francis Nathaniel Clements 1849–70.]
{1857   Attendance 450. 42 communicants.}   {B 32.}
[Francis Clements was the fifth son of the Earl of Leitrim.]

21.15   Church of England, St Cuthbert, Redmarshall (541.4)
Population 1851: 332 (parish) 76 (township)

Name   St Cuthbert's church. Ancient parish church. No
               chapelry in the parish.
Consecrated Before 1800. [Restored 1845–46 and 1893.]
Endowment Tithe £72 6s 3d. Glebe land (six acres and half) £20.
               Fees £1.
Sittings   Free (none). Other 150 to 160. Total 150–160 (besides
               school forms).
Attendance 30 March   Morning 100 + 21 SS. Total 121 or 125 (*sic*).
               Evening 70. Total 70.
Average attendance   Morning 240. Total [240].
               Evening 240. Total [240].
Dated   31 March 1851.
Signed   Thomas Austin, rector [1845–56].
               Rectory, Redmarshall, Stockton-on-Tees.
{1857   Attendance 70. 25 communicants.}   {B 15.}

21.16   Church of England, Holy Trinity, Seaton Carew (541.61)
Population 1851: 728 (township)

Name   Holy Trinity. Church of a district chapelry [created 21
               October 1841 out of the parish of Stranton].
Consecrated 29 September 1831 [by the Bishop of Chester] as an
               additional church. [In 1842 additional seating in the

chancel and gallery provided an additional seating for 246 (of which were free for 140 children).]

Erected   By private benefaction or subscription (of £1,691 14s 7d). Mrs [B. J.] Lawson of Boroughbridge Hall, Yorkshire endowed the church with £2,400 and, with her family, contributed £360 to its building and subsequent enlargement. Total cost *£1,691 14s 7d.

Endowment   Glebe £44. OPE £63 1s. Total endowment, as above, £125 15s.** Pew rents £14 14s. Fees £4.

Sittings   Free 304. Other 201. Total 505.

Attendance 30 March   Morning 172 + 55 SS. Total 227.
Afternoon 106 + 60 SS. Total 166.

Average attendance   Morning 240 + 55 SS. Total 295.
Afternoon 154 + 60 SS. Total 214.

Remarks   *Cost of building the church (in 1831) £819 19s 5d; of enlarging (1842) £871 15s 2d. Under the latter sum a clock (£120) is included, and also the East window stained glass (£70) given by the Rev. J. Lawson. But the cost of an organ (£50) also given by the Rev. J. Lawson, and enlarged by public subscription at the cost of £82 6s is not included under either item.

** The average surplus of pews rents (above the cost of church repairs and expense of maintaining divine service), is given on an average of three years. Fees on a three years average.

N.B. During the bathing season the church is often quite filled with the influx of visitors. Hence the average attendance for the whole year considerably exceeds the number given as attending divine service on 30 March.

Dated   30 March 1851.

Signed   John Lawson, minister [1835–90].
Seaton Carew, Stockton on Tees.

{1857   Attendance 300. 49 communicants.}   {B 18.}

21.17   Church of England, St Edmund, Sedgefield (541.81)
Population 1851: 1,362 (township) 2,192 (parish)

Name   St Edmund's church.

Consecrated   Not known. [Restored 1848–49, 1876–77.]

Endowment   [Not given.] [£1,802.]

Sittings   Free 276 (open sittings includes children's). Other 204.
              Total 480.
Attendance 30 March Morning 202 + 117 SS. Total 319.
                      Afternoon 132 + 117 SS. Total 249.
Average attendance   Morning 225 + 117 SS. Total 342.
                      Afternoons 140 + 117 SS. Total 257.
                      Evening none.
Dated   30 March 1851.
Signed   Thomas James Steele, curate [1847–57].
              Sedgefield, Ferryhill.
Incumbent   [Thomas Linwood Strong 1829–56.]
{1857   Attendance 220. 35 communicants.}   {B 52.}

21.18   Church of England, [St Mary, Embleton], Sedgefield
(541.84)
Population 1851: 113 (township)

Name   Consecrated chapel.
Consecrated Not known. [Chapel of ease from 1553.]
Endowment   [Not given.]
Sittings   None free. Other 70. Total 70.
Attendance 30 March Morning 22. Total 22.
                      Afternoon none.
                      Evening none.
Average attendance   Morning 28. Total 28.
                      Afternoon none.
                      Evening none.
Dated   30 March 1851.
Signed   Thomas James Steele, curate [1847–57].
              Sedgefield, Ferryhill.
Incumbent   [Thomas Linwood Strong 1829–56.]
{1857   Attendance 15. Communion never celebrated. No
              communion table.}

21.19   Church of England Schoolroom, Fishburn, Sedgefield
(541.79)
Population 1851: 261 (township)

Name   Licensed school room.
Licensed   Licensed about AD 1840. Place distant from parish
              church.
Sittings   Free 50. Other 50 [crossed out]. [100.]

Attendance 30 March   Morning none.
                        Afternoon 22 + 25 SS. Total 47.
                        Evening none.
Average attendance   Afternoon 35 to 40 + 24 SS. Total 59–64.
Dated   30 March 1851.
Signed   Thomas James Steele, curate [1847–57].
              Sedgefield, Ferryhill.
Incumbent   [Thomas Linwood Strong 1829–56.]
{1857   'Service every alternate Sunday'.}

21.20   Church of England, Licensed Room, Mordon, Sedgefield
(541.85)
Population 1851: 163 (township)

Name   Licensed room [in a farmhouse] at Mordon.
Licensed   About nine years ago. In a village at distance from the
              church.
Sittings   Free 40. Total 40.
Attendance 30 March   Services on alternate Sundays.
Average attendance   Morning none.
                        Afternoon 33. Total [33].
                        Evening none.
Dated   30 March 1851.
Signed   Thomas James Steele, curate [1847–57].
              Sedgefield, Ferryhill.
Incumbent   [Thomas Linwood Strong 1829–56.]

21.21   Church of England, All Saints, Great Stainton (541.92)
Population 1851: 117 (township)

Name   All Saints church. Ancient parish church.
Consecrated Before 1800. [Rebuilt 1876.]
Endowment   Tithe (commuted) £270. Glebe £80. Total £350.
Sittings   Free 20. Other 60. Total 80 (sittings for children not
              included).
Attendance 30 March   Morning 41 + 23 SS + 7 other children.
                        Total 71.
                        Afternoon 21 + 22 SS + 2 other children.
                        Total 45.
Average attendance   [Not given.]
Remarks   The above represents about the average attendance.
Dated   31 March 1851.

Signed   Thomas Louis Trotter, rector [1841–1892].
              Great Stainton, Bishopton, Stockton-on-Tees.

{B 2.}

21.22   Church of England, St Thomas, High Street, Stockton-on-Tees (541.34)
Population 1851: 10,172 (township)

Name   St Thomas. Built in the reign of Queen Anne [1710–12]
            and then made a separate parish. Previous to that time,
            it formed part of the parish of Norton.
Consecrated   Before 1800. [21 August 1712 and cost £1,600. Restored
            1893–95; enlarged chancel consecrated 19 July 1906.]
Endowment   [£274.]
Sittings   Free 663. Other 947. Total 1,610.
Attendance 30 March   Morning 1,000 + 240 SS. Total 1,240.
                        Evening 800. Total [800].
Average attendance   [Not given.]
Dated   31 March 1851.
Signed   Francis Joseph James, vicar [1847–74].
              Vicarage, Stockton-Tees.
{1857   Attendance 1,200. 110 communicants.}   {B 214.}

21.23   Church of England, Holy Trinity, Park Row, Stockton-on-Tees (541.33)
Population 1851: 10,459 (parish) 10,172 (township)

Name   The district parish church of the most Holy Trinity,
            Stockton-on-Tees.
Consecrated   In 1835 [22 December by the Bishop of St David's].
            In consequence of want of accommodation in the old
            parish church, the pews being mostly private. The
            parish was divided into ecclesiastical districts by
            Order in Council [20 September 1837] and a church
            was built and consecrated by the B[isho]p of Durham,
            who contributed […] to it in […] ch[urch] yard and
            glebe lands.
Erected   By grant from church societies and local subscriptions.
            There was debt upon the church which was taken up
            by 17 individuals […] each £100. In consideration of
            which they book and claim certain pews in the church.
            Subscriptions £5,000 to £6,000. Total cost £5,000 to

£6,000. [Replaced by a new church consecrated on 27 September 1906.]

Endowment Glebe £5. OPE £300 (for clergy ...). Fees, say £2. Easter offering £6 to £10.

Sittings Free 400. Other 800. Total 1,200.

Attendance 30 March Morning 200 to 300 + 200 SS. Total 450 (*sic*) [400–500].
Afternoon 150 + 150 SS. Total 300.

Average attendance Morning 300 + 200 SS. Total 500.
Afternoon 200 + 150 SS. Total 350.

Remarks In consequence of the proximity of the old church, families living in the district parish being allotted and hold pews in the mother church, attend church of the [...] from old associations. The attendance of the new church is small and because other persons had [...] of the church, difficulty of hearing worship to which mistake again [...].

Dated 1 April 1851.

Signed Richard Dutton Kennicott, incumbent of the Holy Trinity church [1845–86].
[Victoria Terrace], Stockton-on-Tees.

{1857 Attendance 700. 110 communicants.}

21.24   Church of England, All Saints, Stranton (541.56)
Population 1851: 4,008 (township)

Name Dedicated to All Saints. An ancient parish church.

Consecrated Before 1800. [Restored 1852, 1889.]

Endowment Land, set 1851 gross amount. Tithe £348 12s. Glebe (house and garden). Fees £17 10s.

Sittings Free 189. Other 230. Total 419.

Attendance 30 March Morning 300 + 80 SS. Total 380.
Afternoon 30 + 70 SS. Total 100.

Average attendance Morning 300 + 80 SS. Total 380.
Afternoon 30 + 70 SS. Total 100.

Remarks The above seems to be a fair return for the past year, but this parish being at the present time in the receipt (almost daily) of fresh inhabitants, at the new docks and harbour, it is impossible to convey an accurate idea of its spiritual wants.

Dated 4 April 1851.

Signed Rowland Webster, vicar of Stranton [1833–51].

Stranton, Hartlepool.
{1857   Attendance 130. 20 communicants.}   {B 126.}

21.25   Church of England, St Cuthbert, Trimdon (541.76)
Population 1851: 1,598 (parish)

Name   St Cuthbert's. Ancient parish church.
Consecrated   Before 1800. [Enlarged 1874.]
Endowment   Glebe £65. Fees (no account) about £5. Other £60 to
                £70.
Sittings   [None free.] Other 150. Total 150.
Attendance 30 March   Not counted.
Average attendance   Not counted.
Remarks   We have not been in the habit of counting our
                congregation, but the usual attend […] in about two
                weeks of the whole.
Dated   31 March 1851.
Signed   George Sproston, perpetual curate [1846–84].
                Trimdon, Ferryhill, Co[unty] of Durham.
{1857   Attendance 70. 16 communicants.}   {B 38.}

21.26   Church of England, St Mary Magdalene, Wolviston (541.49)
Population 1851: 750 (township)

Name   The perpetual curacy of St Mary Magdalen, Wolviston.
Consecrated   It is unknown. In the year 1716 it was rebuilt after
                having lain in ruins for perhaps more than 100
                years. It would undoubtedly be consecrated at first
                as a chapel of ease to the vicarage of Bellingham the
                mother church, from which, however, it has long been
                severed [since 1577] and rendered independent of
                it. [Replaced by St Peter, Wolviston, consecrated 21
                September 1876.]
Erected   I might here state that in 1830 the chapel underwent
                a considerable enlargement, with a gallery and tower
                at the cost of £470, raised by voluntary contributions
                entirely out of and beyond the chapelry. Cost, by
                individuals and societies £470 [of which £50 was from
                the Dean and Chapter of Durham]. Total cost £470.
Endowment   Glebe lands £182 (gross amount). OPE by an annual

rent charge of 9s paid from each farm in the chapelry,
and paid half-yearly, £12. Fees £1 (churching [of
women]).

Sittings   Free 130. Other 136. Total 266.

Attendance 30 March   Morning 57 + 26 SS. Total 83.
                        Evening lecture 87. Total 87.

Average attendance   Morning between 60 & 70 + about 24 SS.
                       Total 90 (*sic*). [84-94].
                       Evening lecture from 75 to 80. Total [75–80].

Remarks   The Sunday scholars do not attend church as such
                   in the evening, altho[ugh] they are assembled in the
                   morning and afternoon at the Sunday school.

Dated   31 March 1851.

Signed   Lancelot Christopher Clarke, perpetual curate [1823–
                   64].
                   Wolviston, Stockon-on-Tees.

{1857   Attendance 160. 30 communicants.}   {B 17.}

21.27   United Presbyterian, Hart Street, Hartlepool (541.71)

Name   United Presbyterian Chapel. [St John's Church
                   1882–83.]

Erected   1839. [Opened 1 January 1840.]

Building   A separate and entire building. Used exclusively for a
                   place of worship.

Sittings   Free [see remarks]. Other 500. Total [500].

Attendance 30 March   Morning 213. Total 213.
                        Afternoon 69 SS. Total 69.
                        Evening 230. Total 230.

Average attendance   [Not given.]

Remarks   Any poor person who applies for a sitting as such
                   may have a sitting (*gratis*) in any part of the chapel
                   that may be regarded most suitable, but no part of the
                   sittings is set apart exclusively for that purpose.

Dated   31 March 1851.

Signed   James Douglas, minister [1843–].
                   Maritime Terrace, Hartlepool.

21.28   United Presbyterian, West Row, Stockton-on-Tees (541.36)

Name   Presbyterian Chapel (Scotch Church).

Erected   1817.

Building   [Separate and entire. Exclusively used for worship.]

Sittings   Free 75. Other 178. Total [253].

Attendance 30 March   Morning 76 + 40 SS. Total 116.
                         Evening 105. Total 105.
Average attendance   Morning 80. Total 80.
                         Evening 140. Total 140.
Remarks   The number present at service last evening being
             from some cause less than usual. I have under the [...]
             an average for the last twelve months from a return
             furnished to me a few weeks ago. J. C.
Dated   31 March 1851.
Signed   James Caldwell, minister [1849–].
             Stockton-on-Tees.

[A secession occurred in 1843 and the congregation met in a room of the Temperance Society until they became the Congregational Chapel **(21.30)**.]

21.29   Independent [Congregational], Darlington Place, Hartlepool (541.70)

Name   Independent or (Congregational) Chapel.
Erected   In the year 1844. [Opened 26 April 1844. Cost £1,000.]
Building   [Separate and entire. Exclusively used for worship.]
Sittings   Free 60. Other 470. Total [530].
Attendance 30 March   Morning 400 + 50 SS. Total 450.
                        Evening 500. Total 500.
Average attendance   [Not given.]
Dated   31 March 1851.
Signed   Samuel Lewin, minister [1841–52].
             Hartlepool.

21.30   Independent [Congregational], Norton Road, Stockton-on-Tees (541.42)

Name   Congregational Chapel.
Erected   1845. [Opened 9 December 1845.]
Building   [Separate and entire. Exclusively used for worship.]
Sittings   Free 50. Other 500. Total [550].
Attendance 30 March   Morning 105 + 78 SS. Total 183.
                        Evening 120. Total [120].
Average attendance   [Not given.]
Remarks   The congregation is now rapidly increasing. Peculiar
             circumstances have hitherto operated to keep the
             number small, so that the adjoining statement
             will not serve as an estimate of the strength of

Congregationalism in the town beyond the present
time. The evening congregation smaller than usual by
some thirty persons.

Dated   31 March 1851.

Signed   John Chisman Beadle, minister.
King Street, Stockton-on-Tees.

[In 1843 the congregation seceded from the United Presbyterian
Chapel (**21.28**).]

21.31   Independent [Congregational], Woodham (541.86)

Name   None.

Erected   1840.

Building   [Not separate and entire or exclusively used for
worship.]

Sittings   All free.

Attendance 30 March   Morning none.
Afternoon 20. Total [20].
Evening none.

Average attendance   [Not given.]

Dated   31 March 1851.

Signed   Ann Thompson [married to Robert Thompson,
farmer].
Woodham Cottage, Rushyford, Durham.

21.32   Baptist, West Row, Stockton-on-Tees (541.37)

Name   Salem Chapel.

Erected   In the year 1840. [Originally a warehouse and
converted to a chapel in 1809.]

Building   [Separate and entire. Exclusively used for worship.]

Sittings   All free sittings. Standing room none.

Attendance 30 March   Morning 55 + 57 SS. Total 112.
Evening 63. Total 63.

Average attendance   [Not given.]

Dated   31 March 1851.

Signed   William Leng, minister [1823–69].
[John Street], Stockton-on-Tees.

21.33   Particular Baptist, Hartlepool (541.67)

Name   None.

Erected   N[ot] k[nown].

Building   Not a separate building. For worship only.

Sittings   Free 220 (free). Other (let) 30. Total [250]. Standing
room, no free space.
Attendance 30 March   Morning 100 + 40 SS. Total 140.
Afternoon 150. Total 150.
Evening 200 + 60 SS. Total 260.
Average attendance   Morning 100 + 40 SS. Total 140.
Afternoon 150. Total 150.
Evening 200 + 60 SS. Total 260.
Remarks   The room for which this return is made is the upper
story (*sic*) of a private building near the Victoria
Dock, Hartlepool. It is used by the Baptists on Sunday
mornings and evenings and for the accommodation
of seamen in the afternoon. The rent is paid by the
Baptists and the Bethel committee.
Dated   28 March 1851.
Signed   John Kneebon, minister.
Saint Hilda St[reet], Hartlepool.
[In 1845 the Particular Baptists in Hartlepool began with seven
members. In 1852 they opened a chapel to seat 500 people, which
cost £600.]

21.34   Particular Baptist Schoolroom, West Hartlepool
(541.58)
Name   None.
Erected   [Not given.]
Building   Not a separate building, nor an entire building, used
for a day school.
Sittings   All free sittings. Standing room none.
Attendance 30 March   Afternoon 35. Total [35].
Average attendance   Afternoon 35. Total [35].
Dated   29 March 1851.
Signed   John Kneebon, minister.
St Hilda Street, Hartlepool.

21.35   Wesleyan Methodist, Billingham (541.51)
Name   Wesleyan Chapel.
Erected   1836. [Cost £150.]
Building   [Separate and] entire building. Exclusively used for
worship.]
Sittings   Free 80. Other 44. Total [124].
Attendance 30 March   Morning 50 + 10 SS. Total [60].
Evening 43. Total [43].

Average attendance   Morning 50 + 30 SS. Total [80].
Dated   31 March 1851.
Signed   Robert Just, trustee [shopkeeper].
                 Billingham, Durham.

21.36 Wesleyan Methodist, Haverton Hill, Billingham (541.50)
Name   [Not given.]
Erected   About 1839.
Building   [Separate and entire. Exclusively used for worship.]
Sittings   Free 60. Total [60].
Attendance 30 March   Afternoon 28. Total [28].
Average attendance   Afternoon 30. Total [30].
Dated   30 March 1851.
Signed   Henry Smallwood, minister [1849–51].
                 Gosford Street, Middlesbrough.
[Henry Smallwood was also the minister of Middlesbrough (**21.79**)
and Picton (**21.80**).]

21.37 Wesleyan Methodist, Bishopton (541.91)
Name   Wesleyan Chapel.
Erected   1836.
Building   Separate building. Exclusively for a place of worship.
Sittings   Free 20. Other 70. Total [90]. Standing room 60.
Attendance 30 March   Evening 70. Total [70].
Average attendance   [Not given.]
Dated   31 March 1851.
Signed   Joseph Leighton, owner [brick maker].
                 Bishopton, n[ea]r Stockton-on-Tees, Durham.

21.38 Wesleyan Methodist, Bradbury (541.88)
Name   None.
Erected   Before 1800.
Building   [Not separate and entire or exclusively used for
                 worship.]
Sittings   Free 60. Total [60].
Attendance 30 March   No service.
Average attendance   Afternoon 60. Total [60].
Remarks   No service on 30 March 1851. Meetings once a
                 fortnight.
Dated   30 March 1851.
Signed   William Moody, manager [farmer].
                 Bradbury, near Sedgefield, Durham.

21.39   Wesleyan Methodist Schoolroom, Cornforth (541.95)
Name   Cornforth Schoolroom Wesleyan.
Erected   Before 1840.
Building   [Separate] and entire building. [Exclusively used for
             worship.]
Sittings   Free 60. Total [60].
Attendance 30 March   Morning 18 + 32 SS. Total 50.
Average attendance   Morning 18 + 16 SS. Total 34 (for each
             Sabbath).
Dated   30 March 1851.
Signed   James Anderson, steward [coal miner].
             West Cornforth Colliery, Ferryhill.

21.40   Wesleyan Methodist, Greatham (541.55)
Name   Wesleyan Chapel.
Erected   1834. [Cost £120.] [Replaced by new chapel,
             foundation stone laid 6 December 1882.]
Building   [Separate and] entire. Exclusively as a place of
             worship.
Sittings   Free 75. Other 53. Total [128].
Attendance 30 March   Afternoon 18. Total 18.
             Evening 19. Total 19.
Average attendance   Unknown.
Dated   31 March 1851.
Signed   Thomas Chrisp, steward [yeoman farmer].
             Greatham, Stockton-on-Tees.

21.41   Wesleyan Methodist, Northgate Street, Hartlepool (541.69)
Name   Wesleyan Chapel. [Northgate Church.]
Erected   Before 1800. [Replaced 1839, cost £1,800. Enlarged and
             reopened 13 November 1864. Cost £1,127 16s 6d.]
Building   [Separate and entire. Exclusively used for worship.]
Sittings   Free 161. Other 421. Total [582]. Standing room none.
Attendance 30 March   Morning 240 + 60 SS. Total 300.
             Evening [260]. Total 260.
Average attendance   Morning 300. Total 300.
             Evening 400. Total 400.
Dated   31 March 1851.
Signed   Matthew Carter, chapel steward (builder). [A trustee of
             the chapel.]
             [Northgate Street], Hartlepool.
Minister   [Thomas M. Fitzgerald 1849–52.]

21.42   Wesleyan Methodist, Hartlepool (541.68)
Name   Wesleyan Branch.
Erected   Since 1800.
Building   [Not separate and entire or exclusively used for
                worship.]
Sittings   Free 80. Total [80].
Attendance 30 March   Morning 80. Total [80].
                        Evening 120. Total [120].
Average attendance   [Not given.]
Remarks   We are seeking reform in Wesleyan Methodism.
Dated   21 March 1851.
Signed   George Middleton, preacher [grocer and tea dealer].
                Northgate Street, Hartlepool.

21.43   Wesleyan Methodist, Mordon, Sedgefield (541.89)
Name   None.
Erected   Before 1800.
Building   Part of a dwelling house. [Not exclusively used for
                worship.]
Sittings   Free 50. Total [50].
Attendance 30 March   Afternoon 37. Total [37].
Average attendance   Morning 50. Total 50.
Dated   31 March 1851.
Signed   Ann Tyson, occupier of the house.
                Mordon, Sedgefield, Durham.

21.44   Wesleyan Methodist, Stockton Road, Norton (541.47)
Name   Wesleyan Chapel.
Erected   1824. [Opened 22 December 1824.]
Building   [Separate and entire. Exclusively used for worship.]
Sittings   Free 80. Other 209. Total [289]. Standing room 50.
Attendance 30 March   Afternoon 153 + 87 SS. Total [240].
                        Evening 115. Total [115].
Average attendance   Morning 140 + 60 SS. Total 200.
Remarks   [In another hand] Norton church missing.
Dated   31 March 1851.
Signed   Peter Samuel, minister [1850–52].
                No 1 Brunswick Street, Stockton.

21.45   Wesleyan Methodist, Seaton Carew (541.63)
Name   Wesleyan Methodist Chapel.
Erected   1830. [Chapel enlarged 1878.]

Building   [Separate and entire. Exclusively used for worship.]
Sittings   Free 108. Other 42. Total [150].
Attendance 30 March   Evening 79. Total [79].
Average attendance   [Not given.]
Remarks   The average number will amount to 100.
Dated   31 March 1851.
Signed   George Dixon, steward [tailor].
                Seaton Carew, Durham.

21.46   Wesleyan Methodist, Sedgefield (541.83)
Name   Wesleyan Methodist Chapel.
Erected   1811.
Building   An entire building for public worship. Exclusively
                a place of worship with the exception of holding a
                Sabbath school in the same.
Sittings   Free 200. Other 104. Total [304].
Attendance 30 March   Morning 6 + 35 SS. Total 41.
                        Afternoon none.
                        Evening 84. Total 84.
Average attendance   Morning [not given]. Total 200.
Dated   30 March 1851.
Signed   Robert Simpson, trustee [teacher].
                Sedgefield, Durham.

21.47   Wesleyan Methodist, Fishburn, Sedgefield (541.80)
Name   Wesleyan Chapel.
Erected   1846.
Building   [Separate and entire. Exclusively used for worship.]
Sittings   Free 74. Other 26. Total [100].
Attendance 30 March   Morning 27. Total [27].
Average attendance   Morning 28. Total [28].
                        Afternoon 36. Total [36].
Dated   31 March 1851.
Signed   John Mann, steward [farmer].
                Bearley Carr, N[ea]r Trimdon, Durham.

21.48   Wesleyan Methodist, Brunswick Street, Stockton-on-Tees
(541.35)
Name   Brunswick Chapel.
Erected   1823. [Opened 31 December 1823.]
Building   [Separate and entire. Exclusively used for worship.]
Sittings   Free 286. Other 672. Total [958].

Attendance 30 March   Morning 405 + 90 SS. Total 495.
                        Evening 406. Total 406.
Average attendance   Morning 475 + 95 SS. Total 570.
                        Evening 560. Total 560.
Dated   31 March 1851.
Signed   William Bolam Brayshay, steward [chemist and
                druggist].
                No 36 High Street, Stockton-on-Tees.

21.49   Wesleyan Methodist, Middleton, Stranton (541.60)
Name   Wesleyan Chapel.
Erected   1835.
Building   [Separate and entire. Exclusively used for worship.]
Sittings   Free 75. Other 127. Total [202].
Attendance 30 March   Afternoon 20. Total [20].
Average attendance   Afternoon 50. Total [50].
Dated   5 April 1851.
Signed   William Jenkinson, chapel steward [slater].
                [Northgate Street], Hartlepool, Durham.

21.50   Wesleyan Methodist, New Trimdon (541.78)
Name   Wesleyan Methodist Chapel.
Erected   1846.
Building   Entire but not separate. [Exclusively used for worship
                in two houses.]
Sittings   Free 100. Other 90. Total [190]. Standing none.
Attendance 30 March   Afternoon 50. Total [50].
                        Evening 64. Total [64].
Average attendance   [Not given.]
Dated   30 March 1851.
Signed   Matthew Caygill, steward [grocer and boot and
                shoemaker].
                [New] Trimdon, Durham.

21.51   Wesleyan Methodist, Wolviston (541.52)
Name   Wesleyan Chapel.
Erected   1829.
Building   [Separate and entire. Exclusively used for worship.]
Sittings   Free 100. Other 48. Total [148]. Standing room 15.
Attendance 30 March   Afternoon 60 + 18 SS. Total 78.
                        Evening 70 + 24 SS. Total 94.
Average attendance   Afternoon 60 + 24 SS. Total 84.
                        Evening 80 + 25 SS. Total 105.

Dated   31 March 1851.
Signed   John Stephenson, leader and superintendent [farmer].
             [White House], Newton Bewley, near Wolviston.

21.52   Wesleyan Methodist, Woodham (541.87)

Name   None.
Erected   Preaching begun in the year 1831.
Building   [Not separate and entire or exclusively used for
             worship.]
Sittings   Free 40. Total [40].
Attendance 30 March   Morning 18. Total 18.
Average attendance   Afternoon 20. Total 20.
Dated   30 March 1851.
Signed   William Boyd [farmer].
             Woodham Burn, near Ferryhill, Durham.

21.53   Primitive Methodist, Ferryhill (541.97)

Name   [Not given.]
Erected   Dwelling house used for worship.
Building   [Not separate and entire or exclusively used for
             worship.]
Sittings   [Not given.]
Attendance 30 March   Morning SS none.
                        Evening 39. Total [39].
Average attendance   [Not given.]
Dated   31 March 1851.
Signed   George Legar.
             Ferryhill, Durham.

21.54   Primitive Methodist, Knowles Street, West Hartlepool
(541.59)

Name   None. [Primitive Methodist crossed out.]
Erected   Since 1800.
Building   [Separate and entire but not exclusively used for
             worship.]
Sittings   Free 90. Other 32. Total [122]. Standing room 30.
Attendance 30 March   Morning 105 SS. Total [105].
                        Afternoon 50. Total [50].
                        Evening 120. Total [120].
Average attendance   Morning 50 SS. Total [50].
                        Afternoon 50. Total [50].
                        Evening 100. Total [100].

Dated   31 March 1851.
Signed   Samuel Russell, leader [joiner].
             Pilot Street, West Hartlepool.

21.55   Primitive Methodist, The Croft, Chapel Street, Hartlepool
(541.65)
Name   None. [Croft Chapel.]
Erected   In 1830. [Enlarged 1833. New chapel in Brougham
             Street, opened in December 1851, cost £2,700.]
Building   [Separate and entire. Exclusively used for worship]
             except for Sabbath school.
Sittings   Free 100. Other 200. Total [300].
Attendance 30 March   Morning 180 + 130 SS. Total 210 (*sic*) [310].
                        Afternoon 130 SS. Total 130.
                        Evening 350. Total 350.
Average attendance   Morning 180 + 130 SS. Total 210 (*sic*) [310].
                        Afternoon 130 SS. Total 130.
                        Evening 350. Total 350.
Dated   31 March 1851.
Signed   John Wilson, minister.
             William Street, Hartlepool, Durham.

21.56   Primitive Methodist, Maritime Street, Stockton-on-Tees
(541.44)
Name   Primitive Methodist Chapple (*sic*). [Ranters' Building.]
Erected   1825.
Building   [Separate and entire. Exclusively used for worship.]
Sittings   Free 140. Other 144. Total [284].
Attendance 30 March   Morning 160 + 60 SS. Total 220.
                        Afternoon 75 SS. Total 75.
                        Evening 260. Total 260.
Average attendance   [Not given.]
Dated   30 March 1851.
Signed   Thomas Corner, society steward [grocer].
             [18] Garden Place, [Maritime Street], Stockton-on-Tees.
[The first Primitive Methodist camp meeting was held in the
area in 1821. Thomas Corner was also associated with the Non-
denominational chapel (**21.61**).]

21.57   Primitive Methodist, Trimdon Grange (541.77)
Name   Trimdon Grange a dwelling house.
Erected   1844.

Building   [Not separate and entire or exclusively used for
              worship.]
Sittings   [None free.] Other 150. Total [150].
Attendance 30 March   Morning 92 SS. Total 92.
                       Afternoon 90. Total 90.
                       Evening 112. Total 112.
Average attendance   [Not given.]
Dated   30 March 1851.
Signed   David Grieves, manager [coal miner].
              No 78 Trimdon Grange.

**21.58   Wesleyan Methodist Association Schoolroom, Darlington
Street, Hartlepool** (541.73)
Name   Mr [George] Bell's Schoolroom.
Erected   1801. [In 1851 the congregation planned to erect a
              chapel to seat about 400 people.]
Building   [Separate and entire but not exclusively used for
              worship.]
Sittings   Free 160. Other none. Total [160]. Standing room 40.
Attendance 30 March   Morning 67 + 42 SS. Total 109.
                       Evening 103 + 26 SS. Total 129.
Average attendance   Morning 65 + 40 SS. Total 105.
                         Evening 150 + 25 SS. Total 175.
Remarks   This place was opened by the above denomination
              for public worship on Sunday, 24th day of November
              1850, and during the four months it has been opened,
              there have been 53 public services held.
Dated   30 March 1851.
Signed   Joseph Richardson, secretary and class leader [over-
              man at lead mine].
              Middleton, Hartlepool, Durham.

**21.59   Wesleyan Methodist Association, Regent Street, Stockton-
on-Tees** (541.38)
Name   Regent Street Chapel.
Erected   1836.
Building   [Separate and entire. Exclusively used for worship.]
Sittings   Free 200. Other 320. Total [520]. Standing room none
              but the isles (*sic*).
Attendance 30 March   Morning 130 + 98 SS. Total 228.
                       Afternoon 76. Total 76.
                       Evening 140. Total 140.

Average attendance   Morning 130 + 85 SS. Total 215.
Afternoon 85 SS. Total 85.
Evening 200. Total 200.
Remarks   No attendance of scholars in the afternoon in
consequence of a Love Feast for the members of the
church, 76 of whom attended.
Dated   31 March 1851.
Signed   Richard Hoskin, minister.
20 East Street, Stockton-on-Tees.
[The Methodist Love Feast was a communal meal of plain cake and
water, with singing and testimony, and based on the Agape of the
early church. The Love Feast was revived by the Moravians and
adopted by the Methodists.]

21.60   Wesleyan Reformers, Pilot Street, West Hartlepool (541.57)
Name   Non (*sic*).
Erected   No. [A chapel to seat 500 was opened on 8 June
1851. It was rebuilt in Church Street to seat 600, cost
£732 and was enlarged in 1862. Another Wesleyan
Reformers' chapel was opened in Mill Lane and had
opened on 6 April 1851.]
Building   [Not separate and entire or exclusively used for
worship.]
Sittings   [Not given.]
Attendance 30 March   Afternoon 80. Total [80].
Evening 90. Total [90].
Average attendance   [Not given.]
Dated   31 March 1851.
Signed   William Marwood, manager (treasurer).
No 30 Pilot Street, West Hartlepool, Durham.

**21.61   Non-denominational, Seamen's Bethel, Finckle Street,
Stockton-on-Tees** (541.45)
Name   Bethel for Seamen and others.
Erected   Before 1800.
Building   [Not separate and entire or exclusively used for
worship.]
Sittings   Free about 100. Total [100].
Attendance 30 March   Afternoon 64. Total 64.
Average attendance   Afternoon 100. Total 100.
Remarks   Of the 64 attending on Sunday, 30 March 1851, about
10 were sailors, 20 sailor's wives. About three fourths

of the no. of persons attending here are members of other churches or frequenters of other places of worship. (The denomination is described as Wesleyan Association, Primitive Methodist, Baptist, Presbyterian and Congregational.)

Dated   [Not given.]
Signed   Thomas Corner, secretary [grocer].
            Garden Place, [Maritime Street], Stockton-on-Tees.

[Thomas Corner was also associated with the Primitive Methodist chapel **(21.56)**.]

21.62   Society of Friends [Quakers], Seaton Carew (541.62)
[On a Nonconformist form]
Name   Friends Meeting House.
Erected   1841. [Opened 8 August 1841.]
Building A separate and entire building. Used exclusively as a place of worship.
Sittings 50 sittings all free.
Usual attendance   Morning from 10 to 30. Total [10–30].
Remarks   [The attendance of between 10 and 30] in summer but none during the winter months.
Dated   [Not given.]
Informant Edward Spence, registrar.
            [Friargate], Hartlepool.

21.63   Society of Friends [Quakers], Mill Lane, Stockton-on-Tees (541.39 and 541.40)
(541.39) [On a Nonconformist form]
Name   Friends Meeting House.
Erected   *Before 1800. [Erected 1814. Cost £1,800.]
Building [Separate and entire. Exclusively used for worship.]
Sittings Free 700. Total [700]. **Standing room.
Attendance 30 March   Morning 53. Total [53].
                        Afternoon 35. Total [35].
Average attendance   Morning 53. Total [53].
                        Afternoon 35. Total [35].
Remarks   *The present Meeting House was built in 1814 in lieu of one not far distant. Built before 1800.
            **All the sittings are free.
Dated   31 day of third mo[nth] (March) 1851.
Signed   Alfred Brady, clerk to the meeting [bank manager].

Stockton-on-Tees.

(541.40) [On a Quaker form]
Erected   Before 1800.
Building   [Separate and entire. Exclusively used for worship.]
Sittings   Floor area 1,830 [square feet].   460 sittings.
              Gallery [area] 960 [square feet].   240 sittings.
                                                     Total 700.
Attendance 30 March   Morning 53. Total [53].
                      Afternoon 35. Total [35].
Dated   11th day of fourth month 1851.
Signed   John Beaumont Pease [woollen merchant].
              of Darlington monthly meeting.
              North Lodge, Darlington.
[John Beaumont Pease (1803–1873) was also involved with several other Quaker meeting houses (**13.59**, **13.60**, **21.92**, **23.30** and **23.56**).]

21.64   Roman Catholic, Middlegate Street, Hartlepool (541.72)
Name   St Hilda.
Erected   1832. [Inscription, 'This building was erected by John Wells, and presented by him to the Roman Catholics, for the use of their religious exercises, at the request of Mary, his wife, AD 1834.' A new church dedicated to St Mary, was opened on 8 August 1851, and cost nearly £4,000.]
Building   [Separate and entire. Exclusively used for worship.]
Sittings   Free 170. Other 200. Total 370. Standing room 60.
Attendance 30 March   Morning 460 + 130 SS. Total 590.
                      Evening 300. Total [300].
Average attendance   [Not given.]
Dated   31 March 1851.
Signed   William Knight, priest [1834–1851].
              Hartlepool, Durham.
[In 1852 the estimated number of Roman Catholics in the area was 1,000.]

21.65   Roman Catholic, Sedgefield (541.82)
Name   St Joseph's Chapel.
Erected   Since 1800. Purchased by the bishop about 12 or 14 years ago, as far as I remember, and built a few years previously.

Building   Separate (but adjoining the priests' residence).
             Exclusively [used for worship].
Sittings   Free* (comfortably) 100.
Attendance 30 March   [Not given.]
Average attendance   Morning on average nearly 80 + 20 SS.
             Total 100.
             Afternoon.**
             Evening about 45 + 15 SS. Total 60.
Remarks   *I have termed them all free sittings, as everyone has
             a seat whether he can pay or not, but all who can pay
             something more or less.
             **As I have two chapels [at Sedgefield and New
             Thornley] and service is alternately at the two
             morning and evening.
             ***I am the parish priest, but strictly speaking [I] am
             administrator of the parish until certain hierarchical
             arrangements are completed.
Dated   29 March 1851.
Signed   Robert Suffield, Roman Catholic priest.***
             St Joseph's Chapel House, Sedgefield, Ferryhill, Co.
             Durham.
[Robert Suffield was also a priest at New Thornley (**17.32**). In 1852
the estimated number of Roman Catholics in the area was 150.]

21.66   Roman Catholic, Norton Road, Stockton-on-Tees (541.43)
Name   St Mary's Catholic Chapel.
Erected   1842. [Opened 7 May 1842. Cost about £7,000.
             Enlarged 1866, 1870, 1908.]
Building   Separate [and entire. Exclusively used for worship.]
Sittings   [All] about 300. Total [300].
Attendance 30 March   Morning 250. Total 250.
             Evening 200. Total 200.
Average attendance   [Not given.]
Dated   31 March 1851.
Signed   Robert Cornthwaite, Roman Catholic priest [1847–52].
             St Mary's, [Major Street], Stockton-on-Tees.
['Robert Cornthwaite (1818–1890)', *ODNB*, vol. 13, pp. 464–465.
He was the Bishop of Beverley 1861–78 and then the first Bishop
of Leeds 1878–90. 'Cornthwaite was regarded not only as an able
administrator but as a man of sanctity and prayer who hid a tender
heart beneath a cool and reserved exterior.' *ibid.*, p. 465.

In 1852 the estimated number of Roman Catholics in the area was 740.]

21.67   Unitarian, High Street, Stockton-on-Tees (541.41)
Name   Unitarian Chapel.
Erected   Before 1800. [1699, rebuilt 1753.]
Building   [Separate and entire. Exclusively used for worship.]
Sittings   Free.* Other 240. Total [240].
Attendance 30 March   Morning 44.** Total 44.
                       Evening 31. Total 31.
Average attendance   Morning 70. Total 70.
                       Evening 70. Total 70.
Remarks   *There are no seats bearing the name of free sittings,
              but one half of them at least are free.
              **The number of attendants this day being so much
              less than those stated as the average arises from the
              congregation being at present without a minister.
Dated   31 March 1851.
Signed   Thomas Richmond, treasurer [retired iron merchant].
              Smithfield, Stockton-on-Tees.
Minister   [James McDowall 1844–51.]

21.68   Latter-day Saints [Mormons] Schoolroom, High Street, Hartlepool (541.66)
Name   Bygate's Schoolroom.
Erected   Before 1800.
Building   [Not separate and entire or exclusively used for
              worship.]
Sittings   Free (free). Other (free). Standing room none.
Attendance 30 March   Morning 30. SS none. Total [30].
                       Evening 40. Total [40].
Average attendance   Morning 50. SS none. Total [50].
                       Afternoon 50. Total [50].
Dated   30 March 1851.
Signed   Robert Collingwood Blackett, elder [shipwright].
              Silver Street Folly, Hartlepool, Durham.

22. Sunderland District (HO 129/549)
72 places of worship
Population 1851: 71,004 (total of Bishopwearmouth, Monkwearmouth and Sunderland)

22.1   Church of England, St Michael and All Angels, High Street, Bishopwearmouth (549.22)
Population 1851: 35,035 (parish)

Name	St Michael. The ancient parish church of Bishopwearmouth.
Consecrated	Before 1800. [Re-ordered 1806–08, enlarged 1849–50 (re-opened 10 March 1850), restored 1872, 1874–75.]
Erected	The church was enlarged in 1850 by private subscriptions and grants from societies. Private £1,750. Total cost £1,750.
Endowment	Tithe £1,293. Glebe £417. Fees £148.
Sittings	Free 546. Other 800. Total 1,346.
Attendance 30 March	Morning 600 + 213 SS. Total 813.
	Afternoon 126 + 210 SS. Total 336.
	Evening 700. Total 700.
	(On average not less than 1,200 people attend the church services during the Sunday.)
Average attendance	Morning 800 + 200 SS. Total 1,000.
	Afternoon 150 + 230 SS. Total 380.
	Evening 1,000. Total 1,000.
Remarks	The church was enlarged in 1850 and 528 free sittings were added for the use of the poor. Another new church [St Paul, Hendon, consecrated 15 November 1852] is also about to be built in the parish. There are three curates in the parish, whose stipends are paid by the rector which, with other outgoings, exceed £800 a year.
Dated	31 March 1851.
Signed	John Patrick Eden, rector [1848–64]. Rectory, [2 High Street], Bishopwearmouth, Sunderland.

{1857   Attendance 1,000. 220 communicants at festivals.
80 ordinary throughout the parish.}   {B 620.}
[An additional 534 new sittings were provided in the enlargement of

1850, and the building was further enlarged in 1933. It became the Sunderland Minster Church of St Michael in 1998. For a map of Bishopwearmouth, Monkwearmouth, Sunderland and the adjoining parishes see M. Meikle and C. Newman, *Sunderland and its Origins* (Chichester, 2007), pp. 42, 82.]

22.2   Church of England, Ryhope Chapel, Bishopwearmouth (549.39)
Population 1851: 475 (township)

Name	Ryhope Chapel. Chapel of ease to Bishopwearmouth.
Consecrated	In [24 July] 1827, as the chapel of an intended chapelry district. [District chapelry created 18 February 1854.]
Erected	By local subscriptions aided by a grant from Queen Anne's Bounty. Total cost about £700.
Endowment	Glebe (house). OPE £100 from the rectory of Bishopwearmouth. Additional £100 from Ecclesiastical Commissioners. Pew rents £10. Fees £2 10s.
Sittings	Free 90. Other 90. Total 180.
Attendance 30 March	Morning 92 + 18 SS. Total [110].
	Evening 70. Total 70.
Average attendance	Morning 85 + 25 SS. Total 110.
	Evening 90. Total 90.
Dated	31 March 1851.
Signed	William Wilson, minister [1843–80].
	Ryhope Chapel, Sunderland.
Incumbent	[John Patrick Eden, 1848–64.]
{1857	Attendance 100. 12 communicants.} {B 16.}

[Replaced by St Paul, Ryhope, consecrated on 10 August 1870.]

22.3   Church of England, St Andrew, Deptford, Bishopwearmouth (549.2)
Population 1851: 6,193 (township)

Name	St Andrew. Church of a district chapelry. [Created on 23 May 1844 out of the parish of St Michael, Bishopwearmouth.]
Consecrated	14 Dec[ember] 1841. As an additional church.
Erected	By grants from Her Majesty's Comm[issioner]s for building churches (£500); from Church Building

Society (£500); from diocesan [church building] society (£50); and by local subscriptions (£1,449 12s 6d). Total cost £2,499 12s 6d.

Endowment OPE £350. Pew rents £10. Fees £6.

Sittings Free 754. Other 305. Total 1,059.

Attendance 30 March Morning 234 + 119 SS. Total 353.
Evening 162. (SS no attendance.) Total 162.

Average attendance Morning 250 + 150 SS. Total 400.
Evening 280. (SS no attendance.) Total 280.

Remarks Out of my income I have £80 to pay towards my curate's salary, to meet a grant from the Curates' Aid Society; besides £10 a year in support of the services of the church, and £25 a year house rent and house, there being no parsonage. The above return is as accurate as I can make it. The attendance on Sunday evening last was much below the usual average. In the morning also both the general congregation and the number of scholars was under the average.

Dated 31 March 1851.

Signed William Henry Bulmer, incumbent [1843–69]. Deptford, Sunderland, Durham.

{1857   Attendance 450. 45 communicants.}   {B 146.}

[From the Church Pastoral Aid Society annual returns (1852–53) the population was 8,000; the income of the living was £366; the stipend paid by the incumbent £30 and with a grant of £50 from CPAS to support a lay assistant.]

22.4 Church of England, St Thomas, John Street, Bishopwearmouth (549.21)
Population 1851: 7,005 (township)

Name St Thomas, district church.

Consecrated 14 October 1829. As an additional church [chapel of ease] to the Parish of Bishopwearmouth. [District created out of the parish of Bishopwearmouth, 23 May 1844.]

Erected I believe and apart from the Church Commissioners [£4,570] and private benefaction and subscriptions. [Total cost £5,576.]

Endowment [£300.]

Sittings Free 500. Other 500. Total 1,000.

Attendance 30 March [Not given.]
Average attendance   [Not given.]
Remarks   These questions I cannot answer satisfactorily not
having kept any account of numbers.
Dated   31 March 1851.
Signed   Richard Skipsey, incumbent [1844–68].
[8 John Street], Bishopwearmouth, Sunderland.
{1857   Attendance 500. 40 communicants.}   {B 69.}

22.5   Church of England, St Mary, South Hylton,
Bishopwearmouth (549.1)
Population 1851: 546 (township) [The South Hylton area was also
called Ford]

Name   South Hylton Church. First a chapel of ease to
Bishopwearmouth, now a district chapelry, separated
by the Ecclesiastical Commissioners in 1849.
Consecrated   About 1820 [15 February 1821 by the Bishop of
St David's], as a chapel of ease to [the] parish of
Bishopwearmouth.
Erected   By Rev. Robert Gray, then curate of Bishopwearmouth,
and late Rector of Sunderland.
Endowment   OPE £100 (and in 3 per cents). Pew rents £12. Fees £6.
Sittings   Free 200. Other 200. Total 400.
Attendance 30 March   Morning 150 + 20 SS. Total 170.
Evening 250. Total 250.
Average attendance   Morning 120 + 20 SS. Total 140.
Evening 140. Total 140.
Remarks   The congregations vary much; but generally much
larger in the evening than the morning. The Sunday
scholars in the morning are few; in the afternoon, the
number varies from 50 to 70; but there is no service
then in the church; in the evening many attend, but
not as scholars.
Dated   1 April 1851.
Signed   Joseph Law, incumbent [1843–72].
South Hylton, Sunderland.
{1857   Attendance 150. 20 communicants.}   {B 48.}
[The building was destroyed by fire on 9 March 1878 and a new
church consecrated on 21 June 1880.
Robert Gray was the curate of Bishopwearmouth 1816–19 and rector
of Sunderland 1819–38. He was the curate to his uncle Robert Gray,

1805–27 (the Bishop of Bristol 1827–34). Robert Gray, the son of the Bishop of Bristol, was vicar of St Thomas, Stockton on Tees, 1845–47 and Bishop of Cape Town 1847–72.]

22.6   Church of England, St Peter, Church Street, Monkwearmouth (549.57)
Population 1851: 3,366 (township)

Name   St Peter's Parish Church, one of the oldest in England [dedicated AD 674.] (Sir Hedworth Williamson Bart MP, patron.)

Consecrated Before 1800. King Ecgfrid built, at the instigation of Abbot Benedict. [Restored and enlarged 1875–76.]

Endowment   Tithe £65 (compensation for Southwick). Glebe £40. OPE £67 17s 10d (Queen Anne's Bounty). Fees £100 (more or less). Easter offerings £8 (more or less). Other £50 (more or less). No parsonage house. Rent and rates from £70 to £80. Towards a curate £20.

Sittings   Free 100. Other 900. Total 1,000.

Attendance 30 March   Morning 300 + 230 SS. Total 530.
                       Afternoon 40 + 240 SS. Total 280.
                       Evening 350 + 150 SS. Total 500.

Average attendance   (winter.)
                       Morning 350 + 224 SS. Total 574.
                       Afternoon 40 + 250 SS. Total 290.
                       Evening 450 + 150 SS. Total 600.

Remarks   The congregation depends mainly on ye weather. When fine, we have 6[00] or 700, but every pew is taken and ye aisles only are free. Ye church is very ancient, and there is a great want of a new one to accommodate an increasing population.
            That the clergyman has no house attached to the living (considering the population and ye work) must be a matter of surprise and regret.

Dated   31 March 1851.

Signed   Benjamin Kennicott sen[ior], minister [1816–66]. [15 North Bridge Street], Monkwearmouth.

{1857   Attendance 500. 50 communicants.}   {B 337.}
[Salem Chapel in Broad Street which had been erected by the Independents 1817, was subsequently purchased for £400 by the Dean and Chapter of Durham, then consecrated and used as a chapel

of ease to Monkwearmouth parish church until the opening of All Saints Church (consecrated on 23 October 1849). Benjamin Kennicott's eldest son, Benjamin Centum Kennicott, was the incumbent of All Saints 1844–86. Kennicott (junior) failed to perform his clerical duties, was charged with drunkenness and from 1880 to 1884 was suspended from the living. He refused to resign and died in post in 1886. He was succeeded by the Pentecostal pioneer Alexander Boddy 1886–1922.

At St Peter's, Benjamin Kennicott's successor was Charles Popham Miles (1810–1891). As the curate of St Michael, Bishopwearmouth, Miles had known Arthur Rees, the then curate of Holy Trinity, Sunderland, who was to secede from the Church of England (**22.23**). At Miles' final sermon at St Michael's on 5 August 1843 there was a congregation of over 3,000. 'The sermon was preached extempore with his usual fervid and impressive manner, and lasted for one hour and fifty minutes.' (H.W. Hodges (ed.), *Antiquities of Sunderland, 1916–17*, vol. 17, p. 58). He then served as the incumbent of St Jude, Glasgow, and was excommunicated from the Scottish episcopal church for his active support of schismatic Evangelical clergy in the episcopal church. During his time in Scotland he trained as a medical doctor. From 1859 Miles was the principal of the Malta Protestant College and when it closed in 1865 the chairman of the committee, Lord Shaftesbury, noted in his diary that 'the Malta College must, on the whole, be regarded as a complete failure ... and we must close it in debt'. (E. Hodder, *The Life and Work of the Seventh Earl of Shaftesbury KG* (London, 1887), vol. 3, pp. 180, 181). Miles returned to England and from 1867 to 1883 was the vicar of St Peter, Monkwearmouth.]

22.7   Church of England, Holy Trinity, Southwick, Monkwearmouth (549.68)
Population 1851: 2,721 (township)

Name	Holy Trinity Church. The church of a distinct and separate parish, consisting of the townships of Southwick and Hylton, separated from the parish of [St Peter], Monkwearmouth under 1 & 2 Vic. c.106 [1838].
Consecrated	[28 July 1845] as the parish church of the parish of Southwick.
Erected	By the Dean and Chapter of Durham, with the aid of the Church Building Society and others. Dean and Chapter £1,400.

Church Building Society and other society £200.
Private £375. Total cost £1,975.
Endowment Land £150. Tithe £115. Pew rents £20.
Sittings [Free 300. Other 300. Total 600.]
Attendance 30 March Morning 175. Total 175.
Afternoon 105. Total 105.
Average attendance Morning 170. Total 170.
Afternoon 100. Total 100.
Remarks In the absence of the incumbent, I cannot supply all the information requested.
Dated 31 March 1851.
Signed John Anthony Pearson Linskill, curate [1850–51].
Southwick, n[ea]r Sunderland.
Incumbent [Lewis Morgan 1847–63.]
{1857 Attendance 450. 30 communicants.}   {B 122.}

22.8 Church of England, Holy Trinity, Church Street East, Sunderland (549.41)
Population 1851: 19,058 (parish)

Name Parish Church of Sunderland.
Consecrated Sunderland was constituted a parish in 1719 [and separated from Bishopwearmouth] and the church was consecrated the same year [5 September 1719 by the Bishop of London. Enlarged 1735.]
Endowment Land £30. OPE £80. Fees £180. Easter offerings £15.
(I pay £100 a year for a curate out of the above sum.)
Sittings Free 562. Other 971. Total 1,533.
Attendance 30 March Morning 1,000 + 34 SS. Total 1,034.
Evening 1,100 + 34 SS. Total 1,134.
Average attendance Morning 1,000 + 34 SS. Total 1,034.
Evening 1,100 + 34 SS. Total 1,134.
Dated 7 April 1851.
Signed Henry Peters, rector of Sunderland [1848–72].
[Church Walk], Sunderland.
{1857 Attendance 1,000. 70 communicants.}   {B 820.}
[An Act for making the town and township of Sunderland a distinct parish from the parish of Bishopwearmouth in the County of Durham. 5 Geo. I c.19. (1719). In 1992 Sunderland became a city.]

22.9   Church of England, St John the Evangelist, Barrack Street, Sunderland (549.42)

Name   St John's Chapel, Sunderland.

Consecrated   In 1768. [5 October 1769.] [Chapel of ease to Sunderland, created a parish in 1875. The upper north gallery was used by the troops from the nearby barracks.]

Erected   By private subscription. Grant and rate not known.

Endowment   Land £220. OPE £84. (I pay £20 towards a curate's stipend out of the above sum.)

Sittings   Free 1,108. Other 657. Total 1,765.

Attendance 30 March   Morning 750 + 356 SS. Total 1,106.
                        Afternoon 340 SS. Total 340.
                        Evening 500 + 50 SS. Total 550.

Average attendance   Morning 700 + 340 SS. Total 1,040.
                        Afternoon 300 SS. Total 300.
                        Evening 520 + 45 SS. Total 565.

Dated   7 April 1851.

Signed   Henry Peters, rector of Sunderland [1848–72].
                 [Church Walk], Sunderland.

{1857   Attendance 400. 30 communicants.}   {B none.}

22.10   Church of England, Episcopal Chapel, Spring Garden Lane, Sunderland (549.52)

Name   Spring Garden Lane Episcopal Chapel in the parish of Sunderland.

Consecrated   Licensed by the Bishop of Durham in the year 1844.

Erected   [Not given.] [1766. In 1843 purchased from the Presbyterians (who moved to Smyrna Chapel) as a chapel of ease to Sunderland and first used by the Church of England, 17 December 1843. Sold by auction 18 June 1855, and then used by other denominations.]

Endowment   No endowment.

Sittings   Free 420. Other 200. Total 620.

Attendance 30 March   Morning 100 + 80 SS. Total 180.
                        Afternoon 120 SS. Total 120.
                        Evening 120 + 40 SS. Total 160.

Average attendance   Morning 100 + 75 SS. Total 175.
                        Afternoon 130 SS. Total 130.
                        Evening 120 + 30 SS. Total 150.

Remarks   (I supply the duties of this chapel by myself and
             curates [of] the parish church.)
Dated   7 April 1851.
Signed   Henry Peters, rector of Sunderland [1848–72].
             [Church Walk, Sunderland.]
[Replaced by St Paul, Hendon, consecrated on 15 November 1852.]

22.11   United Presbyterian, Coronation Street, Bishopwearmouth
(549.32)
Name   Union Chapel.
Erected   In the year 1822.
Building   [Separate and entire. Exclusively used for worship.]
Sittings   Free [none]. Other 700. Total [700].
Attendance 30 March   Morning 450 + 50 SS. Total 500.
             Evening 550. Total 550.
Average attendance   [Not given.]
Remarks   I would remark that, in reference to free sittings, while
             no particular space is allotted, for this purpose, in
             Union Chapel, nor generally in Presbyterian places
             of worship, a considerable number of free sittings are
             allowed to the poor, in different parts of the church.
Dated   31 March 1851.
Signed   James Muir, minister [1831–59].
             21 Tavistock Place, Sunderland.
[In 1870 the building became a Roman Catholic church.]

22.12   United Presbyterian, Borough Road, Bishopwearmouth
(549.36)
Name   Smyrna [Chapel].
Erected   1832. [Previously at Spring Garden Lane (**22.10**).]
Building   Separate and entire. Used exclusively as a place of
             worship.
Sittings   Free (no one compelled to pay for a sitting). Other 550.
             Total [550].
Attendance 30 March   Morning 135 + 95 SS. Total 230.
             Evening 134 + 72 SS. Total 206.
Average attendance   Morning total 250.
             Afternoon 100 communicants
             (Communion four times in the year in the
             afternoon.)
Remarks   Population of the church and congregation: Members
             115. Adherents 97. Children 150. [Total] 362.

Average attendance above 200. A proportion always
at sea. This church removed from Spring Garden Lane
to Smyrna in 1843. The Sabbath school now taught
commenced in that place of worship [in] 1825. See
Sabbath school return.
I communicate religious instruction to three separate
classes during the week. Numbers attending said
classes, 100.

Dated   31 March 1851.

Signed   John Parker, minister [from 1835 at Spring Garden
Lane, and at Smyrna from 1843–78].
28 South Durham Street, Bishopwearmouth.

[From 1889 the congregation met at St George's Chapel, Villiers
Street, and renamed it St James Chapel.]

22.13   United Presbyterian, Hamilton Street, Monkwearmouth Shore (549.64)

Name   Hamilton Street Chapel.

Erected   1827. [Cost £700.]

Building   [Separate and entire. Exclusively used for worship.]

Sittings   Free 100. Other 400. Total [500].
Standing room – none except the passages and a large
singing pew.

Attendance 30 March   Morning 250 + 40 SS. Total 290.
Evening 300 + 20 SS. Total 320.

Average attendance   [Not given.]

Dated   30 March 1851.

Signed   William Tarbitt, manager [printer and bookseller].
Church Street, Monkwearmouth.

Minister   [John Mattison (18 June) 1851–79.]

[In 1872 the chapel was acquired by the Church of England and
became St Cuthbert's church. It closed on 26 October 1903.]

22.14   United Presbyterian, Maling's Rigg, Sunderland (549.47)

Name   Maling's Rigg Chapel.

Erected   Prior to 1800. [1778.]

Building   [Separate and entire. Exclusively used for worship.]

Sittings   Free – the poor have seats allowed them.
Other 360. Total [360].

Attendance 30 March   Morning 140 + 59 SS. Total 199.
Evening 170 + 50 SS. Total 220.

Average attendance   [Not given.]
Remarks   Our average attendance will be from 160 to 240.
Yesterday many were absent from circumstances which
could not be controlled.
Dated   31 March 1851.
Signed   John Morris, minister [1845–78].
4 D'Arcy Street.
[In 1856 the chapel was acquired by the Primitive Methodists.]

22.15   English Presbyterian, Villiers Street, Bishopwearmouth
(549.25)
Name   St George's Chapel.
Erected   In 1825, instead of an old chapel in another part of
the town, now converted into dwelling houses. [Cost
£4,200.]
Building   A separate and entire building, with vestry and
chapel-keeper's rooms as wings. Used exclusively as a
place of worship, very little for the Sunday schools.
Sittings   Free 21. Other 700. Total [721]. Standing room none
excepting the passages.
Attendance 30 March   Morning 456. Total [456].
Evening 415. Total [415].
Average attendance   [Not given.]
Remarks   Being aware that the numbers attending places of
worship when only guessed at are generally over-
rated by at least a third, pains were taken in this case,
both morning and evening, to have them accurately
counted. The chapel, though fitted according to
ordinary measurement to accommodate at least 250
more than were actually present, seemed well-filled
as usual. The Sunday scholars sit with their parents in
their own pews.
Dated   1 April 1851.
Signed   John Thornville Paterson DD, minister [1821–66].
20 Frederick Street, Bishopwearmouth, Sunderland.
[The congregation had previously met in a Presbyterian chapel in
Robinson's Lane (erected in 1739) where the final service was held on
13 November 1825. In 1889 the St George's congregation moved to
Belvedere Road and the United Presbyterians from Smyrna Chapel
occupied the chapel in Villiers Street and renamed it St James. In
1842 John Paterson became the moderator of his denomination.

He resigned from the pastorate in 1866, but continued as minister emeritus until his death in May 1868.]

22.16   Independent [Congregational], Villiers Street, Bishopwearmouth (549.26)
Name   Bethel Chapel.
Erected   1817. [Enlarged 1826.]
Building   [Separate and entire. Exclusively used for worship.]
Sittings   Free 212. Other 638. Total [850].
Attendance 30 March   Morning 260 + 35 SS. Total 295.
                        Evening 505. Total 505.
Average attendance   Morning 400 + 80 SS. Total 480.
                        Evening 600. Total 600.
Remarks   There has been a separation in the congregation of this place of worship within the last two months. The separatists are at present worshipping in Bethany Chapel. [The schism was led by Robert Whitaker McAll (**22.18**) and they moved from Hedworth Terrace to Fawcett Street in November 1852.]
Dated   31 March 1851.
Signed   Thomas Davison, deacon [agent].
                4 Sunderland Street, Bishopwearmouth.

22.17   Independent [Congregational], Hedworth Terrace, Bishopwearmouth (549.37)
Name   Bethany Chapel.
Erected   1849. [Opened 16 September 1849. Cost £1,000.]
Building   [Separate and entire. Exclusively used for worship.]
Sittings   Free 600. Other none. Total [600].
Attendance 30 March   Morning 91 + 28 SS. Total 119.
                        Evening 206. Total 206.
Average attendance   [Not given.]
Dated   31 March 1851.
Signed   John Halcro, minister.
                [28 John Street], Sunderland, Durham
[John Halcro, a layman, seceded from the Church of England, and erected Bethany Chapel. He ministered there for some years before transferring the building to the United Presbyterians. After the death of the minister, John Morris, the chapel was acquired by the Christian Lay Church.]

22.18   Independent [Congregational], Fawcett Street, Bishopwearmouth (549.27)

Name   Ebenezer Chapel in course of erection, worshipping in another place *pro tempore* [at Bethany Chapel. The congregation had broken away from Bethel Chapel.]

Erected   In course of erection 1851. [Opened 6 November 1852. Cost £2,600.]

Building   [Separate and entire. Exclusively used for worship.]

Sittings   Chapel in course of erection to seat upwards of 1,000 persons.

Attendance 30 March   Morning 338 + 153 SS. Total 491.
                         Evening 388 + 53 SS. Total 441.

Average attendance   [Not given.]

Remarks   The congregation at present meets in Bethany Chapel, Hedworth Terrace, Bishopwearmouth, by permission. Of the regular attendants of which chapel a separate return has been made by its minister (**22.17**).

Dated   30 March 1851.

Signed   Robert Whitaker McAll, minister [1851–55]. 34 Villiers Street, Sunderland.

22.19   Independent [Congregational], South Hylton, Bishopwearmouth (549.4)

Name   Ebenezer.

Erected   [Not given.]

Building   [Not separate and entire.] Part of a building [In another hand]. Exclusively [used] as a place of worship.

Sittings   Free 70. Total [70].

Attendance 30 March   Afternoon 23. Total [23].
                         Evening 40. Total [40].

Average attendance   [Not given.]

Dated   30 March 1851.

Signed   Robert Twizell, manager [grocer and druggist]. South Hylton, Sunderland.

22.20   Independent [Congregational], Dundas Street, Monkwearmouth Shore (549.62)

Name   Independent Chapel.

Erected   1832.

Building   Separate entire building. Exclusively as a place of worship.

Sittings   Free 100. Other 500. Total [600]. Standing room 100.
Attendance 30 March   Morning 250 + 111 SS. Total 361.
Afternoon 111 SS. Total 111.
Evening 263. Total 263.
Average attendance   Morning 250 + 110 SS. Total 360.
Afternoon 121 SS. Total 121.
Evening 268. Total 268.
Dated   31 March 1851.
Signed   Samuel Watkinson, minister [1829–55].
21 Dundas Street, Monkwearmouth, Durham.

22.21   Independent [Calvinist], High Street, Sunderland (549.55)
Name   Corn Market Chapel. [Salem Chapel.]
Erected   In the year 1711.
Building   [Separate and entire. Exclusively used for worship.]
Sittings   Free 50.* Other 348. Total [398]. Standing room, none
excepting the isles (*sic*).
Attendance 30 March   Morning 121. Total 121.
Evening 148. Total 148.
Average attendance   Morning 180. Total [180].
Remarks   *I have put down 50 free sittings, for though we have
no part of the chapel appropriated for free seats, yet
we accommodate the poor and strangers with sittings
wherever there is a vacancy; and have many attend
who do not pay.
Dated   31 March 1851.
Signed   Samuel Turner, minister [1810–54].
No 31 Nile Street, Sunderland, Durham.
[The earlier tradition of the chapel had been Church of Scotland,
but it moved away from Presbyterianism and the Rev. William
Platt was a member of the Countess of Huntingdon's Connexion.
Samuel Turner was 'unconnected with any sect, and receiving no
education for the ministry from any university, college, or academy,
he professes to have been called to it by the Son of God, and to
have been taught by the Holy Spirit, under the ministry of the late
Rev. William Huntingdon of London'. G. Garbutt, *A Historical and
Descriptive View of the Parishes of Monkwearmouth and Bishopwearmouth
and the Port and Borough of Sunderland* (Sunderland, 1819), p. 223. The
Corn Market Chapel was sold in 1851 and the congregation moved
to St George's schoolroom, then to St James, Villiers Street (**22.15**).]

22.22   Baptist, Garden Street, Bishopwearmouth (549.5)
[Summary form]
Name   Baptist Chapel. [Garden Street Chapel.]
Erected   [Not given.]
Building   [Separate and entire. Exclusively used for worship
              and] used also as Infant and Sunday school.
Sittings   All free. Total [100.]
Usual attendance   Morning 40 + 40 SS. Total 80.
Dated   [Not given.]
Signed   Sarah Chresle.
              17 Garden Street.

22.23   Baptist, Tatham Street, Bishopwearmouth (549.38)
Name   Bethesda Free Chapel.
Erected   1845. [1844.]
Building   [Separate and entire. Exclusively used for worship.]
Sittings   Free 1,050 (all sittings are free). Total [1,050]. Standing
              room nil.
Attendance 30 March   Morning 550. Total 550.
                      Afternoon 130 SS. Total 130.
                      Evening 1,000. Total 1,000.
Average attendance   [Not given.]
Dated   30 March 1851.
Signed   Arthur Augustus Rees, minister of the chapel [1844–84].
              Chapel House, [70] Tatham Street, Sunderland.
[Arthur Augustus Rees (1814–1884) known as 'the pope of Tatham
Street' had previously been the assistant curate of Sunderland parish
church (**22.8**). He left the Church of England, was baptised by George
Muller of Bristol, and on returning to Sunderland opened his own
chapel in Tatham Street. While he was critical of the Evangelical
Revival of 1859–60, he supported the Moody and Sankey month-
long campaign in 1873.]

22.24   Baptist, Charles Street, Bishopwearmouth (549.20a)
[Summary form]
Sittings   Free 130. Total [130.]
Remarks   The congregation have removed to a new chapel
              known by the name Providence Chapel. The chapel
              in Dunning Street is at present occupied as a dwelling
              house.
Dated   11 September 1852.

Signed   Jonathan Dunn [registrar]. [Page torn.]
             [2 Dun Cow Street, Bishopwearmouth.]
Minister   [F. Hill.]

22.25   Baptist, Halgarth Square, Monkwearmouth Shore (549.63a)
[Shared with Wesleyan Methodists (**22.44**)]
Name   Baptist Chapel.
Erected   1846.
Building   [Separate and] entire building. Used exclusively as a
                place of religious worship.
Sittings   All free 300. Total [300].
                Standing room – the iles (*sic*) will admit 40 or 50
                persons.
Attendance 30 March   Morning about 250. Total *350 (*sic*) [250].
                (About 250 Wesleyans who for a time have
                one service on Lord's Day.)
                Afternoon 5. Total 5.
                Evening about 40. Total 40.
Average attendance   Morning 200. SS none. Total 200.
                **Afternoon 10. SS none. Total 10.
                Evening 200. SS none. Total 200.
Remarks   *The Wesleyan Methodists have one service on Lord's
                Day in this place of worship until they have a capel
                (*sic*) completed that is now in course of erection.
                **The afternoon service is not a public service but
                meeting for Breaking of Bread by members of the
                Baptist Church.
Dated   30 March 1851.
Signed   Joseph Graham, pastor (or minister).
                Chapel House, [Halgarth Square], Monkwearmouth,
                Sunderland, Durham.

22.26   Baptist, Maling's Rigg, Sunderland (549.45)
Name   Maling's Rigg Chapel.
Erected   Before 1800. [Before 1842 used as a Freemasons'
                lodge.]
Building   *Separate [and entire. Exclusively used for worship.]
                [In another hand.] *This is a mistake. The chapel is not
                a separate and entire building for that purpose. But a
                large room above a public house and butcher's shop.
                George Lord, registrar, East district.
Sittings   Free 100. Other 100. Total [200].

Attendance 30 March Morning 100 + 40 SS. Total 140.
                       Afternoon 50. Total 50.
                       Evening 180 + 30 SS. Total 210.
Average attendance   [Not given.]
Dated   31 March 1851.
Signed   George Preston, minister.
             3 Manor Place, [Bishopwearmouth].

22.27   Particular Baptist, Sans Street, Bishopwearmouth
(549.29)
Name   Particular Baptist Chapel.
Erected   Before 1800. [Opened 25 December 1798. Rebuilt 1813
               and 1853. Later used as a church hall for St Thomas'
               church (**22.4**).]
Building   [Separate and entire. Exclusively used for worship.]
Sittings   All free 200. Total [200].
Attendance 30 March Morning [124]. Total 124.
                       Afternoon [70]. Total 70.
                       Evening [157]. Total 157.
Average attendance   [Not given.]
Dated   31 March 1851.
Signed   James Redman, minister.
             24 Pemberton Street, Sunderland.

22.28   Wesleyan Methodist, Sans Street, Bishopwearmouth
(549.24)
Name   Wesleyan Methodist Chapel.
Erected   1793. [Enlarged 1809 and 1824.]
Building   [Separate and entire. Exclusively used for worship.]
Sittings   Free 325. Other 1,030. Total [1,355]. Standing room 700.
Attendance 30 March Morning 419. Total 419.
                       Evening 786. Total 786.
Average attendance   Morning 440. Total 440.
                       Evening 800. Total 800.
Dated   31 March 1851.
Signed   Isaac Woodcock, Wesleyan minister [1850–51].
             24 Frederick Street, Sunderland.

22.29   Wesleyan Methodist, Fawcett Street, Bishopwearmouth
(549.31)
Name   Wesleyan Methodist Chapel.
Erected   1836.

Building   [Separate and entire. Exclusively used for worship.]
Sittings   Free 410. Other 902. Total 1,312. Standing room 200.
Attendance 30 March   Morning 385 + 27 SS. Total 406.
                         Evening 372 + 20 SS. Total 392.
Average attendance   Morning 480 + 30 SS. Total 510.
                         Evening 500 + 20 SS. Total 520.
Dated   31 March 1851.
Signed   Isaac Woodcock, Wesleyan minister [1850–51].
               24 Frederick Street, Sunderland.

22.30   Wesleyan Methodist, East Street, Bishopwearmouth
(549.34)
Name   East Street Methodist Chapel.
Erected   Cannot say. Used as a chapel since 1849.
Building   Part of a house. [Exclusively used for worship.]
Sittings   Free 140. Other none. Total [140]. Standing room 30.
Attendance 30 March   Afternoon 14 + 17 SS. Total 31.
                         Evening 28 + 15 SS. Total 43.
Average attendance   Morning 35 SS. Total [35].
                         Afternoon 30 + 27 SS. Total [57].
                         Evening 30 + 27 SS. Total [57].
Dated   31 March 1851.
Signed   Isaac Woodcock, Wesleyan minister [1850–51].
               24 Frederick Street, Sunderland.

22.31   Wesleyan Methodist Schoolroom, Ayre's Quay,
Bishopwearmouth (549.19)
Name   Laing School.
Erected   [Not given.]
Building   [Separate and entire but not exclusively used for
               worship.]
Sittings   About 150. Other none. Total [150]. Standing room
               none.
Attendance 30 March   Morning 33. Total 33.
                         Evening 56. Total 56.
Average attendance   [Not given.]
Remarks   This building is used temporarily as a Wesleyan
               Chapel in lieu of one of which the Society have been
               deprived. Its original purpose was that of a day school
               and it has been borrowed for the occasion. No return
               can therefore be made of the general congregation.
Dated   31 March 1851.

Signed   Isaac Woodcock, Wesleyan Methodist [1850–51].
             [24 Frederick Street], Sunderland.

22.32   Wesleyan Methodist, Southwick, Monkwearmouth (549.71)

Name   Wesleyan Chapel.
Erected   1822.
Building   Two rooms under the chapel let as a cottage, but now
             unoccupied [unclear and in another hand]. Exclusively
             used for worship.
Sittings   Free 98. Other 80. Total [178]. Standing room 50.
Attendance 30 March   Afternoon 36 + 22 SS. Total 58.
                        Evening 55 + 34 SS. Total 89.
Average attendance   Afternoon 36 + 22 SS. Total 58.
                        Evening 60 + 30 SS. Total 90.
Dated   31 March 1851.
Signed   Isaac Woodcock, Wesleyan minister [1850–51].
             [24 Frederick Street], Sunderland.

22.33   Wesleyan Methodist, High Street, Sunderland (549.48)

Name   Wesleyan Methodist Chapel.
Erected   Cannot say.
Building   Part of a house. [Exclusively used for worship.]
Sittings   Free 140. Other 210. Total [350]. Standing room 40.
Attendance 30 March   Afternoon 25 + 50 SS. Total 75.
                        Evening 23 + 18 SS. Total 41.
Average attendance   Afternoon 40 + 50 SS. Total 90.
                        Evening 60 + 30 SS. Total 90.
Dated   31 March 1851.
Signed   Isaac Woodcock, Wesleyan minister [1850–51].
             24 Frederick Street, Sunderland.

22.34   Wesleyan Methodist, Mill Street, Sunderland (549.44)

Name   Mill Street Methodist Chapel.
Erected   Cannot say.
Building   It is part of a house. [Exclusively used for worship.]
Sittings   Free 90. Other none. Total [90].
Attendance 30 March   Evening 32 + 12 SS. Total 44.
Average attendance   Evening 40 + 12 SS. Total 52.
Dated   31 March 1851.
Signed   Isaac Woodcock, Wesleyan minister [1850–51].
             24 Frederick Street, Sunderland.

22.35   Wesleyan Methodist, East Street, Sunderland (549.49)

Name   East Street Methodist Chapel.
Erected   Cannot say.
Building   Not a separate building but a large room rented.
                [Exclusively used for worship.]
Sittings   Free 75. Other 25. Total [100]. Standing room none.
Attendance 30 March   Morning 42 + 70 SS. Total 112.
                        Evening 72 + 24 SS. Total 96.
Average attendance   Morning 50 + 40 SS. Total 90.
                        Evening 80 + 12 SS. Total 92.
Dated   31 March 1851.
Signed   Isaac Woodcock, Wesleyan Minister [1850–51].
                [24 Frederick Street], Sunderland.

22.36   Wesleyan Methodist, Hylton Ferry, Bishopwearmouth
(549.3)
Name   Wesleyan Methodist Chapel.
Erected   1791.
Building   Separate building. [Exclusively used for worship.]
Sittings   Free 60. Other 140. Total [200]. Standing room none.
Attendance 30 March   Afternoon 77. Total 77.
                        Evening 85. Total 85.
Average attendance   Afternoon 100 + 25 SS. Total 125.
Dated   30 March 1851.
Signed   John Lynn, chapel steward [foreman of the paper mill].
                Ford Paper Mill, Sunderland.

22.37   Wesleyan Methodist, Hope Street, Bishopwearmouth
(549.14)
Name   Wesleyan Methodist Chapel.
Erected   1828.
Building   [Separate and entire. Exclusively used for worship.]
Sittings   Free 130. Other 150. Total [280].
Attendance 30 March   Morning none.
                        Afternoon 60. Total 60.
                        Evening 39. Total 39.
Average attendance   Morning none.
                        Afternoon 120. Total 120.
                        Evening 90. Total 90.
Dated   31 March 1851.
Signed   Andrew Smith, steward [tailor].
                51 Hedley Street, Bishopwearmouth, Durham.

22.38   Wesleyan Methodist, Deptford, Bishopwearmouth (549.18)
Name   Wesleyan Methodist Chapel.
Erected   1833.
Building   [Separate and entire. Exclusively used for worship.]
Sittings   Free 132. Other 94. Total [226]. Standing room none.
Attendance 30 March   Morning 33. Total 33.
                Afternoon no service.
                Evening 20. Total 20.
Average attendance   Morning 100 + 30 SS. Total 130.
                Afternoon no service.
                Evening 150. Total 150.
Dated   31 March 1851.
Signed   John Wilson Phillips, steward [agent to the Wear Glass
                Bottle Company].
                Deptford Cottage, n[ea]r Sunderland.

22.39   Wesleyan Methodist, Ryhope, Bishopwearmouth (549.40)
Name   None.
Erected   1835.
Building   [Separate and entire. Exclusively used for worship.]
Sittings   All free. Other none.
Attendance 30 March   Afternoon 20. Total [20].
                Evening 30. Total [30].
Average attendance   Morning and afternoon 25 + 20 SS. Total 45.
Dated   30 March 1851.
Signed   Thomas James Caincross, steward [agent].
                32 Union Street, Bishopwearmouth.

22.40   Wesleyan Methodist Room, Bishopwearmouth (549.20b)
[Summary form]
The congregation have removed from the schoolroom, Deptford
Terrace lately occupied by them as a chapel. They now meet for
worship in a room in a dwelling house every Monday evening. At
other times the room is used for domestic purposes. The seats are
free. (I think the room will not seat above 20 persons.)
Dated   11 September 1852.
Signed   Jonathan Dunn [page torn] [registrar].
                [2 Dun Cow Street, Bishopwearmouth.]

22.41   Wesleyan Methodist, North Hyton, Monkwearmouth
(549.66)
Name   Wesleyan Methodist Chaple (*sic*).
Erected   1844.

Building   [Separate and entire. Exclusively used for worship.]
Sittings   Free 60. Other 42. Total [102].
Attendance 30 March   Morning 50 + 10 SS. Total 60.
                Afternoon no.
                Evening 29 + 12 SS. Total 41.
Average attendance   Morning 50 + 10 SS. Total 60.
                Evening 60 + 20 SS. Total 80.
Dated   30 March 1851.
Signed   John Raine, chapel steward [chemical manufacturer].
                North Hylton, Sunderland, Durham.

22.42   Wesleyan Methodist, Southwick, Monkwearmouth
(549.69)
Name   Wesleyan Branch Chapel.
Erected   [Not given.]
Building   [Not separate and entire but exclusively used for
                worship.] No school.
Sittings   Free 50. Other [150]. Total [200].
Attendance 30 March   Afternoon 56. Total [56].
                Evening 50. Total [50].
Average attendance   [Not given.]
Remarks   This chapel was only opened four weeks ago. Will
                hold about 200 altogether.
Dated   2 April 1851.
Signed   John Taylor, one of the managers [hosier and dealer in
                fancy goods].
                10 Bridge Street, Sunderland.

22.43   Wesleyan Methodist, Whitburn Street, Monkwearmouth
Shore (549.61)
Name   Wesleyan Methodist Chapel.
Erected   1826. [1761 rebuilt 1826. Cost £2,000.]
Building   [Separate and entire. Exclusively used for worship.]
Sittings   Free 300. Other 900. Total 1,200.
Attendance 30 March   Morning 260 + 87 SS. Total 347.
                Evening 328. Total 328.
Average attendance   Morning 400 + 200 SS. Total 600.
                Evening 600. Total 600.
Dated   31 March 1851.
Signed   Thomas Speeding, trustee [canvas and sail
                manufacturer].
                [Wear Street], Monkwearmouth, Sunderland.

22.44   Wesleyan Methodist, Halgarth Square, Monkwearmouth Shore (549.63b) [Shared with Baptists (**22.25**)]
[Until the chapel is built for the Wesleyan Methodists, they hold their morning service (of about 250) in the Baptist chapel, Monkwearmouth.]
[The Methodist historian Geoffrey Milburn maintained that this congregation were Wesleyan Reformers.]

22.45   Wesleyan Methodist, Union Lane, Sunderland (549.54)
Name   None.
Erected   [Not given.]
Building   [Not separate and entire but exclusively used for worship.]
Sittings   Free 75. Total [75].
Attendance 30 March   Evening 33. Total 33.
Average attendance   Evening 40. Total [40].
Dated   1 April 1851.
Signed   William Calvert, manager [auctioneer and commercial agent].
              160 High Street, Sunderland.

22.46   Methodist New Connexion, Zion Street, Bishopwearmouth (549.33)
Name   Zion Chapel.
Erected   1808. [Opened in 1809. Cost £1,500. Later the congregation moved to Park Road, and the chapel was converted into a bakery.]
Building   [Separate and entire. Exclusively used for worship.]
Sittings   Free 174. Other 326. Total [500].
Attendance 30 March   Morning 263 + 65 SS. Total 328.
                        Evening 397. Total 397.
Average attendance   [Not given.]
Dated   31 March 1851.
Signed   Thomas Rudge, minister.
              30 Ahey Street, Bishopwearmouth.

22.47   Methodist New Connexion, Dame Dorothy Street, Monkwearmouth (549.59)
Name   None.
Erected   Before 1800. [Rebuilt 1854.]
Building   [Not separate and entire but exclusively used for worship.]

Sittings   Free 60. Other none. Total [60]. Standing room none.
Attendance 30 March   Morning no service.
                        Afternoon no service.
                        Evening 35. Total [35].
Average attendance   Morning no service.
                        Afternoon 30 + 10 SS. Total 40.
                        Evening 25 + 10 SS. Total 35.
Remarks   Service generally in the afternoon, but on the
               afternoon of the 30 March, given up.
Dated   30 March 1851.
Signed   William Parkinson, superintendent [grocer].
               Rendlesham Street, Topliffe Row, Monkwearmouth,
               Sunderland.

22.48   Methodist New Connexion, Hatcase, Sunderland (549.50)

Name   A room in a dwelling house.
Erected   Cannot tell. About 15 months ago enter on the
               services.
Building   [Separate and] entire. Place of worship and day school.
Sittings   [All] free.
Attendance 30 March   Evening 20. Total [20].
Average attendance   Evening 10. Total [10].
Remarks   In this place we have had services almost every night
               in the week and sum (*sic.*) much good done among
               abandoned characters, reclaimed and brought to God,
               and are now good citizens and Christians united to the
               Christian church, about 100 which some have join[ed]
               other churches.
Dated   31 March 1851.
Signed   Joseph Cook [waterman] with several others.
               66 Lawrence Street, Bishopwearmouth.

22.49   Primitive Methodist, Hopper Street, Bishopwearmouth (549.12)

Name   Primitive Methodist Chapel.
Erected   1832.
Building   [Separate and entire. Exclusively used for worship.]
Sittings   Free 290. Other 110. Total [400].
Attendance 30 March   Morning 120 + 70 SS. Total 190.
                        Evening 270. Total 270.
Average attendance   [Not given.]
Dated   [Not given.]

Signed   Samuel George Butterwick, minister.
20 North Durham Street, Bishopwearmouth, Durham.

22.50   Primitive Methodist, South Hylton, Bishopwearmouth
(549.7)
Name   Primitive Methodist Chapel.
Erected   1837. [Rebuilt 1880.]
Building   [Separate and entire. Exclusively used for worship.]
Sittings   Free 100. Other 50. Total [150].
Attendance 30 March   Morning 100. Total 100.
Evening 100. Total 100.
Average attendance   [Not given.]
Dated   [Not given.]
Signed   Samuel George Butterwick, minister.
20 North Durham Street, Bishopwearmouth, Durham.

22.51   Primitive Methodist, Low Southwick, Monkwearmouth
(549.70)
Name   Primitive Methodist Chapel.
Erected   1836.
Building   [Separate and entire. Exclusively used for worship.]
Sittings   Free 120. Other 80. Total [200].
Attendance 30 March   Morning 50. Total 50.
Afternoon 90 SS. Total 90.
Evening 60. Total 60.
Average attendance   Morning 56. Total 56.
Afternoon 80. Total 80.
Evening 100. Total 100.
Dated   31 March 1851.
Signed   John Stockdale, trustee [tailor and draper].
[High] Southwick, Sunderland.

22.52   Primitive Methodist, Williamson Terrace,
Monkwearmouth (549.60)
Name   Williamson Terrace Chapel.
Erected   1840. [New chapel 1881. Cost £3,000.]
Building   [Separate and] entire. [Exclusively used for worship.]
Sittings   Free 200. Other 300. Total [500]. Standing room none.
Attendance 30 March   Morning 350. Total [350].
Afternoon 232 SS. Total [232].
Evening 500. Total [500].
Average attendance   [Not given.]

Dated   30 March 1851.
Signed   Roger Walton, manager (blacksmith).
             Monkwearmouth.

22.53   Primitive Methodist, Monkwearmouth Colliery, Monkwearmouth (549.58a)
[Shared with Wesleyan Reformers (**22.64**)]
Name   None.
Erected   [Not given.] [New chapel 1860.]
Building   [Not separate and entire or exclusively used for worship.]
Sittings   Free 150. Total [150].
Attendance 30 March   Morning 140. Total [140].
                        Afternoon 140 SS. Total [140].
Average attendance   [Not given.]
Remarks   The Primitive Methodists in the morning and the Wesleyan Reformers in the evening.
Dated   31 March 1851.
Signed   Thomas Fairley, lay preacher and class leader [coal inspector].
             Railway Cottages, MWM [Monkwearmouth].

22.54   Primitive Methodist, Flag Lane, Sunderland (549.53)
Name   Primitive Methodist Chapel.
Erected   In the year 1824. [Opened 3 September 1824. Cost £1,600.]
Building   [Separate and entire. Exclusively used for worship.]
Sittings   Free 500. Other 700. Total [1,200].
Attendance 30 March   Morning 550 + 130 SS. Total 680.
                        Evening 1,150. Total 1,150.
Average attendance   Morning 600 + 130 SS. Total 730.
                        Evening 1,000. Total 1,000.
Dated   30 March 1851.
Signed   Colin C. McKechnie, minister.
             High Street, Sunderland.
[On the Monday after the chapel opened there was a congregation of 1,500. In a revival in 1849 some 500 converts were added to the Sunderland circuit, some of whom joined the Flag Lane Chapel. W.M. Patterson, *Northern Primitive Methodism* (London, 1909), pp. 247, 253.]

22.55   Wesleyan Methodist Association, South Durham Street, Bishopwearmouth (549.35)

Name   South Durham Street Tabernacle.
Erected   1835 or 1836.
Building   A separate building. Exclusively as a place of worship.
Sittings   Free 244. Other 506. Total [750].
Attendance 30 March   Morning 190 + 100 SS. Total 290.
             Afternoon no service.
             Evening 312. Total 312.
Average attendance   [Not given.] The above is the average.
Remarks   In addition to the 190 in the morning there would be about 100 children belonging [to] the school adjoining. They are brought into chapel every Sabbath morning and the average number of children attending the morning service is about 100.
Dated   30 March 1851.
Signed   William Dixon, managing trustee [chemist].
             18 Tavistock Place, Bishopwearmouth.

22.56   Wesleyan Methodist Association, Ballast Hills, Bishopwearmouth (549.15)

Name   Tabernacle.
Erected   1836.
Building   [Separate and] entire building. [Exclusively used for worship.]
Sittings   Free 140. Other 34. Total [174]. Standing room 50.
Attendance 30 March   Morning 96 SS. Total [96].
             Afternoon 46. Total [46].
             Evening 28 + 20 SS. Total [48].
Average attendance   [Not given.]
Dated   30 March 1851.
Signed   John Todd, class leader [waterman].
             14 Jobling Street, Deptford Hill, Bishopwearmouth.

22.57   Wesleyan Methodist Association, Deptford, Bishopwearmouth (549.16)

Name   Wesleyan Association Chapel.
Erected   1838.
Building   [Separate and entire. Exclusively used for worship.]
Sittings   Free 65. Other 73. Total [138].
Attendance 30 March   Morning 70. Total [70].
             Evening 70. Total [70].

Average attendance   [Not given.]
Dated   30 March 1851.
Signed   Cuthbert Elliott, elder and steward [keelman].
16 Church Street, Deptford.

22.58   Wesleyan Methodist Association, South Hylton, Bishopwearmouth (549.6)

Name   Tabernacle.
Erected   1838.
Building   [Separate and entire. Exclusively used for worship.]
Sittings   Free 102. Other 119. Total [221].
Attendance 30 March   Afternoon 86 + 110 SS. Total 196.
Evening 106. Total 106.
Average attendance   Afternoon 100 + 110 SS. Total 210.
Evening 150. Total 150.
Dated   30 March 1851.
Signed   James Ball, chapel steward.
2 Dawson Terrace, Hylton.

22.59   Wesleyan Methodist Association, Brougham Street, Bishopwearmouth (549.28)

Name   Tabernacle.
Erected   1841. [Cost £2,500.]
Building   [Separate and entire. Exclusively used for worship.]
Sittings   Free 280. Other 550. Total [830]. Standing room [in]
ailes (*sic*) etc. 200.
Attendance 30 March   Morning 116 + 65 SS. Total 181.
Evening 235. Total 235.
Average attendance   Morning 150 + 50 SS. Total 200.
Evening 300. Total 300.
Dated   31 March 1851.
Signed   Thomas B[rown] Young, trustee [ship-broker, owner,
chandler and sail-maker].
[161 High Street], Sunderland.

22.60   Wesleyan Reformers, Fawcett Street, Bishopwearmouth (549.30)

Name   Athenaeum.
Erected   Before 1840. [(*sic*). Opened 1 June 1841. Cost £4,500.]
Building   Part of a building [but not exclusively used for
worship].

Sittings   Free about 800. Other none. Total [800]. Standing room
200.
Attendance 30 March   Morning 450. Total 450.
Evening 930. Total 930.
Average attendance   Morning 400. Total 400.
Evening 870. Total 870.
Dated   31 March 1851.
Signed   Benj[ami]n Armstrong, steward.
128 High Street, Sunderland.
[The firm of Armstrong and Harrison were ironmongers, gas fitters,
tin-plate, iron and zinc workers.]

22.61   Wesleyan Reformers, Ballast Hills, Bishopwearmouth
(549.10)
[Simplified form]
Name   Wesleyan Chapel.
Erected   21 November 1847.
Building   A separate building. [Exclusively used for worship.]
Sittings   Free 60. Other 70. Total [130].
Usual attendance   Morning 100 + 30 SS. Total 130.
Evening 100. Total 100.
Dated   [Not given.]
Signed   James Johnson [master mariner].
Hanover Place, Ballast Hills, [Bishopwearmouth].

22.62   Wesleyan Reformers, Deptford, Bishopwearmouth (549.17)
Name   Shipswrites (*sic*) Hall.
Erected   1850.
Building   Entire building. Carpinters (*sic*) Union.
Sittings   Free 200. Other none. Total [200]. Standing room none.
Attendance 30 March   Morning 100 + 42 SS. Total 142.
Evening 200. Total 200.
Average attendance   Morning 100 + 40 SS. Total 140.
Afternoon 48 SS. Total 48.
Evening 200. Total 200.
Dated   30 March 1851.
Signed   John Greenwood, chapel steward [chemist].
[40 Church Street], Deptford, Bishopwearmouth.

22.63   Wesleyan Reformers, North Hylton, Monkwearmouth
(549.67)
Name   None.

Erected   [Not given.]
Building   [Not separate and entire or exclusively used for
               worship.]
Sittings   Free 50. Other 60. Total [110].
Attendance 30 March   Morning no.
               Afternoon 37. Total 37.
               Evening 40. Total 40.
Average attendance   [Not given.]
Remarks   Commenced to build a Reform chapel at North
               Hylton. Length 25ft, breadth 20ft. Supposed to be
               room for 100 persons.
Dated   [Not given.]
Signed   Joseph Leckenby, chapel steward.
               North Hylton, Durham.

**22.64   Wesleyan Reformers, Monkwearmouth Colliery,
Monkwearmouth** (549.58b)
[Shared with Primitive Methodists (**22.53**). The Primitive
Methodists meet in the morning and the Wesleyan Reformers in
the evening.]
Attendance 30 March   Evening 200. Total [200].

**22.65   Non-denominational, Disciples of Jesus Christ, Charles
Street, Bishopwearmouth** (549.13)
Name   Providence (*sic*) Chapel.
Erected   November 1843.
Building   Separate [and entire]. Used exclusively as a place of
               worship and Sunday school.
Sittings   All free. Total number of sittings 130. Standing room 50.
Attendance 30 March   Morning 16. Total [16].
               Evening 20. Total [20].
Average attendance   Morning 30 + 25 SS. Total 55.
Dated   31 March 1851.
Signed   Francis Hill, pastor [shoe-maker].
               23 William Street, Bishopwearmouth.

**22.66   Non-denominational, Seamen's Bethel, Wear Street,
Monkwearmouth Shore** (549.65)
Name   Seamen's Bethel Chapel. (A general society.
               Sunderland Sailors' Society.)
Erected   1844. [Opened 8 October 1843.]

Building   [Separate and entire. Exclusively used for worship.]
Sittings   All free for about 200. Total [200]. Standing room all
              free.
Attendance 30 March   Afternoon 60. Total [60].
Average attendance   [Not given.]
Remarks   (Not sectarian. A general society. Sunderland Sailors'
              Society.
Dated   31 March 1851.
Signed   James Milne, minister.
              No 7 Frederic (*sic*) Street, Sunderland.

**22.67   Non-denominational, Seamen's Bethel, Church Street,
Sunderland** (549.43)
Name   Seamen's Bethel Chapel. (Not-sectarian. A general
              society. Sunderland Sailors' Society.)
Erected   A century or two ago, and only lately set apart for
              holding religious meetings for the good of seamen.
              [Commenced January 1843.]
Building   [Not separate and entire or exclusively used for
              worship.]
Sittings   All free seats about 500. Total [500].
Attendance 30 March   Afternoon 200. Total [200].
Average attendance   [Not given.]
Dated   31 March 1851.
Signed   James Milne, minister.
              No 7 Frederic (*sic*) Street, Sunderland.

**22.68   Society of Friends [Quakers], Nile Street,
Bishopwearmouth** (549.8 and 549.23)
Name   Friends' Meeting House.
Erected   1822. [Cost £3,000.]
Building   Separate [and entire. Exclusively used for worship.]*
Sittings   Floor area   2,394   Seats   560.
              In the galleries   550   Seats   140.
              Total   2,944   Total   700 (all free).
Attendance 30 March   Morning 136. Total [136].
                         Afternoon 93. Total [93].
Remarks   *The Meeting House has twice or thrice since its
              erection been used for meetings of a philanthropic
              kind.
Dated   30 day of 3rd month (March) 1851.

Signed   Edward Capper Robson (appointed to make this
              return) [corn miller].
              37 Frederick Street, Sunderland.
Footnote   The officer receiving this return will please to take
              notice that I have filled up a duplicate return, to be
              forwarded to Jas. Bowden of Houndsditch, London,
              the agent of the Society of Friends, to transmit the
              same to the Registrar General. E. C. Robson.

22.69 Roman Catholic, Bridge Street, Bishopwearmouth (549.9)

Name   St Mary, Catholic.
Erected   [Not given.] [Opened 15 September 1835. Enlarged
              and re-opened, 3 December 1852.]
Building   [Not given.]
Sittings   Free 50. Other 30. Total [80].
Attendance 30 March   [Not given.]
Average attendance   Morning 95. Total [95].
Dated   [Not given.]
Signed   [Unclear.]
              (Letter sent by registrar.)
Incumbent   [Philip Kearney 1835–56.]
[In 1852 the estimated number of Roman Catholics in the area was
8,000.]

22.70 Unitarian, Bridge Street, Bishopwearmouth (549.11)

Name   Unitarian Chapel.
Erected   1830. [Foundation stone laid 14 May 1830. Cost
              £3,000.]
Building   [Not separate and entire but exclusively used for
              worship.]
Sittings   Free 250. Other 50. Total [300].
Attendance 30 March   [Not given.]
Average attendance   Morning 20. Total [20].
                         Evening 200. Total 200.
Remarks   A missionary chapel, supplied by the North of
              England Unitarian Association. This schedule was
              handed to me yesterday, 30 May.
Dated   31 May 1851.
Signed   Ebenezer Lyme, missionary minister.
              12 Upper Sans St[reet], Bishopwearmouth.

22.71   Synagogue, High Street, Bishopwearmouth (549.56)
Name   None.
Erected   1829. [New synagogue opened May 1862.]
Building   [Not separate and entire but exclusively used for worship.]
Sittings   Free 40. Total [40].
Attendance 29 March   Morning 40 to 60. Total [40–60].
                Afternoon seldom.
                Evening 15. Total [15].
                As Sunday is seldom a day of divine service,
                unless it is a Jewish festival, say Saturday,
                29 March.
Average attendance   Afternoon 100. Total 100.
Remarks   The foregoing is a return of the particulars of our
                place of worship being free for anyone to attend
                divine service. It is a private room in the house
                of Mr Jacob Joseph [in 204 High Street]. And the
                apparent inconsistency of certifying to a congregation
                unrelated is caused by the fact that there actually was
                a congregation of between 15 to 20 on Friday evening
                28th, the commencement of our Sabbath. See remark
                [under attendance].
Dated   31 March 1851.
Signed   David Joseph, reader [watchmaker].
                11 Wear Street, [Bishopwearmouth].
[In 1821 this congregation (known as the 'Israelite' Synagogue)
separated from the Polish Synagogue and was more conservative in
outlook and less anglicised than the older congregation. B. Susser, 'The
Nineteenth-century Constitution of the Sunderland Congregation',
Transactions of the Jewish Historical Society, 40 (2005), p. 4.]

22.72   Synagogue, Vine Street, Sunderland (549.46 and 549.51)
Name   Polish Synagogue.
Erected   In about the year 1781. [Closed in the early 1850s.]
Building   Not a separate building. [Exclusively used for]
                worship only.
Sittings   Free 42. Other 34. Total [76]. Standing room none.
Attendance 29 March   Morning 12. Total [12].
                Afternoon none.
                Evening 13. Total [13].
Average attendance   [Not given.]
Remarks   No president being solely official [except] myself.

Dated   30 March 1851.
Signed   Myers Marks, secretary and [reader].
              154 High Street, Sunderland.
[On Myers Marks see A. Levy, *History of the Sunderland Jewish Community* (London, 1956), pp. 39–41. Marks has been described as 'a man impressed by his own importance'. L. Olsover, *The Jewish Communities of North-East England 1755–1980* (Sunderland, 1981), p. 264.]

23. Teesdale District (HO 129/543)
32 places of worship (and 28 in Yorkshire)

23.1   Church of England, Holy Trinity, Eggleston (543.42)
Population 1851: 636 (township)

Name   The church of the ancient chapelry of Eggleston.
              [District created 9 July 1859.]
Consecrated [Not given. New church opened 12 July 1869.]
Endowment   Land £59 9s. OPE £39 10s. Fees about £1.
Sittings   Free 94. Other 84. Total 178.
Attendance 30 March   Morning 56. Total [56].
              Afternoon 17. Total [17].
Average attendance   Morning 60. Total [60].
              Afternoon 20. Total [20].
Dated   31 March 1851.
Signed   Wilse Brown, perpetual curate [1835–57].
              Eggleston, Barnard Castle.
{1857   Attendance -. 20 communicants.}   {B 16.}
[Wilse Brown was 'the only clergyman in England serving in a volunteer corps'. J.A. Venn, *Alumni Cantabrigienses* (Cambridge, 1940), vol. 1, part 1, p. 411.]

23.2   Church of England, St Mary the Virgin, Gainford (543.14)
Population 1851: 669 (township)

Name   An old parish church, dedicated to St Mary the Virgin.
Consecrated I know not. [Restored and reopened 10 September
              1860.]
Endowment   Land [including glebe] £30 (30 acres). Tithe £1,000.

OPE none. Pew rents illegal. Fees perhaps £5 5s.
Easter offerings, none collected. Paid out to perpetual
curate £50.

Sittings   There are in all 80 pews on an average holding five
each. Sittings for about 400. Besides an undivided
gallery holding about 55. (Number of sittings 450, of
which are free 56. Appropriated 394 sittings.) Total
[450].

Attendance 30 March   Morning 225. Total [225]. } (SS) do not
Afternoon 85. Total [85]. } sit together.

Average attendance   Morning 220. Total [220].
Afternoon 80. Total [80].
Thin congregations on rainy Sundays.

Remarks   Gainford is a very antient (*sic*) parish. Barnard Castle,
Whorlton and Denton are in the parish and have
independent churches.

Dated   31 March 1851.

Signed   George Macfarlan, vicar [1824–62].
Gainford, near Darlington.

{1857   Attendance 200. 40 communicants.}   {B 29.}
[George Macfarlan was also the minister of Bolam Chapel (**13.4**).]

23.3   Church of England, St John the Evangelist, Ingleton
(543.12)
Population 1851: 305 (township)

Name   St John's, Ingleton, a new district church made under
the provisions of the 16th Session of an Act passed in
the 59th year of the reign of his majesty King George
III [c.134] instituted an Act for building additional
churches in populous parishes etc.

Consecrated   On 31 October 1844. As an additional church.
[District created 13 January 1845 out of the parish of
Heighington.]

Erected   By subscription. Private £430. Total cost £430.

Endowment   Tithe £50. OPE £30. Pew rents £4. Fees £2.

Sittings   Free 173. Other 33. Total 206.

Attendance 30 March   Morning 150 + 50 SS. Total 200.
Afternoon 50 + 20 SS. Total 70.

Average attendance   [Not given.]

Remarks   On the annexation of the adjoining township of
Killerby in the parish of Heighington to the Ingleton

district in 1849 [8 January 1850]. Ingleton was constituted a distinct parish having entirely separated from the united parishes of Cockfield and Staindrop.

Dated   31 March 1851.
Signed   Martin Wright, minister [1845–74].
             Ingleton, n[ea]r Darlington.
{1857   Attendance 150. 20 communicants.}   {B 14.}

23.4   Church of England, St Mary the Virgin, Staindrop (543.7)
Population 1851: 2,447 (parish) 1,429 (township)

Name   St Mary's church. Ancient parish church. [Previously dedicated to St Gregory.]
Consecrated Before 1800. [Restored 1849.]
Endowment OPE £80. [From Cockfield (**23.5**).]
Sittings   Free 86. Other 436. Total 522.
Attendance 30 March   Morning 208 + 65 SS. Total 273.
             Afternoon 91 + 56 SS. Total 147.
Average attendance   Morning 305 + 70 SS. Total 375.
             Afternoon 125 + 56 SS. Total 181.
Remarks   Being a wide-spread country parish, the congregation differs very greatly according to the weather. There being sometimes upwards of 400 present in the morning.
Dated   31 March 1851.
Signed   Henry Curteis Lipscomb, vicar [1846–1904].
             Staindrop, Darlington.
{1857   Attendance 300. 25 communicants.}   {B 42.}

23.5   Church of England, St Mary the Virgin, Cockfield (543.1)
Population 1851: 647 (township)

Name   Cockfield Church.
Consecrated Before 1800. [Restored and enlarged 1911.]
Endowment [£354.]
Sittings   Free 19. Other 107. Sunday scholars 60. Total 186.
Attendance 30 March   Morning 73 + 55 SS. Total 128.
Average attendance   Morning 80 + 60 SS. Total [140].
Remarks   Number variable according to seasons and weather.
Dated   31 March 1851.
Signed   Peter Barlow, curate [1851–66].
             Cockfield, Darlington.

Incumbent   [Henry Curteis Lipscomb 1846–1904.]
{1857   Attendance 34. 9 communicants.}   {B 20.}

23.6   Church of England, St Mary, Whorlton (543.34)
Population 1851: 296 (township)

[Summary form]
Name   Whorlton, St Mary.
Erected   Newly erected. [Consecrated by the Bishop of Cape
              Town, 13 July 1853.]
Endowment   [Tithes commuted in 1850. Total £107.]
Sittings   Free 160. Total [160].
Usual attendance Morning about 100 + between 40 & 50 SS. Total
              [140–150].
Informant   Henry Rayson.
Incumbent   [John George Edwards 1849–54.]
{1857   Attendance 100. 20 communicants. Church erected
            three years ago on site of old one.}   {B 9.}

23.7   Church of England, St Andrew, Winston (543.17)
Population 1851: 301 (parish)

Name   The church of St Andrew. An ancient parish church.
Consecrated Before 1800. [Rebuilt 1846–48.]
Endowment   Tithe £496. *Glebe. Fees uncertain but very small in
              amount.
Sittings   Free 20. Other 158. Total 178.
Attendance 30 March   Morning 60. Total [60].
                        Evening 40. Total [40].
Average attendance   Morning 80 + 30 SS. Total 110.
                        Evening 60. Total [60].
Remarks   The church has been extensively repaired, and in part
              rebuilt by private subscription.
              *The glebe is about 29 acres, of which 20 are let for
              £40 per. Ann[um]. The Sunday scholars sit in the
              chancel, on forms, not reckoned in the above number
              of sittings.
Dated   31 March 1851.
Signed   William Webb, minister [1848–62].
              Winston Rectory, Darlington.
{1857   Attendance 50. 14 communicants.}   {B 12.}

23.8   Independent [Congregational], Hall Street, Barnard Castle
(543.37)

Name   Independent or Hall Street Chapel.
Erected   1836. [Opened 18 April 1837.]
Building   [Separate and entire. Exclusively used for worship.]
Sittings   Free 70. Other 380. Total [450]. Standing room none.
Attendance 30 March   Morning 76 + 66 SS. Total 142.
              Afternoon*
              Evening 119. Total 119.
Average attendance   Morning 100. Total [100].
              Evening 150. Total [150].
Remarks   *Prayer meetings are held at 3 o'clock and at ½ past 5
              o'clock during the afternoon. The average attendance
              for 12 months is given below rather above the
              numbers. It was ascertained that from affliction etc.
              more than 40 regular hearers were absent last night.
Dated   31 March 1851.
Signed   James Hardman, minister [1848–55].
              Barnard Castle, Durham.

23.9   Independent [Congregational], Gainford (543.16)
Name   Gainford Independent or Congregational Chapel.
Erected   1849. [Opened 1 January 1850. Cost £350.]
Building   [Separate and entire. Exclusively used for worship.]
Sittings   Free 130. Total [130].
Attendance 30 March   Morning 14 SS. Total [14].
              Afternoon 29 + 15 SS. Total [44].
              Evening 76. Total [76].
Average attendance   Morning 14 SS. Total [14].
              Afternoon 40 + 15 SS. Total [55].
              Evening 90. Total [90].
Dated   31 March 1851.
Signed   William Bowman, deacon [schoolmaster].
              Gainford, Darlington.

23.10   Independent [Congregational], Staindrop (543.10)
Name   Independent Chapel.
Erected   1827. [Opened 23 May 1827.]
Building   Separate and entire building. Exclusively a place of
              worship.
Sittings   Free 50. Other 183. Total [233]. Standing room 40.
Attendance 30 March   Morning 100 + 56 SS. Total [156].

Afternoon 20 + 10 SS. Total [30].
Evening 160. Total [160].
[Combined total for the day] 346.
Average attendance   Morning 150 + 56 SS. Total 206.
Dated   [Not given.]
Signed   John Mountain, deacon (gardener).
               Staindrop.

23.11   Independent [Congregational], Whorlton (543.35)
Name   Independent or Congregational.
Erected   1840.
Building   [Separate and entire. Exclusively used for worship.]
Sittings   Free 90. Other 50. Total [140].
Attendance 30 March   Afternoon 48. Total 48.
Average attendance   Afternoon 50 + 12 SS. Total 62.
Dated   30 March 1851.
Signed   Ferdinand Raine, minister [–1879].
               Little Hulton, Winston, Darlington.

23.12   Baptist, Middleton-in-Teesdale (543.51)
Name   Hude Chapel.
Erected   1826–27. [Opened 21 June 1827.]
Building   [Separate and entire. Exclusively used for worship.]
Sittings   Free 200. Other 140. Total [340].
Attendance 30 March   Morning 200. Total [200].
               Evening 340. Total [340].
Average attendance   [Not given.]
Dated   31 March 1851.
Signed   Charles Forth, minister.
               Middleton-in-Teesdale, Barnard Castle.

23.13   Baptist, Forest, Middleton-in-Teesdale (543.57)
Name   Forest Chapel.
Erected   1833–34.
Building   [Separate and entire. Exclusively used for worship.]
Sittings   Free 200. Total [200].
Attendance 30 March   Morning 150. Total [150].
               Afternoon 150. Total [150].
               Evening 150. Total [150].
Average attendance   [Not given.]
Dated   31 March 1851.
Signed   Charles Forth, minister.
               Middleton-in-Teesdale, by Barnard Castle.

23.14   Wesleyan Methodist, The Bank, Barnard Castle (543.39)
Name   Wesleyan Chapel.
Erected   1822. [Opened 1 January 1823. Cost £1,200.]
Building   [Separate and entire. Exclusively used for worship.]
Sittings   Free 330. Other 430. Total [760].
Attendance 30 March   Morning 231 + 124 SS. Total 355.
                        Evening 326. Total 326.
Average attendance   [Not given.]
Dated   31 March 1851.
Signed   Henry Hine, Wesleyan minister [1850–52].
                Wes[leyan] Chapel Yard, Barnard Castle.
[On 5 June 1763 John Wesley recorded that 'I rode to Barnard Castle, and preached in the evening, but to such a congregation, not only with respect to number, but to seriousness and composure, as I never saw there before … There is something remarkable in the manner wherein God revived his work in these parts.' J. Wesley, *The Journal of the Rev John Wesley* (Dent edition, 1906), vol. 3, pp. 136, 137.]

23.15   Wesleyan Methodist, Middleton-in-Teesdale (543.53)
Name   Wesleyan Methodist Chapel.
Erected   1808.
Building   [Separate and entire. Exclusively used for worship.]
Sittings   [Not given.] [300–400.]
Attendance 30 March   Afternoon 140 + 60 SS. Total 200.
                        Evening 196 + 30 SS. Total 226.
Average attendance   [Not given.]
Dated   31 March 1851.
Signed   Henry Hine, minister [1850–52].
                Barnard Castle, Durham.

23.16   Wesleyan Methodist, Cockfield (543.4)
Name   Wesleyan Chapel.
Erected   1839. [Cost £175.]
Building   An entire building. [Exclusively used for worship.]
Sittings   Free 72. Other 72. Total [144].
Attendance 30 March   Afternoon 45. Total [45].
Average attendance   Morning 30. Total [30].
Dated   30 March 1851.
Signed   Atkinson Lambert, steward [banks man and weigh man].
                Butterknowle, n[ea]r Cockfield, Durham.

23.17   Wesleyan Methodist, Woodland, Cockfield (543.2)
Name   Woodland Chapel.
Erected   AD 1826. [Enlarged 1868.]
Building   [Separate and entire. Exclusively used for worship.]
Sittings   Free 116. Other 24. Total [140].
Attendance 30 March   Afternoon 53. Total 53.
Average attendance   [Not given.]
Dated   3 April 1851.
Signed   John Blackett, steward [boot and shoemaker].
                Woodland, near B[arnar]d Castle.

23.18   Wesleyan Methodist, Eggleston (543.55)
Name   Wesleyan Methodist.
Erected   1828. [Cost £500.]
Building   [Separate and entire. Exclusively used for worship.]
Sittings   Free 122. Other 70. Total [192].
Attendance 30 March   Morning no service.
                Afternoon no service.
                Evening 104. Total [104].
Average attendance   [Not given.]
Dated   31 March 1851.
Signed   William Wall, steward [butcher].
                Eggleston, near Barnard Castle.

23.19   Wesleyan Methodist, Gainford (543.15)
Name   Wesleyen (*sic*) Chapel.
Erected   1834. [Opened 25 December 1834, enlarged 1851]
Building   Entire building. Place of worship and Sunday school.
Sittings   Free 70. Other 70. Total [140].
                (Standing room) free space; 20 feet by 12 [feet].
Attendance 30 March   Afternoon 70. Total 70.
                Evening 100. Total 100.
Average attendance   Morning 90 + 20 SS. Total 110.
                Average a month 440. Total 440.
Dated   30 March 1851.
Signed   Matthew Preston, Wesleyan local preacher (cabinet
                maker) [and ironmonger].
                Gainford, Durham.

23.20   Wesleyan Methodist, Langley Dale (543.6)
Name   Wesleyan Methodist Chappel (*sic*).
Erected   In the year 1813.

Building   Separate dwelling under. Exclusively for worship [in another hand] No [to both sections H.M.].
Sittings   Free 40. Other 40. Total [80].
Attendance 30 March   [Not given.]
Average attendance   Morning 60. Total [60].
Dated   30 March 1851.
Signed   William Lowry, leader (farrier).
          B[arnar]d Castle Moor, near B[arnar]d Castle.

23.21   Wesleyan Methodist, Newbiggin (543.56)
[Simplified form]
Name   Newbiggin Wesleyan Methodist Chapel.
Erected   In the year one thousand seven hundred and sixty.
          [1760.]
Building   A separate and entire building. Used exclusively as a place of worship, except for a Sabbath school.
Sittings   Ninety eight free sittings [98]. Seventy-two sittings let [72]. Total [170].
Usual attendance   Morning 65 + 40 SS. Total 105.
          Afternoon 90 + 15 SS. Total 105.
          Evening 60 + 10 SS. Total 70.
Signed   Jonathan Coatsworth [farmer].
          Newbiggin, near Middleton-in-Teesdale, Durham.

23.22   Wesleyan Methodist, Staindrop (543.9)
Name   Wesleyan Chapel.
Erected   1813.
Building   Separate [and entire] building. [Exclusively used for worship.]
Sittings   Free 120. Other 50. Total [170].
Attendance 30 March   Afternoon 51 + 30 SS. Total [81].
          Evening 94. Total [94].
Average attendance   [Not given.]
Dated   31 March 1851.
Signed   James Railton, Wesleyan leader (saddler) [and harness maker].
          Staindrop, Durham.

23.23   Primitive Methodist, Bowleys (543.54)
[Simplified form]
Name   Bowlees (*sic*) Primitive Methodist Chapel.

Erected   In the year of our Lord eighteen forty-five.
Building   A separate and entire building. Used exclusively as a
              place of worship except for a Sabbath school.
Sittings   Free: one hundred and twenty-five sittings [125].
              Other: fifty-seven sittings let [57]. Total [182].
Usual attendance   Morning (No service in the morning). 76 SS.
              Total 76.
              Afternoon 100 + 25 SS. Total 125.
              Evening 140 + 20 SS. Total 160.
Signed   George Crowther [lead miner].
              Stable Edge, [Newbiggin], Middleton-in-Teesdale,
              Durham.

23.24   Primitive Methodist, Broadgates, Barnard Castle (543.38)
Name   Primitive Methodist Chapel.
Erected   AD 1829.
Building   An entire chapel. Exclusively a place of worship and
              Sunday school.
Sittings   Free 347. Other 153. Total [500].
Attendance 30 March   Morning 191. Total [191].
              Evening 260. Total [260].
Average attendance   Morning 200 + 115 SS. Total [315].
              Afternoon 126 SS. Total [126].
              Evening 350. Total [350].
Dated   30 March 1851.
Signed   William Brining, minister.
              Broadgates, Barnard Castle, Durham.

23.25   Primitive Methodist, Cockfield (543.3)
Name   Primitive Methodist Chaple (*sic*).
Erected   Before 1820.
Building   Part of a dwelling house. Exclusively a place of
              worship.
Sittings   Free 50. Other 50. Total [100].
Attendance 30 March   Evening 60. Total [60].
Average attendance   [Not given.]
Dated   30 March 1851.
Signed   John Liddle, flour dealar (*sic*) [shopkeeper].
              [Cockfield.]

23.26   Primitive Methodist Schoolroom, Ingleton (543.13)
Name   Chapel.
Erected   1815.
Building   [Separate and entire.] Day school and Sunday school
                belonging to the Church of England.
Sittings   Free 100. Other 50. Total [150].
Attendance 30 March   Evening 100. Total 100.
Average attendance   Evening 100. Total 100.
Remarks   This chapel was built by the inhabitants of Ingleton
                for a day school, a part of which is appropriated for
                the Primitive Methodists to hold their meetings on the
                Sunday evening.
Dated   31 March 1851.
Signed   William Young, manager [cartwright].
                Ingleton by Darlington.

23.27   Primitive Methodist, Langley Dale (543.5)
Name   A house occupied by the Primitive Methodists for
                divine worship.
Erected   First occupied in 1838.
Building   A separate house. Used partly as a place of worship.
Sittings   Free 50. Total [50].
Attendance 30 March   Afternoon 18. Total [18].
Average attendance   Afternoon 20. Total [20].
Dated   30 March 1851.
Signed   Joseph Heslop, Primitive Methodist preacher (farm
                labourer).
                Beckside [House], Langley Dale, Durham.

23.28   Primitive Methodist, Middleton-in-Teesdale (543.52)
Name   Primitive Methodist Chapel.
Erected   1825.
Building   [Separate and entire. Exclusively used for worship.]
Sittings   Free 200. Other 350. Total [550]. Standing room 50.
Attendance 30 March   Afternoon 200. Total 200.
                Evening 350. Total 350.
Average attendance   [Not given.]
Dated   31 March 1851.
Signed   Anthony Todd, local preacher [farmer].
                Hood Gate, Middleton-in-Teesdale.

23.29   Primitive Methodist, Staindrop (543.11)
Name   None.
Erected   Before 1800.
Building   [Not separate and entire but exclusively used for worship.]
Sittings   Free 100. Other 26. Total [126].
Attendance 30 March   Afternoon 50. Total [50].
                        Evening 120. Total [120].
Average attendance   [Not given.]
Dated   31 March 1851.
Signed   Thomas Railton, steward [boot and shoemaker].
                Staindrop, Darlington, Durham.

23.30   Society of Friends [Quakers], North Green, Staindrop (543.8)
Name   [Not given.]
Erected   Before 1800. [1771.]
Building   [Separate and entire. Exclusively used for worship.]
Space   Ground floor 819 [square feet]. No gallery.
                Total 819 [square] feet.
                Estimate of number who can be seated 170. Total 170.
Attendance 30 March   Morning 15. Total [15].
                        Afternoon 9. Total [9].
Dated   Eleventh day of fourth month 1851.
Signed   John Beaumont Pease [woollen merchant].
                Of Darlington monthly meeting.
                North Lodge, Darlington.
[John Beaumont Pease (1803–1873) was also involved with several other Quaker meeting houses (**13.59**, **13.60**, **21.63**, **21.92** and **23.56**).]

23.31   Roman Catholic, Barnard Castle (543.36)
Name   St Mary's Chapel, Barnard Castle.
Erected   First used as a chapel in 1847.
Building   Separate and entire. [Exclusively a] place for worship, only.
Sittings   Free 114. Other 80. Total [194]. Standing room at least 100.
Attendance 30 March   Morning 96 + 47 SS. Total 143.
                        Evening 106 + 34 SS. Total 140.
Average attendance   Morning 110 + 40 SS. Total 150.
                        Evening 130 + 40 SS. Total 170.
Dated   31 March 1851.

Signed   William F. Allen BA, Catholic priest [1847–56].
Barnard Castle.
[In 1852 the estimated number of Roman Catholics in the area was 414.]

23.32   Unitarian, Broadgates, Barnard Castle (543.40)
Name   The Broadgates Chapel.
Erected   1760. But it became a chapel for this body only in 1846.
Building   It is a separate building. But not all used as a chapel. The members let off part.
Sittings   All free. The chapel is 11 yards by 9 yards.
Attendance 30 March   Evening 40 + 15 SS. Total 55.
Average attendance   Morning and afternoon 100 + 17 SS. Total [117].
Remarks   (Most of the members profess Unitarian sentiments and are called Christian Brethren and sometimes Unitarians.)
Dated   30 March 1851.
Signed   William Elliott, secretary to the trustees [carpet weaver].
King Street, Barnard Castle.

24. Weardale District (HO 129/544)
37 places of worship

24.1   Church of England, St Edmunds, Edmundbyers (544.23)
Population 1851: 485 (parish)

[Summary form]
Name   Edmundbyers Parish Church.
Erected   Cannot say.
Endowment   [£178.]
Sittings   Free 90. Other 30. Total 120.
Usual attendance   Afternoon 40 + 20 SS. Total [60].
Informant   John Benson, [registrar].
Incumbent   [Joseph Forster 1837–55.]
{1857   Attendance 40. 10 communicants.}   {B 13.}
[In 1990 Edmundbyers was transferred to the diocese of Newcastle.]

24.2   Church of England, St James, Hunstanworth (544.26)
Population 1851: 615 (parish)

Name   St James's, an ancient parish church. Private
             patronage.
Consecrated Before 1800. [Built 1781, rebuilt and opened on 9 June
             1863.]
Endowment   Glebe £32 10s. OPE none. Other £67 10s (from the
             patron) [Robert Capper].
Sittings   All free [200]. Total 200.
Attendance 30 March   Afternoon 50 + 27 SS. Total 77.
Average attendance   Morning 30 + 20 SS. Total 50.
                       Afternoon 60 + 30 SS. Total 90.
Remarks   The services are held alternately, morning and
             afternoon.
Dated   31 March 1851.
Signed   [James] Samuel Payne, minister [1835–56].
             Blanchland, Riding Mill, Gateshead.
{1857   Attendance 90. 7 communicants.}   {B 21.}

24.3   Church of England, St Thomas the Apostle, Stanhope
(544.12)
Population 1851: 8,882 (parish) 2,545 (township)

[Summary form]
Name   Stanhope Parish Church.
Erected   Cannot say.
Endowment   [£4,848.]
Sittings   Free 310. Other 120. Total 430.
Usual attendance   Morning about 200 + about 60 SS.
                      Total [about 260].
                      Afternoon about 100 + about 60 SS.
                      Total [about 160].
                      Evening about 100 + about 60 SS. Total
                      [about 160].
Informant   John Benson, [registrar].
Incumbent   [William Nicholas Darnell 1831–65.]
{1857   Attendance 435. 25 communicants.}   {B 96.}
['William Nicholas Darnell (1776–1865)', *ODNB*, vol. 15, pp. 164–165.
When Darnell was a fellow and tutor at Corpus Christi College,
Oxford, one of his pupils was John Keble, later to become one of
the leaders of the Oxford Movement. Keble dedicated a volume

of his sermons to Darnell, 'in ever grateful memory of invaluable helps and warnings received from him in early youth'. W. Lock, *John Keble* (London, 1893), p. 4. Darnell may well have suggested Keble as the first principal of the University of Durham. In *c*.1836 Darnell opened a chapel of ease at Frosterley, and after it closed it became a girls' school. Subsequently St Michael and All Angels, Frosterley was consecrated on 2 March 1866. Darnell was also responsible for the erection of St Bartholomew, Thornley **(24.9)** where he had an estate. In the 19th century there was much disparity in clerical incomes. A 'Peel district' minister received an annual stipend of £150; the rector of Stanhope nearly £5,000 (making it one of the richest livings in the Church of England); the Dean of Durham £3,000; and the Bishop of Durham £8,000.]

24.4   Church of England, Rookhope Church, Stotfield Burn, Stanhope (544.13)

Name	Rookhope Church or chapel of ease [of Stanhope].
Consecrated	[18] August 1822 [by the Bishop of Oxford. Restored 1884. Dedicated to Holy Trinity 1892. Parish created 16 February 1866.
Erected	By the late Bishop [Shute] Barrington.
Endowment	[Not given.]
Sittings	Free [360]. Total 360.
Attendance 30 March	Morning 56 + 66 SS. Total 122.
	Evening 30 + 40 SS. Total 70.
Average attendance	Morning 30 + 50 SS. Total [80].
Remarks	The evening service of 30 March was occasional. Divine service is performed by the Rev. Rob[er]t Maughan, curate of Stanhope [1844–65].
Dated	4 April 1851.
Signed	John Maddison, schoolmaster.
	Bolts Burn, Stanhope, Durham.
Incumbent	[William Nicholas Darnell 1831–65.]

24.5   Church of England, All Saints, Eastgate (544.14)

Name	Eastgate Church. Licensed chapel built for the convenience of the inhabitants of Eastgate village, and surrounding neighbourhood.
Consecrated	[1 May] 1840, for the convenience of the inhabitants of Eastgate and scattered vicinity who are three miles from the parish church at Stanhope.

Erected   Principally by the rector of Stanhope, and public
subscription. Total cost between £400 and £500.
Endowment   [Not given.]
Sittings   Free 120. Total 120.
Attendance 30 March   Afternoon 44 + 45 SS. Total 89.
Average attendance   Afternoon 50 + 48 SS. Total 98.
Dated   31 March 1851.
Signed   Thomas Moore, clerk [schoolmaster].
              Eastgate, Stanhope, via Darlington, Co[unt]y Durham.
Incumbent   [William Nicholas Darnell 1831–65.]
[A new church was consecrated by the Bishop of Adelaide on 20
December 1888.]

24.6   Church of England, St John the Baptist, St John's Chapel
(544.1)
Population 1851: 4,358 (Forest Quarter)

Name   St John's Chapel in Weardale, dedicated to St John the
              Baptist.
Consecrated Unable to say. [Ancient chapel. Chapel of ease to
              Stanhope. Erected 1752, enlarged 1881–83. Parish
              created 26 February 1866.]
Endowment   (The income is about £170 per annum chiefly derived
              from land, the remainder from Queen Anne's Bounty,
              in what proportion I have no information.)
Sittings   Free 400. Total 400.
Attendance 30 March   Morning – unable to ascertain + 24 SS.
              Total [?].
              Afternoon – unable to ascertain + 20 SS.
              Total [?].
Average attendance   [Not given.]
Dated   31 March 1851.
Signed   James Green, curate [1830–65].
              St John's in Weardale, Darlington.
Incumbent   [Joseph Waite 1821–65.]

{B 25.}

[In 1865 James Green succeeded Joseph Waite, and when Green died
in 1880 he was described as 'the oldest clergyman in the diocese
of Durham', G. Neasham, *The History and Biography of West Durham*
(Durham, 1881), p. 113.]

24.7   Church of England, Heathery Cleugh Chapel, Copt Hill
(544.2 and 544.2a)

Name   Heathery Cleugh Chapel, in parish of Stanhope.
Consecrated   In 1823. [3 September by the Bishop of Oxford.]
                Distance from St John's Chapel, out of which chapelry
                it was formed. [Parish created 20 February 1866.]
Erected   Entirely by the late Bishop [Shute] Barrington.
Endowment   Land £24. Glebe £9. OPE £89 (less expenses etc.).
                Fees £4 per annum.
Sittings   Free 250. Other 10. Total 260.
Attendance 30 March   Morning 12 + 20 SS. Total 32.
Average attendance   Morning 26 + 30 SS. Total 56.
Remarks   None.
Dated   31 March 1851.
Signed   Arthur George Hogarth, curate [1850–54].
                Heathery Cleugh Parsonage, Stanhope, Darlington.
{1857   Attendance 50. 7 communicants.}   {B 63.}
[St Thomas' church that opened on 6 February 1915 was built from
the stone of the previous building.]

(544.2a)
Name   Heathery Cleugh Chapel.
Consecrated   [3 September] 1823. As a district church to St John's
                Chapel.
Erected   Solely by Bishop [Shute] Barrington.
Endowment   Land £24. Glebe £9. OPE about £85. Fees £5.
Sittings   Free 250. Total 250.
Attendance 30 March   Morning 20 + 30 SS. Total [50].
Average attendance   Morning 20 + 30 SS. Total [50].
Dated   7 December 1851.
Signed   Arthur George Hogarth, curate [1850–54].
                Heathery Cleugh, Stanhope, Darlington.

24.8   Church of England, St Matthew, Wolsingham (544.28)
Population 1851: 4,585 (parish)

Name   St Mathew's. Ancient parish church.
Consecrated   Before 1800.
Endowment   [Not given.] [£791.]
Sittings   Free 150. Other 300. Total 450.
Attendance 30 March   [Not given.]
Average attendance   [Not given.]

Dated   31 March 1851.
Signed   John Alexander Blackett, rector [1847–56].
     Wolsingham Rectory, Darlington.
{1857   Attendance 200. 25 communicants.}   {B 42.}
[From December 1855 John Blackett assumed the name Blackett-Ord. The ancient dedication of the church was St Mary and St Stephen. When the church was reopened for worship after being rebuilt on 14 January 1849 (at a cost of £1,200) it was dedicated to St Matthew, and in 1896 the old dedication was restored.]

24.9   Church of England, St Bartholomew, Thornley
[Wolsingham] (544.29)
Population 1851: 2,206 (East Quarter)

Name   St Bartholomew. The church of the chapelry district
     of Thornley, Wolsingham, in the diocese of Durham,
     under the provisions of 59 Geo. III c.134, s.16.
Consecrated   In [12] August 1845, with a view to its becoming the
     church of a new ecclesiastical district. The chapelry
     district of Thornley was assigned to it in 1848 in [31
     January 1844 out of the parish of Wolsingham] by an
     Order of the Queen in Council.
Erected   By means of private subscription [by William Darnell
     (**24.3**)]. Private about £350. Total cost about £350.
Endowment   [£100 a year from the Weardale Iron Company. Fees
     about £10. In all £150.]
Sittings   Free 130. Total 130.
Attendance 30 March   [Not given.]
Average attendance   [Not given.]
Remarks   Divine service is celebrated every Sunday afternoon
     in a licensed schoolroom situated at Tow Law, in the
     above named chapelry district of Thornley.
Dated   31 March 1851.
Signed   Joshua Elliott, minister.
     Wolsingham, Darlington.
Incumbent   [John Alexander Blackett 1847–56.]
{1857   'A church is required at Tow Law'.}   {B 131.}
[Joshua Elliott, who was ordained deacon in 1840 and priest in 1841, was the headmaster of Wolsingham Grammar School 1838–47. The school, founded in 1614, was 'to teach boys the rudiments of Christian religion and grammar'. T.V. Devey, *Records of Wolsingham*

(Newcastle 1926), p. 73. The school moved to new buildings in 1849 and 1911.]

24.10   Church of England Schoolroom, Tow Law (544.30)
Population 1851: About 2,000

[Summary form]
Name   Licensed [National] schoolroom for the services of the
            Church of England.
Licensed   [2 May 1849. Services discontinued July 1856.]
Erected   AD 1849. [Total cost £1,000.]
Sittings   Free 250. Total 250.
Usual attendance   Afternoon (average for the last year) about 70
            + about 75 boys and girls [in SS]. Total about
            145.
Informant   Joshua Elliott, [minister].
            [Wolsingham, Darlington.]
Incumbent   [John Alexander Blackett 1847–56.]
[In 1841 Tow Law was the name of a farmhouse. By 1851 it was a village of 2,000 people. {By 1857 the services had been discontinued.} The church of St Philip and St James was consecrated on 24 July 1869.]

24.11   Baptist, Market Place, Wolsingham (544.34)
Name   Baptist Chapel.
Erected   1830. [Opened 5 May 1831. Enlarged 1889.]
Building   [Separate and entire. Exclusively used for worship.]
Sittings   Free 160. Other 39. Total [199].
Attendance 30 March   Evening 111. Total 111.
Average attendance   Afternoon 50. Total 50.
            Evening 120. Total 120.
Remarks   In this chapel there are two preaching services every
            alternate Sabbath. On 30 March, only one preaching
            service was held, viz. in the evening.
Dated   31 March 1851.
Signed   Thomas Cardwell, Baptist minister.
            [Market Place], Wolsingham.
[Thomas Cardwell was also the minister of Hamsterley (**13.18**).]

24.12   Wesleyan Methodist, Eastgate (544.17)
Name   Methodist Chapel.
Erected   1825.

Building   [Separate and] entire. [Exclusively used for worship.]
Sittings   Free 100. Other 18. Total [118]. Standing room none.
Attendance 30 March   Afternoon 30. Total 30.
                          Evening 25. Total 25.
Average attendance   Afternoon 30. Total 30.
                          Evening 30. Total 30.
Dated   31 March 1851.
Signed   Thomas Phillipson, chapel steward [farmer and butcher].
              Eastgate, Stanhope, Darlington, Durham.

24.13   Wesleyan Methodist, Edmundbyers (544.25)
Name   Wesleyan Chapel.
Erected   Year 1835. [Opened 21 August 1835.]
Building   [Separate and] entire. [Exclusively used for worship.]
Sittings   [All] free sittings.
Attendance 30 March   Morning 24 SS. Total 24.
                          Evening 50. Total 50.
Average attendance   [Not given.]
Dated   31 March 1851.
Signed   John Stokoe, steward [farmer].
              Edmundbyers, Shotley Bridge, Gateshead.

24.14   Wesleyan Methodist, Lane Head, Forest (544.10)
Name   Lane Head.
Erected   1815.
Building   [Separate and entire. Exclusively used for worship.]
Sittings   Free 80. Other 80. Total 160.
Attendance 30 March   Afternoon 60 + 30 SS. Total 90.
                          Evening 20 + 5 SS. Total 25.
Average attendance   Afternoon 120 + 30 SS. Total 150.
                          Evening 45 + 20 SS. Total 65.
Dated   30 March 1851.
Signed   John Carrick, society steward [lead ore miner].
              Stanhope, Durham.

24.15   Wesleyan Methodist, Mill Lane, Frosterley (544.22)
Name   Wesleyan Chapel.
Erected   [Not given.] [Built 1814, enlarged 1861. New chapel opened 21 February 1878.]
Building   [Separate and entire. Exclusively used for worship.]
Sittings   Free 100. Other 48. Total [148].

Attendance 30 March   Morning 57 SS. Total [57].
Afternoon 85 + 57 SS. Total [142].
Evening 40. Total [40].
Average attendance   Morning 70 + 57 SS. Total 127.
Dated   31 March 1851.
Signed   John Bainbridge, chapel steward [farmer].
Willow Green, Frosterley, Darlington.

24.16   Wesleyan Methodist, Lane Head, Heathery Cleugh (544.3a)
[Shared with Primitive Methodists (**24.29**)]
Name   Lane Head.
Erected   1813 or 1814.
Building   [Separate and entire. Exclusively used for worship.]
Sittings   Free 150. Other 70. Total [220].
Attendance 30 March   Afternoon 120 + 50 SS. Total [170].
Evening 60. Total [60].
Average attendance   [Not given.]
Dated   [Not given.]
Signed   Thomas Emerson [mining agent].
[Wellhope, Stanhope.]

24.17   Wesleyan Methodist Schoolroom, Hunstanworth (544.27)
Name   Rainshaw Wesleyan Preaching and Schoolroom.
Erected   1850.
Building   A room erected over the mines stores room. A
weekday evenings school also.
Sittings   Free 250. Total [250].
Attendance 30 March   Afternoon 73 + 49 SS. Total 122.
Evening 119 + 35 SS. Total 154.
Average attendance   [Not given.]
Dated   30 March 1851.
Signed   Thomas Elliott, steward to the society [farmer].
Wagtail, n[ea]r Blanchland, Riding Mill, Gateshead-on-
Tyne, Durham.
[By 1856 the schoolroom at the Derwent Lead Mines was used on
alternate Sundays by the Wesleyan Methodists and the Primitive
Methodists.]

24.18   Wesleyan Methodist, High House, Ireshopeburn (544.5)
Name   High House [Chapel].
Erected   Before 1800 [1760], but enlarged about the year 1806
[and 1872].

Building   [Separate and entire. Exclusively used for worship.]
Sittings   Free 350. Other 350. Total [700]. Standing room 150.
Attendance 30 March   Morning 360. Total [360].
              Afternoon 600. Total [600].
              Evening 90. Total [90].
Average attendance   Morning 350. Total [350].
              Afternoon 650. Total [650].
              Evening 90. Total [90].
Dated   31 March 1851.
Signed   John Phillipson, chapel steward [builder].
              Rigg House, St John's Chapel, Weardale, by
              Darlington.
[High House is reputed to be the oldest Methodist chapel still
holding weekly services.]

24.19   Wesleyan Methodist, Stanhope (544.20)
Name   Wesleyan Chapel.
Erected   1797. [New chapel 1871.]
Building   [Separate and entire. Exclusively used for worship.]
Sittings   Free 200. Other 80. Total [280]. Standing room 30.
Attendance 30 March   Morning 150. Total [150].
              Afternoon 75. Total [75].
              Evening 100. Total [100].
Average attendance   [Not given.]
Dated   31 March 1851.
Signed   Nicholas Emerson, society steward [limestone
              quarryman].
              Stanhope, Darlington, Durham.

24.20   Wesleyan Methodist, Bolts Burn, Stanhope (544.16)
Name   Wesleyan Methodist Chapel.
Erected   1813.
Building   [Separate and] entire. Exclusively [used for worship].
Sittings   Free 60. Other 55. Total [115]. Standing room 85.
Attendance 30 March   Afternoon 40 + 9 SS. Total 49.
              Evening 33 + 6 SS. Total 39.
Average attendance   Afternoon 81 + 30 SS. Total 110 (*sic*). [111].
              Evening 80 + 20 SS. Total 100.
Dated   31 March 1851.
Signed   William Bowman, trustee [lead smelter].
              Rookhope, Stanhope, Darlington.

24.21   Wesleyan Methodist, Westgate (544.8)
Name   Westgate Chapel.
Erected   1790. [Enlarged 1878.]
Building   [Separate and entire. Exclusively used for worship.]
Sittings   Free 300. Other 172. Total [472].
Attendance 30 March   Morning 50 + 30 SS. Total 80.
                        Afternoon 150 + 30 SS. Total 180.
                        Evening 400 + 20 SS. Total 420.
Average attendance   [Not given.]
Dated   30 March 1851.
Signed   Joshua Myers.
               John Imisson, Wesleyan minster [1850–51].
               Westgate.

24.22   Wesleyan Methodist, Wolsingham (544.31)
Name   Wesleyan Chapel.
Erected   Since 1800. [Opened 1776, rebuilt 1835 and 1862.]
Building   [Separate and entire. Exclusively used for worship.]
Sittings   Free 80. Other 350. Total [430].
Attendance 30 March   Afternoon 100 + 30 SS. Total 130.
                        Evening 300 + 20 SS. Total 320.
Average attendance   [Not given.]
Dated   30 March 1851.
Signed   John Imisson, Wesleyan minister [1850–51].
               [Front Street], Wolsingham.

24.23   Wesleyan Methodist, Wolsingham (544.35)
Name   Wesleyan Chapel.
Erected   Nov[ember] 1846.
Building   [Not separate and entire but exclusively used for
               worship.]
Sittings   Free 160. Other 132. Total [292].
Attendance 30 March   Morning 64 SS. Total 64.
                        Afternoon 110. Total 110.
                        Evening 118. Total 118.
Average attendance   Morning 60 SS. Total 60.
                        Afternoon 100. Total 100.
                        Evening 140. Total 140.
Remarks   There is a day school and dwelling house under the
               chapel.
Dated   30 March 1851.
Signed   Michael Soulsby, society steward [schoolmaster].
               Tow Law, by Darlington.

24.24   Primitive Methodist, Brotherlee (544.7)

Name   Chapel.
Erected   1850.
Building   [Separate and] entire building. Place of worship and Sunday school.
Sittings   Free 76. Other 24. Total [100]. Standing room 0.
Attendance 30 March   Morning 52 + 14 SS. Total 66.
Average attendance   Morning 40 + 20 SS. Total [60].
Dated   [Not given.]
Signed   John Dover Muschamp, circuit steward [landed proprietor].
                Brotherlee, Weardale, Durham.

[When Primitive Methodism first came to Weardale in January 1822 the first convert was John Dover Muschamp (1776–1858). Initially he fitted up a barn for services and then, at his own expense, built the chapel at Westgate (**24.33**) for £400. 'This gentleman was a remarkable person and an earnest Christian. He kept a diary of the passing local events, and rendered great assistance to and was an earnest supporter of the Primitive Methodists, when they first missioned Weardale in 1822', W.M. Egglestone, *All Around Stanhope* (Stanhope, n.d.), p. 216.]

24.25   Primitive Methodist, Eastgate (544.18)

Name   None.
Erected   [Not given.]
Building   [Not separate and entire or exclusively used for worship.]
Sittings   Free 36. Total [36].
Attendance 30 March   Morning 20. Total 20.
                        Evening 20. Total 20.
Average attendance   [Not given.]
Remarks   The service is performed in a private dwelling house.
Dated   31 March 1851.
Signed   William Dowson, deacon [ironstone labourer].
                Eastgate, Stanhope, via Darlington, Co[unt]y Durham.

24.26   Primitive Methodist, Edmundbyers (544.24)

Name   None.
Erected   Before 1800 [crossed out].
Building   [Not separate and entire or exclusively used for worship.] Dwelling house [in another hand].
Sittings   [Not given.] Standing room 30 yards.

Attendance 30 March   [No services held.]
Average attendance   Morning 25. Total [25].
Dated   30 March 1851.
Signed   George Rain, steward [farmer].
                Edmundbyers, Shotley Bridge, Gateshead.

24.27   Primitive Methodist, Lane Head, Forest (544.11)
Name   Lane Head.
Erected   1834.
Building   [Separate and entire. Exclusively used for worship.]
Sittings   Free 70. Other 50. Total [120].
Attendance 30 March   Afternoon 51. Total [51].
                        Evening 59. Total [59].
Average attendance   [Not given.]
Dated   31 March 1851.
Signed   James Carrick, elder.
                Wellhope, Wearhead.

24.28   Primitive Methodist, Bridge End, Frosterley (554.21)
Name   Primitive Methodist Chapel.
Erected   In the year 1830. [New chapel 1861.]
Building   [Separate and entire. Exclusively used for worship.]
Sittings   Free 80. Other 70. Total [150].
Attendance 30 March   Morning 105 + 20 SS. Total 125.
                        Evening 190 + 10 SS. Total 200.
Average attendance   [Not given.]
Remarks   It will be observed that the number attending on the
                evening of the 30 March is 50 above the number for
                whom seats are provided, but it is intended to build a
                larger chapel as soon as the society find it convenient
                to do so! T. Calvert.
Dated   30 March 1851.
Signed   Thomas Calvert, society steward [railway station
                master].
                Frosterley, via Darlington.

24.29   Primitive Methodist, Lane Head, Heathery Cleugh (544.3b)
[Shared with Wesleyan Methodists (**24.16**)]
Name   Lane Head.
Erected   1834 (*sic*) [1813 or 1814].
Building   [Separate and entire. Exclusively used for worship.]
Sittings   Free 60. Other 50. Total [110].

Attendance 30 March   Afternoon 50. Total [50].
                        Evening 58. Total [58].
Average attendance   [Not given.]
Dated   [Not given.]
Signed   Edward Baty [lead miner].
               [Wellhope, Heathery Cleugh.]

24.30   Primitive Methodist, Stanhope (544.19)
Name   Primitive Methodist Chapel.
Erected   1847.
Building   [Separate and entire. Exclusively used for worship.]
Sittings   Free 200. Other 200. Total [400].
Attendance 30 March   Morning, Sabbath school meets.
                        Afternoon 78 + 20 SS. Total 98.
                        Evening 147. Total 147.
Average attendance   Afternoon 100 + 20 SS. Total 120.
                        Evening 200. Total 200.
Remarks   The weather being unfavourable on 30 March our
               congregation fell below average, the principal part of
               which having to come from a distance being scattered
               over a rural district.
Dated   31 March 1851.
Signed   Joseph Rain, steward (tailor).
               Stanhope, Darlington.

24.31   Primitive Methodist, Rookhope, Stanhope (544.15)
Name   Primitive Methodist Chaple (*sic*).
Erected   In 1838. [New chapel 1863.]
Building   [Separate and entire. Exclusively used for worship.]
Sittings   Free 65. Other 50. Total [115].
Attendance 30 March   Afternoon 31 + 12 SS. Total 47 (*sic*) [43].
                        Evening 16 + 2 SS. Total 16 (*sic*) [18].
Average attendance   [Not given.]
Dated   30 March 1851.
Signed   Cuthbert Hanless, local preacher.
               High House, Rookhope, Stanhope, Darlington.

24.32   Primitive Methodist, St John's Chapel (544.4)
Name   Primitive Methodist Preaching House.
Erected   It was not erected for a meeting house, but was taken
               by the Primitive Methodists to last May. Cannot say
               when erected. [Enlarged 1852.]

Building   [Not separate and entire or exclusively used for
             worship.]
Sittings   Free 60. Total [60].
Attendance 30 March   Morning 60 + 51 SS. Total [111].
                        Evening 46. Total [46].
Average attendance   [Not given.]
Dated   31 March 1851.
Signed   William Clemitson, minister.
             [Three Elms] Westgate, Weardale, Durham.

24.33   Primitive Methodist, Westgate (544.9)
Name   Primitive Methodist Chapel.
Erected   1823. [Opened 4 April 1823, and cost £400 solely
             provided by John Muschamp (**24.24**). New adjacent
             chapel to seat 600 was opened 29 April 1871, and cost
             £1,650.]
Building   [Separate and entire. Exclusively used for worship.]
Sittings   Free 250. Other 280. Total [530]. Standing room none.
Attendance 30 March   Morning, meeting for prayer.
                        Afternoon 144 + 22 SS. Total 166.
                        Evening 244. Total 244.
Average attendance   Afternoon 200. Total [200].
                        Evening 300. Total [300].
Remarks   This district being a rural one, our congregations
             are much affected by the state of the weather, and
             30 March being a stormy one, accounts for the
             congregation not being so large as it usually is.
Dated   31 March 1851.
Signed   William Clemitson, minister.
             [Three Elms] Westgate, Weardale, Durham.

24.34   Primitive Methodist, Wearhead (544.6)
Name   Wearhead Chapel.
Erected   In 1824.
Building   Separate building. A place of worship and Sunday
             school.
Sittings   Free about 160. Other about 240. Total [about 400].
Attendance 30 March   Morning – Sunday school.
                        Afternoon 130. Total [130].
                        Evening 50. Total [50].
Average attendance   Morning 300 + 110 SS. Total [410].
Dated   31 March 1851.

Signed   Timothy Naltrap, trustee.
                Ireshopeburn, Weardale, Durham.

24.35   Primitive Methodist, Silver Street, Wolsingham (544.33)
Name   Primitive Methodist Chapel.
Erected   About the year 1826. [Converted to cottages 1885.]
Building   [Separate and entire but not exclusively used for
                worship.]
Sittings   Free 150. Other 100. Total [250].
Attendance 30 March   Afternoon 60 + 10 SS. Total [70].
                        Evening 92 + 6 SS. Total [98].
Average attendance   [Not given.]
Dated   31 March 1851.
Signed   William Snowball, chapel steward [stonemason].
                [East End], Wolsingham, Durham.

24.36   Primitive Methodist, Wolsingham (544.36)
Name   Primitive Methodist Chapel.
Erected   1846.
Building   [Separate and entire. Exclusively used for worship.]
Sittings   Free 130. Other 124. Total [254]. Standing room 50.
Attendance 30 March   Morning 60 + 48 SS. Total 108.
                        Evening 200 + 50 SS. Total 250.
Average attendance   [Not given.]
Dated   31 March 1851.
Signed   John Beach, society steward.
                Tow Law Iron Works, Darlington.

24.37   Roman Catholic, Wolsingham (544.32)
Name   Chapel of Saint Thomas of Canterbury. (Holy Catholic
                Church.)
Erected   1849. [New church to seat 800, opened 5 September
                1854. Cost about £2,000.]
Building   [Separate and entire. Exclusively used for worship.]
Sittings   Free 66. Other 93. Total [159]. Standing room 30.
Attendance 30 March   Morning 150. Total 150.
                        Afternoon 40. Total 40.
Average attendance   Morning 150. Total 150.
Remarks   The numbers attending divine service in this
                congregation cannot be fairly presented in a return of
                this kind; because very many of the men are at work

every second Sunday at the neighbouring iron works
and thus are only able to attend on alternate Sundays.

Dated   31 March 1851.

Signed   Thomas William Wilkinson, Catholic priest [1849–59].
Wolsingham, Darlington.

[In 1852 the estimated number of Roman Catholics in the area was
700.]

Summary of All Places of Worship
in County Durham

617 places of worship

13. Auckland District (HO 129/542)   **61 places of worship**

Church of England churches	15
Church of England schoolroom	1
Independent chapel	1
Baptist	
General chapel	1
Baptist schoolroom	1
Methodist	
Wesleyan chapels	17
Primitive chapels	16
Primitive schoolrooms	3
Association chapels	3
Society of Friends meeting houses	2
Roman Catholic church	1

14. Chester-le-Street District (HO 129/548)   **36 places of worship**

Church of England churches	7	
Church of England schoolrooms	3	
Independent chapel	1	
Methodist		
Wesleyan chapels	16	(2 shared with Primitive Methodists)
Wesleyan schoolroom	1	(1 shared with Primitive Methodists)
New Connexion chapels	2	
Primitive chapels	4	(2 shared with Wesleyan Methodists)
Primitive schoolroom	1	(1 shared with Wesleyan Methodists)
Association chapel	1	

15. Darlington District (HO 129/540)   **38 places of worship**

Church of England churches	13
Church of England schoolroom	1
Independent chapel	1
Baptist chapel	1

Methodist
   Wesleyan chapels   12
   Wesleyan schoolroom   1
   Primitive chapels   4
   Association chapels   4
Roman Catholic church   1

16. Durham District (HO 129/545)   **90 places of worship**
Church of England churches   22
Church of England schoolrooms   6
Independent chapel   1
Baptist
   General chapels   2
Methodist
   Wesleyan chapels   25
   Wesleyan schoolrooms   5   (1 shared with Primitive
                                    Methodists)
   New Connexion chapels   3
   Primitive chapels   16
   Primitive schoolrooms   3   (1 shared with Wesleyan
                                    Methodists)
Society of Friends meeting houses 2
Roman Catholic churches   5

17. Easington District (HO 129/546)   **32 places of worship**
Church of England churches   10
Church of England schoolroom   1
Methodist
   Wesleyan chapels   9
   Wesleyan schoolroom   1
   Primitive chapels   7
   Primitive schoolroom   1
   Association chapel   1
Roman Catholic churches   2

18. Gateshead District (HO 129/551)   **65 places of worship**
Church of England churches   12
Church of England schoolrooms   3
Presbyterian
   United church   1
   English church   1
Independent chapels   5

Baptist chapel   1
Methodist
    Wesleyan chapels   15
    Wesleyan schoolroom   1
    New Connexion chapels   9
    New Connexion schoolroom   1
    Primitive chapels   12
    Reformers chapel   1
Roman Catholic churches   3

19. Houghton le Spring District   **37 places of worship**
(HO 129/547)
Church of England churches   6
Presbyterian
    United church   1
Independent chapel   1
Baptist schoolroom   1
Methodist
    Wesleyan chapels   13
    Wesleyan schoolroom   1
    New Connexion chapel   1
    Primitive chapels   7
    Association chapels   5
Roman Catholic church   1

20. South Shields District (HO 129/550)   **49 places of worship**
Church of England churches   12
Presbyterian
    United churches   2
    English churches   2
Independent chapels   3
Baptist
    General chapel   1
    Particular chapel   1
Methodists
    Wesleyan chapels   13
    Wesleyan schoolroom   1
    New Connexion chapels   3
    Primitive chapels   4
    Primitive schoolroom   1
    Association chapels   2
    Reformers chapel   1

Non-denominational chapel 1
Roman Catholic church 1
Latter-day Saints (Mormons) 1

21. Stockton District (HO 129/541)   **68 places of worship**
Church of England churches 23
Church of England schoolrooms 3
Presbyterian
    United churches 2
Independent chapels 3
Baptist
    General chapel 1
    Particular chapel 1
    Particular schoolroom 1
Methodist
    Wesleyan chapels 17
    Wesleyan schoolroom 1
    Primitive chapels 5
    Association chapel 1
    Association schoolroom 1
    Reformers chapel 1
Non-denominational chapel 1
Society of Friends meeting houses 2
Roman Catholic churches 3
Unitarian chapel 1
(Mormons) 1

22. Sunderland District (HO 129/549)   **72 places of worship**
Church of England churches 10
Presbyterian
    United churches 4
    English churches 1
Independent chapels 6
Baptist
    General chapels 5   (1 shared with Wesleyan
                  Methodists)
    Particular chapel 1
Methodists
    Wesleyan chapels 16   (1 shared with Baptists)
    Wesleyan schoolrooms 2
    New Connexion chapels 3

Primitive chapels	6	(1 shared with Wesley Reformers)
Association chapels	5	
Reformers chapels	5	(1 shared with Primitive Methodists)
Non-denominational chapels	3	
Society of Friends meeting house	1	
Roman Catholic church	1	
Synagogues	2	
Unitarian chapel	1	

23. Teesdale District (HO 129/543)　　32 places of worship

Church of England churches	7	
Independent chapels	4	
Baptist		
General chapels	2	
Methodist		
Wesleyan chapels	9	
Primitive chapels	6	
Primitive schoolroom	1	
Society of Friends meeting house	1	
Roman Catholic church	1	
Unitarian chapel	1	

24. Weardale District (HO 129/544)　　37 places of worship

Church of England churches	9	
Church of England schoolroom	1	
Baptist chapel	1	
Methodist		
Wesleyan chapels	11	(1 shared with Primitive Methodists)
Wesleyan schoolroom	1	
Primitive chapels	13	(1 shared with Wesleyan Methodists)
Roman Catholic church	1	

Total summary 617
Church of England churches 146
Church of England schoolrooms 19
Presbyterian
    United churches 10
    English churches 4
Independent chapels 26
Baptist
    General chapels 15
    General schoolrooms 2
    Particular chapels 3
    Particular schoolroom 1
Methodists
    Wesleyan chapels 173
    Wesleyan schoolrooms 15
    New Connexion chapels 21
    New Connexion schoolroom 1
    Primitive chapels 100
    Primitive schoolrooms 10
    Association chapels 22
    Association schoolroom 1
    Reformers chapels 8
Non-denominational chapels 5
Society of Friends meeting houses 8
Roman Catholic churches 20
Synagogues 2
Unitarian chapels 3
Latter-day Saints (Mormons) 2

Numerical Strength 617
Methodist 351
Church of England 165
Independent 26
Baptist 21
Roman Catholic 20
Presbyterian 14
Society of Friends (Quakers) 8
Non-denominational 5
Unitarian 3
Synagogues 2
Latter-day Saints (Mormons) 2

Places of Worship not listed in the Religious Census

This is an incomplete list. County and town directories may indicate the existence of a church or chapel but rarely give the date when the building was opened, and whether or not it was in use in March 1851. Durham cathedral is not included since returns from cathedrals were not compulsory.

Church of England
St Mary, Barnard Castle. {1857 attendance 600. 75 communicants.}
{B 137.}
Shinton, Barnard Castle, schoolroom (from 1850). {1857 average congregation 70.}
Bridgegate, Barnard Castle, schoolroom. {Average congregation 60.}
Blackhill, schoolroom (1847).
Chopwell, schoolroom (from 1845).
St John's, Darlington, schoolroom (1846).
Dunston schoolroom (1847).
Witton Park, Escomb, schoolroom.
St James the Less, Forest and Frith.
Christ Church, West Hartlepool (consecrated 20 April 1834).
St James, Harwood in Middleton (consecrated 7 August 1845).
St Cuthbert, Hebburn.
North Hylton, schoolroom (1850).
St Bede, Jarrow.
St Philip and St James, Kimblesworth.
St John the Evangelist, Merrington. {B 43.}
St Mary the Virgin, Middleton-in-Teesdale. {B 48.}
Monkheselden, schoolroom (1844). {1857 70 well attended.}
All Saints, Monkwearmouth (consecrated 23 October 1849). {B 70.}
Monkwearmouth room (1844).
Softey
(No dedication) Whitworth (erected 1808, rebuilt 1850). {B 20.}
Gibside Chapel, Winlaton.
Woodland, Cockfield schoolroom. {1857 average 40am, 12 pm.}
Wynyard Hall chapel, Grindon (1847). {1857 attendance 40.}

Presbyterian
Ireshopeburn, Stanhope (1687).

Independent [Congregational]
Bishop Auckland (opened 24 November 1822).

Newgate, Barnard Castle (1836).
Felling (1835).

Baptist
Enon Chapel, Barclay Street, Monkwearmouth Shore (1834).
Hartlepool (1845).

Methodist

Wesleyan Methodist
Castle Eden.
Etherley (1829).
Haswell (erected 1849).
Hurworth on Tees (opened 4 Oct 1827)
Loninghead, Heathery Cleugh.
Midridge.
Tow Law (opened 1846).

Methodist New Connexion
Willington (1845).

Primitive Methodist
Collierly (from 1842).
Collierly Dykes [Dipton] (1834, new chapel 1873). 'The Ranters'
     Chapel'.
Easington.
Etherley (erected 1829, enlarged 1840).
Sacriston.
Loninghead, Heathery Cleugh.
Tow Law (1846).

Wesleyan Methodist Association
Leasingthorpe (1847).
Seaham Harbour, Church Street (1837).
Stockton on Tees, Regent Street.

Wesleyan Reformers
Town Hall, Hartlepool.
Monkwearmouth Shore, Dock Street (1851).

Non-denominational
Sailors' Bethel, Victoria Dock, Hartlepool.

Sailors' Bethel, The Docks, Seaham Harbour (opened 20 September 1846).

Society of Friends (Quakers)
Skinnergate, Darlington (1768, enlarged 1793; rebuilt 1846).

Roman Catholic
St Mary and St Joseph, Birtley (opened 8 April 1843).
[In 1852 the estimated number of Roman Catholics in the area was 450.]

Latter-day Saints (Mormons)
The Mormons held open air meetings on Sundays.

YORKSHIRE

Places of Worship included in the Durham Returns

63 places of worship

For the complete returns for Yorkshire see, J. Wolffe (ed.), *Yorkshire Returns of the 1851 Census of Religious Worship*, 4 vols. (York 2000–). The Church of England parishes were located in the adjoining dioceses of York and Ripon (formed in 1836).

15. Darlington (HO 129/540)
10 places of worship

15.39   Church of England, St Cuthbert with St Mary, Barton
(540.4 and 540.3)
Population 1851: 508 (township)

[Summary form]
Name   Barton.
Erected   1840 and 1841. See annexed particulars.
Endowment   [£110.]
Sittings   Free 165. Other 217. Total 382.
Usual attendance   Morning about 150 + 75 or 80 SS.
                        Total [225–230].
                        Afternoon between 80 & 90 + 75–80 SS.
                        Total [155–170].
                        Evening about 130 + about 80 SS. Total [210].
Remarks   In winter the service is in the afternoon. In summer the service is in the evening.
Dated   [Not given.]
Signed   William Raine Atkinson, incumbent of Barton [1835–72].

(540.3) [Supplementary letter]

In the village of Barton, in the county of York and diocese of Ripon within 300 yards of each other stood two very ancient churches or chapels up to the year 1840. They were two district perpetual curacies. The church or chapel of St Mary's, Barton under the vicarage of Gilling. The vicar of Gilling being patron in right of his vicarage. The church or chapel of St Cuthbert's, Barton under the vicarage of St John's, Stanwick. The vicarage of Stanwick being patron in right of his vicarage.

In the year 1840, the two churches or chapels became so dilapidated and also too small for the congregation, as the same congregation attended churches, the duty or service being morning and evening alternately. It was then thought desirable to take down the two existing churches and build one sufficiently large to accommodate both parishes: but before this could be done, it was necessary to consolidate the two benefices into one. The patron (as at that time the same person held both the vicarages, viz., Gilling and Stanwick), the bishop of the diocese, and myself, as incumbent of both parishes, all agreeing, the two perpetual curacies were united into one benefice under an Act holden in the first and second years of the reign of her present Majesty, intituled An Act to abridge the holding of benefices in plurality etc., etc. [An Act to abridge the holding of benefices in plurality, and to make better provision for the residence of the clergy, 1 and 2 Vic. c.106]. The vicar of Gilling and the vicar of Stanwick for the time being to have alternate presentation.

In the years 1840 and 1841 the new church was erected in the old churchyard of St Cuthbert's, Barton, and consecrated, in the month of September 1841. It cost about £1,000 raised by subscription and with the assistance of the Incorporated Society for the Building and Enlarging of churches and chapels, and the Ripon Diocesan Church Building Society, the occupiers of the land giving the leading of materials.

The income of the benefice is derived from the following sources: an immemorial annual payment of £10 from the vicar of Gilling, the like sum from the vicar of Stanwick; from land purchased by grants from the governors of Queen Anne's Bounty, £72 per annum. Interest on £400 in the hands of the governors of Queen Anne's Bounty at 3¼ per cent per annum, £13. Total income £105 per annum. The fees are very small.

W. R. Atkinson, incumbent of Barton.

Barton, 10 December 1851.

15.40   Church of England, St Peter, Cleasby (540.5)
Population 1851: 197 (parish)

Name	Cleasby Chapel. The church of an ancient chapelry, an old foundation. A parish church.
Consecrated	Before 1800. Rebuilt and very slightly enlarged 1828.
Erected	Erected originally by Dr [John] Robinson, Bishop of London in the early part of the 18th century.
Endowment	Land about £180.
Sittings	Free 37. Other 83. Total 120.
Attendance 30 March	Morning 51 + 9 SS. Total 60.
	Evening 37. Total 37.
Average attendance	[Not given.]
Remarks	The congregation may be accounted for by the erection of a Methodist meeting house, and one of the principal occupiers of land being a nonconformist requiring all whom he employs to attend, he employing the majority of the labouring class, they being agricultural labourers.
Dated	30 March 1851.
Signed	Charles Watson, curate [1846–54].
	Cleasby, Darlington.
Incumbent	[Joseph Jameson 1826–76.]

[John Robinson (1650–1723), born at Cleasby. Bishop of Bristol 1710–14, Bishop of London 1714–23.]

15.41   Church of England, St Peter, Croft (540.9)
Population 1851: 750 (parish) 447 (township)

Name	Old Parish Church. St Peter's.
Consecrated	Before 1800. [Restored 1878; enlarged 1887.]
Endowment	Tithe £923. Glebe £56. Fees under £5.
Sittings	Free 25. Other 325. Total 350.
Attendance 30 March	Morning 159 + 84 SS. Total 243.
	Afternoon 97 + 54 SS. Total 151.
Average attendance	[Not given.]
Remarks	There are evening services in the summer as well as in the morning and afternoon, but they have not yet commenced for this season.
Dated	31 March 1851.
Signed	Charles Dodgson, rector [1843–68].
	Croft Rectory, Darlington.

[The high churchman Charles Dodgson (1800–1868) was also an examining chaplain to the Bishop of Ripon (Charles Thomas Longley) 1836–56, and Archdeacon of Richmond 1854–68. His eldest son, Charles Lutwidge Dodgson, is better known as Lewis Carroll. 'Charles Lutwidge Dodgson (1832–1898)', *ODNB*, vol. 16, pp. 420–426. Croft is described as a 'bustling spa and hunting centre' (p. 421).]

15.42   Church of England, All Saints, Manfield (540.2)
Population 1851: 435 (parish) 372 (township)

[Summary form]
Name   All Saints.
Erected   Very old, but repaired and partially restored 1850–51.
                [Restored 1855.]
Endowment [£466.]
Sittings   Free 82. Scholars 55. Other 160. Total 297.
Usual attendance   Morning from 90 to 110 + 52 SS.
                Total [142–162].
                Afternoon from 50 to 70 + 52 SS.
                Total [102–122].
Dated   [Not given.]
Signed   John Swire, vicar [1823–60].

15.43   Church of England, St Andrew, North Cowton (540.12)
Population 1851: 312 (township)

Name   St Andrew's, the church of an ancient chapelry.
                (Reputed to be in the parish of Gilling, but completely
                separated from it.)
Consecrated [Not given.]
Endowment Land £35 5s. Glebe and OPE £13 1s 1d. Fees 10s.
                Easter offerings 10s. Total £49 6s 1d.
Sittings   Free 73 (seats open 34, seats claimed by custom
                39). No faculty. (Other) persons have seats here by
                custom. There is room for additional seats at present
                unoccupied. Total 73.
Attendance 30 March   Afternoon 42. Total 42.
Average attendance   Morning 40. Total [40].
                Afternoon 50. Total [50].

(Only one service a day alternating with
[St Mary] South Cowton.)

Remarks   The parsonage is included in £35 5s and might let for
£4 or £5. The tithe is commuted for £14 7s 9d but a
payment of £3 6s 8d is made to the vicar of Gilling out
of them. A deduction ought to be made from the tithe
on account of averages being in favour of the payers.
(£14 7s 9d – £1 6s 8d = £13 1s 1d.)
(No marriage, no burial during the last year, but three
in this w[ee]k to church, and the fees for churchings
etc. returned to all poor people.)
(It may be required to have a similar statement
respecting South Cowton in which about as many
seats are open as in pews.)

Dated   31 March 1851.

Signed   John Todd, minister [1840–77].
North Cowton, Catterick, Yorkshire.

15.44   Wesleyan Methodist, Barton (540.7)

Name   Wesleyan Chapel.

Erected   1830. [Dated 1829. Restored 1878.]

Building   [Separate and entire. Exclusively used for worship.]

Sittings   Free 120. Other 76. Total [196].

Attendance 30 March   Evening 100 [including SS]. Total [100].

Average attendance   [1,200 crossed out.]

Dated   31 March 1851.

Signed   George Marshall, steward [carpenter].
Barton, near Darlington, Yorkshire.

15.45   Wesleyan Methodist Schoolroom, Dalton-on-Tees (540.11)

Name   Dalton School.

Erected   1834.

Building   [Separate and entire but not exclusively used for
worship.

Sittings   Sittings for about 90. Total [90].

Attendance 30 March   Morning 19 SS. Total 19.
Afternoon 18. Total 18.

Average attendance   [Not given.]

Dated   31 March 1851.

Signed   George Wild senior, steward [schoolmaster].
Dalton upon Tees, near Croft, Yorkshire.

15.46   Wesleyan Methodist, Stapleton (540.8)

Name   Wesleyan Preaching Room.
Erected   Opened in 1848, in lieu of a similar room, occupied say
              20 years before.
Building   Part of a dwelling house. [Exclusively used for
              worship.]
Sittings   Free 45. Total [45].
Attendance 30 March   Afternoon 15. Total [15].
Average attendance   [Not given.]
Dated   31 March 1851.
Signed   George Jackson, superintendent minister [1849–51].
              Wesley Place, Darlington, Durham.
              [George Jackson was also the minister of two chapels
              in Darlington (**15.19, 15.20**) and Sadberg (**15.21**).]

15.47   Wesleyan Methodist Association Schoolroom, Cleasby
(540.6)

Name   School House or Dames School.
Erected   Used as a place of worship since May 1849.
Building   Separate [and entire. Used by] day school, Sunday
              school and place of worship.
Sittings   All free [100 in another hand]. Total [100].
              Standing room 8 yards by 4 [yards].
Attendance 30 March   Morning none.
                       Afternoon 45 SS. Total 45.
                       Evening 60. Total 60.
Average attendance   Morning from 40 to 70 + from 30 to 45 SS.
                       Total [70–115].
Dated   31 March 1851.
Signed   Joseph Johnson, local preacher, class leader and
              superintendent of Sunday school [farmer].
              Cleasby, near Darlington.

15.48   Wesleyan Methodist Association, Croft (540.10)

Name   None.
Erected   [Not given.]
Building   Not separate [and entire. Exclusively used for
              worship.]
Sittings   Free 100. Total [100]. Standing room for 150 persons.
Attendance 30 March   Evening 56. Total [56].
Average attendance   Evening 60. Total [60].

Dated   30 March 1851.
Signed   Henry Tarrant, minister.
[5] Prebend Row, Darlington.
[Henry Tarrant was also the minister of Blackwell (**15.34**) and Darlington (**15.35**).]

17. Easington (HO 129/541)
1 place of worship

17.33   Church of England, All Saints, Easington, Holderness, East Yorkshire (546.18)
Population 1851: 803 (parish) 602 (township)

Name   All Saints, an ancient village church.
Consecrated   Consecrated.
Endowment   Land £61. OPE money payment from the Archbishop
                of York. Other £20.
Sittings   Free 42. Other 358. Total 400.
Attendance 30 March   Afternoon 53 + 10 SS. Total 63.
Average attendance   Morning 20 + 20 SS. Total 40.
                        Afternoon 70 + 20 SS. Total 90.
Remarks   The land was bought by Queen Ann's (*sic*) Bounty.
Dated   31 March 1851.
Signed   Frederick Thomas Wilson, curate [1849–57].
                Easington, near Patrington, Hull.
[This return was incorrectly included with Easington, County Durham (**17.3**).]

21. Stockton (HO 129/541)
26 places of worship

21.69   Church of England, St Mary, Acklam (541.19)
Population 1851: 110 (parish)

Name   Name given to the church on its consecration not
                known. Commonly called Acklam Church.
Consecrated   [Not given. Rebuilt 1765 and enlarged 1874.]
Erected   Not known.
Endowment   [£44.]
Sittings   Free 150 (estimated). Other 50 (estimated). Total 200
                (estimated).

Attendance 30 March   Morning between 80 & 90. Total [80–90].
Afternoon about 50. Total [about 50].
Average attendance   Morning between 80 & 100. Total [80–100].
Afternoon between 40 & 60. Total [40–60].
Remarks   The population is scattered in the parish and the
congregation varies according to the weather and the
time of the year.
Dated   31 March 1851.
Signed   Isaac Benson, incumbent-curate [1823–64].
Acklam, Stockton-on-Tees.

21.70   Church of England, St Hilda, Middlesbrough (541.20)
Population 1851: 7,893 (parish) 7,631 (township)

Name   St Hilda. New church of a distinct and separate parish.
Consecrated   In 1840 [25 September by the Bishop of Durham].
There was no church in the parish [of Ackham] till the
present one was built. [New chancel 1890.]
Erected   By subscriptions and a grant [of £500] from the
Church Building Society. [Total cost £2,500.]
Endowment   Land £34. Pew rents £80. Fees £37.
Sittings   Free 300. Other 300. Total 600.
Attendance 30 March   Morning 250 + 334 SS. Total 584.
Evening 360. Total [360].
Average attendance   Morning 250 + 220 SS. Total [470].
Afternoon 270 SS. Total [270].
Evening 450. Total [450].
Dated   30 March 1851.
Signed   John Peel, curate [1848–53].
[Queens Terrace], Middlesbro[ugh].
Incumbent   [Isaac Benson 1823–64.]

21.71   Church of England, St Martin, Kirk Levington (541.9)
Population 1851: 513 (parish) 44 (township)

Name   St Martin. A small ancient parish church.
Consecrated   Before 1800. [Restored 1883.]
Endowment   Land £35. Tithe £20. OPE £38. Fees £2.
Sittings   Free 120. Other 30. Total 150.
Attendance 30 March   Morning 60. Total 60.
Average attendance   [Not given.]
Remarks   The duty in this church alternates, i.e. in the morning

one Sunday, in the afternoon the following one.
The state of education in this parish is wretchedly
low there being neither day not Sunday school in
connexion with the established church.

Dated   31 March 1851.
Signed   William Putsey, minister [1838–75].
             Kirk Levington, Yarm, North Yorkshire.

21.72 Church of England, St Peter, Stainton (541.15)
Population 1851: 2,485 (parish) 358 (township)

Name   St Peter's.
Consecrated Consecrated in very early times, probably about [the]
               time of [the] Conquest. [Repaired 1810, restored 1861.]
Endowment   Tithe £205. Glebe £93 (gross value). Fees £3. Dues £3.
Sittings   Free 70. Other 130. Total 200.
Attendance 30 March   Morning 124 + 44 SS. Total 168.
                        Afternoon 70 + 50 SS. Total 120.
Average attendance   The figures being averages.
Dated   31 March 1851.
Signed   William Gooch, vicar and rural dean [1833–76].
               Stainton, Middlesbrough-in-Tees.

21.73 Church of England, St Paul, Thornaby (541.31)
Population 1851: 1,759 (township)

Name   Thornaby Church – formerly a chapelry belonging to
               Stainton in Cleveland. [Became a parish in 1844.]
Consecrated [Not given. New church consecrated in South Stockton
               23 September 1858.]
Endowment   [£120.]
Sittings   Total about 80.
Attendance 30 March   Morning 60 + 28 SS. Total 88.
Average attendance   [Not given.]
Dated   31 March 1851.
Signed   Henry William Beckwirth, minister [1850–54].
               Stainton Grange, Middlesbrough.

21.74 Church of England, All Saints, High Worsall (541.7)

Name   Chapel of High Worsall, an ancient chapelry formerly
               in the parish of Northallerton, but having been
               expanded it is now a distinct and separate parish.

Consecrated   Before 1800.
Endowment   Land £54. OPE grant by the Ecclesiastical
        Commissioners £20. Fees 10s.
Sittings   Free (none). Other 68. Total 68.
Attendance 30 March   Morning 20. SS none. Total [20].
            Afternoon 60. SS none. Total [60].
Average attendance   Morning 20. SS none. Total 20.
            Afternoon 20. SS none. Total 20.
Dated   31 March 1851.
Signed   Henry Graves, minister [1832–65].
        Yarm, Yorkshire.
[Henry Graves was also the rector of St George, Middleton St George
(**15.13**).]

21.75   Church of England, St Mary Magdalene, Yarm (541.53)
Population 1851: 1,647 (parish) 493 (township)

[Summary form]
Name   [Not given.]
Erected   Rebuilt in 1730 [with the exception of the tower].
Endowment   [£210.]
Sittings   None free. Other 700. Total 700.
Usual attendance   Morning 57 + 23 SS. Total [80].
            Evening 120 + 12 SS. Total [132].
Informant   George Bradley, sexton of the church [agricultural
        labourer].
Incumbent   [John Winpenny 1840–95.]

21.76   Independent [Congregational], East Street, Middlesbrough
(541.25)
Name   Independent Chapel.
Erected   1838. [Opened March 1839. Replaced by a new chapel
        in Queen's Terrace, opened 14 June 1857.]
Building   [Separate and entire. Exclusively used for worship.]
Sittings   Free 132. Other 234. Total [366].
Attendance 30 March   Morning 134 + 173 SS. Total 307.
            Evening 172. Total 172.
Average attendance   Morning 130 + 160 SS. Total 290.
            Evening 170. Total 170.
Remarks   The school being taught in a separate building, the

scholars do not attend divine service in the chapel in the evenings. No fixed minister at present.

Dated   30 March 1851.
Signed   Stephen Stewart Johnston, deacon.
             Graham Street, Middlesbrough.
Minister   [Charles Bingley 1842–51.]
[Stephen Johnston (aged 24) lodged with William Ainsworth (**21.77**).]

21.77   Particular Baptist, West Street, Middlesbrough (541.24)
Name   Baptist Chapel.
Erected   [Not given.] [Opened as a Unitarian chapel 30 June
             1833, and occupied by the Baptists 1849–63, when it
             returned to the Unitarians.]
Building   [Separate and entire but not exclusively used for
             worship.]
Sittings   Free 100. Total [100].
Attendance 30 March   Afternoon 13 + 18 SS. Total 31.
Average attendance   Afternoon 30 + 15 SS. Total 45.
Remarks   Service only in the afternoon. No regular minister
             residing in the town. Pulpit supplied by the Rev
             W[illiam] Leng, Baptist minister of Stockton. Chapel
             originally built as a Unitarian chapel is a large upper
             room over three tenements, but has no internal
             communication with them. Used also as a day school.
Dated   30 March 1851.
Signed   William Hague Ainsworth, manager [a classical and
             mathematical teacher].
             Graham Street, Middlesbrough.
[William Ainsworth subsequently became the pastor of the chapel.]

21.78   Wesleyan Methodist, Ingleby Barwick (541.17)
Name   None.
Erected   [Not given.]
Building   Part of [a] dwelling house. [Not exclusively used for
             worship.]
Sittings   Free 50. Total [50].
Attendance 30 March   Afternoon 20. Total [20].
Average attendance   Afternoon 22. Total 22.
Dated   31 March 1851.
Signed   Charles Pearson, leader.
             Barwick-on-Tees, near Yarm, Yorkshire.

21.79   Wesleyan Methodist, Market Place, Middlesbrough (541.23)

Name   Wesleyan Chapel. [Centenary Chapel.]
Erected   1838. [Opened August 1838. Cost £800; gallery added 1848.]
Building   [Separate and entire. Exclusively used for worship.]
Sittings   Free 250. Other 650. Total [900].
Attendance 30 March   Morning 351 + 50 SS. Total 401.
                                 Evening 320. Total 320.
Average attendance   Morning 650 + 70 SS. Total 720.
Dated   31 March 1851.
Signed   Henry Smallwood, minister [1849–51].
                 Gosford Street, Middlesbrough.
[Henry Smallwood was also the minister of Billingham (**21.36**).]

21.80   Wesleyan Methodist, Picton, Kirk Levington (541.11)
Name   None.
Erected   [Not given.]
Building   Upper room part of a dwelling. [Exclusively used for worship.]
Sittings   Free 35. Total [35].
Attendance 30 March   Afternoon 30. Total [30].
Average attendance   Afternoon 30. Total [30].
Dated   24 March 1851.
Signed   Henry Smallwood, minister [1849–51].
                 Gosford St[reet], Middlesbrough, Yorkshire.

21.81   Wesleyan Methodist, Stainton (541.16)
Name   Stainton Chapel.
Erected   1840.
Building   Separate building. Exclusively as a place of worship.
Sittings   Free 62. Other 38. Total [100].
Attendance 30 March   Afternoon 23. Total [23].
                                 Evening 42. Total [42].
Average attendance   Morning 50. Total 50.
Dated   31 March 1851.
Signed   William Sherwood, steward and leader [farmer].
                 Thornton-by-Middlesbrough.

21.82   Wesleyan Methodist, Thornaby (541.32)
Name   Stafford Chapel.
Erected   1835.

Building   [Separate and] entire building. Exclusively a place of
              worship.
Sittings   Free 100. Total [100].
Attendance 30 March   Evening 50. Total [50].
Average attendance   [Not given.]
Dated   31 March 1851.
Signed   William Smith, elder.
              Stafford Cottage, South Stockton, Yorkshire.

21.83   Wesleyan Methodist, Yarm (541.12)
Name   Yarm Wesleyan Methodist Chapel.
Erected   Before 1820. [Erected 1763, enlarged 1815, restored
              1873.]
Building   [Separate and entire. Exclusively used for worship.]
Sittings   Free 235. Other 260. Total [495].
Attendance 30 March   Morning 118 + 48 SS. Total 166.
                        Evening 182. Total 182.
Average attendance   [Not given.]
Dated   31 March 1851.
Signed   Richard Appleton, treasurer of the trustees [corn
              miller].
              Yarm, Yorkshire.
[On 24 April 1764 John Wesley recorded that 'I preached ... in the
evening at the new house at Yarm, by far the most elegant in England.
A large congregation attended at five in the morning ... [and] I had
indeed the satisfaction of finding most of the believers here athirst
for full redemption.' J. Wesley, *The Journal of the Rev John Wesley* (Dent
edition, London, 1906), vol. 3, p. 177.]

21.84   Primitive Methodist, Kirk Levington (541.10)
Name   None.
Erected   Before 1800.
Building   [Separate and entire. Exclusively used for worship.]
Sittings   Free 80. Other 20. Total [100]. Standing room none.
Attendance 30 March   Morning 20 SS. Total 20.
                        Evening 40. Total 40.
Average attendance   Morning 20 SS. Total 20.
                        Evening 40. Total 40.
Dated   31 March 1851.
Signed   Thomas Scalfe, steward.
              Kirk Levington, Yarm, Yorkshire.

21.85   Primitive Methodist, Richmond Street, Middlesbrough (541.28)

Name   None.
Erected   1841. [Opened 6 June 1841. Cost £350.]
Building   [Separate and entire. Exclusively used for worship.]
Sittings   Free 252. Other 208. Total [460]. Standing room none.
Attendance 30 March   Morning 180 SS. Total [180].
                 Afternoon 160 + 120 SS. Total [280].
                 Evening 400. Total [400].
Average attendance   Morning 180 SS. Total 180.
                 Afternoon 160 + 120 SS. Total 280.
                 Evening 410. Total 410.
Dated   31 March 1851.
Signed   George Smith, society steward [grocer and tea dealer].
                 Market Place, Middlesbrough, Yorkshire.

21.86   Primitive Methodist, Yarm (541.13)

Name   Primitive Methodist Chapel.
Erected   1836. [Rebuilt 1897.]
Building   Separate [and entire]. Exclusive[ly used for worship].
                 (30 feet by 30 feet.)
Sittings   Free 100. Other 80. Total [180].
Attendance 30 March   Afternoon 100. Total [100].
                 Evening 120. Total [120].
Average attendance   [Not given.]
Dated   31 March 1851.
Signed   Robert Clapham, steward [grocer; sack manufacturer;
                 and rope, line and twine maker].
                 Yarm, Yorkshire.

21.87   Wesleyan Methodist Association, High Leven (521.18)

Name   No name. Wesleyan Association [crossed out].
Erected   [Not given.]
Building   Dwelling house. [Not exclusively used for worship.]
Sittings   Free 45. Total [45].
Attendance 30 March   Afternoon 42. Total [42].
                 Evening 20. Total [20].
Average attendance   Morning 40. Total 40.
Dated   31 March 1851.
Signed   Joseph Featherston. His + mark. Manager.
                 High Leven, near Yarm, Yorkshire.

21.88 Wesleyan Methodist Association, Yarm (541.14)

Name Methodist Association Chapel.

Erected 1838.

Building [Separate and entire. Exclusively used for worship.]

Sittings Free 125. Other 145. Total [270].

Attendance 30 March Morning 100 + 46 SS. Total 146.

Evening 130 + 20 SS. Total 150.

Average attendance Morning 100 + 40 SS. Total 140.

Evening 150 + 20 SS. Total 170.

Dated 31 March 1851.

Signed Thomas Sherwood, steward [watch and clock-maker].

Market Place, Yarm.

21.89 Wesleyan Reformers, Town Hall, Middlesbrough (541.26)

Name Town Hall.

Erected 1846. [Town Hall opened 24 October 1846. Wesleyan
Reformers began meeting in the Town Hall in 1849,
and erected a chapel in Brougham Street 1853,
replacing it with a new chapel in 1871.]

Building [Not separate and entire* or exclusively used for
worship.]

Sittings Free 300. Total [300].

Attendance 30 March Morning 200. Total [200].

Evening 280. Total [280].

Average attendance Morning 280. Total [280].

Evening 300. Total [300].

Remarks *The Town Hall is a separate and entire building, but
is let for other purposes than that of religious worship,
and has been only very recently taken by the Wesleyan
Reformers as an asylum having been expelled by
their paid minister from their own legitimate place
of worship for expressing their sympathies with the
'expelled'. [Probably broke away from the Wesleyan
Methodist chapel (**21.79**).]

Dated 1 April 1851.

Signed Eneas McKenzie, minister [schoolmaster].
[Suffield Street], Middlesbrough-on-Tees.

**21.90 Non-denominational, Christian Mission Room,
Commercial Street, Middlesbrough** (541.22 and 541.21)

Name Christian Mission Room. (Christian Missionary
Society.)

Erected   About 1840.

Building   [Not separate and entire or exclusively used for worship.]

Sittings   Free 200. Other none. Total [200].

Attendance 30 March   Morning 40 + 20 SS. Total 60.

Afternoon 30 SS. Total 30.

Evening 100. Total 100.

Average attendance   [Not given.]

Remarks   Used as a day school during the week.

Dated   31 March 1851.

Signed   Stephen James, minister.

Stockton Street, Middlesbrough-on-Tees.

(541.21) [Simplified form]

Name   Mission Room.

Erected   [Not given.]

Building   [Not separate and entire or exclusively used for worship.]

Sittings   All free. Total [200].

Usual attendance   Morning 20 + 40 SS. Total 60.

Evening 50. Total 50.

Dated   [Not given.]

Signed   Stephen James [Minister].

Stockton Street, Middlesbrough.

21.91   Non-denominational, Town Sailors' Mission Room, Dock Gates, Middlesbrough (541.29)

Name   Town and Sailors' Mission Room.

Erected   1842.

Building   Separate [and entire]. Not exclusively [used for worship].

Sittings   Free 80. Total [80]. Standing room 80.

Attendance 30 March   Afternoon 15. Total [15].

Average attendance   Morning 40. SS none. Total [40].

Remarks   This place is used as a [Terminus?] store] but is allowed to be used on the Sabbaths as a preaching room by the Dock Company. The mission is supported by the various Protestant bodies in the town.

Dated   31 March 1851.

Signed   Deynis Stringer, town and sailors' missionary.

Richmond Street, Middlesbrough.

21.92 Society of Friends [Quakers], Wilson Street, Middlesbrough (541.30)

Erected 1848. [Opened 19 March 1849.]
Building [Separate and entire. Exclusively used for worship.]
Floor area 1,040 [square feet]. No galleries. Total 1,040 [square feet].
Sittings Free 168. Total 168.
Attendance 30 March Morning 50. Total [50].
Afternoon 31. Total [31].
Dated Eleventh day of the fourth month 1851.
Signed John Beaumont Pease [woollen merchant].
Of Darlington Monthly Meeting.
North Lodge, Darlington.
[John Beaumont Pease (1803–1873) was also involved with several other Quaker meeting houses (**13.59**, **13.60**, **21.63**, **23.30** and **23.56**). The meeting house became a police station in 1871 and in 1873 the congregation moved to Dunning Road.]

21.93 Roman Catholic, High Worsall (541.8)

Name Friarage Catholic Chapel.
Erected Before 1800.
Building [Separate and entire. Exclusively used for worship.]
Sittings Free 90. Other 10. Total [100]. Standing room 20.
Attendance 30 March Morning 85. Total 85.
Afternoon 30 to 40. Total 30–40.
Average attendance [Not given.]
Dated 31 March 1851.
Signed John Bradley, Catholic priest.
Yarm, Yorkshire.

21.94 Roman Catholic, Sussex Street, Middlesbrough (541.27)

Name Saint Mary's Chapel.
Erected 1848. [Enlarged 1854 and 1866. The site of the cathedral, consecrated 21 August 1878.]
Building [Separate and entire. Exclusively used for worship.]
Sittings Free 28. Other 280. Total [308].
Attendance 30 March Morning 160. Total [160].
Afternoon 160. Total [160].
Evening 160. Total [160].
Average attendance Morning 108 + 52 SS. Total [160].
Remarks About 500 Catholics in the church of Middlesbrough.
Dated 1 April 1851.

Signed   Joseph McPhillips, Catholic priest [1848–54].
              Middlesbro[ugh]-on-Tees.

23. Teesdale (HO 129/543)
26 places of worship

23.33   Church of England, St Michael and All Angels, Barningham (543.21)
Population 1851: 573 (parish) 333 (township)

Name   St Michael. Parish church.
Consecrated The church was rebuilt on new ground and
              consecrated 1815. [Restored 1891.]
Erected   By sale of pews [total cost] about £800.
Endowment   Land £157. Tithe £420. Fees, dues and Easter offerings
              none.
Sittings   Free [none]. Other 280. Total [280].
Attendance 30 March   Morning 163. Total [163].
                        Afternoon 80. Total [80].
Average attendance   [Not given.]
Dated   5 April 1851.
Signed   William Fitzwilliam Wharton, rector [1840–74].
              Barningham Rectory, Richmond, Yorks[hire].
[William Wharton 'lived much abroad', and died at Mentone in 1893
(J.A. Venn, *Alumni Cantabrigienses*, vol. 6 (Cambridge, 1954), p. 420.]

23.34   Church of England Schoolroom, Scargill, Barningham (543.24)
Population 1851: 99 (township)

Name   Schoolroom.
Licensed   1846.
Sittings   Free 60. Total 60.
Attendance 30 March   Evening 35. Total 35.
Average attendance   [Not given.]
Dated   5 April 1851.
Signed   William Fitzwilliam Wharton, rector [1840–74].
              Barningham Rectory, Richmond, Yorkshire.

23.35   Church of England, St Giles, Bowes (543.30)
Population 1851: 725 (parish) 645 (township)

Name   Bowes, an old church dedicated to St Gyles (*sic*).
              An ancient parish church.
Consecrated No[t] known. [Reopened after restoration 20 August
              1865. Cost £1,500.]
Endowment   Glebe £75.
Sittings   Free [200]. Total 200.
Attendance 30 March   Morning 100. Total 100.
                      Evening 20. Total 20.
Average attendance   Morning 150. Total 150.
                      Evening 35. Total 35.
Dated   30 March 1851.
Signed   Johnson Lambert, incumbent [1823–67].
              Bowes, Barnard Castle.

23.36   Church of England, St Mary, Brignall (543.26)
Population 1851: 173 (parish)

Name   St Mary's. Ancient parish church.
Consecrated AD 1834 [4 September]. In lieu of a previously existing
              church. [Restored 1892.]
Erected   J. B. S. Morritt Esq., lord of the manor; the vicar; a
              donation from the Church Building Society and a small
              rate. Total cost £600.
Endowment   Endowed by tithe and glebe-land. The curate is unable
              to answer as to the aggregate amount. [£300.]
Sittings   Free 120. Total 120.
Attendance 30 March   Morning 70 + 5 SS. Total 75.
Average attendance   [Not given.]
Dated   31 March 1851.
Signed   Robert Parker Bowness, curate [1841–54].
              Brignall vicarage, Greta Bridge.
Incumbent   [Orfeur William Kilvington 1816–54.]
[Robert Parker Bowness was the son of George Bowness, the rector
of Rokeby (**23.40**). John Bacon Sawrey Morritt (1771–1843) of Rokeby
Park was a friend of Sir Walter Scott. Morritt's monument is in St
Mary the Virgin, Rokeby.]

23.37   Church of England Schoolroom, Cotherston (543.44)
Population 1851: 607 (township)

[Summary form]
Name   Schoolroom.
Erected   1834.
Sittings   Free 100. Total 100.
Usual attendance Afternoon 55 (once a fortnight). Total [55].
Informant   John Hutchinson.
[St Cuthbert chapel of ease to Romaldkirk East was erected in 1881.]

23.38   Church of England, St Mary, Great Hutton (543.20)
Population 1851: 189 (township)

Name   Great Hutton Chapel is a perpetual curacy in the
            parish of Gilling and township of Great Hutton.
Consecrated Before 1800. [Rebuilt 1877.]
Endowment [Not given.]
Sittings   Free 26. Other 74. Total 100.
Attendance 30 March   Morning 30. Total [30].
            Afternoon 30. Total [30].
Average attendance   [Not given.]
Remarks   Tithe and glebe belong to the vicar of Gilling, the
            patron. The curate's income of Great Hutton (which
            arises from a fixed annual money payment by the
            vicar; from lands; by parliamentary grant and by
            Queen Anne's Bounties) amounts to £50.
Dated   31 March 1851.
Signed   William Heslop, curate [1800–60].
            Great Hutton, near Greta Bridge.

23.39   Church of England, Laithkirk, Middleton (543.43)
Population 1851: 321 (part of Lunedale township)

[Summary form]
Name   Laithkirk.
Erected   Unknown. Most probably erected before the
            Reformation. [Repaired 1826. Parish created 1845.]
Endowment [£100.]
Sittings   Free 200. Other none. Total 200.
Usual attendance   Morning 150 + 60 SS. Total [210].
            Afternoon about 30. Total [about 30].

Evening 200 + 60 SS. Total [260].

Informant James Relwell.
Incumbent [Leonard Sedgwick 1848–53.]
[Additional unclear note – page torn on edge.]
... able. I give an average as parish exceedingly [...] is distant of 19 miles [incon]veniently population. Much seasonal [...] inclement or weather [...] 150 [...] 50.

23.40   Church of England, St Mary the Virgin, Rokeby (543.27)
Population 1851: 189 (township)

Name St Mary's, Rokeby.
Consecrated Before 1800. [Rebuilt 1778, restored 1877.]
Endowment Tithe commuted. Glebe 5 acres. Fees £10. Easter
offerings £15. [£160.]
Sittings Free 108. Other 12. Total 120.
Attendance 30 March Afternoon [81] + 10 SS. Total 91.
Average attendance [Not given.]
Remarks Owing to the illness of the rector there was no
morning service on 30 March 1851.
Dated 31 March 1851.
Signed George Bowness, rector [1823–58].
Rokeby, Greta Bridge, Yorkshire.
[George Bowness was the father of Robert Parker Bowness, the curate of Brignall (**23.36**).]

23.41   Church of England, St Michael, Startforth (543.28)
Population 1851: 582 (parish)

Name Startforth ancient parish church.
Consecrated Before 1800. [Holy Trinity rebuilt on the same site in
1863. Cost £2,000.]
Endowment Land £34. Tithe £96. Fees £3.
Sittings Free 83. Other 37. Total 120.
Attendance 30 March Morning 70 + 57 SS. Total 127.
Afternoon 38 + 34 SS. Total 72.
Average attendance [Not given.]
Remarks Only 120 persons can be conveniently accommodated
with seats in this church. The open space in the
chancel before the altar-rails is occupied by a portion
of the Sunday scholars.

Dated   31 March 1851.
Signed   Henry Kendall, minister [1826–67].
             Startforth, Barnard Castle.

23.42   Church of England, St Mary, Wycliffe (543.18)
Population 1851: 144 (parish)

[Summary form]
Name   Wycliffe.
Erected   [Not given.] [Restored 1850.]
Endowment [£456.]
Sittings   [Not given.]
Usual attendance   Morning 80. Total [80].
Informant Henry Rayson.
Incumbent [John Headlam 1793–1854.]
[John Headlam was also the Archdeacon of Richmond 1826–54 and
the Chancellor of the diocese of Ripon 1846–54.]

23.43   Independent [Congregational], Cotherston (543.46)
Name   Independent Chapel.
Erected   Before 1770. [About 1748, rebuilt 1869.]
Building   [Separate and entire. Exclusively used for worship]
             and for a Sunday school.
Sittings   Free 84. Other 28 let. Total [112]. Standing room none.
Attendance 30 March   Morning 40 SS. Total 40.
                        Afternoon 54 + 40 SS. Total 94.
Average attendance   No average acc[oun]t taken or kept.
Remarks   43 scholars attended the annual tea party and 5 were
             absent.
Dated   31 March 1851.
Signed   George Chapman, deacon [agricultural labourer].
             Cotherston, near Barnard Castle.

23.44   Wesleyan Methodist, Barningham (543.23)
Name   Wesleyan Chapel.
Erected   1815. [Enlarged 1869.]
Building   Separate [and entire. Exclusively used for worship.]
Sittings   Free 40. Other 75. Total [115].
Attendance 30 March   Morning 49. Total [49].
                        Evening 93. Total [93].
Average attendance   [Not given.]
Dated   31 March 1851.

Signed   George Russell, Wesleyan minister [1848–51].
            Barningham, n[ea]r Richmond.

23.45 Wesleyan Methodist Schoolroom, Scargill, Barningham (543.22)
Name   Scargill School House.
Erected   Before 1800.
Building   [Separate and entire but not exclusively used for worship.]
Sittings   Free 50. Other 80. Total [140].
Attendance 30 March   Afternoon 25. Total [25].
Average attendance   [Not given.]
Dated   31 March 1851.
Signed   George Russell, Wesleyan minister [1848–51].
            Barningham, n[ea]r Richmond.

23.46 Wesleyan Methodist, Bowes (543.31)
Name   Bowes [crossed out] Wesleyan Chapel.
Erected   1822. [Rebuilt 1878.]
Building   [Separate and entire. Exclusively used for worship.]
Sittings   Free 104. Other 84. Total [188]. Standing room none.
Attendance 30 March   Afternoon 70 + 39 SS. Total [109].
                       Evening 72 + 30 SS. Total [102].
Average attendance   Afternoon 70. Total [70].
Dated   26 March 1851.
Signed   Francis Addison, steward (grocer).
            Bowes, Yorkshire.

23.47 Wesleyan Methodist, Hulands, Bowes (543.33)
Name   [Large ink blot.]
Erected   [Not given.]
Building   [Not separate and entire or exclusively used for worship.]
Sittings   Free 40. Total [40].
Attendance 30 March   Afternoon 15. Total 15.
Average attendance   Afternoon 20. Total 20.
Remarks   The day was unfavourable; the average attendance will be as stated in proper column.
Dated   30 March 1851.
Signed   Miles Metcalf, resident at the house [farmer].
            Hulands, near to Bowes, Yorkshire.

23.48   Wesleyan Methodist, Cotherston (543.45)

Name   Cotherston Wesleyan Chapel.
Erected   1777. [Rebuilt 1872.]
Building   [Separate and entire. Exclusively used for worship.]
Sittings   Free 100. Other 30. Total [130].
Attendance 30 March   Evening 73. Total [73].
Average attendance   Evening 55 + 12 SS. Total 67.
Remarks   The attendance at a monthly service on Sunday
              mornings is not entered in this schedule.
Dated   31 March 1851.
Signed   Thomas Raine, steward [shoemaker].
              Cotherston, Teesdale, Yorkshire.

23.49   Wesleyan Methodist, Lunedale, Romaldkirk (543.49)

Name   None.
Erected   1843.
Building   Separate building entirely. [Exclusively used for]
              public worship, expect for Sunday school.
Sittings   Free 100. Total [100].
Attendance 30 March   Afternoon 41 + 17 SS. Total 58.
Average attendance   [Not given.]
Dated   31 March 1851.
Signed   William Longstaff, steward [farmer].
              Greengates, Lunedale, Yorkshire.

23.50   Wesleyan Methodist, Mickleton (543.47)

Name   Wesleyan Chapel.
Erected   1830.
Building   [Separate and entire. Exclusively used for worship.]
Sittings   Free 60. Other 60. Total [120].
Attendance 30 March   Afternoon 40 + 26 SS. Total [66].
                        Evening 30. Total [30].
Average attendance   [Not given.]
Dated   31 March 1851.
Signed   John Tinkler, steward [farmer].
              Mickleton, Teesdale, Yorkshire.

23.51   Primitive Methodist, Barmingham (543.25)

Name   [Not given.]
Erected   [Not given.]
Building   House. [Other details not given.]
Sittings   [Not given.]

Attendance 30 March   Morning 12. Total [12].
                         Afternoon 40. Total [40].
Average attendance   [Not given.]
Dated   3 April 1851.
Signed   George Pearson, local preacher [farmer].
                         Barningham.

23.52   Primitive Methodist, North Bitts, Bowes (543.32)
Name   None.
Erected   [Not given.]
Building   [Not separate and entire or exclusively used for
              worship.]
Sittings   Free 40. Total [40].
Attendance 30 March   Evening 20. Total 20.
Average attendance   Afternoon 30. Total 30.
Dated   30 March 1851.
Signed   John Jackson, respondent at the house [farmer].
              North Bitts, Bowes, Yorkshire.

23.53   Primitive Methodist, Lunedale, Romaldkirk (543.50)
Name   Planting End.
Erected   In the year 1842.
Building   Separate building for public worship. [Used
              exclusively for] public worship only.
Sittings   Free 90. Other none. Total [90]. Standing room none.
Attendance 30 March   [Not given.]
Average attendance   Morning from 28 to 40. Total [28–40].
                         Evening from 40 to 60. Total [40–60].
Dated   31 March 1851.
Signed   Thomas Sayer, steward or local preacher [shopkeeper
              and farmer].
              Lunedale, Yorkshire, Middleton Teesdale.

23.54   Primitive Methodist, Mickleton (543.48)
Name   Primitive Methodist Chapel.
Erected   1843.
Building   [Separate and entire. Exclusively used for worship.]
Sittings   Free 65. Other 60. Total [125]. Standing room 21 feet by
              16 [feet].
Attendance 30 March   Afternoon 43. Total [43].
                         Evening 85. Total [85].
Average attendance   Afternoon 50. Total [50].

Night (*sic*) 90. Total [90].

Remarks	This place of worship is best known as Mickleton Primitive Methodist Chapel.
Dated	30 March 1851.
Signed	Richard Peel, local preacher [grocer]. Bridgegate, Barnard Castle.

23.55   Primitive Methodist, Startforth (543.29)

Name	A house.
Erected	Commenced 25 years ago.
Building	An inhabited house. A dwelling and [a place] for worship.
Sittings	Free 50. Total [50].
Attendance 30 March	Afternoon 17. Total [17].
Average attendance	Morning 20. Total [20].
Dated	[Not given.]
Signed	Henry Whitfield, Primitive Meth[odist] preacher [pauper, formerly labourer]. Boldron, Yorkshire.

23.56   Society of Friends [Quakers], Cotherston (543.58)

Name	[Not given.]
Erected	Before 1800.
Building	[Separate and entire. Exclusively used for worship.]
Sittings	Free 160. Total [160]. Ground floor area 798 [square feet]. No galleries. Total 798 [square feet].
Attendance 30 March	Morning 20. Total [20]. Afternoon 17. Total [17].
Dated	Eleventh day of fourth month 1851.
Signed	John Beaumont Pease [woollen merchant]. Of Darlington monthly meeting. North Lodge, Darlington.

[John Beaumont Pease (1803–1873) was also involved with several other Quaker meeting houses (**13.59, 13.60, 21.63, 21.92** and **23.30**).]

23.57   Roman Catholic, Lartington Hall, Lartington (543.41)

Name	Catholic Chapel [St Lawrence].
Erected	Before 1800.
Building	Domestic chapel [separate and entire. Exclusively used for worship.]
Sittings	Free 150. Total [150]. Standing room 30.

Attendance 30 March Morning 121 + 10 SS. Total 131.

Average attendance 86 [not recorded in any column, but given at the side]. Total [86].

Remarks The persons enumerated in the afternoon are the same as attended in the morning.

Dated 31 March 1851.

Signed Michael Ellis, Catholic pastor.
Lartington, B[arnar]d Castle.

23.58 Roman Catholic, Wycliffe (543.19)

Name St Mary's Catholic Church.

Erected Since 1800. [1848–49.]

Building Separate building. Exclusively as a place of worship.

Sittings Free 30. Other 160. Total [190]. Standing room no free space.

Attendance 30 March Morning 130. Total [130].
Afternoon 60. Total [60].

Average attendance [Not given.]

Dated 30 March 1851.

Signed John Bradshaw, Catholic priest.
[Chapel House], Wycliffe, Darlington.

CUMBERLAND

Registration district of Alston included in the Durham Returns

Though situated in the county of Cumberland, the ecclesiastical parish of Alston (with the chapelries of Garrigill and Nenthead) was located in the diocese of Durham (from 1882 in the diocese of Newcastle). The complete returns for Cumberland and Westmorland (now Cumbria) have yet to be published.

25. Alston (HO 129/564)
19 places of worship

25.1 Church of England, St Augustine, Alston (564.2)
Population 1851: 6,816 (parish) 2,005 (township)

Name   St Augustine.
Consecrated In remote times. [1769–70, replaced by a new building dedicated on 30 August 1870.]
Erected   Cannot now be ascertained.
Endowment   Tithe £6 (commuted). Glebe £123 8s. Other £32. Fees £8. Easter offerings £8. Other £12 12s.
Sittings   Free 140. Other 400. Total 540.
Attendance 30 March   Morning 141 + 37 SS. Total 178. Evening 147 + 19 SS. Total 166.
Average attendance   Morning 150 + 50 SS. Total 200. Evening 200 + 40 SS. Total [240].
Dated   31 March 1851.
Signed   Hugh Salvin, vicar of Alston [1841–52]. Alston, near Penrith.

25.2 Church of England, St John, Garrigill (564.3)
Population 1851: 1,443 (chapelry)

[Summary form]
Name   Garrigill.

Erected   [Rebuilt 1790, restored 1890s.]
Endowment [Not given.]
Sittings   Free 200. Total 200.
Usual attendance   Morning 35 + 26 SS. Total [61]
                Evening 60. Total [60].
Dated   [Not given.]
Signed   George Monkhouse, curate of the chapelry of Garrigill
                [1851–76].
Incumbent   [Hugh Salvin 1841–52.]
[George Monkhouse was the vicar of St Thomas, Heathery Cleugh,
1876–92 **(24.7)**.]

25.3   Church of England, St John the Evangelist, Nenthead
(564.4)
Population: 1,964 (chapelry)

Name   St John's Chapel, Nenthead district church.
Consecrated [14] August 1845, as an additional church. [Restored
                1907. District created out of the parish of Alston 23
                December 1845.]
Endowment Land £3. Fees £5. Easter offerings £3.
Sittings   Free 330. Other 20. Total 350.
Attendance Morning 30 + 16 SS. Total 46.
                Evening 115 + 16 SS. Total 131.
Average attendance   [Not given.]
Dated   5 April 1851.
Signed   Thomas Holme, minister [c.1849–58].
                Nenthead, near Alston, Cumberland.
                                            {B 19.}
[Thomas Holme, who had been the headmaster of Alston Grammar
School 1847–48, was later the perpetual curate of Nenthead 1858–61.]

25.4   Independent [Congregational], Alston (564.6)
Name   Independent Chapel.
Erected   In the year 1804.
Building   Separate building for public worship. [Used
                exclusively for] public worship only.
Sittings   Free 120. Other 300. Total [420].
Attendance 30 March   Morning 84 + 29 SS. Total 113.
                Evening 118 + 29 SS. Total 147.
Average attendance   Morning 160 + 102 SS. Total 262.
Remarks   Short of an average on account of weather. Scholars at

public service. Numbers of Sunday scholars as below. Many of the Sunday scholars do not attend public service.

Dated   30 March 1851.
Signed   Jonathan Harper, minister [1815–58].
            Alston, Cumberland.

25.5   Independent [Congregational], Redwing (564.17)
Name   Redwing Meeting House.
Erected   Before 1800. [1757.]
Building A separate building. In the winter months we worship in a schoolroom to have the benefit of a fire. Used exclusively as a place of worship except for a Sunday school.
Sittings All are free sittings. Total [Not given.]
Attendance 30 March   Afternoon 10 +13 SS. Total [23].
Average attendance   Morning 18 + 20 SS . Total [38].
Dated   30 March 1851.
Signed   Jonathan Harper, minister [1815–58].
            Alston, Cumberland.

25.6   Wesleyan Methodist, Alston (564.7)
Name   Wesleyan Chapel.
Erected   1825 in lieu of one built in 1797.
Building [Separate and entire. Exclusively used for worship.]
Sittings Free 210. Other 231. Total [441].
Attendance 30 March   Morning 150 + 30 SS. Total 180.
            Evening 250 + 50 SS. Total 300.
Average attendance   Morning 150 + 30 SS. Total 180.
            Evening 250 + 50 SS. Total 300.
Dated   31 March 1851.
Signed   Thomas Ballingall, Wesleyan minister [1850–51].
            Alston, Cumberland.
[Thomas Ballingall was also responsible for chapels in the Haltwhistle area (**7.14–16**).]

25.7   Wesleyan Methodist, Ashgill (564.18)
Name   [Not given.]
Erected   About 1820.
Building [Separate and entire. Exclusively used for worship.] A week evening school is taught in it.
Sittings Free 30. Total [not given]. See letter.

Attendance 30 March   Morning 25. Total [25].
Average attendance   Morning 25. Total [25].
Dated   31 March 1851.
Signed   Thomas Ballingall, Wesleyan minister [1850–51].
Alston, Cumberland.

25.8   Wesleyan Methodist, Low Brownside (564.8)
Name   Low Brownside Methodist Chapel.
Erected   1849.
Building   [Separate and entire. Exclusively used for worship.]
Sittings   Free 84. Other 62. Total [146]. Standing room 30.
Attendance 30 March   Afternoon 70 + 10 SS. Total 80.
Evening 38 + 12 SS. Total 50.
Average attendance   Afternoon 70 + 10 SS. Total 80.
Evening 38 + 12 SS. Total 50.
Dated   31 March 1851.
Signed   Thomas Ballingall, [Wesleyan] minister [1850–51].
Alston, Cumberland.

25.9   Wesleyan Methodist, Garrigill (564.20)
Name   Garrigill Wesleyan Chapel.
Erected   Before 1800.
Building   [Separate and entire. Exclusively used for worship.]
Sittings   Free 180. Other 120. Total 300. Standing (free space for
120). 36 feet by 21 feet.
Attendance 30 March   Morning 25. Total 25.
Afternoon 135. Total 135.
Evening 145. Total 145.
Average attendance   Morning 102 (*sic*). Total 102 (*sic*).
Dated   31 March 1851.
Signed   Thomas Ballingall, Wesleyan minister [1850–51].
Alston, Cumberland.

25.10   Wesleyan Methodist, Nenthead (564.11)
Name   Wesleyan Chapel.
Erected   1827.
Building   [Separate and entire. Exclusively used for worship.]
Sittings   Free 258. Other 162. Total [420].
Attendance 30 March   Morning 34. Total 34.
Afternoon 46 + 65 SS. Total 111.
Evening 55 + 43 SS. Total 98.
Average attendance   Morning 50. Total 50.

Afternoon 100 + 70 SS. Total 170.
Evening 140 + 60 SS. Total 200.

Dated   31 March 1851.
Signed   Thomas Ballingall, Wesleyan minister [1850–51].
Alston, Cumberland.

25.11   Wesleyan Methodist, Nest (564.14)

Name   Nest Chapel.
Erected   1844.
Building [Separate and entire. Exclusively used for worship.]
Sittings Free 70. Other 20. Total [90]. Standing room 30.
Attendance 30 March   Afternoon 44 + 20 SS. Total 64.
Average attendance   [Not given.]
Dated   31 March 1851.
Signed   Thomas Ballingall, Wesleyan minister [1850–51].
Alston, Cumberland.

25.12   Wesleyan Methodist, Tynehead (564.15)

Name   Tynehead Chapel and School.
Erected   1821.
Building [Separate and entire. Exclusively used for worship.]
Chapel and school.
Sittings Free 140. Total [140].
Attendance 30 March   Morning 40 + 6 SS. Total 46.
Afternoon 50 + 8 SS. Total 58.
Average attendance   Morning 40 + 6 SS. Total 46.
Afternoon 50 + 8 SS. Total 58.
Dated   31 March 1851.
Signed   Thomas Ballingall, Wesleyan minister [1850–51].
Alston, Cumberland.

25.13   Wesleyan Methodist, Nentbury (564.10)

Name   Nentbury Wesleyan Chapel.
Erected   1825.
Building [Separate and entire. Exclusively used for worship.]
Sittings Free 108. Other 156. Total [264].
Attendance 30 March   Afternoon 68 ⎰ Total 138.
Evening 70 ⎱
Average attendance   Morning 90 + 30 SS. Total 120.
Evening 60 + 30 SS. Total 90.
Dated   30 March 1851.
Signed   Thomas Holmes, chapel steward [carpenter].
Gressfield, Alston, Cumberland.

25.14   Primitive Methodist, Alston (564.5)
Name   High Chapel.
Erected   1825.
Building   An entire building. Exclusively [used for worship.]
Sittings   Free 180. Other 120. Total 300. Standing room 160.
Attendance 30 March   Afternoon 130 + 74 SS. Total 204.
                        Evening 215 + 42 SS. Total 257.
Average attendance   [Not given]
Dated   30 March 1851.
Signed   John Davidson, steward [lead miner].
              [Town Head], Alston, Cumberland.

25.15   Primitive Methodist, Blaggill (564.9)
Name   None.
Erected   [Not given.]
Building   [Not separate and entire nor exclusively used for worship.]
Sittings   [Not given.] Room.
Attendance 30 March   Evening 41 + 19 SS. Total 60.
Average attendance   Evening 45 + 20 SS. Total 65.
Dated   30 March 1851.
Signed   John Hobues, manager.
              Blaggill, Alston, Cumberland.

25.16   Primitive Methodist, Greathead (564.16)
Name   Greathead Chapel.
Erected   1825.
Building   [Separate and entire. Exclusively used for worship.]
Sittings   Free 140 + 160 SS. Total [300].
Attendance 30 March   Afternoon 81 + 34 SS. Total 115.
                        Evening 220. Total 220.
Average attendance   [Not given.]
Dated   30 March 1851.
Signed   Daniel Gates, minister.
              Bolts, Alston, Cumberland.

25.17   Primitive Methodist, Hayring (564.13)
Name   Hayring Chapel.
Erected   1828.
Building   [Separate and entire. Exclusively used for worship.]
Sittings   Free 58. Other 68. Total [126]. Standing room 50.
Attendance 30 March   Afternoon 51 + 31 SS. Total 82.

Evening 80 + 17 SS. Total 97.

Average attendance   Afternoon 50 + 30 SS. Total 80.

Evening 80 + 20 SS. Total 100.

Dated   30 March 1851.

Signed   William Wailes, chapel steward [lead miner].

Haggs Foot, near Alston, Cumberland.

25.18   Primitive Methodist, Nenthead (564.12)

Name   High Chapel.

Erected   1823.

Building   [Separate and entire. Exclusively used for worship.]

Sittings   Free 120. Other 140. Total [260]. Standing room 50.

Attendance 30 March   Afternoon 230. Total 230.

Evening 258. Total 258.

Average attendance   [Not given.]

Dated   30 March 1851.

Signed   John Walker, chapel steward [lead miner].

[Holmes Foot], Nenthead, near Alston, Cumberland.

25.19   Society of Friends [Quakers], Alston (564.19)

Name   [Not given.]

Erected   Before 1800. [1732.]

Building   [Separate and entire. Exclusively used for worship.]

Sittings   Ground floor 38 [feet] x 14 feet. 530 [square feet].

Galleries 15 [feet] x 14 [feet]. 211 [square feet].

Total 741 [square feet].

Capable of seating 200.

Attendance 30 March   Morning 6. Total [6].

Average attendance   [Not given.]

Dated   Seventh day of the fourth month 1851.

Signed   William Wilson [clogger and shoemaker].

Allendale Town.

Appendix 1

Consecrations of Anglican Churches and Chapels

The consecration documents exist for some of the churches and chapels in Northumberland (Northumberland Archives, Wood-horn, NRO 1875), marked (N) below; and County Durham (DUL, ASC, DDR/EA/CHC/1 and 3), marked (D). Until the creation of the diocese of Newcastle in May 1882 the Bishop of Durham was responsible for the consecration (unless he delegated the responsibility to another bishop), and before 1836 Hexhamshire was the responsibility of the Archbishop of York. Some churches and mission churches were not consecrated, nor generally were those churches that were rebuilt on the same site.

Numerous church plans from the archives of The Incorporated Church Building Society (f.1818) may be seen at Lambeth Palace (www.churchplansonline.org), and in the library of Durham Cathedral is a collection of seventy-four church plans in the archdeaconry of Durham that pre-date the wholesale destruction carried out by the Victorian 'restorers'.

Consecrations before 1791
1668 Jul. 5   Christ Church, North Shields
1712 Aug. 21 St Thomas, Stockton on Tees
1719 Sep. 5   Holy Trinity, Sunderland   Bishop of London
1746 Oct. 26 All Saints, Penshaw   Bishop of Gloucester
1754 Oct. 18 Chapel of Infirmary, Newcastle (N)
1764 Jul. 4   St Mark, Ninebanks   Archbishop of York
1764 Jul. 6   St Helen, Whitley Chapel   Archbishop of York
1766 Aug. 10 Beadnell Chapel, Beadnell
1768 Sep. 8   St Ann, Newcastle
1769 Oct. 5   St John the Evangelist, Sunderland
1789 Nov. 17 All Saints, Newcastle (N)

Consecrations between 1791 and 1882

Bishop Shute Barrington 1791–1826   [21 churches]

1791 Nov. 2	St Bartholomew, Longbenton (N)	Bishop of Peterborough
1797 Jul. 20	St Cuthbert, Haydon Bridge (N)	
1801 Jul. 8	St Francis, Bryness (N)	
1809 Apr. 27	St Peter, Wallsend (N)	Bishop of St David's
1810 Aug. 7	St Edmund's, Gateshead (D)	
1812 Jul. 30	Gibside Chapel, Winlaton (D)	
1818 Jul. 29	St Thomas, Westoe (D)	(Later church consecrated 11 Oct. 1877)
1818 Aug. 8	St Aidan, Thorneyburn (N)	Bishop of Oxford
1818 Aug. 9	St Luke, Greystead (N)	Bishop of Oxford
1818 Aug. 10	St Michael, Wark (N)	Bishop of Oxford
1818 Aug. 11	St Peter, Humshaugh (N)	Bishop of Oxford
1819 Jul. 30	St Hilda, South Shields	Bishop of Oxford
1821 Feb. 15	St Mary, South Hylton (D)	Bishop of St David's (Later church consecrated 21 Jun. 1880)
1822 Aug. 6	St Mary, Heworth (D)	Bishop of Oxford
1822 Aug. 18	Rookhope Church, Stotfield Burn, Stanhope (D)	Bishop of Oxford
1823 Sep. 3	St Thomas, Heathery Cleugh (D)	Bishop of Oxford
1824 Aug. 31	St George, Mickley (N)	Bishop of Oxford (Later church consecrated 30 Nov. 1886)
1825 Aug. 29	St Mary, West Rainton (D)	Bishop of Oxford (Later church consecrated 21 Apr. 1864)
1825 Aug. 30	St John the Evangelist, Gateshead Fell (D)	Bishop of Oxford
1825 Sep. 1	St Peter, Falstone (N)	Bishop of Oxford
1825 Sep. 23	West Allen Chapel, Carrshield, Allendale	

Bishop William Van Mildert 1826–1836   [19 churches]

1826 Sep. 23	St Mary the Virgin, Shincliffe (D)	(Later church

		consecrated 1851 Aug. 5)
1827 Jul. 24	Ryhope Chapel, Bishopwearmouth (D)	(Later church consecrated 10 Aug. 1870)
1828 Sep. 9	St Paul, Winlaton (D)	
1828 Sep. 11	St Cuthbert, Greenhead (N)	
1829 Oct. 14	St Thomas, Bishopwearmouth (D)	
1829 Oct. 19	St Luke, Ferryhill (D)	(Later church consecrated 20 Sep. 1853)
1830 Oct. 19	St Thomas, Newcastle (N)	Bishop of Carlisle
1831 Sep. 29	Holy Trinity, Seaton Carew (D)	Bishop of Chester
1831 Sep. 30	St Andrew, Sadberge (D)	Bishop of Chester
1832 Oct. 8	St James, Benwell, Newcastle (N)	Bishop of Bristol
1832 Nov. 15	Holy Trinity, Hetton-le-Hole (D)	Bishop of Bristol
1832 Nov. 24	St Cuthbert, Etherley (D)	Bishop of Bristol
1834 Jan. 14	St Paul, North Sunderland	Bishop of Carlisle
1834 Apr. 20	Christ Church, West Hartlepool	
1834 Sep. 9	St John, Shildon (D)	
1834 Sep. 18	Holy Trinity, South Shields	Archbishop of York
1835 Mar. 5	Holy Trinity, Usworth (D)	Bishop of St David's
1835 Oct. 23	St Matthew, Dinnington (N)	Bishop of Carlisle (Later church consecrated 6 Dec. 1886)
1835 Dec. 22	Holy Trinity, Stockton-on-Tees (D)	Bishop of St David's

Bishop Edward Maltby 1836–1856   [61 churches]

1836 Oct. 21	Holy Trinity, North Shields (N)
1836 Oct. 22	St Bartholomew, Cresswell (N)
1837 Aug. 30	St John, Snods End, Shotley (N)
1837 Oct. 9	Holy Trinity, Dalton
1837 Oct. 10	Holy Saviour, Sugley (N)
1837 Oct. 12	St Alban, Earsdon (N)
1838 Sep. 25	All Saints, Girsby, Sockburn (D)
1838 Oct. 11	Holy Trinity, South Hetton (D)
1838 Dec. 6	Holy Trinity, Darlington (D)
1839 Aug. 5	St Cuthbert, Shadforth (D)
1840 May 1	All Saints, Eastgate, Stanhope (D)
1840 Sep. 8	St Cuthbert, Herrington (D)

1841 Jul. 13   St James, Coundon (D)   (Later church
                                               consecrated
                                               8 Jul. 1873)
1841 Aug. 4   St Thomas, Collierley [Dipton] (D)
1841 Aug. 11   Holy Saviour, Tynemouth (N)
1841 Aug. 31   St Paul, Westgate Hill, Newcastle (N)
1841 Oct. 21   St John the Evangelist, Seaham Harbour (D)
1841 Oct. 22   Holy Trinity, Wingate Grange (D)
1841 Dec. 14   St Andrew, Deptford, Bishopwearmouth (D)
1842 Aug. 25   St Alban, Windy Nook, Heworth (D)
1842 Oct. 24   Holy Trinity, Pelton
1843 Feb. 23   St Peter, Newcastle (N)
1843 Aug. 8   St Bartholomew, Thornley [Kelloe] (D)
1843 Aug. 17   Holy Trinity, Cambo (N)
1843 Aug. 23   St Peter, Scremerston (N)
1843 Sep. 12   St Catherine, Crook (D)
1844 Sep. 17   Holy Trinity, Matfen (N)
1844 Sep. 18   Holy Trinity, Horsley (N)
1844 Oct. 31   St John the Evangelist, Ingleton (D)
1845 Feb. 7   St George, East Boldon (D)   (Later church
                                               consecrated
                                               8 Dec. 1923)
1845 Jul. 10   St Peter, Byers Green (D)
1845 Jul. 15   St Paul, Hunwick (D)
1845 Jul. 28   Holy Trinity, Southwick, Monkwearmouth (D)
1845 Aug. 7   St James, Harwood in Middleton (D)
1845 Aug. 12   St Bartholomew, Thornley [Wolsingham] (D)
1845 Aug. 14   St John the Evangelist, Nenthead, Alston
1845 Aug. 25   St Cuthbert, Stella [Blaydon] (D)
1846 Sep. 24   St Bartholomew, Croxdale (D)
1846 Oct. 13   St Stephen, South Shields (D)
1846 Oct. 15   St James the Great, Morpeth (N)
1846 Oct. 16   St Paul, Alnwick (N)
1848 Feb. 22   St Anne, Bishop Auckland (D)
1848 Mar. 16   St Cuthbert, Bensham, Gateshead
1848 Aug. 23   Christ Church, Walker (N)
1848 Oct. 17   St John the Evangelist, Lynesack (D)
1849 Jul. 21   Holy Trinity, Seghill (N)
1849 Aug. 9   St John the Evangelist, Birtley (D)
1849 Oct. 23   All Saints, Monkwearmouth (D)
1849 Nov. 6   Holy Trinity, Grindon (D)   (Later church

		consecrated 17 May 1887)
1850 Sep. 12	St Cuthbert, Benfieldside (D)	
1851 Aug. 5	St Mary the Virgin, Shincliffe (D)	(Also 23 Sep. 1826)
1851 Aug. 7	St Matthew, Newbottle	(Later church consecrated 1 Jun. 1886)
1852 May 25	Holy Trinity, Hartlepool (D)	
1852 Nov. 15	St Paul, Hendon (D)	Bishop of Cape Town
1853 Jul. 13	St Mary, Whorlton (D)	Bishop of Cape Town
1853 Jul. 16	St John the Evangelist, Darlington	
1853 Sep. 20	St Luke, Ferryhill	(Also 19 Oct. 1829)
1854 Apr. 20	Christ Church, West Hartlepool (D)	
1854 Jul. 11	St Saviour, Shotton (D)	Bishop of Moray & Ross
1854 Sep. 6	St Thomas, Eighton Banks (D)	Bishop of Exeter

Bishop Charles Thomas Longley 1856–1860   [10 churches]
1857 Jan. 7   St Stephen, Willington (D)
1857 Sep. 18   St John the Evangelist, Greenside (D)
1857 Oct. 15   St Mary Magdalene, Belmont (D)
1857 Oct. 27   St John the Evangelist, Otterburn (N)
1858 Apr. 22   St James, Riding Mill (N)
1858 May 25   St Paul, Spennymoor (D)
1858 Nov. 8   St Mary, Berwick-upon-Tweed (N)
1859 Apr. 30 Blessed Virgin Mary, Etal (N)
1859 Sep. 30 St Paul, High Elswick, Newcastle (N)
1859 Nov. 29 St Mary the Virgin, Rye Hill, Newcastle (N)

Bishop Henry Montagu Villiers 1860–1861   [6 churches]
1860 Sep. 11   Holy Trinity, Whitfield (N)
1860 Sep. 13   St John, Healey (N)
1860 Sep. 13   St James, Newton Hall (N)
1860 Nov. 21   Christ Church, New Seaham
1861 Jan. 14   Jesmond Church, Newcastle upon Tyne (N)
1861 Jun. 14   St Mary, Cowpen (N)

Bishop Charles Baring 1861–1879   [98 churches]
1861 Nov. 12   Christ Church, Shieldfield (N)
1861 Nov. 13   Christ Church, Great Lumley (D)
1862 Mar. 11   St Michael, Byker (N)
1862 Jun. 10   St John, Chevington (N)

1862 Sep. 10   St John the Divine, Acklington (N)
1862 Sep. 11   St James, South Charlton (N)
1862 Oct. 22   St Mary, Tyne Dock, South Shields (D)
1862 Dec. 31   St John the Baptist, Brandon   (Later church
                                               consecrated
                                               2 Jul. 1905)
1863 Aug. 27   St Cuthbert, Durham (D)
1863 Sep. 15   St John the Baptist, Escomb
1864 Apr. 21   St Mary, West Rainton (D)   (Also 29 Aug. 1825)
1864 Jun. 14   St Mary, Blyth
1864 Jun. 16   St Michael and All Angels, Hawthorn (D)
1864 Aug. 31   St Peter, Low Town, Tynemouth (N)
1864 Sep. 2   St John Percy, Tynemouth (N)
1864 Sep. 3   St Paul, Whitley [Bay] (N)
1865 Jul. 5   St James the Less, Gateshead (D)
1865 Dec. 23   St John the Evangelist, Haverton Hill (D)
1865 Dec. 29   St Peter, Cambois (N)
1866 Mar. 2   St Michael, Frosterley (D)   (Later church
                                              consecrated
                                              27 May 1869)
1866 Apr. 26   Christ Church, Felling (D)
1866 May 22   Holy Innocents, Tudhoe (D)
1866 Jun. 22   St James the Great, Duddo (N)
1866 Aug. 2   St Peter, Sacriston (D)
1866 Nov. 15   Christ Church, Consett (D)
1866 Nov. 16   St Paul the Apostle, Choppington (N)
1866 Dec. 19   St Cuthbert, East Rainton (D)
1867 Jul. 1   St Paul, Haswell (D)
1867 Mar. 8   St John the Evangelist, Castleside
1867 Aug. 15   St Peter, Harton (D)
1867 Sep. 12   St Ives, Leadgate (D)
1867 Sep. 18   St Paul, Evenwood (D)
1868 Jan. 30   St Paul, Cassop cum Quarrington (D)
1868 Feb. 20   St Stephen, Low Elswick (N)
1868 Feb. 25   St Barnabas, Burnmoor (D)
1868 May 11   St James, Stockton-on-Tees (D)
1868 May 12   St Nicholas, Cramlington (N)
1868 May 14   St Mary the Virgin, Coxhoe (D)
1868 Aug. 27   St Anthony, Byker (N)   Bishop of Ripon
1868 Sep. 21   Holy Trinity, Cornforth (D)
1868 Oct. 27   All Saints, New Shildon (D)
1869 Mar. 31   All Saints, Cleadon

1869 May 27	St Michael, Frosterley (D)	(Also 27 May 1869)
1869 Jul. 12	Holy Trinity, Eccleston	
1869 Jul. 24	St Philip and St James, Tow Law (D)	
1869 Jul. 29	St Andrew, Westgate (D)	
1869 Oct. 5	Christ Church, Jarrow Grange (D)	
1869 Oct. 22	St Mary the Virgin, Fir Tree (D)	
1869 Dec. 14	St James, West Hartlepool (D)	
1869 Dec. 28	St John, Killingworth (N)	
1870 Jan. 13	St John the Evangelist, Holmside (D)	
1870 Aug. 4	Venerable Bede, Monkwearmouth (D)	
1870 Aug. 10	St Paul, Ryhope (D)	(Also 24 Jul. 1827)
1870 Sep. 22	St Michael and All Angels, Lyons, Houghton-le-Spring (D)	
1870 Oct. 15	St Cuthbert, Amble (N)	
1871 Feb. 27	Holy Saviour, Milbourne (N)	
1871 Apr. 13	St Lawrence, Middleton St George (D)	
1871 Jun. 28	St John the Evangelist, Spittal, Tweedmouth (N)	
1871 Oct. 31	St Mary the Virgin, Stannington (N)	
1872 Apr. 30	St Mark, Millfield, Bishopwearmouth (D)	
1872 May 28	St Mary, Sherburn (D)	
1872 Jun. 26	St Matthew, Silksworth (D)	
1872 Sep. 19	St Paul, Darlington (D)	
1872 Nov. 6	Christ Church, Bensham, Gateshead (D)	
1872 Nov. 28	St Peter, Bishopwearmouth (D)	
1873 Jul. 8	St James, Coundon (D)	(Also 13 Jul. 1841)
1873 Jul. 10	St Philip, High Elswick (N)	
1873 Aug. 12	St Lawrence, Piercebridge, Gainford (D)	
1873 Nov. 20	St James, Burnopfield (D)	
1874 Jun. 30	St John the Baptist, Stockton on Tees (D)	
1874 Aug. 27	St Luke, Pallion (D)	
1874 Nov. 3	St Margaret, Castle Town, Hylton (D)	Bishop Vincent Ryan
1874 Nov. 4	St Hilda the Virgin, Lucker (N)	Bishop Vincent Ryan
1874 Nov. 5	St Cuthbert, Hebburn (D)	Bishop Vincent Ryan
1875 Apr. 20	St Peter, Bishop Auckland	
1875 May 26	St Mark, South Shields (D)	
1875 Jun. 22	Christ Church, Bishopwearmouth (D)	
1875 Jul. 6	St John the Baptist, Hamsteels (D)	
1875 Dec. 27	St John the Evangelist, Brandon (D)	
1876 Jan. 13	St Barnabas, Hendo, Sunderland (D)	
1876 Feb. 3	St Paul, Howdon Panns (N)	
1876 Feb. 3	St Paul, Willington Quay	

1876 Apr. 26   Christ Church, Dunston (D)
1876 Jul. 6   St Mary the Virgin, Willington (N)
1876 Jul. 20   St Andrew, Chilton Moor (D)
1876 Aug. 15   Christ Church, Darlington (D)
1876 Aug. 29   St Helen, Low Fell, Gateshead (D)
1876 Aug. 30   St James the Great, Darlington
1876 Sep. 14   St John the Evangelist, Longhurst (N)
1876 Sep. 21   St Peter, Wolviston (D)
1876 Nov. 7   St John the Evangelist, Alnmouth (N)
1876 Dec. 26   St Andrew, Beamish (D)
1877 Feb. 13   St Thomas Apostle and Martyr, Stanley (D)
1877 May 18   St Paul, Witton Park (D)
1877 Jun. 1   Holy Trinity, East Murton
1877 Oct. 11   St Thomas, Westoe (D)   (Also 29 Jul. 1818)
1877 Nov. 15   St Cuthbert, Marley Hill (D)
1879 Jan. 31   St Stephen, Ayers Quay,   Bishop Vincent Ryan
               Bishopwearmouth

Bishop Joseph Barber Lightfoot 1879–1889   [45 churches]
1879 May 27   St Edmund, Bearpark
1879 Jun. 23   St George, Fatfield (D)
1879 Jul. 22   St Mark, Eldon (D)
1880   St John, Monkheselden
1880 Jun. 9   St Paul, West Pelton (D)
1880 Jun. 14   St Matthew, Newcastle (N)
1880 Jun. 21   St Mary, South Hylton (D)   (Also 15 Feb. 1821)
1880 Jun. 28   St John, Stillington (D)
1880 Jul. 17   St Cuthbert, Monkwearmouth (D)
1880 Jul. 20   St Simon, Tyne Dock, South Shields (D)
1880 Oct. 9   All Saints, Duddo (N)
1880 Dec. 29   St Philip, Auckland Park
1881   St Andrew, Boulmer
1881 Jan. 18   St Cuthbert, Newcastle (N)
1881 Jun. 29   St Peter, Jarrow (D)
1881 Oct. 13   St Peter, Stockton on Tees (D)
1882 Feb. 2   St Michael and All Angels, South Westoe, South
               Shields (D)
1882 Feb. 17   St Nicholas, Hedworth (D)
1882 Apr. 26   [St James], Castle Eden Colliery

In May 1882 the diocese of Newcastle was created and, during the remaining seven years of his episcopate, Bishop J. B. Lightfoot consecrated a further twenty-six churches in the diocese of Durham.

Appendix 2

Bishops and Archdeacons

Bishops of Durham
1787–1791	Thomas Thurlow
1791–1826	Shute Barrington
1826–1836	William Van Mildert
1836–1856	Edward Maltby
1856–1860	Charles Thomas Longley
1860–1861	Henry Montagu Villiers
1861–1879	Charles Baring
1879–1889	Joseph Barber Lightfoot
1890–1901	Brooke Foss Westcott
1901–1920	Handley Carr Glyn Moule

Bishops of Newcastle
(the diocese was created in 1882)
1882–1896	Ernest Roland Wilberforce
1896–1903	Edgar Jacob
1903–1907	Arthur Thomas Lloyd
1907–1915	Norman Dumenil John Straton

Archdeacons of Durham
(until 1832 the archdeaconry was annexed to St Mary the Virgin, Easington)
1791–1808	Benjamin Pye
1808–1831	Richard Prosser
1831–1862	Charles Thorp
1863–1882	Edward Prest
1882–1922	Henry William Watkins

Archdeacons of Auckland
(the archdeaconry was created in 1882)
1882	Henry William Watkins
1882–1907	Robert Long

Archdeacons of Northumberland
(until 1842 the archdeaconry was annexed to St Michael and All
Angels, Howick)

1792–1812	Robert Thorp
1812–1826	Reginald Gideon Bouyer
1826–1842	Thomas Singleton
1842–1853	William Forbes Raymond
1853–1880	George Bland
1880–1882	Henry William Watkins
1882–1905	George Hans Hamilton

Archdeacons of Lindisfarne
(the archdeaconry was created in 1842 and annexed to St Maurice,
Eglingham)

1843–1844	Charles Thomas Bigge
1844–1853	George Bland
1853–1865	Richard Charles Coxe
1865–1882	George Hans Hamilton
1882–1904	Henry John Martin

Appendix 3

Dissenters' Places of Worship 1853

Returns made to the House of Commons, 11 February 1853 (23 February 1853), pp. 36, 50. 'Temporary' includes houses or rooms used as a temporary place of worship. 'Permanent' includes chapels, buildings and meeting houses. The denominations include Presbyterians, Independents (or Congregationalists), Baptists (General and Particular), Society of Friends (Quakers), Methodists (Wesleyan, Primitive and other Arminian Methodists), Roman Catholics, specified denominations and unspecified denominations.

| | Northumberland | | Durham | |
	Temporary	Permanent	Temporary	Permanent
1731–1740	1			
1741–1750	1			
1751–1760	2			
1761–1770	2	1	4	
1771–1780	7	3	17	4
1781–1790	14	12	30	5
1791–1800	21	24	46	22
1801–1810	18	16	46	22
1811–1820	56	35	75	44
1821–1830	26	31	108	68
1831–1840	12	36	22	59
1841–1850	13	35	19	61
1851–1852	2	7	2	18
	175	200	369	303

Sum of temporary totals   544
Sum of permanent totals   503

For the returns of registered meeting houses in the diocese of Durham 1825–52, see DUL, ASC, DDR/EA/NCN/3. Chapels were registered under the Toleration Act of 1688, and the Places of Religious Worship Act of 1812, but from 1852 it was no longer necessary to register meeting houses in the bishops' registers.

Appendix 4

Workhouse Attendance 1851

The *Census of Great Britain 1851, Population Tables I, Vol. 2, Numbers of the inhabitants* (London, 1852). County Durham, pp. 11–23; Northumberland, pp. 23–43.

Alnwick	78
Belford	26
Bellingham	31
Berwick	139
Castle Ward (Ponteland)	75
Glendale (Wooler)	56
Haltwhistle	30
Hexham	185
Morpeth	61
Newcastle upon Tyne	458
Rothbury	29
Tynemouth	278
Auckland	60
Chester-le-Street	51
Darlington	69
Durham (Durham, 96; Lanchester, 46)	142
Easington	26
Gateshead	185
Houghton le Spring	28
South Shields	147
Stockton (Hartlepool, 42; Sedgefield, 242)	64
Sunderland	296
Teesdale (Barnard Castle)	60
Weardale	34
	(total 2,608)

Appendix 5

The Maltby Fund

In 1850, Edward Maltby, the Bishop of Durham, deposited thousands of pounds with the Ecclesiastical Commissioners for the building or repairing of parsonage houses in the diocese. The returns are from the appendices to the Annual Reports of the Ecclesiastical Commissioners for England, 1851 to 1861 (in £s).

	1851	1852	1853	1854	1855	1856	1857
Auckland, St Helen			400				
Barnard Castle	400						
Beadnell						300	50
Belmont				300	50		
Benfieldside	400						
Berwick upon Tweed					300	50	
Billingham				300			
Birtley (Co. Durham)	300		100				
Birtley (Northumberlamd)			150				
Byers Green	280	70					
Byker (St Michael)							400
Byrness			300		50		
Bywell (St Peter)		200					
Collierly (Dipton)						400	
Crook		300					
Darlington, St John				350		50	25
Darlington, Holy Trinity				300			100
Deptford, St Andrew		400					
Elswick, St Paul		400					200
Escomb		300					
Etherley		150					

	1851	1852	1853	1854	1855	1856	1857
Hartlepool, St Hilda				300		100	
Hartlepool, Holy Trinity					400		
Hamsterley		200					
Hetton-le-Hole							300
Heworth, St Albans	300					100	
Hunwick		400					
Ingleton	350						
Jarrow		400					
Kelloe			288	111			
Kyloe			200				
Lesbury		200					
Lucker				200			
Monkwearmouth, All Saints		350				50	
Monkwearmouth, St Peter				200	100		
Muggleswick			200				200
Newcastle, St John				400			200
Newcastle, St Andrew					400	200	
Newcastle, St Peter					300	100	
Newcastle, All Saints						400	
Newcastle, St Ann							600
Penshaw	400						
Seaham Harbour		200					
Seghill					300	100	
Shildon		100					
South Hylton						300	100
South Shields, Holy Trinity	400						
South Shields, St Stephen	300						
Southwick			150	50			300
Stockton-on-Tees, Holy Trinity		300					
Stella	100						
Thornley (Kelloe)			350				
Thornley (Wolsingham)		300	100				
Usworth				400			

	1851	1852	1853	1854	1855	1856	1857
Walker					400		
Wallsend			300				
West Hartlepool						400	
Whitley			150				
Wolviston							
Total	3150	4970	2688	3361	2000	2000	2525

The Maltby Fund (continued)

	1858	1859	1860	1861
Auckland, St Helen				
Barnard Castle				
Beadnell		50		
Belmont			200	
Benfieldside				
Berwick-upon-Tweed, St Mary			400	100
Billingham				
Birtley, Co. Durham				
Birtley, Northumberland				
Byers Green				
Byker (St Michael)				
Byrness				
Bywell, St Peter				
Collierly (Dipton)				20
Coniscliffe			200	
Cramlington		200		
Crook				
Darlington, St John				
Darlington, Holy Trinity				
Deptford, St Andrew				
Dinnington				100
Edmundbyers	200	100		
Egglestone		300		
Elswick, St Paul				

	1858	1859	1860	1861
Elton			300	
Escomb				
Etherley				
Grindon			300	
Hartlepool, St Hilda				
Hartlepool, Holy Trinity				
Hamsterley				
Hendon			300	
Hetton-le-Hole			100	
Heworth, St Albans				
Howden Panns				400
Ingleton				
Jarrow				
Kelloe				
Kyloe				
Ledbury				
Lucker				
Meldon			200	100
Monkhesleden			300	
Monkwearmouth, All Saints				
Monkwearmouth, St Peter				
Muggleswick				
Newcastle upon Tyne, St John				
Newcastle upon Tynne, St Andrew				
Newcastle upon Tyne, St Peter				
Newcastle upon Tyne, All Saints	200			
Newcastle upon Tyne, St Anne				
Newcastle upon Tyne, St Nicholas			400	
Newbanks	50			
Penshaw				
Seaham Harbour			200	
Seghill				
Shildon				
South Shields, Holy Trinity				

	1858	1859	1860	1861
South Shields, St Stephen				
Southwisk				
Stockton-on-Tees, Holy Trinity				
Stella				
Thornley (Kelloe)				
Thornley (Wolsingham)				
Usworth				
Walker				
Wallsend				
West Hartlepool				
West Rainton			400	
Whitley				
Widdrington				300
Willington, St Stephen				200
Wolviston				
Total	450	650	3000	1520

Appendix 6

The Lord Crewe Charity

Taken from the will of Lord Nathaniel Crewe (1633–1721), the Bishop of Oxford 1671–74 and Bishop of Durham 1674–1721, dated 24 June 1720 and codicil 17 September 1721. From his extensive estates in Northumberland and County Durham the annual income was £1,312 13s 5d. Over the years this increased and by 1830 it was £8,126 8s 4d. The charity was regulated by schemes drawn up in 1876 and 1896. The income was held in trust and paid by Hoare, the London banker, to various worthy causes that included an annual payment of £20 to the Rector and £10 to each of the twelve fellows of Lincoln College, Oxford, together with an annual payment of £20 each to twelve boys entering the college from the diocese of Durham, and a further sum of £10 each to eight poor scholars at the college. Other educational provision was made in providing £20 for a schoolmaster at Newbold de Verdun, Leicestershire, and £20 a year for a schoolmaster to teach thirty boys in the parish of Bishop Auckland. In the city of Durham and in the surrounding area provision was made to support apprentices and in the support of the residents of four almshouses; apart from some smaller provisions, the rest of the charity went on supplementing clerical stipends. Two large payments of £40 a year were for the incumbent of St Aidan, Bamburgh, and £30 for the incumbent of St Andrew, Auckland. The twelve poor livings in the diocese of Durham that each received £10 a year were:

St Helen, Auckland
St Mary, Barnard Castle
St James, Castle Eden
St Cuthbert, Darlington
St Mary-le-Bow, Durham
Holy Trinity, Grindon
St James, Hamsterley
St Hilda, Hartlepool
All Saints, Lanchester

St Lawrence, Pittington
St Andrew, Shotley
St Philip and St James, Witton-le-Wear

There were five trustees, one of whom was to be the Rector of Lincoln College, Oxford, where Crewe had been a student and later the Rector, 1668–72. The trustees met when they had business to conduct, and three of them were considered to be a quorum. In practice the Rector of Lincoln College rarely attended any of the meetings and the business was conducted by the clergy-trustees of the diocese of Durham. In the mid-nineteenth century they were:

Charles Thorp, Archdeacon of Durham 1831–62
James Thompson, Rector of Lincoln College, Oxford, 1851–60
William Nicholas Darnell, rector of Stanhope, 1831–65
Henry George Liddell, rector of Easington, 1832–72
John Dixon Clark, of Belford Hall, and previously the curate of
    Belford 1837–41

Crewe was very much a man of his time and seemingly more interested in power and influence at court than in his diocesan responsibilities. A near contemporary described him as 'a most accomplished gentleman as well as a pious and vigilant prelate ... His charity towards man was equal to his piety towards God' [DUL, ASC, DDR/EA/CHC/1/1]. But a later historian was far less effusive and more forthright in his opinion. 'Crewe is a remarkable instance of a man whose posthumous munificence has done much to outweigh a discreditable career' (M. Creighton, *Dictionary of National Biography* (London, 1888), vol. 13, p. 80).

[W. Whellan, *History of the County Palatine of Durham* (London, 1856), pp. 103–104. For Crewe's will, see C.E. Whiting, *Nathaniel Lord Crewe, Bishop of Durham 1674–1721, and his Diocese* (London, 1940), pp. 332–358. See too F. Whellan, *History, Topography and Directory of the County Palatine of Durham* (London, 1894), pp. 210–211.]

Appendix 7

The Newcastle Daily Chronicle Census of 1881

In 1881 various provincial newspapers in some eighty towns in England and forty in Scotland conducted their own religious census, the first of which took place in Newcastle and Gateshead. These locally conducted censuses provided an invaluable means of comparing the patterns of church and chapel growth and decline during the thirty-year period 1851 to 1881. The annual Anglican Church Congress met twice in Newcastle, in October 1881 and in September 1900. On the Sunday morning before the 1881 Congress opened *The Newcastle Daily Chronicle* conducted a census of church and chapel attendance in the two Tyneside towns.

Attendance in Newcastle in 1851 and 1881

Denomination	1851	1881	Increase	Decrease
Church of England	7,202	6,441		761
Presbyterian	2,499	3,053	556	
Congregationalist	826	1,200	464	
Baptist	1,072	805		267
Wesleyan Methodist	1,270	3,345	2,075	
Methodist New Connexion	210	369	159	
Primitive Methodist	806	997	171	
Bible Christian		200	200	
United Methodist Free Church	630	1,145	515	
Non-denominational	8	245	235	
Catholic Apostolic		150	150	
Danish Church		70	70	
Society of Friends	217	124		93
Roman Catholic	3,399	3,845	456	
Jews	50	255	205	

Unitarian	461	220		241
Swedenborg	70			70
Total	18,710	22,534	5,256	1,482

Attendance in Gateshead in 1851 and 1881

Denomination	1851	1881	Increase	Decrease
Church of England	1,583	2,045	462	
Presbyterian	290	670	380	
Congregationalist		330	330	
Baptist		175	175	
Wesleyan Methodist	516	1,272	756	
Methodist New Connexion	630	320		310
Primitive Methodist		522	522	
United Methodist Free Church		131	131	
Non-denominational		24	24	
Roman Catholic	500	510	10	
Plymouth Brethren		140	140	
Salvation Army		122	122	
Total	3,519	6,261	3,052	310

In the thirty years 1851 to 1881 the population had increased but the church and chapel attendances had barely kept in step. In 1851 the population of Newcastle was 87,784 and in 1881 it was 145,359; in 1851 the population of Gateshead was 25,568 and in 1881 it was 65,100. While there had been an increase of 70% in the population of Newcastle, the attendance at places of worship had only increased by 20%. 'In 1851 the percentage of worshippers to population was twenty-one, but in 1881 the percentage had fallen to fifteen.' By way of contrast in Gateshead the population had increased by 154% and the attendance at places of worship had been 77%. However, whereas the percentage of worshippers to population had been 13% in 1851, it had fallen to 9% in 1881. 'If we estimate the adult population of the two towns at least one half the grand total, it may be said that less than one third of those who might go do go to church or chapel on Sunday morning. Newcastle appears to be much more of a church-going town than Gateshead, for while 15% of the people of this town went to places of worship on Sunday morning last, only 9% of

Gateshead people attended. In 1881 three Anglican clergy refused to co-operate (one in Shieldfield and two in Gateshead) and estimates were made for them and also for three small Methodist chapels. With these reservations we claim for our returns that they are fair and complete, and on the whole quite as reliable as the figures given in the census of 1851.'

[All of the information and quotations are from *The Newcastle Daily Chronicle*, 5 October 1881.]

BIBLIOGRAPHY

Manuscript Sources

Berwick on Tweed Record Office
Mss. *Index of Presbyterian Churches in England: Northumberland*, n.d., C4/9

Dr Williams Centre for Dissenting Studies
The Surman Index Online, http//surman.english.qmul.ac.uk

Durham University Library
Clergy Discipline 1846–56, ASC, DDR/EJ/CLD/2
Consecration deeds, ASC, DDR/EA/CHC/3
Consecration deeds, Northumberland Archives, NRO 1875
Consecration documents, ASC, DDR/EA/CHC/1/1
Durham Diocesan Book 1856, ASC, DDR/EV/VIS/7/1/5
Episcopal Act Books 1826–56, ASC, DDR/EA/ACT/1/5
Extracts from Clergy Returns for the Bishop's First Visitation, September 1857, ASC, AUC/1/142
Huddleston, C.R., Biographical card index of clergy, ASC
Letters testimonial, ASC, DDR/EA/CL1/2
Return of baptisms in the diocese of Durham, 1851, ASC, DDR/EA/PBT/5

Tyne and Wear Archives
The analysis of the population of the townships of Benwell and Elswick including the workhouse population in the parish of St James', Benwell, DX 678/1

Printed Sources

Addleshaw, G.W.O., *The Pastoral Organisation of the Modern Dioceses of Durham and Newcastle in the Time of Bede* (Jarrow, 1963)
Anderson, M., *Northumberland and Cumberland Mining Disasters* (Barnsley, 2009)
(Anon.), 'Biographical Sketch of the Late Bishop of Durham (the Rt Rev Charles Baring DD)', *Newcastle Daily Journal*, 16 September 1879

(Anon.), *Local Records of South Durham from 1819 to 1827* (Darlington, 1866)

Antiquities of Sunderland, 17 vols. (Sunderland, 1900–17)

Atlay, J.B. *The Life of the Right Reverend Ernest Roland Wilberforce* (London, 1912)

Baring, C. *A Charge delivered at his Primary Visitation of the Diocese, October 1862* (Durham, 1862)

Baring, C. *A Charge delivered to the Clergy of the Diocese of Durham, at his Third Visitation, October 1870* (Durham, 1870)

Baring, C. *A Charge intended to have been delivered to the Clergy of the Diocese of Durham, at his Fourth Quadrennial Visitation, September 1874* (Durham, 1874)

Bates, C.J. 'The Dedications of the Ancient Churches and Chapels in the Diocese of Newcastle', *Arch. Ael.*, new series, xiii (1889), pp. 317–345

Bebbington, D.W. *Evangelicalism in Modern Britain* (London, 1989)

Bellenger, D. 'The French Exiled Clergy in the North of England', *Arch. Ael.*, fifth series, x (1982), pp. 171–177

Binfield, J.C.G. 'The Building of a Town Centre Church: St James's Congregational Church, Newcastle upon Tyne', *Northern History*, xviii (1982), pp. 153–181

Black, J. *Presbyterianism in Sunderland and the North* (London, 1876)

Blair, R. *The Communion Plate and Church Bells of Northumberland and Durham*, 3 vols. (South Shields, 1891) [includes plans and elevations of many of the churches in the two counties]

Boag, G.W. 'Congregationalism in Northumberland and Durham', *Transactions of the Congregational Historical Society*, vol. 4 (1909–10), pp. 79–91

Bossy, J. *The English Catholic Community 1570–1850* (London, 1975)

Bossy, J. 'Four Catholic Congregations in Rural Northumberland 1750–1850', *Recusant History*, ix, no. 1 (January 1967), pp. 88–119

Bossy, J. 'More Northumbrian Congregations,' *Recusant History*, x (January 1969), pp. 11–31

Bourn, W. *Whickham Parish, its History and Antiquities* (Carlisle, 1893)

Boutflower, D.S. (ed.), *The Registers of Sherburn Hospital, in the County of Durham* (Newcastle upon Tyne, 1914)

Braithwaite, M. *History of Methodism in the Bishop Auckland Circuit* (Bishop Auckland, 1885)

Brockett Booklets, 2 vols. (Gateshead, 1864)

Brockie, W. *Sunderland Notables: Natives, Residents and Visitors* (Sunderland, 1894)

Brown, C.G. *Religion and Society in Twentieth-century Britain* (Harlow, 2006)

Bruce, J.C. *Handbook to Newcastle on Tyne* (Newcastle, 1863)

Bruce, S. 'Methodism and Mining in County Durham, 1881–1991,' *Northern History*, xlviii (2011), pp. 337–355

Burgess, J. *A History of Cumbrian Methodism* (Kendal, 1980)

Burnside, F. (ed.), *The Official Yearbook of the Church of England 1885* (London, 1885) [church extension in the Diocese of Durham, pp. 15–18]

Butler, D.M. *The Quaker Meeting Houses of Britain*, 2 vols. (London, 1999)

Cameron, N.M. De S. *Dictionary of Scottish Church History and Theology* (Edinburgh, 1993)

Carter, G. *Anglican Evangelicals. Protestant Secessions from the Via Media, c.1800–1850* (Oxford, 2001)

Catherall, G.A. 'The Baptists of North Northumberland', *Baptist Quarterly*, xxi (1966), pp. 169–173

Census of Great Britain 1851, 4 vols. (London, 1852–54)

Census of Great Britain. Religious Worship. England and Wales. Report and Tables (London, 1853). Reprinted in the Irish University Press series of *British Parliamentary Papers. Population*, vol. 10, 1970

Charleton, R.J. *A History of Newcastle on Tyne* (Newcastle, n.d.)

Charlton, E.M. *Methodism in the Allen Dales* (Nenthead, Cumbria, n.d.)

Clark, B.F.L. *The Building of the Eighteenth-Century Church* (London, 1963)

Coad, R. *A History of the Brethren Movement* (Exeter, 1968)

Coleman, B.J. *The Church of England in the Mid-Nineteenth Century* (London, 1980)

Collier, C. and Stewart, L.A. *Wooler and Glendale. A Brief History* (Wooler, 2006)

Collinson, J. *A Farewell Sermon, preached at Gateshead, in the Chapel of the Holy Trinity, in the Morning, and in the Evening, on Sunday, 29 December 1839* (Newcastle upon Tyne, 1840)

Colls, R. (ed.) *Northumbria. History and Identity 547–2000* (Chichester, 2007)

Colls, R. and Lancaster, B. (eds.) *Newcastle upon Tyne. A Modern History* (Chichester, 2001)

Cookson, G. (ed.) *A History of the County of Durham* (Woodbridge, 2005)

Cooter, R. *When Paddy Met Geordie. The Irish in County Durham and Newcastle 1840–1880* (Sunderland, 2005)

Coxe, R.C. *A Charge delivered to the Clergy of the Archdeaconry of Lindisfarne, June 1855* (London, n.d.)

Coxe, R.C. *A Cursory Survey of the Churches and Church Buildings within the Archdeaconry of Lindisfarne* (London, 1860)

Cranfield, R. 'An "Indefatigable Chaplain": the Rev George Hans Hamilton, Durham Prison, 1848–54' (Part One), *Durham County Local History Society*, Bulletin 58 (November 1998), pp. 25–42. (Part Two), *Durham County Local History Society*, Bulletin 60 (November 1999), pp. 36–63

Davies, J. *Christian Worship: its object and essential requisites. A Discourse preached before the University of Cambridge, at St Mary's Church* [June 1844] (London, 1844)

Davies, J. *The Ministry of the Church considered with respect to its influence on Society. A Sermon on behalf of the Church Building Society preached at St Mary's Church, Gateshead, on Sunday, 12 March 1843* (London, 1843)

Davies, J. *The Subdivision and Re-arrangement of Parishes. A Letter addressed to the Rt. Hon. Lord Ashley MP* (London, 1849)

Davies, J. *A Sermon, occasioned by the re-opening of St Mary's Church, Gateshead* (Gateshead, 1855)

Davies, R. and Rupp, G. (eds.) *A History of the Methodist Church in Great Britain*, 4 vols. (London, 1965–88)

Davis, C.D.W. *The Great Parish of Simonburn from Hadrian's Wall to Carter Bar* (Newcastle, 1972)

Davison, W. *Descriptive and Historical View of Alnwick* (1822, reprinted 1973)

Devey, T.V. *Records of Wolsingham* (Newcastle, 1926)

Dissenters' Places of Worship, House of Commons, February 1853

Dixon, D.D. *Upper Coquetdale* (Newcastle, 1903)

Dixon, D.D. *Whittingham Vale, Northumberland. Its History, Traditions and Folk Lore* (Newcastle, 1895)

Dodd, W. *A Sermon preached on the evening of 8 January, at the Parish Church of St Andrew, in aid of the Building Fund of the Proposed New Chapel of St Peter* (Newcastle, 1843)

Drysdale, A.H. *History of the Presbyterians in England. Their Rise, Decline and Revival* (London, 1889)

Durham Diocesan Calendar, Clergy List and Church Almanack for 1873 *(Durham, 1873)*

Egglestone, W.M. *All Around Stanhope* (Stanhope, n.d.)

Fergusson, J. *Mitford Church. Its History, Restoration and Associations* (Newcastle, 1884)

Field, C.D. 'The 1851 Religious Census of Great Britain: A Bibliographical Guide for Local and Regional Historians', *The Local Historian*, xxvii (November 1997), pp. 194–217

Fordyce, T. *Local Records or Historical Register of Remarkable Events*, 2 vols. (Newcastle, 1867)

Fordyce, W. *The History and Antiquities of the County Palatine of Durham*, 2 vols. (Newcastle, n.d. [c.1855])

Foster, J. *Alumni Oxonienses*, 2 vols. (Oxford, n.d.)

Friedman, T. *The Georgian Parish Church* (Reading, 2004)

Gailiunas, P. 'The Hawks Family and the Progress of Church Music on Tyneside before the Oxford Movement', *Arch. Ael.*, fifth series, xxxvi (2007), pp. 309–323

Garbutt, G. *A Historical and Descriptive View of the Parishes of Monkwearmouth and Bishopwearmouth and the Port and Borough of Sunderland* (Sunderland, 1819)

Gay, J.D. *The Geography of Religion in England* (London, 1971)

Gill, R. *Competing Convictions* (London, 1989)

Gill, R. *The Myth of the Empty Church* (London, 1993)

Gregory, J.V. *Church Dedication-Names in the Diocese of Newcastle* (Newcastle, 1884)

Harbottle, S. *The Reverend William Turner. Dissent and Reform in Georgian Newcastle upon Tyne* (Newcastle, 1997)

Hartley, T.G. (ed.) *Hall's Circuits and Ministers. An Alphabetical List of the [Wesleyan Methodist] Circuits in Great Britain … 1765 to 1912* (London, [*c*.1912])

Hawkins, F.H. *The Presbytery of Durham* (South Shields, [*c*.1973])

Heesom, A.J. 'Problems of Church Extension in a Victorian New Town: The Londonderrys and Seaham Harbour', *Northern History*, xv (1979), pp. 138–155

D. Hempton, *Methodism. Empire of the Spirit* (New Haven, CT, 2005)

Hilton, J.A. 'Catholicism in Elizabethan Northumberland', *Northern History*, xiii (1977), pp. 44–58

Hiscox, R. *Celebrating Reader Ministry* (London, 1991)

A History of Northumberland [six editors], 15 vols., (Newcastle, 1893–1940)

Hodgson, G.B. *The Borough of South Shields* (Newcastle, 1903)

Hodgson, J.C. 'A Survey of the Churches of the Archdeaconry of Northumberland [1663]', *Arch. Ael.*, xvii (1895), pp. 244–262

Hole, C. *The Life of the Reverend and Venerable William Whitmarsh Phelps MA*, 2 vols. (London, 1871, 1873)

Inglis, K.S. 'Patterns of Religious Worship in 1851', *Journal of Ecclesiastical History*, xi (April 1960), pp. 74–86

Jackson, G. *Wesleyan Methodism in the Darlington Circuit* (Sunderland, 1850)

Judd, S. and Cable, K. *Sydney Anglicans* (Sydney, 2000)

Kelly, B.W. *Historical Notes on English Catholic Missions* (London, 1907)

Kirby, M.W. *Men of Business and Politics* (London, 1984)

Kirkwood, […] *Memoir of the Rev Alexander Kirkwood of Berwick-upon-Tweed* (London, 1856)

Larsen, T. *A People of One Book. The Bible and the Victorians* (Oxford, 2011)

Lee, R. *The Church of England and the Durham Coalfield, 1810–1926* (Woodbridge, 2007)

Levy, A. *History of the Sunderland Jewish Community* (London, 1956)

Lightfoot, J.B. *Primary Charge. Two Addresses Delivered to the Clergy of the Diocese of Durham in December 1882* (London, n.d.)

Lillie, W. *The History of Middlesbrough* (Middlesbrough, 1968)

Livingstone E.A. (ed.) *The Oxford Dictionary of the Christian Church* (Oxford, 3rd edn, 1997)

Low, J.L. *Diocesan Histories. Durham* (London, 1881)

MacEwen, A.R. *Life and Letters of John Cairns* (London, 1898)

Mackenzie, E. *An Historical, Topographical and Descriptive View of the County of Northumberland*, 2 vols. (Newcastle, 1825)

MacRaild, D.M. (ed.) *The Great Famine and Beyond. Irish Migrants in Britain in the Nineteenth and Twentieth Centuries* (Dublin, 2000)

Mallia, S. 'The Malta Protestant College', *Melita Historica*, x (1990), pp. 257–282

Maltby, E. *A Charge delivered to the Clergy of the Diocese of Durham at the Visitation in July, August and September 1849* (London, 1850)

Maltby, E. *A Charge delivered to the Clergy of the Diocese of Durham at the Visitation in July and August 1853* (London, 1853)

Manders, F.W.D. *A History of Gateshead* (Gateshead, 1973)

Mason, A.J. *Memoir of George Howard Wilkinson*, 2 vols. (London, 1909)

Matthew, H.C.G. and Harrison, B. (eds.) *Oxford Dictionary of National Biography*, 60 vols. (Oxford, 2004)

Maynard, W.B. 'Pluralism and Non-Residence in the Archdeaconry of Durham, 1774–1856: the Bishop and Chapter as Patrons', *Northern History*, xxvi (1990), pp. 103–130

McCollum, M. 'Changes in the Patten of Ecclesiastical Jurisdictions in and connected with the Diocese of Durham during the Nineteenth Century, with a note on the location of the Records of these Jurisdictions', *Transactions of the Architectural and Archaeological Society of Durham and Northumberland*, new series (1982), pp. 61–65

Meikle, M. and Newman, C. *Sunderland and its Origins* (Chichester, 2007)

Middlesbrook, S. *Newcastle upon Tyne. Its Growth and Achievement* (Newcastle, 1968)

Milburn, G.E. 'Catholicism in Mid-Nineteenth Century Northumberland', *Tyne 'n Tweed*, no. 32 (Autumn 1978) pp. 16–22

Milburn, G.E. 'The Census of Worship of 1851', *Durham County Local History Society Bulletin*, no. 17 (July 1974), pp. 3–20

Milburn, G.E. 'The Census of Worship of 1851 and its Value to the Local Historian', *Tyne 'n Tweed*, no. 29 (Spring 1977), pp. 3–13

Milburn, G.E. 'Religion in Sunderland in 1851', *Durham County Local History Society Bulletin*, no. 18 (April 1975), pp. 3–21

Milburn, G.E. *Religion in Sunderland in the Mid-Nineteenth Century* (Sunderland, 1982)

Milligan, E.H. *British Quakers in Commerce and Industry 1775–1920* (York, 2007)

Moore, H.E. *Our Providential Way. Methodism: Its Gospel and Growth in Darlington* (Lancaster, 2005)

Morgan, A. *Victorian Panorama. A Visit to Newcastle upon Tyne in the Reign of Queen Victoria* (Newcastle, 2007)

Morris, M. and Gooch, L. *Down Your Aisles. The Diocese of Hexham and Newcastle 1850–2000* (Hartlepool, 2000)

Munden, A. *A Light in a Dark Place. Jesmond Parish Church, Newcastle upon Tyne* (Newcastle, 2006)

Munden, A.F. 'The First Palmerston Bishop: Henry Montagu Villiers, Bishop of Carlisle 1856–60 and Bishop of Durham 1860–61', *Northern History*, xxvi (1990), pp. 186–206

Munden, A.F. 'The Origin of Evangelical Anglicanism in Newcastle upon Tyne', *Arch. Ael.*, fifth series, xi (1983), pp. 301–307

Neasham, G. *The History and Biography of West Durham* (Durham, 1881)

Neil, D.F. *The Baptists of North East England* (Houghton-le-Spring, 2006)

Newton, D. and Pollard, A.J. *Newcastle and Gateshead before 1700* (Chichester, 2009)

Nichol, J. *A Short Account of the Presbyterian Church, Harbottle, Northumberland* (Alnwick, 1913)

Norwood, H. 'William Stephen Gilly, 1789–1855', *Tyne and Tweed*, no. 55 (2001), pp. 34–45

Oliver, T. *Reference to a Plan of the Borough of Newcastle upon Tyne and parts of the Borough of Gateshead* (Newcastle, 1844)

Olsover, L. *The Jewish Communities of North-East England 1755–1980* (Sunderland, 1981)

Orde, A. 'William Van Mildert, Charles Thorp, and the Diocese of Durham', *Northern History*, lx (March 2003), pp. 147–166

Page, W. (ed.) *The Victoria History of the County of Durham*, vols. II–III (London, 1907, 1928)

Patterson, G. 'The Religious Census – a Test of its Accuracy in South Shields', *Durham County Local History Society Bulletin*, no. 21 (April 1978), pp. 14–17

Patterson, W.M. *Northern Primitive Methodism* (London, 1909)

Pevsner, N. *The Buildings of England. County Durham* (Harmondsworth, 1953)

Pevsner, N. *The Buildings of England. Northumberland* (Harmondsworth, 1957)

Pevsner, N. *The Buildings of England. Yorkshire. The North Riding* (Harmondsworth, 1966)

Pickering, W.S.F. *A Social History of the Diocese of Newcastle 1882–1982* (Stocksfield, 1981)

Plummer, M. *A Letter to the Lord Bishop of Durham in reference to the late proceedings in the Parish of Heworth* (Newcastle, 1852)

Pollard, H. *John Wesley in Northumberland* (London, 1949)

Port, M.H. *Six Hundred New Churches. The Church Building Commission 1818–1856 and its Church Building Activities* (London, 1960; Reading, 2006)

Post Office Directory of Yorkshire (London, 1857)

Potts, R. 'Presbyterians, Congregationalists and other Dissenters', *Tyne and Tweed*, no. 58 (2004), pp. 2–21

Prins, S. and Massingberd-Mundy, R. *The Newcastle Diocesan Gazetteer. A Guide to the Anglican Churches in Newcastle upon Tyne and Northumberland* (Newcastle, 1982)

Purvis, G. *Churches of Newcastle and Northumberland* (Stroud, 2006)

Raine, J. *The History and Antiquities of North Durham* (London, 1852)

Raine, J. *A Memoir of the Rev John Hodgson*, 2 vols. (London, 1858)

Record of Benefactions for the improvement, endowment or support of churches, chapels, oratories and schools, made by the Dean and Chapter of Durham from 1750 AD to 1857 AD (Durham, 1858)

Reid, H.G. (ed.) *Middlesbrough and its Jubilee* (Middlesbrough, 1881)

Report of the Commissioners appointed by the Right Reverend the Lord Bishop of Newcastle, to Examine into the Spiritual Wants and Requirements of Certain Parishes in the Diocese of Newcastle (Newcastle, 1883)

Report, Rules and Regulations of the Society for the Relief of Distressed Clergymen and their Widows and Families commonly called the Society of the Sons of the Clergy in the Diocese of Durham (Newcastle, 1843)

Reports of the Ecclesiastical Commissioners for England, 1851 to 1861

Richardson, W. *History of the Parish of Wallsend* (Newcastle, 1923; reprinted 1998)

Richmond, T. *The Local Records of Stockton and the Neighbourhood* (Stockton, 1868)

Rowdon, H.H. *The Origins of the Brethren, 1825–1850* (London, 1967)

Rowen, W. *Methodism in the Hartlepools and Whitby and Darlington District* (West Hartlepool, 1913)

Ruscoe, J.E. *The Churches of the Diocese of Durham* (Durham, 1994)

Scott, J. *Berwick upon Tweed. The History of the Town and Guild* (London, 1888)

Sharp, C. *History of Hartlepool* (Hartlepool, 1851)

Short, C.C. *Durham Colliers and West Country Methodists* (Kidderminster, 1995)

Snell, K.D.M. and Ell, P.S. *Rival Jerusalems. The Geography of Victorian Religion* (Cambridge, 2000)

Stell, C. *An Inventory of Nonconformist Chapels and Meeting Houses in the North of England* (London, 1994)

Stranks, C.J. *The Charities of Nathaniel, Lord Crewe and Dr John Sharp 1721–1976* (Durham, 1976)

Sunman, W.R. *The History of Free Methodism in and about Newcastle upon Tyne* (Newcastle, 1902)

Susser, B. 'The Nineteenth-century Constitution of the Sunderland Congregation', *Transactions of the Jewish Historical Society*, xl (2005)

Sykes, J. *Local Records and Historical Register*, 2 vols. (Newcastle, 1866)

Tate, G. *The History of the Borough, Castle and Barony of Alnwick* (Alnwick, 1869)

Thorp, C. *A Charge to the Clergy of the Archdeaconry of Durham and the Officiality of the Dean and Chapter, delivered at Durham, 21 July 1846* (Durham, 1846)

Tibbetts, K. 'Methodism in Berwick upon Tweed', *Proceedings of the Wesleyan Historical Society*, xxxiii (December 1982), pp. 161–169

Tyerman, L. *The Life and Times of the Rev John Wesley MA*, 3 vols. (London, 1890)

Van Mildert, W. *A Charge delivered to the Clergy of the Diocese of Durham, 1827* (Oxford, 1828)

Van Mildert, W. *A Charge delivered to the Clergy of the Diocese of Durham, 1831* (Oxford, 1831)

Varley, E.A. *Last of the Prince Bishops. William Van Mildert and the High Church Movement of the Early Nineteenth Century* (Cambridge, 1992)

Venn, J.A. *Alumni Cantabrigienses*, 6 vols. (Cambridge, 1940–1954)

Vickers, J.A. (ed.) *A Dictionary of Methodism in Britain and Ireland* (Peterborough, 2000)

Wakefield, G. *Alexander Boddy. Pentecostal Anglican Pioneer* (London, 2007)

Ward's North of England Directory (Newcastle, 1851)

Ward's Northumberland and Durham Directory (Newcastle, 1850)

Wesley, J. *The Journal of the Rev John Wesley*, 4 vols. (Dent edition, London, 1906)

Whellan, F. *History, Topography and Directory of the County Palatine of Durham* (London, 1894)

Whellan, W. *History of the County Palatine of Durham* (London, 1856)

Whellan, W. *History, Topography and Directory of Northumberland* (London, 1855)

Whiting, C.E. *Nathaniel Lord Crewe. Bishop of Durham 1674–1721 and his Diocese* (London, 1940)

Whiting, C.E. *The University of Durham 1832–1932* (London, 1932)

Wilson, F.R. *An Architectural Survey of the Churches in the Archdeaconry of Lindisfarne* (Newcastle, 1870)

Wilson's Handbook to Morpeth (Morpeth, 1884, reprinted 1996)

Wolffe, J. 'The 1851 Census and Religious Change in Nineteenth-century Yorkshire', *Northern History*, xlvi (March 2008), pp. 71–86

Wolffe, J. *The Religious Census of 1851 in Yorkshire* (York, 2005)

Wolffe, J. (ed.) *Yorkshire Returns of the 1851 Census of Religious Worship*, 4 vols. (York, 2000–)

Woodman, W. 'The Presbyterian Church at Morpeth', *Arch. Ael.*, third series, ii (1906), pp. 163–167

Yates, N. *Buildings, Faith and Worship* (Oxford, 1991; revised edn 2000)

Yates, N. 'Urban Church Attendance and the Use of Statistical Evidence, 1850–1900', *Studies in Church History*, xvi (1979), pp. 389–400

Yeo, A. 'Towards a History of Protestant Dissent in Hexham', *Hexham Historian*, no. 20 (2010), pp. 50–70

Together with numerous mostly anonymous church and chapel histories

Theses

Cooter, R.J. 'The Irish in County Durham and Newcastle, c.1840–1880', University of Durham MA, 1972

Shuler, J.C. 'The Pastoral and Ecclesiastical Administration of the Diocese of Durham 1721–1771 with particular reference to the Archdeaconry of Northumberland', University of Durham PhD, 1975

Willett, G.T. 'The Durham Episcopate of Charles Baring (1807–1879)', University of Durham MA, 1982

INDICES

Northumberland: Index of People

Northumberland: Index of Places

County Durham: Index of People

County Durham: Index of Places

Yorkshire: Index of People

Yorkshire: Index of Places

Cumberland: Index of People

Cumberland: Index of Places